מסורה

ArtScroll® Series

Rabbi Nosson Scherman / Rabbi Gedaliah Zlotowitz
General Editors
Rabbi Meir Zlotowitz ז״ל, *Founder*

Published by

ArtScroll®
Mesorah Publications, ltd

PENSON FAMILY EDITION

The Rebbetzin

THE STORY OF REBBETZIN

ESTHER JUNGREIS

HER LIFE, HER VISION, HER LEGACY

RABBI NACHMAN SELTZER

FIRST EDITION
First Impression … March 2020
Second Impression … April 2020

Published and Distributed by
MESORAH PUBLICATIONS, LTD.
313 Regina Avenue / Rahway, N.J. 07065

Distributed in Europe by
LEHMANNS
Unit E, Viking Business Park
Rolling Mill Road
Jarrow, Tyne & Wear NE32 3DP
England

Distributed in Australia & New Zealand by
GOLDS WORLD OF JUDAICA
3-13 William Street
Balaclava, Melbourne 3183
Victoria Australia

Distributed in Israel by
SIFRIATI / A. GITLER — BOOKS
POB 2351
Bnei Brak 51122

Distributed in South Africa by
KOLLEL BOOKSHOP
Northfield centre, 17 Northfield Avenue
Glenhazel 2192, Johannesburg, South Africa

ARTSCROLL® SERIES
THE REBBETZIN
© *Copyright 2020, by* MESORAH PUBLICATIONS, Ltd.
313 Regina Avenue / Rahway, N.J. 07065 / (718) 921-9000 / www.artscroll.com

---

ISBN 10: 1-4226-2567-2 / ISBN 13: 978-1-4226-2567-5

Typography by CompuScribe at ArtScroll Studios, Ltd.

Printed in the United States of America.
Bound by Sefercraft, Quality Bookbinders, Ltd., Rahway, N.J. 07065

לֵךְ כְּנוֹס אֶת כָּל הַיְּהוּדִים
"Go, assemble all the Jews..." (*Megillas Esther* 4:16)

We are humbled to dedicate this book
in memory of the unforgettable
REBBETZIN ESTHER JUNGREIS ע"ה
הרבנית אסתר בת הרב אברהם הלוי ע"ה

How apropos it is that **THE REBBETZIN** is released during the month of Adar, the time when we read in the *Megillah* about Queen Esther's mission to "assemble all the Jews" in order to spare them from the evil decree of Haman.

No one in the past century personified the mandate of "assemble all the Jews" more than our beloved Rebbetzin Esther Jungreis.

A survivor of the Holocaust/*Churban Europa,* the Rebbetzin arrived on these blessed shores and worked relentlessly to battle the surging tides of assimilation, intermarriage, and abandonment of faith, and to recommit myriads to the path of Torah and mitzvos.

The Rebbetzin had an insatiable desire to ignite the flame of the *"pintele Yid"* in everyone whose life she touched.

The *hakaras hatov* that we have for the Rebbetzin
cannot be adequately expressed.

Our family would not be what we are today
without her nurturing us every step of the way.

The Rebbetzin brought us to a life of Torah; she was always there for us.

The Rebbetzin will forever be our spiritual Ima,
and the Bubby to our children.

Our gratitude extends as well to the Rebbetzin's children,
Chaya Sora, Rabbi Yisroel, Slovie, and Rabbi Osher,
for all that they have taught us, which helped shape our present
— and our future.

May the Rebbetzin's memory be a blessing, and may she continue to daven for all of her children — both biological and spiritual — who gained so much from her precious years with us.

With eternal gratitude and appreciation,
Andrew and Shannon Penson and family

Rebbetzin Esther Jungreis ע״ה had a secret.

It wasn't her voice that touched your soul.
Or her intelligence that fed it.
Or her passion that set it on fire.
Those talents were well known to everyone.

The Rebbetzin's secret was simple: she meant it.
She meant each and every word she uttered.
She had no veneer, no mask.
The Rebbetzin shared her pure love of Hashem
and His people straight from the heart.
That was her secret weapon.
And she was ours.

Renee and Philip Pilevsky

In memory of my spiritual mother
Rebbetzin Esther Jungreis ע״ה

May her memory always be for a blessing.
Thank you for bringing Torah into my life, home and heart.
I am forever changed.
Through your teachings, I see life through a Torah lens
and appreciate that everything comes from Hashem.
Your teachings will live on in my children and, *b'ezrat Hashem*, in their children.
I am eternally grateful to you for your love, devotion, courage,
persistence and passion!
With deep appreciation and love,

Debbie August

In memory of
our beloved Rebbetzin Esther Jungreis ע״ה

who inspired and guided me to Hashem.
Prior to the Rebbetzin awakening my *neshamah*, I was just a Jewish guy.
Thanks to her, now I am a real Jew ... a Yid!
My respect, appreciation and gratitude for the Rebbetzin are boundless, forever.

Shmuel (Marc) Levine
Houston, Texas

Table of Contents

Foreword and Acknowledgments   11
Introduction   15

Prologue

Chapter One: The Prime Minister's Prayer   21

Part 1: 1972-1974

Chapter Two: The Challenge   35
Chapter Three: Hineni — Here Am I!   46
Chapter Four: *"Tzvei Shtick Fleish"*   56
Chapter Five: Madison Square Garden   67
Chapter Six: Footsteps in the Snow   75
Chapter Seven: The Girl From L.A.   87
Chapter Eight: The Reverend's Letter   105

Part 2: 1967 – 1980

Chapter Nine: The American Singer   115
Chapter Ten: In the Tower of the YMCA   124
Chapter Eleven: The Midnight Cry of King David's Harp   130
Chapter Twelve: A Tale of Two Bands   138
Chapter Thirteen: The Hineni Medallion   152
Chapter Fourteen: The Shofar of Bergen-Belsen   160

Part 3: 1806-1939

Chapter Fifteen: The Chasam Sofer's Letter 171
Chapter Sixteen: The Angelic Prescriptions 180

Part 4: 1943-1956

Chapter Seventeen: The Csenger Tefillin 199
Chapter Eighteen: The Belzer Rebbe's Mandate 208
Chapter Nineteen: The Beis Medrash Maternity Ward 212
Chapter Twenty: Zeide's One Request 219
Chapter Twenty-One: The Boxer's Return 235

Part 5: 1955-1980

Chapter Twenty-Two: The Rabbi's Secret 247
Chapter Twenty-Three: The Rebbetzin's Viewpoint 261
Chapter Twenty-Four: Camp Naarah 269
Chapter Twenty-Five: The Tongue Reader 275
Chapter Twenty-Six: The Syrian Connection 287
Chapter Twenty-Seven: Sandwich in the Sky 295
Chapter Twenty-Eight: The Question
    That Wouldn't Go Away 300
Chapter Twenty-Nine: Ava'leh 315
Chapter Thirty: The Key to Kiruv 324
Chapter Thirty-One: The Actress 330

Part 6: 1980-1995

Chapter Thirty-Two: The Breakup Artist 337
Chapter Thirty-Three: The Marriage Counselor 346
Chapter Thirty-Four: The Lebanese Purim Party 354
Chapter Thirty-Five: My Rebbi the Rebbetzin 366
Chapter Thirty-Six: The Little Csenger Sefer Torah 386
Chapter Thirty-Seven: Seder Night Story 400
Chapter Thirty-Eight: *"V'nafsho Keshurah V'nafsho"* 405

Part 7: 1987-1996

Chapter Thirty-Nine: *New York Magazine* 411
Chapter Forty: "Good Morning America" 424
Chapter Forty-One: A Tale of Two Promises 434
Chapter Forty-Two: The Taxi Driver's Rebuke 451
Chapter Forty-Three: The Reporter 460
Chapter Forty-Four: Four Mitzvos 466
Chapter Forty-Five: *"Kumu L'avodas HaBorei"* 473
Chapter Forty-Six: A Perfect Man Prepares 481
Chapter Forty-Seven: The Bride and Groom Arrive 490
Chapter Forty-Eight: Salute of the Ducks 496

Part 8: 1998-2016

Chapter Forty-Nine: The Chaim Shlomo Siddur 507
Chapter Fifty: Getting on Jackie's Nerves 512
Chapter Fifty-One: The Presidential Invite 520
Chapter Fifty-Two: The Equestrian 531
Chapter Fifty-Three: The Struggle 541
Chapter Fifty-Four: "Jewish Ammunition" 552
Chapter Fifty-Five: Whisper of Love 562
Chapter Fifty-Six: "T" Is for Tiffany 568

Part 9: 1995-2016

Chapter Fifty-Seven: Visits to a World Long Gone 585
Chapter Fifty-Eight: Family First 594
Chapter Fifty-Nine: The Unexpected Bris 612

Part 10: 2012-2016

Chapter Sixty: The Ballerina 623
Chapter Sixty-One: *Hazos* Rebbetzin Jungreis? 633
Chapter Sixty-Two: The Zeide's *Yaaleh* 646

Afterword 650

Photo Credits

Menachem Adelman

Bottom Line Marketing Group

Calligraphix

C-SPAN

Mrs. Barbara Handler Goldgraben

Golding Design

Shimon Golding

Hineni Archives

Mrs. Debby Jacobs

Mrs. Barbara Janov ע״ה

The Jerusalem Post

The Jewish Press

Rabbi Dov Ber (Beryl) Jungreis

Mrs. Goldie Jungreis

Rabbi Yaakov (Jacob) Jungreis

Ken Lieberman Laboratories

Nassau County Police Department

The Natural Lens

Yisroel and Leah Neuberger

Mrs. Marilyn Salem

Mishpacha Magazine

The White House

Foreword
and Acknowledgments

*I*t's hard to believe that over three years have passed since the *petirah* (passing) of our beloved mother, our teacher, our source of light, our inspiration.

To us, Rebbetzin Esther Jungreis was our biological Ima; to tens of thousands throughout the world, she was their spiritual Ima, she was **THE REBBETZIN**. Countless people have told us that with the passing of the Rebbetzin, they too feel like they lost *their* Ima, their Torah Ima, their Bubby.

How proud we were as young children — and even later in life — to be introduced as the Jungreis children. People would always ask, "As in the Rebbetzin?" And we would proudly answer, "Our mother!" And they would universally respond, "How lucky!" Indeed, we were. What a *zechus* to grow up in a home where our Abba, Harav Meshulem HaLevi *zt"l*, and our Ima *a"h* gave us a *derech hachaim*, a path in life, and created "footprints" not just for us, but for our children and grandchildren.

Despite our Ima's exhaustive schedule and worldwide travels to awaken Am Yisrael, she was never too tired to listen to each of us with all her heart, to make us smile, and to give us the strength that each of us needed during challenging times. How eternally grateful we will always be for Ima's devotion, compassion, commitment, advice, and — most importantly — her berachos and her tefillos.

Our Ima was the bedrock of our family. She was a strong link in the *mesorah* of our holy Zeides and Bubbas. She made us understand from where we came, and our responsibility to carry on in the holy traditions of our ancestors.

Over the past few years, so many friends and admirers of the Rebbetzin have reached out to us, to share their stories about how the Rebbetzin transformed their lives through her singularly unique blend of charisma, warmth, love, and teaching. They encouraged and inspired us to undertake this monumental project of chronicling the Rebbetzin's life, her vision, her historic achievements, and the legacy that she left all of us.

This book is not merely a biography. Through the amazing stories in this book, you will connect yourself to the precious legacy that the Rebbetzin left us. It lays out in simple yet majestic words how much one person can accomplish when dedicated to a mission that one totally believes in, and follows through as if one's life depends on it. In this case, it was not just Ima's life that depended on it; it was also the lives of tens of thousands of searching *neshamos* who needed to be brought back to Torah and Yiddishkeit. We have no doubt that Hashem chose to spare our Ima from the horrors of the Holocaust so that she could come to these shores and save thousands of *Yiddishe neshamos* — and all of their future generations — from disappearing as a result of assimilation and the spiritual Holocaust that was engulfing our people.

It is our privilege to bring our Ima's story to the broader public. However, for a project like this to progress from concept to reality does not just happen on its own. It took the collective efforts of numerous individuals — each bringing his or her skillset of talents and passion to the project, and combining them into a beautiful harmony of ideas, words, and finally, a book.

We have tremendous *hakaras hatov* (gratitude) to all of our partners who helped bring this book to fruition. We know that our Ima is looking down from her lofty place in the eternal world; that she joins us in extending *hakaras hatov* — a *middah* (trait) that was so fundamental to her and permeated everything that she did.

We thank **Rabbi Nachman Seltzer**, one of the most celebrated writers of our time, for truly bringing to life our Ima's very essence, her vision, her accomplishments and her legacy. Although Reb Nachman never interviewed the Rebbetzin in person, through his painstaking research, extensive interviews with scores of individuals, and creative and inspiring writing style, the Rebbetzin's story comes "alive" with radiant fullness on every page in this book. While we had never met Reb Nachman prior to collaborating together on this book, we are delighted that we have found a new friend, and created a meaningful and enduring bond.

We are grateful to **Andrew and Shannon Penson** for dedicating **THE REBBETZIN**. The Pensons' ongoing appreciation to the Rebbetzin for igniting the *pintele Yid* in their entire family's *neshamos* knows no limits. We thank **Philip and Renee Pilevsky, Glenn and Debbie August, and Shmuel (Marc) Levine**, each of whom have been deeply affected by the Rebbetzin's love, guidance, and teaching, for their major dedications that enabled this project to go forward. **We are grateful to all of those who chose to dedicate chapters in this book**, as a measure of gratitude and respect for everything the Rebbetzin has meant to their lives. **We are thankful to all those who gave of their time to be interviewed**, who shared stories and vignettes, all of which helped shape the final product that we are so proud to present.

It is difficult to commit to words the appreciation that we have for the premier Jewish publishing house, **ArtScroll/Mesorah**, and in particular for its President, **Rabbi Gedaliah Zlotowitz,** and the entire ArtScroll team. From the moment that the concept of producing a biography of our Ima saw the light of day, it was Reb Gedaliah who jumped on it and encouraged us with unrelenting enthusiasm to move ahead. We sensed the passion in his voice, the zeal, the urgency, and the imperative to tell the story of our Ima's life — from her birth in Szeged, her suffering through the Holocaust and of her triumph over evil as she arrived in the United States and blazed a path of reconstructing that which was destroyed in Europe.

Thanks to **Reb Sheah Brander and Reb Eli Kroen** for their masterful creative and design skills, for executing a most striking and imaginative cover, and for bringing out the best in the many photos that are included in this book. **Reb Mendy Herzberg** ably shepherded this project through its many technical and production steps until completion. We are grateful to **Mrs. Estie Dicker** for typesetting the manuscript with care and precision and for being available at any time, during the day or night, for the numerous edits and revisions. Thanks also to **Mrs. Rivka Weiss**, who assisted in the typesetting. The editing skills of **Mrs. Judi Dick and Mrs. Esther Feierstein** added greatly to the richness of the final product, as did the proofreading of **Mrs. Tova Finkelman**. And, we greatly appreciate the advice and counsel of our good friend, **Reb Avrohom Biderman**. It has been an elevating experience working with every member of the ArtScroll team.

Thanks also to **Reb Menachem Adelman**, photographer extraordinaire, for his creative photography and for supplying several photos from his archives.

This project could not have been undertaken and brought to completion without the unwavering support of our families. **We thank our spouses, Rabbi Shlomo, Rivki, Mendy, and Yaffa**, for their guidance, encouragement, and insightful advice through the many months of work that went into bringing this book to the finish line. Truthfully, they are also our "siblings," as Ima always considered them equally as children, and those feelings were mutually felt by all. We are especially grateful to Shlomo, whose decades of administrative and organizational skills as Executive Vice President of Agudath Israel of America, combined with his intense involvement with every phase of this project, enabled it to move along in an efficient and well-organized manner.

Lastly, we are deeply grateful to Hashem for giving us the privilege of bringing this masterful work to the broader world. We know that our Ima's shoes are impossible to fill. As one of the *gedolim* (Torah giants) of our time related to us when we were sitting *shivah*, "The Rebbetzin was not just a *yechidah* (singularly unique individual) in this generation. She was a *yechidah bekamah doros* (in many, many generations)." Yet, we have been mandated by our Ima to strengthen ourselves to perpetuate her life's work by continuing to build, reach out, and teach. With Hashem's help, and the ongoing inspiration provided by so many whose lives our Ima touched, we will succeed, and this will be not only her legacy, but her greatest *nachas* as well.

We are confident that many, many thousands will gain from this book, and will learn from our Ima's life story, so richly told on every page, to emulate her ways, and in particular her boundless love for every Jew. We pray that in this *zechus*, may it bring an *aliyas neshamah* (eternal merit) to our dear Ima, and in the merit of her transformative life's accomplishments, may the coming of Mashiach be hastened, speedily, in our days.

With blessings of friendship and gratitude,

Chaya Sora Jungreis Gertzulin   *Rabbi Yisroel Jungreis*
Slovie Jungreis Wolff   *Rabbi Osher Jungreis*

Rosh Chodesh Adar 5780
February 2020

Introduction

I visited the United States to conduct interviews for the Rebbetzin Jungreis biography during February 2019. It was snowing on the day I arrived and it was snowing on the day I left. On the second to last day of my visit, Chaya Sora Gertzulin, the Rebbetzin's oldest child, suggested that we drive to Beth David cemetery in Elmont, Long Island, so that she would be able to introduce me to her mother and tell her that I would be writing the book about her life.

I thought that was a wonderful idea.

We drove out to the Island on Tuesday morning. It was a frigid day and it was difficult to stay outside for longer than a few minutes at a time. We made good time to the cemetery, driving through its narrow intersecting streets until we reached the plot of land containing the final resting places of the Rebbetzin's parents, Rav Avrohom HaLevi and Rebbetzin Miriam Jungreis, as well as the Rebbetzin and her husband, Rav Meshulem HaLevi Jungreis.

We said Tehillim by the *kevarim*, the icy wind buffeting us from every direction, reddening our cheeks and numbing our faces. Chaya Sora introduced me to her mother and said, "Ima, this is Rabbi Nachman Seltzer. He will be writing the book about your life."

"Rebbetzin, Rav Meshulem, Zeide and Mama," I said to them, "it is a great privilege for me to have been chosen to write your book. I will do my best."

We left Beth David shortly afterward.

In the car we discussed the fact that it happened to be Purim Kattan, the day in Adar I on which Klal Yisrael remembers Mordechai and Esther — one month prior to Purim.

The significance of it being Queen Esther's day was undeniable, as was virtually every detail of the entire trip.

I have been fortunate to write many books. I have met numerous people from all walks of life. But there was something incredibly unique about working on **"The Rebbetzin."** When Rabbi Gedaliah Zlotowitz and Reb Shmuel Blitz first approached me with the possibility of working on this project, it was obvious how excited they were about it.

As was I.

The excitement continued unabated through every step of the way. I met Rabbi Shlomo Gertzulin and his wife Chaya Sora — the Rebbetzin's daughter and son-in-law — in Israel for a preliminary interview. Ten minutes later we had already become good friends. It was beautiful to see their commitment to preserving the Rebbetzin's legacy and the memorable way she lived her life.

As I stated earlier, it was snowing outside when I landed in America, but the warmth I encountered everywhere I went dispelled the cold. Each person I spoke with and interviewed (and there were dozens) was overcome with emotion at the opportunity to discuss and commemorate the Rebbetzin's undeniable impact on their lives.

Seeing the Rebbetzin's family up close and meeting the rest of her children was a wonderful experience. It was crystal clear that the "Hineni" vision lives on in every facet of the Jungreis family — immediate and extended. Meeting the Rebbetzin's children — Chaya Sora, Rabbi Yisroel, Slovie and Rabbi Osher (and their children and grandchildren) — brought home to me what truly amazing role models the Rebbetzin and her husband both were to have raised a family that feels such extraordinary responsibility for the Jewish nation.

But there was more to come.

Each person I met clearly felt that their relationship with the Rebbetzin was one of the most pivotal components of their lives.

As for me, I felt honored to have been chosen to write about such a legendary individual, the esteemed woman known throughout the world as **The Rebbetzin.**

As I boarded my return flight to Eretz Yisrael, I couldn't help but reflect over the previous whirlwind week and a half. It had been an incredible experience for me as I interviewed many of those who had been so close to the Rebbetzin throughout her life. There was no question in my mind that Rebbetzin Esther Jungreis had been one of the most phenomenal people to grace our nation in the last century. She wore her mantle with grace, charm, nobility and righteousness — changing the lives of thousands in the process.

Since the Rebbetzin is no longer with us, I was able to interview her through her beautiful books, gleaning much vital information about her life, the people who influenced her, her *hashkafah*, her worldview and her decision-making process. *The Jewish Soul on Fire, The Committed Life, The Committed Marriage,* and *Life Is a Test* were all invaluable resources, as were several of her columns from *The Jewish Press*, all of which provided me not only with her history and stories, but more so a window into Rebbetzin Jungreis' pure *neshamah*.

Many of the names mentioned in this book have been changed. An asterisk beside a name serves as an indication for when that is the case.

The Rebbetzin passed away in 2016 at the age of eighty. The founder of Hineni and a pioneer of the worldwide *kiruv* (outreach) movement, she was a prolific writer of articles and author of books, a media personality, a Torah teacher, confidante, friend to many, *shadchante* par excellence, newspaper columnist, counselor of wise advice, wife, mother, grandmother and great-grandmother.

She was one of the most fascinating, charismatic and spiritually inspiring individuals in recent history.

It was now time to write her story.

The story of **The Rebbetzin**.

Rabbi Nachman Seltzer

February 2020 / אדר תש״פ
Ramat Beit Shemesh

Prologue

My brothers and I agreed that the one word that stands out most in our minds from our Holocaust experiences was "Schnell." The Nazis were constantly yelling, "Schnell! Schnell! — Quickly! Quickly!"

We had to leave our homes quickly.

We had to climb into the cattle cars quickly.

We had to march from the railroad station to Bergen-Belsen quickly.

We had to ready ourselves for roll call every morning quickly.

And they stuffed and shoved millions of our people into the gas chambers — quickly.

Oy Tatte Zeese, if it was so urgent for those terrible reshaim to quickly bring about our demise, then surely, Almighty G-d, Tatte Zeese, it should be even more urgent for You to bring us, Schnell! Schnell! — Quickly! Quickly! — to our redemption speedily in our day.

We, Your children, are very tired — two thousand years is a very long time.

With love of Torah and Israel,

Rebbetzin Esther Jungreis
from "Life Is a Test"

I might be the Rebbetzin of Bnei Brak, but you, Rebbetzin Jungreis, are the Rebbetzin of the world.

Rebbetzin Batsheva Kanievsky

CHAPTER ONE
The Prime Minister's Prayer

*T*he Rebbetzin traveled to Eretz Yisrael on numerous occasions. Every trip brought her in contact with more people and made her more of a well-known personality throughout the land.

During the 1982 Lebanese War, the Rebbetzin was invited by the Israeli Army to give *chizuk* to the soldiers at various IDF outposts in Lebanon. While in Lebanon, the call came from Yechiel Kadishai, reaching out to her from the office of Prime Minister Menachem Begin.

The Rebbetzin with Prime Minister Menachem Begin

The Rebbetzin with Rebbetzin Batsheva Kanievsky

"The Prime Minister would like to see the Rebbetzin," he said.

"She'll be there as soon as possible," the driver replied.

A day later, their jeep finally reached the outskirts of Yerushalayim. The Rebbetzin, Slovie and Barbara Janov (who had accompanied the Rebbetzin to Lebanon as she always did) insisted on returning to their hotel before driving over to meet Prime Minister Begin. It was one thing to visit an array of army bases after traveling in a jeep for days on end. But for a visit to the Prime Minister of Israel, the Rebbetzin (and the rest of them) needed to go back to her hotel and change.

A few hours after returning to Yerushalayim saw the Rebbetzin, her daughter Slovie and Hineni's Executive Director, Barbara Janov, exiting

The Rebbetzin with Prime Minister Ariel Sharon

the Plaza Hotel and being driven to the Prime Minister's office in the Rechavia section of Jerusalem, not far from the hotel.

That very morning they had been driving through the north, past the scenic views and tall trees, past the hiking trails and rushing waterfalls. Now they were back in the city. It was a different world. Homes were homes. There were gardens and cars. Here lived the businessmen and the politicians, the diplomats and the famous intellectuals and writers. It was an old neighborhood with a fascinating past.

The Prime Minister was waiting for the Rebbetzin. He welcomed her into his office, showing her tremendous respect, telling her, "*Kavod HaRabbanit*, Am Yisrael needs you and Eretz Yisrael needs you."

They conversed for a while, their fascinating conversation meandering in numerous directions.

"*Kavod HaRabbanit*," the Prime Minister said at last, "I want to share my most personal tefillah (prayer) with you. When I daven to Hashem in my most serious moments, I always make sure to use the words of Tehillim, asking and beseeching the Master of the world with the prayer, '*V'ruach kadshecha al tikach mimeni.*'

"I beg Hashem, and I tell Him, 'This is my greatest tefillah and my greatest wish. Really, it's the only thing I ask of You — *v'ruach kadshecha al tikach mimeni* — please, please do not remove the spirit of Your holiness from me.'"

The Rebbetzin with Prime Minister Benjamin Netanyahu

The Rebbetzin with Knesset Speaker Yuli Edelstein

The Rebbetzin understood him. It took so much out of Menachem Begin to serve in the position of prime minister. He was a man with integrity, a man who possessed a measure of *yiras Shamayim* (fear of Heaven), a man who did his best for his country and was appreciated and revered by many.

The Rebbetzin would never forget the Prime Minister's prayer.

Neither would Slovie Jungreis Wolff.

After all, it's not every day that a teenage girl from the Five Towns has the opportunity to meet with the Prime Minister of Israel.

The Rebbetzin with Jerusalem Mayor Uri Lupolianski

The connection between the Prime Minister and the Rebbetzin was deep enough that she sent him an invitation to Slovie's wedding a few years later.

The return telegram was especially warm and personal, filled with blessings to Slovie and her chassan Mendy Wolff, and concluding with a wish for *nachas* for the entire family for all time, and signed, *Menachem Begin*.

On another occasion, the Rebbetzin traveled to meet with Prime Minister Begin at Blair House in Washington, D.C.

Mazel tov telegram from Prime Minister Menachem Begin to Slovie and Mendy Wolff upon their wedding

It was after he'd been at Camp David and was subjected to the most intense pressure imaginable by President Jimmy Carter and Egyptian President Anwar Sadat.

"Rebbetzin," he said, "I just returned to Washington from being tortured."

He was referring to Camp David and the fact that he'd been bullied into giving up control of the Sinai for peace. It was a mark of his great esteem and respect for her that he chose Rebbetzin Jungreis as the person to whom he was able to unburden his heart.

The Rebbetzin had just concluded that first meeting with Menachem Begin and was leaving his office when she was asked to make yet another stop that day. This time the call was not for a tour of army bases or government offices. This time it was a completely different request — a request for the Rebbetzin to come speak to the prisoners at the Ramle Prison for Women.

"Rabbanit," the army officer who was driving her interjected, "this is one invitation you should turn down."

"Why should I turn it down?"

"You just walked out of a meeting with Menachem Begin. A visit to a Ramle Prison for Women is beneath your stature."

"Nothing is beneath my stature," the Rebbetzin retorted. "The girls in Ramle prison are *bnos Yisrael* — Hashem's daughters. I would never turn down such an opportunity!"

"If you insist," he replied dubiously.

They transferred from the jeep to a vehicle that had been sent by the National Prison Authority of Israel. Their group drove out of Jerusalem and down Highway 1 in the direction of Tel Aviv, taking the exit for Ramle — a dusty, half-forgotten city that lies just a hop, skip and a jump from the country's most prestigious neighborhoods, but which might as well have been on a different planet for the endlessly deep chasm that separated the economic classes.

Slovie, who was seated in the back of the van — in the area where prisoners were normally kept under lock and key — would always remember the feeling of shame (despite the fact that she had done nothing wrong) that she experienced when sitting behind bars, though it was a short ride and she was let out as soon as they arrived. There may have been no reason for it, but the shame was still there. The memory of her ride in the prison van would help her have empathy for people in the days and years to come.

Ramle was a city where Jews and Arabs lived together, mainly in squalor. It was a poor city, a city that seemed to have been forgotten by one and all. They drove through the streets, past hordes of children playing in the rubble and the neighborhood peddlers trying to make a sale. It wasn't long before they arrived at their destination.

The Rebbetzin in an Israel Prison Authority paddy wagon on the way to visit Ramle Women's Prison

The Ramle Prison for Women was located in an old stone building that was shaped like a square with a large courtyard in the center. It had been used by the British military as a prison when they ruled the country and it was now being used for the same purpose. Everything was the same — only the masters had changed. If you sniffed the air you could smell the stench of fear. The fear of prisoners. The fear of authority.

It was a scorchingly hot day and they could barely breathe in

the stifling air. Barbara Janov walked beside the Rebbetzin carrying the heavy equipment that she used to record every one of the Rebbetzin's meetings, speeches and classes for future radio use. She was none too happy about where they were, exhausted from the last few days and mumbling to herself in protest.

The Rebbetzin was deep in thought at the time and couldn't respond to her friend because she was at a loss as to what to say to the prisoners and didn't know how she was going to handle the upcoming speech. What could she say to them that would resonate with women and girls who had been through so much in life?

It didn't happen often — but Rebbetzin Esther Jungreis was at a real loss for what to say. Try as she might, she had no idea what to tell the prisoners.

They reached the prison's front gate. Barbara rang the bell. The large gate slowly rolled open, and the Rebbetzin and Slovie stepped over and into the shadowy forecourt. Barbara started forward as well but didn't manage to see the iron bar at the bottom of the gate (due to all the equipment in her arms) and tripped.

The next few moments happened in excruciatingly slow motion.

It was difficult to watch. Barbara went flying over the bar and fell flat on her face, the equipment leaving her arms and going off on a flight of its own. It was all made a thousand times worse by the fact that all the prisoners had been sitting in the courtyard waiting for the speaker, arms crossed and eyes narrowed. The guards rushed forward to help Barbara, who rose from the ground with difficulty, brushed the dust off her clothing and tried to cleanse the scrapes to the best of her ability. If she had been upset before, now you could practically see the smoke emerging from her ears in two thick clouds.

Yet while the Rebbetzin felt a rush of sympathy for her friend, in Barbara's great moment of embarrassment there was a silver lining, for the perfect speech had suddenly entered the Rebbetzin's head, prepared down to the tiniest detail and ready for delivery.

"I would like to introduce you all to my right-hand woman, Mrs. Barbara Janov," the Rebbetzin said to the assembled group of female prisoners when everything had calmed down. The girls sat in the square and met her gaze. They hadn't been expecting the excitement of the last few minutes and weren't quite sure what to make of it all. Who was this woman who had come to speak to them? What did she want? Why had she come?

Barbara Janov pointing to the steel bar on which she tripped at the Ramle Prison

"Let me tell you about Barbara," the Rebbetzin continued. "She is a highly educated woman who has worked in numerous top-level positions. She is also a concert violinist who has performed on some of the most prestigious stages around the world. She is a brilliant woman who is the executive director of my organization. In all honesty I don't know what I would do without her."

Here the Rebbetzin paused.

"In all the years we have been working together, I have never, ever seen her fall, much less take a spill like the one she just took now. But maybe," the Rebbetzin continued, "maybe it was meant to happen right now, right in this very place, to show you all that it is possible for a person to fall — yes, for anyone in the world — and while it is uncomfortable and embarrassing and we try to avoid falling, that's not the important thing.

"The important thing is that when a person falls, that they get back up again, dust themselves off, get up and keep on running.

"That's the important thing and that's my message for today.

"I will now take questions."

The Rebbetzin later said that out of all her programs and speeches in Israel that summer, her brief off-the-cuff speech in the dusty square of the Ramle prison was perhaps the most moving speech of all.

The female prisoners were full of questions for the Rebbetzin. Somehow, despite the language barrier, she had managed to get through to them and they were touched. In the minutes that followed her speech, some of the girls told the Rebbetzin that they wanted to start Torah classes at the prison. Most of all, they were filled with the desire to find their way back to G-d.

But there is always at least one person who remains cold, who doesn't feel the excitement. There was one girl named Sari* who stayed out of the discussion, merely staring at the Rebbetzin with a contemptuous glare on her pretty face.

"This is all fancy talk," she burst out angrily. "Nobody will ever give any of us a second chance. This is our life and this will always be our life! All of you are wasting your time listening to her! Do you really think we will ever be able to repent for the things we've done? Get *real*!"

At that moment another idea miraculously surfaced in the Rebbetzin's mind and she decided to tell the story of Reish Lakish to the prisoners. And so, there in the middle of a boiling hot day in the courtyard of a prison for women, Rebbetzin Esther Jungreis told the group of angry and hurt girls about a famous robber who had met a great rabbi and how their meeting had led to the robber's repentance from his evil ways. The Rebbetzin explained to all the girls that Judaism understood that sometimes human beings are weak — and that they fall — but Judaism also makes it very clear at the same time that a person can always, always return, no matter what — even if he was known throughout the land as the worst bandit and thief!

The message resounded across the courtyard. It was as if she had been speaking through the most powerful microphone — though she had been using nothing other than her natural voice.

"Each and every one of you sitting here today can do teshuvah if you desire. It's up to you. There's a formula to follow just like with everything important in life."

"What's the formula?" one of the girls wanted to know.

So the Rebbetzin explained three components of doing teshuvah as noted in the *machzor* for the Yamim Noraim: teshuvah, tefillah, and tzedakah (repentance, prayer and charity).

"Repentance means taking a good look at yourself in the mirror, admitting where you went wrong, feeling remorseful about your behavior and resolving to never repeat the wrongful act again. In addition, it means that you are willing to make a general commitment to keeping Hashem's commandments, observing Shabbos and living a life of integrity."

Next she explained to the prisoners what prayer was all about, telling them how it worked and that it was supposed to be done on a daily basis, morning, afternoon and night. They had lots of questions and the Rebbetzin had lots of answers.

"You may not even realize it," the Rebbetzin said, "but your *neshamos*, your souls, are very hungry. Your souls need to eat just like your bodies do. The difference is that while food sustains your body, it is tefillah that satisfies your *neshamah*."

The women listened to her every word. You could see from their faces that they were connecting to her on the deepest level. Many of them were crying. The hard looks were gone from their faces, having been replaced with a softness that had been long missing from their eyes. Gone were the tough girls who had sat with arms folded and antagonistic body language when she'd first entered their lives. The Rebbetzin had gone from not knowing what to tell them to finding a connection that would remain with them long after she had returned home.

One of the girls had a question.

"I understand how we can repent and turn to Hashem in prison," she said, "but how will we be able to give charity to others when we have no money of our own?"

The Rebbetzin loved the question; it meant that her words were burrowing deep into the hearts of her listeners, who were seriously considering how to make them part of their lives.

"I will tell you how you can give charity anywhere," she told the girl, and proceeded to explain that giving charity didn't necessarily mean helping others with money, that it was also possible to give tzedakah in other ways. There are so many ways to help.

"You can do volunteer work with troubled girls," she told them. "That is just one way of turning the negative experiences of your life into something positive for someone else, and it is one hundred percent tzedakah."

The conversation between the Rebbetzin and the prisoners at Ramle prison continued for a long time. Somehow, every one of the girls in the prison couldn't get enough of their visitor. Even the girl who had screamed at her fellow prisoners to pay no attention to their visitor had had a change of heart and was now listening to the Rebbetzin with bright eyes, nodding along with everything she said. It was a classic Rebbetzin Jungreis scene.

When it was finally time for them to leave, Sari — the girl who had originally thought the entire discussion a waste of time — approached Slovie, a crumpled piece of paper in her hand.

"Can you do me a favor?" she asked her.

Slovie was more than happy to oblige.

"The girls wanted to ask your mother, but we felt it would be too much of an imposition for such a busy person so we decided to ask you instead."

"It's not an imposition for me and I'm sure my mother would feel the same way. But what do you want me to do for you?"

It was funny talking to these girls, some of whom were much older than her.

"I was a free person for the majority of my life," Sari said pensively, "yet I never managed to find the time to visit the Kotel. I don't even know how to pray. After hearing your mother's words, however, I wrote a note — can you please take it and slip it into one of the cracks in the Kotel in Yerushalayim?"

"I'd be honored to slip your note into the Kotel," Slovie assured the girl.

"Thank you very much," she replied, "but I'd feel much better if you opened my note and read what I wrote. I just want to make sure that it's a good enough tefillah to be put in the Kotel."

Slovie opened the note.

There were three words written inside.

"*Elokim selach li* — Hashem, please forgive me."

The Kosel, with myriad prayer notes in its crevices

"Is that *b'seder*? Is it okay?"

There was a shy, almost pleading look on her face. Slovie was able to see how important this was to her.

"It's more than *b'seder*," she told her. "It's perfect."

Slovie took her note. Later, she would slip it into a crack in the Kotel HaMaaravi and daven for the girls she had met in the Ramle prison on the day her mother taught them about the three steps of repentance: teshuvah, tefillah and tzedakah.

As for the Rebbetzin, she left the prison with Barbara, making the reverse journey over the metal bar that had given her the perfect message, and entered the prison van that would drive them up the steep hills to Yerushalayim and a well-deserved rest.

And as the wheels of their van rolled over the highways of the country she loved so much, the Rebbetzin's mind filled with the incredible images of the last few days and the fantastic journey that had preceded it. And she remembered how it had all begun.

Part 1
1972-1974

We sang there. The Felt Forum was packed! She brought the house down!

Country Yossi

I attended the rally at Madison Square Garden — a teenager who traveled in from Connecticut — and I will never forget that event. How she spoke about the pintele Yid and how I cried like a baby.

Rabbi Hanoch Teller

As she walked onto the darkened stage and stepped over to the microphone, Rebbetzin Esther Jungreis knew that her life would never be the same again — and that she had been born to follow in the illustrious footsteps of her father, grandfather and great-grandfather.

Then the spotlight hit her and she was blinded. For a millisecond she froze, and then her nervousness disappeared and she started to speak. It was as if an angel had descended to earth from heaven — such was the beauty and power of her words.

"You are a Jew..."

CHAPTER TWO

The Challenge

*I*t was rare to walk into the Jungreis kitchen in North Woodmere without finding the homey room filled with all manner of people, young and old, men and women, complete strangers and members of the community. As the people conversed and sought her advice on the widest array of subjects, the Rebbetzin kept busy, moving from task to task, cooking, baking, frying and preparing for Shabbos, a perpetual smile on her face, words of Torah flowing constantly from her lips. It was Yiddishkeit in action, family, children, school, learning, homework, town politics, gefilte fish, and the myriad details involved in establishing what was essentially the first Orthodox shul in the area.

And then everyone at the table would be handed a slice of cake, along with a cup of coffee or juice and a sparkling smile that said, "You are the most important person I know."

That's the way it was in the Jungreis house.

It was the late '60s and the Hineni movement had already begun (in an unofficial capacity) around the Rebbetzin's kitchen table. It was a simpler time, but the cake was delicious, the community was growing and the laughs abounded. Who would have believed that their Rebbetzin was standing poised on the cusp of international stardom? Did anyone dream that the Rebbetzin of a small shul from a neighborhood with but a handful of *shomer Shabbos* families would soon find herself standing and addressing audiences from the most famous stages in the world?

And yet, Rebbetzin Jungreis made the transition from her kitchen table to Manhattan's Madison Square Garden and Jerusalem's Binyanei Ha'uma Convention center as if it were the most natural progression in the world.

Because in all honesty, Esther Jungreis had been preparing herself for her future role every day of her life. And when the time came there was no stopping her.

It began with a beautiful moment that could have been skillfully crafted only by the Master of the World — and it happened at the legendary Pine View Hotel in the Catskill Mountains.

Many of the family's summers were spent with the Rebbetzin lecturing at various Catskill Mountain hotels and resorts. This afforded the Rebbetzin the ability to not only take her immediate family away for the summer, but also allowed her to bring her parents and grandfather Rav Tzvi Hirsch Cohen along as well. Having her parents with her at the hotel gave Esther Jungreis endless pleasure.

The crowds of guests at the hotel were treated to a broad range of lectures from the young and charismatic rebbetzin, who was already then becoming more and more well known for her golden tongue and ability to convey the most complex and compelling ideas using terminology that entered every heart. She was like a surgeon who knew exactly where to make an incision — her operations objects of beauty that changed her listeners' lives without them even understanding when or how. But it wasn't only her speeches that had an effect on the people around her. A lot of the Rebbetzin's magic began when people saw the way she treated her parents.

With the Shabbos candles burning brightly on the sideboard, Esther Jungreis would walk

The Rebbetzin's parents, Rav Avrohom HaLevi and Rebbetzin Miriam Jungreis, known to all as Zeide and Mama

through the Pine View dining room, weaving her way through the tables — all while holding firmly onto the hands of both her father and her mother — as if to testify without speaking, "This is where I come from… This is the well from which you drink…"

To this day, guests of the hotel make a point of mentioning how touched they were by the incredible honor that she bestowed upon her father and mother. And when it came to her speeches — while there were always surprises, some things never changed.

She never began a speech without directing her gaze heavenward and uttering the words, *"Hashem sefasai tiftach u'fi yagid tehilasecha —* Hashem, open my lips, and my mouth will offer Your praise."

That was a prerequisite for sharing her thoughts with others. It came from the Rebbetzin's deep-seated knowledge that ultimately man can only be successful if it is willed from Above. If she wanted her words to emanate from her heart and touch the hearts of her listeners, they had to be preceded by a sincere request.

If you stood beside her in the final moments before she walked over to the microphone, you would see her lips moving in silent prayer as she beseeched the Ribono shel Olam (Master of the world) to allow her words to breach even the most hardened of hearts.

Her pre-speech tefillah was a given.

But there was another definite. And that was the fact that she was seemingly incapable of giving a speech without mentioning the full names of her parents and husband and without giving them credit for her unique abilities to inspire. She didn't view herself as someone who stood alone, but rather as a link in the chain of the Jungreis mesorah — a *yichus* and tradition spanning some of the most distinguished and erudite names in the history of Hungarian Jewry.

On the way home from delivering her speeches she'd inevitably ask Barbara to detour off the quickest route back to North Woodmere, and to drive via Canarsie where her parents lived. It didn't matter if she was driving back from the city or anywhere else. It didn't matter if it was one or two in the morning. She'd always say, "Brooklyn is on the way home. We're stopping off by Mama and Zeide."

As busy as she was, there would always be a detour through Canarsie, to home and parents. It was quite simply the essence of who she was. Home is where the heart lies — so how could it have been otherwise?

Before there was a Hineni building in Manhattan, the Rebbetzin

Zeide's yeshivah, Ateres Yisroel in Canarsie, Brooklyn

delivered her weekly Chumash class at her father's shul, Ateres Yisroel on East 87th Street in Brooklyn. But always at the end of the class — and this was part of her way of fulfilling the mitzvah of *kibbud av* (honoring one's parents) — she'd request that her father stand up and give a berachah to everyone in the room. And even though the people in the room didn't speak Yiddish, Zeide would deliver a short *dvar Torah* and give them a berachah — all in Yiddish. Somehow his words were able to penetrate every heart. It didn't matter that he spoke Yiddish and they spoke English. It didn't matter in the slightest because while the words

The Rebbetzin teaching at the original Hineni School in Zeide's shul in Canarsie, Brooklyn

The Rebbetzin and Zeide at a Hineni School Chanukah Program

he was speaking might have been Yiddish, he was communicating to them with the language of love.

That was the Zeide — a tzaddik who knew how to hug a Yid until he broke through whatever walls they had managed to erect.

The summer months at the Pine View were magical days for the still youthful Jungreis family. Halcyon days. Days of happiness and relaxation. The giant trees swayed in the Catskill breeze and the hills were lush with the greenest grass. The Rebbetzin didn't want to be compensated for her job as the senior lecturer at the hotel. All she wanted was to be surrounded by her family, her entire being glowing when that occurred.

It was the early 1970s and Klal Yisrael was experiencing a rejuvenation. The Holocaust was behind them and thousands of Jews were streaming to the mountains for vacation and plain old family fun. If you would have looked at the people relaxing on the lawn chairs as their children ran like the wind and swam in the lake, you would be forgiven for assuming them the products of a placid American upbringing. But in truth, so many of the vacationers had suffered greatly not that long before in a land across the sea, and their free and easy attitude belied the

Rav Meshulem and Rebbetzin Esther Jungreis in the Pine View Hotel

deep wounds that were hidden just beneath the surface.

For Esther Jungreis, the Holocaust would never be ignored or forgotten. She never failed to utilize her memories from the darkest days in Bergen-Belsen, and of her childhood before that, as a spiritual arrow that allowed her to pierce the armor that was holding people back from growth.

Years later, the Rebbetzin would spark her daughter Slovie's speaking career at the same Pine View hotel where her mother had given so many Shabbos afternoon speeches. Naturally very shy, Slovie had neither the desire nor the inclination for public speaking, but the Rebbetzin knew it was time.

"You're going to give a *shiur* at the hotel," she told her daughter.

"Are you kidding me? There's just no way!"

Slovie was in twelfth grade at the time and the last thing she wanted to do was give a *shiur* at the hotel.

"Ma, I'm not a speaker and I never get up and talk in front of people. I can't do it!"

The Rebbetzin was not fazed by her daughter's reaction.

The Rebbetzin speaking with college students at the Pine View Hotel.

"You have what to give and you will give. This is who we are."

And Slovie found herself standing at the front of a room at the hotel, giving a *shiur*. And the moment she began, she knew that her mother was correct and that she did have what to give and that she would give. Because this was who they were and this was what they did. This was what it meant to be a daughter of Rav Meshulem and Rebbetzin Esther and this was what it meant being a granddaughter of Rav Avrohom HaLevi Jungreis — teachers of Torah all.

Yisroel Jungreis celebrated his bar mitzvah on *Parashas Eikev* in the summer of '72. As on every Shabbos afternoon, the hotel guests rose from their sweet Shabbos naps and straggled out of their rooms and over to the tea room for slices of cake and tall glasses of steaming tea. Then, properly fortified, they made their way to the sweeping lawn where Rebbetzin Esther Jungreis delivered her weekly "Lecture on the Lawn" Shabbos afternoon speech.

Picture the scene.

Over a hundred people sitting on chairs or on the grassy lawn, the sun beginning to descend into the trees, a calm breeze rippling through the leaves — and the ethereal sound of the Rebbetzin's voice as she put forth her weekly message from the Torah.

"It is *Parashas Eikev*," she began. "The word *eikev* means heel. However, it can also refer to a person's footsteps."

Slowly but surely she built a beautiful edifice aimed at illustrating her point: Klal Yisrael's collective obligation to follow in the footsteps of their ancestors. It was a clarion call to everyone listening to her, her wish and berachah for them; and at the same time, it was a message to her son, the bar mitzvah boy, to follow in the ways of his parents and grandparents — to seize the torch and hold it high for others to follow.

"As a Holocaust survivor," she said, and total silence instantly reigned on the great lawn, "I cannot tell you how much I am pained by what I see happening all around us. We lost so many millions of Yidden in Europe to the Nazi murderers. But instead of rebuilding our nation, instead of our fellow Jews returning to their Father in Heaven — so, so many of our brothers and sisters are being lost to assimilation. I cannot describe the pain this causes me. It goes beyond all words! It's a Holocaust of the soul!"

Her words hung in the resort air, resolute, uncompromising, authentic

— committed to telling the truth in the most honest way.

There was a very large crowd of people listening to her speak that Shabbos afternoon. Many of them were students belonging to a well-known organization, an organization with considerable financial resources at its disposal. She looked at them from where she stood. A group of young people: confident, self-assured, concerned with the future of the Jewish people. And Rebbetzin Jungreis felt a crushing surge of sadness.

"I see you sitting here," she said to them, "and I don't understand. Don't you see what's happening around you? Don't you see how many members of the Jewish people are disappearing before your very eyes? Don't you know that the American intermarriage statistics will end up rivaling the numbers of the Holocaust if nothing is done about it!"

The words were tough and they hit hard.

There was complete silence on the lawn for a few seconds as the students allowed the Rebbetzin's words to percolate.

Finally one of them responded.

"Clearly you want us to do something," he said, "but I'm at a loss to understand what. What would you like us to do?"

"If I had your organizational clout, if I had your power... Let me tell you what I would do, my friend. I would get on a train and travel to Manhattan where I would book a venue like Madison Square Garden.

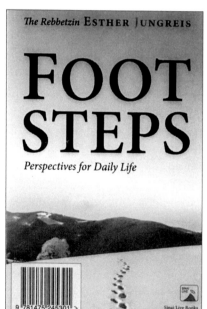 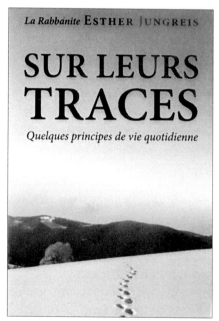

The Rebbetzin's book *Footsteps*, English and French editions

And then, once the Garden was booked, I would advertise like crazy and invite the entire Jewish world to attend the event — and I wouldn't even charge them to come — because I know how Jewish people feel about having to pay to go to shul. That's what I would do if I had the resources!

"The event I would organize, if only I had the means, would be completely free! I would advertise in all the papers and let the Jewish world know that our doors are open and all are welcome! Can you imagine how incredible it would be if thousands of Jewish people would be able to gather together and say as one that we are here to fulfill the word of G-d and to keep the Torah and do Hashem's mitzvos? Can you imagine the spiritual power of thousands of Jewish people reciting the prayer of *Shema Yisrael* in unison? Could such a gathering, such an event, fail to change and alter the universe as we know it?"

Of course, nobody was able to ignore the truth in what the Rebbetzin was saying.

Her passion was genuine and just and everyone believed that she would do exactly as she'd said, if only she were able. They all wanted to help — they were excited too. But she knew that their excitement would fade and they would forget all about her major speech by the time Motza'ei Shabbos rolled around and they wanted to go out and buy pizza.

She finished speaking soon afterward and the crowd dispersed slowly, the effect of her powerful words still lingering on every face. The men headed to the hotel shul for Minchah and everyone's thoughts turned toward the third meal of the day. It had been a grand speech as usual. The Rebbetzin was something else.

And so it all came to an end.

But the reality was completely different. Because everything was about to begin. The pile of coals had been arranged. Now the only thing needed was for someone to strike a match.

Yisroel's afternoon bar mitzvah affair was scheduled for a few weeks later at Terrace on the Park in Queens, New York. While Rabbi and Rebbetzin Jungreis would come to know an incredible number of people over the next forty-odd years, even at this point, the guest list was very full, with a very nice showing from their North Woodmere Ohr Torah shul. The band was in full swing and the guests took to the dance floor where they energetically surrounded the bar mitzvah boy, singing along to the Jewish musical hits of the '70s.

And then the ballroom was filled with the catchy chords of Reb Shlomo Carlebach singing his brand-new rollicking hit *"Yisrael Betach BaShem"* (the Nation of Israel trusts in Hashem). It was especially apropos considering the name of the bar mitzvah boy. The room was on fire with the power of a tune that is still being sung so many decades after its initial release. The music swirled to a crescendo, but nobody wanted to stop dancing. This was their way of showing gratitude to their beloved Rabbi and Rebbetzin — the spiritual leaders who guided them, charting a clear course for them to follow. Who among them hadn't benefitted from the smiling wisdom of their beloved Rav Meshulem? Who among them hadn't sought guidance or solace at one time or another around the Rebbetzin's kitchen table?

The Jungreis family had given them so much and nobody wanted the dancing to stop. But eventually it came to an end and the guests began leaving the dance floor, still on a high from the lively music, everyone in the best of moods.

They were sitting at the round tables when they heard Reb Shlomo Carlebach making an announcement. It was obvious that he had something important to say.

"Mazel tov to the Jungreis family," Reb Shlomo announced with a radiant smile. "I just wanted to let everyone know that the Rebbetzin is going to be gathering all the Jewish people together at a major event in the near future!"

The room was filled with a shocked silence.

Nobody had been expecting such an announcement in the middle of Yisroel's bar mitzvah — least of all the Rebbetzin, who hadn't asked anyone to announce anything and wasn't sure how to react.

However, Reb Shlomo wasn't finished.

"As everyone knows, the Jewish people don't push off doing mitzvos. That's why," he paused, "the first meeting to kick off the Rebbetzin's major upcoming event will be held this very evening — tonight, after Yisroel's bar mitzvah — at the Jungreis home in North Woodmere. Everyone is invited!"

The Rebbetzin's first reaction to the announcement was one of amusement. It hardly seemed like a serious idea.

But as Esther Jungreis looked around Terrace on the Park's crowded ballroom, she saw the expressions on the faces of those around her:

Sunday, April 10, 2022

A VERY SPECIAL HAPPY HOUR WITH MUCH TO CELEBRATE
NEXT WEDNESDAY APRIL 13, 2022 AT 4:30 PM.

Let us join together outside if weather permits or at the Arbor
Cafe to celebrate Jean Simm's 91st birthday which was last
Wednesday and the fact that Kitty Gregg is back at Broadmead
in Hallowell.

If the table is out by the Burton bench, we're good to go outside.
Either way bring yourself, something to drink and a treat to share
if you like.

Willy Sydnor
R5
443-240-9355

surprise, followed by a great eagerness for such an event. Knowing instinctively how to read people, she could sense a true yearning for the kind of gathering they knew she could provide, as if this was the very thing for which they had all been waiting.

The Rebbetzin was used to being asked to scrutinize other people's souls, other people's *neshamos*. Yet on that sweltering Labor Day weekend in 1972, she peered into her own soul, into her own *neshamah*, and she asked herself, "Could it be that the time has really come?"

Rav Meshulem HaLevi Jungreis

She looked at her husband, the soft-spoken tzaddik Rav Meshulem, the tall man with the ever-present shy smile, and he gave her a look — telling her without words that he was fully committed to sharing her vision, and would stand by her side every step of the way. She sought her father's eyes next, finding them amid the tangle of people. He too gave her a look — a look that contained his every hope for his daughter and his absolute confidence and knowledge that she could go on to change the world if she only tried.

And Rebbetzin Esther Jungreis squared her shoulders, pulled herself up to her full height of 4'9", and took the next step toward the pivotal moment that was soon to come. She had spoken many times before. She had addressed packed auditoriums on many occasions. But now it was happening in her home town — and there was no way in the world that she would stand in its way.

It was a go.

The sky was the limit.

CHAPTER THREE
Hineni — Here Am I!

*I*t is not easy for people to get away for bar mitzvahs, weddings and sheva berachos, the celebrations of happiness that make up the fabric of our lives. And even when we do get away, in many cases, we are waiting for the moment when we can wish the *baal simchah* mazel tov, collect our cars and go home.

Not that night.

In an astounding turn of events, instead of leaving Terrace on the Park and returning home after a long afternoon of celebration, the guests gravitated toward the Jungreis home. It was already nighttime but nobody was tired. There was no time to be tired. Something big was happening and nobody was thinking about sleep. They sat around the kitchen table — yes, the very same kitchen table where it had all begun — and got to work.

"Aren't you tired?" the Rebbetzin asked her visitors, offering them coffee and tea. Nobody was hungry — not after the bar mitzvah celebration just a few hours earlier.

"Tired?" someone asked her incredulously. "How could we be tired? We're sitting down to begin planning 'The Jewish event of the century.' There's no time to be tired! We'll be tired when it's all over!"

That was the feeling in the air. This was going to be very big. The Rebbetzin had been talking about something like this for a very long time. It seemed like her dreams were finally about to come true.

"Before we begin," someone else spoke up, "I think we need a name. Rebbetzin, you are basically on the verge of creating a brand-new organization — and every organization needs a name. Don't you agree?"

She did.

Looking around the table, she waited to see if anyone had any suggestions for a name.

"I have an idea," one of the men said.

"Go on."

"We want to form a brand-new entity — completely independent of everything else that has already been established. The name should be brand new. I suggest 'Hineni.'"

"Hineni?"

"Yes, Hineni, meaning, 'Here Am I.'"

The Rebbetzin considered the name for a few seconds. And the more she thought about it, the more she loved it. It was original and fresh, yet ancient and traditional. It combined old and new, past and present. So many of the greatest and most famous leaders of the Jewish people had used that word. Avraham, Yitzchak and Yaakov had said it to Hashem. So did Moshe. So did Shmuel HaNavi. All of those tzaddikim — those great, great tzaddikim — had been challenged by Hashem to stand up for their people and taken the step without hesitation.

Now it was her turn.

Was she willing to join the legendary lineup of leaders who said "Hineni"?

The Rebbetzin looked up toward Heaven and said, *"**Hineni, Here Am I.**"*

The Rebbetzin so connected with the idea of Hineni that she asked Mordechai Ben David (MBD) to compose an English song devoted to the concept, thereby crystalizing the meaning of the message via the *olam haneginah* (the world of song). MBD accepted the challenge and composed the famous tune that he would eventually use to headline his iconic album "Hineni" (his first major album). The lyrics were written by Leah Reiss and the album was arranged by the incomparable Yisroel Lamm. With hit songs like *"Ki Lo Yitosh,"* the legendary *"Shema Yisrael"* and the '70's most popular version of *"Od Yeshama,"* MBD's Hineni album put him on the musical map and showed the world he was here to stay.

As always, Rebbetzin Jungreis knew whom to ask.

From the *Hineni* album, released in 1974:

> *Our father Abraham was called by G-d to sacrifice his son,*
> *With the cry of Hineni the deed was done.*
> *Now what will become of our father's devotion?*
> *If we won't say Hineni in our every emotion.*
>
> *Our forefathers smiled as they died in peace,*
> *But the cries they began will never cease,*
> *The words they cried shook the heavens above*
> *They said Hineni, we are here with love.*
>
> *So my brothers, put your faith in the Above,*
> *Say "Hineni," I am ready to serve You with love.*

The song's lyrics touched on the Rebbetzin's personal journey through the valleys of Nazi gehinnom and suffering — from which she emerged determined to say "Hineni" despite it all. Quite simply, it encapsulated her world vision and ensured that the message of "Hineni" would live on forever.

And in the words of MBD himself:

> *"This song was written in 1972 at the request of Rebbetzin Esther Jungreis as she embarked on her mission to spread the light of Hashem and ignite the spark of light in every Yiddishe neshamah, with the founding of the 'Hineni' organization. She traveled the*

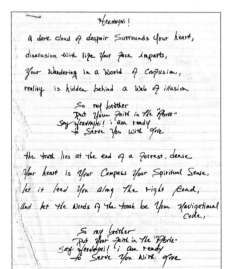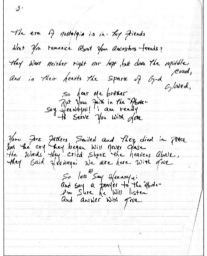

Some of the original handwritten lyrics of the Hineni song

world with the passionate messages she so eloquently delivered, bringing so many lost souls back to their roots."

Rebbetzin Jungreis was also ready to stand before Hashem with the same firm commitment made by so many of her ancestors. At the same time, however, she couldn't possibly take what was happening too seriously.

"Do you know how much it costs to rent a major venue like Madison Square Garden?" she asked the committee.

They hadn't really given it much thought.

Esther Jungreis might have been a dreamer, but she was an extremely pragmatic and practical person at the same time.

A silence filled the homey kitchen as the committee began to realize the unlikelihood of their newfound dream materializing. Madison Square Garden was out of their league. They didn't have a chance.

"Rebbetzin," one of them protested. "You know so many people. Can't you think of someone who would be willing to back you on this?"

But she couldn't.

Slowly but surely the people who had been so excited rose from the table and got ready to leave.

"What about asking Joe Wohl?" one of the group threw out as she left the house. It was a good idea. Joe Wohl was an extremely charitable man who was known to support a wide range of causes. He lived in a beautiful home in Lawrence and there was no question in anyone's mind that Joe Wohl possessed the financial means to back such an event. The only question was whether he would.

"Do you know Mr. Wohl?"

The Rebbetzin shook her head. Though she had of course heard his name, they had never been introduced.

The evening was over. Everyone left the house. Soon only Barbara Janov was left. Barbara Janov — her confidante, the close friend who would stay at the Rebbetzin's side for nearly fifty years. The two of them looked at each other. It had been a long day and night and they were exhausted.

"What do you think?" Barbara asked her mentor, Rebbetzin and dear friend. "Should we try and approach Mr. Wohl?"

The Rebbetzin nodded. "I'll call him tomorrow."

Wishing the Rebbetzin a good night, Barbara went home, leaving

Esther Jungreis sitting at the kitchen table. It took her a long time to fall asleep that night.

Everyone needs a right-hand man. In the Rebbetzin's case, the right-hand man was a woman and her name was Barbara Janov. Janov had been serving as the president of the United Parent-Teachers Association of the Board of Jewish Education of New York when she heard Rebbetzin Jungreis speak. Touched on a deeper level than she had thought possible, Barbara sought out the Rebbetzin. Thus began a relationship spanning almost half a century.

Barbara was not satisfied with paying lip service to the idea of becoming a better Jew. It was more of the *"Naaseh v'Nishma"* (we shall do and we shall listen) variety, and the Janov household experienced a series of major changes as their wife and mother, along with their devoted father Dr. David, led them forward into an authentic Torah life. In a short time, the entire family was frum, the kids had been transferred into religious schools and Barbara was walking around wearing a sheitel!

And she didn't stop there.

Knowing from the second they'd met that her destiny was intertwined with that of Esther Jungreis, Barbara Janov convinced her husband to put their home on the market, and to move into North Woodmere, to a home located a mere three blocks away from that of the Jungreis family. She then quit her teaching position at Queens College

The Rebbetzin with Hineni Executive Director Barbara Janov

and began another job — one that would last for the rest of her life — as the Rebbetzin's devoted assistant, confidante and mentee.

When the Rebbetzin dictated her thoughts for her weekly column in *The Jewish Press*, it was Barbara Janov who typed them and sent them in. When the Rebbetzin began crisscrossing the globe to address Jewish audiences worldwide, it was Barbara Janov who gave out her books. When the Rebbetzin traveled throughout Israel visiting army bases to talk to the soldiers, it was Barbara Janov who videoed the incredible response for posterity in the Hineni archives.

In the case of Barbara Janov, one speech changed not only her life, but the lives of her entire family.

Rebbetzin Jungreis would be able to rely on her friend Barbara for the rest of her life.

The Rebbetzin dialed the number of the Wohl family with trembling fingers. Normally it was the other way around. People usually called her with their needs. But now she needed something from someone else.

The phone rang.

"Hello?"

"Is this Mr. Wohl?"

"Speaking. Who is this?"

"My name is Rebbetzin Esther Jungreis. My husband and I are the Rabbi and the Rebbetzin of the Ohr Torah synagogue in North Woodmere."

"What can I do for you, Rebbetzin Jungreis?"

"There is something of great importance that we need to discuss. When can I make an appointment to see you?"

"What is this about, Rebbetzin?"

"Mr. Wohl, I would like to discuss the future of the Jewish people with you. Is that possible?"

"I'm very busy."

"Even so. It won't take much time and it's very important."

He was silent for a few seconds.

"Okay," he said at last, "I will meet you at my home."

They agreed on a time. Before she hung up the phone, he said, "Please don't be late."

When she got off the phone, the Rebbetzin called Barbara.

"We're in."

"He agreed to a meeting?"

"Yes, this Sunday afternoon."

"What should we do to prepare?"

"Daven, there's nothing else we can do."

They parked outside the Wohl home. Every blade of grass on the spectacular lawns was mowed to precision and the garden was filled with a delightful array of flowers in every color of the rainbow. Barbara and the Rebbetzin exited the car and the two of them walked up the shrub-lined path to the front door. They exchanged a quick smile and then Barbara rang the bell. Moments later, they were being ushered into the living room, where tall windows let in lots of sunlight.

Joe hadn't let the Rebbetzin know that his wife Ronne would be at the meeting — it is very possible that she just decided to take part on the spur of the moment. Whatever the case, it didn't take Ronne Wohl long to make up her mind about Rebbetzin Jungreis. That's the way it is sometimes. You meet a person and you just know that this is someone you want in your life. It was a common reaction people had when they met the Rebbetzin (there was something magical about her), and Ronne was no exception.

Pleasantries taken care of, Joe got right to the point. A successful businessman, he had no time for playing around.

"Okay, Rebbetzin, here we are. On the phone you made it sound as if the future of civilization is hanging on the outcome of this meeting. I'll admit to being curious as to what you have in mind."

"Mr. and Mrs. Wohl," the Rebbetzin began, "thank you for agreeing to see us. I will keep it short. I was born in Hungary and experienced the horrors of the Holocaust along with the rest of my family at a young age. We were given front-row seats at the greatest demonstration of man's basest appetites. Many members of my family did not survive. My parents, siblings and I were sent to Bergen-Belsen, where we suffered terrible degradation, starvation and abuse. Yet through it all, I dreamed of a day when we'd be freed and given the chance to rebuild the beautiful Jewish world that was lost in the killing grounds of Auschwitz, Treblinka and Chelmno.

"It took us a few years until we were able to leave the blood-soaked earth of Europe for the friendly shores of the United States."

Esther Jungreis was crying now. A genuinely emotional person, she was moved to tears very easily. Now too, she couldn't help herself as she recounted her memories from the years of suffering. In most cases her tears moved people and broke through any resistance they may have had to her message. She didn't cry on purpose — the tears emanated from her *neshamah*.

Struggling to get her emotions under control, she continued speaking despite the tears.

"In America things were mostly different, even though my father's shul was set on fire, breaking our hearts all over again. But for the most part, we were given the opportunity to start afresh and to rebuild our lives, while helping the Jewish community in our midst. My parents have had a shul for years. My husband and I are doing the same thing.

"But for a long time now I have been wanting to do more. To reach more Jewish people. To help stem the tide of assimilation. How is it possible that we are losing millions of Jews to intermarriage after our terrible losses during the Holocaust! It's a tragedy beyond all words!"

She was speaking with urgency now.

"You asked me to tell you why I am here."

She looked at her hosts.

"I have come here to meet with you because I want to create an event that will bring Jews together. Not a little event in a neighborhood social hall. I want to book a venue like Madison Square Garden in Manhattan. We will advertise everywhere. People will stream to the event. It will be like nothing that was ever done before. And it will be free. No charge. It's bad enough that Jewish people have to pay for the privilege of attending services on Rosh Hashanah and Yom Kippur. This event will be completely free.

"And when the hall is filled with Jewish people, I will speak to them and share my message, and I hope that G-d will grant me the right words — words that will bring my fellow Jews back to their Creator. I am ready to do whatever I can for the Jewish people. In fact, that's what we will be calling this new organization — '*Hineni*, Here Am I' — in the spirit of the great Jewish leaders who stood before G-d and made the same proclamation in the generations going back to the time of Avraham Avinu and Moshe Rabbeinu!"

She paused for a second before continuing.

"Mr. Wohl. In order for me to turn this dream into a reality, I need a backer. Someone who will take financial responsibility for booking the venue. I am not a wealthy person. If I was, I wouldn't hesitate to do it myself. But I need help.

"Mr. and Mrs. Wohl, will you join me on this historic journey? Will you agree to partner with me to help return the Jewish nation to its Father in Heaven?"

The Rebbetzin was done. She had made her plea. The matter was out of her hands. But looking at Joe Wohl and the unconvinced look on his face, Esther Jungreis felt that she hadn't succeeded in conveying the message. She had done her best, but she feared that in this case, her best wasn't good enough.

She was right.

"I'm sorry, Rebbetzin," Mr. Wohl said. "I'm afraid I won't be able to join you in this venture, but I wish you much success."

Incredibly enough, Joe Wohl was impervious to her charm. Rebbetzin Jungreis would go on to meet international business leaders, media titans, presidents and prime ministers. All loved her. All bought in to her vision.

But the man she was hoping would partner with her on this — her inaugural project in the United States — wasn't seeing it. She was extremely disappointed.

Yet much like in the Purim story, help would come from an unexpected source. Ronne Wohl was not okay with her husband's decision.

"Joe," she said, "if you don't agree to back the Rebbetzin, I will take every piece of jewelry that I own, sell them, and give the Rebbetzin the money myself to back her event! I like the Rebbetzin, I feel connected to what she's doing, and I will make sure her dream gets off the ground, no matter what!"

What could Joe Wohl say after such a speech? Turning to his guests, he said, "You've got yourself a backer."

Joe Wohl wasn't just talk. In the aftermath of that fateful meeting, he would indeed go on to not only cover all the expenses of the original Hineni event at Madison Square Garden with a "blank check," but both he and Ronne became major supporters of both the Rebbetzin and Hineni. In fact, the Jungreis children came to know Mrs. Wohl as "Momma Ronne."

More than that, the support for Hineni didn't stop with Joe and Ronne, who quite simply fell in love with Rabbi and Rebbetzin Jungreis. Their eldest daughter, Elinor, went on to found the Hineni Women's League and served as its president for many years. Elinor and her sisters also opened their homes in Manhattan and hosted events and *shiurim* for many of the Manhattan socialites who would have never had the opportunity to be exposed to Torah. Yet they came and they were amazed by what they heard and nobody left quite the same as they arrived. It would have been impossible.

All that, however, was yet to come.

This chapter has been dedicated
in memory of Mrs. Elinor Wohl ע״ה
Anonymous

CHAPTER FOUR

"*Tzvei Shtiek Fleish*"

*F*inancial backing in place, events began moving in dizzying fashion over the next twelve months. It started with Rebbetzin Jungreis and Barbara Janov taking the Long Island Railroad into Manhattan to get a good look at the hall they would be renting for "the Jewish event of the century." After meeting with officials at Madison Square Garden, Rebbetzin Esther Jungreis signed a contract booking Madison Square Garden's Felt Forum for November 18, 1973. Picking up a pen to sign her name on the contract's dotted line, she felt her hand shake ever so slightly as she scrawled her signature.

"What if nobody comes," a little warning voice shouted in her head. "What if you prepare and advertise and then the room is empty? What then!?"

She wasn't the only one who was nervous.

Chaya Sora Jungreis was in tenth grade at the time and couldn't believe that her mother was actually going ahead with the event.

"Ma," she'd say, "are you sure about this? What if we get to the hall on the day of the event and it doesn't fill up?"

It was a valid fear for a tenth-grader.

(Chaya Sora's fears would prove groundless. Among the overflow crowd were none other than the majority of her classmates from TAG (Torah Academy for Girls), who would never forget what they witnessed that night. In fact, if you happen to chance upon a copy of her twelfth-grade yearbook and open it to Chaya Sora Jungreis, you will see a caption reading, "Say 'Hineni' to CSJ.")

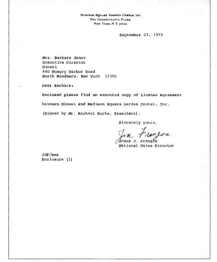

Cover letter from Madison Square
Garden Hineni Contract

Signature page of MSG contract
for Hineni event

By this point, the Rebbetzin was already a prominent figure on the Jewish American national scene. She was the author of a widely read column in *The Jewish Press*, the most popular Jewish newspaper in the country; was a beloved lecturer and speaker; and served as mentor and surrogate mother to everyone in her community and to many elsewhere.

But as busy and popular as the Rebbetzin was, she was still her children's mother, and it was difficult for them to envision her making the monumental leap from her "kitchen table" to one of the most iconic stages in the world.

As for the Rebbetzin herself, she would later recount how she felt after signing her name on the contract that changed everything about her life forever.

"In all honesty, I do not know how I was able to bring myself to sign that contract! I was scared. I was more than scared. I was terrified. This was such a giant step, such an awesome leap into the unknown. So I did what I always did when I had a question. I turned to the great men in my life and asked them for their opinion.

"My father heard me out. His face was calm and comforting, his demeanor strong, his eyes sympathetic. And when he spoke, the words that emerged were exactly what I needed to hear.

"'My dearest child,' he began. 'I want to remind you of something written in the Torah. Think about this verse and you will no longer be afraid. The Torah clearly states: *He shall bless you in everything that you shall **do**.*

"'What do those words teach us?

"'Simply that we do not need to be afraid — the only thing being asked from us is that we *do*. The moment we start doing for Hashem, the heavens will open up and blessing will come raining down on us!'"

The Rebbetzin's husband Rav Meshulem also had something to say.

"Remember the story of Basyah, daughter of Pharaoh, king of Egypt," he said to his wife.

"What do you mean?"

"The Torah tells us that she went down to the river to bathe and she caught sight of a basket floating in the distance. She saw the basket and she had a feeling that she knew what lay hidden within. She wanted to see what was inside the basket, but there was one problem: it was out of her reach; it was humanly impossible for her to pull it to her side. But she stretched out her arm and tried to reach the basket even though there was no way for her to accomplish the goal. And then a miracle happened — Basyah's arm grew longer and longer, and she was able to reach across the wide expanse of water and to take hold of the basket in which Moshe Rabbeinu lay.

"What do we learn from this beautiful story?" Rav Meshulem asked his wife. "The answer is simple. We learn that the only thing demanded of us is to stretch out our arms as far as they can go. The moment we do our part, Hashem will take care of the rest."

And the Rebbetzin calmed down.

She knew the things they were telling her. She knew the stories and the messages. But sometimes it helps to hear it all again. Suddenly she was infused with a fresh dose of confidence that Hashem was going to be on her side and that she was making the right decision and need not be even a little bit afraid.

Was she doing the right thing?

The little voice inside her heart told her yes.

And so she booked the hall and prepared herself mentally and emotionally. Somehow everything she had been worried about simply fell by the wayside with no trouble at all.

Sometimes at night she dreamed of walking out onto the stage — only to find that nobody was in the audience. Sometimes she imagined what it would be like if the crowd didn't connect to her message.

All of those worries, however, paled beside her greatest fear — the fear that she wouldn't succeed in conveying to the audience the reason she had summoned them in the first place. That was her biggest fear.

So it went in the Jungreis home in the weeks leading up to the big event.

There was something else that needed to occur before she'd feel ready to give the most important speech of her life. It was important to the Rebbetzin that people understand that Esther Jungreis did not stand alone. That she was not operating in a religious vacuum.

In the weeks prior to the event, the Rebbetzin asked her father to accompany her to various *gedolei Yisrael* (Torah Sages). She had a very simple reason for doing this. Although she sensed that the idea of establishing Hineni was correct and on track, there was no precedent or procedure for doing such outreach. She would be groping in the dark and laying the groundwork for others who would follow. But was this the right thing to do?

For her holy mission to succeed, the Rebbetzin needed the support and blessings of the greatest Torah leaders of the day.

Rav Yosef Henkin was the oldest sage of that time. He was also the head of Ezras Torah (a prominent tzedakah organization) and a major Torah personality.

"When should we go see Rav Henkin?" the Rebbetzin asked her father.

Her father, Rav Avrohom Jungreis, explained that the Rav was very old and frail and that it would best if they went to see him as soon as possible. Leaving the hotel where she was staying, she took a bus from South Fallsburg and met her father at the housing project where Rav Henkin lived on the Lower East Side of Manhattan. It was summertime, and it felt as though they were standing on the sun itself. It was hot enough that day to fry an egg on the pavement. Summertime in the scorching city.

Rav Avrohom was waiting for her when she got off the bus.

"Don't be shocked, my child, when you see Rav Henkin," he warned her.

"How bad is it?"

"The Rav is very sick and has lost his eyesight."

Standing in the hallway of the apartment building, father and daughter knocked on the door and waited until Rav Henkin's aide let them in.

"Please have a seat, Rav Henkin will be with you momentarily."

The room was simple — humble. The furnishings were meager. But the bookcases were packed with well-used *sefarim*. Off to the side the Rebbetzin could see a simple, wooden *aron kodesh* (ark) for Rav Henkin's Sefer Torah.

"The Rav has a minyan in the house?"

"Only after he became sick."

Rav Henkin entered soon after. It was very difficult for him to walk, yet he made his way across the room, intent on his destination. Rav Avrohom and the Rebbetzin stood up. It was difficult to see a respected person in such a state. But Rav Henkin had no time for self-pity. It was clear that he was still focused, still busy, still accomplishing.

Rav Henkin and Rav Jungreis embraced. It was clear that they were close friends and felt exceptional warmth for each other. After Rav Avrohom had greeted his old friend, the Rebbetzin's father introduced his daughter to Rav Henkin, explaining that she was in the process of forming a new organization whose goal would be Jewish outreach, and that she had come to the Lower East Side to ask for his blessing for success and *siyata d'Shmaya* (Heavenly assistance).

"My daughter, Rebbetzin Esther, is in the process of organizing a major event at Madison Square Garden," Rav Avrohom explained. "We are hoping that thousands of Yidden will come hear her speak and be drawn closer to Hashem."

Rav Henkin's pale face erupted in a wide smile.

"Any project undertaken for the sake of Hashem will surely succeed. Hashem will be with you and bless you in all your undertakings."

He then veered off script, his next words coming as a surprise. They were directed toward the Rebbetzin and there was no mistaking the urgency of the powerful message.

"Rebbetzin," he said, "I would like you to do one thing for me. When you speak, please tell people what you saw here today. Tell them how you met a rabbi who is old and blind. Tell them that his eyes are no longer able to see and have become '*tzvei shtick fleish* — two pieces of flesh.' Tell them that my body no longer functions. Whatever I know, whatever knowledge I have, I acquired when I was still able to see. Rebbetzin, remind them that the years pass very quickly, and one day every person will find themselves in a similar situation — a situation where their body just disintegrates. I am begging you to share this message. Tell the people to study while they still have the energy and the tools with which to learn Hashem's wisdom."

The Rebbetzin listened carefully to Rav Henkin's message.

"Rebbetzin Jungreis," he concluded, "I give you a berachah that you should be able to teach the Jewish people to have *rachmanus* (compassion) on their souls. People today are always thinking about their health. They are obsessed with being healthy. They exercise and watch their diets. But one day after one hundred and twenty years, we are all going to stand before Hashem for judgment. There will be no body at that time, just our soul 'standing,' as it were, before Hashem. How will our soul be able to stand without a body? Will it have the spiritual muscles it needs?

"May you teach the Jewish people to use their years on earth to strengthen their souls with the proper diet of Torah and mitzvos, so that all of us will be able to stand before the One Above with dignity and pride."

Berachah given, Rav Henkin and Rav Jungreis began to learn together. The Rebbetzin watched as two Torah scholars exchanged words and ideas — one raising a question, the other responding, back and forth, rapid fire. It was like watching two prophets of old learning together as fire danced above them in the sky! And then it happened. Rav Henkin did something he had done a million times before. He reached over, picked up a *sefer* and opened it to the page he needed. That wasn't the interesting part. The interesting part was the fact that he did this without being able to see the words. He couldn't see, he didn't have use of his eyes, and yet he still knew exactly where he was — down to the smallest word on the bottom line.

As if to underscore his earlier statement, Rav Henkin commented, "You have to study while your eyes still see so that you have something to remember when they grow dim."

The Rebbetzin never forgot that conversation or the message he repeated, relating his words in countless speeches over the years.

"Hashem gifted us with an incredible present — the gift of time. It's worth more than anything in the world because it allows us to accomplish our goals and to make a difference. And yet, not only do we not take advantage of the time we are given, we throw it away, as if it's not worth anything. How absolutely tragic!"

Together with her father, the Rebbetzin visited other great rabbis as well. Since it was during the summer and many people were in the mountains, she went to meet Rav Moshe Feinstein in Swan Lake, asking the venerable Rosh Yeshivah for a berachah, which she received.

"Not only will I give you a berachah for success at Madison Square Garden," said the undisputed *gadol hador*, "I will also send my talmidim to assist you on the big night itself!"

It was obvious from his words that Rav Moshe trusted the Rebbetzin implicitly and wanted her to succeed. She was very moved — both by his warm words and by his offer to help her. With a tzaddik like Rav Moshe on her side, could there be any question that she was actively fulfilling the will of Hashem?

The Rebbetzin's visit to Rav Moshe would long be remembered in the Jungreis family, not only because of the gracious manner in which the *gadol hador* welcomed her and the berachah he bestowed, but also due to a series of events that would occur long after his passing.

As a child, Shaindy Wolff accompanied her grandmother the Rebbetzin on a number of her Hineni trips to Eretz Yisrael. Of course, every trip included a visit to the *kever* of Rav Tzvi Hirsch Cohen (the Rebbetzin's mother's father and the author of *Likutei Tzvi*) on Har HaMenuchos. Before leaving Eretz Yisrael at the end of her year in seminary, Shaindy decided to go daven for a shidduch at her great-grandfather's *kever*. She took the bus to Har HaMenuchos. But upon her arrival, she was unable to find the *kever*. Try as she might, and despite having been at the *kever* a number of times, she was unable to locate the grave she was seeking.

With time running out, Shaindy made the decision to daven at a different *kever* instead. It so happened to be that the section she was searching in (the section where her Zeide's grave was located) was near the area where many great rabbis, including Rav Moshe Feinstein *zt"l*, were buried. With the clock rapidly ticking away the minutes until she had to leave, Shaindy decided to daven for a shidduch at the *kever* of the legendary Rav Moshe Feinstein — the *gadol hador* who had given her grandmother a berachah for success at Madison Square Garden decades earlier.

Minutes later, prayers completed, Shaindy left the cemetery and returned to her dorm to catch the taxi to the airport.

Not long after she returned to the United States, a shidduch was suggested for Shaindy by two shadchanim working in tandem — Rebbetzin Esther Jungreis and Rebbetzin Shelia Feinstein, Rav Reuven Feinstein's wife — two wonderful friends who wanted only the best for one another.

Matzeivah of the Rebbetzin's grandfather, Rav Tzvi Hirsch Cohen, on Har HaMenuchos

The chassan? None other than Reb Shlomo Eisenberg, a great-grandson of Rav Moshe Feinstein at whose *kever* she had davened just before leaving Eretz Yisrael.

Rebbetzin Shelia was a young wife when Rebbetzin Jungreis came with her father to ask Rav Moshe for a berachah. She had never forgotten that moment and her father-in-law's incredible berachah to the Rebbetzin. Now with the Jungreis/Eisenberg engagement, everything had come full circle.

As always, the Zeides were unquestionably helping things along.

When the Rebbetzin went to see Rav Yosef Ber Soloveitchik, Rosh Yeshivah of RIETS — Rabbi Isaac Elchanan Theological Seminary (the Rabbinical School of Yeshiva University), he phrased his response to her request for a berachah in a very interesting way. Instead of just giving her a straightforward berachah, Rav Soloveitchik told her that he didn't generally give berachos. He then followed that statement with a berachah that he classified as an *eitzah* (suggestion), using the powerful words, "*Nobody will be able to stop you.*"

(In the years to come, his words rang true for the Rebbetzin on numerous occasions. There were many times throughout the years when the Rebbetzin was nervous before a speech, unsure how her words would be accepted or if the crowd would allow her to speak at all. But her words were always accepted with love and every speech was a success.)

Rabbi Soloveitchik wasn't content with giving her his wonderful *"eitzah."* He had a suggestion to make as well.

Crowd entering Madison Square Garden

"Can I make a recommendation, Rebbetzin?"

"Of course, please do!"

"Here's what I am picturing at the Garden. People will walk inside. There will be a large open space and corridors too — right outside the hall. What if the corridors were lined with booths?"

"What kind of booths?"

"The kind that matter. Mitzvah booths. Every booth will be devoted to teaching the visitors about another important mitzvah. A booth for tefillin, a booth teaching about the mitzvah of mezuzah, a booth about Shabbos. What do you think?"

"I love it."

The Rebbetzin did in fact implement Rav Soloveitchik's idea on the great night in the Garden, where the wide, spaced hallways of the Felt Forum were in fact lined with exactly the kind of booths he had envisioned.

Learning about mitzvos in the Garden lobby

"My talmidim will be at MSG on the great night to help assist your staff at the event," Rav Soloveitchik promised, making the same promise as Rav Moshe Feinstein. And indeed, his students were there just as their rebbi promised, helping to direct people to their seats and to take care of the thousands of details that needed to be dealt with. Most importantly, they were there to answer any questions people had about the mitzvos they were learning about for the first time in their lives.

Three *gedolim*, three different answers.

Rav Henkin gave the Rebbetzin a beautiful berachah and a mission.

Rav Moshe gave her a beautiful berachah and an offer of assistance.

Rav Soloveitchik gave her a beautiful berachah and contributed a groundbreaking idea of his own.

But the Rebbetzin's father still wasn't done. There was someone else they needed to visit before they could go to the Garden. For their last visit to a renowned *gadol*, he took his daughter to see the Satmar Rebbe, the famous Rav Yoelish, who lived in Williamsburg. This wasn't the first time the two of them had met, having shared the same barracks during the years of gehinnom in Bergen-Belsen, in what seemed like a lifetime earlier. Who would have believed that they would not only survive the Nazis, but that little Esther — from the barracks in Bergen-Belsen — would grow up to organize such an event!

Rav Avrohom explained what his daughter wanted to do and the Satmar Rebbe took a great interest in the young rebbetzin's dream of doing kiruv on a grand scale. He then joined the rest of the *gedolim*, giving her a heartfelt berachah of his own as she charted a course through what were still unfamiliar waters.

Only then — having received the blessings and warm wishes of Rav Yosef Henkin, Rav Moshe Feinstein, Rav Yosef Ber Soloveitchik and the Satmar Rebbe — was Esther Jungreis finally ready to make her move.

It took her time and a lot of thought before she was able to decide on the theme of the evening. Eventually, however, she settled on the concept of *Shema Yisrael* — six of the most powerful words known to Klal Yisrael.

But how to bookend the evening with the theme?

The answer when it dawned on her was simple. She would bind it all together with the immense power of music. An Israeli singer/ songwriter named Zvika Pick had introduced his song "*Shema Yisrael*" at the Chassidic Song Festival in 1972, and it had become an instant hit around the country and abroad. It was "*Shema Yisrael*" that the

Rebbetzin chose as the theme song for the first Hineni event, the song that Mordechai Ben David would go on to record and that is still sung around the world today.

Esther Jungreis loved that song.

More importantly, she loved the concept of thousands of Jewish people singing the eternal words of the Shema; and, in essence, it was those simple words that would create a bond between every person in the audience — a bond that was both indescribable and everlasting. The bond of the six magic words of *Shema Yisrael*.

As a *bachur*, Rabbi Moshe Katz (today of Chicago) learned in Yeshiva Chaim Berlin.

"With the news spreading around Brooklyn of the Rebbetzin's upcoming event at Madison Square Garden, there was a major tumult in the yeshivah world. An event the likes of what the Rebbetzin had planned had never been done before."

(As an aside, Rabbi Katz related that he was once in a car with the wife of Rav Avigdor Miller. During the course of the car ride Rebbetzin Jungreis' name came up in conversation. Rebbetzin Miller then told the other people sitting in the car, "My husband respects Rebbetzin Jungreis tremendously, because she accomplishes so much.")

As did Rav Moshe.

And the Satmar Rebbe.

And Rav Henkin.

And Rav Soloveitchik.

They were all on her side. They respected her and supported her — because she had the power to change Klal Yisrael for the better and was willing to do whatever was needed.

And she kept her word. As they believed she would.

This chapter has been dedicated
in memory of Rebbetzin Esther Jungreis ע"ה

Zvi and Judy Klein

CHAPTER FIVE
Madison Square Garden

*T*he day of the event finally arrived. The Rebbetzin woke early, davened a lengthy *Shemoneh Esrei* (the Amidah prayer, which she did every time she prayed) and recited her daily quota of Tehillim.

The phone didn't stop ringing. At some point she stepped out of the picture, leaving the final details in the hands of the very competent Barbara, who was a multitasker par excellence before the word was invented. The evening was to be recorded live and released on record, and Barbara was in touch with the sound engineers who were setting up on site.

The mitzvah booths were in place. The hallways were ablaze with the colors of the booths and the attractive signs explaining the significance of every booth and the mitzvah it represented. The Rebbetzin had been in touch with numerous schools and asked them if they wanted to take

Entrance ticket to Hineni event at Madison Square Garden

part in the program with their own booth. Many institutions had taken her up on the offer. She dubbed the line of booths "A Smorgasbord of Jewish Ideas." And couldn't wait to see and hear how that part of the evening would play itself out.

In addition to everything else they had planned, every person would be given a "Hineni Shopping Bag" upon entering the Felt Forum. The hallway of booths was like a mall filled with mitzvah stores, and the people were being encouraged to take out their "wallets" and go shopping for the treasure of Jewish heritage.

Barbara had been in touch with the orchestra and singers who would be providing the evening's musical interludes, making sure that they knew when to arrive at the hall and that they would have sufficient time for one final rehearsal before the show.

Through it all, the Rebbetzin sat and recited Tehillim, davening for *siyata d'Shmaya*.

Finally it was time to leave for Manhattan. Esther Jungreis got in to the car. She was lost in thought. Usually she had so much to say. But this was not a normal day. This was the culmination of decades of hope and prayer and the dreams of a little girl lying on her bunk in a filthy barracks in Bergen-Belsen.

They entered the city. Traffic was heavy and it took time for them to reach their destination. At last they were pulling up at the world-famous entertainment venue. They found the entrance they needed.

"Who are you?" the security guard asked.

"This is Rebbetzin Esther Jungreis."

The guard checked his list of names and held open the door and they entered the hall. It was still early in the day and the corridors were more or less empty. Here and there a group of boys worked on a booth display. From far away, they could hear the orchestra tuning up on the stage.

The Rebbetzin entered the auditorium and looked at the thousands of empty seats, imagining them filled in a few hours' time. Would the people come? This was it — the outcome of her challenge to the group of students on the Shabbos of Yisroel's bar mitzvah at the Pine View Hotel. Her words had been heard upstairs and in the blink of an eye, nature had turned itself inside out. The result — a frum woman, a rebbetzin — was about to stand up on stage and talk to her nation about

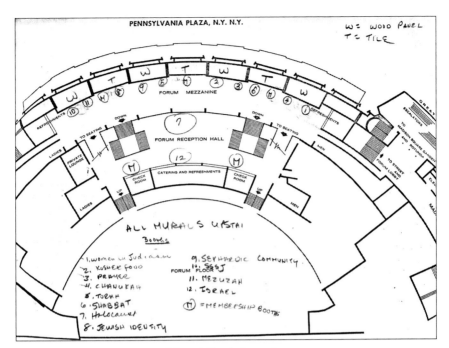

Mitzvah Booth floor plan

belief in G-d and the meaning of life! Who would have believed such a thing possible? They had done their best, but only Hashem could fill the cavernous room. It was up to Him and no one else.

With a silent prayer on her lips, she turned and left the Felt Forum. Barbara accompanied her friend to her dressing room.

"Try to relax," she advised the Rebbetzin, "it's going to be a big night."

Then she turned and left, leaving Esther Jungreis all by herself.

Yet in truth, she was never all by herself. All it took was one look in the mirror and she could see all of them — the Zeides and Bubbas, and their fathers and mothers — hovering over her shoulder like guardian angels, whispering words of wisdom into her ear and enveloping her in their arms with protection and love.

The hands on the clock moved forward rapidly. If there's any one constant in life, it's the inevitability of the passage of time. Esther was sitting in her dressing room when her father knocked on the door.

"Come in."

He entered the room — Barbara was there as well — and she could tell that something was amiss.

"There are many people waiting outside — too many," Zeide said. "The security guards are not allowing them into the building. You must do something, my child; those people must be allowed to participate."

The Rebbetzin looked at Barbara for confirmation.

"The rules at the Garden are very strict," Barbara explained. "Since all the seats have been filled, letting more people in will create a fire hazard."

While on one hand the Rebbetzin was filled with joy — they had succeeded in their mission, the hall was full — another part of her knew there was no way she could get up on the stage and speak with the knowledge that Jewish people, eager to hear words of Torah, had been denied entrance.

No. Zeide was right, something had to be done immediately.

"Barbara," the Rebbetzin said, "please ask the floor manager to come and see me."

Barbara rushed out of the dressing room in search of the manager. She returned a few minutes later, manager in tow. The man radiated a sense of stern professionalism. You could tell that he did his job well and that he did it by the book. This was a person who didn't cut corners. But on the night of "The Event of the Century," he would have to rise above himself.

"My father tells me there are many people waiting outside who want to come in," she said to him.

"Yes, ma'am, your father is correct."

"Sir, I need those people to be allowed into the hall. Many of them have traveled vast distances to be here tonight and it will simply be catastrophic if they are turned away!"

She spoke with all her power and the passion that comes from knowing the truth is on your side.

"Mrs. Jungreis, I have to apologize. I would love to accommodate you here, but there is no getting around the law in this case. The aisles and floor must be kept clear, and only those holding tickets will be allowed to enter the Garden."

Esther took a deep breath while inwardly asking Hashem to put the right words in her mouth.

"Sir, do you believe in G-d?"

"I haven't missed church on Sunday yet," he answered her question, "but what does that have to do with anything?"

Overflow crowd at Hineni event with people sitting on the Garden floor

"On the contrary," she said, "it has everything to do with tonight's event. This is no ordinary event. It's not entertainment and we are not here tonight to have fun. We have assembled our people for a specific purpose, to reaffirm G-d's Covenant. You know your Bible. Surely you know that we, the Jewish people, are bound by a promise to keep the Commandments and become a blessing to all of mankind."

"Yes, I know all of that," the man burst out, "but what do you want me to do?"

"I want you to let them in. Every single person standing outside Madison Square Garden. Let them in and I promise you that you will share in our history. One day when you will stand before G-d's Throne, you will tell this story and receive your reward."

The manager considered her words for a minute. It was one of the longest minutes in her life.

"I must be crazy for agreeing to break the rules," he said at last, "but all right, let them all in! Some of them will have to sit on the floor in front of the stage — and if they disturb you, don't blame me!"

Later, much later, the Rebbetzin would speak of that moment in time. It was at that very second that her earlier fear returned with a vengeance.

"What if someone from the audience starts screaming at me," she wondered. "What if they throw me off course? What if I forget what I wanted to say? What if they laugh? Will all of this be for nothing?"

Yet scared or not scared, she knew that every single person standing outside the Felt Forum had to be allowed inside. It was that kind of night. A night where every single member of Klal Yisrael was welcome.

Like an honored guest.

And that was exactly what occurred.

The hands on the clock were moving even faster. Now the crowds (the sheer volume of people!) were passing through the doors, walking down the hallways, stopping at the booths, asking questions — so many questions — wanting to know more and more about the mitzvos they were encountering, many of them for the first time ever.

Inside the Garden, the crowd was already being treated to a musical celebration. A group of talented young singers were singing *Shema Yisrael* on the stage. Many of them would go on to become well known in their own right.

Their voices resounded throughout the Felt Forum — youthful, powerful and confident, as they sang the eternal message of *Shema Yisrael* over and over. The children of the post-Holocaust generation.

The last few people standing in the aisles were seated. Everyone was excited and there was a sense of exhilaration in the air. Suddenly the music stopped. The song was over. The air crackled with spiritual electricity and the Rebbetzin, still in her dressing room, knew that the event was about to begin.

There was a knock on the door. It was Barbara, accompanied by Garden security.

"It's more than we could have ever hoped for," Barbara said to her lifelong friend, her voice filled with a kind of profound wonder. "Everybody is waiting for you. Go with mazel."

The Rebbetzin looked at Barbara and thought about how lucky she was to have such a devoted friend — a friend who was willing to do everything in the world to turn their dreams into reality. Barbara had gone without sleep, had worked so hard, had asked for so little and given so much — and now they were finally here, standing on the threshold of making history!

This was it. The reason they'd worked so hard. Nobody had ever attempted such a thing. They were the first. Would it work? Would she be able to connect with every *neshamah*? Would her message go over well? Would she succeed in providing inspiration to a room filled with thousands of Jews — who had come to listen, learn and hopefully accept and change?

The Rebbetzin could hear them — the thousands of people, all of them waiting for her. She could feel the energy in the room, hear the laughter and sense their willingness to be inspired. With at least five thousand people in the room, after having spent months running around the tri-state area speaking at every high school, university and community event to raise awareness for the Hineni event — it had boiled down to this. She was exhausted. She was exhilarated.

The Rebbetzin and her father

And then a moment of crisis as the Rebbetzin realized that she didn't recall a single word she had been planning to say! Her mind was blank! She — a fantastic speaker who never used notes — couldn't remember a single thing she had wanted to talk about. What would she say to all those thousands of people?

Now what?

From her vantage point in the wings, she looked up and down the hall, her eyes hoping that her father would sense her need for his assurance. They had always possessed that special bond; he had always known when she needed him most. And then she saw him. It was a sudden movement. One second he hadn't been there, the next he was making his way toward his daughter. His eyes burned with an internal

Some of the Hineni literature distributed at Madison Square Garden

Chapter Five: Madison Square Garden □ 73

flame, his mouth curved upward in a smile, and he uttered words she would never, ever forget, even as he gently placed his hands on her head — the way Jewish parents have been blessing their children for thousands of years.

"May angels of mercy accompany you, my precious child," he whispered. "May the One Above give you the words with which to reach every heart."

It was incredible, but the words were back — poised on the tip of her tongue.

Suddenly it was time for the final walk. To the stage and the crowd — waiting and sizzling with anticipation.

And the Rebbetzin whispered the words she always said before addressing an audience: *"Hashem sefasai tiftach, ufi yagid tehilasecha."*

This chapter has been dedicated
in memory of our dear parents and grandparents
Pearl and Morris Latt ז״ל
Laurie Latt Wolff and Richard Wolff and Family

CHAPTER SIX
Footsteps in the Snow

As she walked the final corridor to the Felt Forum stage, the Rebbetzin's mind traveled back in time. One second she was in Madison Square Garden and the next she was a child of five on the way to her paternal grandparents' home in the Hungarian town of Nadudvar. Picture a little girl on a train. She travels with the knowledge that every minute of the journey brings her closer to her destination — the home of Bubby and Zeide. The fact that her parents elected to make such a journey through Hungary at precisely such a time of danger could not be explained. On the other hand, if they hadn't traveled when they did, they would have never seen them again.

The Rebbetzin electrifies the Garden with her fiery speech

Esther studied her father. She saw a long black coat, a high black yarmulke, a distinguished beard and smiling lips, and knew there was no mistaking her father for anything other than what he was.

Those were dangerous times and a Jew who looked like Rav Avrohom Jungreis could easily find himself being tossed from a moving train or beaten for no reason at all. Yet her parents made the decision to travel in spite of all the dangers. They were going to Bubby and Zeide and that was it.

Esther was young enough that she didn't really understand all of this. On the other hand, even the smallest child could feel and sense the fear, and even the smallest child knew when to keep silent and when to cry.

Esther and her brothers, Yaakov and Binyomin, alighted when the train finally came to a full stop. Esther loved the hustle and bustle of the porters and the sound of the train's whistle as it warned the boarding passengers to hurry up and board before it was too late.

Leaving the station, her father found a horse-drawn carriage for hire and gave the driver the address. Heaving their luggage aboard, the driver motioned for the children and their parents to climb up and take their seats. Only then were they off, into the coldness of the Hungarian winter day.

The frozen trees seemed to glide past them as the horses clip-clopped down the muddy road. They passed a lake where children skated, their coats a flash of color as the shadows lengthened. Soon they had entered the village itself. They turned a corner and the driver pulled the horses to a stop before a rambling house, a house with many rooms and hidden corners. Luggage tumbled down, children jumped to the ground, money was exchanged.

And then, Esther caught sight of them — the Bubby and Zeide she loved so, so much! They stood outside in the snow, waiting stoically, their faces lighting up when the carriage came into view.

Bubby's embrace. Pure heaven.

Esther was already looking forward to the hours she would spend with Bubby in the kitchen, partaking of all her delicious dishes. More than that, she was looking forward to the moment when she would climb down the staircase in the morning when the world outside slept, and make her silent way down the hallway and into the Zeide's study. She knew he would be there. It went without saying. And then she would climb onto his lap and he would hold her tight and stroke her cheek and all would be right with the world…

"My *tayere kinderlach*, my precious little ones, what would you like to eat? Everything is ready!"

They might have been tired just moments before, but the heavenly

Zeide's father, Rav Yisroel HaLevi
Jungreis, *Hy"d*, Rav of Nadudvar

Zeide's mother, Rebbetzin Slova Chana
Jungreis, *Hy"d*

aromas wafting from the pots on the stove roused them and they came alive with a sense of contentment that lasts forever.

Is there anything more wonderful then arriving at your Bubby's house and seeing the pots bubbling and boiling on the stove?

Can anything compete with a slice of freshly baked cake at a Bubby's kitchen table?

The memories were more than memories. It was as if she had just gone back in time and was silently making her way down the hallway on padded feet.

"I adored the visits to Zeide's study," the Rebbetzin would say. "I loved to sit at his feet, playing my silent games to the rhythmic sound of his sweet voice chanting passages from the holy books. And how very special I felt when he would interrupt his studies for a moment, pour himself a cup of hot tea and beckon me to bring the plate holding the sugar cubes to him.

"Thank you, my precious little one," he would smile, as he took the plate from my hands and lifted me onto his knee. "It's time for you and me to have some refreshments."

Can anything compare to the exquisite first taste of your Zeide's sugar cube? Is there anything in the world to compare with the sweetness?

And the stories that he told…

He radiated a sense of peace and she would nod off as he learned, the sweet *niggun* helping her drift off to sleep, though she had risen not long before. Yes, a visit to Bubby and Zeide's house was a five-year-old's dream come true — a visit for all five senses. Truly a magical experience to be held close by a saintly tzaddik.

Such sweet memories. A world long gone.

But the internal world of the mind remains — even after everything else has been destroyed.

It was still very early when Esther awoke. It took her a few seconds to remember where she was, but then all at once it came back to her — the journey was over, and they were finally at her grandparents' home. Slipping out of bed, Esther flew down the stairs and knocked gently on Zeide's study.

"Come in," he called out.

Pushing open the door, she walked inside — and there he sat, his head turned in her direction, welcoming her with a great big smile.

So it went every morning.

And then… There came a morning like every other. She rose and went downstairs, eagerly awaiting a glass of tea and a few sugar cubes. The taste — how good it was. Outside, the world was silent, covered in a blanket of snow and ice. Inside, all was peaceful and warm. She pushed the door open and entered the study. The shelves of *sefarim* gazed down at her, smiling at the five-year-old who had come to "study" with her Zeide.

One look at her Zeide, however, and Esther knew there was something terribly wrong.

Zeide was in the chair the same as every day. There were *sefarim* opened in front of him. But unlike every day, the tune of his Torah study was interrupted by an incessant cry.

But it got even worse.

His shoulders heaved with silent sobs, his face was crumpled and incredibly sad.

Esther could not bear the sight. Turning away from the terrible sight, she ran to find her father, sure that he would be able to explain what she had seen.

"Tatty, Tatty," she blurted out, "something terrible must have happened! Zeide is crying!"

Instead of smiling broadly at her and telling her that she was mistaken and that everything was going to be okay, her father's face became extremely sad — and he too began to cry. This was too much! The fact that Zeide was crying was bad enough. But to see her own father with tears streaming down his cheeks and into his long beard was the most distressing sight in the world.

Her father took his little daughter by the hand.

"Come, my sweet child," he said, his deep comforting voice never failing to make her feel better, even as he wiped the tears from his eyes.

"Put on your coat and boots, I want to take a walk outside with you, just the two of us."

As her father helped his five-year-old daughter put on her winter clothing, she could see that his eyes held a kind of terrible and evocative sadness. A perceptive child, Esther was filled with a sense of apprehension. Why was everyone so upset? Why were they all crying?

Rav Avrohom opened the front door and they walked outside onto the porch and then down the steps and onto the ground. The going was slow. The snow was very deep and it was impossible to move at a quicker pace.

"Esther, walk behind me," her father said. *"Follow in my footsteps."*

And so they walked. The going was difficult. But her father pressed down on the snow and created a footprint into which she was able to place her boot. The air outside was bracingly cold, and Esther felt her eyes water.

Her father didn't go far. It wasn't long before he had stopped in his tracks and turned back to face her.

"My dear child," he asked, "do you know why I walked ahead of you?"

"Yes," little Esther confidently replied. "You didn't want me to fall in the snow. You wanted me to be able to follow in your footsteps."

Her father gave her a bright smile. He loved her answers — he always had.

"My sweetest child," he continued, "it is not only in deep snow that a parent must make a path for his children. There is another road, a road that you, my child, are not familiar with just yet. It is a road laden with challenges, a road which many start to take, only to find themselves unprepared for the difficulties that come upon them. Although it is a road on which you will fall many times, more than anything, it is the road that Zeide is preparing for us with the power of his tears."

Esther listened very carefully to the lofty words and ideas emanating from her father's mouth.

"When your Zeide studies the holy books, he not only studies for himself, but he studies in order to pave the way for us, his children, and for all Jewish children. He utters a prayer and sheds a tear so that all of us — all the Jewish people — should merit to study Torah.

"Soon the snow is going to be very deep and you will fall, but every time you fall, remember that Zeide made a path for you. And then you will be able to stand up and keep walking on that path, following in his footsteps."

Esther was just a child at the time of that conversation. She did not fully grasp the import of her father's words, but the poignantly shocking memory of the tears of both her father and grandfather never left her. And it wasn't long before she discovered that the snow was deeper than she could have ever imagined. In the difficult moments that lay ahead, she would hear her father's voice whispering and encouraging her onward, as he said, "Esther, you can do it. Your Zeide already paved the way for us. You have only to follow in his footsteps."

As the Rebbetzin walked that final corridor to the stage, she remembered her grandparents: Zeide and Bubby who were sent to Auschwitz along with so many of her cousins and cast into the flames; Zeide who refused to abandon his grandchildren and with his final breath tried to shield them from the poisonous gasses. There was no question in her mind that just as her holy Zeide did his best to shield his grandchildren — so had his tears continued to fall as he paved the way for yet another generation.

Those final few steps were incredibly difficult for her to take.

And as she walked onto the darkened stage and stepped over to the microphone, Rebbetzin Esther Jungreis knew that her life would never be the same again — and that while she would never forget her kitchen table or the Shabbos afternoon speeches on the lawn of the hotel and everything that happened there, she had been born to follow in the illustrious footsteps of her father, grandfather and great-grandfather.

To follow them in the snow, so that her children and grandchildren (both biological and otherwise) should have footsteps of their own to follow while trudging through the snow.

Then the spotlight hit her and she was blinded. For a millisecond she froze, and then her nervousness disappeared and she began to speak. It was as if an angel had descended down to earth from heaven — such was the beauty and power of her words.

You are a Jew…

Esther Jungreis stood on the stage at Madison Square Garden and felt as if her very heart had stopped beating. Her voice quavered for a second or two, but she mustered all her courage and continued.

You are a Jew. You have created civilizations. You have been a citizen of every nation. You have given birth to every ideal that has shaped mankind. Justice, peace, love and the innate dignity of man have all had their genesis in your Torah.

But above all, you have been given the unique mission of proclaiming the Oneness of G-d!

A throbbing electricity coursed through the auditorium. The words emanating from her mouth ceased being just words and became something much greater than the sum of their individual parts. With every line and every thought, she was creating a spiritual ladder connecting her brethren to their heritage: to the world of Avraham Avinu standing at the edge of Nimrod's fiery pit; to Yitzchak Avinu, bound on the altar, prepared to be brought as an offering to Hashem; to Yaakov Avinu, encountering his brother Esav, his wives and children behind him.

The Rebbetzin at Madison Square Garden

First and second recordings of the Rebbetzin's Madison Square Garden
"You Are a Jew" speech

Anyone who was there when the Rebbetzin delivered her soul-stirring *"You are a Jew"* speech will count that moment as one of the greatest and most memorable moments of their lives.

And it was all the more powerful by virtue of the fact that the individual speaking was a Jewish woman — a wife, mother, daughter and sister. At that moment the Rebbetzin connected to every Jewish mother throughout history, joining them as they exhorted their children to never forget who they were and what they could become. She spoke from her soul, every word committed to memory, no paper before her, no notes on a lectern. Just her thoughts and her words piercing every individual — right in the heart.

Her voice was soft, yet powerful. Piercing and pleading at the same time. She spoke quietly, yet every syllable rang forth, entering every heart and demolishing barriers.

You are a Jew.

You have traveled the four corners of the earth. You have become a part of every people, and yet you have remained a people apart. You have known oppression. You have experienced every form of persecution. Your body has been scorched by fire.

You have forgotten your past.

But there is one prayer, one little prayer that you cannot forget, a prayer that speaks of your own mission in life. It is a prayer that has been a beacon of faith throughout the centuries of darkness, a prayer that has brought you back to the faith of your ancestors, a prayer that speaks of your own mission in life.

Her voice rose. Triumphant. Majestic. Eternal.

"Shema Yisrael — Hear, O Israel, Hashem our G-d, Hashem is One!"

The crowd erupted with spontaneous applause, while the singers lifted their voices and sang the song *"Shema Yisrael"* with uplifted glory — joined by every voice in the great room. The applause went on and on. They weren't clapping for the Rebbetzin. They were clapping for her words, for her message, for the concept she had presented with such talent and charisma.

The Rebbetzin touching the *"pintele Yid"* in everyone

At that moment Esther Jungreis became "The Jewish mother," a composite of Sarah, Rivkah, Rachel and Leah.

"Shema b'ni mussar avicha, v'al titosh Toras imecha — Listen, my son, to your father's guidance, and do not turn away from the Torah of your mother."

For years, she had spoken to so many around her kitchen table, but had never ceased dreaming of the day when she would be able to spread the word of Hashem in a truly outstanding way.

The audience hanging on to every word of the Rebbetzin's speech

"Shema Yisrael — Hear, O Israel, Hashem our G-d, Hashem is One!"

Unscripted and without prompting or a prior request, the entire audience — thousands and thousands of Jews — repeated the immortal words of *Shema Yisrael*. Their voices rang forth with those six words of power — the secret of the Jewish people. They uttered the words that were first proclaimed by Yaakov Avinu, words through which the Jewish nation have sanctified the Name of Hashem throughout the millennia.

Shema Yisrael resounded throughout the Garden!

The very walls seemed to quiver and tremble with the song of our people. It was a spontaneous affirmation of faith.

Suddenly everyone was singing, *"Shema Yisrael, Hashem Elokeinu, Hashem Echad* — Hear, O Israel, Hashem our G-d, Hashem is One!"

She spoke of the way things were at the dawn of time and how Avraham Avinu had heard the call and answered G-d by crying, *"Hineni,* here am I! Let me serve You! Let me elevate my every deed through the acceptance of Your mitzvot!"

She spoke of the Holocaust.

And the singers sang *Ani Maamin.* It was so powerful. So real. It was impossible to have been there and to have remained untouched.

She described an old man waiting on line to be sent to the fires of death. And how he took his last few drops of water, and instead of using the precious liquid to quench his thirst, poured the water over his

Garden crowd breaking out in spontaneous dance
following the Rebbetzin's speech

hands to purify them — and then recited the timeless words: *"Yisgadal v'Yiskadash Shemei Rabba!"*

(Here her voice rose to the ceiling of the Felt Forum, while the singers sang *"Achakeh lo b'chol yom sheyavo* — I will wait for him [Mashiach] on every day that he may arrive.")

She spoke for a long time. It was more than a speech. It was a manifest, a mandate, a passing of the torch. It was the epitome of storytelling, the epitome of education, of *chinuch* and mesorah.

And when she was finished, when she had said everything she came to say and the singers had sung every song they had prepared — there was a surprise.

Because it was at that moment that the crowd started to dance.

They danced in the aisles, they danced at the back of the room. They danced wherever they found the space.

They danced with fervor, with passion. It was the dance of a million Simchas Torahs wrapped into one, the dance of happiness at having been chosen for a special mission, the dance of joy at having been reminded of who they were and why they were a nation who dwelled alone. They danced and they sang — whirling around in circles. The music swelled, the singing grew stronger. It was something akin to receiving the Torah and mitzvos anew, to the feeling of *"Ashreinu mah tov chelkeinu* — How fortunate we are, how beautiful is our portion…"

The holy and inspiring words of *Shema Yisrael* were sung over and over again, growing louder every time, by Jewish people — some of whom had never heard those words before — until it seemed as if the roof itself was going to fly off the building and disappear into the night.

Nobody who had the good fortune to have been part of that event would ever forget what he saw. It was not possible. It was also a night that could never be duplicated or accurately copied. It could not be replicated because it was the most unique of moments — one with its own DNA and branding.

More than anything, the event that night at Madison Square Garden heralded the beginning of a movement.

A movement named Hineni.

CHAPTER SEVEN
The Girl From L.A.

*I*n the aftermath of the Hineni phenomenon, everyone began reaching out to the Rebbetzin at the same time. Everyone wanted to hear her speak, everyone wanted her to fly to their communities — everyone wanted a piece of the action. It was like Madison Square Garden had been a match — a match that lit a flame, which began small, only to turn into a raging bonfire. Cities around North America called and begged the Rebbetzin to fly to speak to their people. And everywhere she went — from Miami to Toronto — Hashem showed her favor and placed the right words into her mouth.

But although the phenomenon had begun with a flood of kiruv, it wasn't long before the phone was ringing with other types of requests. The '70s was a decade when many Jewish children across America were lost to cults and alternative religions, and the Rebbetzin would play a major role in helping many of those Jewish children escape and return home. Meanwhile, the parents called and asked to speak with the Rebbetzin who had acquired a reputation for being able to achieve miracles.

One day a woman called and asked to speak with the Rebbetzin.

Introducing herself, she told Rebbetzin Jungreis that she lived in L.A., had heard what she was capable of, and had a problem that only the Rebbetzin could solve.

The Rebbetzin's message reached audiences
around the world

Reaching out to a Jewish cult member. Note name badge — "Chaya"!

"We have a daughter Rachel* to whom we have given everything we could. We raised her with every luxury and provided her with the finest clothing and vacations. But she rebelled against us. Not only did she show us as clearly as possible that she rejects us and everything that we stand for, but she ran away from home and joined a cult."

"Which cult did she join?"

"Jews for J," the mother answered and broke down in a torrent of sobs, which sizzled through the phone lines and promptly buried themselves in the Rebbetzin's heart.

Now the sobs intensified and the mother said, "She didn't just join Jews for J. She's one of their star recruits. The other members listen to every word she tells them."

The picture was turning bleaker and bleaker, but the Rebbetzin knew very well what it meant to do the impossible. Besides, a Jewish mother was in pain. How could she possibly turn away?

It so happened that Rebbetzin Jungreis was scheduled to give a major speech at the Hollywood Palladium in L.A. a few days later.

"I want to help you heal your daughter," she told the mother.

"However, in order for me to be able to try, I need to meet her. That's the only way. Here's what I suggest. Meet me at the Palladium when I'm in L.A. and bring your daughter with you. I will meet her and we will see what happens."

On the night of the event, the Rebbetzin waited for the mother and daughter to come see her after the event, but in the end only the mother put in an appearance, explaining that her daughter must have figured out that she wanted to introduce her to the Rebbetzin and simply didn't show up.

"The game isn't over yet," the Rebbetzin said. "She didn't come here, but there's nothing stopping me from waiting for her at your house."

Disregarding the fact that she hadn't slept in many hours and forgetting all about jetlag, Rebbetzin Jungreis accompanied Rachel's mother to her house and waited into the early hours of the morning, but Rachel never showed.

While the two of them would eventually meet, there was still no opportunity for conversation due to the fact that Rachel came fortified with her entire group of fellow Jews for J along with their non-Jewish minister. The group was hoping to debate the Rebbetzin, but they were in for a disappointment, since the Rebbetzin had a firm policy against debating anyone. She was not a confrontational person and knew that her strength and power stemmed from love and warmth and not from arguing religious beliefs with people who had been brainwashed by charismatic cult leaders.

Rachel would not agree to speak with the Rebbetzin privately, which meant that they found themselves caught in a catch-22. In the end Rebbetzin Jungreis and Barbara left L.A. without having managed to achieve a private conversation.

The story, however, was just beginning.

Springtime approached and in Jewish homes around the globe everyone was busily cleaning the chametz out of every pocket and shelf and from the deepest recesses of every closet.

But the Rebbetzin couldn't clean in her normal lighthearted way. She tried to get into it, tried to do the tasks she did every year, but this year she couldn't concentrate.

How can you possibly sit down at your Pesach Seder this year knowing that a Jewish child is still ensnared?

A minute later she was on the phone with Barbara.

"We're flying to L.A.," the Rebbetzin informed her friend and Hineni's executive director.

"What are you talking about?"

Barbara was taken aback. After all, Pesach was just around the corner.

"We didn't succeed in getting through to that girl Rachel last time we were there, and I won't be able to sit down at my Seder table without trying again."

Barbara knew when she could argue and more importantly, Barbara knew when it was a lost cause.

"I'll book us two seats on tonight's flight."

Rav Meshulem and Rebbetzin Esther at a family simchah

"Thank you."

While she did her best to always make it home for the kids — even taking the red-eye flight whenever she could — getting through to Rachel was a case of *pikuach nefesh* (a matter of life and death), and that year, the dishes were changed over and Pesach was prepared by the Rebbetzin's mother — and by her daughters, all overseen by the unassuming tzaddik with the golden smile, Rav Meshulem; everything was ready for the Rebbetzin when she walked through the door.

The Jungreis family worked like a team and made sure that everything would be ready for their wife and mother when she returned from saving yet another *neshamah*. While the normal saying goes, "Behind every great man stands a great woman," in the Jungreis home the line went slightly different: "Behind the greatest woman stands a fully complete and supportive man."

Esther Jungreis used to say, "My husband's name is Meshulem and the name Meshulem means complete."

Rabbi Jungreis was so completely at peace with himself and who he was as a person that he enjoyed introducing himself, with a twinkle in his eye, as "the husband of Rebbetzin Jungreis."

And he was so, so proud of her.

FRANCE

BRAZIL

EUROPE

EUROPE

HUNGARY

92 □ THE REBBETZIN

SOUTH AFRICA

VENEZUELA

PHILLIPINES

EUROPE

MEXICO

Chapter Seven: The Girl From L.A. □ 93

Throughout the flight Rebbetzin Jungreis asked herself how to handle the upcoming situation. In the end, she had to admit that she had no idea what to do or say, and that He Who had carried her this far would continue to do so.

Of course, the moment she arrived in L.A., she was asked to deliver a speech at one of the local schools. The Rebbetzin was making her way up to the podium when one of the community rabbis approached her.

She could tell that something was making him very nervous.

"What's going on?"

"Rebbetzin, the girl that you were hoping to meet is here."

"Here?"

"Yes, here. She's standing at the back of the room right now, handing out missionary leaflets to the kids and attempting to convince them to convert. How do you want me to handle this? Should I get rid of her?"

"How did she get in?"

"She sneaked in. Nobody realized who she was until she started handing out her literature."

"Leave her alone," the Rebbetzin replied. "Don't allow her to hand out any of her material, but do not ask her to leave. I want her to stay. Let her listen to the speech."

The Rebbetzin was hoping that she'd have a chance to talk to Rachel after the speech, but once again, by the time she was finished speaking, Rachel had slipped away. The Rebbetzin, however, remained unfazed. If Rachel was stubborn, so was she. Rachel might be determined, but so was the Rebbetzin.

Rachel didn't know it yet, but she had met her match.

That evening, Rebbetzin Esther Jungreis returned to Rachel's house for a second time. Time passed and once again the teenage girl didn't show up. The Rebbetzin stared at the hands on her watch ticking the hours away and wondered if there would ever be a happy ending for this child. By the time the clock hit two in the morning, no real hope remained. Rachel's parents went to sleep and Barbara dozed off in an armchair. But the Rebbetzin remained awake and alert in the semi-darkness. Something told her that Rachel was going to return home. She didn't know how she knew, but she knew.

Call it intuition. Call it whatever you want. Sometimes a person knows something and the Rebbetzin knew that the door to Rachel's heart was about to open up.

She wasn't surprised when she heard the front door open and close a few minutes later. Rachel stood in the doorway — a young Jewish kid, a beautiful *neshamah* who had once stood at Sinai together with the rest of Klal Yisrael, but had lost her way.

The Rebbetzin looked at her. And she loved her.

She wanted to envelop her in her arms and hug her like a mother.

"I have been waiting for you," she finally said, "and your people have been waiting even longer. Here is a prayer book of your fathers. Let's open it together and may G-d help us both."

The two of them stayed up talking for the rest of the night.

In a fascinating turn of events, two had flown in to L.A. Yet when they left the next morning, they were three.

In essence, Rachel was brought back with a combination of love and the generations of tzaddikim who accompanied the Rebbetzin wherever she went.

Most mothers would have called home to let the family know that a new sister was about to join their household. Rebbetzin Jungreis did not.

"It never occurred to me to ask my husband or children whether they would be willing to accept a new addition to the family," she said. "It was obvious to me that they would welcome this young girl with open arms." And so they did.

From Hungary to New York, nothing had changed for the Jungreis *mishpachah*.

When Chaya Sora returned home from high school later that day, she walked into her room and discovered that she had a new sister, who would be sharing the high-riser and the shelves in her closet. But it didn't stop there. The Rebbetzin instructed her daughter to teach Rachel everything that she learned in school. This developed into a super beautiful friendship that was as close to sisterhood as possible.

Rachel's story was completely out of the ordinary.

— Raised with all the comforts of life.

— Left it all behind.

— Joined Jews for J.

— Enter the Rebbetzin.

When Rachel left L.A. it was a major blow for Jews for J, both in California and in New York. Losing a potential leader of Rachel's caliber and family pedigree hurt their image terribly and they were left reeling from the shock. Her flight couldn't have come at a worse time for the cult. They had been planning major events in L.A. and wanted to hold a gigantic event of their own at Madison Square Garden (they had even established a "Hineni for J!" to confuse people), but Rachel's "kidnaping" threw the entire leadership into a frenzy and they were filled with a terrible rage at Rebbetzin Esther Jungreis for the harm she had caused them.

There was an Erev Pesach custom on Hungry Harbor Road in North Woodmere. At about ten o'clock in the morning, the entire Jewish community began to gravitate toward the Jungreis backyard where the Rabbi waited for them, a roaring fire burning in a metal garbage can. Shlepping bags, boxes and cartons filled with leftover cereal, loaves of bread and half-eaten donuts, the members of the shul, and anyone else who so desired, would hand their chametz to Rabbi Jungreis to dispose of. In the middle of the noise and hustle and bustle, the Rebbetzin said to her new daughter, "Come, Rachel, it is time for you to burn your chametz."

Rachel hadn't arrived from L.A. empty-handed. She might have acquiesced to the inevitable and joined the Jungreis family, but she'd arrived with baggage — including literature extolling the benefits of joining Jews for J.

This was the chametz that the Rebbetzin had to convince her to burn.

As her pamphlets and brochures were tossed into the flames and went up in smoke, a change came over Rachel. There was no question that shedding that part of her past was a huge watershed moment in her life. Sometimes the mere symbolic act of burning one's spiritual chametz can have a genuine effect on a person. As she watched her *tereifah* literature go up in flames, Rachel underwent a spiritual rejuvenation. By the time the fire died down, she had become a different person.

Slowly but surely the flames died down and the people began to disperse to their homes after shaking the Rabbi's hand and wishing the Jungreis family a *"chag kasher v'same'ach."*

The Rebbetzin and her family were eager to take care of the numerous last-minute tasks that still had to be done before the Seder that evening. The house was filled with the once-a-year aromas of Pesach food. A gigantic pot of chicken soup was bubbling on the stove, Rabbi Jungreis was grating the marror (while wiping away the tears from his eyes), and the long, elegant table was being set for what promised to be a delightful Seder, especially because Rachel would be joining her new family to discuss the story of leaving Mitzrayim (Egypt).

There was a knock at the door.

One of the kids went to answer.

A UPS delivery truck was parked outside the house and the driver was standing on the doorstep with a large box.

"Delivery for Esther Jungreis."

The box was brought into the kitchen and all gathered round, curious as to what it contained.

Rabbi Jungreis cut through the tape and opened the flaps. What followed was one of the most shocking sights of their lives. There was a letter addressed to the Rabbi and his wife. But that was nothing compared to the other item.

It was a hog's head. Bloody.

A large pink pig's head complete with bulbous snout and little eyes in the Jungreis kitchen on Erev Pesach! Rabbi Jungreis opened the letter. It had been written by members of Jews for J and it contained a threatening missive for the Rabbi and his wife, denouncing them for having ruined the cult's plans for New York and promising to take revenge.

As a child standing in her mother's kitchen, Slovie would always remember that scene as the moment when she truly comprehended the code of *mesirus nefesh* (self-sacrifice) that encapsulated her parents' life. It was one thing to address huge audiences on the grandest stages of the world and to rub shoulders with the leaders of society. No doubt people thought her mother's life was all fun and games.

But the truth was different.

Because the Rebbetzin was willing to travel to the far ends of the world to bring her people back to Hashem and His Torah. Even if it meant putting herself in danger, or being threatened or having a freshly slaughtered and bloody pig's head sitting in the middle of her kitchen on Erev Pesach.

None of that was important. As long as the Jewish people returned to their Creator.

It wasn't long before Rabbi Moshe Weitman, the principal of TAG, gave Rachel permission to attend any classes that she wanted. After a few weeks in the Jungreis home, Rachel acted and was treated exactly like the rest of the children. The Rebbetzin loved her and treated her like a daughter; the children, like a sibling. When the Rebbetzin traveled to South Africa to give a series of lectures, she returned with a gift for Chaya Sora and an identical gift for Rachel.

Rachel would go on to become completely frum.

Of course — this being the Jungreis family — when Zeide felt it was time, the Rebbetzin's father made Rachel's shidduch.

While dancing at Rachel's wedding a few years down the line, Esther Jungreis traveled back in time to a major speech in L.A.... Waiting for hours for Rachel to come home... Leaving L.A. empty-handed... Returning to the West Coast a few days before Pesach... Making a second nighttime attempt... And the triumphant journey home, brand-new daughter in tow.

After experiencing such a story, the Rebbetzin would never think a mission impossible. There was always a way. You just had to be granted the *siyata d'Shmaya* to open the door.

The rest would fall into place by itself.

The Rebbetzin looked into Rachel's eyes and smiled. Then she wiped away a tear.

And in Rachel's own words:

> With tears in my eyes and pain in my soul from recollecting the past, I want to share with all my brothers and sisters about how I came back to G-d. It is a hard story for me to write since it involves thinking again of all the pain I went through. While it may seem to some that it was very simple for me to come back to Hashem, in reality it was the hardest thing for me to do. But it is worth bringing this all back to memory, in order to help someone else who is suffering. The most painful experience is to realize that one's life has been wrong; it is hard to accept this.
>
> After many years of searching for the truth and struggling, I

finally found the purpose, the fulfillment and the only answer for my existence — the Torah. The Rebbetzin and the entire Jungreis family welcomed me and comforted me through the many tests which I had to overcome. I owe much to Chaya Sora who helped teach me Hebrew, and to Rabbi Jungreis who always explained with patience and love. I can only thank Hashem for helping me to find my way back to Him, for strengthening the Rebbetzin to do her holy work, and also for helping my parents to endure the many years they suffered because of me.

Baruch Hashem, I have come home.

The Rebbetzin made a point of staying away from debates. She had long come to the realization that there was a much better and more effective way of breaking down barriers and bringing people home. Instead of arguing, she did her best to expose the wandering Jew to the beautiful world of mitzvos — handing them their heritage along with a massive dose of love and kindness. It could be experiencing a Shabbos, learning Torah or sitting in the succah.

"Once a person starts doing mitzvos," the Rebbetzin would say, "the callus around the *neshamah* — that hard, tough callus — automatically begins to soften up and it becomes possible to reach them."

But not through debate. You could be the best, most accomplished debater in the world. Yet no matter how good you were, there was a better way to make inroads to another person's soul — and that was by injecting them with a lot of Torah, endless loads of mitzvos and buckets overflowing with love. Put those three ingredients together and there wasn't a person in the world who could withstand their power.

Proof?

The results were immediate. Time after time her way proved itself. And that was why she did her utmost to refrain from the types of debates on which others thrived. For her it was always about the Torah, mitzvos and love.

Susan* was another girl who fell prey to the world of the cults. A nice Jewish kid, her parents never imagined the fate awaiting their daughter when they sent her to university. To their shock and dismay, Susan met a group who identified themselves as "Messianic" missionaries. It didn't take them long to reel her in.

Susan, like so many other Jewish kids, didn't know anything about her heritage. She was fair game. For the missionaries, it was like taking candy from a baby.

Thanksgiving was in the air.

Though already regarding herself as a member of the cult, Susan still had feelings for her family. In her mind, there was no reason not to take a break from school for a few days. It would give her a chance to see her parents and to catch up on the family news. It would also give her the opportunity to take a seat at her parents' dining room table — to enjoy a piece of turkey with stuffing and all the trimmings. The whole thing was no big deal. Return home, eat a good meal, have a nice conversation or two, and back to university and her newfound friends and beliefs.

In most cases, the cult leaders would have told Susan that she wasn't allowed to leave the campus right then. The truth is, Susan wasn't ready to go off on her own. She was still vulnerable and unprotected. But a "mistake" was made and when she asked if she could go home, she was given permission to leave. Heads would roll, but by then it was too late.

It was a statistical improbability, but it happened.

Off Susan went, back to home and hearth and a giant slab of turkey and cranberry sauce.

As she boarded her train and found a seat beside the window, Susan admitted to herself that she was extremely relieved to be leaving the campus. There was a reason for this. Though she hadn't admitted her true feelings to any of her new "friends," the truth is, Susan wasn't one hundred percent sure she was making the right move by joining the "Messianic Jews." She found much of their beliefs strange, they made her uncomfortable, and if she was totally honest with herself, something deep inside her soul kept on insisting that her new way of life was just plain wrong.

While still on campus there hadn't been anything she could do about her doubts (she was in too deep), but now that she was returning home, she told herself that it might be a good idea to seek out her local rabbi for a conversation. Maybe she was being hasty? Maybe she was making a mistake?

The train flew down the tracks. Some of the homes she passed had light emanating from their windows. Others were dark and shuttered.

"What kind of home do you want?" she asked herself.

It was time to find out.

Her father was waiting for her at the station, bundled up in his parka. Yet the hood couldn't block the huge smile on his face when he caught sight of his daughter heading his way.

"Susan, over here!"

Grabbing her suitcase, her father led her out of the station and over to the nearby parking lot. Soon they were driving through the familiar streets of her old neighborhood.

"Dad?"

"Yes, honey?"

"Could you do me a favor?"

"Sure, what do you need?"

"There's something I want to talk about with the rabbi down at the temple."

Her father was taken aback.

"You want to meet with Rabbi Schoen*?"

Susan nodded and said, "You sound surprised."

"I am surprised. You never ever had any interest in talking to the rabbi before."

"Things change."

"I see that. I'll tell you what. I'll give the rabbi a call as soon as we get home and ask him when would be a good time for you to go see him at the temple."

"Thank you, Daddy."

Her father stared at her for a second, really looking at her.

"Are you sure you're okay?"

She nodded and didn't meet his gaze.

Susan laid all her cards on the table. She wasn't there to make it easy for him. She had questions — a lot of questions — and she wanted real answers. The rabbi was taken aback. He knew Susan's parents, and nothing about them and their approach to Judaism could have helped him anticipate what he would be facing when she walked into his office.

Twenty minutes into the conversation, Rabbi Schoen knew that he was ill-equipped to answer Susan.

"I'm going to be honest with you," he said to her. "I'm the wrong man to help you out. Your questions are strong — too strong for me."

"What are you saying?"

The Rebbetzin at her weekly Chumash class in the early years of Hineni

"I'm saying that I don't know how to answer you."

Susan's face closed down like a mask.

"That doesn't mean there are no answers. It just means that I don't know them."

Susan looked at him. It was a challenging stare.

"So, here's what I think you should do. There's a woman named Rebbetzin Esther Jungreis whom you should meet. She will be able to answer every single question you have and a thousand more that you never thought of. That's my advice."

And he gave her the Rebbetzin's contact information.

Although she knew that her cult leaders would not want her visiting someone like the Rebbetzin, Susan decided that what they didn't know wouldn't hurt them. She had managed to stump her parents' rabbi; surely a rebbetzin would pose no great challenge.

The Rebbetzin would never forget the way Susan looked at her when she entered the room. The Rebbetzin was giving a class at her father's shul that night, and hadn't been expecting anything out of the ordinary. But the look on Susan's face hit the Rebbetzin hard. She stared at Susan's eyes. They appeared dead to the world.

The Rebbetzin wasn't surprised. She'd seen the look many times before. It was the look of someone who'd been brainwashed. Someone who had been worked over and hung out to dry. Many times it was too late for people like that. They were too far in. On the other hand, the girl had come to see her. That meant that her brain was still working. There was still someone to talk to.

For her part, Susan was faced at that moment with a host of warring emotions. She could hear the missionaries back on campus promising her the world. She heard her own voice reminding her of all the doubts. The good and the evil — fighting one another.

Susan stared at the Rebbetzin.

Who was this woman who held the key to her life? Who knew all the answers?

She liked her and didn't like her. She wanted to know her and she wanted to run the other way.

She wanted to smile, but she could only scowl.

"You already know the truth… Why did you even come to this place?"

It was the voice of the cult leader yelling at her.

"Go to Rebbetzin Jungreis," the rabbi had said. "She'll be able to answer all your questions."

Anger, hatred, pain and hope all merged into one.

Nobody could save her. It was too late.

"It's not too late," argued the voice that had compelled her to visit the rabbi in the first place.

Suddenly she was standing before the Rebbetzin.

The scene that followed happened much faster than it takes to write. People usually imagine that saving a life takes time, a long time. Not always. Sometimes saving a life can be done in an instant.

That's what happened that night.

Susan glared at the Rebbetzin, who asked, "What is your Jewish name, sweetheart?"

Susan was not ready for such a line, but she would not allow it to break down her defenses. She might have a good relationship with her father and mother, but she wouldn't allow this rebbetzin to think that she could call her sweetheart and get away with it. Who did this lady think she was anyway, asking her about her Jewish name!?

"I don't have one."

It was like the ice queen had spoken.

"I'm sure you have one," the Rebbetzin replied. "Maybe you forgot."

"I don't have a Jewish name."

(Unspoken were the words, "I will not let you move me. I will not let you find a way into my heart." And all the time she could hear the sound of the cult leader back at school warning her...)

But the Rebbetzin wouldn't give up. Meeting Susan's gaze, she said, "Didn't you ever have a Zeide who called you 'Sara'le'?"

That was it.

From somewhere deep within her heart, a volcano shot upward — a volcanic eruption sending a sea of lava up, up, up and out, out out.

Her eyes became moist and the tears hit her a second later. Susan never had a chance. Crying hysterically, she stepped into the Rebbetzin's arms and loving embrace.

The whole conversation lasted maybe ten seconds.

Did the Rebbetzin debate Susan?

She did not. Not even for a second.

Instead the Rebbetzin hit her like a Sherman tank with the image of her Zeide — and the memory of a kind face whispering, "My Sara'le, my *zeese*, sweetest Sara'le."

That was it; the war was won.

If you happen to meet Sara'le today you would never, ever imagine that she had once been involved with a cult. No trace remains of the girl with the glazed eyes and blank look. She has been replaced with the mother of a large family who smiles broadly and smiles often.

And to think that the whole picture changed in a ten-second conversation...

This chapter has been dedicated
in blessed memory of Rebbetzin Esther Jungreis ע״ה
and in honor of our dear children
Jonathan David • Alexandra Nina
Jacob Abraham • Joshua Nouriel
Randy and Michele Lee Fine

CHAPTER EIGHT

The Reverend's Letter

*T*he story of Michael Kransky* was another fascinating example of the *siyata d'Shmaya* that had been granted to the Rebbetzin from above. Kransky had been an average American Jew — didn't know anything about religion and didn't care enough to try to find out. No doubt he would have carried on that way his entire life, were it not for the fact that he joined the U.S. Army. Once stationed in Alaska — in the middle of nowhere — Michael became close friends with his new army buddies. Yet while he looked at the friendship as a social outlet, they looked at him as a religious mark.

Out on patrol in the middle of nowhere, Kransky and his "friends" had lots of time to talk. And talk they did. It didn't take them long to try to convince the Jewish soldier that he should consider looking into another religion.

It wasn't that Michael didn't try to put up a fight. He asked questions and put up a halfhearted resistance. But he was no match for the guys in his platoon who put all their efforts into "saving" his soul.

At the end of the day, Michael could not stand up to them and he knew it. By the time he was released from army service, Michael had not only converted to a different faith, he had donned the mantle of clergy as well. He was now a reverend — leader and spiritual guide to his American community. Here too the story might have ended were it not for the fact that Michael was still uneasy about his adopted religion. While he stood up and preached to his congregation, deep down, Michael knew there were many things that just didn't make sense.

It was a time of seekers and Michael was no exception. While thousands of young American Jews left the shores of America for the ashrams of India and the monasteries of China and Tibet, Michael picked up a pen and some paper and began writing letters instead.

Rather than write to the spiritual guides of his new faith, Reverend Kransky chose to write to rabbinical leaders instead, spilling out his questions, worries and anxieties and asking the rabbis to please respond to his questions. Knowing better than to be drawn into a debate with a clear heretic, none of the rabbis responded to Mike. Being stonewalled by his own people made him even more nervous and upset than he'd been before he started writing, and it reached a point where he really didn't know what to do.

"It would have been one thing," he said to himself, "if I had never learned about another religion and just remained a Jew. However, I changed my entire life around for what I thought was the truth. Now I don't know any longer. I need someone to answer my questions before I lose my mind completely!"

Lucky for Mike, someone was about to answer his questions.

Someone who really knew what she was talking about.

It was 1974 when Michael Kransky picked up a copy of *The Jewish Press* for the first time in his life. Mike had never heard of that particular newspaper, but it looked interesting and he was bored at the time — so why not? He sat down with a cup of coffee and read the paper from beginning to end. One specific column jumped out at him, grabbing him and holding him firmly in place. It was titled "The Rebbetzin's Viewpoint," and after perusing a few of the questions that had been sent to the Rebbetzin (whoever she was) to be addressed, he could see why people found her advice worth listening to. She reminded him of a religious "Dear Abby" type of column and he was intrigued.

She was obviously intelligent — that was clear. More importantly, it wasn't hard to tell that she was empathetic and caring, not to mention sincere. On top of all that, the woman was clearly a scholar. Knowing it was a long shot, but past caring, Reverend Michael Kransky picked up his pen once again and wrote a letter to Rebbetzin Esther Jungreis — care of "The Rebbetzin's Viewpoint" at *The Jewish Press*.

> *Dear Rebbetzin,*
>
> *My name is Reverend Kransky.*
>
> *I was born a Jew. These days I am the spiritual adviser and leader of a non-Jewish congregation. I have many, many questions — and cannot seem to find the answers, try as I might.*
>
> *I really want to understand why the Jewish religion rejects everything I have been taught and the religion I have chosen to accept upon myself. I was raised as a Jew and am intimately familiar with the emptiness of the Jewish lifestyle.*
>
> *Why would any sane person willingly choose to remain in such an existence?*
>
> *On the other hand, I do not seem to be able to make peace with my adopted religion either, due to a long list of questions which I cannot seem to shake.*
>
> *Please do not think that I am trying to pick a fight. I am merely trying to figure out the truth.*
>
> *Sincerely yours,*
> *Reverend Michael Kransky*

When he finished writing his letter, he sat at the table for a while staring at the piece of paper. He found an envelope and a stamp, placed the letter in the envelope and went to drop it in the mailbox on the corner.

Then he sat back and waited to see if his luck was about to change.

We are spoiled today. Whereas it used to take time for mail to make its way from place to place (at times it even got lost), today we send our emails from one side of the world to the next with the mere click of a button. But Reverend Kransky was living in the '70s and back then the only option was "snail mail." You can therefore imagine his happiness when he opened the mailbox one morning and found an envelope there from the Rebbetzin.

He asked himself why he was so nervous, and concluded that he was hoping that her answer would help him find himself. No wonder he was nervous. Removing the piece of paper from within, he unfolded it and began to read.

> *Dear Reverend Kransky,*
>
> *I read your letter a number of times and would like to help you*

find the answers that you seek. The only way to do such a conversation justice is face to face.

Therefore, I would like to extend an invitation for you to join me and my family at the Pine View Hotel in the Catskill Mountains for a Shabbos weekend. This will give us plenty of opportunity to discuss all your issues and to hopefully help you resolve them once and for all.

Having questions is a good thing. Having them answered is even better. Let us hope that we will be able to achieve the latter.

Please let me know if you will be taking me up on my offer.

Rebbetzin Esther Jungreis

Michael wasted no time reaching out to the Rebbetzin. They set a tentative date, and then, plan of action in place, Mike was finally able to relax. In anticipation of all the upcoming arguments, he invited a student of his named Alan to join him at the hotel, and the two of them headed to the Catskills geared for battle.

Parking the car in the hotel lot, Mike and Alan checked in and, after depositing their luggage in the room, went in search of the Rebbetzin.

Main building and front lawn of Pine View Hotel

When they found her, they introduced themselves and Mike told her how eager he was to get down to business.

"Mr. Kransky," the Rebbetzin said, "there will be plenty of time to discuss everything on your mind. Right now, however, is not that time. Shabbos will be here soon and I have much to do before candle lighting."

(This was part of the Rebbetzin's strategy. She never began with the debate. It was always, "Come hear words of Torah," or "do a mitzvah," or "keep Shabbos." There was a reason for this. She firmly believed that these actions would help soften the person's *neshamah* and open them up to being able to accept the truth.)

"So when do we sit down and get it all out on the table?"

He was a little disappointed.

"Tomorrow night. Once Shabbos is over, we will sit down and I will give you the opportunity ask me anything you want for as long as you want. Okay?"

It sounded okay to the reverend. And so Michael Kransky went to get ready for his first Shabbos. And what a Shabbos it was.

From the davening on Friday night in the shul, where his soul felt as if it were almost lifted out of his body, Michael couldn't get over what he was seeing, feeling and experiencing. Standing near Zeide, Michael couldn't help feeling loved — for the first time in a really long time. Zeide had this magical effect on people and Reverend Kransky was no exception.

He didn't recognize any of the songs, but he did his best to sing along anyway. When the entire shul suddenly stood up and prayed qui-etly, Mike stood up along with them and tried to follow along. He had no idea what was taking place, but he loved it.

When the davening was over, everyone in the shul wished one another "Good Shabbos" with a great big smile, and Michael and Alan shook countless hands until they were hoarse from repeating the same greeting over and over.

A few minutes later found the two of them in the dining

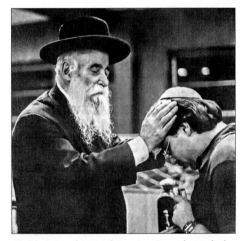

Zeide was always there to give a berachah

room sitting around the table with the Rebbetzin and her family. The meal was delicious, every course fit for a king. Singing spontaneously erupted from time to time. It would start at one table and spread, until the entire dining room was joined by glorious song. Of course their table was the best of all, because Zeide was there and he knew how to create an atmosphere. There was singing and dancing with the grandchildren. There were stories and Torah thoughts. Chicken soup, roast chicken, potato kugel and chocolate cake. It was all so special and beautiful — and Michael would have been happy if the meal had lasted for another six hours.

But of course it wound its way to an end, and after everyone recited some blessing from a whole batch of little books, some of the people went for a walk, others gravitated toward the couches in the lobby, and still others said "Good Shabbos" once again and retired for the night. It had been a long week and they were tired.

As was Mike, but he couldn't just go to sleep. Not when his brain was churning like a washing machine. It took the reverend a long time to fall asleep that night, and when he finally nodded off, his dreams were unique and peaceful.

Zeide's Havdalah at the Pine View Hotel

And so it went. Mike and Alan spent a real Shabbos with real Yidden for the first time in their lives, and instead of waiting for it to end, they were actually sad when it was time to make Havdalah. Mike inhaled the aroma of the spices and it hit him deep in his *neshamah.*

What a Shabbos it had been.

So many firsts.

The first davening of his life.

The first time he'd heard Kiddush.

The first time he sang "*Yom Zeh Mechubad.*"

Most importantly, it was the first time in a really, really long time that Michael Kransky had been happy and at peace with himself — and that was a big, big deal.

It goes without saying that the Rebbetzin hadn't forgotten their deal. In fact she approached them and asked them if they were ready for the big conversation of 1974.

Funny thing — they were no longer keen on hashing it out. There was no real reason for the lack of interest — except for the fact that they had just experienced their first Shabbos. Clearly, however, that was enough, because neither Michael nor Alan was even a little bit in the mood for a debate. In fact, not only was the whole debate thing off the table, the Rebbetzin was able to convince them that it would be a good idea to burn the books they had brought with them to the hotel. People crowded around and watched the scene, wishing the two of them "Mazel Tov" when their literature had been burned to a crisp.

When they were ready to leave, things were thrown slightly off course by Alan, who told Zeide that he would have to go say goodbye to his non-Jewish girlfriend before transferring to a yeshivah.

But Zeide would have none of that.

As always, Zeide spoke from his heart. Despite his broken English, Zeide's words pierced Alan's *neshamah*.

"You cannot go," he told Alan. "If you go, the girl will cry. Then you feel bad. Then you cry. Before you know it, you change your mind and then we never see you again. No. You stay here with us. We care for you and we want the best for you. If you must speak to the girl, you call her on the phone."

And Alan stayed.

And so the story of Reverend Michael Kransky and his faithful sidekick Alan wound its way to a happy ending. Alan would end up moving in with the Neuberger family (much more about Yisroel [Roy] and Leah [Linda] Neuberger later), who took good care of him and treated him like a son. In good time, Alan was introduced to a Jewish girl and he married her. They have raised a beautiful, Torah'dik family and have several kids.

As for Reverend Mike, the letter-writer — it took him time, but he got there in the end as well. If you would happen to run into Mike and Alan today, you would never guess what their lives were like before they met the Rebbetzin, Zeide, and the rest of the family. This small group of people changed lives through their unique brand of love, warmth, sensitivity and an incredible ability to accept people for who they were, without judgment or criticism.

And the recipe worked.

Oh, how the recipe worked.

This chapter has been dedicated
in loving memory of Steven Elmowitz ז״ל
Stanley, Judith and Alan Elmowitz

Part 2
1967-1980

Jews urged to recall heritage — woman revivalist seeks to stir religious, ethnic pride — like a prophetess.
Los Angeles Times

I spoke to the soldiers at West Point. They asked me to explain why the Jewish people went like sheep to the slaughter.

I responded by asking them if they had studied Israel's miraculous military campaign during the Six Day War.

"When G-d wants it, we are like sheep," I said to them. "But when G-d wants it otherwise, the sheep become lions."

Rabbi Yaakov Jungreis,
the Rebbetzin's brother

CHAPTER NINE

The American Singer

When the Jungreis children were sitting *shivah* for their mother, one of the women who came to be *menachem avel* made the following comment:

"If I were summing up your mother's life, I'd say she was a *gilgul* (reincarnation) of Esther HaMalkah (Queen Esther). The Rebbetzin was the most regal and aristocratic person I have ever met. She carried herself as if she was pure royalty. And," she continued, "it wasn't only the fact that she looked like a queen.

"The Megillah records Queen Esther telling Mordechai, '*Leich kenos es kol haYehudim* — Go assemble all the Jews together.'

"Your mother did exactly the same thing throughout her life, establishing Hineni with a giant gathering of thousands of Jews — where they declared *Shema Yisrael* with one voice and in unity. For me, the Rebbetzin will always be a modern-day Queen Esther."

The woman wasn't finished.

"Some may ask why Esther HaMalkah had to return to this world in a *gilgul*. There's a simple explanation for that.

"Esther HaMalkah had no children. It's true that she gave birth to Daryavesh (Darius), but he was the son of Achashveirosh (Ahasuerus) and lived his life as a non-Jew. But your mother — she had thousands and thousands of children — real Jewish children."

It was true. On any given Erev Shabbos there were numerous people calling to wish the Rebbetzin "Good Shabbos," many of them referring to her as their "Torah Ima."

From the time she arrived in the United States as a young girl, Esther Jungreis was involved in outreach among those who knew less than she. She invited her friends to her apartment to meet her parents and to experience authentic Jewish life, and she herself was very effective at relaying Torah lessons. After her marriage to her third cousin — Rabbi Meshulem Jungreis — a genuine *talmid chacham* (Torah scholar) and a special person, the young couple would spend their lives as the Rav and Rebbetzin of Ohr Torah in North Woodmere. Here too, the Rebbetzin led the women of her community by practical example.

Slowly but surely, she became more and more well known on the national scene, until events finally exploded with the launching of Hineni at Madison Square Garden in November of 1973.

Yet all the while that so many exciting events were taking place in the United States, the Rebbetzin never forgot her passion for Eretz Yisrael. She was a living example of *"Libi BaMizrach"* (my heart is in the East), a person who possessed an intense love for Eretz Yisrael from the time of the Holocaust. Perhaps that was why Hashem directed her footsteps across the ocean to the land of her forefathers, where she continued spreading the message of Hineni — Here Am I — to answer the call from above and to draw her brethren back to their Creator. She didn't do it on her own. There were always dedicated messengers who appeared at the right time, shared her vision and were willing to do whatever it took to help her carry the torch.

In Israel, first and foremost among them was Rabbi Yisroel Gellis.

I visited Rabbi Yisroel Gellis in his modest apartment in the Ezras Torah neighborhood of Yerushalayim. A man of many talents and an acclaimed expert on the history of the holy city, Reb Yisroel is also a famous author, journalist, prominent radio personality and tenth-generation Yerushalmi. In addition, he was also Rebbetzin Jungreis' man in Yerushalayim for decades. Strewn across his dining room table were Hineni memorabilia from the '70s — most notable were the records that he had produced of her most famous appearances in Eretz Yisrael.

Rabbi Gellis remembers the Rebbetzin well. After all, they worked together for some forty years.

The Rebbetzin with Rabbi Yisroel Gellis in Yerushalayim

"This record," he said, pointing at the old-fashioned square record cover, "is from the Rebbetzin's first major appearance in Israel, which took place in Beit Ha'am (a prestigious venue in Yerushalayim) in 1972. That was followed by her Madison Square Garden/*Shema Yisrael* event in November of 1973, and then by another very successful event in Binyanei Ha'uma in Yerushalayim on July 18, 1974. I ordered fifty thousand copies of the recording that I made of that event for distribution around the country. We didn't charge a cent for them. That wasn't her way. The only thing she wanted was for as many Jews as possible to hear her message, and we distributed them in army bases and kibbutzim — anywhere where they would reach unaffiliated Jews."

Rabbi Gellis relates:

> I first met the Rebbetzin in 1972. At that point Hineni had not yet been established in a serious way, even in the States. While she was the Rebbetzin of a shul in North Woodmere and already giving speeches, she was not yet a national star, although she was beginning to earn a reputation as an incredibly charismatic speaker.
>
> That, however, was all in America.
>
> In Israel she was an unknown entity. At the time of our first meeting, my father worked for the Jerusalem municipality. He was in charge of what is called "Machlakah L'Tarbut Toranit" — the section of city hall whose responsibility it was to arrange cultural

The Rebbetzin meeting with Jewish Agency Director Aryeh Dulzin

events for the religious community. The Rebbetzin had crossed paths with a man named Aryeh Leon Dulzin who held important positions in the Sochnut (Jewish Agency) and served in the Knesset as a minister without portfolio. It was Dulzin who arranged the introduction between my father and Rebbetzin Jungreis. The Rebbetzin had been to Eretz Yisrael. She had had dreams of living here after the war in 1948. But Hashem sent her to America. Maybe they needed her more over there.

When she and Mr. Dulzin met, the Rebbetzin shared her dream of traveling to Eretz Yisrael to speak.

"Rebbetzin," he told her, "there's a Jew who works for the Jerusalem municipality named Rabbi Yaakov Gellis. He's in charge of the section that deals with arranging cultural events for the religious population. Get in touch with Reb Yaakov. He'll be able to arrange venues for the kind of speeches that you want to give."

But Aryeh was wrong, because the Rebbetzin wasn't only interested in speaking to religious people. She also very much wanted to be given the opportunity to address the non-religious as well.

The Rebbetzin did as Aryeh Dulzin suggested and contacted my father at City Hall.

At first my father was a little taken aback.

Who was this rebbetzin from America who wanted to fly to Israel and give speeches to the *chilonim* (unaffiliated Jews)? She could

Aryeh Dulzin (bottom right) listening intently to the Rebbetzin at Beit Ha'am

barely speak a word of Ivrit! He didn't really understand what she wanted. But as the head of the Tarbut Toranit, it was his job to set up events and *shiurim*. In addition, he had connections with municipalities around the country and within the military. He spoke to her for a few minutes and came to the realization that she was the real deal. A frum Rebbetzin — the Rebbetzin of a shul, married to a *talmid chacham* and the daughter, granddaughter and great-granddaughter of talmidei chachamim. If she was ready to drop everything on her side of the ocean to come and speak Torah to the masses, then my father would do everything in his power to help her.

After meeting the Rebbetzin and finding himself singularly impressed by her sincerity and *yiras Shamayim* (fear of Heaven), he decided that instead of launching her visit with a bunch of small events, he would make a major event at one of the city's most prominent auditoriums — a hall called Beit Ha'am, which was located on Rechov Betzalel near the center of town. It was the type of venue that was generally booked for important concerts and plays. No doubt my father got a kick out of using what was a very famous cultural spot for something so out of the ordinary. It is very possible

The Rebbetzin at Beit Ha'am

that the Rebbetzin's speech was the first time anyone delivered a Torah *shiur* in that hall.

I watched in wonder (and did everything I could to assist her) as she prepared for the event. Nothing even remotely similar had ever been done in Yerushalayim before. There was a choir that accompanied her throughout the speech, singing softly as she spoke. From time to time, she stopped speaking and then the choir would break out into full-throated song. It was something to see. No detail was left to chance. Everything was special.

The music. The lighting.

It was precisely done and incredibly well produced — and as I said, Yerushalayim had never seen anything like it. Israeli productions were far, far behind America at that point in time, and the Rebbetzin was ready to treat her audience to an evening they would never forget.

Beit Ha'am was packed on the night of the Rebbetzin's speech. Every seat was taken and people sat in the aisles and perched on the stairs. The audience was a huge mix, with every segment of the population represented. Everyone had come to hear Rebbetzin

Packed house at Beit Ha'am

Jungreis from America. It was a major attraction. My father had done significant advertising and the city was abuzz with news of the American "singer" who had traveled so far to give a free performance in the capital.

The ways of Hashem are fascinating.

The ads that had been plastered around the city featured a picture of Rebbetzin Jungreis, microphone in hand. From the ads, one could be forgiven for assuming that Rebbetzin Jungreis was a singer who had come to give a musical show. However, the misunderstanding on the part of the Jerusalem population proved to be a wonderful thing. Because it meant that the Rebbetzin had a full house for her first legendary speech in Eretz Yisrael. They had all heard of the 'Singing Rabbi from America' and naturally assumed that she had come to do the same thing. They couldn't have been more wrong. Because she wasn't there to sing a note.

She was introduced. Rebbetzin Jungreis walked out onto the stage. The audience saw a slight yet regal woman. The spotlight illuminated her and she took her place before the microphone.

The audience waited for the "show" to begin. For the singer to open her mouth and wow them with her vocal gymnastics.

It didn't happen.

Instead of singing, the Rebbetzin began to speak. And the

The Rebbetzin's first best-selling book, *The Jewish Soul on Fire*,
Hebrew and English editions

people in the audience looked at one another and didn't understand what she was doing.

"When is she going to start singing? We came to hear a singer; why is she talking?"

Being Israelis, they were none too shy about vocalizing their feelings. They had come to spend their evening listening to a famous American singer — but she was no singer. All she was doing was talking about the fact that they were Jews — a fact that they already knew!

The people were confused and unhappy. They were just beginning to get a little rowdy and antagonistic (who knows what would have happened next?) when the Rebbetzin's emotions came to the fore and she began to weep. The moment her voice broke and the tears began to flow it was over — she had the audience in the palm of her hand.

They were hers. The rough-voiced soldiers who had fought in Syria and Egypt. The upper-class intellectuals from Rechavia. The housewives who had come to Beit Ha'am for a night of music and culture.

Inexplicably they were all hers.

The crowd listened to everything she had to say that night. They listened, even though she wasn't completely fluent in Ivrit. It didn't matter. From one second to the next they were hers. She might have stood small, but her personality was larger than life. She conquered the hall and the Israeli audience belonged to her.

I watched her reach their hearts and I knew that I would do whatever I could for the Rebbetzin from America.

This chapter has been dedicated
in memory of the Rebbetzin ע"ה and my dear aunt Cecelie ע"ה
whom I will love and remember always
Shari

CHAPTER TEN

In the Tower of the YMCA

When the Rebbetzin finished delivering her first speech in Israel, she exited the stage to thunderous applause. Though she hadn't known what to expect at the beginning of the night, she was warmed by the fact that she had managed — with the help of Hashem — to reach their souls. The wind was cool on her face as she walked the streets of Yerushalayim, looking around her with joy, gratified to be back home.

The Rebbetzin had been there before.

Her thoughts took her back in time to 1948 and the incredible happiness that had been experienced around the world by every Jew who survived the Holocaust. She remembered that time well. She remembered how determined she was to help build the brand-new country across the ocean. She remembered trying to help raise money for Israel — even as she struggled with a European accent. When people are young, they feel incredible passion for the causes they believe in. That's the way it was for Esther Jungreis whenever the subject of Eretz Yisrael arose.

She knew one thing.

As soon as high school was over, she was moving to the land of the Jews.

At least that was the plan.

There was nothing simple about the plan. She belonged to a close-knit family and they would never get over her leaving. Maybe if they hadn't been Holocaust survivors things would have been different. But they did go through the war together. As a result their bonds were incredibly strong.

How could she just leave them and travel across the world — to a land beset by war? Could she just say goodbye to her father and mother? What about her two brothers? They'd been through so much together! They loved one another with all their hearts! How could she just board an Israel-bound ship not knowing how long it would be before she would see them again?

Yet despite her love for her family, Esther knew that this was something she had to do. In everyone's life there are times when they need to make choices. This was one of those times.

"How can you leave them all behind?" she asked herself.

But the answer was simple. She wasn't traveling to Paris or London to see the sights. She wasn't flying to South Africa to search for diamonds. She was going to Eretz Yisrael, and there was no question in her mind that not only would they not prevent her from going, but that they would even understand her motives and agree with her.

And she was right.

Though of course not a day would go by when they didn't think of their daughter and talk about her.

"I left the United States in 1953," the Rebbetzin later recalled. "My route took me from New York to Marseilles in France. There I boarded an Israeli ship. I will never forget the day in Marseilles when I stood on the French dock and first set eyes on the Israeli Star of David flying proudly in the fierce sea breeze. To think that a person such as I — a person who had been one foot away from the gas chambers — was about to step aboard a ship bound for Israel — a ship staffed by Jewish people; it was like a dream come true.

"And then we arrived. Sliding slowly in the Haifa bay.

"I looked at Eretz Yisrael.

"It was early morning. Dawn. It was as if a talented artist had touched the scene with a magical brush. Every house was a palace. Every street was paved with gold. I felt a rush of emotion so powerful that it could not be contained. Exquisite rays of golden sunlight brushed the top of the Carmel and through it all ran the words of *Tehillim* (125:2): *As the mountains surround Jerusalem, so Hashem enwraps His people, from this time forth, forevermore.*"

High up on the hillside, Esther could see rows of houses with red roofs. Even from afar she could see the flowers and trees of Haifa, and as she stepped off the boat and onto the holy ground of Eretz Yisrael, she got down to kiss the land and recite the blessing of *Shehechiyanu*, thanking the One Who had brought her to such a day.

The pushing and the demands of everyday living pulled her back to noisy reality.

"*Sherut, sherut!* (Taxi, taxi!)"

People were yelling at one another as they manhandled their luggage from spot to spot. Everything was happening all at once and Esther was just content to allow the sounds and sights to wash over her — there — in her first hour in the Holy Land.

"*Hineni!* I am here," she sang silently. "I am here. Thank You, Hashem, for helping me reach this moment."

Esther had come to Eretz Yisrael to study and to learn. At the same time she wanted to get to know the land. She boarded buses and went everywhere. There was no part of the country that was not exciting or interesting, nothing that wasn't worth seeing.

Here was the spot where Eliyahu HaNavi (the prophet Elijah) challenged the prophets of Baal and proved the veracity of Hashem to the Jewish nation.

Esther listened closely. It seemed to her that she could still hear Eliyahu calling out to the people, "*Hashem Hu HaElokim!* Hashem, He is G-d!"

The land drew her to it.

She reveled in its feel and texture.

Here was the spot where David fought Goliath the giant. She could picture him raising his slingshot, see the stone flying through the air and striking the giant…

She saw fields ripe with wheat and vineyards filled with grapes. Farmers worked the land and soldiers rode the buses and wherever she went she couldn't help thinking over and over, "I am home. *Baruch Hashem,* I am home."

Esther with some friends on a seminary outing in Eretz Yisrael

Of course Yerushalayim was greatest of all. It occupied a place in her mind and heart that would not, could not, be eclipsed by anything else. Unfortunately it was still divided, but she knew that the day would come when the walls separating the Old City from the sprawling new neighborhoods that were being built in every direction would finally be accessible for good.

Meanwhile, however, the city was divided.

And yet how could she not see the Kosel?

Esther asked around and was told where to go.

There were a few spots in Yerushalayim that provided a view of the Western Wall — from a distance. One of these was the tower on the roof of the YMCA building, located across the street from the iconic King David Hotel — the hotel where kings, queens and presidents stayed when they visited the State of Israel.

Esther climbed the stairs of the tower. Standing at the highest spot, she looked out at the beautiful city and studied the Kosel through a pair of binoculars she had brought with her. There it was. The last vestige of the Beis HaMikdash. The sole remainder of the once-grand edifice that had called the Jewish nation from around the world to serve Hashem. Now, it was all that remained.

A billion stars twinkled in the sky above.

As the wind rustled through the trees and spoke to her in a high-pitched song of hope, the young girl recalled the not-so-distant past and the days in Bergen-Belsen. Here she was, standing at the top of the

Tower of the YMCA in Yerushalayim

world — not far from the Temple Mount — such a far cry from the bar-racks of Bergen-Belsen. It seemed to her that nothing was impossible, no dream that couldn't be achieved. Not if her life was an example. A sense of *hakaras hatov* (gratitude) welled up within her and the tears of thanks came gushing forth as she looked up at the heavens — so close — and pondered from where she had come and to where she was headed.

Meeting new people was a constant. Some of them were of Yemenite background. She became friends with a young Yemenite girl. The two shared their hopes and dreams.

"Tell me about your life before you came here," Esther would say, and her friend would describe life in Aden and Sa'ana and how her people had never seen a car. She told of the dust and the persecution and how her brothers, sisters and parents had left their homes and followed their dreams to Eretz Yisrael, flying on a plane though they could not com-prehend how such a device might lift off the ground.

"But if you were afraid of the plane, how did you bring yourselves to board?" Esther asked.

The girl stared at her, seemingly surprised by the question.

"Because the Torah tells us that this is so," she replied.

"What do you mean?"

"Doesn't it say, 'I will fly you on eagles' wings to your land'?"

And Esther had to admit that it did indeed say that, and that of course there was no reason to fear boarding a plane when Hashem Himself had promised such a means of transportation.

As time passed, Esther realized that if given the opportunity, she would like nothing more than to spend her life teaching children and teenagers — just like her new friend. She could see herself in the class-room — Morah Esther — teaching the children Chumash and Navi. She was a born teacher; how wonderful it would be to instruct and inspire. To help a child see the greatness within themselves.

But it was not going to happen.

Not in Israel. And not right then.

Though she would spend much of her life teaching, instructing and guiding, it would not be as a teacher in a classroom in the cities or moshavim of Eretz Yisrael.

Here too, Hashem had a plan for the young woman, and the plan includ-ed returning to the United States, to her parents, her Zeide and her brothers.

One day she came down with the measles. She got sick the way she did everything else — all the way. Her parents learned of her illness and of the fact that their beloved daughter had been sent to the hospital. At that moment, her parents made up their minds. Esther was coming back to America.

Her father spoke and she gave in.

Esther was saddened when she learned of her parents' insistence that she return. And yet part of her understood. This was her father — the man who had taken her outside with him in the snow. The man who had stood tall and unafraid in the darkest and most frightening places. The man who had fed his children crumbs of bread on Friday night, magically creating the Shabbos atmosphere in Bergen-Belsen. She was his daughter and their love for one another was larger than life.

Was it any wonder that he needed and wanted her back at his side — especially if she was ill?

This was her mother. The woman who had fed and cared for hundreds and hundreds of Hungarian Jewish boys, who had mothered them, loved them and comforted them when they needed it most. The woman who sewed contraband into the pockets of her children's garments because the Jewish prisoners needed it desperately. The woman who remained upbeat and positive — even while being degraded. The woman who remained a role model for her daughter through thick and thin.

Was it any wonder that she needed her daughter back at her side — especially if she was ill?

It was not.

And so, despite her desire to stay in Eretz Yisrael more than anything, and despite doing her utmost to turn her dreams into reality, the trajectory of Esther's life moved in a different direction than she planned. But that was okay, because Hashem had another plan for her. She was destined for greatness — destined to spread the Name of Hashem throughout the world.

Meanwhile, however, the Ribono shel Olam wanted her back in America — back in her family's embrace.

The Midnight Cry of King David's Harp

Years went by. In November 1955, Esther married her husband, Rabbi Meshulem Jungreis. He was her third cousin and they shared the same family name. The two of them were determined to rebuild the lost world they had left behind by helping the Jewish people return to their roots. Rabbi Jungreis taught Torah to everyone he met. He had a ready smile and an easy warmth — the kind of warmth that endeared him to all.

In the months leading up to the June 1967 Six Day War, the news from Yerushalayim became more and more menacing. And when the war finally broke out it sent an electric shock straight through the heart of the Jewish community. In every shul, school and yeshivah, all everyone talked about was the upcoming war and the situation in Israel. Suddenly every single Jew was connected and on the same page. Fear for their Israeli brethren brought everyone close and made them forget the tiny imperfections that divide us.

Suddenly everyone prayed. Wherever you went, prayer was in the air. Every Jew was intent on taking a part in easing the burden, in doing whatever they could for their brothers across the sea. People donated money. Others streamed to the Israeli consulate and offered to be inducted into the IDF so they too could fight. It was a moment of supreme togetherness and *achdus* (unity). There was beauty within the pain. It was classic Jewish survival. It was Am Yisrael.

It was incredible. It was a miracle. The war had been won and the Jews were back in the reunited city of Jerusalem. The barbed wire that had separated the two sides so effectively had been ripped down. It was gone. The door stood open, inviting in anyone who wanted to enter. Bullets hadn't stopped the Jewish soldiers. Nothing had been able to hold them back — not on the day when Hashem had made it possible for His people to return home.

The soldiers pushed their way through the Magreb Gate, and suddenly they stopped in their tracks, thunderstruck. They were taken by surprise to find themselves standing before the Wall. It was gray. It was not as large as one might have thought, yet spiritually greater than they'd imagined. They laid their hands on the stones and wept.

Chief Rabbi of the IDF, Rabbi Shlomo Goren, made his way through the Old City, "armed" with a shofar and a siddur. When he reached the Kosel, the Chief Rabbi sounded the shofar in a moment of triumph and

Rabbi Shlomo Goren, Chief Rabbi of the IDF, blowing the shofar at the Kosel upon liberation of Yerushalayim in 1967

Chapter Eleven: The Midnight Cry of King David's Harp   □   131 joy. His enthusiasm infected every soldier and they were all caught up in the moment.

But the shofar didn't only sound in Yerushalayim.

It may have started in the holy city, but its call reached Jewish hearts in the four corners of the world. The effect was magical. The Jewish nation became spiritually rejuvenated. Even those who had never believed felt something fresh and strong stirring in their hearts. The Wall called out to them and despite themselves, they felt the need to respond — to touch its stones, to place a note with a prayer in its crevices, to pour out their hearts and cry.

That's the way it was for the Jewish people, collectively and individually. We were coming home.

Back home in North Woodmere, Rav Meshulem and Rebbetzin Esther Jungreis made a decision. There was no way in the world they could possibly remain in the United States at such a critical juncture of Jewish history. And so, taking their four children with them, the Jungreis family boarded a plane and flew to Israel, kissing the ground with great emotion when they landed.

After spending some time with family in different parts of the country, the Jungreis family traveled to Yerushalayim. It was Friday afternoon when they arrived.

The city was utterly congested and there wasn't a hotel room to be found. Everything was taken.

For a moment Esther grew very scared — what were they going to do — but then her husband reminded her of the Talmud's lesson: "*V'lo amar tzar li hamakom…*" In Yerushalayim, no one ever complained of discomfort; in the city of Hashem, every man had a place, everyone was welcome.

Suddenly she knew that they would also find a place to lie down and go to sleep. Eventually they managed to find the hotel room that Hashem had set aside for them.

Time was of the essence. The Shabbos Queen was about to arrive in Jerusalem. Everything began slowing down. Shutters were pulled down on the stores. The buses stopped running. Shabbos was almost here. And then a shiver ran down every spine as the sound of the siren rang, heralding the onset of Shabbos. And then a silence descended on the holy city of Yerushalayim.

Throughout the city, in homes on every street, women lit Shabbos candles, moving their hands through the air, as they covered their eyes and prayed for their families. Rav Meshulem, Rebbetzin Esther and their four children walked the streets as if in a dream. And as they walked, as they made their way through the narrow alleyways and broad avenues, they were joined by more people and then more — until they had become a throng, a crowd, a group, a force — and finally a procession.

It was an ingathering of the masses, and it seemed to come straight out of the books of Tanach, straight out of the pages of history.

The people came from every direction — so many people, so different yet so alike. Tall men with long beards and hats, and tall men with white knitted kippot on their heads. Some were still in uniform, others had never worn a uniform in their lives. Some of the women wore scarves, others sheitels, still others had never heard that a married woman was supposed to cover her hair. Young children strode alongside elderly men. Religious and unaffiliated, people of the shtetl and men of the world — everyone was in this together — everyone was here because of the call. All of them — and the six members of the Jungreis family — rushing and running to the same place, to the Wall.

The Rabbi and his wife didn't know how to get there. After all, they had never been there before. The last time Esther saw the Wall had been when she stood at the top of the tower of the YMCA.

But now it was real.

Now the dreams were coming true. It boggled the imagination.

They walked, part of the huge crowd and yet apart — and the scenes of her life merged in her mind, like a movie playing in slow motion.

The Rebbetzin was lost in her thoughts, in the memories, the pain, the suffering — and the redemption.

> *Trains speeding down the tracks bound for the concentration camp.*
> *The hatred on every face.*
> *The Hungarian girl grabbing her doll right out of her arms.*
> *The Nazis yelling, hitting, beating them.*
> *Her father hugging them as Shabbos entered Bergen-Belsen.*
> *"Footsteps in the snow, my daughter, footsteps in the snow."*
> *The Israeli ship sailing into the Haifa harbor.*
> *The majestic mountains of Israel.*
> *Teaching Torah to students in America.*

Chapter Eleven: The Midnight Cry of King David's Harp □ 133

The Yemenite girl laughing as she tells Esther about flying to Israel on eagles' wings.

Teaching Torah to the children on her block.

Sitting on her Zeide's lap sucking on a sugar cube.

Staring at the Kosel from high up in the sky in the tower of the YMCA, as day turned to night and a million stars took over the cosmos.

The Jungreis family followed the crowd, became one with them — were swallowed up by them. They were home — with their family. This was the land of their fathers and it was suddenly impossible to feel alone. The Rebbetzin's heart beat faster and she clutched her children's hands tightly.

She saw tears in Rav Meshulem's eyes.

He was crying.

Of course he was.

They were in Yerushalayim — going to the Kosel. How could he not cry? How could anyone not be crying at such a time, at such a moment?

They could hear the glorious songs of Friday night davening.

"Mizmor shir l'yom haShabbos."

"Tov l'hodos laShem u'lezamer l'shimcha elyon."

Song bursting forth from every window, from every balcony. The notes were filled with pleasure — dancing on the wind, flying on the breeze.

Their steps grew more rapid. A sense of momentum overtook them. It was almost Biblical in its intensity. Could it be that they were actually walking in such a place, down the stone staircases, through the narrow alleyways, on the cobblestones of ancient history?

It was almost too marvelous to comprehend.

Yet it was true.

They made their way through the darkened paths. Past the shuttered Arab shops and the soldiers cradling guns in their arms.

The Rebbetzin's son tugged at her arm.

"Ima," he asked, "how did our soldiers do it? How did they liberate the city? How did they get through these gates, these alleys?"

"Jerusalem's time had come," she answered him, "and Hashem Himself opened the gates."

And the little boy nodded, because he knew it was true.

They walked a little farther and the Rebbetzin couldn't help but recall a precious man with a long white beard who had lifted her onto his lap and shared his sugar cubes with his granddaughter. She searched for the man who had cried on that long-ago day when she entered his study early in the morning — crying because he was begging the One Above to help his children follow his footsteps through the deepest snowdrifts. She searched for him in the sky above and it seemed to her as if she could discern his smiling face peering down at them from between the clouds.

To see the Wall on such an evening was a sight a person would never forget.

It was larger than life, yet a mere memory of what had been. Words could not do it justice, songs could not convey its significance. It was magnificent and alluring, lustrous and immovable. Most of all, it was ours.

We had returned. We were back.

We stood there as if in a trance (the Rebbetzin would later write in her first book, *The Jewish Soul on Fire*), *my husband, my children and I. We could not speak. There were only tears. For two thousand years we had waited for this moment. Our ancestors had prayed for this day. What they would not have given to stand here, even for a fleeting second, and yet they were denied the privilege. How strange that we who were unworthy, we — who were wanting in faith — were the ones to stand here in the presence of sanctity! How, I wondered, could we ever prove ourselves worthy of the merit? How dare we approach this holy place?*

I looked up at the heavens and searched for my grandfather. Surely the angels had gathered his ashes from Auschwitz and brought them as an offering to this very spot.

"Zeide, Zeide," I cried into the night, my voice merging with the sound of a million other voices, "please walk with me, for here I cannot stand alone!"

Time was passing. How nice it would have been had everything just stopped for a few hours — trapped in the moment. But no. Time will never stand still, not even for the most wonderful happenings. People were leaving, returning home for the *seudas Shabbos*, and the Jungreis family also turned back in the direction they had come, hungry now, and more than ready to partake of a delicious Shabbos meal. And as they walked, Rav Meshulem spoke to them as he always did. And since it was a special day, his words held even more meaning than usual — for it was at that wonderful moment that he shared the story of Dovid HaMelech (King David) and his glorious harp.

"Before the king lay down at night," he told his children, "he placed his harp on the windowsill. At first, silence filled his room and he would sleep for a short while. But he never slept for long. Because at midnight a wind would start to blow through the window and David's harp would start to play a tune on its melodious strings.

" 'It is time for you to wake up,' the harp would call out to the king. 'Stand up, rise up, Your Majesty, and sing praises to Hashem!'

"At that moment, the king would jump out of bed, rising like a lion. He would take hold of his beloved harp — the instrument that accompanied him throughout his life — and then he would compose yet another song of praise to the One Above."

The children gazed at their father in wonder. The picture he was verbally painting for them was so powerful they could actually visualize the scene down to the minutest details.

"Though many years have passed since those evenings in the king's chamber," the Rabbi went on, "there are those who still possess the ability to hear the sound of David's harp. They know when to listen and they know how to hear."

"When does the harp play its song?" the children wanted to know.

"Legend has it, the winds return to play their song at midnight."

The children were silent, digesting this piece of information.

"What if we were to return to the Kosel at midnight," one of them asked, "would we be able to hear the song of the harp as well?"

Rabbi Jungreis smiled at his children.

"Abba," they said to him, "please bring us back here at midnight. We want to hear the song of the harp!"

And so it came to be that every night at midnight, every night during that glorious visit to Yerushalayim, they stood at the Wall, the entire family — Abba and Ima, Chaya Sora, Yisroel, Slovie and Osher Anshil — and heard David's song:

One thing I asked of Hashem, that I shall seek: Would that I dwell in the House of the Hashem all the days of my life... (*Tehillim* 27:4).

One night the children and their parents met a soldier. They asked him his story. He told them of battles fought and how it had felt to be among the soldiers who liberated the Kosel.

Sometimes people do not want to speak about what they saw, what they suffered. But the soldier must have felt among friends, for he bared his heart and told them of his sorrow. He described a battle and how his best friend had been among those who fell. He told them how he tried to save his friend, but there had been nothing to do for him.

"What happened next?" they asked the soldier.

"What happened? I began to weep and cry for my friend. Yet suddenly I heard a sound that made me stop crying."

"What did you hear?"

"I heard the sound of a donkey."

"A donkey?"

"Yes. He was braying loudly, as if he too was suffering greatly, as if he too was in pain. It was almost as if the donkey were begging Hashem to allow it the merit of carrying Mashiach into Yerushalayim on its back."

There was nothing to say after such a story.

Maybe that was what their father had meant when he said you could hear the sound of David's harp?

"The Six Day War could have served as the harbinger for the end of days," the Rebbetzin would later say. "We could have risen up and made it happen. After all, hadn't everyone witnessed the miracles? Hadn't there been a national realization after seeing the mighty hand of Hashem?"

But no. The people wavered and the opportunity was lost.

All too soon, the poignant call of the donkey was lost in the annals of time, gone as if it had never even happened.

But for the Rebbetzin that moment would prove pivotal. Though many others might have shrugged and moved on, she made a momentous decision at that very moment. Though she didn't know where her life would lead her, she was going to try to bring her people back to their Creator — to lead them and help them and to be there for them. She would do her best, for can any more be expected of a person?

So it went at midnight at the Western Wall.

This chapter has been dedicated
in honor of Slovie Wolff and Rabbi Osher Jungreis
for charting our children's path to Torah
and in memory of our Rebbetzin Esther Jungreis ע"ה
Bari and Troy David

CHAPTER TWELVE
A Tale of Two Bands

The Hineni event at Madison Square Garden was the turning point in the Rebbetzin's life. In the days following the event that had touched so many people and made such a difference, she received a call from Shlomo Levin, then serving as the Israeli consul in New York.

"Rebbetzin," he began, "I was one of the people who had the good fortune to be in the audience at Madison Square Garden and I have a question for you. Would you be able to come see me at my office?"

When they were sitting across the desk from one another, the Israeli consul said, "Here's the thing, Rebbetzin. While I was sitting in the audience at Madison Square Garden listening to your amazing speech, a fantastic idea popped into my mind."

"What's that, Mr. Levin?"

"I think you should travel to Israel to address the soldiers of the IDF."

The Rebbetzin didn't understand and told him so.

"What exactly are you saying? You want me to get on a plane and go teach Torah to the IDF? How is that going to work?"

As much as she would have loved to do such a thing, the Rebbetzin didn't see his request as something in the realm of possibility and she turned him down.

Regretfully.

But once again Esther Jungreis would learn that there was a plan and that when something was supposed to happen, it would happen — whether she thought it was possible or not.

The Rebbetzin reaching out to Israeli soldiers accompanied by an American jazz band

Shlomo Levin had already sent a publicity shot of Rebbetzin Jungreis to the Israeli Army Entertainment Corps. It was a picture of Esther Jungreis, standing on stage with a microphone in her hand, and upon receiving the picture, the army entertainment corps mistakenly thought she was a singer. The follow-up call came from an army office based out of Tel Aviv a few weeks later.

The voice on the other end of the line was Israeli and spoke English with a very heavy accent.

"Iz diz Esther Jungreis?"

The Rebbetzin asked the caller to identify himself.

"I calling from Israeli Army."

Somewhat taken aback, the Rebbetzin asked what she could do for him.

"We want know how many shows you do in Israel?"

Not understanding that they were contacting her as an entertainer, the Rebbetzin found herself incredibly moved by the invitation — the Israeli army wanted her to come teach them Torah!

There was no way for her to refuse. After accepting the offer and settling on a tentative date for the trip, the Rebbetzin sat down to figure out the logistics and how everything would work.

"For this to actually make sense," she told herself, "I'm going to need to replicate what I did at the Garden. Before speaking at the Garden there was music — which means I'll need to have music with me at the army bases as well." The talented group of singers who had accompanied her at the Garden were local and clearly not an option. Yet if not them, who?

In the Rebbetzin's life, challenges had a way of working themselves out, and here as well she received a call from a Miami-based lawyer she had met in Florida not long before.

"Rebbetzin, I hear that you're off to Israel."

"You heard correctly."

"That's very exciting news. Lucky soldiers. The reason I'm calling is because my sons and I would like to join you on this trip."

"You want to join me? In what way?"

"As your band."

Rebbetzin Jungreis was very amused.

"You want to be my band? What kind of music do you play?"

"Well, in all honesty, we're into jazz, but I'm sure we'll be able to play whatever type of music you want!"

Picking up the dubious silence from her end of the line, the man said, "Rebbetzin, we would really appreciate being given this opportunity!"

The Rebbetzin would have much preferred a band that was familiar with Jewish music and knew all the hits of the '70s. But with no other musical options in sight, she convinced herself that it just might work. Truthfully, she had no choice but to make it work. Otherwise there would be no music and the event would not be the same.

The Rebbetzin flew to Israel accompanied by Barbara Janov and the jazz band from Miami. Her first program had been arranged at the Ramat David air force base. It was a very large base, with hundreds of soldiers, and just thinking about speaking to such a group was enough to make even the Rebbetzin nervous. Though she had already spoken at Beit Ha'am in Yerushalayim, there the crowd had been an older and more mature audience. Now she was addressing soldiers and she had a sneaking suspicion that if her audience wasn't happy with the speech, they would feel one hundred percent free to let her know it. She had no interest in being pelted by tomatoes at her first event for the IDF.

However, it was too late to do more than worry.

The jazz players from Miami were warming up the crowd as the Rebbetzin waited on a side stage for her turn. She could hear them banging, thumping and tootling away; when they were done, the evening's MC thanked them over and over, remarking that if they were the warm-up act, how excited he was to listen to the "singer" who had flown all the way from New York to join them at Ramat David.

At that moment Rebbetzin Jungreis suddenly realized how the mistake occurred.

"They are expecting me to sing," she said to herself. "Ribono shel Olam, they are expecting me to sing!"

Though the same misunderstanding had occurred at Beit Ha'am, she hadn't known about it at the time. Now she suddenly grasped why the army had come calling. Shlomo Levin had sent them a picture and they had erroneously assumed she was a singer.

Now what?

She tried to recall her father's blessing from the Madison Square Garden event.

"May angels of mercy go with you, my precious child. May Hashem give you the words to reach every heart!"

If there was ever a time when she needed that blessing, it was right then.

"Ladies and gentlemen, please give a warm welcome to the famous singing sensation Esther Jungreis — all the way from America!"

"I heard them announce my name," she'd say years later, "and I

The Rebbetzin giving *chizuk* to Israeli soldiers at an army camp

Chapter Twelve: A Tale of Two Bands ☐ 141

wanted to run. I wanted to escape. But it was too late. I had no choice but to walk out onto that stage and face my audience."

"*Hincha Yehudi*! You are a Jew!"

They didn't know what she was talking about. They had been expecting a singer and here some lady was standing on the stage telling them they were Jews. Looks of perplexity covered every face, as the soldiers attempted to figure out what was going on.

She ignored the confusion. She had come all the way from the United States for a reason, and whether she would be successful or not was ultimately in the hands of Hashem and nobody else.

And so she began to speak. She told the soldiers about our history, the story of our nation. She told them how it all started and that even though we are a small nation, we have never ceased to have an impact on the world. She spoke about the fact that we had been away from our Land for so long, and how incredibly wonderful it was that we were finally back where we belonged, in the land of our forefathers Avraham, Yitzchak and Yaakov.

And then something happened.

There was silence in the room. A silence filled with the sound of thousands of voices from the past, begging her to find a way to inspire the young soldiers.

She continued speaking. She spoke and spoke, trying to help them connect with their past, trying to help them imagine the future — a future in which G-d played a major role.

As she looked out over the audience, she knew she had reached them. She knew this because they were staring at her with wide-open eyes. And in those eyes she saw tears — the tears of people who had been touched, touched despite themselves. Shlomo Levin was right, it was she who had been wrong. He had foreseen their reaction from that first moment at Madison Square Garden, and he deserved much of the credit for going out of his way to make it happen.

The Rebbetzin did something wonderful for the Israeli army. They were used to rabbis — rabbis in long coats and black hats, rabbis with serious expressions on their faces. They were used to religion being something unrelatable and unapproachable. Yet here she was and it was completely different, brand new and exciting. Suddenly they realized that religion could be relevant and enjoyable.

Of course there was a major problem.

The Rebbetzin had been invited to Israel by the IDF office which managed the army's entertainment corps. The entertainment corps never exposed the soldiers to Torah lectures. That was not their style. Yet by bringing the Rebbetzin, they had done just that — albeit in error.

Repercussions were on the way.

Early the next morning, the Rebbetzin was visited by an officer.

"I am very sorry," he began, "but there is no way I can allow you to continue your tour at our army bases."

The Rebbetzin was not surprised. Deep inside, she knew that it would come to this. On the contrary, she would have been surprised if it went smoothly.

"The soldiers connected to me very much, did they not?"

He nodded.

"I can't argue with you. They did like your presentation. It was original, young and fun. But you can't do what you're doing through the entertainment corps. This is the kind of thing that needs to be organized through army chaplaincy — not entertainment. I wish it wasn't this way, but this is the situation. *Ein mah laasot* — sorry, but there's nothing we can do!"

The Rebbetzin, however, did not want to be speaking to the soldiers under the chaplaincy umbrella, because then she would be speaking to soldiers who were already religious. Her target audience was the crowd from the previous night, and she wanted to be able to continue impacting non-religious soldiers like them.

"Look," he went on, "I am very sorry about how this whole thing turned out. I know you came here from America — and there's no question that you're clearly a celebrity... But it's all out of my hands. Believe me. If they find out what you've been selling the troops — Avraham, Yitzchak and Yaakov — people will say that you're trying to influence them, that you're trying to turn them into a bunch of Chareidim."

"So?"

"I will get in trouble. I could even be stripped of my officer's bars."

He was kind of joking, but not really.

For Rebbetzin Jungreis the conversation she was having was almost a replay of what had taken place in her dressing room with the manager in Madison Square Garden. Yet she had won at the Garden and she was going to win again.

She looked at the officer and then she spoke. From her heart.

"I appreciate what you are telling me and the fact that this could harm your career. On the other hand, you are an officer and I'm sure you want to do the best thing for your soldiers. Be honest with yourself for a second. Are you going to stand there, look me in the eye and tell me that you want to deny these young Jews a chance to connect to their heritage? Are you truly prepared to make such a decision? This is an opportunity for your boys to hear ideas and concepts that they should have been learning about for years — ideas that have been denied to them.

"Hashem sent me to speak to the army. The fact that I am here goes against all the odds. Are you going to be the one to stop this from happening? Are you prepared to live with the consequences?"

"But what am I going to do if they find out what you've been telling the troops?"

"Don't say anything. Tell anyone who asks that you had nothing to do with booking me or bringing me to the bases. Tell them that Shlomo Levin sent me here and if they have any questions they should speak to him!"

And like the manager at Madison Square Garden before him, the officer gave in, and told her that he wouldn't stand in her way.

When the Rebbetzin left American shores she had no expectations. She wasn't proficient in the Hebrew language and wasn't familiar with army culture. How successful could she be? And yet, she walked onto the stage of base after base and every single time the response was incredible. They applauded for her and asked for more, appreciated the gifts she had brought them from America and didn't want her to leave. They lined up to speak with her when she finished and sang along with the hastily learned songs of the band. Night after night she was living her dream — bringing young Jews back to their heritage and Hashem. She traveled across the land and spoke and spoke and spoke.

And then it was over and she was supposed to leave.

To return home to her husband in North Woodmere.

Funny thing — the army asked her to stay. Invitations were pouring in from all over the country. Everyone wanted to hear the Rebbetzin who came to teach them Torah. Now what? Could she give up such an opportunity?

She did the thing she would do many times throughout her life. She got on the phone and called her husband.

"How did it go?" he asked her from New York.

"Meshulem, it was a miracle. In the beginning they told me that I would not be able to continue speaking to the soldiers, but I argued with the officer and in the end he promised to let me continue."

"And?"

"And it just got better and better. I was able to touch so many *neshamos*. For so many of them, it was the first time in their lives that anyone talked to them about Torah and the mesorah. I never imagined such *hatzlachah*!"

"That's wonderful," he said warmly. "Rebbetzin Jungreis does it again!"

"Yes, but there's something I need to ask you."

"Go on."

"They want me to stay. I've been getting invitations and offers to speak from all over the country. Every speech means reaching more Yidden. Every talk means another priceless opportunity to introduce Jews to their Father in Heaven."

"If they are asking you to stay, there's no question that that is what you should do."

"But you are home by yourself!"

"Exactly. The kids are away in camp, and there's no pressure at all. Stay. Teach Torah to Klal Yisrael and do your best to continue making a *Kiddush Hashem*!"

The "perfect" man had spoken, and his wife listened.

Of course there was another problem: the fact that the jazz band had to leave and return home. Though later in her life the Rebbetzin no longer felt the need to have music at her speeches, back then, she put a lot of emphasis on that aspect. She needed a band to play music for her audiences before she spoke. She told her husband about this as well. And once again he reassured her and reminded her that it was all going to work out — as it always did.

And she felt calm and went about changing her ticket, while deep inside her mind, that little voice asked her yet again, *Yes, but what about the band?*

To which she replied, *He who sent me the jazz band from Florida will no doubt be able to send me another band to take their place.*

And with that, the Rebbetzin carried on.

Friday night at the Plaza. It had been a grueling ten days and she was finally able to sit down and catch her breath. Sitting in the hotel dining room dressed in Shabbos finery, the Rebbetzin was filled with a sense of profound gratitude to the Ribono shel Olam for what had transpired all across the country.

Suddenly the maître d' interrupted her train of thought.

"Rebbetzin Jungreis?"

She looked up at him.

"Yes?"

"You have some visitors outside in the lobby."

"Thank you."

Rising from her place at the table, the Rebbetzin exited the dining room and went to greet her visitors, who were sitting on some couches waiting for her. They rose as she approached.

"Good Shabbos," she greeted them, "what can I do for you?"

"Rebbetzin," said the boy who seemed to be the self-appointed spokesman of the group, "we have come to the hotel to offer you our services."

"What kind of services?"

"We have a band."

"A band?"

"Yes, and we would like to accompany you around the country when you speak. It would be a real honor to play music for you!"

"In that case," she replied, "it will be a real honor for me to have such a *chashuve* band!"

The *bachurim* were very excited.

American yeshivah boys coming together to provide music
at the Rebbetzin's programs

The Rebbetzin was about to return to the dining room, but she noticed that the band leader had something else on his mind.

"I just wanted to tell you a story," he explained.

"I love stories," she replied.

And then, sitting in the lobby of the Plaza Hotel in Yerushalayim, the Rebbetzin heard a truly beautiful story.

"Not long ago," the band leader began, "I was not a religious Jew. The only thing I cared about was music. I thought about music morning, afternoon and night and dreamed of traveling abroad to further my musical studies. Though I am learning now in Eretz Yisrael, I had been planning on moving to Europe where I hoped to immerse myself in the music and culture.

"One day, however, everything changed."

"What happened?"

"I saw an accident happen. I was walking down Kings Highway in Flatbush, minding my own business and thinking about something I needed to take care of, when I suddenly heard the sound of screeching brakes and squealing tires. It was the sound of a car trying to stop, and failing. There was a tremendous crash and the sound of shattering glass. Having been yanked out of my daydream by all the noise, I turned in the direction of the accident and saw an old man with a beautiful white beard lying on the ground in a spreading puddle of blood.

"I ran over to the man. He was out of it and I began talking to him, trying to get him to focus, knowing that there was nothing good about him losing consciousness. He was clearly experiencing terrible pain. I held his hand and talked to him and just tried to get him to hang in there, and eventually the police showed up and the emergency personnel moved him from the street onto a stretcher."

He paused for breath, and carried on telling his story.

"As the old man was being moved into the ambulance, I could see that he wanted to tell me something. I leaned in close to his mouth so I could hear what he was trying to say.

"'Are you Jewish?' he asked me.

"In all honesty I was shocked that he was asking me such a question at that time.

"'Yes,' I whispered.

"'There is something you have to do.'

"There was a sense of urgency to his words and I was filled with curiosity about the mission he was about to send me on.

"'What do I need to do?'

"'You need to leave this country and go to study at a yeshivah in Jerusalem.'

"His English was not great, but I understood his words, I understood them perfectly well.

"'Do you hear me?'

"I nodded.

"As they moved the saintly Jew into the ambulance and drove off, sirens blaring, I knew that I had just met an incredible person. He didn't care about himself at all. He was in real pain, but he didn't pay attention to it. All he cared about was making sure I understood what I needed to do. And that is how I ended up leaving America to come learn Torah here in Eretz Yisrael. Maybe one day I'll reach a fraction of that man's greatness."

He had come to the end of his story and waited for the Rebbetzin's reaction.

It wasn't long in coming.

"I want to tell you a secret," she said to him.

He was taken aback.

"What do you mean?"

"I mean that I know who that old man was."

Now the band leader became excited.

"Who?" he demanded.

"My father, Rav Avrohom HaLevi Jungreis. I will never forget how badly he was hurt when that car hit him. I went to visit him in the hospital and spent as much time with him as possible. The moment he was well enough to speak, he shared the story of your meeting, telling us about the special young man who ran to his side and held his hand in his moment of suffering. My father asked us to try to track you down —

Rav Avrohom HaLevi Jungreis
… always with a warm smile

and we did try — but we had no idea where to look for you. Eventually we gave up the search.

"And yet here you are — right on my doorstep!"

Finally the Rebbetzin was able to thank the band leader on behalf of the entire Jungreis family for his part in helping their father.

It was Shlomo HaMelech (King Solomon) who wrote, "Cast your bread upon the waters — and in days to come, you shall find it" (*Koheles* 11:1).

Kindness for others is like a boomerang. Send it out and watch as it returns.

The tour was a huge success. The Rebbetzin spoke and spoke. And her words were lapped up thirstily by the people fortunate enough to hear her speak. She spoke in Tel Aviv and Yerushalayim. She spoke in the Sinai. She spoke at moshavim and kibbutzim, in cities and villages. Finally it was her last night and last speech. She was introduced and spoke for an hour — entreating and explaining — making them

The Rebbetzin speaking to a packed crowd at Gan Hapa'amon in Yerushalayim

laugh, think and want to grow and become better people and better Jews.

She was about to get off the stage when the officer appeared.

It was the same man who had wanted to send her home after her first speech for the IDF. There was something in his hands.

"This is for you," he said, handing it to her.

She opened it.

There was a citation of thanks inside. From the army.

She would treasure that piece of paper for the rest of her life. It taught her that no matter how distant a person was from the truth, things could always change — and hope should never be lost.

Or as the saying goes: "As long as the candle burns..."

Her experience with the IDF taught the Rebbetzin to trust herself and to do what she felt was right when giving a speech. It didn't matter what the organizers wanted. She had a mission, and the message had to come across to the people who needed to hear what she had to say.

On one occasion the Rebbetzin was invited to give a speech in an official government capacity at Binyanei Ha'uma in Yerushalayim. Before going on stage, she was warned not to focus on Hashem, perhaps because the evening was intended to be devoted to the founding fathers of the State — and not to the One Above. Of course, the moment she walked onto the stage and began to speak, the Rebbetzin directed her speech in the opposite direction from which she had been told. Down below the stage, the security guards were doing their best to get her attention — to no avail — as she firmly delivered a real *dvar Torah* to those assembled.

"Ori, over there," she said to the crowd while pointing at the security guard, "he wants me to stop talking about Hashem and His Torah to all of you. But I need to tell you about our Real Father — our Father in Heaven…" and on she went, talking about Hashem, while the riveted audience waited to hear what she was going to say…

She knew it would be okay. The soldiers hadn't thrown tomatoes at her and neither would these people.

If anything, the opposite was true.

They were thirsty. And she gave them water to drink.

The best, thirst-quenching water in the world.

CHAPTER THIRTEEN
The Hineni Medallion

*I*f the Six Day War was the epitome of victory for the State of Israel, then the Yom Kippur War took the nation's pride in victory and smashed it into smithereens. So confident was the IDF in its abilities to prevent their myriad enemies from attacking the country that they disregarded top-level intelligence suggesting Egypt's intent and abilities. In the end, many of the highest army officers would resign, as did Prime Minister Golda Meir. All that, however, was scant comfort for the people who were left bleeding and traumatized from the surprise attack.

The Hineni necklace always proudly worn by the Rebbetzin

The Rebbetzin wanted to do something for them so that they should at least feel that Jewish people around the world cared about what was happening in Israel. The Rebbetzin assembled a design team and had them create various souvenirs with the Hineni logo. There were bumper stickers and even T-shirts. But the Hineni medallion was the most popular of all.

Designed by Rabbi Jungreis himself, the logo/medallion spelled the word Hineni in Hebrew artistically displayed in the shape of a flame, reminding everyone who saw it of the Rebbetzin's ultimate goal — to set the Jewish world ablaze with Jewish feeling.

Now armed with her medallions, the Rebbetzin set off for Eretz Yisrael to visit the wounded and injured in hospitals around the country. A jeweler who frequented Hineni offered to design the Israeli batch of medallions in silver, and the Rebbetzin accepted the offer.

And so she left the United States yet again, off to give *chizuk* (encouragement) to those who had given everything to save their people.

Years later, a man began attending the Rebbetzin's *shiurim* at Hineni, eventually becoming religious. One day he asked the Rebbetzin if he would be able to have one of the Hineni medallions. Of course she gave him one.

A few weeks later he returned holding a small jewelry box in his hand, which he presented to her, saying, "This is for you."

"What is this?" she asked him.

"It's the medallion. I'm returning it."

"But I gave it to you for keeps."

He smiled and told the Rebbetzin to open the box. She did and found a diamond-encrusted Hineni medallion inside.

"I deal in diamonds," he told her, "and I had this made for you. I cannot repay you enough for changing my life, but this is a small token of my appreciation."

The Rebbetzin was touched beyond words and always wore the medallion from that day on. In fact you can see the medallion in virtually every picture of her. There was something about that medallion that she loved very much. It is not difficult to understand why. It bore the name of Hineni, the organization to which she had devoted her life — and it had been designed by her husband, the man she credited with her success.

Once again the Rebbetzin took to the air. She was a frequent flyer before there was such a concept. She was accompanied by Barbara and by her daughter Chaya Sora, who was just finishing high school.

The truth of the matter is, Chaya Sora was hesitant to go. Regents exams were coming up and Chaya Sora, a conscientious student, knew that traipsing around Israel from top to bottom would not allow her to study for the Regents.

"Ma, I can't go."

"Why not, *sheinkeit*?"

"I have Regents right when we get back!"

"So you'll study on the trip."

"There's no way I'll be able to study. We'll be traveling from army base to army base. There's no way. I know what it's going to be like. As much as I want to go, I don't think it's the right thing to do."

But the Rebbetzin didn't think like other people. Other mothers might have been proud of their child for being willing to forfeit an incredible trip to Israel so as not to get a bad grade on an important test. But the Rebbetzin wasn't happy with her daughter's decision.

"This is not the way I raised you," she told Chaya Sora. "I raised my children to care about Klal Yisrael. Tests are important, but not as important as visiting soldiers who were injured saving Jewish lives!"

Seeing her mother so passionate about the trip, Chaya Sora gave in and agreed to come.

"I hope I get a good mark."

"You'll be fine. Everything will work out with the test."

And off they went.

Of course Chaya Sora was right. There was no time to study and during the rare moments when she wasn't busy, she was too exhausted to try to memorize the Periodic Table of Elements and the various algorithms of Trigonometry. For her part, Chaya Sora made peace with the situation. Her mother was right. She was there to give *chizuk* to Jewish heroes who had risked their lives for their country and she wouldn't worry about the exams.

The hospitals were full. The suffering was intense. You could hear the cries of the wounded as the nurses did their best to ease their pain and grant succor even in the slightest way. It was a tough scene, made even worse by the sight of the wives and children of some of the soldiers, who sat by their bedsides and looked at the world with eyes that saw nothing. The only thought on their minds was the soldiers, and they were attuned to their every twist, turn and cry. The scene in every hospital could have been summed up with the one-word caption: War!

The Rebbetzin didn't arrive alone. She brought a group of musicians along with her, and as they played and sang, filling the wards with the cheerful sounds of happy songs, Chaya Sora distributed drinks and

The Rebbetzin speaking at a rehab center for wounded Israel soldiers

cakes to anyone healthy enough to enjoy. When the Rebbetzin spoke, it was as if a special fire would fill her soul. She told the soldiers stories and gave them *chizuk*. Her visits were a unique blend of music, speech and love. At the conclusion of her speech, the Hineni medallions would be handed out, one per soldier. The soldiers at the gatherings were injured — some grievously so — but they enjoyed the speech, sang along with the music as best they could, participated as much as their injuries permitted and thanked the Rebbetzin both for coming to see them and for the silver medallions.

But there were some soldiers who were too badly wounded to leave their private rooms, and the Rebbetzin paid them each a private visit, knowing full well how challenging it would be to put a smile on the faces of men who had been through a form of gehinnom on earth.

It was in one of the rooms that the Rebbetzin came across a soldier who lay in bed and didn't move at all. He was wrapped in bandages and looked like a mummy. Pulling the Rebbetzin over to the side, a nurse quietly explained that the patient had been severely burned in a tank battle and was having an extremely difficult time recuperating. The Rebbetzin greeted him warmly, but the soldier did not respond.

Chapter Thirteen: The Hineni Medallion ☐ 155

"I've come to thank you for your heroic service for Klal Yisrael," she said.

Still the soldier had nothing to say. He lay still in the dimly-lit room and pretended he couldn't hear a word she said. Clearly he was not in any mood for conversation. Then again, he had never met the Rebbetzin.

"Please tell me your name."

Silence.

"I know what you're thinking," she said to him. "You think I cannot possibly understand what you are going through. You are thinking that there's no reason for me to come here and that I should leave you alone to suffer in silence. I know what you're thinking and I know how these visits seem. But I want you to know that I mean every word I'm saying. You're a hero and you should know it!

"I also brought you something as a little gift. It's small but I hope you like it," and she showed the young and badly burned soldier the Hineni medallion she had brought for him.

If she had been hoping to wake him up, she succeeded. The soldier who had refused to say a word suddenly went on the attack.

"Take the medallion and leave. I don't want it, I have no use for it, and I will never have any use for it! Take it out of here and leave!"

His words were clipped, his tone filled with anger.

The Hineni medallion that the Rebbetzin distributed to Israeli soldiers

"I know that you are in pain. I know how much it hurts. I know that you don't think you need the medallion, but I am going to leave it with you anyway — just in case. You never know. There may come a day when you will remember the medallion I tried to give you and wish you still had it."

"Why would I ever feel that way? Why would I ever need a medallion?"

It was a shot in the dark, but it worked. If her earlier words to him served to shake him out of his lethargy, her next line threw him for a loop and got him even angrier.

"You want to know why you would possibly need this," she

said. "I'll tell you why. To save as a present for your kallah when you get engaged."

She would never know why she had uttered those exact words. All she knew was that Hashem had placed them into her mind at that exact second — and that they had appeared for a reason. She had spoken to enough people in pain by that point in time to know that Hashem had a way of sending her the words she needed.

The next second he reacted. His reaction shook her to the core.

He opened his mouth and laughed. Laughed. A bitter laugh. The laugh of a person who has lost all will to live.

"You talk to me about getting engaged. You dare talk to me about marriage! Lady, do you not see who I am and what I have become? Nobody will agree to marry me. No girl will look twice at me. I have no chance of living a normal life. I'm no longer a *ben adam* (man)! So please, please, take your medallion or whatever you want to call it, and leave my room!"

The Rebbetzin was silent for a few seconds. It was almost as if she had left the room. But she was still there, looking thoughtfully at the figure in the bed.

"You are so right when you say you are not a *ben adam*," she said to him. "Because that's the truth. You made the ultimate sacrifice for your people. You are not a *ben adam*! You are a *malach Hashem*, an angel of Hashem! You are a special person and I am sure you will find happiness in your life.

"We have a tradition that every person has someone destined for them. This is true for you as much as for everyone else. Do not fear. You will see that you too will meet the girl who is right for you. When that happens, be sure to tell her of our meeting — and how a rebbetzin came to see you and told you that you have tremendous *zechusim* (merits) that you are prepared to share with her.

"Tell her everything. Tell her the whole story. And make sure to explain to her that the medallion I left for you here at the hospital is a reminder and a symbol of everything I said."

He looked at her.

"Rebbetzin, I can't imagine saying any of this to a girl. She'll think I'm out of my mind."

"You're wrong. She won't think that at all. You will see. You will find the perfect girl — and remember, all you need is one — and when you find her, tell her that when you get married, the two of you are going to share your portion in Olam Haba (the World to Come)."

After giving this speech, Rebbetzin Jungreis placed the Hineni medallion on the night table beside his bed.

"Shalom," she said.

Then she left the room, the medallion resting on the night table.

The Rebbetzin returned to Eretz Yisrael one year later. By now the majority of the soldiers had already been released from many of the hospitals. There were, however, many soldiers who had been transferred to recuperation centers around the country. They were taken care of by devoted nurses who taught them the skills they would need to get back on their feet. Once again the Rebbetzin didn't stop. She visited many places and gave much *chizuk* to hundreds of soldiers.

At one recuperation center (this was in Haifa) the Rebbetzin stood on a stage and spoke from her heart to a receptive audience who appreciated her sentiments and applauded her warmly when she finished. She was still standing on the stage when some of the staff helped a soldier in a wheelchair up onto the stage. He was holding a bouquet of flowers in his lap, which he wanted to present to her as a token of their gratitude.

She looked at the soldier.

He looked at her.

"Do you recognize me?"

"I'm not sure," she replied. "You look familiar."

(This was her standard answer when someone asked her whether she recognized them — something that occurred about ten times a day…)

"You came to see me in the hospital last year."

She stared at him. Tears came to her eyes.

"I was wrapped like a mummy."

"I remember."

"You left me a gift, though I told you to take it away."

"Yes," she whispered.

"Rebbetzin," he said, "I'd like you to meet my wife."

And so saying, he introduced her to the nurse standing behind his chair — a young, smiling Yemenite woman.

That alone would have been more than enough. But that wasn't the end of the story. For around the woman's neck was a chain on which none other than the Hineni medallion was suspended. And then Esther Jungreis cried.

But what about Chaya Sora and the Regents?

When the tour came to its successful conclusion and they had returned to New York, Chaya Sora's earlier fears came rushing back to her young heart in a torrential downpour. This was it, she was going to fail. She never had time to study. It was a very sad young woman who went to sleep, knowing there was no way she would ever receive a decent mark.

And then something incredible happened.

On June 15, 1974, the *New York Times* went to print with the headline: *"Four Regents Tests Canceled After Discovery of Thefts."*

The Times went on to explain that for the first time in ninety-six years, the tests would not be taking place as scheduled due to the fact that a few students, having managed to get their hands on the tests, had sold them to thousands of other students throughout New York.

"In the end the Regents were canceled that year," Chaya Sora said with a smile. "Once again, my mother was proven right. As always."

This chapter has been dedicated
in memory of Jeffrey Silverman ע"ה
loving and devoted father and friend
The Feinsod Family
The Sealove and Laskowitz Families

CHAPTER FOURTEEN

The Shofar of Bergen-Belsen

"After the Rebbetzin's initial meeting with my father," Rabbi Gellis said, "she decided that he was a tzaddik and would be able to help her actualize her dreams. She realized that he was well connected with everyone — religious, secular and even within the military — and hoped that he would use those connections to have her speak across the country, from Metulah to Eilat. I was my father's chief of staff, as it were, so I soon found myself designated as the Rebbetzin's man in Israel. When she told me that she wanted to speak at the army bases, I was the one who made the calls and set up the events. I called the air force and the navy on her behalf and drove her to many places that were off the beaten trail — places that the average citizen never saw or even imagined existed."

Rabbi Yisrael Gellis continues:

Watching the Rebbetzin in action was always fascinating. The soldiers were used to entertainment. Many of the country's finest singers had a practice of making the rounds of the bases to give live performances. Many of them had been in the army entertainment unit themselves and were happy to return 'home.' Chava Alberstein used to come on a regular basis. So did Ofra Hazah. These were the names that were familiar. And then along came the Rebbetzin, and not only wasn't she a singer — she talked Torah to them! Like I said, it was a sight to behold. Every single place she went — she somehow managed to captivate the audience. I don't know how she did it.

It was almost supernatural.

I took the Rebbetzin to speak to the tank units at their bases, and to the soldiers standing guard on Israel's borders — up and down the length and breadth of the country. She was never tired, always ready for another adventure. And whenever she finished speaking, the soldiers wouldn't let her go. They'd line up to talk to her, each one sharing his personal challenges with her… Practically speaking, there was not much she was able to do for any of them. She didn't live in the same country as them. But she did one thing for them and she did it well — she listened to them.

That alone was crucial.

And so many times I watched as tough, burly, battle-scarred soldiers lost control and cried to her — and she shared in their sorrow and cried with them.

Our normal method of communication back then was via letters. I'd walk into my father's office and find a letter from overseas with the Rebbetzin's name on the front. I still remember opening those letters and reading about the next thing she wanted to do.

Dear Rabbi Gellis,

As you know I was recently zocheh to do an event at Madison Square Garden in New York. Baruch Hashem, many thousands of people attended the event and it was a genuine Kiddush Hashem. There was singing and dancing and many Yidden were able to draw closer to their Creator.

I would like to replicate the success of that evening in Eretz Yisrael. Would you be able to arrange funding from the municipality for a major event at Binyanei Ha'uma in the near future?

Please let me know as soon as possible.

Esther Jungreis

My father was in charge of funding for all of the city's Torani events. He'd decide where to allocate the funds and how much money to devote to any particular event. It was his prerogative to pay for an entire event or to fund it partially.

When it came to the Rebbetzin, he couldn't do enough. The municipality paid for everything: for the hall, advertising and music. He believed in her and knew that everything she did was *l'sheim Shamayim*, for the sake of Heaven.

In those days the Jerusalem municipality had access to roughly one hundred billboards in different neighborhoods on which posters and advertisements were pasted.

"Reb Yisroel," she said to me, "one hundred poster boards is not enough. By tomorrow, someone else will come along and cover our posters with an advertisement for some other event."

"So what should we do?"

"We will have the municipality paste posters on all the boards — and we will hang our own posters as well."

"We?"

"Yes, I'm coming with you. We will hang the posters in the middle of the night."

I rented a car for the night, filled the trunk with posters and off we went together with Barbara and another helper. Our first stop on the night of the great poster-hanging ceremony was at the home of Noach Klepper who lived on Rechov Hoshea in the center of Geula. Klepper's specialty was preparing the special glue used by the municipality to adhere the posters to the poster boards. Klepper prepared his glue from a mixture of wheat and water and it was known to be long lasting and impervious to weather. In Yerushalayim, where the rain sometimes came down in buckets, using the right kind of glue was vital.

We picked up the glue from Klepper and off we went.

All went well for a while as the four of us found our rhythm. Hang, swipe with glue, hang, swipe with glue. And so on. We hung posters all over the city for a few hours, undisturbed.

I was hanging a batch of posters on Rechov Ramban in Rechavia at four in the morning when a police car appeared. The cop got out of his car in a clearly confrontational and aggressive mood.

"What are you doing here?" he challenged me. "This is a residential neighborhood! Do you have a permit to hang posters on this street?"

The Rebbetzin, who had been sitting in the car at that moment, opened the door and approached the police officer.

The next few minutes were priceless.

I watched as she gave the cop a speech about Am Yisrael and saving the Jewish nation and the Holocaust and *mesirus nefesh* (self-sacrifice) and Israeli soldiers and *Shema Yisrael* and "*Oorah Yisrael* — wake up, Israel!"

(In general the words "Oorah Yisrael" were her war cry. I can't tell you how many times I heard her calling out that particular phrase with all her heart! "Wake up, Klal Yisrael, wake up!")

And then, standing in the middle of Rechov Ramban at 4:15 in the morning talking to an Israeli policeman, Esther Jungreis started to cry.

In all truthfulness, the cop never had a chance. The moment she started to cry it was all over.

The end of the story — the cop helped us finish hanging the batch of posters on Rechov Ramban, right in the heart of Rechavia — and without a permit.

"*Tatzlichi* (much success) with your *derashah* (speech)," he told the Rebbetzin before getting back into his cruiser and driving off into the night, his aggression gone.

Of course the Rebbetzin wouldn't let him go without giving him a berachah, and then another one for his wife and kids. By the time we parted, there was no question in my mind that he would remember his encounter with the Rebbetzin for the rest of his life.

Establishing a branch of the Rebbetzin's organization in Givatayim was a logical choice. The city was completely secular — which meant there were people to work with and teach. Once the office was up and running, however, they needed to find a way to fund themselves. Help appeared in the form of an individual named Menashe Hoss.

Menashe Hoss was a man of means — he owned a string of successful art galleries and had been in the audience at the Rebbetzin's speech at Beit Ha'am in 1972. Hearing about the launch of the new Hineni office, Hoss got in touch with Gellis and told him to rent an office and get to work — and that he would pick up the bill.

Once the operation had been set up the question became — what next?

It was the mid-1970s and kiruv operations were few and far between.

The Rebbetzin loved the fact that we were turning Hineni into an international operation, and gave us free rein to be as creative and out-of-the-box as possible. And so it came to be that Hineni Israel held its first seminar for secular people on Chol HaMoed Succos in Kibbutz Ramat Rachel. I am still in touch with the people who became religious at that seminar.

I called the Rebbetzin a week before Succos and gave her a full report about what we were planning for the seminar. She loved it, and went so far as to record a message to the attendees that she sent to me from America and that I aired at the seminar.

But to my way of thinking, Hineni was best epitomized by the Rebbetzin — not by other speakers. It was the Rebbetzin who stepped onto the stage at Madison Square Garden, the Rebbetzin who addressed the crowd in her broken Ivrit at Beit Ha'am, and the Rebbetzin who cried at army bases around the country. Bringing other speakers wasn't the same and didn't have the same effect.

So we organized a special event at Rav Dovid Brodman's shul in the exclusive Savyon neighborhood in Tel Aviv, and the Rebbetzin made plans to fly in from America to attend the event.

On the night of the Rebbetzin's speech, the shul was filled. The audience was not religious. Some were traditional, others had no connection — and the one common denominator among the crowd was that virtually all of them were upscale and sophisticated. Her speech went over very well, with the crowd growing openly emotional despite the fact that they were of Ashkenazi descent and not prone to displays of emotion in public. Upon hearing the Rebbetzin's words, however, they were unable to control themselves and within a short time, there was a beautiful shul filled with people from the upper echelons of the country who were wiping tears from their eyes — along with the Rebbetzin herself, who was never quite able to subdue her heartfelt emotions.

The Rebbetzin was a master orator.

Every speech held some of the same elements, yet every speech was different.

In every speech she shared a few of her memories from her Holocaust experiences. I remember at that speech that she told the story of the three hundred cigarettes and the shofar of Bergen-Belsen.

I watched them sitting and listening to her, and as her words pierced their hard exterior shells the audience became different people. Gone were the million-dollar homes and luxury cars, the designer suits and fancy vacations. She had transported them back to the snow, back to the striped uniforms, back to the shaven heads. They were the same people, yet completely different. As the Rebbetzin described the scene, the people sitting in that well-appointed shul left their seats and tiptoed over the barbed wire fences and into hell on earth.

"In the days leading up to Rosh Hashanah," the Rebbetzin began, "there were many meetings as the camp's rabbinical leadership tried to determine if there was any chance in the world for them to get hold of a shofar and a machzor for the Yamim Noraim. Many people will no doubt ask why on earth they were even thinking about such things when people were dying right and left, but of course the opposite is true — because what is life worth without being able to hear the shofar being blown on Rosh Hashanah? In their minds, there was no question that the sacrifice was worth the price.

"It was eventually determined that it would cost them as much as three hundred cigarettes (a form of concentration camp currency) to obtain both a shofar and a machzor through the very active Bergen-Belsen black market. And so it was done — done with incredible *mesirus nefesh* on the part of the Jews — who had nothing and yet managed to somehow collect three hundred cigarettes!"

Every face in the shul was turned in her direction. I watched the feelings and emotions playing over their lips, the looks in their eyes — the expressions on their faces. They were completely immersed in her story.

"It goes without saying that news of the shofar's arrival spread like wildfire. Somehow every Jew felt that having a shofar with them portended great things to come. All waited anxiously for the otherworldly moment when the *baal toke'a* would put the shofar to his lips sounding the blasts, begging Hashem to forgive His people."

The Rebbetzin took a breath and continued her story.

"Near our camp was another camp, for Polish Jews. They too knew about our shofar, and they too wanted — no, needed — to hear the sound of the shofar blasts: the *tekios*, *shevarim* and *teruos*. But the shofar was in our hands. So they did what every Jew might have done, yes, even in the concentration camps. They crawled up as close as possible to the barbed wire fences separating our camps and waited for the moment when the piercing sound of the shofar would be heard.

"And then it happened.

"The *baal toke'a* lifted the shofar to his lips. Seconds later the sound of the shofar rang out loud, plaintive, childlike. The young men lying beside the gate were transformed from concentration camp inmates into Yidden back in shul on Rosh Hashanah. Yidden listening to the shofar. Yidden, the way they'd been years before the Nazis destroyed their world.

"But the sound of the shofar sounds like a siren. And the second the Nazis heard that siren sound, they came running from all directions. They were fast enough to catch the young men at the fence, fast enough to make sure they didn't get away. Up went the clubs high in the air, and then down they came on the prisoners, again and again, harder and harder, yet no matter how they were beaten, they paid no attention. The Nazis had been reduced to nothingness as the shofar drove every other thought out of their minds — and they cried out with every fiber of their being, '*Baruch Atah Hashem, Elokeinu Melech ha'olam, asher kideshanu b'mitzvosav v'tzivanu lishmoa kol shofar* — Blessed are You, Hashem, our G-d, King of the universe, Who has sanctified us with His commandments and has commanded us to hear the sound of the shofar.'"

The shul in Savyon was completely silent. Here and there, someone broke down, their sobs a testimony to the memories they evoked.

"And what about the machzor," she went on. "Didn't we need a machzor if we were to daven as a *tzibbur* (congregation) on Rosh Hashanah? But three hundred cigarettes didn't buy you machzorim for an entire camp. It bought only one.

"One machzor.

"How was that going to help a few hundred people?

"In the end Zeide and the other rabbanim decided that everyone in the camp should learn at least one special prayer, one tefillah by heart. But which one? They discussed it for a while before making a decision. And so in the days leading up to Rosh Hashanah the Yidden of Bergen-Belsen memorized the prayer of '*L'bochen Levavos* — [Let us pray] to He Who searches hearts on the Day of Judgment,' by heart.

"There is no question," the Rebbetzin concluded, "that when Hashem came down to our camp that year and heard our prayer — there is no question that He searched our hearts, exactly as the prayer says, and knew that we had never wavered in our love for Him. Not even then. Not even in the darkness of Bergen-Belsen."

But the story wasn't over yet.

Many years later the Rebbetzin was again in Eretz Yisrael. One of her many speeches took place in a town called Ginat Shomron. There she spoke at a shul in a neighborhood called Neve Alizah, named in memory of the wife of Prime Minister Menachem Begin.

Summer was coming to an end as the Rebbetzin stood up in that shul to speak. Elul was on its way. And suddenly the Rebbetzin decided to tell the gathering the story of the shofar from Bergen-Belsen — the shofar that had impacted so many lives — the shofar that had sparked such incredible *mesirus nefesh*.

She spoke and of course there was not a dry eye in the room, as the audience relived the experience with her. It was as if they themselves were transported from Neve Alizah, over the mountains of the Shomron — and into the world of barbed wire and brutality.

She finished her speech. There was a collective intake of breath.

Suddenly a woman stood up in the middle of the audience.

"That shofar," she said.

"Yes?"

"I know that shofar. I know exactly what you're talking about!"

People looked at one another, then back at the Rebbetzin.

"Please explain."

"My father," the woman said, "my father was the Rabbi in the Polish section right beside yours. I do not know if anyone ever told you what happened after that first day of shofar blowing."

The Rebbetzin shook her head.

"What happened?"

"The shofar, the precious shofar, was smuggled out of your side of the camp and into ours. It had been smuggled into the camp in the bottom of a very large pail filled with a coffee-like liquid and was blown by my father in our side of the camp on the second day of Rosh Hashanah."

The two of them stared at one another. There were no words.

"Rebbetzin, I still have that shofar. It's here. Right here in Neve Alizah. I'll never forget how we blew that shofar after liberation and took it with us, away from the horrors of Europe."

She left the room. A few minutes later she returned — the shofar of Bergen-Belsen clutched tightly in her hands. Only then did they lose control — two women — two daughters of men who had risked everything to blow the shofar on Rosh Hashanah, though it put their lives at risk.

The Rebbetzin hadn't seen the shofar in many years. Holding it in her hands, she looked at it, running her hands over its smooth sides. That moment in the Shomron was nothing less than a reunion.

When the Jungreis family was sitting *shivah* for the Rebbetzin, countless people came to be *menachem avel*. One woman sat down in front of Chaya Sora and Slovie and proceeded to make a comment that brought no comfort to them at all.

"Your mother made a point of constantly repeating her story about the shofar the Satmar Rebbe blew in Bergen-Belsen."

They nodded at her.

"I was also an inmate in Bergen-Belsen and I have to tell you, I have zero recollection of hearing anyone blow the shofar on Rosh Hashanah! In fact, I don't know what your mother was talking about!"

Chaya Sora and Slovie exchanged glances and had no reply, at a loss to understand what the woman wanted of them. She left a few minutes later, leaving a stunned kind of silence behind her. There was little time to dwell on the visit, however, because the door kept on opening with new visitors arriving to take the place of those who had left.

Another woman slipped into the chair just vacated by the woman who had come to cast doubt on the validity of the shofar of Bergen-Belsen.

In fact, as the first was leaving, the second took her seat.

It was that close.

After exchanging a few words, the newcomer told the family that she had made a point of attending the *shivah* because she wanted to talk to them "about the shofar of Bergen-Belsen!"

"What about it?" they asked her, still slightly stunned from the previous encounter and somewhat wary now.

"I live in Neve Alizah," she began, "and my mother-in-law was the woman who ran back to her house to bring your mother the shofar of Bergen–Belsen. Today that shofar is proudly displayed in my house…"

Two women.

The opposite of comfort and the epitome of comfort — a few minutes apart. Life. How fascinating it is.

This chapter has been dedicated
in tribute to the Rebbetzin's ever-presence
and in honor of Slovie Jungreis Wolff and her family
for continuing to light the world with wisdom and love

David and Lisa Sakhai

Part 3
1806-1939

The Jungreis family, Csenger, the Menuchas Osher—
that was her life... And she never stopped striving to
help the mishpachah remember who we are...

Harav Yitzchok Dov (Berel) Jungreis,
the Gorlitzer Rebbe
a cousin of both Rav Meshulem and
Rebbetzin Esther Jungreis

CHAPTER FIFTEEN

The Chasam Sofer's Letter

No doubt people wondered what type of mother the Rebbetzin was. After all, how could a woman who filled the role she did to such accolades on the international stage possibly find the time to juggle the much less acclaimed role of mother as well? And yet, they would be completely wrong.

The Rebbetzin continually wrote notes to her children — notes filled with warm messages and expressions of her love for them — inevitably signed with the words "*V'nafsho keshurah b'nafsho* — our souls are eternally intertwined."

There was, of course, a reason she signed that way. It had to do with her experiences in the Displaced Persons (DP) camp, in Switzerland after the war. Sleeping in a dorm with other orphans and separated from her parents, Esther suffered frightful nightmares. There was one bright spot, and that was the fact that her father, Rav Avrohom, would often come to say *Shema* with her and her roommate before they went to sleep. After he finished saying *Shema* with his little girl, he would have to leave. But before he left her for the night, Zeide would bend down and whisper in her ear, "*V'nafsho keshurah b'nafsho*."

Esther Jungreis grew up to become a prominent powerhouse, and the words "*V'nafsho keshurah b'nafsho* — our souls are eternally inter-twined" never left her. She knew without a shadow of a doubt that she was her father's daughter, that unmistakable and undisputable fact of life shaping her world vision on numerous levels. While Esther would grow up to become a legendary force, her power could be compared to

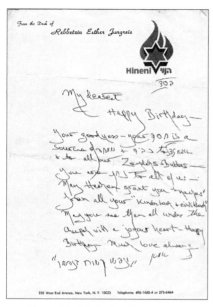

The Rebbetzin's signature ending
"V'nafsho keshurah b'nafsho" on a
birthday letter to one of her children

that of a bullet leaving a gun. The tip of the bullet is what enters the target, but it is the force of the gun that gives the bullet its ability to penetrate and conquer. So it was with her. She was the speaker and the person everyone wanted to listen to. But her power stemmed from her father and mother, from her incredible husband and from the long line of Zeides — the Menuchas Osher especially — to whom she felt eternally connected.

Esther Jungreis might have been the bullet.

But there was a whole line of eminent tzaddikim behind her pressing the trigger and giving her unique bullet the velocity and power it needed to shatter the apathy she faced in her quest to make the world aware of the modern-day spiritual Holocaust.

One cannot truly appreciate who a person is until you know his background and family history. For Rebbetzin Esther Jungreis, family was paramount. She didn't think of herself in terms of a single entity, but rather as another link in the glorious Csenger dynasty.

And the time has come to tell that part of her story, the story of the Csenger Zeide, Harav Osher Anshil HaLevi Jungreis — the Menuchas Osher — the tzaddik revered by all of Hungary, and the stories of the Zeides who followed the Csenger. There are many stories, but they are intertwined.

There were many factors in her relationship with her ancestors.

But the main thing to remember is this:

There are three words that sum it up best of all.

"V'nafsho keshurah b'nafsho."

If we are looking for a starting point for today's Jungreis family, it would probably be a good idea to begin with the Menuchas Osher and his father Rav Shmuel. Rav Osher Anshil was a respected leader of Hungarian Jewry in the early 1800s, a great-grandfather of both Rav Avrohom HaLevi Jungreis, the Rebbetzin's father, and her husband Rav Meshulem. Rav Shmuel HaLevi Jungreis (father of the Menuchas Osher) had a Chumash in which he recorded the dates of his children's births inside the front cover. This is how we know the birthday of his son, the Menuchas Osher.

The Csenger Tzaddik, known as the Menuchas Osher, Rav Osher Anshil Jungreis

The first thing you have to know about Rav Shmuel is that he was offered the position of Chief Rabbi of Budapest and he turned it down, explaining that life in a small town would be much healthier for his family from a Torah perspective.

"I want to educate my children without outside influences."

Acting accordingly, Rav Shmuel HaLevi served as rav in the town of Csecse, located about an hour from Budapest, where he was able to keep his family out of the public eye.

Not only did he succeed in raising them to be ehrliche Yidden (pious Jews), they went on to become one of the most famous rabbinic families in Hungary. Before the war there were eighty-five Jungreis rabbanim serving Jewish communities all across the country. All but a handful of the family were brutally murdered by the Nazis. The fact that even a few remained alive was an open miracle.

The Jungreis family traces its origins to the renowned historical city of Prague. This was where Rav Shmuel HaLevi Jungreis lived, learned and taught. But when people thought of him, it was difficult for them to remain focused on his erudition and piety. This was due to the fact that Rav Shmuel Jungreis was extremely good looking. Ultimately, his good looks would have major ramifications for the tzaddik who just wanted to be left alone to learn.

Sefer written by Rav Shmuel HaLevi
Jungreis, father of the Menuchas Osher

As a leader of the Jewish community, Rav Shmuel was once invited to the royal palace to plead the case for his kehillah. There he was seen by the queen, who invited the Jewish rabbi to her private apartment, claiming that she wanted a chance to have a conversation with him undisturbed.

Once in the queen's quarters it didn't take Rav Shmuel long to understand that he had erred by allowing himself to go with her. When she excused herself for a minute and left the room, Rav Shmuel hurried to the window and parted the drapes, trying to ascertain how high up he was and whether it was possible to jump from her quarters.

To his chagrin he found that he was stranded on one of the palace's highest floors. Far below he could see the Charles River. It was dark and forbidding and there was no question in his mind that jumping from where he was, down into the river, could very well mean instant death. On the other hand, he didn't see any alternative. There was no way for him to flee the palace other than through the window.

Rav Shmuel took a deep breath and climbed up on the windowsill. Down below, the river moved swiftly forward, chunks of ice floating past in the inky blackness. There was no time to lose. Mumbling the words of *Shema*, Rav Shmuel looked heavenward, and leapt off the ledge and into the river. He survived the plunge, but the river tried to pull him into the undertow, though he managed to outswim the vicious currents. Using every last bit of strength, Rav Shmuel swam against the pull of the river and somehow reached the shore, where he collapsed for a few seconds.

He knew, however, that he couldn't lie there indefinitely. Though the queen would think he died (if she even believed that he jumped from such a high floor), he couldn't allow passersby to see him lying there. Summoning vestiges of strength from deep within his soul, Rav Shmuel rose to his feet and ran from the river bank, his freezing wet clothing sheathed against his shivering body.

Leaving the spot of his miracle, Rav Shmuel went to the home of the city's Chief Rabbi where he asked his advice, wondering whether it was still possible for him to remain in the city.

"Leave tonight," he was told. "Leave before the queen learns that you survived."

Taking his family, Rav Shmuel abandoned their life in Prague for an unknown future. Yet heaven would not forget what he did and the incredible risks he took by jumping out the palace window and into the river, and he was rewarded with noteworthy descendants. The Jungreises became one of the premier rabbinic families in Europe.

Matzeivah of
Rav Shmuel HaLevi Jungreis

Rav Shmuel had many sons, all *chashuv* (worthy).

But there was one son who rose above them all. His name was Osher Anshil and he would grow up to become known far and wide as the Menuchas Osher.

The Menuchas Osher was born on Erev Shabbos, 26 Shevat 5566/1806, at two in the morning. From the time he was a very young child, it was obvious to his parents that this boy had an exceptional future ahead of him. One Motza'ei Shabbos his father was sitting at the dining room table eating Melaveh Malkah and singing *zemiros* to bid farewell to the Shabbos Queen. Meanwhile Anshi'le was sleeping in his room. Suddenly, Rav Shmuel heard laughter emanating from his son's bedroom. Rising from his seat at the table, he entered the room and found his son in bed, clearly having been laughing in a dream.

"What happened, Anshi'le?"

"I just had a dream," he told his father. "I saw Avraham Avinu in one corner of the room I was in. Yitzchak Avinu was in the second corner. Yaakov Avinu was in the third corner. Eliyahu HaNavi was in the fourth corner."

The father waited for his precocious son to get to the point.

"I didn't know who to say *Shalom Aleichem* to first. Should I approach Avraham Avinu? After all, he was the oldest of everyone in the room. On the other hand, it says about Eliyahu HaNavi: '*Ashrei mi she'raah Eliyahu HaNavi b'chalom v'nasan lo shalom, v'hechzir lo shalom* — Praised is he who sees Elijah the prophet in a dream and greets him with *Shalom Aleichem*, which Eliyahu returns.'

"I didn't know the right move to make."

"What did you do?" his father asked him curiously.

"I gave Eliyahu HaNavi *Shalom Aleichem* first. I figured that Avraham Avinu is a good father and he will forgive me for greeting him second."

As Osher Anshil matured, it was evident that he was highly intelligent. From his bar mitzvah until he was fifteen years of age, the Menuchas Osher learned at the yeshivah of the Maharam Ash in the city of Ungvar. At a certain point, the young *bachur* began displaying miraculous abilities. When the Maharam Ash understood that his *talmid* was involving himself in the world of miracles — giving blessings to people that were actually coming true — he called him into his office and told him that it was still not time for him to be involved in such matters.

"There is a time and a place for everything in life," the brilliant Maharam Ash told his student, "and now it is your time to be completely immersed in the sea of Torah."

The Menuchas Osher obeyed his rebbi and curtailed that aspect of his personality and abilities.

At least for the time being.

When Osher Anshil turned fifteen, the Maharam Ash decided that the time had come for his student to leave his yeshivah and to enroll in the yeshivah of Rav Koppel Charif (the sharp one) in Verbo. Osher Anshil was miles above everyone else. His brain was like a live wire. He possessed unique abilities when it came to learning. More than anything, his brain was sharp — sharper than a razor-edged knife. He obviously needed to be constantly challenged to prevent boredom. And so the Maharam Ash informed his star pupil that he would be moving on to further his growth in Torah and *avodas Hashem* (service of G-d).

The Menuchas Osher would never forget his years with the Maharam Ash.

Later in life, Rav Osher Anshil wrote in a letter about his rebbi and his methodology in serving Hashem.

When I was younger, I studied under the Maharam Ash for two years. My rebbi used to fast three times a week and studied Torah in holiness and purity. He was completely proficient in Shas and Poskim, in *Alfas, Shulchan Aruch* and *Arba'ah Turim, Safra, Sifri, Tosefta*, Yerushalmi, Midrashos, Agaddos, *Sifrei Mussar* and *Sifrei Kabbalah*; and when he davened, it was with all the inner meanings of the Arizal.

Somehow, the young teenager knew exactly what type of *kavannos* (concentrations) his rebbi had while davening; and the Maharam Ash, like all truly amazing educators, knew when his student was ready to move on, and didn't keep him in his yeshivah despite the prestige of having such a student.

It was time to leave, and the Maharam Ash sent him on to the next level, where he remained for the next five years.

The story of the Menuchas Osher's shidduch is the stuff of legends. Rav Meir Almasher was the Rav in the city of Mattersdorf (then in Austria). Having a daughter of marriageable age, the Mattersdorfer Rav sent a letter to the Chasam Sofer — who was Rosh Yeshivah of one of the most prestigious yeshivos in Hungary — asking him to choose one of his best students as a shidduch for the Rav's daughter Nucha. The Mattersdorfer Rav made it clear in the letter that he was searching for a boy with the sharpest of minds. This made sense, considering that the Rav himself was brilliant.

The Chasam Sofer did exactly as he was asked. Scrutinizing the best boys in his yeshivah, he chose a *bachur* who fit the criteria. At the end of the winter *z'man* (term), when the *bachur* was leaving to return home for Yom Tov, the Chasam Sofer handed him a letter to be delivered to the Mattersdorfer Rav. Making a stop in Mattersdorf would of course necessitate delaying his return trip home, but the *bachur* was honored to be asked to do his rebbi a favor and accepted the mandate, no questions asked.

In the letter, the Chasam Sofer wrote that the person bringing him the letter was a genuine *talmid chacham* with an incredibly sharp mind, and that he warranted being chosen as the Mattersdorfer Rav's son-in-law.

It so happened that Osher Anshil Jungreis was also returning home at that time, and the two *bachurim* "happened" to cross paths in an inn along the way. Being of friendly disposition and on their own, the two boys elected to seat themselves at the same table, where they shared a meal and conversation. There Osher Anshil confided in his new friend that he was toying with the idea of moving on to go learn under the world famous Mattersdorfer Rav.

"You're going to the Mattersdorfer Rav," rejoined the *bachur*, "maybe you can do me a favor?"

"Sure, what do you need?"

"I have a letter from my Rebbe the Chasam Sofer that he asked me to deliver to the Rav. I had planned on making a major detour to Mattersdorf. But if you are traveling to the Rav in any case, maybe you could take the letter instead of me. What do you say?"

"It would be my pleasure."

So it came to be that the letter from the Chasam Sofer to the Mattersdorfer Rav changed hands. In the morning the *bachurim* parted ways, wishing one another a warm farewell. Osher Anshil arrived in Mattersdorf a short while later, where he asked to see the Rav. Sitting in the Rav's study, Osher Anshil explained that while he had been learning under Rav Koppel Charif for the last five years, he was ready to move on to the Mattersdorfer Rav's yeshivah.

The Rav needed no second invitation to converse in learning with a sharp mind, and witnessing the boy's seriousness and desire for greatness, he began a deep Talmudic conversation which traversed the width and breadth of Shas. By the time they were finished, the Rav found himself more than happy to welcome Osher Anshil into his circle of select students.

Before he could get any further, however, the twenty-year-old *bachur* remembered the letter he had been given. Removing it from his bag, he handed it to the Rav, telling him it was from the Chasam Sofer.

The Mattersdorfer Rav opened the letter and read the lines penned by the Chasam Sofer extolling the virtues of the letter's bearer and informing the Rav that he had been hand-picked by the Chasam Sofer for his daughter.

"Are you coming to me from Pressburg?" the Rav asked Osher Anshil, not comprehending how the letter had ended up in his hands.

"No."

"Then how are you the bearer of this letter?"

Osher Anshil was more than happy to clarify the matter.

"I met a *bachur* from Pressburg at the inn where I stayed on the way here. When he heard that I was planning on coming here for a *bechinah* (test), he asked me to deliver the letter for him."

To the Mattersdorfer Rav, the *hashgachah* (Divine Providence) seemed impossible to ignore, and he decided to tell Osher Anshil what the Chasam Sofer had written in the letter. Completely taken aback by the incredible turn of events, the *bachur* told the Rav that he would have to return home and discuss the whole sequence of events with his father.

Which he did.

Rav Shmuel HaLevi and his wife Miriam Yittel agreed with the Mattersdorfer Rav's appraisal of the situation, and it wasn't long before the shidduch came to be, with the Menuchas Osher engaged to the daughter of the Mattersdorfer Rav — setting the stage for his future role as the miracle worker of Hungarian Jewry.

This chapter has been dedicated
in memory of our beloved
Abba Zeide זצ״ל and Bubba ע״ה
Rav Meshulem and Rebbetzin Esther Jungreis
JJ and Rivkie Bistricer and Family

CHAPTER SIXTEEN
The Angelic Prescriptions

*T*he Menuchas Osher was appointed rav in the city of Csenger four years after his marriage. It was at that point that he left his father-in-law's home and began earning a reputation as a future Torah giant and leader throughout the country.

In the introduction to their father's *sefer Menuchas Osher* (a Talmudic work so respected in its day that a Talmudic student's ability to expound on a piece of Torah from the *sefer* was seen as an indication of his being a genuine *talmid chacham*), his children wrote that for the family's first

An heirloom copy of the first edition of the *sefer Menuchas Osher*

Recently reprinted editions of the *sefarim* of the Menuchas Osher

eight years in Csenger, they lived in abject poverty. Their father's salary was not adequate for the family's needs, and in consequence they suffered. Csenger was not a big city with *baalei batim* (laymen) who could afford to pay the Rav the type of salary he deserved. But the Menuchas Osher didn't want to move to a bigger town. Like his father before him, Rav Osher Anshil turned down a life of affluence for small village life and the opportunity to educate his children in the *derech* of Yisrael Saba, the path of generations past.

Yet even while they were living in relative obscurity, an interesting incident took place.

It was so cold in their home that the children and their father were forced to learn beneath the covers so that they wouldn't freeze. It didn't faze the Menuchas Osher. Nothing did.

One day the Menuchas Osher was learning with his children when he looked up for a second and noticed a man standing in the room. There was no reason for a stranger to be there. In fact, he shouldn't have been able to be there, because the door was locked! The man stared at the tzaddik and his children.

"All of you are shivering," he pointed out. "Why don't you put some firewood in the grate and heat the room?"

The Menuchas Osher looked at the man and replied, "I have no money for firewood."

Matzeivah of the Menuchas Osher

"Let me give you an idea," the stranger said. "You should offer visitors medical advice. The money they pay you will help you support your family. Right now all you have is what your town pays you for being their rav. If you combine the two livelihoods, you should have enough money for your needs."

"The most important thing is that I learn," the Menuchas Osher told the stranger. "If lines of people come to seek my advice for their medical problems, what will become of my learning?"

But the stranger wasn't listening. Leaving the Menuchas Osher's side, he took out a pen and began writing on the dining room table. Nobody knew what, but upon closer examination they began to understand.

The man was writing cures. Cures for a host of medical ailments.

There was a cure for epilepsy. And a cure for strokes. There was even a cure for headaches.

Soon the entire dining room table was covered by the man's medical scrawlings.

When he was finished, he turned and left — leaving a family behind who still didn't understand how he had entered their home in the first place.

The moment he was gone, the Menuchas Osher asked his wife to please clean the table and get rid of the "medical" scribbles.

Yet try as she might, they wouldn't come off. She tried and tried.

Nothing worked. The writing adhered to that table and despite all her efforts stubbornly refused to come off. Eventually the Menuchas Osher understood that his visitor had been none other than the Malach Raphael, the Angel Raphael. He then took out a pen and a notebook and copied all of the stranger's cures from the table and into his new "doctor's" miracle book. Only then, when the last of the cures had been written down — only then — was the Rebbetzin able to erase the writing.

From that moment on, a steady stream of people began making their way to Csenger where they pleaded with the Menuchas Osher to intercede with the Ribono shel Olam for them — and to diagnose their medical ailments.

With results came fame.

More people streamed to the town, and the Menuchas Osher became known as a medical miracle worker, able to assist people whom the greatest doctors had turned away due to the doctors' lack of knowledge. Having been "mentored" by an angel, the Menuchas Osher always knew what to do and what medicine to prescribe. With the passing of time, Rav Osher Anshil became more and more famous as the most extraordinary *baal mofes* (miracle worker) in the country.

Though there were other rabbis who were also known as miracle workers, it was the Menuchas Osher to whom the *gedolim* turned when they themselves needed a *yeshuah* (salvation). For example, Rav Yosef Shaul Nathanson, the Lemberger Rav (one of the famed rabbanim in Galicia), wrote a letter to the Menuchas Osher requesting that he daven for him. The fact that a *talmid chacham* of the caliber of the Lemberger Rav would send a letter to a Rebbe was a novelty. But given the Menuchas Osher's reputation, it made complete sense. The Lemberger Rav's letter is quoted in the *sefer Menuchas Osher*, referenced for all future generations.

But it wasn't only the Lemberger Rav who turned to his young colleague. In a fairly short time, the Menuchas Osher had become the miracle worker of the miracle workers!

In those days, railroads in Europe offered different accommodations for their passengers. Most travelers couldn't afford first or second class; consequently, third class was usually the fullest. Of course, traveling in third class was no great pleasure due to the inevitable presence of gypsies who harassed their fellow passengers. One day several *bachurim* were traveling together (as there is safety in numbers) when an elderly conductor suddenly entered their compartment and called out, "Is there anyone here named Jungreis?"

It so happened that Rav Yaakov Tzvi HaLevi Jungreis (later known as the Fehergyarmat Rav) was on the train and he identified himself as a member of the Jungreis family. Seeing the apprehension on his face, the old man told him not to be afraid.

"My father used to be the mayor of the Csenger area," he told the *bachur*, "and he made it his business to make life miserable for the Jews living in his district. It got so bad that people started traveling to the Menuchas Osher to complain about the mayor and how he was making their lives unbearable with all his decrees.

"One day my baby brother came down with an illness. My mother tried everything she could think of to nurse him back to health, but nothing worked and my brother became weaker and weaker. In desperation, my mother asked my father to take the baby to the Menuchas Osher for a berachah.

" 'Everyone goes to see the Rabbi,' she told her husband. 'He has blessed many non-Jews and they have also been healed. Please take the baby to him tonight.'

"But there was no way my father would ever consider such a thing.

The *ohel* of the Menuchas Osher in Csenger

He hated the Jewish people and he hated their rabbis.

"Meanwhile my brother grew weaker by the day. One night my brother's fever began to rise. Red spots broke out on his cheeks like splotches of paint. In desperation my mother wrapped the baby in a blanket and ran to the home of the Menuchas Osher without waking my father or letting him know what she was about to do. She was shown in to the Rebbe, who asked her why she had come.

"In response, she showed him the baby and asked him for a berachah for a speedy recovery.

"'Yes, yes," the Menuchas Osher responded, 'but you must bring your husband to see me first.'

"My mother wasted no time. Running home, she marched into the bedroom, woke my father and informed him that she had taken the baby to the home of the Menuchas Osher for a berachah, but that the Rabbi had refused to acquiesce to her request unless her husband accompanied her as well!

"'You are getting out of bed this instant,' she ordered him, 'and coming with me to see the Rabbi.'

"With no choice, my father rose from his bed, dressed and left his home for the short walk to the home of the Menuchas Osher.

"'You evil man,' the Menuchas Osher addressed the mayor in Hungarian, 'what do I need to do to get you to my home?'

"My father had nothing to say.

"'If you promise me that from now on, whenever you see a Jewish man you will do what you can to help him, your baby will remain alive. If you will not accept my offer, your child will die.'

"Having no choice, my father promised the Menuchas Osher that he would mend his ways.

"I am that child's brother," the elderly conductor said, "and I was brought up with the knowledge that a rabbi by the name of Jungreis saved my brother's life. I therefore made sure to find out if there was anyone on the train from his family. Don't worry about the gypsies or anyone else. I will make sure you will be perfectly safe."

Many years later, the Rebbetzin's father, Rav Avrohom HaLevi Jungreis, was traveling by train on a mission to visit Jewish people throughout Hungary. It was 1943 and Hungarian Jewry was being persecuted all over the country. It was extremely dangerous for a Jew to travel alone, but Rav Avrohom felt he had no choice but to visit different communities and give them *chizuk.*

On the train was a squad of Hungarian gendarmes, the military police. Though the Germans had yet to make an appearance in Hungary, the brutal gendarmes were virtual clones of the Nazis and exulted in beating Jews whenever they had the opportunity. Upon seeing Zeide, they forced him into their compartment and began interrogating him, wanting to know where he was going and why. The situation was dire and Zeide davened silently that none of them would decide to pull out his beard and peyos (as happened later).

Suddenly the door of the compartment opened and a high-ranking Hungarian officer entered.

Everything stopped.

Surveying the scene, he asked the members of the militia, "What's going on here? You found a Jew?"

They nodded.

"But why are you being so nice to him?"

The gendarmes kept quiet, knowing they had let the high-ranking officer down.

"Get out of here," the officer ordered Zeide, who rose from his seat and followed the officer through the train until they arrived at the officer's private compartment.

"Go in."

Rav Avrohom HaLevi went in.

Once they were inside the room, the officer's demeanor changed. He didn't threaten or yell at Rav Avrohom and he didn't hurt his Jewish prisoner.

"Rabbi," he addressed Zeide, "I want to apologize for how I talked to you earlier. If I had acted any differently, the other officers would have been suspicious. I screamed at you because I had no choice if I wanted to get you away from them unharmed."

Zeide stared at the man, confused by the turnaround.

"I know you are shocked by my behavior," the gentile officer told him. "Let me explain. It all has to do with a family tradition that has been passed down from father to son in my family. A tradition that began when we experienced a miracle at the hands of a great Jewish miracle worker, known as the Menuchas Osher.

"My great-grandfather was the son of an extremely wealthy and influential nobleman who hated the Jewish people with a passion. But when my great-grandfather became extremely ill, the nobleman, seeing that his son was about to die, swallowed his loathing and went to beseech the Menuchas Osher for a miracle. After spending time with the nobleman's son, the Menuchas Osher promised him that he would recover and return to his former self. The nobleman could not help but be filled with overwhelming gratitude to the Jewish rabbi who saved his son. He offered to pay the Rabbi for the blessing, but the Rabbi refused all offers of remuneration.

צורת רבינו הקדוש, צדיק יסוד עולם, מופת הדור והדרו,
אור ישראל ופארו, שר התורה, מאור הגולה, לי דמיה תהלה
מרן רבינו **אשר אנשיל הלוי יונגרייז** וצוקללה"ה, אב"ד
ור"מ דק"ק טשענגער תע"א, בעהמ"ח ספרי מנחת אשר,
בהגה"ק מרן שמואל הלוי זצוק"ל. נפטר ה' בסלו תרל"ה.

The Menuchas Osher

" 'I ask one thing of you and one thing only.'

" 'What's that?'

" 'I want you to tell your son the story of how his life came to be saved and I want your son to tell the story of his salvation to his own son, when he has one. I want this story to become part of your family history — to be passed from generation to generation.'

"And so it was.

"This story has been a part of my life ever since I can recall. Ever since I was a small child, my father told me what happened and warned me to treat every Jew I met with respect and kindness.

"I hope that I have passed the test today. I feel as if the fact that I managed to save you from the hands of the other officers will go a long way in helping to repay my family's debt to the Menuchas Osher."

When Rav Avrohom HaLevi identified himself as a Csenger grandchild, the officer was even more overcome, and the two of them parted warmly. And so the story came full circle on a train in the middle of anti-Semitic Hungary 1943, as the Menuchas Osher had foreseen decades earlier.

A young man who was suffering from rheumatism came to see the Menuchas Osher and to ask him for a berachah.

"Show me where you have pain," the Menuchas Osher said to him.

The patient showed the Rebbe the painful points.

"My sister is also suffering from rheumatism."

"Where?"

He showed the Rebbe the sensitive points.

"This is for your sister," the Rebbe told him, placing his hand gently on the spots he had been shown.

"And this is for you," and again the Menuchas Osher placed his hand on every pain-filled spot he had been shown.

Neither of them ever suffered from rheumatism again.

The Menuchas Osher used to write his "prescriptions" on a piece of paper and tell the people who had come to him for a *yeshuah* to take the prescription to the town druggist. There the druggist filled the prescription and it wasn't long before the patients would recover. He used a mixture of the power of *segulah* (spiritual remedy) and the power of prayer. Whatever the cause, the Menuchas Osher possessed the touch, and people who were suffering from life-threatening ailments were cured against all odds after ingesting the medicine he prescribed.

This was a direct outcome of the moment the stranger entered his home and wrote the list of cures on the Rebbe's dining room table. But

The original *cheder* in Csenger

the Menuchas Osher kept the miracles hidden within a prescription, insisting that any patient who wanted medicine had to leave his home and travel to Csenger. There, away from the public eye, the Menuchas Osher saw tremendous *siyata d'Shmaya* in putting people back on their feet.

When the Csenger druggist grew older, he decided to retire and move to Budapest. There was no shortage of people interested in purchasing his pharmacy — after all, his medicines had a proven track record. It didn't take him long to conclude the deal. The druggist then packed his bags and moved to the big city.

Two years later, he returned to Csenger for a visit. Naturally he dropped in at his pharmacy to say hello to the new owner and ask about the business.

"Business is terrible," the new druggist told him.

Shocked, the druggist tried to figure out why that would be the case. "Is the Rebbe no longer alive?"

"No, he's still alive."

"What's the matter? Did he stop sending you prescriptions?"

"No. He still sends me prescriptions."

"If that's the case, business should be booming like it was when I ran the store! What on earth could have possibly gone wrong? The pharmacy was like a license to print money!"

"I'll tell you the problem. The Rebbe constantly varies what he writes on the prescriptions. If he'd always prescribe one particular medicine for patients, I'd make sure to stock up on that medication. But every day someone else comes in with another prescription for yet another medicine! I can't keep up with him! In all honesty, I don't know what to stock."

The previous owner looked at the current druggist and asked him, "Tell me, have you lost your mind completely?"

The druggist was taken aback by his words.

"What do you mean?"

"I'll tell you what I mean. Do you know what I used to do when the Rebbe sent me a prescription? I'd go into the back of the pharmacy, take any medicine off the shelf, mix in some coloring, put it in a bottle and give it to the patient. That's what I did and it worked every time! The whole point of the medicine was just to serve as a camouflage for the miracles the Rebbe was doing! From now on, stop bothering to read the prescription, open a bottle of medicine, and do what I did."

So it went in the pharmaceutical business in Csenger.

The Rebbe's prescriptions worked so well — so outstandingly well — that it reached a point where almost every single family in Hungary had experienced a personal miracle through the Menuchas Osher.

The Makover Rav related how when he very young he met an elderly rabbi in Budapest. Upon learning that he was a grandchild of the Menuchas Osher, the Rabbi wouldn't let him leave without first sharing a story about his holy grandfather.

"When I was young," he began, "I was diagnosed with a growth in my head. The doctors told my father that there was nothing to do and no medicine to take. My father chose not to give up on me. Instead of waiting for me to pass away, he took me to the train station and we rode the train from Budapest all the way to Csenger — quite a journey in those days.

"When we arrived at the home of the Menuchas Osher, the Rebbe examined me and then did something very interesting. The Menuchas Osher sent a child to the shul and asked him to return with a large hand-ful of candle wax. This was prior to the days when electric lighting was typically used — especially in a Hungarian village. Instead, the shul was illuminated with candles. The child was back a few minutes later,

The Rebbetzin at the *kevarim* of her great-grandparents, Rav Avrohom HaLevi and Rebbetzin Esther Jungreis, son and daughter-in-law of the Menuchas Osher

The Rebbetzin davening at the *kever* of Rav Moshe Nosson Nota HaLevi,
son of the Menuchas Osher, and grandfather of Rav Meshulem

his hands filled with freshly melted wax. The Menuchas Osher, working
with his hands, fashioned a yarmulke out of the wax and instructed me
to wear it on my head in place of my usual yarmulke.

"'Wear this,' he said, 'and you will live a long life.'"

Though it was many, many years later, the elderly rabbi still had the
wax yarmulke and was able to show it to the Makover Rav.

There was a consensus among the tzaddikim that looking at a picture
of the Menuchas Osher was a *segulah* for *yiras Shamayim*. He was such
a tzaddik, such a learned man, that just gazing at his holy face would
enable a person to reach great spiritual heights. Though a photographer
never actually snapped a picture of the Menuchas Osher, an artist was
commissioned to draw a portrait of the holy tzaddik at one of the major
rabbinical gatherings of his day. It is cherished by his descendants, who
go out of their way to connect themselves to the righteous man who
managed to inspire an entire country even while remaining in the shadows of a small European town.

Young Meshulem (back row, center) pictured with his family before the war. Only he and one brother survived.

The Menuchas Osher had a number of sons. His son Rav Avrohom, the Rebbetzin's great-grandfather, assumed his esteemed father's position in Csenger, serving in that capacity for thirty years after his father passed away, although he stated most emphatically that he was not deserving of replacing his father.

The rabbanim of the time decreed, however, that he had to step into his father's position.

With no choice, Rav Avrohom HaLevi accepted their decision. But his was a quiet reign, a far cry from the incredible miracles that characterized his father's court on a daily basis.

Another son, Rav Moshe Nosson, was the author of a *sefer* called *Toras Moshe Nosson*, and was also the grandfather of Rav Meshulem HaLevi Jungreis, rabbi of Ohr Torah in North Woodmere.

Rav Avrohom's second son, Rav Yisroel, was the Rebbetzin's paternal grandfather, whom she met when she was five years old on her family trip to Nadudvar just prior to the onset of the Holocaust. Rav Yisroel

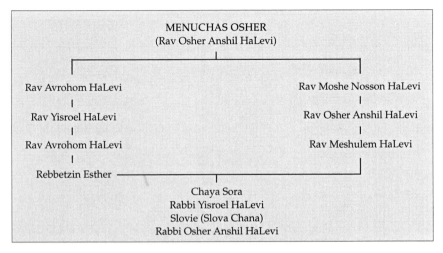

MENUCHAS OSHER
(Rav Osher Anshil HaLevi)

Rav Avrohom HaLevi

Rav Yisroel HaLevi

Rav Avrohom HaLevi

Rebbetzin Esther

Rav Moshe Nosson HaLevi

Rav Osher Anshil HaLevi

Rav Meshulem HaLevi

Chaya Sora
Rabbi Yisroel HaLevi
Slovie (Slova Chana)
Rabbi Osher Anshil HaLevi

Family tree from the Menuchas Osher through the children of
Rav Meshulem and Rebbetzin Esther Jungreis

called his son Avrohom, after his own father, which completes the chain
of the Jungreis family down to the Rebbetzin herself.

Rav Yitzchok Dov (Berel) Jungreis lives in Boro Park. He is a cousin
of both the Rebbetzin and Rav Meshulem — all of them descended from

Rav Berel Jungreis, a cousin of the Rebbetzin,
at the rededication of the *cheder* in Csenger

Siddur of the Menuchas Osher

the Menuchas Osher. One of the crowns of his huge collection of *sefarim* is the siddur that belonged to the Menuchas Osher. Rebbetzin Jungreis used to make a practice of visiting her cousin's house in Brooklyn. She'd sit down at the dining room table and begin filling out *kvitlach* (personal petitionary prayers written by a supplicant to his spiritual leader), mainly the names of her children and grandchildren, which she'd insert between the pages of the Zeide's siddur.

"When the Rebbetzin was admitted to the hospital for an operation," Rav Yitzchok Dov related, "she gave the doctor a berachah that the Angel Raphael should be at his side."

He thanked her and accepted the blessing graciously, and she was left with a good feeling about the operation.

"When I accompanied my husband to the hospital for surgery," the Rebbetzin told her cousin, "I gave his doctor the same berachah, blessing him that the Angel Raphael should stand by his side and assist him in his work. But unlike the doctor who had been assigned to me, my husband's doctor looked me in the eye and said, 'I don't believe in that.'"

"When the Rebbetzin heard the doctor talking that way," said Rav Yitzchok Dov, "she knew the surgery wouldn't be successful. Not with a doctor like that."

She was correct. The surgery was not successful and her beloved husband of forty years passed away a short while later.

Davening on the yahrtzeit inside the *ohel* of the Menuchas Osher in Csenger

How had she known?

The truth is, there's really no question at all.

She was a granddaughter of the Menuchas Osher — and possessed a direct link to the endless chain of miracles performed by the Zeides.

If she said she knew, then she knew. That's how connected she was. To the Csenger Zeide and to all who followed.

But there was another element that built her and turned the Rebbetzin into the person she became.

I am referring to the Holocaust, which she would talk about and discuss for the rest of her life. And whereas some people's minds and spirits were irrevocably altered after the trauma they experienced, the Rebbetzin took it all — every last experience — and used them to rebuild her nation.

This chapter has been dedicated
in honor of Slovie Jungreis Wolff

William and Suzanne Plotch

Part 4
1943-1956

Soon, my sweetest child, the snow is going to be very deep and you will fall, but every time you fall remember that Zeide made a path for you. And then you will be able to stand up and keep walking on that path.

Rav Avrohom HaLevi Jungreis

We didn't survive the Holocaust. We triumphed over the Holocaust.

Rebbetzin Esther Jungreis

CHAPTER SEVENTEEN

The Csenger Tefillin

"*My name is Esther Jungreis. I lived before the war, during the war and after the war. I was like Noach who lived before the flood, during the flood and after the flood.*"

Those were words the Rebbetzin consistently said.

They summed up who she was and the incredibly powerful experiences that would shape the way she looked at and related to the world for the rest of her life.

The Jungreis family lived in Szeged where Rav Avrohom HaLevi Jungreis served as the city's chief Orthodox rabbi. Szeged was the second-largest city in Hungary and Rabbi Jungreis' mandate was extensive, as was his sense of responsibility to his people. It was a dark time for the Jewish people, and although the German army would not be seen in Hungary until almost the end of the war, the Hungarian people did a fairly good job of torturing their Jewish citizens — all on their own. Calling the police to report a crime against a Jew was a foolish move and would result in the police joining the criminals and harming the Jew who had reported a crime.

In those years, Jewish boys were conscripted into slave labor battalions and sent to work for their country. Very often, being sent to those battalions meant death. Szeged, being a major city in Hungary, was used as a staging point from where many of the boys were sent away to the

Rav Avrohom HaLevi,
as a young Rav in Szeged

Bor copper mines, which was in effect a slave labor camp.

The rabbi of the city was determined to help them. The question was how.

Rav Avrohom was a smart man. He possessed the razor-sharp, analytical brain of the true *talmid chacham* and he put his intellect to work trying to come up with a plan. Finally he hit on an idea.

The Hungarian people were very frightened of becoming infected with dangerous diseases. They were especially fearful of contaminating their soldiers. Rav Avrohom decided to use that fear against them. He consulted with a number of physicians and asked them to suggest the kinds of remedies that if ingested would give a person symptoms of illness without actually making him sick. There were many ideas and Rav Avrohom implemented the two remedies that were both easiest to concoct and most effective.

The first idea was very simple.

Injecting a person with raw milk straight from the cow induced a

The Rebbetzin as an infant

mysterious fever that came suddenly and disappeared not long afterward.

The second idea was also quite simple. It involved a paste made from soybeans, which when smeared onto a person's eyelids simulated symptoms of trachoma.

Stage one had been accomplished. Rabbi Jungreis and his rebbetzin had a way to help the Jewish boys mimic illness. The question now became — how to get them their medicine?

They found a way.

As the rabbi of the community, Rav Avrohom was given permission to visit the Jewish boys incarcerated in his city. Just because he had permission, however, didn't mean he was free to come and

A young Rebbetzin Miriam Jungreis, the Rebbetzin's mother, affectionately know to all as "Mama"

go as he pleased. He was still a Jew and not trusted, and the soldiers always searched him before allowing him entry to the boys he'd come to visit. Keeping this in mind, there was no way for Rabbi Jungreis to hide the concoctions on his person. But there was another way, and it was Rebbetzin Miriam — the Rebbetzin's mother — who thought of it.

She sewed pockets into the lining of the coats of her children, Yaakov and his younger sister, Esther. She then hid the potions inside those pockets along with a few candies and messages from home. Then, with the difficult part accomplished, all that was left was for Rav Avrohom to visit the boys, taking along his son and daughter to cheer them up. They usually made the visits once or twice a week. Once inside the barracks, the medicine was distributed to one and all, and nobody ever discovered why the Rabbi insisted on bringing his children with him when he went to visit the prisoners.

There was no question that Rav Avrohom's behavior put them all in danger. Yet as the rabbi of the city, there was no way he could possibly sit back and watch so many young Jewish men being sent to almost certain death.

One afternoon the children accompanied their father to visit the

Jewish boys. As always, their secret pockets were filled with illegal concoctions and medications. Normally, while their father was searched, the kids were let right in. This time, however, an officer stopped them as they were walking into the compound. Clearly he had seen them before and his suspicions had been raised.

This was the first time they were stopped and they turned pale with fright. There was no telling what would happen to them if they were caught trying to help the Jewish boys.

"I knew why we were familiar to him," Rabbi Yaakov Jungreis, the Rebbetzin's older brother, explained. "The officer had seen us when we went to say goodbye to the Jewish boys at the pier, before they were taken by a boat to the copper mines in Bor. My father took a number of coins with him — a type of Hungarian coin that had a hole in the center — put a string through them and gave each boy a coin to hang around his neck (like a *kamei'a*, amulet), while blessing them with the words '*Ki malachav yitzaveh lach* — may the angels accompany you on your way...'

"The Hungarian officer had been at the pier when the boat left, had seen us then — and here we were again a short while later. No wonder he stopped us in the hallway.

"But the truth is, the officer wasn't trying to get us in trouble. He had another reason for stopping us. Something else entirely. Turning to my father, he said, 'Do you remember the officer who was with me on the day I met you at the pier?'

"My father nodded. He had a good reason for remembering the officer. His mind went back to a different visit a short while earlier. As he met with all the boys, my father distributed the coins he had brought — a coin for every boy — and he blessed them, trying to reassure them even as they were being sent away for slave labor. It was at that moment that another officer approached them. Stopping in his tracks, he studied my father and saw what he was doing. He understood that my father was going out of his way to help the boys and make them feel loved before their journey into the unknown.

"And then that evil Hungarian man began to laugh at my father. He laughed and he laughed, as if what my father was doing was the funniest thing in the world.

" 'It's not going to help them, rabbi, nothing is going to help.'

"He acted as if the coins my father had prepared for the boys was one big joke.

"Of course my father remembered the Hungarian officer. It is hard to forget someone who dances around you and makes jokes at your expense.

" 'I remember him well,' he said to the officer who had stopped us.

" 'Well, rabbi, you should know that something happened to him. Something bad!'

"My father was having difficulty reading the look on the Hungarian's face.

" 'What are you talking about?'

" 'He accompanied the Jewish boys, as did I, on the boat ride to Bor. When we arrived and the boat docked, the boys were taken away to their labor brigade and the officer who treated you with disrespect decided to go for a swim. He jumped into the water and was enjoying himself when he was caught in the undertow and drowned.'

"My father was shocked.

" 'Yes, rabbi, the officer who made fun of you drowned.' "

For Rabbi Jungreis and his children, it was as if Hashem was giving them a sign and letting them know that He was looking out for them. They could see a bright light in the darkness.

The Rebbetzin would relate these stories — as did her brothers — many times in the years and decades to come. On one occasion, while giving a speech to an audience in New Jersey, she told the story of their travails in Hungary and how she and her brother had put their lives on the line smuggling medicine into well-guarded military enclosures.

Suddenly someone from the audience made it clear that he had a question for her.

"Rebbetzin?"

"Yes?"

"How old are you?"

The entire room gasped.

Hearing the audience's reaction, the man realized he'd just made a faux pas and quickly corrected his mistake by explaining that he hadn't meant to make her uncomfortable.

"It is just that your story reminded me of something my father told me many times."

"What did your father tell you?"

The Rebbetzin was intrigued.

"He told me that he was saved from being sent away because of a rabbi. The rabbi's name was Jungreis and he visited them along with his children. He also said that the children smuggled homemade pastes made from soybeans that when used correctly made a person appear sick for a short time — but long enough to help them get set free — so as not to 'infect' the other prisoners."

Now the Rebbetzin was staring at the man. It was obvious that she recognized something in his face.

Suddenly she called out, "Are you the son of Miklos Aaron?"

The room erupted in an outpouring of emotion, which culminated with the young man's suggestion that they phone his elderly father in Belgium on the spot and give him the opportunity to speak with his savior there and then. People held their breath as the phone rang, and when Miklos answered and the Rebbetzin identified herself, it was a long-distance reunion that defied all sense of emotion. The awe in Miklos' voice was something incredible. It was very special. But then there were many incidents that routinely happened to the Rebbetzin on any given day — events that would have been the highlight of a "regular" person's life — yet for her were just part of her blessed existence.

Rav Avrohom and Rebbetzin Miriam didn't content themselves with smuggling "magic" potions to their boys. That was not enough for them. In their eyes, the boys had become their own children and were to be treated as such. Every time the Hungarians shipped another round of boys into Szeged from all over the country, the boys ended up at the Jungreis home. On average, there were about fifty people a week sleeping in their home — and this went on for years. It was understood by all the people in the city that this was so, and the city's drivers picked up any Jewish passengers from outside the city's central train station, dropping them off outside the Jungreis house without a word — knowing the destination would become self-explanatory the moment they met their new family.

There Rebbetzin Miriam cooked for them, took care of them, made sure they ate a good meal and washed their clothing. Before they were taken away, she prepared packages for every boy. The packages were filled with delicious honey cookies, which stayed fresh for days and whose taste would be long remembered even after every last crumb had disappeared. She would jump out of bed at the crack of dawn and start her day. There was no time to waste and much to do.

She did the same thing during the family's time in Bergen-Belsen. They were Polish boys instead of Hungarians, but the premise was the same. They were Yidden, they were frightened and they were emaciated — and the Rabbi's wife adopted them and called them *"sheifelah"* and *"yingele"* and did everything in her power to bring a smile to their lips.

Her response to crises: find someone to assist and do it well. If you are suffering, surely someone else is suffering just as much and needs your help. She would never change, not then and not until the end of her life.

For people who had survived the Holocaust, every family simchah in the post-war years was cause for great celebration. There was no such thing as missing a family gathering, even for a good reason. Klal Yisrael had suffered so much for so long; it was now time to thank the One Above for His incredible bounty.

One evening in the early '70s, Zeide and Mama Jungreis were visiting the Rebbetzin in Long Island for a family *simchah*. It was a cold winter night, but inside the house all was warm and inviting. Suddenly the phone rang. It was just a phone call and nobody guessed that the caller was about to shatter their evening with terrible news.

"Is this Rebbetzin Esther Jungreis?"

"Speaking. Who is this?"

"I am your parents' neighbor in Canarsie. I tried reaching your parents, but they weren't home and someone suggested I try you instead."

"What's the matter?"

"Your father's shul is on fire!"

Rav Avrohom's beloved shul — the shul he had put his heart and soul into — was burning.

"How can that be?" she gasped.

"It was arson, Rebbetzin."

"Ribono shel Olam, why would they do such a thing?"

That, however, was exactly what happened.

It was a clear case of arson, with the fire begun by a group of young criminals who had broken into the shul with gasoline and hate. It was a catastrophe, made a million times worse by the excruciating memories a burning shul evoked in Zeide and his rebbetzin.

They left the house minutes later. The drive went quickly at that time of night. Nobody spoke; there was total silence in the car. Every person was immersed in their own thoughts. This was America, not Hungary.

People were not supposed to burn down shuls in the United States.

Zeide, you see, was thinking about the one worldly possession he treasured most in the world.

His tefillin.

Rav Avrohom's tefillin were especially precious. They came with a pedigree, having belonged four generations earlier to none other than the Menuchas Osher of Csenger, Rebbetzin Esther's great-great-grandfather. At Rav Avrohom's bar mitzvah, his father, the Zeide from Nadudvar, presented his son with the tefillin and bestowed a powerful blessing on him at the same time, begging the One Above that the tefillin remain with his son and protect him throughout his life, no matter where he might find himself.

Miraculously, the tefillin would survive the war untouched and unharmed and make their way across the ocean, where they were again worn every day in the Jungreis family shul in Canarsie, Brooklyn. And on the day when his shul and yeshivah were burned down, Zeide stood in the darkness and stench of burning ashes and searched through the ruins, looking for something, unwilling to leave. His children tried their best to convince him to return home, but he remained adamant in his refusal to leave his beloved shul until he had found what he was looking for.

"*Tatta zeesa,*" they said to him, "please come home and go to sleep — you've been here for hours."

But he wouldn't leave, no matter what they said.

In the early hours of the morning, after an entire night of sifting through blackened wood and rubble, he turned to his children and said, "Everything will be all right; I have found what I was searching for. I can finally go home."

As he spoke, Rav Avrohom HaLevi Jungreis showed his children the tefillin of the Menuchas Osher, which he had always kept hidden away in the *aron kodesh* (ark).

The *aron kodesh* had been destroyed in the flames that engulfed the sanctuary, but somehow, miraculously, the tefillin survived: as they survived through Bergen-Belsen — as they survived life in America.

"We shall rebuild," Zeide said. "Our shul will be great again!"

And so they did.

But what about Mama? Where was she; what was she doing while Zeide was busy searching through the ashes for his tefillin?

The Rebbetzin and Mama

As in every moment of her life, now too, Mama had no time to waste. She was in the house, standing in the kitchen. She was doing what she knew how to do best: baking cookies and taking care of people.

She stood at the counter and started baking cookies. Baking and crying, rolling the dough and crying, mixing all the ingredients together and wiping the tears from her eyes.

The Rebbetzin found her mother baking the cookies.

"Mama, what are you doing? Why are you baking cookies right now?"

"People are going to come and help us now that the shul burned down. They're going to be hungry. You'll see, every cookie will be eaten."

It was that simple.

Some people dwell on their misfortunes. Others turn everything around and comfort those in pain, even as their own hearts are breaking on the inside.

That was Mama. It was the way she acted back in Szeged, and in Bergen-Belsen and in Canarsie.

CHAPTER EIGHTEEN

The Belzer Rebbe's Mandate

*T*he story of the Belzer Rebbe's escape from Poland to Hungary reads like an exciting novel. Smuggled across the border — beard shaved and peyos gone — the Rebbe would eventually reach Hungary, where he went into hiding once again. When Rebbetzin Esther's father, known as the Szegedeiner Rav, heard that the Rebbe was in Hungary, he knew that he had to visit him. It wasn't easy for him to get to Budapest. Just taking the train ride meant putting his life in danger. But Rav Avrohom HaLevi Jungreis was not afraid. He was a messenger for his people and he fully intended to carry out his mission.

Part of the reason he had felt it was so important for him to visit the Rebbe was because of a case filled with *kvitlach* that he brought with him — scraps of paper on which Yidden had scrawled their requests for berachos from the Rebbe. There were many righteous Jews in Hungary, but the Belzer Rebbe was in a league of his own and everyone wanted a berachah from him.

Upon his arrival at the Belzer Rebbe's hiding place, Rav Avrohom made his way around the corner of the building and to an open window leading into the basement. Making sure that nobody was watching him, Rav Avrohom lowered himself through the window and down into the basement, gratified that he would momentarily be finding himself in the Rebbe's presence. But his joy was marred by tremendous pain the moment he caught sight of the Rebbe.

The Belzer Rebbe had the appearance of an old, old man. He was weak and emaciated, pale and drawn. He looked like a person who had been through the worst things in the world — and had still not managed to reclaim his former strength. His journey through Poland had been extremely difficult for him and the two rabbanim who had accompanied him. There were times — many times — when they were sure they would not survive. At the same time, numerous miracles occurred that saved them and proved that Hashem wanted the Rebbe to live.

It was quite a story.

Yet worse than all of that — worse than the journey and worse than having to elude the Nazis who had been on the lookout for him for so long — was the fact that his family had been killed by the Nazis. The terrible sights that he saw in Poland would remain in the Rebbe's memory for the rest of his life.

At a loss as to what to do for the Rebbe, Rav Avrohom handed him the case.

"Rebbe, these are the *kvitlach* that were sent by Yidden desperate for the Rebbe's berachah."

"Szegedeiner Rav, I have no *koach* to give berachos."

Now what?

"*Heiliger* (holy) Rebbe," Rav Avrohom Jungreis replied, "what should I do with all the *kvitlach* I was given by Klal Yisrael?"

"I am appointing you my *shaliach*, my representative, to give Yidden berachos. When someone asks you for a berachah, you will be able to bless them in my name. From now on, you will serve as my *shaliach*."

Rav Avrohom HaLevi Jungreis left the Belzer Rebbe shortly after that conversation. He returned home spiritually richer than he had left, having been gifted with an ability that had previously belonged to the leader of one of the largest chassidic dynasties in Poland. That power would prove very useful in the dark days to come. Though the Belzer Rebbe would eventually regain his strength, Rav Avrohom had been granted something incredible that day. From that moment on, he would begin giving Yidden as many berachos as he could. After all, it was the Belzer Rebbe's mandate.

During those days of terror, rumors abounded. Nobody knew what was real and what was make-believe. Were the Nazis as bad as everyone was saying they were? Were they worse? Nobody knew the truth.

There were times when Polish refugees managed to sneak across the border and tell the people what they had seen. Yet even then, the Jews of

Hungary were unable to bring themselves to accept the words coming out of their mouths. One evening a Polish Jew appeared in the Jungreis home.

"I must tell you of the things I saw."

They stopped what they were doing and listened.

The man's hands shook, but he forced himself to continue speaking.

"In the camps, there are little buildings which the Nazis call 'gas chambers.' Hundreds of Jews are forced into the buildings and when every single inch of space has been filled, canisters of gas are released into the interior and they are killed — choked to death.

"All it takes is a few minutes and everyone inside the gas chambers is dead."

The people around the table stared at the man wide-eyed.

"There are also ovens. These are used to burn people alive."

Esther's mother couldn't accept what he was saying. She argued with him, pointing out that Germany was the most cultured nation in Europe.

"You are right. They were. But they have sunk lower than all the animals," the man said quietly. "They turn our fat into soap and our skin into lampshades. Our bones they use to fertilize their fields. Nothing is wasted."

His words were all the more powerful by how quietly they were stated.

But the people at the table couldn't believe him. It hurt too much.

Esther Jungreis was in first grade when she awoke to the most terrifying sound in the world. It seemed to the little girl that she was hearing thousands upon thousands of boots marching through the city streets. The sound was incredibly frightening, every collective thump sending another shock wave to the ground — waves that reverberated and echoed in every direction, creating a clanking, marching sound on the cobblestones outside that would never leave her memory.

She ran to the window and peeked through the curtain. She saw the waves of German troops. She saw the helmets and the bayonets, and she began to tremble uncontrollably. Suddenly she felt her parents' arms around her. Looking up at her mother, she saw tears in her eyes. Looking at her father, she recognized new lines etched around his eyes and mouth and the sorrow emanating from deep within his *neshamah*. Suddenly she recalled their conversation on a winter day outside her grandparents' house in a small Hungarian village. She remembered putting on her coat and boots and leaving the house with her father. She remembered the snow and how he had walked before her, making indentations in the snow so she would be able to walk.

She looked at him and remembered every word of their conversation, and Esther knew that her father's words had come true and that the snow was indeed becoming very, very deep.

A young Esther Jungreis in Szeged

CHAPTER NINETEEN

The Beis Medrash Maternity Ward

The Nazis' grand entrance to the city was followed by a spate of announcements plastered all over the streets. Every day there was a new edict. One morning the Jews of the city woke up to find the streets of the city plastered with yet another sign that stated: *From now on, all Jews must wear yellow stars for identification purposes. Any Jew found without a yellow star will be killed!*

After that bad things began happening very rapidly.

Jewish schools were forced to shut their doors.

A few days later Jewish businesses were forced to stop operating.

That was followed by an edict informing the Jews of Hungary that Jewish doctors, lawyers and other professionals were no longer allowed to practice.

All that, however, was merely the prelude to the fact that the Jews were soon ordered to leave their homes and relocate into a ghetto in the center of the city. The Jungreis home was situated in the center of the ghetto. It wasn't only the people of the city who were sent to live in the Szeged ghetto. The Germans transported many others into the city as well, causing the already crowded ghetto to be filled beyond capacity.

Rav Avrohom and Rebbetzin Miriam saved numerous individuals without thought to possible consequences or repercussions. Among the many people who were taken to the Szeged ghetto was a woman, married for just a few months, who was expecting her first child.

Rav Avrohom was a doer. If there was a problem, he worked at it until he came up with a solution. That was the way he approached life. With a woman who was soon to have a baby, Rav Jungreis had no choice but to think of a solution to the challenge at hand. He knew that the moment she gave birth the Germans would be on the way and the baby would be murdered.

What to do?

How to protect the mother and child from the all-seeing eyes of the Nazis?

In the end, Rav Avrohom arrived at a novel and seemingly unorthodox solution.

The mother would be moved into the shul.

Who would have thought that the Rabbi's solution would be to turn Szeged's main shul into a maternity ward?

But Rav Avrohom knew how to think outside the box. He knew that such a move would keep the Germans away — even if just for a few days.

Those days were filled with unique sights. But even people who had become used to seeing the unnatural knew they would never forget watching the giant bed being carried into the shul, where it was deposited directly in front of the *aron kodesh* — the only area in the room where it fit.

The woman was moved into the "maternity ward" right after davening, and at twelve o'clock that night, Esther's older brother Yankie saw his mother getting ready to leave their house to go deliver the baby, who was born a few hours later.

The actual bris took place at the mikveh. It was celebrated on time. The Zenta Rav was the *sandek*. Rav Avrohom himself served as *kvatter*.

It might have been a *simchah*, but many of the people who took part in the baby's bris didn't look at it that way.

"This baby has virtually no chance of survival — and that's without having a bris," they screamed at Rav Avrohom. "Are you trying to make sure the Nazis kill him? Why give him a bris now? Wait until this is over! If he's still alive after the war, he can have a bris then!"

Rav Avrohom didn't argue with them. Arguing with one who is angry is a pointless exercise. Besides, there were so many angry people then. The only thing the Rav could do for them was hear them out and ease their pain.

A newborn needs many things. At that moment he had nothing — not even a diaper.

What to do?

Once again there was a challenge, and the Jungreis family acted to solve it. The task of purchasing everything the baby needed was handed over to Yankie Jungreis, who was quick and efficient. Yankie was given a list of items to purchase and the money to pay for them. Removing his yellow star, Yankie made his way over to the end of the ghetto and jumped the fence, running three blocks to the nearest store. There was no question that he was risking his life. If even one non-Jew recognized that he was a Jewish boy, he could be beaten black and blue or even sent away forever. But Hashem was at his side and he managed to sneak into a store, find everything on the list, pay for the goods, and return to his family in the ghetto. The memory of removing his yellow star and jumping the ghetto wall would be etched into Yankie Jungreis' mind for all time.

Yet despite the fact that Rav Avrohom had endangered his life by turning his shul into a maternity ward, and despite the fact that Yankie had endangered his life by removing his yellow star and entering the non-Jewish part of the city on a mission of mercy, the Jungreis family didn't look for praise or recognition.

It was sufficient for them that another Jewish child had been entered into the covenant of Avraham Avinu — even in the darkest of times.

Were they tzaddikim?

They didn't even have time to think about the question. They were too busy saving yet another life. And then another. And then another.

Postscript: As an adult living in Canarsie near his parents and working alongside his father in the Jungreis shul and their yeshivah, Ateres Yisroel, Reb Yaakov and his wife, Rebbetzin Shifra, ate with his parents every Shabbos. At *every single Shabbos meal*, Rav Avrohom and his rebbetzin would raise the topic of how they had sent their son over the fence and out of the ghetto — filled with guilt, and not comprehending how they had willingly put their Yankele in danger. This was the main topic of discussion every single Shabbos for decades.

And yet, at the time, they didn't hesitate and neither did he.

A short while after the bris, mother and baby were deported from Szeged to a little-known concentration camp near Vienna called Strasshof. Nobody expected to ever see them again.

But the story wasn't over yet.

Rudolf Kastner — the Zionist leader who organized the Kastner Train from Hungary, thereby saving more than 1,000 Jews, including many world-famous rabbinical figures — used to visit Strasshof once a month to pay the Nazis protection money for the Jewish prisoners. While at the camp, he had the opportunity to get to know some of the people there. There was a rabbi in the camp — only one: the sole rabbinical figure in the camp. His name was Rav Tzvi Hirsch Cohen, the Rebbetzin's maternal grandfather. One day, Kastner approached Rav Tzvi Hirsch and told him that he had some good news.

"What do you mean when you say 'good news'?

"Exactly that. I am in the process of negotiating with the Nazis for a truck that will be allowed to carry twenty-four rabbis out of Nazi-occupied Europe — to freedom. I want you to be one of the rabbis on this truck!"

It was the offer of a lifetime.

When the truck arrived at Strasshof, Rav Tzvi Hirsch thanked Rudolf Kastner for offering him such an incredible opportunity. He then did something unimaginable. He turned Kastner down.

"You are offering me a seat on the truck and I thank you for that. But I want you to give my seat to someone else. Send someone else in my place!"

Mama's father, Rav Tzvi Hirsch Cohen,
as a Rav in Patterson, New Jersey

Sefer Likutei Tzvi, written by the
Rebbetzin's grandfather,
Rav Tzvi Hirsch Cohen

Mama's mother, Rebbetzin Rivka Cohen, Hy"d, who perished in the Holocaust

Kastner couldn't believe his ears. Who on earth was willing to give up a chance to live? It didn't make any sense!

"Whom do you want me to give your seat to?"

Rav Tzvi Hirsch told Kastner that he wanted his seat to go to the woman who had given birth in Szeged — and to her newborn baby boy. Rav Tzvi Hirsch spoke and Kastner agreed. The woman and her baby son left Strasshof on the truck, the Stropkover Rebbe sitting nearby. She was a very young girl at the time and the Stropkover was already an elderly man. But when they arrived in the United States after the war, the woman on the truck eventually married the Stropkover Rebbe; after his *petirah* (passing), she married the Tzeilimer Rav, who was also significantly older than she.

The little baby who celebrated his bris in the Szeged mikveh was adopted by the Rav and grew up to become the current Tzeilimer Rav. In years to come, he would write the story of how a young boy named Yankie Jungreis removed his yellow star and jumped the ghetto fence — selflessly placing his life in danger to buy a newborn baby diapers and a pacifier — and included it in his *sefer*.

When Rebbetzin Miriam Jungreis passed away, the Tzeilimer Rav came to the *levayah* with an entourage of chassidim.

When he was asked by the family to what they owed the honor of his presence, he explained.

"I am here to give honor and thanks to the woman who personally took care of my mother in Szeged. I have come to thank the woman who risked her life and helped bring me into this world."

The *hesped* (eulogy) he delivered was not only beautiful, but personal and emotional.

That's the way it is when you speak at the *levayah* of the woman who brought you into the world.

He came to show his gratitude to the Jungreis family — *hakaras hatov* on his part to the family who saved his life, turning their beis medrash into a maternity ward.

It was very difficult for people to know what to do during those insane days of darkness. The greatest people were struck with blindness.

One evening Rav Avrohom heard knocking on his front door. He ran to answer. There was a man standing there, a member of his shul. He knew the man well and was surprised to see him there. After all, nobody was allowed outside after curfew. The man had endangered his life to come to his rabbi.

"What happened?" he asked him.

"Rebbe, I need your advice."

"Yes?"

"I have been given an opportunity that might save my son's life."

"What are you talking about?"

"I am talking about a chance for my son to be baptized. Once baptized, the Nazis will leave him alone because in their eyes he will no longer be a Jew."

(This was not true in any event. It was false hope. The Nazis never let a Jew live just because he'd been baptized.)

Hope shone from the man's eyes. At the same time, Rav Avrohom could see how much it hurt the man to even mention the words baptize and son in the same sentence.

"Rebbe, tell me what to do. I am begging you. Give me guidance!"

Rav Avrohom studied the man.

"Rebbe, help me. I'm desperate. I have one son. I don't want him to die! Please Rebbe, tell me what to do!"

Rav Avrohom was silent for a very long time. When he spoke you could hear the anguish in his voice.

"You want your child to live," he said at last. "Is there anyone in the world who doesn't want their son to grow up and live a good life? Of course you want your child to have every chance at life.

"But tell me something. If your son is baptized, if your son is not a Jew, will he live? If he's not a Jew, living a Jewish life, can he possibly be alive?"

That was it. Rav Avrohom had spoken. It was just a few words, but they were words of undeniable truth — words that couldn't be ignored.

"I know, I know," the man whispered, his face ashen. "The entire time

I knew the *emes*, the truth. I knew it when I left my home this evening and sneaked through the streets to come here. Forget I said anything. You are right. Of course I will never do such a thing. My son will either live as a Jew or he will die as a Jew!"

The next moment both of them were embracing — Rebbe and talmid. The man had come for advice and he'd received it.

It was guidance at its finest.

The truth was the truth.

A Jew must live like a Jew. Otherwise, what was the point of life?

This chapter has been dedicated in honor of
Rabbi Shlomo and Chaya Sora • Rabbi Yisroel and Rivki
Mendy and Slovie • Rabbi Osher and Yaffa
who are keeping the Rebbetzin's legacy alive

Moshe and Ariella Wolfson

CHAPTER TWENTY
Zeide's One Request

And then the Nazis came.

They arrived in the middle of the night, breaking down the front door, shouting like animals. They were accompanied by their dogs, who wouldn't stop barking. It was a terrifying experience, made all the worse by the presence of the Germans' beasts.

"Juden, Juden, schnell, schnell, move it, move it, you lazy good-for-nothing Juden, get out of here, leave now!"

They barely had time to take anything with them. But the real question was — what to take? Rav Avrohom made his choices.

First his tefillin.

The Csenger tefillin.

There was no question in his mind that the tefillin that had been handed down from one Jungreis to another, all the way back to the Menuchas Osher, needed to accompany him! He packed quickly, filling a small bag. In went the tefillin. In went his tallis. In went a number of unpublished manuscripts written by his great-grandfather Rav Mordechai Benet — who wrote on *Mesechtos Shabbos, Berachos* and *Gittin* — and the *Be'er Yitzchok*, written by another grandfather, Rav Avrohom Yitzchok Glick, on *Mesechte Kiddushin*.

Was that the smartest course of action?

Maybe he should have taken something to eat? Something to drink? What about money, or another form of currency?

No. Zeide packed the things that were the most important in the world.

Matzeivah of Harav Mordechai
Benet

Sefer authored by
Harav Mordechai Benet

It made no sense. There was no way for the tefillin, tallis and manuscripts to survive! And yet they did. In a truly incredible turn of events, everything would survive the war and the manuscripts would be published one day in the future, handed over to the talmidei chachamim (Torah scholars) of Klal Yisrael to learn and cherish.

As for Esther, she left her home holding her doll in her arms. Though she had been forced to leave everything behind, at least she had her beloved doll for comfort. They were about to leave when a little Hungarian girl named Bridgee, the daughter of their building's superintendent, stepped over to her. Esther thought she wanted to say goodbye.

Instead of wishing her well, the girl reached over and plucked Esther's doll from her unsuspecting arms.

Shocked to her core at having her doll stolen from her very person, Esther looked toward the girl's father to see if he would make his daughter return the doll. Eyes as hard as granite, the man spat at Esther Jungreis and said, "Where you're going, you won't be needing a doll." Every word he said was seared onto her heart forever.

That was the way they left their home.

The snow was almost too deep to bear.

There was a brick factory located at the edge of the city. They were marched from their homes and herded into the deserted room. As they were forced through the streets at gunpoint, the Hungarian citizens of Szeged emerged from their homes to laugh, jeer and point.

It would get worse.

The Jewish patients were removed from the city's psychiatric hospital and moved through the streets locked in a cage, the Nazis going out of their way to show that the Jewish people were really animals.

It was impossible to look at them.

Nobody would be able to forget the scene of the patients fighting with one another over a crust of bread from inside the cage. It was hell on earth.

The factory was freezing cold. The ground was filthy, made all the worse by the fact that there were no facilities for so many people. There is no imagining the pain of that situation. Whatever you can imagine — it was worse. They were to be kept in the factory until the Nazis had the number of Jews they needed for a transport. Only then would they be moved.

There are no words.

It was Tishah B'Av every single day.

The night before they boarded the trains, the Jews slept outside in the fields. Tents were provided. They didn't provide protection against the wet ground, but at least the rain wasn't falling directly onto their faces. As the hours passed, Esther developed a high fever and her breathing became ragged and uneven. She coughed and coughed and her fever climbed until her forehead was extremely hot and her face flushed. Rav Avrohom left his daughter's side and walked around for hours, asking everyone he met whether they had any aspirin. Three hours later he returned empty-handed. There was no aspirin to be found anywhere. Esther's mother and brothers, hearing the bad news, began to cry.

For the next few hours, Esther's parents took turns cradling their eight-year-old daughter in their arms, crooning to her and sponging her burning face with cool water, as they mumbled words of Tehillim and davened for a miracle. Through it all, Esther lay limp and unresponsive, with no idea that her parents were crying bitterly for their little girl. So it went the entire night.

At eight o'clock in the morning the sun finally emerged through a crack in the thick layer of clouds blanketing the sullen sky, and Esther's fever broke. The family's relief was indescribable. The Rebbetzin's brother Reb Yaakov put it best.

"When the fever broke and my sister opened her eyes, it was like my *neshamah* had been returned to me."

Shortly afterward everyone was ordered to line up at the train station.

Those were Esther's final memories of the city where she had been born and raised.

It was May 1944, and the Nazis' death operation was well oiled and in full swing.

Have you any idea what it was like to be stuffed into a cattle car? There was no air to breathe, or food to eat. The train stopped here and there, but there was one particular stop that Esther Jungreis would never forget.

It happened in Linz.

Linz, Austria.

There the people on the train were stripped of their clothing and their heads were shorn of every last hair. Esther didn't know what to do with her eyes. How could she possibly look at her beautiful, holy Mama in such a state of degradation?

They were then stuffed into a shower — a shower that was also a gas chamber. The people knew it was a gas chamber and by that time they were no longer so naïve as to imagine that the Nazis wouldn't dare kill innocent people. They saw the canisters of poison gas and wondered if they would soon be breathing their last. Standing, stuffed together in the gas chamber, they stared at the shower heads and waited for the poison gas to emerge and suffocate them.

But it didn't happen.

For whatever reason, the Nazis chose to use the shower on that particular day and not the gas chamber. What made them do that? Why was one group of people killed and another allowed to live? There is but one answer to that question: It was Hashem's Will.

Bergen-Belsen did not have its own railroad station, so their cattle car stopped at a town called Celle. The family was famished and so utterly weak that they could barely stand up and would have collapsed on the spot, but they were ordered to their feet by the screaming guards and forced to walk ten miles to the concentration camp. How can a person walk after being stuffed in a cattle car for days on end without air or food? How was anyone alive after such a ride?

And then they were there.

Bergen-Belsen.

Piles of dead bodies lying in the streets. Living people who were not living. People who had had the life sucked out of them and were tottering around on matchstick legs.

Yet even here, even in the worst place on earth, Rav Avrohom Jungreis remained the same tzaddik of a Yid. The same wonderful father, the same incredible human being. He knew that the main thing was to keep his family from giving in to despair — to give them something to hold onto, to give them hope.

But what form of hope was to be had in a hell on earth like Bergen-Belsen?

The answer was clear.

He would give them Shabbos. They would hold on to Shabbos and Shabbos would sustain them and grant them life. And so Zeide instructed his children to count the days — "five more days, four more days, three more days, two more days, one more day — and then, children, my precious children," he'd tell them, "soon it will be Shabbos."

But what would they eat when Shabbos finally came to the barracks?

Somehow, Rav Avrohom managed to put aside a tiny piece of stale bread every single day. He saved his food, surviving on the barest minimum imaginable. He'd recite the berachah *Hamotzi* on a few crumbs — that was his reason for eating — but the rest, the rest was put aside for Shabbos.

And when Shabbos came, Esther's parents would gather the children together in the middle of the night, in the midst of all the terror on earth, and her father would say to them, *"My precious lights, my beautiful kinderlach, close your eyes, close your eyes. We are at home. Mama baked the most delicious challah. It's fresh and hot."*

Then he would take out the crumbs he had saved during the week. Those precious crumbs. And he would distribute them among his family and start to sing *Shalom Aleichem*, welcoming the angels of Shabbos.

One Friday night, Esther's younger brother, Binyomin, turned to his father and said, "*Tatty, ich zeh nisht kein malachim* — I can't see any angels! Where are the Shabbos angels?"

And Rav Avrohom Jungreis, tears rolling down his sunken cheeks, stroked his young son's face and replied in his warmest and most comforting voice, "You, my children, you are the angels of Shabbos."

That was how the Jungreis children became angels of Shabbos in the wastelands of Bergen-Belsen.

But Shabbos came only once a week. The rest of the week was pure misery.

At five o'clock every morning, Esther stood outside for roll call. It mattered not if it was warm outside or bitterly cold. It made no difference if there was two feet of snow on the ground. The prisoners were forced out of the barracks and made to stand in lines, without moving. And the Nazis would come with their whips and their pistols to count them, shouting and screaming, "Jewish pigs!"

And as young as she was, Esther looked at them, the "gentlemen" of the "Master Race," and said to herself, "*Baruch Hashem*, blessed be Hashem, that I am not the daughter of your people — that I am the daughter of my father and my mother, the daughter of a nation that stood at Sinai and heard the voice of Hashem and lives by the covenant that Hashem gave us — and not the daughter of a nation of brutes and murderers."

Even in the depths of hell there were rays of light.

One such ray was the fact that Yankie's bed was situated directly opposite the bed of Rav Yoel Teitelbaum, the Satmar Rebbe. The Rebbe's *gabbai*, Reb Yossel Ashkenazi, slept in the adjacent bed, and for the rest of his life Reb Yaakov Jungreis would recall the incredible *mesirus nefesh* Reb Yossel exhibited for his Rebbe, taking care of him to the best of his abilities and making sure the Rebbe had everything he needed — even in Bergen-Belsen. Yankie's relationship with the Rebbe didn't end when liberation arrived and they ceased being roommates, because Yankie was then chosen to serve as the Rebbe's *haus bachur* (attendant) when they were living in the DP camps.

The Rebbetzin would never forget what she saw in Bergen-Belsen.

She would never forget the evil that humans were capable of inflicting on one another for the basest of reasons.

At the same time, she would never forget the ability people possess to ease the pain of their fellow man and to make them feel better.

How could she forget such things when she'd seen them each and every day with her very own eyes?

She would never forget waking up to the sight of her father standing in the barracks in the gray light of the early-morning dawn, the sleeve of his shirt pushed up his arm, the Csenger tefillin held in his hand.

Would you forget such a sight?

There he stood. Like an angel.

And then the tefillin slid onto his arm and he recited the berachah and his face took on an expression of holiness that was simply otherworldly.

But he couldn't keep them on for long. Because there were so many other Yidden who wanted — no, needed — to put them on as well.

The Rebbetzin would often ask, "Can you understand this, my friends? Can you grasp such an idea?"

Starving and miserable, weak and disoriented — yet nothing mattered, besides being given the opportunity to slip the tefillin onto your arm and head, to recite the berachah and revel in the fact that you were born a Jew — a prince of the King — infinitely higher than your enemies would ever be!

To say *Shema Yisrael.*

To live like Rabbi Akiva and the *Asarah Harugei Malchus* (the Ten Martyrs of Israel whom the Roman rulers executed in gruesome fashion).

"All my life I wondered when I would be given the chance to give my life for Hashem..." (the words of Rabbi Akiva).

Hearing *Shema Yisrael* in the middle of a place like Bergen-Belsen ensures that those words and their message are seared onto a person's heart and soul forever. It helps explain why Rebbetzin Jungreis chose those six words and that specific song as the awesome message of her historic event in Madison Square Garden decades later. Yet all that was only in decades to come.

The nights in Bergen-Belsen lasted an eternity.

Esther heard the rats scurrying endlessly from here to there and back again, the patter of their feet on the wooden floorboards filling her sensitive child's heart with terror. There were foul odors in the room and the crying and wailing never stopped. Lying there on her bunk, she would allow her creative imagination to soar — leaving the barbed-wire fences of Bergen-Belsen behind and soaring through the sky to visit the city of Jerusalem in all its glory. She was able to picture it to the point where she could actually taste and feel it. She did this night after night, as the seasons changed and the Nazis were defeated in battlefields across the European continent.

And then one unforgettable day, the Jungreis family, who had lived (if you could call it living) in the hell of Bergen-Belsen for eight misery-laden months, were finally liberated.

What did they want now after suffering so much?

They wanted Eretz Yisrael.

They wanted Mount Hermon with its snowcapped peak.

They wanted the mystic city of Tzfas, long beloved by the nation's Kabbalists.

They wanted the sun-drenched Lake Kinneret and the tombs of Rabbi Meir Baal HaNess and Rachel, Rabbi Akiva's wife.

They wanted the red roofs of Haifa, and the orange groves that grew everywhere, and the sound of Hebrew being spoken and the mystique of being a Jew in the holiest spot on earth.

Most of all, they wanted Yerushalayim: Meah Shearim, the Old City, the Churva Shul and the Western Wall.

They wanted to live the dream that got them through the worst of times.

They wanted Eretz Yisrael.

But the British were in control and the visas never arrived.

With the war over, survivors across the European continent began searching for any family members who had survived the inferno. Zeide asked the same poignant questions of everyone he met.

"Did you see my father? My mother? My brothers, my sisters?"

The answer was always the same.

"No, we didn't see any of them."

And then one day Zeide met a man he had known as a child, a man who had been part of his father's kehillah in Hungary. He asked the man the same questions he asked everyone he met. This time, however, the answer was a different one.

With a trembling voice and tears rolling down his cheeks, the man finally got the words out…

"Yes," he whispered, "I did see them. I saw your father, the tzaddik, and his rebbetzin, his *eishes chayil* (woman of valor). I saw the entire family: the children, the babies, your nieces and nephews. They stood in line at the gas chambers.

"You are the sole survivor of the glorious rabbinic house of Harav Hagaon Yisroel HaLevi Jungreis, *Hashem yinkom damo* (may Hashem avenge his blood). Everyone else was murdered."

That was it. The answer Zeide had been searching for with such determination. His hopes and dreams lay shattered on the floor.

Esther's mother heard the news and screamed out, "No, no, it cannot be! Ribono shel Olam, it just cannot be! They cannot all be gone!"

But it was true. The dark, horrific reality was merciless and inescapable.

It was at that moment that Rav Avrohom HaLevi Jungreis stood up to his full height and spoke in a shaking voice — but one that was laden with an unshakable resolve.

Crying out in Yiddish, Rav Avrohom said, "*Ribono shel Olam! Ich beit nur eine zach. Nor eine zach! Az alle meine kinderlach, alle meine doros, alle Yiddishe kinder zolen bleiben bei Torah* — I beg of You, Hashem, only one thing. Only one thing. That all my children, all my descendants, and all Jewish children, should remain committed to Torah."

Those were his words at the moment of his incredible loss, as he processed the absence of the world he had known and loved and the arduous journey that lay ahead.

In later years, the Rebbetzin would quote her father's words to numerous audiences around the world, inspiring them with the following message.

"We, the Jewish people, understand — as we have understood through the millennia — that 'there is only one thing.' Even as my father prayed for 'only one thing' — that all his descendants should cling to Torah — so too did our Zeides throughout the centuries have the same hope and beseech Hashem with the same prayer.

"Knowing my Zeides, I can assure you that in the Heavens above they organize a special minyan of Jungreis Zeides and all the Zeides who preceded them, who cry out three times a day, '*Nor eine zach, Hashem* — only one thing, Hashem: Torah!'"

In later years, Zeide would rebuild his life, teaching Torah to his kehillah in Canarsie. When the Yamim Noraim would arrive, Rebbetzin Esther would send her children to their grandfather for Rosh Hashanah and Yom Kippur.

"My Zeide davened for the *amud* in two shuls every Yom Kippur — one for Shacharis, the other for Mussaf," Rabbi Yisroel Jungreis related. "I'd accompany him from one to the other. When we arrived at the second shul, I remember seeing a line stretching around the corner. There must have been a couple of hundred people waiting on that line.

" 'Zeide, what are all those people waiting for?'

" 'I will tell you,' he replied. 'We are in America. There are different types of Jews. There are Jews who come to shul every day of the year; there are Rosh Hashanah and Yom Kippur Jews, and there are Yizkor Jews. These are Yizkor Jews.'

" 'Zeide, what do you think about that?'

" 'What do I think? *Oich git* — also good, as long as a person does something.' "

That was Zeide, a man who was only capable of seeing the positive in another human being.

"I'd stand beside my Zeide throughout the entire davening. Zeide was an extremely inspirational *baal Mussaf,* and when he reached the part of the davening that described the execution of the *Asarah Harugei Malchus,* he would break down and cry bitter tears. He didn't cry during the rest of the davening, but at that one spot, he cried as if he would never stop, as if a faucet had sprung a leak, explaining to me that when he came to that point in Mussaf, and read the description of how the greatest rabbis of all time had been murdered, he'd see his own Zeides in the gas chambers being killed *al Kiddush Hashem* (sanctifying the Name of Hashem) — and then he couldn't stop himself from breaking down…"

The weeks turned into months and the months into years. When they were first liberated, it had been 1945. Yet now it was 1947 and nothing had changed. They were ready to move on with their lives, but it didn't seem as if the world was ready for them to do that.

But the waiting was only one part of the problem. A family that had managed to remain together in the Hungarian ghetto and in Bergen-Belsen had been separated, and for a little girl named Esther Jungreis, life became unbearable.

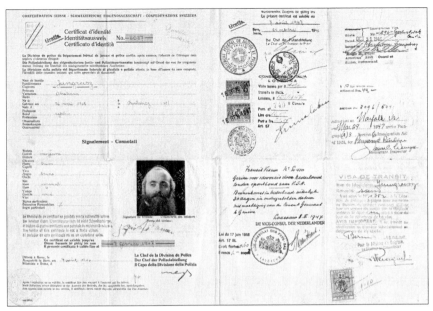

Zeide's post-war identity card

It was in a DP camp in Les Avants, Switzerland, that Yankie had his bar mitzvah. It was a major celebration for the young survivor. There was little in the way of food, but that didn't matter in the slightest to the

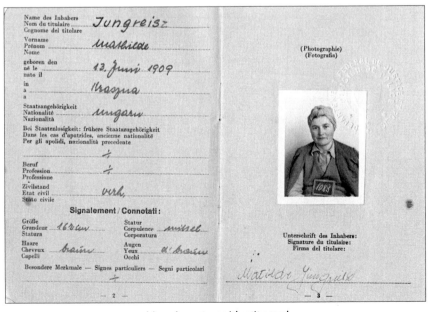

Mama's post-war identity card

fifteen hundred people who turned up to celebrate with Rav Avrohom HaLevi and his *mishpachah*.

At the bar mitzvah, all the children banded together and presented the bar mitzvah *bachur* with a huge box. Excited, Yankie tore into it and found a smaller box within. Opening the smaller box, he found yet another box. So it went, until he opened the final box and found a fruit he had never been introduced to before but would soon come to appreciate.

It was a banana — and Yankie considered it an extremely fine bar mitzvah present, though he didn't know what to do with it. Not knowing that bananas needed to be peeled before eating, Yankie was about to bite into it, but was quickly informed that it might be a good idea to first remove the peel. The next few minutes were spent slicing the banana into enough tiny slices so that every single guest his age could receive a piece.

It was a pretty good bar mitzvah all in all.

For Esther, meanwhile, the separation from her beloved family in the DP camp was sheer torment. Not being with her beloved father

Zeide in a Swiss DP Camp following their liberation

and mother was torture. Her father was able to come to her room and say *Shema* with her, but after he finished reciting the precious words, he would have to leave.

She would watch him leave knowing that nightmares lay ahead. She wanted to beg him to stay with her, but she knew that he would get in trouble if he tried. She had no choice but to be brave. For everyone's sake.

The nights were the worst of all. She went to bed in a state of abject terror. As a state of darkness descended on the room, Esther saw Nazi soldiers everywhere. The chairs were Nazis. The table was a Nazi. Everywhere she looked, all she saw were Nazis. She wanted to scream, but the sounds were caught in her throat. She wanted to cry out, but her voice was trapped. And so she lay in her bed, lying in a pool of sweat, waiting for the sun to rise and crying and weeping silently for her parents. At least there were some other refugee children with her in the room, other children who had been through similar situations and were able to understand.

Then, as if things weren't bad enough, they got worse.

Most of the children in the dorm had already been resettled. The rooms were emptying out at a rapid pace as families reunited and left the country in search of new homes abroad. Soon Esther was left without friends, with nobody to talk to and nobody to cry with when the nightmares hit. When her father came to visit from the camp where he was forced to stay, she told him the truth. That she was scared to death. How she lay awake at night and saw Nazis everywhere. That she was friendless and alone.

Rav Avrohom cradled his daughter in his arms for the longest time. His eyes were closed and Esther could tell that he was in deep thought. Finally he looked at her and declared, "Although our dream had been to go to Eretz Yisrael, the visas from the British were not forthcoming. But your aunt in New York has sent us visas. We shall leave for America on the first available ship."

A signed card by Esther Jungreis saved and treasured by a young roommate in a DP Camp

Esther broke out into a great big smile. Her first real smile in a while. "You mean it?"

"Yes, *mein kindt*, my dear child, it's time for us to be a family again."

Years later, Rebbetzin Esther Jungreis was invited to speak to the Jewish community in Budapest, Hungary.

The Rebbetzin's mother told her daughter, "I am going to accompany you on this trip."

Both had the desire to visit the gravesites of their ancestors, all distinguished rabbanim in Hungary. At the same time, they hoped to return to the shtetl where her grandparents had lived, to the shtetl where the Rebbetzin's father had taken his five-year-old daughter for a walk in the snow.

When they drove into her grandparents' town, the Rebbetzin found an elderly peasant and said to him, "Do you remember the Jews who used to live here? Do you by any chance remember the Rabbi?"

"Yes," the man replied, nodding his head. "I definitely remember

The Rebbetzin with Mama at *kever avos* in Hungary

him. He was a good man who used to give me the chickens that weren't kosher."

"I am his only surviving granddaughter," the Rebbetzin said to the peasant.

He looked at her as if to say, "How come you're still alive; I thought you were all killed?"

She chose to ignore his look.

"Tell me," she said to him, "is the house where my grandfather lived still standing?"

He nodded his head.

"What about the cemetery where my great-great-grandfathers were buried?"

"Yes."

"Can you show us the house?"

He led the Rebbetzin and her mother toward the house. They walked side by side, holding hands. They arrived at the street. And as soon as she stood on the street, Esther Jungreis recognized the house. It was just as she remembered it. Nothing had changed.

As they came very close, Rebbetzin Miriam broke down and wept, crying in Yiddish, "Mama, Mama, please, Mommy, open the door! Angyuka, Angyuka (Hungarian for Mother dear), please open the door. The children have arrived! Please open the door!"

The door opened and a peasant emerged from within.

She looked at them and asked, "What do you want? Who are you looking for?"

What did they want? Who were they looking for?

No one. There was no one to look for.

They turned away from the house and went to the cemetery, where they found the gravestones of their holy great-grandfathers. There the Rebbetzin told the Zeides everything that had happened to their family. She then requested of her great-great-grandfather to please find the Zeide on whose knees she had sat and to please relay her heartfelt gratitude to him — her heartfelt thank you to him for the path he made for her in the snow.

"Tell him that I fell many times. Tell him that the snow was very deep. But also tell him that I always found the path in the end and that I stood up and carried on walking. Tell him that today I have children and grandchildren who are following the path.

"Tell him I established Hineni so that every Jew should be able to follow the path. Tell him that I wrote my books so that every Jew should be able to follow the path. Tell him that I share my story with Jews the world over, so that each and every one of them will remember their own Zeide — the Zeide they used to have, who wept for them and learned for them and made a path for them. Tell him that I never stop reminding all those Jews that they must never forget their Zeides and the paths that were made for them to follow — through the deepest, thickest snow."

Then the Rebbetzin and her mother turned around and left the cemetery — as the Hungarian wind howled through the alleyways and the leaves on the trees swayed and danced in the frigid breeze.

This chapter has been dedicated in memory of
Paula Pilevsky ע״ה, who held us up.
A Holocaust survivor and former partisan,
she led her family with strength, wisdom and love.
Despite the many obstacles she came across along the way,
her arms never got tired.

Renee and Philip Pilevsky and Family

CHAPTER TWENTY-ONE
The Boxer's Return

*I*t was 1947, and Mama's younger sister Zissi and her husband, Rav Laizer Cohen, facilitated the family's exit from Europe to the United States. Esther was ten years old.

Their four-week journey aboard a freighter was an absolute nightmare.

The smell of diesel fuel was everywhere.

They were so seasick Esther's mother actually feared she was going to die and said goodbye to her husband and children.

Rav Avrohom would have none of that.

"*Chas v'shalom*, Mommy dear. You are not allowed to say such a thing."

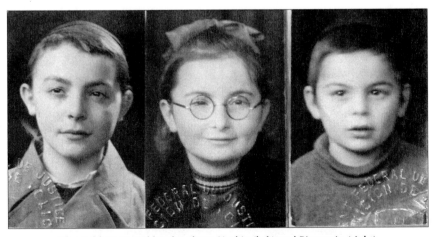

The Rebbetzin and her brothers, Yankie (left) and Binyomin (right)

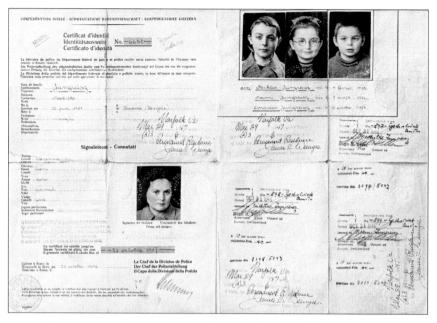

Swiss travel document issued to Mama and the three Jungreis children

Finally, finally they spotted land and the captain announced that they were docking at Norfolk, Virginia.

It was very exciting news, tempered slightly by how sick they were.

It was January when they docked, and bitterly cold. None of them had any idea that Norfolk was quite a distance from New York and their relatives. To them America was America — a notion that they would rapidly come to learn was simply untrue. And so they stepped off the freighter and onto American soil: penniless, famished and with nowhere to go.

Seeing their predicament, someone called the local police, who kindly got in touch with the head of the local Jewish community. The man rushed to the port as soon as he heard about the family waiting, and took them to his home, offering them a meal and assuring them that everything was kosher. Literally starving, the family polished off three loaves of bread and two dozen eggs in no time at all. Then they were temporarily satiated and feeling a tiny bit better after their nightmarish journey. The kind Jew from Norfolk purchased train tickets for them to New York and sent them on their way, speeding down the tracks on their way to the big city and their future life.

When they arrived at Penn Station, the same scenario repeated itself.

Once again they had no idea where to go — once again someone called the police. This time, the policeman who arrived at the scene took one look at the bedraggled family of refugees, and addressed them in Yiddish!

Hearing a policeman speaking to them in Yiddish, all five of them burst into tears, not being able to reconcile the fact that the man was both a policeman and a Jew. A police uniform was something they had always associated with brutality, and they couldn't get over the fact that in America one could be a Jew and also wear a badge. The Jewish policeman bundled the family into a cab and paid their fare! As the taxi drove through the congested streets of the Big Apple, they looked out the window and marveled at the blessed land where even the policemen were benevolent and compassionate — and sometimes Jewish.

Thus they arrived at the residence of Esther's aunt and uncle in Brooklyn, New York.

While Tante Zissi and Uncle Laizer were very warm and hospitable, the Jungreises wouldn't remain in other people's homes for long, moving into their own apartment in East Flatbush, Brooklyn, the neighborhood that was home to many other Jews at the time. Everyone on the block had already been in America for a while and was familiar with

Zeide and Mama in front of their home in East Flatbush

the language and mentality. Purely out of the interest of their hearts, the neighbors made it their business to advise Rav Avrohom to keep his children out of anything resembling a yeshivah if he wanted them to grow up into *mentchen*.

Purely out of the interest of his own heart, Rav Avrohom paid them no need. He thanked every well-meaning neighbor for their advice and then initially sent his boys to Yeshiva Torah Vodaath in Williamsburg, and eventually to Yeshiva Rabbi Chaim Berlin which was much closer to their home.

When it came to the matter of Esther's education, there was only one high school that fit the appropriate criteria for a Jungreis daughter, and that was Bais Yaakov of Williamsburg, which had

Esther's high school
graduation picture

been established under the aegis of Rebbetzin Vichna Kaplan, an original *talmidah* of Sarah Schenirer.

Though she had arrived in the United States without knowing any English, it wasn't long before Esther was at the top of her class — along with the future Rebbetzin Sara Freifeld and Rebbetzin Bruria David — participating vocally in every discussion; already someone whose presence couldn't be overlooked. In later years, her teacher, Rebbetzin Basya Bender, would fondly recall the impression Esther made on her.

The children might have been in school, but their father made it clear to them that he had no interest in raising a family of professionals. No. Zeide had other dreams for his kids. He hoped they would be interested in spending their lives rebuilding the world that had been brutally snuffed out of existence by the Nazis.

Rav Avrohom didn't waste any time getting to work. With his keen intuition, he recognized his Esther's talents and gave her her first job.

"Esther, I want you to go outside and invite every single Jewish child on this block to our apartment for Shabbos."

Esther was mortified by the idea that she would have to confront the lion in its den. The kids on the block ran through the fire hydrant spray on summer Friday nights. How on earth was she supposed to communicate with them when she didn't even speak the language?

The language barrier was just one part of the challenge. Esther's parents had no money to buy nice clothing for her. She didn't look like the other kids or speak like them. Yet her father expected her to walk right up to them, look them in the eye and invite them into her home — the home of a European rabbi with a long beard and black hat. She didn't see how it was possible to do what he asked.

On the other hand, the request was coming from her father.

And Esther loved her father with all the love in her young heart. If her father was asking her to do something for him, she would try. She didn't know if she would succeed, but she would give it her best shot.

Off she went.

Every child she met she invited to their home for a Shabbos visit. To her great surprise, they smiled at her and accepted gratefully. And that was how the Jungreis Shabbos table became the place to be Friday night.

In every neighborhood there are people who do not fit in. They live on the edge of society and are treated like outcasts — and that's if people even notice them at all. In Esther's neighborhood, one of those people went by the name of Goldberg*. He was the kind of person whom kids made fun of as he passed them in the street.

In his younger years, Goldberg's life had been different. He had been a successful boxer and fought many successful fights. But climbing into the ring as a boxer means being on the receiving end of many a blow. One day he agreed to a fight with a sharp young boxer. Goldberg was already older by then and past his prime. His reflexes weren't what they had once been. The young boxer managed to get past his fist and hit him in the head, shaking him up inside.

By the time the fight was over, Goldberg was a different person. From that day on, he sat outside on the street and muttered to himself.

It was very sad.

Most people ignored him, walking by quickly when they chanced upon the confused man.

But Rav Avrohom Jungreis was not most people. He was a man who cared about others. And not just those who "had it all together." No. He cared about the down-and-outs and the hapless individuals whom society had rejected. Rav Avrohom picked up Goldberg from the street, dusted him off and brought him home for a meal at the Jungreis kitchen table.

The children were not at all thrilled with this development. Goldberg was a gruff man and spoke in a coarse manner. The children were not used to people acting this way and had no interest in having someone like him around.

Worst of all was when Goldberg would yell at their father and order him around.

"Bring me a cup of coffee, Rabbi," he'd growl at Rabbi Jungreis — who carried out his every wish, treating him like an honored guest.

It bothered Esther very much to see the way Goldberg treated her father and she complained to him, asking him to get rid of the man from their home.

"You are wrong," he told her. "Goldberg is not being disrespectful to me. He simply doesn't know any better. He is a lost soul and we must try to help him."

"But Tatty," she protested, "do you have to be his waiter? You are a *talmid chacham* and he knows nothing. How can you serve a person like that?"

"*Meine lichtige kindt* (my precious child)," he replied, "don't worry about my *kavod*. Didn't Avraham Avinu serve every guest that came his way? Didn't he leave Hashem mid-conversation to go take care of a group of dusty travelers? If he could leave Hashem to do this, surely I can take care of a fellow Jew!"

To this argument, Esther had nothing to say.

But that wasn't enough for her father. He wanted his daughter to be personally involved in "Project Goldberg."

"Please take Mr. Goldberg into the kitchen and show him how to properly wash his hands for bread."

"Esther, please bring Mr. Goldberg a nice hot cup of coffee and some soup."

"Esther, please show Mr. Goldberg where to sit today."

Esther did everything her father asked of her. And somehow after a while she stopped minding.

Goldberg came to their home for years on end and Rav Avrohom taught him how to read the Hebrew alphabet.

He taught Goldberg how to recite the blessings over food.

He taught him how to pray.

Basically Rav Avrohom taught Goldberg how to act like a Jew.

That was just the beginning. Because Rav Avrohom wanted Goldberg to feel like a *mentch*. He accomplished that by letting everyone know that Mr. Goldberg was going to celebrate his bar mitzvah in Rav Avrohom's shul.

Who can forget the sight of Goldberg the boxer being called up to say the blessings and read from the Torah?

Who can forget the sight of tough Goldberg from the street, breaking down and crying — at having been granted such a beautiful gift!

It was proof to Rav Avrohom's life philosophy: Never give up on a person. It doesn't matter how he looks. There is someone hiding inside who is worth reaching and connecting with. It was an eye-opening moment for the congregation.

The moment he celebrated his bar mitzvah, Goldberg was a different person. He took part in everything going on at the shul. He was there every morning for minyan. Whereas with some people there was a question whether they would come on time, with Goldberg there was no question at all. He lived and loved the shul and his rabbi and would do anything for both.

One morning Goldberg didn't show.

Zeide knocked on the door. Nobody answered.

He called the super.

They opened the door.

Goldberg the boxer was on the floor. He had passed away.

Yet even in his final moments on earth, Goldberg taught them all a lesson.

On his night table there was a siddur. It was still open. It was the siddur from which his friend, the Rabbi, had taught him how to find himself — how to uncover the *pintele Yid* (Jewish spark) that had been long hidden. Goldberg loved that siddur. To him it represented new opportunities and new life.

Once again Rav Avrohom taught his daughter how to give by personal example. For the rest of her life, the Rebbetzin would follow in his footsteps and live by his example. Sometimes people would come to her *shiurim* from the streets. They were disheveled and forlorn. It mattered little to the Rebbetzin. She'd hug them with all her strength and allow them into her heart.

And as she wrapped her arms around a crying woman who could barely communicate, Esther Jungreis would recall a boxer who had taken one too many hits to the head — and how her father's love had turned his life around and given him meaning and self-respect.

After the war was over, almost nobody remained alive from the town of Nadudvar, the town where Esther had walked in her father's footsteps in the snow. One man managed to return. But he did more than just return. The man found a candlestick that Esther's Zeide had buried in his yard. There was no question in his mind that the candlestick needed to be returned to its family.

It took the survivor time, but eventually he reached the shores of America and tracked down Rav Avrohom and his family in their new home.

It was nighttime when he knocked.

Esther's father answered the door.

"What can I do for you?" he asked the stranger standing there.

The stranger explained. About surviving the war. And returning home. And finding a Jungreis candlestick. And wanting to return it to its rightful owners.

You can imagine Rav Avrohom's reaction to the whole story.

He was overcome. It was almost as if his parents were reaching out to him from their grave: talking to him, reassuring him that he was not forgotten and that the Jungreis family — and all of Klal Yisrael — would go on.

The *leichter* originally lit by Zeide's mother, Rebbetzin Slova Chana

"I made a promise," the man said. "I made a promise that I would give this candlestick back to its owners. This is the *leichter* your mother lit every Friday night. I have come to keep my promise."

The candlestick was handed over.

On it Rav Avrohom was able to make out an inscription.

He read the words Slova Chana. It was his mother's name.

He saw the man to the door, thanking him

over and over from the bottom of his heart for giving him back some of the missing pieces of his heart.

Years later Esther Jungreis would marry and have children. She had two daughters. The first was named Chaya Sora. She named the second Slova Chana.

This was a sign for Esther's father to give his daughter the candlestick.

When the Rebbetzin passed away in 2016, the candlestick was passed on to Slovie Wolff — the little girl who was named after the candlestick's original owner — ensuring the continuation of the family chain.

But more on that later.

This chapter has been dedicated
in memory of Celia and Moses Eisenstein ע״ה
Malkah and Chaim Levy ע״ה • Harry Levy ע״ה
and in honor of Toby Levy
Howard, Sonya, Talia and Hannah Levy

Part 5
1955-1980

He walked into my house. I was sitting down. Rabbi Jungreis approached me. Not a word out of his mouth. He just reached over to me and he encircled me in his arms. He hugged me with his entire being. Rebbetzin, there were tears streaming down his face. Do you understand what that did for me? Can you understand what it meant to see the Rabbi, the special rabbi, crying for me and with me?

A grieving father
from the North Woodmere community

You may not feel like you have a reason to smile, but smile anyway, and Hashem will give you a reason.
Rav Meshulem Jungreis

Survivor of Nazi horrors urges all Jews to "Come home to our G-d." She knows her faith, her culture and her people...
Boston Evening Globe

CHAPTER TWENTY-TWO
The Rabbi's Secret

*I*t was Rav Tzvi Hirsch Cohen's idea to match his granddaughter Esther with her cousin Meshulem Jungreis. Meshulem and his older brother Amrom were the sole survivors of a large and illustrious family that had been completely obliterated.

It was like bringing together two diamonds.

History was about to be made.

The wedding took place in November 1955 and was well attended by anyone even remotely related to the Jungreis family and by many others who were not related at all, but who rejoiced nevertheless with the young couple — a couple who survived and started anew. Rav Meshulem was tall and handsome. He was a Torah scholar. Esther was petite, pretty and charismatic. In addition, she had something to say on every subject and was able to quote from the Torah with ease.

They were smart enough to have

At the wedding of Rav Meshulem and the Rebbetzin. Rav Meshulem, flanked by Zeide (right) and the Rebbetzin's grandfather, Rav Tzvi Hirsch Cohen

taken any path in life and made a success of it. But they didn't want any path. They wanted to help their people.

Rabbi Meshulem Jungreis' first position was in the city of Patterson, New Jersey. Their apartment was located directly above the shul. There were to be two more shuls along the way (Bethpage and Valley Stream) before the young rabbi would establish the first Orthodox synagogue in the soon-to-be blossoming community of North Woodmere.

It was 1962 and a spiritual desert was about to bloom.

Rabbi and Rebbetzin Jungreis were a team. It would be that way with everything they did in life, be it at their shul Ohr Torah in North Woodmere or with the Hineni organization. The Rabbi began teaching the men in his congregation and encouraged his wife to do the same for the women of the shul.

But how? It wasn't easy to convince non-religious women to attend Torah lectures.

The Rebbetzin soon found a way.

It wasn't long before the women of North Woodmere were informed that the Rebbetzin was starting a class in her home.

As she folded laundry or prepared dinner for her family, she would tell stories from the Bible to those gathered around her kitchen table. She'd tell them about Miriam HaNeviah (Prophetess) and how she led the women in song at the Red Sea. She spoke of Yael and Devorah — of great prophetesses, and how the women were the first to accept the Torah when it was given to the Jewish nation by Hashem at Mount Sinai.

From time to time she'd stop in the middle of whatever she was doing, child in her arms, and give her students a powerful stare.

"Promise me you will never forget the past," she'd beg them.

Her husband, fully appreciating the unusual abilities of his wife, encouraged her to spread her wings and to expand her activities beyond the confines of their synagogue.

"Esther," he'd say to his rebbetzin, "it's not enough. Hashem gave you the gift of speech. You must try to reach the people in every community, not just here in North Woodmere. I am fully committed to my shul, my people and my *shiurim*. But you should speak everywhere people want to hear your voice."

"What about our children?"

He smiled at her.

"I will be here to watch them. They will fall asleep as I rock their carriage with one hand and turn the pages of my Gemara with the other."

"It's nice that you believe in me. But who says I'm cut out for this?"

"I have met many people," Rav Meshulem told his wife. "In most cases people have no interest in listening to what other people have to say. In some cases, they find themselves moderately interested. And then there are those — and they are one in a million — to whom people are drawn. Those are the people who take on leadership roles and do big things. You have that quality. A genuine star quality. When you talk, people quiet down and listen to you. You have all the natural components to become a true success, most importantly because you'll be doing it for the right reasons. It's not about you and it never was. All you care about is Klal Yisrael — just like your father before you and his father before him — all the way back to our Zeides back in Hungary. And that's why I won't give up until I see you using your talents to be *mekadesh Sheim Shamayim,* sanctify the Name of Heaven in this world."

She heard his words and was convinced.

With such conviction, it was impossible not to be.

So it began, slowly at first. Schools heard of the young rebbetzin and invited her to come and address their students. She was asked to speak at dinners, and for organizations and community centers. Slowly but surely, her name began to spread and people began talking about Rebbetzin Esther Jungreis.

But for Rav Meshulem Jungreis it still wasn't enough — not when his wife was capable of much more. And he resolved to do whatever he could to introduce her to the world. Because he knew that she had what it takes to make a major difference.

At the same time, the Rabbi and his wife went out of their way to involve their entire family in their work — bringing every child on board and turning them into an integral component of the Jungreis operation. The children were raised in a neighborhood where hardly anyone was religious. Many people ask them today, "How could your parents have chosen such a path?"

Of course the children attended fine yeshivos that gave them a classic Jewish education. But it was much more than that. Because the Jungreis kids developed a pride in who they were from a very young age.

One of the reasons this was true was due to their names. Every

Kiruv at a young age. Osher Jungreis (left) befriended a neighborhood boy, who enrolled in a local yeshivah

one of the children had been named after someone special who had been murdered in the Holocaust. Chaya Sora, the oldest child, was named after Rav Meshulem's mother. Yisroel was named after the Nadudvar Zeide, Zeide's father. Slovie had been named Slova Chana after Zeide's mother. Osher Anshil, their youngest child, was named after Rav Meshulem's father, who carried the name of the Menuchas Osher.

One of the ways Zeide showed his appreciation to Hashem for saving his immediate family from the jaws of certain death was by reciting the blessing *Shehechiyanu* every time the entire family got together at a Melaveh Malkah or Chanukah party in years to come. With grandchildren frolicking around him, Zeide would wipe the tears from his eyes and fervently recite the berachah with supreme *kavannah* (concentration).

The fact that the Rebbetzin's parents both survived the war was an open miracle and she didn't content herself with being grateful. Instead, she connected her family to the previous generations in the most powerful way imaginable. Spending time with the grandparents was considered a privilege. Zeide was treated like a king, Mama like a queen. They were the leaders — loved and respected — and that connection helped the Jungreis kids form the kind of roots that were so deeply entrenched in Jungreis soil that no wind would be able to shake

Collage of the Jungreis ancestry, with the Menuchas Osher in the center, which the Rebbetzin gave to all her children and grandchildren

them from who they were or what they believed.

For the Rebbetzin, the Zeides were a major part of life. She had oil paintings made of all the Zeides, which lined the wall — a focal point of the decor — providing a certain intangible element to the house. Anyone who walked into the Jungreis home couldn't help but notice them. In fact, on one occasion Chaya Sora saw a friend of hers sitting on the couch quietly staring at the portraits.

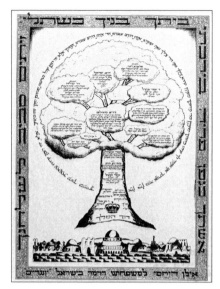

Jungreis family tree

"What's the matter?" she asked her.

"How can I say anything in front of the holy men? Is it even proper to talk in front of them? All those great rabbis are looking at us! There's an aura of holiness in the room — it just doesn't feel right to talk!"

The Zeides accompanied the family wherever they went. On the eve of Chaya Sora's wedding, her father could tell that his oldest child was suffering from an acute case of nerves. Rav Meshulem chose his words carefully, words he knew would make all the doubts disappear.

"You will be okay," he said reassuringly.

"How do you know?"

"Just think, all the Zeides are walking with you — and all the Bubbas. When you walk, they're walking. And all of them are giving you their berachos."

And off Chaya Sora went to get married.

And it was good — just as Rav Meshulem said.

Establishing a shul is a daunting enterprise. And that's true even in a kehillah where the members of the shul see eye-to-eye with their rav. In Ohr Torah it wasn't always that way. The fact that Rav Meshulem Jungreis was the Rav of a kehillah whose members were for the most part not yet religious meant that he had to possess a combination of kindness, strength, willpower and plain common sense to ensure that

Hosting a Hineni Women's Group in the Rebbetzin's succah in North Woodmere

the shul never failed to operate according to halachah and didn't deviate from the straight and narrow.

There were epic battles when it came to the shul's kosher *mechitzah*, a battle that would forever be remembered by anyone who was there. Some who opposed the *mechitzah* were extremely vocal, but the Rabbi wouldn't budge. The female members of the kehillah tried enlisting the Rebbetzin (she was after all a truly progressive woman) to take their side. She told them that the *mechitzah* would remain and that there was nothing to discuss. There would be no compromising in Ohr Torah. Torah was Torah and halachah was halachah — no matter what.

It took the members of the shul time to understand what their Rabbi and Rebbetzin were all about — but they got there in the end. The outcome of the journey was pleasant, but the traveling conditions were not easy for the young Rabbi and his wife. Not easy at all.

Yet they persevered. And when they grew weary (as people inevitably do), the two of them thought of the precious candlestick that had been hand-delivered to Rav Avrohom Jungreis from the courtyard of the shul in Nadudvar — and they remembered their mission and how it was up to them to spread the light of Torah and Yiddishkeit through the desert of North Woodmere.

Then they took a deep breath, squared their shoulders and strode forth to do battle in the Name of Hashem.

Rav Meshulem teaching about the lulav and esrog to Ohr Torah members
in the Jungreis succah

The results are there for all to see. Today, North Woodmere is a vibrant and bustling frum community in every sense of the word. Nothing worthwhile happens, you see, without people who are willing to give of themselves selflessly and completely for the cause.

Halloween came to North Woodmere. The streets were filled with kids in costume, knocking on doors and making the rounds hoping for a good candy haul. The year Yisroel was ten, Halloween fell on a Friday night. The family was sitting down at the Friday night *seudah* when the doorbell rang. Shabbos meals were a big deal in the Jungreis home. The Rebbetzin loved when her family sang *zemiros* and insisted that they sing — a lot. In fact, if they happened to sing a *zemer* (song) when she was out of the room, she made them sing it all over again.

"Ma, we sang it already," they'd protest.

"Yes, but I wasn't here to hear it."

Yisroel was just a kid but he knew how things went in their house. That was why he wasn't surprised when his mother told him to go see who was ringing the bell. Nobody was ever turned away from their front door — even someone who should have known not to ring the bell on a Friday night.

Yisroel went to see who was ringing the Rabbi's bell. He looked

The Rebbetzin conducting a Chanukah party for the children of Ohr Torah

outside. There were a bunch of neighborhood kids standing there.

Returning to his seat at the table, he told his parents, "It's a bunch of kids out 'Trick or Treating.'"

"Open the door," his mother said.

"For who?"

"Yisroel, these are Yiddishe *kinderlach*. You have to open the door. Go get the candy."

There was always candy in the house and Yisroel went to get some candy bars for the visitors. Opening the door, he found himself looking at a group of kids all dressed up. There was Batman and Robin, Snow White and other characters.

"Trick or treat!"

"Good Shabbos," the Rebbetzin called out, warmly greeting the surprised kids.

They had no idea what was going on.

"It's Shabbos today. Do you know what that is? Are any of you Jewish?"

Most of them answered, "I'm Jewish," except for one girl who replied, "My mother told me I'm half-Jewish."

"I want every one of you to take a candy, and I'm going to teach you how to make a berachah."

The kids followed her lead and recited berachos on their candies.

"Tell your parents that tonight is the Sabbath and that you came to the Rabbi's house and the Rabbi's wife gave you yummy candy! Can you do that? And tell them that we have a Hebrew school in our shul and they should send you there to learn about what it means to be a Jew! Can you give them the message?"

The kids nodded.

One of the kids actually followed through, informing his parents of the evening's events and about the Hebrew school at the Rabbi's shul. His parents registered him — and believe it or not, he became religious!

Rabbi Yisroel Jungreis met the man not long ago.

"I'm probably one of the only people in the world who became religious because of Halloween," the man told Rabbi Jungreis.

On a different year Slovie remembers sitting in the kitchen as a group of neighborhood children came knocking on the Jungreis door, chanting "Trick or treat!"

The Rebbetzin gave every one of the visitors a special smile.

"Are you Jewish?" she asked the kids.

"Yes," most of them nodded.

"Listen to me," she said. "This is the Rabbi and Rebbetzin's house. If you're Jewish we have a much better holiday than Halloween. It's called Purim. On Purim every kid dresses up in a costume and there are parties in the shul and at our house and kids receive more candy than they can possibly eat — and it's just the funnest day ever!"

"We never heard of Purim."

So the Rebbetzin told them a little more about Purim and the day it would fall and invited them all back for the festivities.

Rav Meshulem Jungreis was a phenomenal *talmid chacham* — he had been granted *semichah* at a young age back in Hungary — and could have delivered a *shiur* that would challenge the sharpest yeshivah students, but he chose to dedicate his life to teaching basic halachah to the members of his community. Although he was man who possessed a command of the entire Talmud at his fingertips, Rabbi Jungreis was mostly appreciated for his unique kindness, his extraordinary devotion to his community and his homespun quips and anecdotes. Even now, years after the Rabbi passed away, his witticisms are still fondly remembered.

He enjoyed using lines like, *"You may not feel like you have a reason to smile, but smile anyway, and Hashem will give you a reason,"* and

Rav Meshulem — always with a grandchild on his shoulder

another of his favorites, *"You don't have to hear everything. Hashem gave you two ears — in one ear and out the other."*

Simple lessons, but they sunk in and made an impact.

"If I visualize Rabbi Jungreis," Sheila Pilevsky Chess said, "I always see him with a child or grandchild on his arm. Warm and open and giving — just like he'd always been from the time I first came to know him as a child in his shul. He was constantly busy. Busy bringing a package of food to someone who was sick or a challah to brighten a person's day, or tutoring kids who needed help."

"That was our rabbi." And that was why Sheila told the Rebbetzin when she came to be *menachem avel*, "I lost my best friend."

A minute later someone else came in to the *shivah* house and said, "I feel like the Rabbi was my best friend."

That was the way many people felt: that he was their best friend — and would do just about anything for his people.

"When we were sitting *shivah* for my father," Chaya Sora recalled, "an incredible number of people came to be *menachem avel*. There were so many people there, it was almost impossible to even reach my mother's side. All of a sudden one of the members of the shul walked into the room with her child, and a few minutes into the conversation, the little girl started to cry — and all she wanted was to get close to my mother. My mother looked at

Rav Meshulem at the bris of a grandson

the little girl — she must have been around eight years old — and said, "Why are you crying, *sheifelah*?"

The girl looked into the Rebbetzin's eyes and said with a kind of profound sorrow that shook the bystanders to their collective core, "Who is going to do Hebrew homework with me now that the Rabbi is gone?"

This child was the daughter of baalei teshuvah parents whom the Rabbi had convinced to enroll their daughter in a yeshivah. They were unable to help their daughter with her Hebrew homework.

The Rebbetzin hadn't even known about her husband's "tutoring job" — just another kindness from a man with a giant heart; a man who helped and helped and never looked for any recognition.

Within a short time after moving to North Woodmere, Rabbi Jungreis was appointed a chaplain of the Nassau County Police Department, respected and loved by every member of the force, who valued his opinion and trusted his advice.

Under the Jungreis' leadership, North Woodmere became an extremely warm and welcoming community, with Rabbi Jungreis personally visiting any home that needed him to kasher their oven or for any other reason. Nothing was too difficult for the Rabbi and his wife.

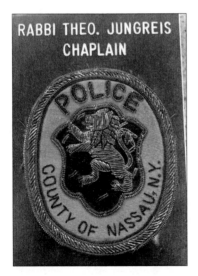

Rav Meshulem's Nassau County
Police Department chaplain ID

Rav Meshulem's official chaplain
badge presented to the family
after his passing

Rav Meshulem conducting a "model Seder" for Jewish officers of the
Nassau County Police Department in Congregation Ohr Torah

Most of all, however, they taught their people Torah.

Many of the members of Ohr Torah had been through the war. Some were no longer religious. Where a person was up to in his religious observance made no difference to the way he was treated in Rabbi Jungreis' shul.

In the early years, the shul was right next door to the Rabbi's house. Which meant that everyone saw the Jungreis living room as an extension of the kiddush hall, showing up after davening and staying for hours.

And that was exactly how Rabbi and Rebbetzin Jungreis wanted it to be.

One day the Rebbetzin ran into a man she knew who had lost a child.

"Rebbetzin," he said to her, "I have to tell you something. Your husband was the one who pulled us through our moment of great loss. It was him, more than anyone else!"

Needless to say, the Rebbetzin was very curious. What did he tell them? What message had he used to help them retain their sanity?

Later that evening, the Rebbetzin sat down with her husband and remembered the conversation that she'd had with Mark Brander.

The Rebbetzin enjoying Rav Meshulem's words at a family gathering

"Meshulem, I ran into Mark. You know, you went to his house and spoke to him and his wife when they lost a child. He said that you helped them more than anyone else. How did you do it? What words did you use?"

"I didn't do anything," he replied. "What could I do? What could I say? What could anyone say to people in such pain?"

The whole thing was a mystery to the Rebbetzin.

Here was Mark, saying that her husband saved their lives.

On the other hand, there was her husband, claiming that he hadn't done anything, hadn't said a word.

The Branders came to see the Rabbi a few weeks later. After serving the couple drinks and cake, the Rebbetzin returned to their earlier conversation.

"When we met last," she began, "you told me that the Rabbi was the one who helped you most in your hour of need."

"Rebbetzin, your husband didn't help us. He saved us. There is no question in the world that we would have drowned without him."

"How did he save you? Can you tell me what he said?"

Mark stared at her and thought for a few seconds.

"Rebbetzin, he didn't say anything. Not one word.

"But he did something else. Something more important.

"He walked into my house. I was sitting down. Rabbi Jungreis approached me. Not a word out of his mouth. He just reached over to me and he encircled me in his arms. He hugged me with his entire being. Rebbetzin, there were tears streaming down his face. Do you understand what that did for me? Can you understand what it meant to see the Rabbi, the special rabbi, crying for me and with me?

"He didn't speak.

"But there was no reason for him to speak. I didn't need him to speak. I needed him to cry with me."

And then the Rebbetzin understood her husband's secret.

It wasn't about what her husband had said.

It was about what hadn't been said.

It was about his silence.

For in that silence lay a world of incredibly powerful empathy — so strong that it would be remembered for all time. And yet again, she marveled at the intense emotion — the passion — that Rav Meshulem Jungreis exhibited and that bubbled right beneath the surface. And when it emerged, it roared forth like a gigantic wall of flame — liquid Torah fire — from the Rabbi's extra-sensitive heart to his fellow Jew. Once you understand what that heart was all about, can there be any question of how and why the spiritual desert that was North Woodmere sprouted and bloomed and became what it did?

CHAPTER TWENTY-THREE

The Rebbetzin's Viewpoint

*S*ummer time. Time to get out of the house and go travel. Time for the sweet feel of the breeze sweeping through the trees and the deliciously cold water of the swimming pool. All over New York, Jewish people made arrangements to leave their homes and go to the Catskill Mountains. The Rabbi and his wife did the same. Destination: the Pioneer Hotel in Greenfield Park, New York.

The hotel was packed with guests: numerous people from all walks of life. Rich, poor, anonymous, and famous and influential. The hotel belonged to Leo and Gerti Gartenberg and it was the place where the Agudah and many other Jewish organizations held their big events. Basically, the Pioneer was the place to be.

As the owner and editor of *The Jewish Press*, Rabbi Sholom Klass had a major say in setting the agenda of what religious Jews read in those days. He would never forget the phone calls he received from Rav Moshe Feinstein and a number of other rabbinical leaders. At the time,

"The Rebbetzin's Viewpoint" column in *The Jewish Press*

The Morning Journal was closing shop and they asked Rabbi Klass to start a newspaper for the Orthodox community — in Yiddish.

Naomi Klass Mauer remembers when her father came home from the meeting and said to her mother, "I'm going to do it — but I'm going to do it in English. I want to reach all the young people."

So Rabbi and Mrs. Klass founded *The Jewish Press*, and it was very difficult in the beginning. Having received his rabbinical ordination from Yeshiva Torah Vodaath, he was able to obtain the yeshivah's mailing list. That helped. From its simple beginnings, the paper's popularity grew, until it began spreading throughout the United States. Countless people all across America attribute the fact that they are religious today to *The Jewish Press* and its weekly effect on their lives.

One Motza'ei Shabbos in the early '60s, Rabbi and Rebbetzin Jungreis were in the Pioneer lobby. Zeide was there too. From inside the rec hall came the sound of the evening's entertainment and everywhere you looked, people were having a good time.

Rabbi and Mrs. Klass and their daughter had also come down into the lobby and were enjoying a pleasant conversation with the devoted young rabbi of North Woodmere's Ohr Torah, his popular Rebbetzin and Zeide, who loved "talking Torah" with the editor of *The Jewish Press*.

All of a sudden, Rav Meshulem Jungreis looked Rabbi Klass in the eye and said, "You know something, you need someone to write an advice column. Not just someone, a woman."

"Yes, but who?" replied Rabbi Klass.

"My wife. She's great at giving advice."

The words were said with decisiveness laced with humility (in classic Rabbi Jungreis style), and they hung there in the delicious nighttime country air.

Rabbi Klass nodded. He liked the idea.

The Rebbetzin, however, wasn't so sure.

"I don't know if I can do it," she said, a little shyly, the idea of writing a weekly national column sounding somewhat ambitious — even for her.

"Of course you can," Irene Klass interjected. "I'll help you. Just start it."

Rebbetzin Jungreis considered the matter for a few seconds.

"Okay," she said, warming to the idea, "I'm going to call my column 'The Rebbetzin's Viewpoint.' I want people to be proud of being a rebbetzin — a rebbetzin has a very strong and powerful position in the Jewish world and I want those incredible women to stop thinking, I'm just the Rabbi's wife. Because you're not just the Rabbi's wife. You're the Rebbetzin!"

In a similar vein, people from out-of-town communities remember the Rebbetzin coming to town to speak in their communities, and how she made wearing a sheitel "in." She'd stand up on the stage in front of a thousand people in one of the stately old shuls of the American south, and it was something these women had never seen before — a with-it young woman wearing a sheitel…

Many people were able to connect to who she was and what she said because of how she looked, her elegance, and yes, her sheitel — which was an absolute rarity in their world. And just as she turned the title Rebbetzin into something to be proud of, she also proved that a woman could have a trendy and sophisticated look, yet always conform with the requirements of *tznius* (modesty).

The fact is, her look literally changed countless lives.

Writing in *The Jewish Press* was another turning point in the Rebbetzin's life, because with the advent of her initial column, she went from being a sought-after speaker on the local level to a national and later international superstar. And yes, the word rebbetzin took on a whole new meaning, just as she'd intended.

"The Rebbetzin's Viewpoint" would remain a steady feature of the paper for the next half a century. The Rebbetzin never missed a column, not even when she fell, not when she broke her hip, and not when she was busy preparing her speech for the Republican National Convention.

And even though the Rebbetzin was offered many opportunities to write for some of the religious publications that were established in the decades to come, she turned them down, explaining to Naomi Mauer, "I just have to picture your father and your mother and I know why I'm writing for *The Jewish Press*. I remember sitting with your parents in the lobby of the Pioneer Hotel, I remember when my husband made the suggestion, and I remember how your parents jumped on it."

She had tremendous *hakaras hatov* to the Klass family for giving her the vehicle through which to enter the homes of so many Yidden.

During those early years, many thousands read her column at their Shabbos tables every week. It was a time when there was almost nothing else to read — and nobody coming to tell Klal Yisrael the proper way to look at current events or what our *hashkafah* (worldview) was regarding this or that development. "The Rebbetzin's Viewpoint" stepped into the breach and gave countless people a taste of what it meant to be truly connected to the mesorah of the Csenger Zeides and Bubbas of yester-year. So many people had no idea what the Torah's position was on any given topic, and the Rebbetzin was there to explain it to them — in the simplest and easiest-to-grasp manner.

Her column became incredibly popular — virtually overnight. Thousands of people began sending letters to Rebbetzin Jungreis, care of *The Jewish Press*. She answered them all with a certain savvy skill, wit, and insight into the human condition that kept her readers coming back hungrily for more. Stacks of letters would arrive at the paper's office — stacks of letters filled with people's problems, dilemmas and challenges — all of them hoping she would choose to focus on their letter for her column. The Rebbetzin was making a huge impact singlehandedly.

And it wasn't just letters. Many times, the Rebbetzin would use her column as a springboard to introduce ideas to the community. She would share with her readers the events of her fascinating life and tell them about speaking around the world and how it felt to travel by jeep up a mountain to a secluded army base to give *chizuk* to the soldiers. She would describe the scene at Madison Square Garden and the thousands of Jews who had come to hear her speak and the cry that had emanated from her soul.

She used the column for kiruv — long before kiruv was a household word — and to talk about Hineni, which was still in its infancy. Soon people began to understand that the Rebbetzin's organization was doing outreach and that maybe they should consider getting involved and doing some kiruv themselves. Often she devoted her column to commenting on various world and political events, showing her readers how to view them through a Torah lens.

Many, many people wrote to tell the Rebbetzin that her words in the paper changed their lives. One thing led to another. In many cases, people read her column in the newspaper, felt like they knew her and decided to go and hear her speak at Hineni. Then, she'd meet them in person and help them find a shidduch — and so on and so forth. Which meant that "The Rebbetzin's Viewpoint" ceased being just a column in the paper and became something much greater than that.

For someone to be able to do what the Rebbetzin did, one would need to have support from the people closest to him or her. She had that support — in spades.

When she arrived at the breakfast table every morning, Rav Meshulem had already cut up a grapefruit for his wife in perfectly concentric slices — just the way she liked it. And of course there would be a stack of newspaper clippings, articles he knew she'd like and maybe use in her speeches, and interesting topics and ideas for the two of them to discuss.

In a sense it was her husband Rav Meshulem who made it all happen. He believed in her and knew that she had what it took to change the world. He was extremely fine, a brilliant thinker and scholar, and he couldn't have been prouder of his wife. And he let her know how he felt — each and every day of their lives.

From her early days of local rebbetzin-hood, Esther Jungreis would soon go on to become a celebrated speaker who was constantly flying around the country to address various religious communities across America. One of these was the community in Chicago, which accorded her a very warm welcome every time she flew in to the Windy City.

It was Rabbi Moshe Katz, director of a kiruv organization called the "Chicago Torah Network," who brought her to Chicago and introduced the Rebbetzin year after year.

The first time he introduced her, Rabbi Katz told the assembled that his relationship with Rebbetzin Jungreis spanned the last thirty years.

"No doubt, the Rebbetzin was thinking to herself, *Who is this man? I have never met him before and have no idea who he is!*"

The truth is, she didn't know who he was and the two of them had never met until that day.

Rabbi Katz explained what he meant:

> While my mother grew up with a religious background, my father did not. My parents met one another in 1947 and when my father showed interest in marrying my mother, she informed him that while she was interested in him as well, there were some deal breakers.
>
> "What type of deal breakers?" he wanted to know.
>
> "Shabbos, kashrus and a few other major mitzvos," she said.
>
> As my father always said, he saw a good deal and he went for it, committing himself to living an observant lifestyle. Yet while he did his best to follow the rules of a Jewish life, he had very

little Jewish education. And it wasn't as if he could just go into a frum bookstore and buy a pile of books back then. In the '50s and '60s, there was a dearth of quality Torah literature for a person who didn't know how to read Hebrew. ArtScroll had not yet been born, and there was a genuine scarcity of available English *sefarim*, which meant that our entire tradition inevitably remained a closed book to anyone who hadn't been educated within the system. They were left on the outside, wistfully looking in.

The only English *sefer* I remember in the house was a copy of the *Kitzur Shulchan Aruch* (Code of Jewish Law) with an English translation. Which meant that there was really nothing inspirational for my father to read and sink his teeth into. Here he was, married to a religious woman and committed to living a religious life — yet unable to study Judaism on his own!

As the years passed, there was one invaluable resource that my father was able to tap into — a column in *The Jewish Press* called "The Rebbetzin's Viewpoint."

I'll never forget the sight of my father sitting at the dining room table reading the Rebbetzin's column. It was as if the Rebbetzin herself was sitting at the table with him saying, "My dear Mr. Katz, let me teach you about Torah values."

And my father, who had come across many rabbis in his life, but was unable to connect to any of them, found the Rebbetzin, read her thoughts and felt connected and inspired. Somehow she was able to light the fire within his heart through her well-chosen words — words that flew out of the newspaper every week and entered his heart. She would make him laugh and cry, uplift him and prod him to grow in his Yiddishkeit.

Everything she gave him ultimately served as factors in the person he eventually became. Today my parents have hundreds of descendants — every one of them a *shomer Torah u'mitzvos* — and it's not even a slight exaggeration to refer to the Rebbetzin as their Bubby because it was she who taught our family what it meant to be strong, proud Jews.

Years later, my father overheard someone making a disparaging remark about *The Jewish Press*.

He let them have it. Boy, did he let them have it.

"Excuse me," he said, "did you teach me about Judaism, or did Rebbetzin Jungreis teach me about Judaism — in the pages of *The Jewish Press*?"

My father had exceptional gratitude to the Rebbetzin for teaching him how to think like a Jew, and for living her life the way she did. If you think about it, the fact that the Rebbetzin was able to accomplish the things she did was an outright miracle.

Here was a girl who came to America without knowing a word of English. She spent no time mourning her losses. Instead, she buckled down and became sufficiently proficient in English to be able to eloquently address Americans (and even their president) and to write an extremely popular newspaper column, which she used as a vehicle to inspire Jews across the United States for over half a century.

That's not a miracle?

A little foreign refugee turned superstar. A kid rescued from the ashes of Bergen-Belsen, finding the words to connect with a native-born American from Chicago.

Not miraculous?

The Rebbetzin used her column to inspire and teach an entire generation about what it meant to be a Jew. At the same time, she also used the column to share the stories that happened to her in the course of her extensive travels lecturing to communities across the globe. She was a master connecter, and the column gave her an effective way to turn all her readers into family. Every week she updated her global "*mishpachah*" with the "family" news. If she traveled somewhere, she let them know about it. When she returned from Eretz Yisrael, she shared her conversations with Prime Minister Menachem Begin. That's the kind of column it was.

When Osher Jungreis was a *talmid* in Rabbi Yaakov Bender's class at Yeshiva Darchei Torah in Far Rockaway, his rebbi made sure to read the Rebbetzin's column every single week. Though he would eventually become the Rosh HaYeshivah, at the time Rabbi Bender was still an elementary school rebbi, and for an entire year he made sure to keep himself abreast of everything the Rebbetzin wrote about in her column.

The Bender/Jungreis relationship had begun long before when Rebbetzin Bender (Rabbi Bender's mother) had taught Esther Jungreis in Bais Yaakov as a young girl. In subsequent years, the Rebbetzin would visit her teacher in Boro Park after she published her first two books, inscribing them with a warm message: "To my Morah, Rebbetzin Bender."

Rebbetzin Bender genuinely appreciated her student's gesture, confiding in her son that Esther Jungreis was the best student she ever had.

One week, the Rebbetzin told her readers of an incident that occurred on her flight from L.A. to New York. There was a young Jewish man on the plane and she went out of her way to draw him close to Judaism.

"As a way to initiate conversation and to break down his defenses," she wrote, "I offered him a piece of cake from a bakery called 'The Famous Hungarian Bakery in L.A.' Obviously my offering led to a conversation and I was able to begin the process of returning yet another Jew to his roots."

That was the article. A great story about how a piece of cake could bring a Jew closer to Hashem.

Rabbi Bender came to school that Sunday morning and said to his *talmid*, "Osher, tell your mother that I also want a piece of cake from The Famous Hungarian Bakery in L.A."

Osher didn't know what his rebbi was talking about and asked for clarification.

"None of your business, Osher," Rabbi Bender replied with a smile. "Just go on home and tell your mother that I also want a piece of cake from The Famous Hungarian Bakery in L.A."

"Rebbi, I don't know if I can do that."

"Osher, I'm the rebbi and you're the *talmid*. Give your mother the message."

Osher came into the classroom the next morning with a big smile on his face. His mother had obviously taken the time to elucidate his rebbi's bizarre request, and he found it highly amusing.

In April, six months after the article and his subsequent comment/joke to the Rebbetzin's son, Rabbi Bender entered his classroom one morning and found a huge box of cake sitting on his desk. On the box was written, "The Famous Hungarian Bakery in L.A."

As always, the Rebbetzin remembered.

CHAPTER TWENTY-FOUR
Camp Naarah

*I*n 1967, the Rebbetzin spent the summer at Camp Naarah in Liberty, New York.

Wanting Chaya Sora to be able to attend what was then one of the best camps for religious girls at the time, the Rebbetzin accepted a position there, giving a daily *shiur* to the girls. Owned and operated by the Stubenhaus family, Camp Naarah had a noted reputation that drew hundreds of girls to their spacious grounds summer after summer. Though the camp is no longer in existence, then-director Barbara Handler Goldgraben is continually receiving regards and meeting women who spent memorable summers at Naarah and love nothing more than rehashing the good times of long ago.

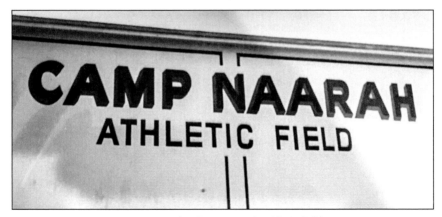

Sign over the Camp Naarah athletic field

The Rebbetzin with R' Akiva and Mrs. Rose Stubenhaus

Ask any camper about those summers and watch her eyes light up with memories of late-night barbecues, frogs on the mossy banks of the nearby lake, oars falling off the boat and into the water, singing with teammates during color war — a red sash across her shirt, a hastily painted cardboard hat precariously perched on her head — pillow-fights, raids, camp plays, salamanders and skunks; and singing, always singing. In the dining room, the shul and during activities. It's difficult to explain what makes camp so memorable. But the intangible magic of the summers of our youth is not to be denied.

Barbara's parents, Rabbi Akiva and Mrs. Rose Stubenhaus, would visit the homes of prospective campers before agreeing to register them to come to Naarah for the summer. They wanted to see the kinds of homes their girls were coming from, and what better way than a personal home visit where they would be able to meet the parents and the rest of the family. After a productive meeting, they'd show the family a slideshow of a summer at Camp Naarah — and that usually helped to clinch the deal.

After watching the slideshow, the Rebbetzin knew she wanted her daughter to go to their camp, but being the wife of a community rabbi, it was a luxury not easily affordable. So it was decided that she would be appointed "sheiyur" counselor at Naarah with special shiurim for the staff. Barbara Handler remembered the Rebbetzin well from Bais Yaakov High School on South 8th Street — Rebbetzin Kaplan's school — and was more than happy to have her aboard.

However, the Rebbetzin came with a condition.

"The only way I can commit to being part of Camp Naarah," she told the Stubenhaus family, "is if my parents can come up to the mountains every Shabbos."

The directors agreed and the deal was struck.

The Rebbetzin would hold the position for only one year — Camp Naarah closed after that summer — but to this day, wherever Chaya Sora Jungreis Gertzulin goes, she meets women who fondly recall her mother's *shiurim* from that summer: a summer that impacted everyone in camp, changing their perceptions on life forever. More than that, the connection between the Rebbetzin and Barbara Handler Goldgraben would develop into something deep and everlasting — both there for each other in their respective hours of need.

Rebbetzin Jungreis moved into her bungalow and within five minutes it was as if she had always been part of Camp Naarah. Suddenly, camp was even more awesome than it had been every other year. Her *shiurim* were dynamic and dramatic, exciting and informative, and the kids loved spending time with her. And when Shabbos came and the Jungreis family took their seats at the head table in the dining room — the Rebbetzin, regal and glowing with the joy of Shabbos, Rav Meshulem with his warm smile, Zeide with his long white beard and *hadras panim* (saintly and beatific expression), and Mama, with an eye on every camper, making sure that every single girl felt warm and protected — was it any wonder that the entire camp was uplifted?

One afternoon Rebbetzin Jungreis discovered a bird's nest that had fallen to the ground from one of the towering trees. Picking it up, she showed it to the girls and said, "Look at the twigs, girls. Do you see how they are intertwined? Do you see how the mother bird instinctively knows how to weave the grasses together with the twigs? Can you imagine how hard that mother bird worked to make this nest?"

The girls nodded.

"Girls," the Rebbetzin said, "that's your parents. Your parents work just as hard to make a home for you."

The campers of Camp Naarah never forgot the lesson of the bird's nest and returned home filled with the kind of appreciation to their parents that never fades — all from the Rebbetzin's bird's nest lesson. As any veteran camper will tell you, it's never about the bells and the whistles. A true camp personality can turn even the simplest bird's nest into a lesson that will be forever remembered.

It was the summer of '67, and the Six Day War had just been won. The Rebbetzin couldn't help but share her thoughts and feelings on the miracles of the war with the campers and how there was no question in her mind that Mashiach was not far away. She was magical as always, and the girls sat on the grass in the Catskill Mountains and happily took their seats in her world, entranced by her language, immersed in the pictures she painted.

That Tishah B'Av, the Rebbetzin gave a never-to-be-forgotten *shiur* about the Beis HaMikdash — bringing every single girl to tears. She told the girls a story about an Israeli soldier who had lost his arm in the fighting and didn't know how he was going to be able to put on his tefillin.

She didn't just tell the story.

She told the story with all of her considerable powers, as the girls sat on the floor and the candles cast flickering shadows on the bunkhouse walls. Everyone cried. The girls became extremely emotional, but Rebbetzin Jungreis wasn't disturbed, clearly feeling it was important for them to truly understand what had happened across the ocean, during the battles that had shifted borders and altered Israel's status.

She concluded her speech that night with a line that went down in the annals of Naarah history, speaking so quietly the girls had to strain their ears to hear her. "And if you're quiet," she said so softly it was almost a whisper, "you can hear the footsteps of Mashiach coming."

Miriam Liebermann, a camper at the time, remembers this scene vividly.

The girls couldn't fall asleep for the rest of the night. Every sound outside their bunkhouses — every cricket chirping or wind blowing through the trees — clearly heralded the footsteps of Mashiach as he made his way from the outskirts of Rome, stopping off at Camp Naarah on his way to Yerushalayim.

Nobody ever forgot that line. Even today, decades later, Naarah campers find themselves remembering that line on Tishah B'Av night. And then they are quiet, listening carefully, as they wait to hear the footsteps of Mashiach…

Every single thing that came her way was an opportunity for a lesson that would be remembered for the rest of the listeners' lives. This was especially true in camp, where the memories and friendships children form remain with them well into adulthood and beyond.

Today — half a century after the Rebbetzin taught Torah at Camp Naarah — the girls who had the good fortune to hear her speak to them still recall the words she used, as if it all took place a few weeks ago. Though they are grandmothers and great-grandmothers today, when they think of their time at camp, the years and decades fall away and they revert to the young girls they were — sitting on the grass, hugging their knees and listening with wide-eyed interest to the warm words and messages of the charismatic Rebbetzin who captured their interest like nobody else.

In 1968, Barbara Goldgraben's first husband, Reb Baruch Handler, had a heart attack at the very young age of thirty-three, and the family decided to close Camp Naarah, bringing a wonderful era to an end.

My first husband Baruch was *niftar* several years after Camp Naarah closed. Beginning from the time I got up from *shivah*, Zeide would call us every Erev Shabbos to *bentch* my children. And on Erev Rosh Chodesh and Erev Yom Tov.

"Vi bist du, mein kindt, vos tist du, mein kindt?" (How are you, my child, how are you doing?)

How I loved the sound of his kind voice. How I waited for that call.

You have to understand something. After my husband's passing I was alone for four and a half years, marrying off two children during that period. When I got engaged to my second husband, the Rebbetzin threw a beautiful Melaveh Malkah for us, reveling in our happiness, as Zeide smiled his glorious smile, his pure heart filled with *simchah* for me and my chassan. And at the wedding, Zeide gave a short speech under the chuppah and was honored with the recitation of all seven berachos.

We knew that Zeide loved us and we loved him right back. When he looked at you with those warm, wise eyes… you couldn't help but feel that things were going to be okay. We never lost touch with Zeide — we were his *kinderlach* and *einiklach* just as much as the rest of the family. How we mourned him when he was *niftar*!

"I can still see her now — that tiny figure bravely standing all alone
on that gigantic stage..." *Barbara Handler Goldgraben*

Barbara remained extremely close with Rebbetzin Jungreis. When the Rebbetzin founded Hineni and held her first major event at Madison Square Garden, Barbara was right there in the front row, giving her friend *chizuk* and cheering her on.

I can still see her now — that tiny figure bravely standing all alone on that gigantic stage, pouring out her heart to Klal Yisrael, begging them to say *Shema Yisrael*...

What a night that was! And I was there, watching my dear friend as she made history! Who would have believed that just a few years earlier, the Rebbetzin had been at my camp, giving *shiurim* to the girls on the lawn?

That night at the Garden made history. She had become a superstar and I couldn't have been prouder of the fact that Rebbetzin Esther Jungreis was part of the Camp Naarah family and would remain so forever.

CHAPTER TWENTY-FIVE

The Tongue Reader

*I*t took time, but within a few years funds had been raised by the grateful congregants of Ohr Torah to build themselves and their rabbi a beautiful shul. The building was located a few short blocks from the Jungreis home. It was from this pulpit that Rabbi Jungreis addressed his congregation for the rest of his life, where he established a Hebrew school for the children, conducted shalosh seudos (complete with a host of beautiful melodies from pre-war Europe) with the members, and taught Torah. In a very short time, Ohr Torah had become a focal point for North Woodmere's religious life.

Shabbos morning in North Woodmere was particularly wonderful. The neighborhood women left shul with their arms linked, walking down the street to visit with the Rabbi and the Rebbetzin before heading home. They chatted, but it was more than chatting. It was family. And even though there was no real reason to stop at the Rabbi and Rebbetzin's house after davening, their home was full every Shabbos with people who made themselves comfortable on the couches, drank a cup of coffee or three, and had a few slices of cake or a bowl of cholent from a pot that never seemed to empty no matter how many people ate from it.

The sanctuary of the original Ohr Torah was an octagon-shaped room. The moment the new "building" was operational, the Rebbetzin contacted NCSY (National Conference of Synagogue Youth) and invited the organization to hold a Shabbaton for high school students at the shul in North Woodmere. NCSY agreed and a few weeks later Ohr Torah proudly hosted its first Shabbaton. Shabbos passed in a frenzy

Congregation Ohr Torah, North Woodmere

of speeches, delicious meals with an abundance of food, and singing and games galore. Even after Havdalah the kids remained, because the Rebbetzin had arranged a special Motza'ei Shabbos extravaganza at the shul complete with music and dancing.

But while everyone was inside the shul dancing away the night, nobody realized that the weather was preparing a surprise for them — because it had begun to snow. It came down softly at first, but as the hours passed, the snow started falling more heavily, blocking the doors of the shul and effectively locking everyone in. At 11:30 when the music came to a stop and the kids tried to leave, they found that the doors, which opened outward, were impossible to open. NCSY was trapped in the shul. There was no way to let anyone in the outside world know what had occurred. The phone lines were down because of the storm (and it was pre-cell phone days). It took them some time to digest the reality of the situation, and when they did, there was an outburst of mass hysteria.

It had been a long, long night. Every kid, having danced for a good couple of hours, was exhausted and more than ready to go home. But they couldn't leave. Worse, it was becoming cold in the shul, with a frigid wind blowing through the as-yet-unfinished walls of the not-as-yet-completed building. If this had occurred anywhere else it would have turned into a catastrophe. But the Rebbetzin was with them and that made all the difference.

"I want everyone on their feet," she ordered them. "If you thought that we danced before, you haven't seen anything yet!"

What followed was the longest spate of dancing any of them would ever do, as the members of NCSY danced through the night until dawn broke over a snowy world and they were finally rescued from their holy confines. Throughout the dancing, the Rebbetzin would deliver her special brand of inspiration, with stories, *chizuk* and encouragement. It might have been freezing outside, but their hearts were warm. Nobody who was at that NCSY Shabbaton with the Rebbetzin would ever forget the hours of dancing and singing, as she encouraged them to keep up the good feelings of the past twenty-seven hours and not give in to the weather.

"My family and I still make Havdalah to the same tune that I heard at the Hineni Shabbatons as a kid," recalls Sharon Dobuler Katz. "It's the most beautiful Havdalah tune in the world; and if that was the only thing the Rebbetzin and her family bequeathed us — *dayeinu*. But they gave us so much more. By virtue of changing my life, she changed the lives of my children, my grandchildren and all future generations. Our outlook, the way we accept other people, the way we do our best to make Torah shine — all of that is from the Rebbetzin."

The only time Ohr Torah had a really huge crowd in the early years was during Rosh Hashanah and Yom Kippur. That was when the shul set up what was tantamount to a Big Top tent, which reminded the community kids of a day of circus fun.

That, however, was only during the Yamim Noraim.

During the winter months, Ohr Torah had a difficult time gathering a minyan — even on Erev Shabbos. Many of the congregants were not yet *shomer Shabbos* in those years and with Shabbos beginning at 4:30 in the afternoon, many were still at work. And yet, the shul needed a minyan.

Rabbi Jungreis decided to get his minyan from the students at Woodmere Academy, Lawrence High School and Hewlett High School. It was a good idea, so the next question became how to convince the high school kids to help put together the minyan.

"I have a secret weapon," Rabbi Jungreis told his son Yisroel, "that's going to bring them in."

"What's the weapon?"

"It's called seven-layer cake."

Zeide marching with Ohr Torah members to dedicate a new Sefer Torah for the shul

Rabbi Jungreis stocked up on seven-layer cake and soda and Ohr Torah's Friday night minyan became a popular place virtually overnight. Being artistic as well (it was the Rabbi who designed the Hineni medallion), he hung a beautiful poster on the wall on which he penned the words "Minyanaire Club." There was a list of names on the poster, and any boy who came to shul had his name checked off. With seven layers of chocolaty cake, ice cold soda and a little recognition, the Friday night minyan flourished. Once again, Rav Meshulem's creativity and ingenuity paid off.

Sharon Dobuler was raised in North Woodmere. Her family moved into the neighborhood when she was eight years old and joined Ohr Torah. When they arrived, North Woodmere was a pile of sand (it was as if the Rabbi was teaching Torah in a desert) with a few intersecting streets and not much more. The Dobuler family considered themselves traditional Jews — they weren't religious or anything like that, but they loved being Jewish and wanted their children to develop a strong Jewish identity. When their neighbors told them about the brand-new shul they attended, Mr. and Mrs. Dobuler decided to join as well. They didn't give it much thought. They just made the move — a decision that would completely alter the trajectory of their lives and the lives of hundreds of others.

Chaya Sora Jungreis was two years younger than Sharon, and the two of them became great friends.

Sharon credits Chaya Sora and her mother for making her frum.

"I was a Jungreis family project," she explained. "I was treated like a member of the family and along the way I became a religious Jew."

It was especially nice for the two of them to have someone close in age to be friends with because there were hardly any other kids around. Chaya Sora went to TAG and Sharon attended the local public school. When she returned home, Chaya Sora would teach her friend what she'd learned in school that day. Of course it wasn't all about the learning. Sometimes they'd just pal around in the den like any two good friends.

The den opened to the Rebbetzin's office, giving the girls a perfect view of the action.

The Rebbetzin was always doing something. Late at night she'd be sitting in her office on the phone giving advice to a member of the community or a complete stranger. The action was non-stop. It was: "Welcome to the Jungreis home — Life happens here!"

Sharon called Rebbetzin Jungreis "Big R." The name developed in reference to her size (she was tiny) as well as the fact that Sharon couldn't get used to calling the Rabbi's wife "Rebbetzin" (it was way too official for her), and she certainly wasn't about to refer to her by her first name as her mother did. So she called Rebbetzin Jungreis "Big R" and everyone was satisfied.

One day Sharon went to see the Rebbetzin.

"Can I ask you something, Big R?"

"Whatever you want, *sheifelah*."

"I know that people are starting to ask you to speak in different places, right?"

The Rebbetzin nodded.

"Well, I wanted to know if you would be willing to come and give a speech at Lawrence High."

The Rebbetzin accepted the invitation graciously.

But as Sharon walked out the door, having accomplished what she'd set out to do, she was suddenly hit by a surge of second thoughts.

"What did I just do?" she asked herself. "How can I have invited a religious rebbetzin to Lawrence High of all places? What is she going to say to them?"

"Rebbetzin," she said, retracing her steps back to the "Big R." "I just realized something."

"What's that?"

"You have to be very careful about what you say at my high school."

And she started listing all the topics the Rebbetzin should avoid.

Later on in life, Sharon discovered that she wasn't the only one who tried to tell the Rebbetzin what to talk about and what to leave out of her speeches. People would say to her, "Don't talk about religion," and the Rebbetzin would soothe their worries, saying, "Don't worry, it's going to be okay."

Generals in the IDF would approach her before she addressed their troops and tell her in no uncertain terms to stay far away from Torah and religion.

"Don't worry, it's going to be just fine," she'd tell them reassuringly.

And then she would go right ahead and give her speech and deliver whichever message she felt was right for her audience. Somehow it always worked out despite the fact that she never failed to include a blatant Torah message.

That was what happened at Lawrence High that afternoon as well. As the Rebbetzin delivered her trademark speech, every single student in the room sat there listening to her, absolutely mesmerized. Yes, mesmerized and absorbed, as the Rebbetzin discussed what it meant to be a Jew living in America, and what every single person in that room could do to become closer to Hashem.

The bell rang but nobody stood up.

Let me repeat that: The bell rang but nobody stood up.

Usually, the second the bell rang everyone was out of their seats and running to their lockers. Not that day. The bell rang and nobody stirred. Every eye remained on the Rebbetzin, wanting more. Wanting to hear what they needed to do to become a good Jew.

Sharon Dobuler never forgot that day.

The speech was classic "Rebbetzin in action." Because the Rebbetzin never allowed an opportunity to pass her by. And even when people told her, "Don't discuss intermarriage because so and so is in the audience and he or she is married to a non-Jew," the Rebbetzin would go right ahead and talk about intermarriage because that was what the audience needed to hear. She was simply fearless and unintimidated — no matter how important or wealthy her listeners were. And people respected her for the fact that she was true to herself no matter what. Ironically, instead of her bluntness pushing people away, it drew them closer. It was a fascinating paradox. Nobody likes being lectured to. But for some reason, they were more than willing to listen when it came from the Rebbetzin.

When Sharon left home for the University of Rochester, the Rebbetzin sat her down for a heart-to-heart talk, entreating her to remember everything she had received at home and at the shul as she left for the big world. On her first visit home, one of Sharon's first stops was at the Jungreis home.

"Sarah Leah," the Rebbetzin said to her (the Rebbetzin called everyone by their Hebrew name) — "open your mouth."

Sharon opened her mouth.

"Has anything non-kosher been in there? I have to make sure your mouth is clean!"

Baruch Hashem, Sharon's mouth was as pure then as it was when she left (she'd eaten dinners at the Hillel House, countless PB&J sandwiches and bags of carrots), but that action on the Rebbetzin's part was a wakeup call to her to stay on the straight and narrow because someone was really watching her and would never let go.

On a similar note, Rabbi Yisroel Jungreis recalls what happened when one of his friends from the neighborhood was getting ready to leave North Woodmere for university.

"I'm warning you, Darren*," the Rebbetzin said to him, "don't you dare go out with a non-Jewish girl! I will know if you do!"

Darren came to visit during Thanksgiving break.

The moment he walked in the door, he was accosted by the Rebbetzin who ordered him to open his mouth.

"What are you doing?" he asked her nervously.

"I'm checking your *neshamah* to make sure it's still holy."

He opened his mouth and she peered inside.

"I see *shmutz*. You are dating a non-Jewish girl!"

"How on earth do you know that?"

"I know. I'm warning you, Darren — stay away from non-Jewish girls if you know what's good for you!"

Darren grew up to become a doctor. He lives in Florida today, is religious and yes, has married a Jewish girl. Having the Rebbetzin take an in-depth look into your mouth was a memorable experience and made an impression.

The Pilevsky family were major supporters of the Rabbi and his wife. But it was more than just supporters. They were like family. When their son Phil got engaged to Renee in 1970, his parents insisted that the bride-to-be meet the Jungreis family.

The Rebbetzin took one look at Renee and said, "You have to have at least four children. The Jewish people need to make up for the children who were lost to us."

The future Mrs. Pilevsky was slightly taken aback, having just met the Rebbetzin.

"But guess what," Renee says with a laugh, "I had four children, just like the Rebbetzin ordered. She was very disarming and had the power to achieve results from every type of person. She was street-smart and could speak to the simplest person and to the most brilliant of minds and had the right words for both without having to think twice. It was an incredible gift and she wielded it with dexterity.

"No matter who the person was, she had the message he needed to hear — and possessed the necessary words to make a connection. I came over to visit her one morning when she was expecting a new bed to be delivered. Soon enough there was a knock on the door.

" 'Who is it?'

" 'Bed delivery guys.'

"The Rebbetzin opened the door and found two strapping men in the doorway with the bed she had ordered. They were big, burly and rough and clearly in a rush to deliver the bed and move on to the next stop on their route. The Rebbetzin, however, would have none of that.

" 'What's your name?' she greeted them.

" 'Jibril Mustafa.'

" 'And you?'

" 'Aba Machmoud Ibn Kalifa.'

"'Do you know what the name Aba means?' the Rebbetzin asked the mattress delivery man in delight. 'It means "father" in the Hebrew language! What a wonderful name to have!'

"The man's face lit up! It was almost as if he had just acquired a new and profound respect for the name he'd always had. By the time the men left her home that day (after manhandling the bed up the stairs and exactly where it needed to go), everyone had become best of friends. Aba Machmoud even gave the Rebbetzin his private cellphone number and told her to make sure and be in touch if there were any problems at all with the bed or mattress."

She possessed a golden tongue.

"The Rebbetzin was walking down West End Avenue one day," Heidi Pilevsky Leifer (daughter of Renee and Phil) related, "when she crossed paths with the well-known actor Dustin Hoffman.

"'Rebbetzin,' I said to her, 'that's a famous actor.'

"'Really, what's his name?'

"'His name is Dustin Hoffman.'

"Hoffman had already passed her by, but without missing a beat, the Rebbetzin turned around and called out in a ringing voice, 'Dovid!'

"Hoffman stopped in his tracks and turned back in her direction — and she initiated a conversation."

They parted with a smile.

And she was able to do that with everyone she met.

After her incredible success at Madison Square Garden's Felt Forum, the Rebbetzin felt that her job was just beginning. She therefore established a brand-new learning center at her father's shul in Canarsie, calling it Hineni School, where she gave *shiurim* throughout the year. Her involvement with her father's shul and yeshivah would remain ongoing throughout her life. If there was ever any way she could be of assistance to him, it would be done. Notable among her accomplishments for his yeshivah was her success in convincing a wealthy man who used to visit her home on a regular basis to co-sign the yeshivah's mortgage.

For the Rebbetzin and her father, it was truly a case of "*V'nafsho keshurah b'nafshah* — and his heart was interconnected with hers."

The Rebbetzin's father, Rav Avrohom HaLevi Jungreis — aka Zeide — would attend every single class, sitting in the back of the room and listening intently to every word his daughter said. Many of

The Rebbetzin and Zeide at Hineni School in Canarsie

the girls who davened at Ohr Torah came to hear *shiurim* at the Hineni School on a regular basis. While it was true that thousands of Jews had been part of the massive Hineni launching at Madison Square Garden, it was now time to grow the organization from the ground up — and that would happen only through delivering Torah *shiurim* week in and week out.

And while the Rebbetzin's girls from North Woodmere came to hear her Torah, they also served in the welcoming committee, finding seats for everyone who entered the room, making every person feel very much at home, and encouraging the audience to ask questions if there was anything they didn't understand.

Of course the Rebbetzin wanted Sharon (who was back from Rochester) to begin shidduchim, but she felt that Sharon needed to acquire a little sophistication in the fashion department first. This was accomplished with a major shopping expedition to Orchard Street on the Lower East Side, then the clothing capital of Manhattan. The Rebbetzin was a busy woman with a million things to do. But she and Barbara took Sharon from store to store to store — for an entire day — outfitting her with a shidduch wardrobe. Only then was she given the green light to date, and the Rebbetzin began setting her up with suitable young men.

One evening a young man showed up to her *shiur* with his uncle. Over the years and decades of its existence, Hineni would come to be known far and wide not only as a place to study Torah, but also as a place where the Rebbetzin and her family sincerely tried to set people up for marriage. Many hundreds of shidduchim would be made by the Rebbetzin and her children. Yet even then, in the very beginning of Hineni, the moment an eligible young man entered the room things began to happen.

And so it was that Zeide took one look at the new arrival and decided on the spot that he would be perfect for their very own Sharon.

The idea worked and the two married.

It is now many decades and grandchildren later — including the first baby girl to be named Esther after the Rebbetzin's passing — and things have turned out very good for Mr. and Mrs. Izzy Katz, who have lived in Eretz Yisrael for the past few decades. But that was Zeide's way. Figure out who fit with another — and get them married.

And the Rebbetzin learned from her father.

Sharon's grandmother who lived in the neighborhood became very ill at the end of her life and moved into the Dobuler home. Rav Meshulem, Rebbetzin Esther and whichever Jungreis children were around used to come visit with her every Shabbos afternoon. The Rebbetzin shared many serious conversations with her.

One Shabbos as they were conversing, Sharon's grandmother confided to the Rebbetzin how sad she was.

"I'm not ready to leave yet," she told her visitor tearfully. "But that's not even the saddest thing."

"What's the saddest thing?"

"The saddest thing is that my granddaughter is about to have a baby and I won't be around for the birth."

"When is the due date?" the Rebbetzin wanted to know.

"Around Shavuos time. This baby will be my second great-grandchild, but it doesn't look like there's any chance of me being around to meet my great-grandchild."

"Mrs. Block," the Rebbetzin said, "let me ask you something. Is there any mitzvah that you never managed to fulfill which you would be able to accept on yourself now? Any mitzvah you can think of that you can add into your life at this crucial moment?"

Sharon's grandmother thought for a few seconds.

"I never managed to count Sefiras HaOmer from the second night of Pesach all the way to the end," she said at last. "I always wanted to do it — I thought about actually committing to the count many times, but somehow, I never got through it."

"If you will count Sefiras HaOmer every day," the Rebbetzin told Mrs. Block, "you will still be with us — *im yirtzeh Hashem* (G-d willing) — when we are celebrating Shavuos!"

Sharon's family began counting Sefiras HaOmer with their

grandmother on the second day of Pesach and continued, the patient never missing a night. In the beginning she was still able to count the days herself, but as the illness progressed she was no longer able to actually say the words, doing her best to mouth them instead. She was still alive at the very end of Sefiras HaOmer that year — making it all the way through for the first time in her life.

When Shavuos arrived, Rabbi and Rebbetzin Jungreis came to visit Mrs. Block with their children. Rabbi Jungreis held one of Ohr Torah's Sifrei Torah in his hands. He raised the Torah to the old woman's lips and she kissed it reverently on its soft velvet mantle, overcome at being granted such an opportunity at that stage in her life.

She then uttered the words "Naaseh v'Nishma" ("we will do and we will listen" — the iconic term uttered by the Jewish nation at Mount Sinai) and slipped peacefully into a coma.

Mrs. Block passed away right after Shavuos and her brand-new great-grandchild was born right after the shivah was over. It was a girl and they named her after her great-grandmother — the Bubby who so wanted to meet her.

And so it was that the Rebbetzin's promise came true and a terribly ill patient lived to accept Hashem's Torah on herself on the very festival when it all began — thousands of years earlier at Mount Sinai.

This chapter has been dedicated
with love and gratitude to the Rebbetzin ע״ה
and the Jungreis Family

The Torah Sisters
Lisa Brandes • Louise Braver • Harriet Cook
Janet Davis • Susan Drucker • Susan Friedman
June Gottlieb • Barbara Katz • Carol King • Sheila Lambert
Judi Leal • Sandy Marrow • Carol Roman

CHAPTER TWENTY-SIX

The Syrian Connection

Marilyn Salem is a member of the Flatbush Syrian community. She enjoyed reading "The Rebbetzin's Viewpoint" in *The Jewish Press* every Shabbos and the more she read, the more she said to herself, "I would really like to meet this rebbetzin!"

At first she didn't see it happening. She wasn't the sort of individual to just drive out to North Woodmere to meet someone she didn't know, even if that person did write a fantastic column in her favorite newspaper. But then one week she read in the paper that the Rebbetzin was going to be speaking at someone's house in Boro Park. This was closer to home. If she was halfway as good a speaker as she was a writer, Marilyn couldn't wait to hear her.

She decided not to go on her own. Taking both her sister-in-law and the president of the Magen David Yeshivah sisterhood with her, Marilyn drove to the address in Boro Park on the day of the *shiur* and found seats in the rapidly filling basement. Apparently, they weren't the only ones enamored with the Rebbetzin from North Woodmere.

Here is Marilyn's story in her own words:

> I expected to see an elderly woman. From the way she wrote and her clarity and wisdom, I figured she'd probably be around seventy-five years old. But when the MC introduced her and I saw a young woman, I found myself filled with happiness. She walked to the front of the room with a beautiful smile on her face, and I was suddenly looking forward to hearing her even more than I'd been

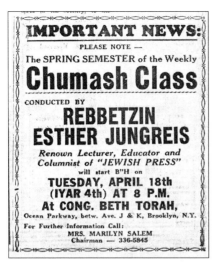

Announcement of the Rebbetzin's
Sephardic Women's Class — 1970s

five minutes earlier. Her unique look had captured me before she even began her speech.

The room quieted, the noisy babble of conversation replaced by a silent expectation as everyone waited to hear her words. From the second she started to speak, I knew that this was exactly what I needed to hear — and that I was going to bring her to the book club where I was a member. After everyone finished thanking her and the room was finally free of people, I approached her and introduced myself.

"Rebbetzin Jungreis, my name is Marilyn Salem. I'm from the Syrian Sephardic community in Brooklyn. Have you ever heard of us?"

"No, I'm sorry, but I have not," the Rebbetzin replied.

(This was in the late '60s, and the Syrian Sephardic community was not yet "on the map" outside Brooklyn.)

"In that case," I said, "little by little you are going to meet our community and learn about our customs and way of life."

The Rebbetzin waited to hear what I wanted from her.

"Rebbetzin, I belong to a book club. We meet and discuss every culture and every 'ism,' but we never talk about Jewish culture or Judaism. The president of the book club is away and I was asked to replace her temporarily until she returns. I would really appreciate it if you would join us at my house for the meeting. Come in through the back door, so to speak, but say whatever you want, because these girls really need a shot in the arm!"

She smiled at me warmly, pleased by my concern for my fellow Jews.

"What book are you girls reading these days?"

"*The Chosen* by Chaim Potok."

"Don't you worry, Marilyn," the Rebbetzin promised me with a twinkle in her eye. "I'll be there."

At the time I lived on East 5th Street between Avenues O and P, right off Ocean Parkway, and as my living room began to fill with the book club members, I wondered how they'd get along with the soft-spoken yet hashkafically immutable Rebbetzin Esther Jungreis.

I need not have wondered, for the women were entranced. It was love at first sight. She spoke about *The Chosen*, but she devoted a lot more time to debunking many of their superstitions about the Ashkenazi community. For the first time in their lives, the Syrian women of Brooklyn were given the opportunity to ask a truly knowledgeable person anything they wanted — with the Rebbetzin going out of her way to make sure they really understood her answers. They left my home with a fresh perspective on many things they'd always taken for granted.

Since her foray into our world had been so successful, I decided to introduce the Rebbetzin to the sisterhood of Magen David Yeshivah. She spoke to both the sisterhood and the students on the same day and was a huge hit. It was clear to me that the Rebbetzin's appeal cut across all ages and demographics. It didn't matter if a person was six or sixty, everyone loved her. She possessed that intangible factor, the charisma that draws people to certain individuals and turns them into stars. She was a born celebrity though she never acted that way.

The best thing about her was that she didn't hesitate to set the Syrian girls and women straight. Many of the teenagers in the community didn't have mothers to raise them with a Torah *hashkafah* or to teach them how to act in public or date, telling them what they needed to improve without hesitation or fear of their reaction. And they loved her for her honesty.

"Know who you are," she'd exhort them. *"You are a daughter of Israel and you have to act accordingly!"*

By now I became all fired up with wanting everyone I knew to hear her message. I brought her to Yeshiva of Flatbush, where she spoke to both Sephardim and Ashkenazim. Then we set up a weekly *shiur*. We tried a number of locations for the *shiur*, eventually settling on Shaarei Zion on Ocean Parkway. The Syrian girls needed someone they could relate to and the Rebbetzin was the right person at the right time.

That summer I was expecting my daughter Debra Esther, and I sent my son to a day camp not far from home. One afternoon they called me from the camp.

"Mrs. Salem, your son is coughing and not feeling well. You need to take him to the doctor as soon as possible."

I took him to a pediatrician as soon as he got home. It wasn't his regular doctor — he was away on vacation — and the elderly physician who examined him told me that my son had come down with pleurisy. Pleurisy sounded extremely serious to my untrained ears. I became very nervous and started to feel severe cramps in my stomach. A young doctor who overheard what happened tried to calm me down, telling me that his colleague was mistaken and that my son had only a mild form of bronchitis, but by then I was beyond listening to reason — and my labor pains continued to intensify.

The Rebbetzin always found time for the children after speaking at school events.

It was summertime, and most of our community was away in Deal, New Jersey. My husband was at the office in the city and I told him that I had gone into early labor. Then I called my doctor.

"The doctor is too far away to get to the hospital right now, Mrs. Salem, but his assistant will meet you at Maimonides Hospital immediately."

Feeling lonely and vulnerable, I picked up the phone one more time and called the only other person I wanted to speak to right then — Rebbetzin Jungreis.

"Rebbetzin," I told her, "I'm on my way to the hospital right now; please say a prayer for me."

I reached the hospital soon afterward. My husband got there as soon as possible, and the doctor who examined me confirmed I had gone into premature labor.

At some point one of the nurses walked into the room and said, "Some woman came to see you. We couldn't let her in, but she gave me this book to give to you."

She then handed me a Tehillim the Rebbetzin had left for me, along with a note that read, "They may not let me in to see you. Everything will be fine."

Touched beyond words by the fact that she'd come to visit me and left me a gift, I picked up the Tehillim and began to read. The moment I started reading the words, I began feeling better. Someone was praying for me. Not just someone. A rebbetzin was davening to Hashem with me in mind! Though I was still in physical pain, mentally I was feeling much better. I kept the Tehillim under my pillow. It made me feel warm and safe and taken care of.

The truth is I still have her Tehillim today.

From time to time I still read her inscription to me:

G-d be with you always. I'm praying for you, I love you.

Esther Jungreis

I was in a lot of pain. At the same time I was supremely touched by her gesture.

The Rebbetzin called me

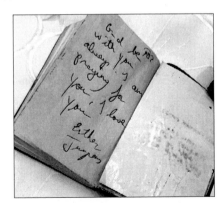

Tehillim inscribed by the Rebbetzin for Marilyn Salem

up a few days later, when I was back home.

"Marilyn," she said, "don't you worry. In two months you're going to have the baby, and everything will be fine."

A personal note the Rebbetzin left for Marilyn Salem

I never forgot her actions during that time of crisis. There was no question in my mind that I would forever remember what she did for me.

When my baby daughter was born — healthy and well — I said to my husband, "I want to name the baby after the Rebbetzin."

"But Ashkenazim don't name after people who are alive."

"Jesse, I have an identical twin sister called Esther. My maternal grandmother's name was Esther. That name is important to me. I'm going to call the Rebbetzin and ask her permission to name our baby after her. I hope she allows me to do so, even though she's Ashkenaz."

I called her up and said, "Rebbetzin, look, I know that you're as Ashkenaz as can be."

She laughed.

"I want to name my newborn daughter Debra — because in my mind the name Deborah signifies strength. But Rebbetzin, you came to the hospital for me when I needed you most, and I'll never forget what you did for me. That's why I want to name my daughter Esther after you, because of your kindness and giving nature."

"Go right ahead," the Rebbetzin said, giving me permission.

Which is how my newborn daughter came to be called Debra Esther.

Slowly but surely I got to know the Jungreis family better. This was still in the pre-Hineni days, before the Rebbetzin had become a household name. She was popular and had a fine reputation due to her column in the paper, but she was still nowhere near as famous as she would soon become.

In those days — the late '60s and early '70s — the Jewish

The Rebbetzin with members of the Syrian Sephardic community at a rally in Washington, D.C. in support of Eretz Yisrael

community was very involved in the political issues of the times, the hottest of which was Soviet Jewry, of course. There were millions of Jewish people living in Russia with no hope of escape. Jewish people made a point of protesting in front of the Russian Embassy. There were major rallies being held in Manhattan. It was something you heard on the news and saw on television.

A few of the Brooklyn Syrian women decided that we in the Syrian Jewish community needed to show our solidarity with our brothers and sisters trapped behind the Iron Curtain. We therefore organized a community-wide event, advertising it as "A Solidarity Conference for Soviet Jewry."

I invited the Rebbetzin to be the keynote speaker.

She accepted and gave a passionate speech to a full house. There were other speakers there as well, but it was the Rebbetzin who brought the house down. She electrified and mesmerized the people; they couldn't get enough. She brought them to tears and made them laugh — and by the time she finished, there was not one person in the audience who didn't comprehend the enormous tragedy that had befallen the Jews trapped in the Soviet Union.

Her popularity mushroomed.

She was invited to address the community in the Deal Synagogue and then to give lectures at private homes throughout the community. The more she spoke, the more *nachat* I had, because I knew the positive influence that she was having on so many people who had come to admire her as a role model.

And then suddenly we were all gearing up for her big debut at Madison Square Garden — and nothing was ever the same after that moment, because that was when the Jewish world suddenly understood who was living in their midst. But we in the Syrian community would always pride ourselves on the fact that we had understood who the Rebbetzin was from the moment we met her.

It was never just about a job or a class with the Rebbetzin. If she was part of a camp staff, she gave it her all and her stories were remembered for the next fifty years. In her role as Rebbetzin of her shul, she gave one thousand percent and her door was always open. And in her role as spiritual mentor to the Syrian women of Brooklyn, she gave of herself to the point where they wanted to name their children after her. The relationship was all-encompassing, unique — and cherished by those lucky enough to have been blessed with the Rebbetzin's presence in their lives.

CHAPTER TWENTY-SEVEN

Sandwich in the Sky

*E*very member of the family knew that theirs was an open house — open to guests, open to new brothers and sisters, and open to the entire Hineni family. There was no such thing as a Chanukah party or a Purim *seudah* with just the Rabbi, Rebbetzin and their children.

Purim was fantastic. The Rebbetzin prepared mishloach manos for the entire congregation and the four Jungreis kids trooped up and down the streets making deliveries. Like everything else, it was a family project. That's the way they were raised — to take part in the Jungreis kiruv initiatives.

When the Rebbetzin *bentched licht* (lit Shabbos candles) every Friday night and before the children recited *Shema* before retiring for the night, she would tell her children to daven for different members of the shul, always keeping other people in mind. One Friday night she told them to daven for a little girl who wasn't feeling well. The Jungreis kids knew the girl and they were all feeling sad for her. One of the women from the shul happened to have been visiting at the time. (It was a rare moment when a shul member *wasn't* there…)

"Rebbetzin," she chastised reproachfully, "you're making the children cry! Why do you have to tell them such sad stories? Why do you have to tell them about other children their age who are sick?"

"All children cry at times," the Rebbetzin replied with trademark clarity. "Some children cry for candy, some children cry for toys, my children are going to cry for their fellow man."

That was the way they were raised — to care, even when it hurt.

When Chaya Sora was in high school, her mother told her that she wanted her to start giving a Shabbos afternoon *Pirkei Avos* class for the women of Ohr Torah.

"Ma, I'm a high-school girl," Chaya Sora protested. "Who's going to listen to me?"

"If you prepare well and really work on your content and delivery, people will listen to you."

Chaya Sora gave in (go fight the Rebbetzin!) and began to prepare. And the *shiur* grew and people listened — even though she was only a high-school girl.

(She's still giving *shiurim* to this day.)

And always there were shidduchim happening. Making shidduchim was Zeide's thing — a vital part of his life that the Rebbetzin adopted. It was after the war and the future would be comprised of new families and children. Making shidduchim was a major part of what went on at Hineni. Many people came to Hineni because they wanted to get married, and ended up becoming frum in the process. The fact is, people need help with shidduchim — the process leading to the chuppah is seldom easy — and the Rebbetzin and her family were ready to do their part. Not only did they make shidduchim, but once a couple was engaged, Rabbi and Rebbetzin Jungreis would invite them over to the house and give them the 1960s version of chassan/kallah classes.

It was late at night when the Rebbetzin and Barbara boarded their flight in Portland, Oregon. Catching the red-eye flight meant that the Rebbetzin made it home in time to serve her children breakfast in the morning, and that was extremely important to her. Saving the world is a wonderful thing, but not at the expense of one's children.

Earlier, the Rebbetzin had spoken to the community for a few hours and met with many of the people in the audience who sought her advice. It was her policy to remain in the hall after a speaking engagement for as long as possible (this gave her the opportunity to meet with everyone who wanted to) and Portland was no exception. It was a long night. She was terribly exhausted.

She was close to dozing off when she heard a voice talking to her.

The voice belonged to a young man.

Part of her wanted to tell him that she couldn't talk right then. She wanted to apologize and explain that she would have loved to have a conversation but it was very late, she was incredibly tired, and a plane ride was a wonderful opportunity to catch some sleep. However, she couldn't bring herself to do this for one simple reason. The young man might be a Jew — and if he was, she had an obligation to talk to him just in case she would be able to change his life.

"You live in Portland?"

"No, I was just in town to give a speech."

"At what venue?"

"A synagogue."

"Not for me," he immediately said.

That came fast enough to clarify matters. There was no question that here was a Jewish man. It was equally clear that he had no interest in connecting to his heritage.

"You look like a nice Jewish boy, am I right?"

"Only because I was born into a Jewish family. It's not like I had a choice in the matter. Some people are born Muslim, some are born Hindu. I was born into a Jewish home. Don't worry, I don't allow that part of my life to get in my way. Not even a little bit."

It was at that point that the flight staff began distributing meals.

The stewardess handed the Rebbetzin a kosher meal. Then, turning to the young man, she asked him what he wanted to eat.

"Ham and cheese," he said promptly.

The Rebbetzin, however, was having none of that. Not on her flight. Not when G-d had sent this poor Jewish boy straight into her life. The young man had no way of knowing that he had just virtually guaranteed himself to be on the receiving end of a kiruv seminar for one.

"You can't have that sandwich!"

"What do you mean? I eat ham and cheese all the time!"

"You just told me that you were born a Jew, did you not?"

His eyes narrowed.

"So what?"

"So put that sandwich down and ask the stewardess for something else. Ham and cheese is not for you!"

"I do not practice the Jewish religion. I do whatever I want. Stop telling me what to do."

"It isn't me telling you what to do. It is you."

"What?"

"You heard me. You signed a binding contract which doesn't allow you to eat a ham and cheese sandwich."

"I don't understand what you're saying. When did I ever sign a contract?"

"You signed a contract, when you, along with every other Jewish soul, stood at Mount Sinai. That was when you promised that you wouldn't eat certain foods. You were there."

He'd had enough.

"You know something," he yelled at her, *"you're nuts! I mean it! You are out of your mind!"*

They did not converse at all for the remainder of the flight. In fact, he pretended that they had never exchanged a word. When the plane landed at JFK, they disembarked and happened to run into one another again at the baggage carousel, where he took the opportunity to throw one last dagger at her.

"Lady, you know — you are one crazy person!"

The Rebbetzin didn't bat an eyelash.

"My name is Esther Jungreis," she said. "This is my card. Take it. Call me when you're ready. Better yet, come and visit me at my office. I have an organization called Hineni, where I help guide people just like you. Come and see me when you're ready."

He was staring at her as if he couldn't figure out if she was serious or joking. She didn't seem to be joking, but on the other hand, how could she possibly be serious? Who talked this way in America?

She held his gaze, completely calm and self-assured. Where most people would have been at least slightly ruffled from being called crazy to their face, she wasn't reacting at all. He couldn't help being impressed by her self-control — even if she was out of her mind.

"I'm serious," the Rebbetzin said. "Everything I'm telling you is documented. In fact, I'll be happy to give you a guided tour of your religion and heritage. Just a little bit of learning and your entire life will change!"

With that, they parted ways, the Rebbetzin and Barbara to North Woodmere and the young man to wherever he was going. The Rebbetzin had a million things to do; before long, she had completely forgotten about the encounter.

A number of years passed since the day Rebbetzin Jungreis reminded a young Jewish man about the time they had both stood at Sinai.

One day she was teaching a class when a stranger entered the room, dressed like a real yeshivah *bachur*. The Rebbetzin stared at him from time to time, trying to place him.

"Rebbetzin," he said at last, "don't you remember me?"

"You look familiar," she replied. It was her standard response for anyone she didn't recognize.

"How about a conversation on a plane? A conversation about a sandwich?"

He was smiling now. So was she.

In a flash it all came back to her. The conversation and the ham sandwich. Being called a nut in front of the entire plane. Meeting him at the luggage carousel. Giving him her card and telling him about Sinai.

"You can't be the guy from Oregon!"

"None other. I won't lie to you. I was angry at first. But in the end I couldn't get your words out of my brain. Finally I had to see if you were telling the truth. Guess what? You were."

He paused.

"Rebbetzin, can you do me a favor?"

"What's that, *sheifelah*?"

"Can you find me a girl to marry who also signed that document at Sinai?"

It goes without saying that the Rebbetzin did as he asked.

This chapter has been dedicated
in appreciation of the Rebbetzin ע״ה
who spread the wisdom of Torah throughout the world
and helped so many with her blessings
David and Carol Feinberg

CHAPTER TWENTY-EIGHT

The Question That Wouldn't Go Away

*R*eb Yisroel (Roy) and Leah (Linda) Neuberger met the Rebbetzin in Newburgh, New York, in the spring of 1974. The meeting could have easily not taken place; in fact, from a statistical perspective it shouldn't have occurred, and yet it did, with miraculous results.

Back in those days, Roy Neuberger was super allergic to the Jewish religion and incredibly embarrassed to have anything to do with Judaism at all. This shouldn't come as a surprise, considering the type of Jews with whom he grew up and with whom he went to high school. His old friends won't even talk to him today if they happen to run into one another at a class reunion. There could be seventy or eighty people in the room. But they'll take one look at him and Leah — obviously religious Jews — and turn the other way, as if they don't exist. That was his reality. So yes, the fact that Roy and his wife Linda (whom he met in high school) ended up not only becoming religious, but going all the way, is more than a statistical improbability and more like a complete miracle.

Growing up on Park Avenue, Roy pushed away everything Jewish. He didn't know what a rebbetzin was — had never even heard the term — and the idea of going to hear one speak was not in the realm of possibility.

Things started to change for Roy and Linda after they had spent a lot of time (years and years) trying out every other way of life, before coming to the realization that none of them were close to true.

For Roy, a moment of breakthrough happened on a night in 1966 at the University of Ann Arbor. At that moment, a thought flashed through his mind and he said to himself, *"Maybe there really is a G-d?"*

It was after that moment that everything started to change, but it would be a long, arduous and painful process, especially considering the fact that he still had no interest whatsoever in being a Jew. He turned to Hinduism, Buddhism and Christianity, hoping that salvation lay in one of those, but everything fizzled out in the end. One by one everything was rejected, because they were just not right.

That part of the search took another eight years.

Roy and Linda were already married for years when the incident occurred. Having returned to New York from Oxford, England, the Neubergers were searching for a place to live. They eventually settled on a town in upstate New York called Cornwall. After working for the government for a number of years, Roy decided to purchase a weekly newspaper that had been founded in 1885. He became the publisher, editor, writer, photographer and print shop manager — doing every job that needed to be done. Cornwall was not far from West Point and Bear Mountain. There were a few Jewish families living in the town, but they were extremely liberal with no hint of or connection to religion.

Wanting to turn his newspaper into the greatest paper in the area, Roy got in touch with "The National Newspaper Association," which is the American trade association of weekly newspapers around the country. At the time, the president of the organization was a man by the name of Walter Grunfeld. The organization comprised hundreds of newspapers throughout America, and Walter was the director of the entire association. He was a brilliant speaker and a wonderful human being, and it wasn't long before Roy and Linda had become friends with him.

One day, on a whim, Roy picked up the phone and called Walter at home.

"It's Roy Neuberger."

"How's everything, Roy?"

"Things are fine. But I wanted to know if Linda and I could come over and pick your brain. I've never been a newspaper publisher before and I have a million questions for a man with your experience."

"Not a problem," Walter told him agreeably, and invited them to his home.

They drove to Binghamton, New York, a few days later. Walter owned three newspapers in the city and he was very prominent in the publishing business. They spent the day in Walter's office enjoying hours of intelligent and informative conversation. Walter was able to answer every question Roy had and his advice was golden. At the end of the day, they swung by the Grunfeld home before leaving town. It was 6:30 in the evening and Walter turned on the TV to watch the news.

The reason Walter had to watch the news was because the State of Israel was fully engulfed in the Yom Kippur War right then. Until that point in time, the war had been going badly for the IDF, but somehow the Israelis "managed" to turn the corner and now the momentum was heading in the opposite direction. For the first time since the war broke out, the Egyptians were finding themselves on the defensive.

Standing in front of the television set, Walter Grunfeld broke down in a torrent of tears.

"I can't believe it, I can't believe it," he repeated over and over, his relief palpable. "A week ago Israel was finished, it was all over, and now look at it — General Sharon just crossed the Suez Canal and he's got the Egyptian army surrounded! They're marching on Cairo! Israel's saved!"

Walter was overcome with emotion, his *Yiddishe hartz* (Jewish heart) experiencing true joy at Israel's salvation.

Roy, feeling like he needed to contribute something to the moment, made a comment like, "Oh, yeah, I read something in the paper about the war in the Middle East," but the way he spoke the words, indicating that he obviously couldn't care less, made Walter stop what he was doing and take a new look at his visitors. There he was, looking at Roy, and you could see that Walter realized that the two Jews standing in his living room were completely clueless about the fact that Israel was even involved in a war, never mind whether it was winning or losing!

The next second, Walter Grunfeld began screaming at Roy Neuberger at the top of his lungs. There were tears rolling down his cheeks and he was yelling at his guests with every particle of passion he possessed.

"What kind of a Jew are you! Are you made of stone? Don't you have a heart?"

For Roy, it was a watershed moment.

Standing there in the living room of a man he respected but barely knew, Neuberger heard himself being berated and a question thrown at him that he couldn't have answered for all the money in the world.

"What kind of a Jew are you, Roy?"

And all Roy Neuberger could think of was, "That's a beautiful question, Walter, because in all honesty, I have no idea what kind of a Jew I am! In fact, I have no idea what being a Jew even means in the first place!"

And Neuberger stood there in front of the blaring TV set and had nothing to say in response to the emotional question that was being shot at him.

When he left Grunfeld's home that night, the question Walter shot at him — the question that had emanated straight from the heart — kept on replaying itself in his mind.

"What kind of a Jew are you? What kind of a Jew are you?"

"I don't know," he said to himself. "I wish I knew the answer to that question. But the truth is, I just don't know."

("It's now over forty years later," Reb Yisroel said with a smile, "and I still wonder about that question from time to time.")

The question would continue to reverberate in Roy's mind for the foreseeable future.

Six months after Grunfeld yelled at him, Roy had a meeting with one of the paper's main advertisers, a wonderful man named Bob Ushman. Ushman, who owned a hardware store in Cornwall and advertised in the local paper, lived in the town of Newburgh, New York, where he was a member in good standing of the local Orthodox shul.

Roy met his friend Bob Ushman for lunch. Still bothered by Walter Grunfeld's question, Roy opened up to Ushman.

"I'm thirty-one years old," he began, "and I have completely exhausted every religious option which I thought might be the truth. There is absolutely nothing left!"

Roy brought the slice of pizza he was holding in his hand to his mouth, then dropped it down on the plate.

"Bob," he said, almost pleading — the six-month-old question rattling around his brain — "What on earth does it mean to be a Jew? I was never even in a synagogue! What goes on there?"

Bob listened sympathetically.

He called Roy back that evening.

"Listen," Ushman told him. "I checked out the program at my shul and there's this woman, a Rebbetzin, coming to speak on Thursday night. They're billing her as the 'Jewish Billy Graham.' Maybe come on over and hear what she has to say."

Roy was silent for a few seconds.

"Look, you want to know what it means to be a Jew. Maybe she can help?"

And in the end Roy and Linda Neuberger decided to go hear the Rebbetzin speak. Because hey, you just never know in this world. Besides, Roy really, really wanted to know what it meant to be a Jew. Maybe the Jewish female version of Billy Graham held the answer in the palm of her hand?

Having no idea what a rebbetzin was, Roy Neuberger had no idea what to expect. In his mind, he had zero expectations from the evening and didn't anticipate the speaker saying anything he would find worthwhile or relevant to his life or the questions plaguing him. The Neubergers would never forget the moment Rebbetzin Jungreis entered the room. They had been expecting a "rebbetzin," a religious Jew with no connection to modern times or fashion. But the woman who entered the room was extremely put together and well dressed — it was difficult for them to reconcile their previous notions with the reality that stood before them.

"This is crazy," Neuberger remembers thinking, "it doesn't make sense!"

From one moment to the next all preconceived notions were shot and everything had to be realigned.

The second the Rebbetzin began to speak, all their thoughts flew out the window, because Roy and Linda were completely awestruck by what she was saying. This wasn't long after the Rebbetzin's first major event at Madison Square Garden, and many of the elements of her talk that night came from her Madison Square Garden speech.

"You are a Jew. You have created civilizations. You have given birth to every ideal that has shaped mankind. Justice, peace, love and the innate dignity of man have all had their genesis in your Torah.

But above all, you have been given the unique mission proclaiming the Oneness of G-d!

Every word was powerful. Every word hit home. Every word entered their minds and touched them deep inside, right in their souls. It was a moment of awakening. They didn't know how or why, but all of a sudden Roy and Linda found themselves crying! They who had traveled the world, who had seen it all, who had grown up in the most cultured environment — they were overwhelmed and couldn't control themselves. The tears just kept on coming and wouldn't stop, no matter how they tried. It was inconceivable, yet true. It was like a bolt of lightning had struck their *neshamos* with a direct hit!

The Rebbetzin on a Hineni tour with Leah Neuberger and her children at the *kever* of Rabbi Shimon Bar Yochai in Meron

Suddenly they came to the realization that there was a whole world that existed that they had never known about and that was inviting them inside. It was as if they had been living in an alternate reality for their entire lives — only to wake up and recognize what was happening just as the two worlds suddenly collided with a fantastic explosion! They were so utterly overwhelmed by what the Rebbetzin had said, so out of their depth and out of context, that they couldn't even talk to her after the lecture — because they lacked the necessary words to articulate their feelings and had nothing to say!

Before leaving that night, they purchased a record of the Rebbetzin's address at Madison Square Garden that was for sale and then they left Bob Ushman's shul awestruck and speechless.

Roy Neuberger was someone who, when overwhelmed by something, couldn't say a word. Instead, he needed to sleep on it and would usually find himself with more clarity come morning. When he woke up the next day he knew one thing — he needed to investigate what he had heard the night before. Something huge had occurred, he had no idea how to deal with it, and he needed to expend the effort to figure it out. He wasted no time. That morning he sat down at his desk and wrote a letter to Rebbetzin Esther Jungreis.

To his utter amazement, the Rebbetzin answered him, explaining that she wanted Roy and Linda to be in touch and that more than anything else they needed to learn Torah.

Later Roy would learn that the Rebbetzin wasn't even supposed to have come speak at the shul the night before. She had been slated to speak at the Newburgh shul during the month of December. But the Rebbetzin came down with laryngitis and the speech had to be postponed to March 1974. Had the speech taken place when planned (before Roy's conversation with Bob Ushman), he and Linda would have missed meeting the Rebbetzin. It would become crystal clear to Roy Neuberger that the meeting between them and Rebbetzin Jungreis was orchestrated by heaven — to the millisecond.

A day before or after — and it would almost definitely not have happened.

The truth is, Barbara Janov hadn't been keen on rescheduling the speech in Newburgh at all.

"Why do we need to go to Newburgh," she'd asked the Rebbetzin. "To speak to two cows and a chicken? What's the point?"

But the Rebbetzin wouldn't change her mind. If Jewish people wanted to hear her in Newburgh — she would go and speak to them in Newburgh.

At the precise moment when the Neubergers met Esther Jungreis for the first time, all the crazy ideas of the past disappeared and they were suddenly receptive to learning the truth about what it meant to be a Jew and his role in the world — something which they would not have been capable of a short while earlier. For Roy and Linda, it was like the fog had just cleared and they were able to see Mount Everest in front of them. The Divine Providence in the timing could not be denied.

The Neubergers began driving in to Brooklyn once a week to hear the Rebbetzin speak. At the time she gave a weekly class to the Syrian community at Shaarei Zion. For the Neubergers, attending the *shiurim*

meant a two-hour drive in each direction. It was the height of the energy crisis at the time, which meant waiting in line at the gas station to fill the tank of their blue Chevy (four doors, tail fins and seemingly twenty feet long), and getting a babysitter for their two little kids, but they were determined to do what it took.

The newspaper was another challenge because the paper needed to be put to bed on Tuesday and the Rebbetzin's *shiur* was also on Tuesday, which meant that they were juggling a lot of balls in the air at the same time. Which they didn't mind doing — because they loved hearing her speak.

Sitting in the Rebbetzin's classes became the highlight of their week. For the first time, Roy and Linda Neuberger were learning the secrets of a happy marriage, how to raise their children, and quite simply, how to understand and relate to the world around them — from a Torah perspective. It was as if Moses had come down from the mountain and was speaking to the people himself. They'd been searching for so long for meaning and purpose; materialism was clearly not enough and could never fill the void — but what then?

Their search had been in progress since Roy was sixteen and Linda was fifteen! Here they were thirty and thirty-one and it was finally happening! They'd been major students, studying night and day, both in the honors program at the university, and when they heard the Rebbetzin teaching Torah, all the literature they used to spend so much time analyzing became completely empty compared to the Torah, where every single word held incredible and deep meaning.

More than that, they realized that a person didn't have to exile himself to a far-away mountaintop to live a spiritual life; that it was possible and in fact recommended to live among likeminded people in a Torah community, and that that was the best way to live a life of genuine spirituality.

Another thing — the Rebbetzin told Roy and Linda that they needed to tell their story and share it with the world around them.

"To declare the miracle," was the way she put it.

So the Neubergers wrote their personal story, which Rebbetzin Jungreis published in her column in *The Jewish Press* for six consecutive weeks. This was one of the ways the Rebbetzin made it clear to them that just as she had inspired them and changed their lives, now it was their turn to do the same for other Jewish people, passing the torch along.

Yisroel Neuberger at home making Havdalah for his family and Hineni Shabbos guests

Things moved along rapidly for the Neubergers, and they decided to sell the newspaper. Two weeks before Rosh Hashanah 1974 they moved to North Woodmere, buying a house in close proximity to Rabbi and Rebbetzin Jungreis on Hungry Harbor Road.

And when they did, the Rebbetzin asked them to become official Hineni Shabbos hosts for the myriads of guests that came along and needed a place to experience the beauty of Shabbos for themselves in a non-threatening and accepting environment.

Needless to say, they accepted.

It was the Rebbetzin asking, after all.

For the next forty years, Yisroel and Leah Neuberger would go on to host thousands of Hineni Shabbos guests.

In fact, they still do.

Sometimes the Rebbetzin would ask them to have people come and live with them — the visits lasting anywhere from a week to a few years. Many of their guests went on to become *shomer Shabbos*, and still express their gratitude to them every time they cross paths — even now, many decades later. Then the Rebbetzin asked Leah to teach the Hineni brides, so she became a kallah teacher.

Reb Yisroel Neuberger served as congregational president of Ohr Torah for twelve years, while Leah was voted sisterhood president for the same twelve years. It was a slow and steady process with the Rebbetzin guiding them skillfully, helping them progress when they were ready and giving them room to breathe when they were just starting out.

The end result: The Neubergers worked hand in hand with Rabbi and Rebbetzin Jungreis, and the entire Hineni family, and continue to do so to this day.

And that is an incredible thing.

It was eleven o'clock on a Sunday night in February 1975 when Yaffa Neuberger first got sick. Roy was at home with their older daughter Sarah, who was about five at the time, while Linda took Yaffa to their family doctor.

Suddenly the phone rang.

Roy answered. The doctor was on the line.

"This is Dr. Hoberman*."

Roy waited to hear what the doctor wanted.

"Your wife just fainted. I can't get a pulse. I think she had a heart attack. You'd better come over immediately. I'm a pediatrician. I can't do anything for her! She's lying on the floor of my office right now. Call an ambulance and take her to the hospital!"

Roy Neuberger almost went out of his mind.

What to do? Should he call the ambulance, like the doctor said? Rush over to the doctor's house? What about Sarah, asleep in her bedroom?

Suddenly another voice entered his mind.

"Call the Rebbetzin," it said to him. And Roy picked up the phone and dialed the familiar number — a number that people knew could be called any time of the day or night.

The Rebbetzin and Barbara were just walking through the door from an event when the phone rang. Barbara answered. Roy told her everything the doctor said and clarified that he was alone in the house with his older daughter.

"Stay home," Barbara told him in her usual decisive tones. "I'll go to the doctor right now!"

She was about to hang up when he heard a voice in the background saying, "Barbara, give me the phone!"

The next second the Rebbetzin got on the phone. She was super calm.

Roy recalls the words she said to him that night as if the conversation happened yesterday. He still chokes up when he tells this story.

"Yisroel, Yisroel!" (Roy hadn't even had a Jewish name until the Rebbetzin had started calling him Yisroel the previous year.) "Mazel tov! Your Leah is pregnant. She's going to have a beautiful Hineni baby!"

(There was no doubt in her voice — as if she knew beyond a shadow of a doubt that what she was saying to the distraught husband was completely accurate.)

"Barbara will be over momentarily to watch Sarah and you will go to the doctor's office. Everything will be fine!"

Roy was left with the receiver in his hand, reeling from the impact of the Rebbetzin's words.

It turned out the Rebbetzin was right. They'd had no idea that Leah was expecting a baby and that was the moment they discovered the wonderful news. When he arrived at the doctor's office, Roy found himself taking care of the doctor, who was shaking like a leaf. He, on the other hand, was completely calm. After all, the Rebbetzin had already diagnosed the patient and there was no reason to worry.

"Dr. Hoberman, can I get you a cup of coffee?"

He settled the doctor and it wasn't long before his wife came to. Her pulse had been there all along. In his nervousness, the doctor hadn't been able to find it.

Roy never asked the Rebbetzin how she knew what was really going on with his wife. He just accepted the fact that she possessed certain spiritual abilities. Bottom line — there was no questioning the Rebbetzin.

Miriam was Neuberger child number three. Now Roy and Linda had three girls and were anxiously awaiting a boy.

The Rebbetzin and Zeide at the bris of Ari Neuberger

Roy came into shul one Shabbos morning. It was still prior to davening and the Rabbi approached him the moment he entered the sanctuary.

"Good Shabbos, Yisroel."

"Good Shabbos, Rabbi Jungreis."

"Yisroel, I have to tell you something."

Yisroel was curious.

"What's that, Rabbi?"

"I had a dream last night."

"What about?"

"I dreamt last night that you have another baby on the way."

Leah went to the doctor that Monday, where she learned that they were indeed expecting another child. But the truth is, they didn't need to go anywhere because the Rabbi had already told them. That's how they found out about their son Aharon Yaakov.

Yaffa Neuberger was three years old when she fell off the monkey bars in nursery school and broke her arm. It was a terrible break — that was obvious even to the untrained eye. The school called Mr. and Mrs. Neuberger, who rushed over — and Roy, who had been trained as an EMT, took one look at the break and knew that they were in serious trouble. It was purple and bulging and needed immediate attention. They moved Yaffa onto a board and into the back of a car that took her to the hospital. (This was pre-Hatzolah days.)

Unfortunately, someone at the school had given her apple juice to drink, never guessing that that was the worst thing they could have done. Before going into surgery, the nurses asked how long it had been since Yaffa had had something to drink, and when they learned that she had been given a cup of apple juice just prior to her arrival, the Neubergers were informed that the surgery was temporarily on hold until it was safe to operate.

Meanwhile, two top orthopedic surgeons examined the little girl and informed Roy and Linda that the chances of a successful surgery were very slim.

"She doesn't have a pulse right now and there's no blood flowing through her right arm. We're sorry to have to tell you this, but it's very possible we won't be able to save her arm."

This was a huge blow for Yaffa's parents, who stared at their beautiful little girl and almost went out of their minds with grief.

The Rebbetzin was in South Africa on a speaking tour at the time (from there she was headed to Israel), but Roy called Rabbi Jungreis immediately to keep him informed of the developments with Yaffa.

(Interestingly enough, Yaffa Neuberger would grow up to marry Osher Anshil Jungreis — which meant that with his call, Roy was giving his daughter's future father-in-law a progress report...)

The moment Rabbi Jungreis understood what happened there was silence on the other end of the line.

And then, Rav Meshulem began to sob.

Roy could hear his friend the Rabbi sobbing on the other end of the receiver. When Roy heard the Rabbi break down, it hit him hard. He hadn't even felt the pain until the Rabbi felt the pain. Then he broke down as well and the two of them cried together over the phone.

By the time Yaffa went into surgery, it was nine o'clock in the evening. Of course, Rav Meshulem and the Rebbetzin's brother Rabbi Yaakov Jungreis were there for the surgery, having arrived at the hospital as soon as possible to give strength and encouragement to the Neubergers in their hour of need. The two of them sat in the waiting room and recited Tehillim, their presence a balm for the brokenhearted parents whose daughter's arm hung on a thread.

At one o'clock in the morning the doctors emerged from the operating theater. Both were non-religious and both were completely nonplussed at what had transpired that evening.

Little Yaffa Neuberger after her hand surgery

"We're at a loss to explain how the operation was a success," they began. "It was like working on the inner mechanism of a watch — that's the kind of delicate touch we needed to reattach all the tiny bone fragments in your daughter's arm."

Yaffa was extremely fine boned and very petite, and the doctors knew what a miracle it was. Of course, there was no question of her leaving the hospital any time soon. But every morning at six o'clock Yaffa Neuberger had a visitor — Rav

Meshulem Jungreis. Nobody was allowed in to see the patients at that hour, but rabbis were above the normal rules and could come and go as they pleased. He did this for an entire week, spending every morning with his future daughter-in-law. When Yaffa was finally released from the hospital and able to return home, she had a very special visitor who had just landed from Eretz Yisrael.

The Rebbetzin came straight from the airport to see Yaffa. She was wearing her coat and when she saw Yaffa she said, "I've just come here from Eretz Yisrael — I still have my coat on and I'm going to give you a hug with the air of Eretz Yisrael that's on my coat and a berachah from Eretz Yisrael!"

And the Rebbetzin enveloped the three-year-old Yaffa in her arms, hugging and kissing her and showering her with love.

Somehow Yaffa still remembers that moment.

That was in the spring.

In the summer the Neubergers had been planning to go Eretz Yisrael with the Rebbetzin. That year, however, they were unsure whether the family would be able to join the tour due to their daughter's broken arm and the long recovery.

"You will come," the Rebbetzin told them emphatically, "and you will see that Yaffa'le will do great things with her arm in Eretz Yisrael!"

The Rebbetzin had spoken and that was that. They were going.

And Yaffa'le was about to do very great things with her arm.

It was the summer of 1975. The Rebbetzin spoke all around the country and the members of the Hineni tour accompanied her from place to place, caught up in the emotional atmosphere and intense experiences that occurred everywhere they went.

Although the 1973 Yom Kippur War was behind them, one of the places the Rebbetzin visited was a rehabilitation center for IDF troops who had been badly wounded in the war. The rehab center was located at Tel HaShomer and when they arrived, they were shown into a large room filled with soldiers, many of them grievously wounded. The Rebbetzin was on fire as always when addressing a crowd who had sacrificed so much for Klal Yisrael. When she finished her speech, she surprised everyone in the audience by inviting three-year-old Yaffa Neuberger to join her on the stage.

The three-year-old girl made her way to the stage, all eyes following her progress. She was adorable and the soldiers couldn't help smiling at the Rebbetzin's helper.

Pointing at Yaffa's arm, which was still in a sling, the Rebbetzin said to the soldiers, "Do you see this little girl? She had an injury that the doctors claimed was impossible to heal! But look at her now!"

Turning to Yaffa, the Rebbetzin said in a soft voice, "Yaffa'le, can you lift your hand and show the soldiers how much better it is now?"

Yaffa did as the Rebbetzin requested. She lifted her hand as high as she could and showed the soldiers how she was beginning to have the ability to wiggle her fingers again…

"This child experienced an incredible miracle," the Rebbetzin told the silent room in a voice that brooked no argument, "and *b'ezrat Hashem* the same will happen with every one of you!"

One of the soldiers sitting in the room had been shot in the elbow and had been diagnosed with an injury similar to Yaffa's break. He was in despair as a result of the damage that had been done to his arm, and terribly depressed.

After the speech, Yaffa was introduced to the wounded soldier. They looked at one another — the three-year-old girl and the wounded soldier. And then for the first time since he'd been injured, the soldier found that he was able to move his arm — just a little bit. There was no rhyme or reason, no way to explain what happened. Before they met, he hadn't been able to move his arm even a fraction of an inch. Yet suddenly he'd been granted flexibility from up Above. It was a miracle — pure and simple — and there was not a dry eye in the house.

Yaffa still remembers that moment.

Wouldn't you?

This chapter has been dedicated
in honor of our beloved Rebbetzin Esther Jungreis ע"ה
who inspired and guided us and countless others
to a life of Torah and mitzvos.
May her light shine forever.

Yisroel & Leah Neuberger & Family

CHAPTER TWENTY-NINE

Ava'leh

When my family moved to North Woodmere in the '60s from Crown Heights," Avi Dobuler began, "we were not religious."

Avi Dobuler recalls seeing the men and boys in dark suits and black hats but he didn't realize that they were Orthodox or chassidim. At some point the Dobulers moved out to the Island, seeking respite from the city's noise and frenzy in the serenity of the suburbs. There they joined the fledgling Ohr Torah community. Avi had minimal contact with the Rabbi and Rebbetzin during their first year in North Woodmere. He had just turned bar mitzvah before the move and was very much still a kid.

He remembers the shul as an amalgam of types. There were the European Holocaust survivors, many of whom had a yeshivah/*cheder* background but were not really religious (possibly due to their experiences during the war). Then there was the American-born population — people who had not been raised in observant homes and had no idea what it meant to live a Torah lifestyle.

Rabbi Jungreis was a man of peace and love and he stayed above the politics, tending to the rabbinical aspect of his position and being there for everyone in the community regardless of whether or not they had voted for him at the board meetings. The politics would never quite disappear. There were arguments between the members who wanted a lower *mechitzah* and those who wanted no *mechitzah* at all, mixed seating or no mixed seating. Should they try to attract more people like them (not really religious) or go for the more Orthodox crowd?

Those were just a handful of the hundreds of questions that arose in the early years. Yet gentle as he was, when it came to matters of halachah you couldn't budge the Rabbi. Not an inch.

He was gentle, yes.

His personal honor was not a big deal and he ignored all slights. But the community would quickly learn that he was immovable when it came to what he perceived as the important things.

If Avi wanted to see his mother when he came home from school, he knew he'd probably find her sitting with the Rebbetzin at the Jungreis kitchen table. It was rare to find the Rebbetzin alone. It was always exciting and always action packed. Through it all, Avi was friendly to everyone — but not more than that; he was a teen, after all.

Then something happened that changed his entire life.

When Avi was fifteen years old, his father was electrocuted in the backyard of the Dobuler home, and nothing was ever the same.

In his early teenage years Avi was rather rebellious. Back in Crown Heights he'd gotten involved with the JDL (Jewish Defense League) and been in a few fights trying to protect the neighborhood. Nothing was easy. Not his life at home, not the fighting on the streets, and not moving into a new neighborhood. Swimming was one thing father and son enjoyed doing together. That was why his father decided to have a pool installed in the back yard. Unfortunately, the wiring installed by the local utility had not yet been covered up and was still exposed. One afternoon his father entered the unfinished pool and touched the live wires with a vacuum he was using to clean out the pool.

One second, Avi had a father who went out of his way to build him a pool. The next second, his father was no longer alive. The guilt was crushing to a kid who had been giving his father a hard time.

Avi wasn't there when the accident occurred. He'd been visiting family on the Island and his aunt drove him back to the house as soon as they heard the news. He reached home just as the ambulance was taking away his father's body. It was August 1965.

From one second to the next Avi's life as he knew it was over.

Suddenly the almost-fifteen-year old kid was sitting *shivah* on a low stool, listening to friends and family share their stories and memories of the man he'd called Dad. Rabbi Jungreis was very involved with the halachic aspect of the mourning period, and both he and the Rebbetzin spent a lot of time comforting the family. Avi's sisters and his mother needed to be cared for, and he was the man — barely grown up but suddenly thrust into the role of the man of the family. He sat on the stool and felt a terrible sense of guilt engulf him. The fact is, he'd been a tough kid and now he would never have the chance to tell his father how sorry he was for everything he'd said and done. He felt hollow inside, as if all the happiness had been scooped out of him, leaving nothing but an empty shell behind.

One afternoon during the *shivah*, Avi had to get away from it all. He left the room and went to sit by himself — away from the crowds of people who filled the Dobuler home. He wanted to be alone — alone with his grief and his feelings of pain and the throbbing knowledge that he would never be able to atone or make it up to his Dad.

Suddenly the Rebbetzin entered the room. She was looking for him.

She took a seat nearby and they sat in silence for a few seconds.

"Ava'leh," she said at last. (She always called him Ava'leh.)

He nodded.

"Look," she told him, "I know how you're feeling."

Being close to the family, she knew that things had been rough between Avi and his father during the last few months — and that the guilt was eating him up inside.

"But Ava'leh, you now have an opportunity — a really major opportunity — to do something for your father."

"What do you want me to do?"

"If you say Kaddish every day for your father's *neshamah*, for your father's soul, it will give you the ability to reconnect with him in a very close, spiritual way. He will have *nachas* from you, his son, and his *neshamah* will rise up

Rav Meshulem delivering a *dvar Torah*

in heaven. Do you understand me? You can lift his soul into a better place in heaven. Nobody else can do it as effectively as you can. You can make it up to him."

The concepts she was telling him were basically foreign to Avi Dobuler. It wasn't the way he'd been raised (though his grandmother was observant), but here the Rebbetzin was telling him in the clearest way possible that it was time to straighten out his life — and that yes, he could make amends with his father if he cared enough to do so.

"Ava'leh, you have to ask yourself what life is for, what it's about. You've been wild, but it's time to get serious. You have a role now. You're the man of the house."

The Rebbetzin's request was not an easy one. North Woodmere was still a spiritual desert. There was a minyan every Shabbos and sometimes there was a minyan in the evening, but no regular services. How was he supposed to say Kaddish for his father if there wasn't a minyan in the neighborhood?

Still, the Rebbetzin had given him a mandate — and a way to pay his father back. So Avi went to the Jungreis home every day. The Rabbi had a list of all the shul members and would tell him who to try — day in and day out — calling ten men for Maariv at night and asking them to return for Shacharis the following morning.

It was a very tough job and it demanded perseverance and a healthy tolerance for rejection. By the time the year was over, Avi had missed saying Kaddish maybe a handful of times — which was a pretty good track record for a kid who wasn't religious and had never done that kind of thing before. In the beginning of the year Avi could barely read the words of Shacharis and he broke his teeth. But the Rabbi advised him to serve as the chazzan, and with time he grew more fluent and at ease. There was no question in his mind that it was the Rebbetzin's words that convinced him to make the commitment — and he kept to it, going out of his way and doing his best to make it happen, while the Rabbi stood by his side and gave him encouragement.

And while Avi didn't actually become religious, he did become sensitized to religion and shul and spirituality and what it meant to commit to something for a greater purpose. He would never forget the gift he'd been given by the Rabbi and Rebbetzin — because there was no question that saying Kaddish for his father had been a real gift.

Avi married Fern Kazarski in 1971, with Rav Meshulem Jungreis officiating at the ceremony. In 1975 two very important events occurred. First, Avi and Fern learned that they were expecting their first child. Second, Avi's grandmother — the only really religious person in the family — found out that she had cancer. The cancer was extensive and the decision was made to keep her at home, rather than have her spend her last few months in the hospital. During her final few weeks of life, Avi's grandmother kept on extracting promises from her family to do more and more things for her *neshamah*.

"Maybe you'll go to shul more often?"

"Yes, Grandma, I will."

A few days later: "Maybe you'll keep kosher in the house?"

By that point she couldn't hold a siddur in her hands and they'd have to help her with it. Soon she wasn't able to see the words any longer and her children recited them aloud with her. She passed away on the day after Shavuos, and on the night the *shivah* was over, Fern Dobuler gave birth to their first child — a baby girl.

Avi's grandmother's final request from her family was: "Maybe you'll be a little more Yiddish?"

She didn't ask for them to become religious — she figured that was too much. But she did want them to make Yiddishkeit a bigger element in their lives.

So Avi called up the Rebbetzin.

"What am I supposed to do?" he asked her. "One of the final requests she made of us was that we'd be a little more Yiddish — and I feel like I want to do something but I don't know what."

Avi had already decided that he would recite Kaddish for his grandmother every day, but the Rebbetzin went in a different direction this time.

"Ava'leh," she said to him in response to his question, "I think it's time for you to start keeping Shabbos."

"What should I do?"

"Keep what you know. Give me a call after Shabbos and let me know how it went."

He called her up after Shabbos.

"*Nu*, Ava'leh, how did it go?"

"It went really well, Rebbetzin. It was one of the first times I didn't work on Shabbos. Fern and I were home for the baby's first Shabbos and we watched some John Wayne movies on Channel 5. It was so good to be resting and not to have to work…"

"Ava'leh," she replied, "I'm glad you had a nice time. But you may remember that we are not supposed to turn lights on and off on Shabbos — and the same thing goes for the television."

"Right, Rebbetzin, now I remember…"

He called her the next Motza'ei Shabbos.

"We watched John Wayne again this Shabbos — except that this time I put the television on a Shabbos clock! We didn't turn on anything, it was terrific!"

"I'm so happy you had a nice time, Ava'leh, but leaving the TV on — even if it's on a timer — is not exactly in the spirit of Shabbos…"

Avi was silent, listening to her.

"Look," she said at last. "There's a book on Shabbos that just came out that I think you should read. Get ahold of the book. The author is a man named Rabbi Donin and I think you will really enjoy his book and get a lot out of it. It will take you on a guided tour through Jewish life. Read a chapter next Shabbos and call me afterwards if you have any questions."

Rabbi Donin's book gave them clear guidance. They learned about the Friday night Kiddush, the Shabbos morning Kiddush and how to hold a lulav and esrog. There was a bibliography at the end of every chapter, and between that and their weekly consultations with the Rebbetzin, things were moving along. Fern especially never took anything at face value, and whenever she read anything new she had to really understand what it meant.

"How do we turn our home into a really kosher home?"

One thing led to another, and soon Avi and Fern were traveling to attend the Rebbetzin's classes every week at her father's shul in Canarsie. Her father not only looked like a tzaddik — he was the real thing in every way. He dressed like a chassid and spoke like an angel, and the great reverence that the Rebbetzin accorded her parents was obvious if you just spent five minutes in their presence.

But Avi knew that the Rebbetzin was larger than the local community. He had not been at all surprised when life led her to Madison Square Garden, where she electrified thousands of Jews with her message.

Yet at the same time, she didn't neglect her people back in North Woodmere just because she'd been catapulted to national stardom virtually overnight. She continued teaching her classes — and those lectures, *shiurim* and the Hineni Shabbatons were all formative in the Dobuler family's development.

She would return from a trip across America, sleep for three hours, and be back at the kitchen table sharing anecdotes from her trip and wise counsel to those in need. There was something unique about her way of never seeing herself as above everyone around her — though she was an iconic figure in every way and was treated as such by the media, both Jewish and not. Here was a woman who was rubbing shoulders with the most famous people in the country and delivering speeches from the most prestigious stages; yet she'd return home, roll up her sleeves and teach the women of North Woodmere Torah, as she prepared Shabbos in her kitchen.

The Jungreis motto: "You are always a member of the family — the door is always open. Just come on in for a cup of coffee, a piece of cake and some good, practical, realistic advice."

The Dobuler family became one hundred percent frum in 1976. Although Avi had promised his grandmother that he would go in the direction she wanted, his wife had made no such promise; this was the cause of tension, which required sage diplomacy on the Rebbetzin's part.

"I was ready for Kabbalah," was how Avi put it, "while my wife wasn't ready to cover her hair."

The Rebbetzin's guidance was skillful; she would tell the young couple when to move forward and when to slow down. The entire time, she did her best to motivate Fern to find Hashem in her own life and to want to grow on her own — not only because her husband had made a promise to his grandmother on her deathbed, but because it was the right thing for a person to do.

It was not easy.

When you're used to going to any restaurant you want and eating whatever you want to eat — the restrictions are tough. And what about your friends and social life? You don't want to lose your friends — whom you've known from high school and college! Yet the progress was undeniable. They were never allowed to just give up the fight. There had to be constant movement, even if they took only baby steps. And they were encouraged to try to bring their friends along.

The Rebbetzin encouraged the young couple to recite the words of

Shema Yisrael together before retiring for the night and to say the words of *Modeh Ani* together when they arose in the morning. This practice solidified their relationship and gave them a practical way in which to express the gratitude they felt for G-d. It brought them closer together and gave them a true appreciation for each and every day. (After Fern passed away and Avi remarried, this tradition was one of the first things he made sure to do with his second wife as well.)

Though he'd worked as an accountant back in the States, Avi became a licensed tour guide after the Dobuler family made aliyah, and it was Avi who led the Hineni tours whenever the Rebbetzin brought a group of Jews to Israel. Seeing him — a true Torah Jew — in action brought the Rebbetzin incredible *nachas*. His favorite sites were the Biblical archeological sites — places that brought the Torah alive. He loved leading tours to Chevron — not only to Me'aras HaMachpeilah, but to numerous archeological sites in the area, and to Kever Rachel and Shiloh and Shechem.

Fern Dobuler passed away in 2016.

Avi and Fern had been married for forty-five years, and Fern's passing was a devastating blow to the entire family. When it was time to erect her *matzeivah* (tombstone), Avi remembered an incident that he'd heard from the Jungreis family many times.

When Rabbi Jungreis passed away, the Rebbetzin was in deep grief at having lost her life partner. One day, while cleaning out his drawers, Slovie found a note in her father's handwriting. The message the note contained provided great comfort to the Rebbetzin.

These were the words written on the note.

"A long life may not be good enough, but a good life is long enough."

Recalling the story and the comfort it had brought to Rebbetzin Jungreis and her children, Avi did the same with his own grief-stricken family, sharing the words that Rabbi Jungreis had penned and left for his family.

When it came time to choose the words to write on Fern's tombstone, the family decided to use the Rabbi's words as a testimony for their mother and the way she had lived her life.

Today, if you should pass by the grave of Mrs. Fern Dobuler, stop for a moment and read the words engraved on her *matzeivah* — words that emanated from Rabbi Jungreis' soul and entered into the *neshamos* of a young couple trying to find their way in a complicated world. There you will see Rav Meshulem's timeless message: *"A long life may not be good enough, but a good life is long enough."*

Because, you see, that is the truth. A long life may not be good enough, but a good life is long enough.

CHAPTER THIRTY

The Key to Kiruv

Rabbi David Aron is the Rosh Yeshivah of Orayta and the founder of Israel Light, a kiruv organization.

He recalls:

I met the Rebbetzin over thirty years ago. At the time, I was an aspiring young rabbi teaching part time for Aish HaTorah in the Old City of Jerusalem. Having heard that the Rebbetzin was visiting Israel at the time, I asked Rav Noach Weinberg, z"l, if I could arrange a meeting between a number of rabbis I knew who were looking to get into the world of kiruv. Rebbetzin Jungreis, who as everyone knew was an unparalleled success in the field of outreach would be able to give our group helpful tips and guidance on how best to reach Jews today.

Rav Noach thought it was a great idea and our group met with the Rebbetzin at the Plaza Hotel. There were about ten of us sitting around that table: ten young rabbis (all baalei teshuvah) who were eagerly hoping to become educators and outreach professionals.

When everyone had arrived, I asked the Rebbetzin if she could share with us some key principles and techniques for reaching Jews today.

She pointed at one of the guys sitting there and asked, "How did you get involved in Judaism?"

"I happened to attend a class given by a rabbi and it made a lot of sense, so I saw the truth and I embraced it."

The Rebbetzin didn't accept his answer at face value and began to poke holes in his story, somewhat akin to a lawyer questioning a witness on the stand.

"You mean, you just walked in and it made sense?"

"No, I walked in, heard the class — and returned five months later."

"What happened after those five months? You just moved into yeshivah?"

"No," he admitted. "I actually went down south to Eilat for three additional months and eventually I returned to Jerusalem and yeshivah."

The Rebbetzin accepted his answer. Then she turned to the rest of us and began subjecting everyone around the table to their own interrogation. Time and again, we heard the same story. Every one of us told of how we had seen and heard the truth and felt connected to it. But as she began challenging us in her sweet way, we all admitted that it had taken us a long time to get to where we were today and that the journey and process had been filled with intellectual and emotional struggles and confusion galore.

The Rebbetzin did this for about an hour, and we all began feeling disturbed by the fact that she was sitting and playing lawyer games with us, without even answering the question we had asked her in the first place!

After an hour, in which she managed to manipulate every one of us into admitting that we had been confused kids whose journey back to Judaism had been time consuming and difficult, she said, "Well, I hope that I helped you," making it clear that she considered the meeting to have reached its natural conclusion.

We looked at one another, devastated by her approach and not comprehending what she was talking about or why she felt her interrogation had answered the question we had come to discuss with her.

It was at that point that I spoke up.

"Rebbetzin," I said, "forgive me, but I must have miscommunicated the purpose of our visit. We came to hear your insights, techniques and guidance on how to reach Jewish people in this day and age..."

The Rebbetzin looked directly at me and replied, as if puzzled, "But I thought that I just shared with you the most important concept you need to know."

Chapter Thirty: The Key to Kiruv □ 325

None of us knew what she was talking about and she must have understood that from the blank looks on our faces.

"Listen," she said at last. "I wanted all of you to understand something important. While it is true that each and every one of you embraced Judaism, it is equally true that each and every one of you has a difficult time now admitting that you went through a period when you were confused and had questions, and that the journey was slow and challenging.

"I want you to understand, to internalize the fact, that just as it was that way for you, it's the same for everyone else who returns from the outside world. Everyone has questions and everyone is confused and nobody likes admitting that when they finally succeed in working everything through and achieving true clarity.

"So this is what I want you to understand.

"In order to reach people and help them become religious, you need to be genuine, sincere, and there for them — truly and honestly there for them. When they feel they can trust you, and that you care about them, then maybe they will open up to you with the real questions that are sitting on their hearts, and then maybe you'll be able to begin a real dialogue with them — the kind of dialogue that leads to change."

That was it. That was what she wanted to tell us. And I remember that we all walked out of that meeting feeling kind of challenged and also wondering how valuable her insight would end up being for us in the future.

The following week I flew out of Ben Gurion to Toronto, Canada, where I was about to begin my first official rabbinical position. On the plane I met a group of very wealthy women that didn't seem to be searching for anything or to have any deep questions at all. They appeared to be blithely going through their lives, happily doing as they pleased.

As the plane took off, I suddenly heard the Rebbetzin's voice in my head saying, "Everyone has a question, everyone is seeking, just give them the opportunity to trust you and open up."

So I began a conversation with one of the women sitting a few seats from me, who turned out to be the leader of that group. And while we talked, I found myself judging her to be a superficial person and questioning the Rebbetzin's premise that everyone is searching and everyone wants to know the truth.

But as the time passed, our conversation grew deeper and suddenly she said to me, "You know, I'm curious about something. You're about to become a rabbi — you actually seem very young to be a rabbi — but maybe you can explain to me why so many of our youth are being drawn into the cults?"

I turned back to her and gave her the following answer:

"I believe that the answer to your question has to do with the fact that deep in their hearts everybody is seeking, deep in their hearts everybody has questions and that deep in their hearts everybody is searching for meaning in their lives."

The woman looked at me (the woman I had erroneously judged to be happily set in her ways and irreligious lifestyle) and said to me with the most genuine sincerity imaginable, "I'm looking, too, rabbi, I'm seeking, too."

And then we had this incredible conversation and I realized that the Rebbetzin was right. In retrospect, her guidance that day at the Plaza had a profound effect on me throughout my years as an educator and as someone who has been involved in outreach. And I also learned another important lesson at that meeting with the Rebbetzin — that there are no real techniques.

Stop searching for the perfect trick, she was telling us, and instead start being a genuine person who cares. This will allow you to create the kind of environment where people feel they can be open, explore, share, and genuinely ask their questions without feeling judged or that you have something to sell them.

At the end of the day the Rebbetzin taught me that it's not about technique. It's about being true and trustworthy.

It was a lesson Rabbi Aron would never forget.

And sometimes it was Rabbi Jungreis, aka "The Gentle Giant," who turned everything around — in one conversation.

When Rabbi Chanina Herzberg *z"l*, the *menahel* of Yeshiva of South Shore, was in a rehab center, his wife stayed with him for weeks on end. One day she got into a conversation with one of the security guards, who started telling her about his sister who was married to a rabbi.

"Really," she said to him, surprised, "who is your sister married to?"

"His name is Rabbi Nota Schiller."

Mrs. Herzberg was completely taken aback at that bit of news.

"Rabbi Schiller is your brother-in-law? He's a major rabbi!"

The security guard nodded.

"How did they come to get married?"

"It's like this. When my sister graduated high school she went around the city with my father looking into different colleges. While they were walking around the city, they ran into a rabbi and started talking to him.

" 'Where do you live?' he asked them.

" 'Lynbrook.'

" 'I live in North Woodmere,' the Rabbi told my father and sister. 'It's not too far from Lynbrook. Would you possibly be able to give me a ride back to the Island?'

" 'No problem.'

"So the Rabbi joined them in the car — and during that journey he managed to convince my sister to go to Stern College, where she became religious and eventually ended up marrying Rabbi Schiller."

There's no question that Rabbi Jungreis never knew the effect that he'd had on the girl whom he convinced to go to Stern. No doubt there are numerous people whose lives were touched and changed forever by his kindness and humility — and which remained unknown to him. To him that wasn't important. It was all about doing his part in the great mission assigned him by the One Above.

And it wasn't only Jews who felt that way. The Rabbi treated every person he came in contact with as a human being who deserved to be treated with genuine respect.

One afternoon during the *shivah* for Rav Meshulem, a woman entered the room where Chaya Sora and Slovie were sitting *shivah* with their mother. She was African-American and wore a nurse's uniform. The sisters looked at one another and back at the nurse, not recognizing her as one of the team who had taken care of their father, and were surprised to see her there.

The woman wound her way through all the people sitting in the room, until she was close enough to the mourners to talk to them. After introducing herself, she explained that she worked as a baby nurse in their part of Long Island.

"Families hire me by word of mouth," she explained. "One woman would have a baby and I'd work for her. Then when she learned that one of her friends was about to have a baby, she'd recommend me to her. That's the way it went, with me moving from one family to the next."

The woman was silent for a few seconds before continuing her story.

"I was sitting in the kitchen this morning at the home where I am currently employed when I heard them discussing the fact that Rabbi Jungreis passed away. When I heard the news, I asked my employers if I could have some time off to come and see you here. I have to tell you something about the Rabbi."

The Rebbetzin and her daughters leaned forward, instinctively understanding that this was going to be worth hearing.

"I was the baby nurse for many families who used to pray at the Rabbi's synagogue in North Woodmere," she said. "Every single time there was a bris at the synagogue, it would be my job to watch the baby, while the family and guests went off to the social hall for the party. And every single time, Rabbi Jungreis would come to where I was sitting, carrying a full plate of food for me and a cup of hot coffee."

She paused, swallowed hard and continued.

"The Rabbi would look at me and say, 'You are such a special lady — you have a holy job, you are taking care of a Jewish baby, a Jewish soul.'

"That's what he used to say to me.

"I want you to know that I was never treated like that by anyone else. For everyone else I was just the nurse sitting in the back room — there to do a job and nothing more. Nobody brought me food and when the party was over, I'd have to find something for myself. But not when the party was at Rabbi Jungreis' synagogue."

The nurse met their eyes and said, "I will never forget the Rabbi who thought that a baby nurse is a special person!"

So North Woodmere was blessed.

CHAPTER THIRTY-ONE
The Actress

The Rebbetzin first met Nechamah* at the Hineni Chanukah party. There were lots of people there. Many were religious, many not, and many would soon make major changes. That's the way it was at any Hineni event. Nechamah had a striking appearance and stood out from the rest of the crowd.

"I don't think we've met," the Rebbetzin said to her.

"We haven't."

There was tension in her voice.

"What's your name?"

"Nikki."

"Nikki?"

"My name is Nicole, but everyone calls me Nikki."

"And what is your Jewish name?"

"Nechamah," she replied, but the Rebbetzin could hear the sharpness in her tone.

"I love that name," she exclaimed, but Nikki cut her off.

"I'm happy that you love that name, but I don't! That's why I changed it to Nicole."

The Rebbetzin had met many people by that point in her life. Some of them had the ability to speak nicely, while others were so full of hurt that they couldn't bring themselves to speak with *derech eretz* (respect).

The Rebbetzin wasn't fazed by Nikki.

"If you knew the significance of your Jewish name, you wouldn't feel that way," she said with assurance.

"That's where you're wrong. I know the significance, I've heard it a hundred times, and it does nothing for me."

Nikki was proving something of a hard nut to crack.

"Maybe if you heard about your name for the hundred and first time, you'd like it better," the Rebbetzin joked. "Meanwhile tell me a little bit about yourself. What do you do?"

"I'm an actress."

"Where do you act? Broadway? TV, film?"

"I've had some parts in a few off-Broadway performances — but I'm still waiting for my big break."

The Rebbetzin at her desk in the Hineni Heritage Center

"While you're waiting, maybe you'll consider trying our Torah classes here at Hineni," the Rebbetzin suggested.

"I don't think so. Been there, done that."

"What are you talking about?"

"I was born into a religious home. I grew up frum. I went to a Jewish school."

Nikki told the Rebbetzin the name of her family. It was a well-known name and the Rebbetzin remembered hearing how one of their daughters was struggling with her faith.

"Do me a favor," she said to Nikki.

"What, Rebbetzin?"

"I know that you think you've heard it all and seen everything there is to see. But I would appreciate it if you would give it one more try and come study Torah with me."

Nikki wouldn't commit.

The Rebbetzin cupped the girl's face between both of her hands and drew her close.

"Do it as a favor to me," she said, gazing straight into Nikki's eyes.

Although she'd really given it her best shot, the Rebbetzin hadn't been expecting Nikki to show up, but there she was the following Thursday; and once she began attending the classes, she never stopped. It didn't take her long to develop a relationship with the Rebbetzin, and once she opened up, it was as if a faucet had been turned on and wouldn't close.

She confided in the Rebbetzin and told her the truth about her seemingly glamorous lifestyle. While she'd had a few parts on stage, it wasn't sufficient to pay her bills, and she had to supplement her stage income by waitressing in a restaurant.

"I don't want to get into the relationships, Rebbetzin — I'm sure you can figure out that I haven't met anyone worth dating. Anyone I had a relationship with left me scarred and hurt.

"The truth is" — she paused, and the Rebbetzin could see how difficult it was for Nikki to admit what she was about to say, "I made a huge mistake when I left my family. I was so stupid, so dumb for running away. The kids I went to school with are all married by now — most of them are mothers — while I'm just wasting my life doing nothing and running after empty dreams that keep on slipping away!

"I don't even understand what got into me! Why I left in the first place! But now it's too late. There's no going back, no turning back the clock. I guess I'll have to live my life knowing I made the worst mistakes a person can make."

The Rebbetzin listened to Nikki. And when she finished, she gave her a major "Rebbetzin Jungreis" look.

"Sweetheart (that word held a universe of depth), of course you can start over! Who told you otherwise? That's the miracle of life — a person can make mistakes, even bad mistakes, and climb up and out of the hole they've dug for themselves and change, and become a different, better person!"

"I wish it were that simple."

"It *is* exactly that simple," the Rebbetzin told the weeping girl, giving her a warm hug. "Hashem wants His children to return home. He has no interest in distancing them from Him. He wants them close by. The fact that you want to close the door on your past is all He wants from you. Let go of the past — take all the pain and suffering of the last few years and convert it all into living a more meaningful life."

Nikki cried.

"Do you remember the first conversation we had? I asked you if you know the significance of your name. Remember that?"

She nodded.

"Your name, Nechamah, means comfort. Live up to your name. Give comfort, give *nechamah* to others, and more than anything else — give comfort to yourself!"

"What should I do?"

"I'll give you an idea. Pesach is coming. In a few weeks, we will be sitting down at the Seder. Tell your parents that you are coming home for the Seder this year."

Nikki looked at the Rebbetzin and shook her head dejectedly.

"There's no way in the world I can ever tell them that!"

"Why not?"

"Why not? I'll tell you why not. My father doesn't want to talk to me. He knows the things I've done and the places I've been. Trust me, he does not want to see me walking through his front door."

Nothing the Rebbetzin said was able to convince Nechamah to call her parents, so the Rebbetzin picked up the phone and called them herself.

Nechamah's father answered the phone.

"Who is this?"

"This is Rebbetzin Esther Jungreis," she said. "Many people have told me about the *hachnassas orchim* (hosting guests) you and your wife do and I was wondering if you would be willing to help Hineni by taking some guests for the Pesach Seder?"

"I'll ask my wife, but it shouldn't be a problem. How many guests are we talking about?"

"One girl."

"That's fine. How old is she and what is her name?"

"She's twenty-five years old and her name is Nechamah."

The silence that came across the line was as powerful as an ocean wave.

"Is this some sort of joke?" the father asked when he was finally able to get himself under control.

"*Chas v'shalom,*" the Rebbetzin replied, "no joke. Your daughter has been attending my classes. She is not the same person you used to know. In fact, she's a completely new girl. She wants to come home for Pesach. At the same time she's afraid that you won't want her to come. She's afraid to call you."

The Rebbetzin could hear weeping at the other end of the line. The pain was palpable. This father missed his daughter intensely.

"This is the plan," the Rebbetzin said. "I would like for you and your wife to come to Hineni next week. When you arrive, go directly to my office and after the class, I will bring Nechamah to speak with you. You will see that everything will be okay."

The reunion was something to see.

Nechamah walked into the Rebbetzin's office the next week and, seeing her parents standing there, she turned ashen. For a moment the three of them just stood like pillars, like statues, staring at one another, unable to say a word, barely able to breathe.

Her mother started sobbing, and her father's eyes were wet with tears.

"Mommy, Tatty," she called out, and rushed into their arms.

That year Nechamah went home for the Seder.

The comfort was awesome, just like her name.

This chapter has been dedicated
in memory of my "Torah Mommy," Rebbetzin Esther Jungreis ע״ה
I am grateful that I knew to cherish
every moment with the Rebbetzin,
who was the role model of the woman I aspire to be.

Faygie Zakheim

Part 6
1980-1995

Very often in interviews with the media, I would be asked, "How do you do it? What's your formula? How do you influence people to become observant Jews?"

"I have a secret weapon," I would respond, "I bring them to Zeide."

Rebbetzin Esther Jungreis

Kevod HaRabbanit, Am Yisrael needs you and Eretz Yisrael needs you.

Prime Minister Menachem Begin

Rebbetzin Revivalist — The Rebbetzin seeks not to convert gentiles, but rather to bring fallen Jews back to a fundamentalist faith.

Newsweek

CHAPTER THIRTY-TWO
The Breakup Artist

*J*n the years that followed the incredible success of her initial speeches, the Rebbetzin returned to Eretz Yisrael numerous times. She stayed in the Plaza Hotel and relied on Rabbi Gellis to arrange speeches for her in as many army bases as possible.

Every time she arrived, she brought an array of special gifts for the soldiers with her. One time it was a thousand specially designed yarmulkes to be distributed to the soldiers of the IDF. In a fascinating twist, those yarmulkes were donated by the Satmar Rebbetzin (Rav Yoelish's wife) who had them manufactured for Hineni.

The Rebbetzin distributing yarmulkes with the Hineni emblem to Israeli soldiers

The Rebbetzin in conversation with Israeli soldiers proudly wearing their Hineni yarmulkes

In those years, the Rebbetzin, Barbara Janov and Rabbi Gellis were frequent visitors to the Israeli army bases in the Sinai Desert, before it was all returned in the American-brokered peace deal between Prime Minister Menachem Begin and the President of Egypt, Anwar Sadat. One particularly memorable trip took them beyond the Sinai and over the Suez Canal, to a place called Goshen. Rabbi Mordechai Halpern, a *talmid chacham* and a medical doctor, had established a yeshivah there — in the spirit of the yeshivah that had been established thousands of years earlier by the sons of Yaakov Avinu (our Patriarch Jacob).

Gellis remembers his conversation with the Chief Rabbi of Israel: telling him about the Rebbetzin, how she possessed a unique ability to stir people to repentance and how he should throw the formidable resources of his office behind her.

"Many people do teshuvah after hearing her speak," he told the Chief Rabbi. "I feel it's very important that you send her everywhere possible."

"She doesn't sing, right?"

"Not even a note. It's all talking."

That conversation led them to the most incredible places.

For that Sinai excursion, they took off in a helicopter from the Sde Dov Airport and landed in the north of the Sinai Desert about a kilometer from the Suez Canal. Down below, the sand shimmered beneath the sun, as it had for thousands of years. An army jeep met the helicopter and drove them to Goshen.

In an interesting turn of events, Rav Shlomo Wolbe (the legendary mashgiach) and Rabbi Avrohom Ravitz (he was a rebbi in Ohr Somayach prior to joining the Knesset) were visiting Goshen as well, also there to address the soldiers.

The three Torah personalities spoke.

It was absolutely fascinating, especially when you compared the difference in style between the way Rav Wolbe and the Rebbetzin answered the same question.

One of the soldiers had a question that was bothering him.

"*Kevod Harav*, why does a Jew need to wear a kippah on his head? Where does it say in the Torah that you need to cover your head?"

Rav Wolbe answered him without missing a beat: "If you want the food that you're cooking to turn out well, you cover the pot. A trash bin is left uncovered."

It was a brilliant response, and from the look on the soldier's face, Rav Wolbe's reply hit home.

When it was the Rebbetzin's turn to speak, she too addressed the kippah question. "First you need to understand why you need a head," she said to the questioner with a sincere smile. "Then you can move on to why you need to cover it. First understand who you are, and what makes you — you. You need to understand what you are fighting for and who you're fighting for! The moment you understand all that, you'll know what your head is all about. Then you'll have no problem understanding why you need a kippah."

Rav Wolbe had answered the question logically. It was a knockout answer.

Rebbetzin Jungreis answered the question emotionally — and knocked them out again. They had no chance. It was a two-pronged attack.

As in the United States, the Rebbetzin wanted to meet with the *gedolim* in Eretz Yisrael, to let them know what she was doing and to receive their berachos. Consequently, she requested that Reb Yisroel introduce her to as many *gedolim* as possible.

Rabbi Yisroel Gellis introduced her to the Admor of Sadigura, the Admor of Ozerov, the Admor of Bohush and to Rav Berel Povarsky, Rosh

Yeshivah of Ponovezh. But her meeting with the Admor of Sadigura was most poignant for Gellis. It happened to be that Rabbi Avraham Yosef (Munia) Shapira (legendary Knesset member for Agudas Yisroel, chairman of the finance committee and owner of Carmel Carpets) was at the meeting as well, as was his son Reb Yitzchok Shapira. Munia Shapira was a *mechutan* of the Sadigura Rebbe (one of his children was married to one of the Rebbe's) and was visiting at the Rebbe's home when they arrived. Of course, he remained for the meeting.

They began to converse and the Rebbetzin told the Admor (Rebbe) about her great-great-grandfather Rav Osher Anshil Jungreis — the Menuchas Osher — patriarch of Hungarian rabbanim, and about her family history and all her efforts in Eretz Yisrael. She also told the Rebbe about her experiences during the war as a child in Bergen-Belsen and the horrors she had witnessed.

In the middle of the conversation, the Admor of Sadigura put his head down on the dining room table and began to cry.

"By this point in time," Rabbi Gellis said, "I was already used to seeing the effect the Rebbetzin had on the people in the audiences at her speeches. I had seen it a hundred times. She possessed a unique ability to draw people in, to connect with them and to instill a desire within them to want to do teshuvah and return to Hashem. But to see the conversation between the Rebbetzin (who sat at the far end of the table) and the Admor of Sadigura was a different matter completely.

"As for Munia Shapira — he was a man who had seen it all, a man who had sat in on a thousand government meetings and dealt with hundreds of emergencies. On the surface, nothing got him excited. But when the Admor of Sadigura laid his head down on the table and began to cry, Munia Shapira lost control and had to find a handkerchief to wipe away the tears. The man who was always composed couldn't stop the tears."

Rabbi Gellis also set up meetings for her with many of the ministers in the Israeli government. She met with Pinchus Sapir, Yitzchok Shamir and Yigal Yadin, the legendary archaeologist. She would meet with Prime Minister Menachem Begin on a number of occasions. Every time these meetings would become extremely emotional. This made sense, considering that both Begin and the Rebbetzin were emotional people who were easily moved to tears and were not embarrassed to wear their feelings on their sleeves.

"I had actually met Menachem Begin years earlier," Reb Yisroel related.

"It was a different world back then in Israel. Much less official. Back then, come Monday morning, Prime Minister Begin used to go have a cup of coffee and a piece of apple strudel or cheesecake at the Gerlitz coffee shop in Geula. He'd be accompanied by his loyal secretary Yechiel Kadishai, and was accessible to anyone in the coffee shop who wanted to question him on matters of national policy. (How things have changed since those days!)

"One day I found myself enjoying a cup of coffee at Gerlitz when Begin walked in and sat down. I couldn't help myself and approached the prime minister, telling him that I had read his book, *HaMered* (*The Revolt*), and how it was extremely popular in the Chevron yeshivah.

" 'It's been read by so many *bachurim*,' I told him, 'that the pages are simply coming out of the binding.'

"Begin smiled at my depiction of his book's popularity.

"The next week we met again at Gerlitz. When he saw me, the prime minister showed me that he had brought a new copy with him to the coffee shop. He then removed a pen from his pocket and inscribed the book:

> *To the Ben Torah, Yisroel Gellis.*
> *Menachem Begin.*

"From then we had a connection.

"Now, whenever the Rebbetzin wanted to see the Prime Minister, I was able to set up a meeting for her at his office in Rechavia.

" 'I heard about you from many people,' he told her the first time they met. 'There's no question you are doing important work for Klal Yisrael. If you need government assistance of any kind, I will help you. It goes without saying that we will take you anywhere you want to go or visit.'

"He treated her with incredible *kavod*.

"The Rebbetzin responded by telling the Prime Minister about the Jungreis family — how there had been eighty-five rabbanim named Jungreis in Hungary before the war and how they were decimated in the ovens and gas chambers of Auschwitz.

"Both of them started to cry.

"She then related an incident involving her father, moving him even further. The conversation was conducted in Yiddish, which they both spoke fluently and were comfortable speaking. They met a number of times. There was a genuine connection between them, and true respect.

"But the truth is, everyone whom the Rebbetzin met was given the feeling that she loved them with her entire heart — just because they were Jews. She met people from across the entire spectrum of Judaism, and she loved them unconditionally — precisely because they were Jews and she considered them her brothers and sisters, no matter what.

"And whenever she talked about the Holocaust, she'd never call herself a survivor. No. Her father had taught her that they were not survivors — they were fighters, who had emerged victorious over the Holocaust and had lived to tell a tale of heroism and *Kiddush Hashem*."

Wherever she went, she showed the world what it meant to be a real rebbetzin — a rebbetzin with genuine halachic standards. She'd make sure to announce at the conclusion of her speech that she was happy to take questions and to meet with anyone in the crowd.

After every speech, the Rebbetzin made her way to the Kosel, gift-wrapping her speeches with spirituality. Sometimes she'd decide on the spur of the moment that she simply had to travel to Kever Rachel as well, to pour out her heart to Mama Rachel and to ask for *siyata d'Shmaya* at the final resting place of the woman who has been crying and praying for her children, for us, for thousands of years.

There she'd talk with Mama Rachel and tell her what she was doing,

The Rebbetzin with children in Chevron in front of the bus donated through Hineni

The Rebbetzin davening at Kever Rachel
before one of her speeches

The Rebbetzin with the armored bus
donated to residents of Chevron

and about the special connection she'd managed to forge with the soldiers and how there was a chance that many of them would find their way back to the Master of the World. It went without saying that she didn't allow a trip to pass without making sure to visit the Avos and Imahos (Patriarchs and Matriarchs) at the Me'aras HaMachpeilah in Chevron. She possessed this absolute connection with her ancestors and talked to them as if they were still alive and right beside her in the room. Seeing her daven was a unique experience.

The Rebbetzin's concern for the residents of Chevron was demonstrated in a very tangible way as well. Being fully aware of the dangerous situation in which they found themselves — particularly when traveling between Chevron and other parts of Eretz Yisrael — the Rebbetzin raised the funds through Hineni and donated a beautiful, modern armored bus to Chevron. The bus is still in use to this day, and has been greatly appreciated by the local community.

There were always surprises.

Rabbi Gellis would review her speeches after she wrote them, correcting the grammatical errors and making sure the tenses were accurate.

"Many times, I'd meet her at a speech and hand her the corrected pages. She'd thank me and say, 'I just arrived here from Kever Rachel and I feel a special sense of inspiration right now. I have to change the entire speech, right now!'

"Then she'd sit down and literally rewrite the entire speech on the spot."

Sometimes people were moved by her words beyond all expectation.

Once, in the midst of a speech in Tel Aviv, a young man stood up in the crowded room and announced that he had something to say. Seeing that he was in an extremely emotional state of mind, the Rebbetzin gave him the floor and waited to hear what he wanted to tell her.

"I have a non-Jewish girlfriend. She is here with me tonight. When I came here this evening I had no intention of changing my life in any way. But after listening to you speak, I realize that I no longer know what to do!"

The Rebbetzin listened to his every word. She was the ultimate Yiddishe Mama.

"You will come and see me after the speech," she told him, "and we will take care of this immediately."

And nobody sitting in the room had any doubt that the matter was going to be resolved in the best way possible.

After the speech was over, the Rebbetzin asked the non-Jewish girlfriend to wait outside the room. She then sat down with the Israeli boy, who waited to hear the magic words that would convince him to throw away his life and prospective wife.

But the Rebbetzin didn't say a word. Not a word.

Instead, she started to cry. She cried for a long time. Finally she spoke.

"I could understand if you were a Jewish boy living in America," she said to him at last. "If you lived in the States and went to a non-Jewish school it would make sense that you were dating a non-Jewish girl. But you live here — in Eretz Yisrael! How could it be?"

And once again she broke down in a torrent of bitter tears — crying with him as if she were his mother or grandmother. They sat together for three-quarters of an hour. When she finished "talking" to him, the boy rose from his place and walked out of the room. There he found the girl waiting for him. He said a few words to her and then they parted — breaking up on the spot!

Seeing her that night was to witness the Rebbetzin at her absolute best.

Through the years the Rebbetzin would become known as the address for those who had nowhere else to turn. A couple reached out to the Rebbetzin, asking her to meet their son, who was dating a non-Jewish girl.

"Bring him to my class," she told them, "and I will meet with him afterward."

In that particular case, the ex-*yeshivah bachur* arrived at Hineni to meet the Rebbetzin, girl in tow.

The Rebbetzin didn't bat an eyelash at his unorthodox behavior.

Turning to the girl, she said, "Sweetheart, I want you to understand something. Just like this boy is planning to abandon his religion to marry you, he's going to abandon you as well one day."

It goes without saying that the girl said goodbye to her "chassan" — who while at first very angry at the Rebbetzin for "ruining his life," eventually came around and realized that she had saved him with a few sharp and well-chosen words.

The Rebbetzin made shidduchim — many of them — but she was equally adamant in taking a strong stand against intermarriage as well. She would smile at a person and break his heart — to save his life.

CHAPTER THIRTY-THREE
The Marriage Counselor

After every class, numerous people waited on line to speak with the Rebbetzin.

One day an older single waited to speak with her at an event.

"Rebbetzin, I need some advice."

"My pleasure, *sheifelah*," the Rebbetzin told the woman. "Let's have a conversation in a quiet spot, while I gather my things and get ready to go home."

When they were in a spot where nobody would overhear their conversation, the Rebbetzin turned to the woman and asked her what was on her mind.

"I've been dating for years, but I feel as if I'm still not getting anywhere. I am still single after years of trying… I've gone out again and again, but it always boils down to nothing in the end."

The Rebbetzin thoughtfully studied the woman sitting beside her.

"Can you handle me being blunt?" she asked.

"Tell me whatever you feel I need to hear."

"I will be happy to do that. I want to tell you something and I want you to listen carefully."

The woman nodded.

"You need to change!"

"What do you mean?"

"I'll tell you exactly what I mean. I am known to tell things as they are. If girls need to improve their makeup, I tell them to go for a makeover.

If they have bad breath, I tell them to make sure to brush their teeth and suck on a mint. If they don't know how to dress, I tell them that they need to ask advice from someone who does and then buy a new wardrobe. So now I'm going to tell you something — you need to change."

"I don't understand," the woman said. "I try very hard to take really good care of myself. I dress well. I know how to put on makeup. What change are you referring to?"

"I am referring to something other than looks. It's your attitude that needs changing."

"My attitude? Why do you say that? What's wrong with my attitude?"

"You are giving off an extremely tough vibe."

"I don't understand."

"I'll give you an example. The entire time I've been speaking with you, you sat there with your arms folded. I know people, and I am telling you that you need to soften up. You're giving off a tough attitude and it's not good for dating or marriage."

"But that's how I sit!"

"*Sheifelah*, I'm telling you that I've been a Rebbetzin for many, many years. I see things. If you are willing to be honest with yourself, you will know what I'm talking about."

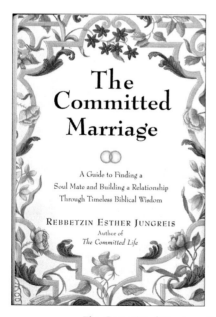 

The Committed Marriage, English and Spanish editions

The woman went home after her conversation with the Rebbetzin. She closed the door of her apartment and sat by herself for a long time. She might have even cried a little because she realized that the Rebbetzin was right.

She was tough. Too tough.

The truth was, she had been dating a sweet and wonderful guy for a while. And she had ruined it. Just that week, just a few days before she'd met the Rebbetzin, she broke off the shidduch.

Sitting across from him, she'd said, "Look, it's not going to work out between us. You're great, but you're just too nice. I can't relate to such a super nice guy."

Now she sat at home after having been fed the truth and asked herself, "What on earth were you thinking?"

That night was her moment for soul-searching. Eventually she called the man she'd broken up with and asked him if he wanted to try again.

It's been ten years now, and they're still happily married. They have adorable kids and her husband is the best a girl could ask for. But this would never had happened were it not for the fact that the Rebbetzin came along and woke her up. Telling her in no uncertain terms that she needed to change her attitude was the best advice she ever got.

The Rebbetzin saved numerous marriages with her wisdom and wise words. She was able to change complex marital situations with a few words — relationships that everyone else (including the people themselves) considered beyond salvation.

A young woman came to see the Rebbetzin. She had been married for a few years and had two children, but she wanted out of the relationship. The reason was simple. Before their marriage, her husband, then a *yeshivah bachur*, had been on a hike and fallen off a cliff, landing on his head. The fall had caused him to experience seizures from time to time — medical information he hadn't shared with his future wife. The young couple had been married for a year when the husband had a seizure in front of his wife. Understandably, she was shocked and dismayed by the news that her husband had a medical condition, and was especially upset by the fact that he hadn't seen fit to share the information with her.

The first seizure was followed by others. The seizures were unexpected and the young wife felt like she was living her life on a knife's edge — and she had no interest in being married to someone like that. Many people tried talking to her and convince her not to throw her life away, but she wasn't swayed by any of their arguments.

And then someone suggested that she go to talk to the Rebbetzin.

She was told that she had to attend the Rebbetzin's *shiur* before they could have a conversation. (Torah learning equaled clarity and a much better chance of being willing to accept good advice.) So she took the train to the Hineni Center in Manhattan, and listened to a *shiur*, after which she was given an appointment with Rebbetzin Jungreis.

Sitting at the semi-circular desk in the Rebbetzin's office on the fourth floor of the Hineni brownstone, the young woman looked around the comfortable room: at the pictures of the Rebbetzin meeting with famous people, and the special portrait of the Jungreis Zeides displayed in a place of honor, looking down at every visitor from just above the Rebbetzin's head.

"What's on your mind?" she asked her visitor, offering her some candies and a drink.

"I want to get divorced."

The semi-circular desk in the Rebbetzin's office in the Hineni Heritage Center, at which she met with countless people into the very late hours of the night

"Why do you want to get divorced?"

"Because I was tricked into getting married in the first place. I was tricked. Duped. Nobody told me I was getting a defective husband — someone who would fall down and start to shake without any warning."

She talked for a long time, and the Rebbetzin listened without passing judgment. Finally she ran out of steam.

"I'm trying to understand something," the Rebbetzin said at last. "Why did you marry your husband? What's wrong with you that you agreed to marry such a person?"

"I didn't agree," she protested. "I was tricked. I would have never married a person like that. I have no interest in living such a life! It's not for me!"

"But how could you have failed to miss all the problems you're describing?"

"There was no way for me to know. The seizures are in his head — how could I have guessed?"

"I want to ask you something," the Rebbetzin said to the distraught woman. "Is your husband kind? Does he have good character? Is he a good person?"

"Yes," the woman replied.

"Remember the reasons you married him in the first place. Remember his good qualities that impressed you. I know a lot of people who are divorced. Unfortunately, at times there is no other option. Of course, every situation is different. But many times, divorce just leads to loneliness. Worse than that, the children suffer beyond all comprehension. You feel as if you picked a lemon. Make yourself a cup of sweet lemonade. People have been known to enjoy lemonade."

Somehow the Rebbetzin's words succeeded in penetrating the wall she had erected and she decided to remain with her husband — and to make the most delicious lemonade in the world. Her husband changed his doctor soon afterward. The new doctor prescribed new medication. It wasn't long before he stopped having seizures.

Many years have passed since that conversation with the Rebbetzin in her warm and cozy office on the fourth floor of Hineni. Many years filled with hundreds of cool glasses of sweet and tangy lemonade. The couple was blessed with a beautiful and large family: their girls goodhearted and kind, their sons exceptional *bnei Torah* — *talmidei chachamim* and wonderful people.

Seven children were born to them after that conversation. Children who would have never entered this world were it not for the Rebbetzin's simple sweet lemonade advice.

Can anyone deny that they are Rebbetzin Jungreis' grandchildren? Not biological, perhaps — but grandchildren in every other way.

One Thursday a surprise awaited the Rebbetzin at her evening class. There in the audience she caught sight of a mother and daughter, as different from one another as was possible. The mother was dressed in chassidic attire from head to toe. The daughter wore clothing too, but hers was an entirely different look. They waited until very late that night to meet with the Rebbetzin. When they were finally seated in the Rebbetzin's office, Rebbetzin Jungreis greeted the pair warmly and offered them some cookies and drinks.

After a few sips of water, the mother said somewhat urgently, "Rebbetzin, we need your help!"

"What's the matter?"

"The matter is that my daughter is a kallah — a kallah whose wedding was scheduled for a few weeks from now. But my daughter changed her mind. She doesn't want to marry her chassan anymore. Worse, she doesn't want to be frum any longer!"

"What does she want to do?"

"She wants to become a model."

The words hung there in the silence of the fourth-floor office.

She wants to become a model. She wants to become a model.

The Rebbetzin turned to the girl.

"First of all," she said to her, "you must not hurt your poor chassan. He didn't do anything to you and doesn't deserve to suffer the pain of a life with a wife who is trying to figure herself out. Break off the engagement immediately. In your current situation there is no way for you to be the kind of wife a young religious man needs. It will be better for all concerned if you break it off now before everyone involved really gets hurt."

"Should we do it tonight?" the mother asked.

"No," said the Rebbetzin, shaking her head. "No. It's Thursday night. Don't spoil his Shabbos. Wait until after Shabbos and do it then."

The Rebbetzin was silent for a few seconds, staring at the kallah, a look of kindness in her eyes.

"*Sheifelah*, about becoming a model…"

The girl's head lifted and she met the Rebbetzin's gaze.

"It's the absolute worst thing you can do for yourself. You have no idea what you are getting into!"

"I just want to model my face!"

But the Rebbetzin wouldn't budge from her stance, repeatedly insisting that no matter how she played it, living the lifestyle of a model was the worst thing a Jewish girl could do to herself!

The Rebbetzin backed her argument with examples and stories and explained exactly how and why she had developed her opinion.

"But I don't want to do anything else!"

The Rebbetzin thought about that for a second.

"You know something," she said, "I want you to come and work for me."

The girl considered the offer for a few seconds. Then she broke into a smile and agreed.

The would-be model went to work for Rebbetzin Jungreis. It wasn't long before she had become a settled person — the kind of person people like and with whom they connect, the kind of person who can be relied upon.

Rav Meshulem had one brother, Rav Amrom, who survived the war. His son, Rav Osher Anshil, married Blimi Meisels, the daughter of the Liezher Rav of London. On one occasion, Blimi hosted the Rebbetzin for a round of speeches. Needless to say, her schedule was completely filled and she barely had a second to breathe. One of her engagements was at the home of Lord Chief Rabbi Immanuel Jacobovits, whose wife, Lady Amelie, was hosting a private by-invitation-only luncheon for tzedakah.

Not long before it was scheduled to begin, Rebbetzin Blimi, who had been invited to serve as MC and introduce her aunt, received a phone call from a member of the community who asked her if she could arrange for her aunt to meet with a young girl.

"Who is the girl?"

"It's the daughter of Mr. Blumenthal*."

Paul Blumenthal had been a prominent member of the community. A man known far and wide for always being ready to help anyone in need, he had passed away unexpectedly and his family was having a difficult time assimilating the fact that they were suddenly fatherless. It was difficult for all the children, but for Shira Blumenthal it was hardest of all.

She had been in the process of going out with a fine young man when the tragedy occurred; having been incredibly traumatized by the loss of her father, she was finding herself unable to commit to getting engaged.

"She needs to meet with the Rebbetzin. Nobody else has been able to get through to her!"

Rebbetzin Blimi Jungreis called Barbara Janov to ask her if it was possible to squeeze Shira in. Barbara studied the Rebbetzin's calendar and informed her that it was totally booked. But when the Rebbetzin heard about the situation she told Blimi to give the Blumenthals the okay.

"Tell her I will see her whenever she arrives."

Shira knocked on the door in the middle of the luncheon. She was so frightened and nervous — a teenager entering one of the most prestigious homes in London, all compounded by the loss of her father.

The Rebbetzin left the dining room in the middle of the luncheon and went to the hallway to meet her visitor. The girl cried and the Rebbetzin cried — both standing and crying together. To this day, Blimi Jungreis doesn't know what her aunt said to Shira Blumenthal to put a smile on her face, but five minutes after they'd met, the girl had the happiest expression on her face. She left the home of the Chief Rabbi and went back to her house, where, a few hours later, she got engaged.

CHAPTER THIRTY-FOUR
The Lebanese Purim Party

*T*he Rebbetzin wasn't the kind of person who just went off and did her own thing. No. Whatever she did became a family affair. Which was why she always wanted her children along if it were at all possible. This way they would be able to learn from her firsthand how to do what she did.

Which explains how Slovie Jungreis ended up joining her mother on a tour of the IDF outposts in Lebanon circa 1982. After it had been decided that she was setting off on what would prove to be an incredible (and somewhat dangerous) experience, the Rebbetzin had a question for her daughter.

"Do you want to come with me to Lebanon, *sheifelah*?"

The teenage Slovie nodded her head.

It was summertime. War was raging and the Rebbetzin was embarking on yet another journey to give *chizuk* to the soldiers.

From Ben Gurion Airport, the Rebbetzin's entourage was driven to an army base, where they were assigned a jeep and soldiers to accompany them on the unique mission to war-torn Lebanon via the rubble-strewn streets of Beirut — a city that had once been called the Paris of the Middle East, but was now a shell of its former self. Beirut itself was mired in traffic and the soldiers stayed on the perimeter roads outside the city, driving their esteemed visitors from outpost to outpost on

The Rebbetzin at the Beaufort Castle in Lebanon shortly after the 1982 war

mountainous, twisting roads overlooking the sea of honking cars and trucks in the city below. You should have seen the soldiers' faces when their jeep pulled up in front of their tents and the Rebbetzin emerged. There wasn't a lot of time — there were many army outposts to visit — and the Rebbetzin would have them gather round for a few words from the heart.

"*Hincha Yehudi* — You are a Jew, and Hashem is with you," she'd declare. "You must never give up the fight!"

Almost immediately the soldiers' eyes would gleam and some of them would find themselves surreptitiously wiping away a tear, while others couldn't help themselves and broke down. By the time she finished speaking, every single soldier felt that he was fighting a war for his people and that his mission was the most important and vital assignment ever given to the Jewish nation. The Rebbetzin would finish with berachos galore for every soldier.

It was almost as if the entire scene was a mirage that had appeared out of nowhere — and they couldn't help rubbing their eyes as they tried to figure out if the whole thing was a dream. No doubt the dream theory was reinforced by the cameramen who had been assigned to film the entire trip, recording every stop along the way for posterity.

Israeli policeman reading a copy of *The Committed Life*

They traveled from outpost to outpost; along rocky mountain roads filled with refugees, along with donkeys and camels and a hundred little Arab boys who perched on their backs and prodded their transportation with the sharp end of the stick and an occasional yell. They were taken to visit the Beaufort Castle, a former PLO stronghold. It had been captured by the IDF, who showed the Rebbetzin and her daughter the terrorists' previously unobstructed view of a large portion of Israel from the castle turrets. Way down below the mountains were brown tents amid sun-baked grass and a jumble of stones. Even further down, one could see the houses spread out across the valley — an endless array of the homes of rich, poor and those in between. The Rebbetzin and her party visited the majority of the outposts, giving *chizuk* at every stop along the way.

The Rebbetzin distributing the Hebrew edition of *The Committed Life* to Israeli soldiers

Distributing the Hebrew edition of *The Committed Life* to Israeli soldiers

On the way down from the north toward Yerushalayim, the Rebbetzin visited the bases of every major division of the IDF, from the air force to the paratroopers to the navy. She spoke to the soldiers — hundreds of them — sitting before her in row after row on the benches of the base's amphitheaters. She used a microphone, her voice amplified so that

The Rebbetzin bringing *chizuk* to Israeli soldiers

every last soldier could hear her words — words of Torah and *kedushah* — words that had rarely been spoken in their bases before.

They drove along the winding roads lined by tall trees and lush bushes, and the Rebbetzin looked out the window and couldn't stop smiling because she was back in the country she loved so.

The Rebbetzin gave a lot of thought to the religious needs of the soldiers. And because she loved Eretz Yisrael to such a degree, she wanted to do something for her husband's memory that had to do with the Holy Land. One day she informed Rabbi Gellis that she was sending six Sifrei Torah from America — all being donated for the soldiers in memory of her husband Rav Meshulem Jungreis.

All eyes were upon the Rebbetzin's son-in-law, Rabbi Shlomo Gertzulin, as he made his way through security at JFK carrying one of the Sifrei Torah in his arms. It was prior to 9/11, so it was still possible to carry the Sefer Torah directly to the plane. As they walked up the staircase, they were met by the El Al pilot who informed Rabbi Shlomo that he insisted on having the Sefer Torah with him, in the cockpit, for the duration of the flight.

"I want it with me for added protection," he explained.

The Sifrei Torah arrived at Rabbi Gellis' house a few days later, and he arranged for them to be delivered to the office of the Chief Rabbi of the IDF for a special procession to the south. But there was something unique about the Torah scrolls the Rebbetzin had sent, because the donor was not only donating Torah scrolls — but also "shuls on wheels" as well! The concept was simple but extremely vital.

The army units are transported where they need to go and are then followed by the logistics unit who work quickly to set up a kitchen and shul. With the arrival of the Hineni mobile shuls, the soldiers wouldn't have to wait until a "field" beit

Israel Army Chaplaincy Corps welcoming new Sifrei Torah donated by Hineni

Delivery of a Hineni mobile shul
to an army base in the South

The Rebbetzin dedicating
a Hineni mobile shul
to Army Chaplaincy Corps

Memorial plaque in
memory of Rav Meshulem
inside a Hineni mobile shul

Sifrei Torah donated by Hineni
supporters to the mobile shuls

Joyously celebrating the
dedication of Sifrei Torah
to the Israeli Army

Interior of a mobile shul donated by Hineni
to the Israeli Army

haknesset was operational, because they would already have a shul to use!

A shul-bus.

The Rebbetzin had the "shuls-on-wheels" constructed in America with a lot of thought and consideration to every detail. The shuls were very much in the tradition of the trademark beauty and grace of everything done by Hineni. Entering the shul-bus one saw a *bimah*, benches for seating, and a large assortment of *sefarim* as befitted a shul… And while the donor had underwritten the project, it was the Rebbetzin who was involved in the design and didn't rest until they had been turned into the most beautiful mobile shuls imaginable.

There were six Sifrei Torah and three mobile shuls.

The Sifrei Torah and the mobile shuls were moved to an army base near Ramle, and the parade set out with soldiers, the Sifrei Torah in their arms, dancing around the shuls — which drove slowly — the soldiers singing and dancing as they were transported down the highway. And then the three mobile shuls split up — each one driving off in a different direction — each shul assigned to another section of the country: north, south and the central region. The mobile shul unit even had its own commanding officer, whose responsibility it was to make sure that the shuls were sent to wherever they were most needed at the time. That hachnassas Sifrei Torah dedication event was a true highlight for everyone involved, and the mobile shuls were used by the army for years to come.

That wasn't the only Hineni vehicle. At one point the Rebbetzin designed a custom-made Hineni van that was used to drive to college campuses. The sides were painted with gigantic murals of Kabbalas HaTorah (receiving of the Torah) on Mount Sinai, and the van was equipped with a state-of-the-art sound system capable of playing music or providing amplification for an impromptu speech. That van gave a whole new meaning to the concept of "college kiruv."

Slovie was at Camp Chedva in the late '70s, and she will never forget the camp director letting her know, with a smile on his face, that "your mother is here."

It wasn't visiting day, but you could hear the music playing from across the grounds. The Rebbetzin stepped out of the van and the entire camp surrounded her as if she were the biggest star in the world (which in a sense she was).

Slovie drove with her mother to Florida in that van, making stops at many college campuses along the way.

"The Rebbetzin is here," would come the announcement over the van's loudspeaker, and she would step out of the van, stand on the attached stage, and deliver an off-the-cuff speech to the crowd of students who'd inevitably gather to listen to the awesome Rebbetzin from New York.

On another occasion the Rebbetzin decided that she wanted to visit an army base located in the middle of a battle zone in Lebanon.

"Reb Yisroel," the Rebbetzin said, "there are a lot of troops stationed in Lebanon and we have to go there to encourage them!"

Arranging the trip was no problem — he had the necessary connections. The issue was something else entirely. It was the Fast of Esther, and Rabbi Gellis wasn't sure it was the best idea in the world to travel for half a day into the middle of a battle zone on a fast day.

"Rebbetzin," he tried to protest, "it's a fast day today! Not such a great day to go for a long, long drive up north!"

"We're going."

There was no stopping the Rebbetzin — or Barbara Janov, for that matter. Once their minds were made up about something, it was as good as done.

Off they went. They drove in a car from Yerushalayim to Rosh Hanikra. At Rosh Hanikra, an army vehicle was waiting to drive them across the border into Lebanon. They arrived in Sidon. Evening was fast approaching as they drove into the army base.

"Rebbetzin," Reb Yisroel said, "it's Purim night. We have to hear the *Megillah*!"

The army base in Sidon was located very close to the *kever* of Yissachar and Zevulun, sons of Yaakov Avinu.

Gellis got on the driver's two-way radio and asked, "Is there anyone on the base who has a *Megillas Esther*?"

"I have one," someone replied. "Where are you?"

"Next to the *kever* of Yissachar and Zevulun."

"I'll be there in half an hour."

Twenty-five minutes later the soldier arrived with his *Megillah*. But he didn't come by himself. He was accompanied by a large group of soldiers.

The Hineni van – Always on the go!!

At the port on the way to Israel

Neither snow nor rain...
stops the Hineni van

The Rebbetzin
and Barbara

Reaching out on a college campus

Reaching out to Jews in Eretz Yisrael

At rallies for Israel in Washington

At rallies for Israel in Washington

The Hineni van at a rally at City Hall

The Rebbetzin speaking up for Am Yisrael. Standing alongside the Rebbetzin is Rav Meshulem, always supportive of the Rebbetzin's accomplishments.

The Rebbetzin with Israeli soldiers on the Lebanese border

Having heard on the radio that someone was reading the *Megillah*, they had come to take advantage and fulfill their Purim obligations.

Fifteen minutes later, Rabbi Yisroel Gellis *leined* the *Megillah* on the roof of Kever Yissachar and Zevulun. The Rebbetzin listened from downstairs with Barbara, who documented the entire event with pictures from every angle. When the *leining* was over, the Rebbetzin climbed onto the roof and delivered a speech that hit every soul right where it counts.

You could have heard the whisper of the wind as she broke down sobbing in the middle of Lebanon.

She talked about what it meant for a person to risk his life for Klal Yisrael, and she compared what they were doing on a daily basis to the self-sacrifice Mordechai and Esther had exhibited in the royal palace in Shushan thousands of years earlier.

She was on fire that night!

And the soldiers sat there and were galvanized by her words and message. It was as if they really understood for the first time what they were fighting for. It was an absolutely fantastic night and the perfect way to segue into Purim.

On a different trip, they were driving back to Jerusalem on Highway 90 when shooting started from the Jordanian side of the border. Of course, the second the terrorists started shooting from Jordan, the Israelis responded with gunfire of their own from the Israeli side of the border. In Reb Yisroel's mind there was no choice but to stop the jeep, get out, and look for shelter until the shooting stopped.

The Rebbetzin felt otherwise.

"Keep on driving," she instructed the driver. "Hashem is with us and there's no reason to be afraid!"

He tried to reason with her.

"Rebbetzin, this is a war zone. Both sides are shooting at one another. You can see the tracers flying through the air above our heads!"

The Rebbetzin remained unperturbed.

"Keep on driving," she told the driver, and that's the way it went for the next forty kilometers.

There was no question in her mind that they were driving with Hashem. There was no reason to stop. Not for bullets and not for terrorists. She might have been a very small person physically, but she possessed the courage of a lioness determined to protect her young. And so they rode through the night, the Rebbetzin holding on to the merits of her holy ancestors — the Zeides and the Bubbas — serene and secure in the knowledge that she was stepping in the footsteps of her father and grandfather, exactly as the Zeide had davened and cried for when she was just a girl of five in the Hungarian village her grandparents called home.

CHAPTER THIRTY-FIVE
My Rebbi the Rebbetzin

*J*ennifer Gross relates:

My husband and I were honored at one of the Hineni dinners. Since we were the honorees that evening, many of my friends were in attendance, and I had gone on and on about the Rebbetzin's incredible speaking abilities and how they were about to hear the speech of their lives.

I was somewhat taken aback, however, when the Rebbetzin rose and took her place at the podium. Because for whatever reason, her speech that night was about the rooster and its greatness! At that point in time, I was still not familiar with the blessing we say in morning prayers — "*Asher nasan lasechvi vinah,* Who gives understanding to the rooster" — and I couldn't fathom why the Rebbetzin had chosen this topic as the theme of her speech.

"It is very important to be like a rooster," she said, in her charismatic way, as my friends stared at her blankly, not comprehending why it was so important to be like a rooster, of all things.

The Rebbetzin went on.

"The rooster knows that he has to wake up every morning to crow like he's supposed to. You will never see the rooster waking up and asking himself, 'Am I too tired to crow right now?' He'll never say, 'You know something, I'm just not in the mood to crow today!'

"The rooster does what the rooster is supposed to do, and that's how a Jew is supposed to live his life!

"You don't wake up and say, 'I'm not in the mood to keep kosher' — we keep kosher! We don't wake up and question the Sabbath or all the other things we do that make us different from everybody else!"

Not being familiar with the blessing she was referring to, I was confused and found myself asking, "What's with the rooster? I don't understand why the Rebbetzin is making such a big deal about roosters!"

It was pretty ironic: I was being honored at the dinner, yet had no real idea of what the Rebbetzin was talking about!

But the speech was the speech.

When I finally learned the blessing of the rooster, I suddenly realized what an important message the Rebbetzin had delivered at the dinner — a message I had missed at the time, and only grasped later on — that Jews have to be the best roosters they can possibly be, every single day of their lives!

In my mind, the Rebbetzin's speech at the dinner ended up ranking among the most important lessons I ever learned! We are Jews, and as Jews, we need to be the best roosters in the world! When I recite the morning blessings these days, I remember the Rebbetzin and how there are no excuses. Basically, I remember the lesson of the rooster and how it changed my life.

Sheila Lambert had her son circumcised in the hospital shortly after he was born. There was no official ceremony, no *mohel* with doctor's bag, no bagels and lox afterward. She never really gave it much thought until one day when the Rebbetzin began teaching her class about our father Abraham being commanded by G-d to undergo circumcision. She remembers sitting in the class and thinking, "Oh, my goodness, what have I done?"

By that time, her son was already twelve years old, no simple age to consider a revision on a bris milah done in the hospital at the time of birth.

After the class Sheila approached the Rebbetzin and asked her how to rectify the situation.

"You will do something called *hatafas dam bris*," the Rebbetzin explained, "which entails using a *mohel*, but is not a major procedure."

Rabbi Yisroel Jungreis arranged "Bris take two." There was a *mohel*, Sheila's son was given an official Jewish name — and Sheila knew that she'd been given an opportunity to fix history.

She also knew that the only reason the entire story had played out the way it did was because she was a friend and student of the Rebbetzin — and the Rebbetzin never ceased teaching her people the truth about life.

Stephanie Mark recalls:

> One of the important lessons that the Rebbetzin taught us is that Hashem gives us all a mission. She called me once to relay how proud she was of my husband and myself for the Torah path we had taken. When I expressed concern that we did not live in a neighborhood where it was easy to be observant, the Rebbetzin taught me that where I was living was not a coincidence. The Rebbetzin explained that if we were to live in a more observant neighborhood, we would merely be one of many families living there as observant Jews, but by opening our home for Torah in a neighborhood that needed spirituality, we were making a much bigger impact on the Jewish people. The Rebbetzin reminded me that Hashem has a plan for each one of us. Although it would not always be easy, we were fulfilling a huge responsibility — "Making Lemonade Out of Lemons" — and it would always give us the merit to be a part of her family. From that moment on, she referred to herself as my bubby. My children to this day say that Rebbetzin Jungreis was their bubby.

The Rebbetzin had a lot of great lines. She used to say to Cheryl Minikes, a long-time Hineni student: "Torah isn't a history lesson," referring to the fact that what she was teaching them was meant to be taken as a practical guide book and not merely as a cultural or historical book of wisdom.

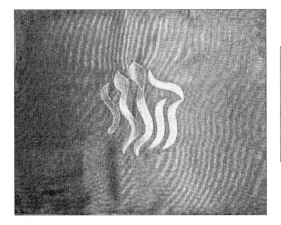

Challah cover created by Lilly Mark (daughter of Stephanie and Ira) and distributed to Hineni families with an inscription on the reverse side in memory of the Rebbetzin

Some of the many tefillah (prayer) cards widely distributed by Hineni

Chapter Thirty-Five: My Rebbi the Rebbetzin ☐ 369

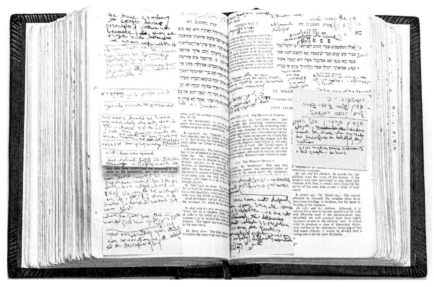

The Rebbetzin's Chumash — every word a Torah lesson

When they met, the Rebbetzin would say, "Okay, what mitzvah are we taking on now?"

"She was always challenging me," Cheryl admitted, "because I didn't pray enough.

"She would ask me, 'Don't you realize that G-d wants to hear from you! When are you going to talk to Him?'

"That was the kind of relationship we had. My husband and I were some of her earliest supporters — she was always trying to help us grow — and we were very close.

"Once a month we hosted a Torah class in our house for couples who had never studied before," Michael Minikes added. "I used to sit at the table and look at her Chumash and laugh because it was so old and filled with so many notes that it was falling apart — and inevitably we wouldn't get past the first line because she was so deep and ended up giving a full class on a few words.

"I used to say to her jokingly, 'You don't know how it ends, do you? You have no idea how this *parashah* ends, do you, Rebbetzin?'

"But all joking aside, her classes were incredibly profound and they helped us grow — maybe not at the rate she would have wanted, but by constantly taking small steps in the right direction."

Dr. Richard Seaman practices dentistry in Cambria Heights, New York. But he also has another passion — Jewish music. So much so that he has become known through countless YouTube musical videos as Dr. Music Tooth.

Richard was introduced to the Rebbetzin through his mother, Mrs. Ina Seaman, who had been attending the Rebbetzin's classes for many years.

Dr. Seaman relates:

> Knowing that I have a passion for singing and composing, the Rebbetzin gave me a blessing and encouraged me to write meaningful Jewish-themed songs that will bring joy to those who hear them. I truly believe that that blessing lit a fire in my soul to begin composing songs, with lyrics about Shabbos, the holidays and finding one's way back to Hashem.
>
> Being asked to sing at Hineni gatherings what the Rebbetzin referred to as "The Shabbos Song" — lyrics I wrote to Paul Simon's classic "Sounds of Silence," renamed "Sounds of Shabbos" — was always a humbling experience. I knew it was the blessing from the Rebbetzin that inspired and enabled me to write those lyrics and many others.
>
> More than anything else, the Rebbetzin was the most sincere, "real" person I knew. She gave 100% of herself 100% of the time. It is said that "words that issue from the heart enter the heart" — the Rebbetzin's words always came from the heart, and they are alive today within the hearts of those who were privileged to hear them; whether in person or through her books, recordings or videos.
>
> The Rebbetzin's boundless energy and insatiable desire to help bring every Jew of every background in every corner of the world back to their roots through Torah study was remarkable.
>
> Personally, the Rebbetzin changed my life without exerting pressure or offering enticements, but simply by setting the best example

The Hineni logo — designed by a student and admirer of the Rebbetzin

— together with her children Chaya Sora, Rabbi Yisroel, Slovie and Rabbi Osher — of the beauty of living a committed Torah-based life.

There was a majesty to the Rebbetzin, an uplifting energy, a light that shone so bright and continues to illuminate our minds and bring nourishment to our souls to this very day and will continue as long as we heed her call, lovingly share the messages and continue to "turn the pages."

Shmuel (Marc) Levine remembers:

Prior to our beloved Rebbetzin awakening my *neshamah*, I was just a Jewish guy. Thanks to her, now I am a real Jew — a Yid! My respect, appreciation and gratitude for the Rebbetzin are boundless, forever. In the course of teaching me how to live a Torah life, the Rebbetzin would say: "We are *mishpachah*. I am your bubby and you are my *einikel* (grandchild)." And during her last few months with us, she continued to inspire and guide me to Hashem. And then, and I can't explain how, the Rebbetzin made sure that my Torah studies would continue with her beloved son Rabbi Osher. *Baruch Hashem!*

Kaila* recalls:

So much is known about the power of prayer. The Rebbetzin always taught us that sincere prayer heals. It creates a special bond between the person praying and Hashem. It can reverse even the most difficult and painful decree.

Several years ago, I had a thorough medical workup and based on multiple MRIs, I was diagnosed with cancer and was scheduled for surgery. I saw what appeared to be cancer illustrated on the scans. I had been in constant contact with the Rebbetzin, who gave me continuous support and many, many berachos.

A few days before the scheduled surgery, the Rebbetzin called and asked me to come to Hineni so that she could give me a berachah "in person" after the *shiur*. After receiving the berachah, the Rebbetzin asked me and my husband to daven in front of the *aron kodesh* that contained several Sifrei Torah, including one that had been returned to the family after the Holocaust. The Torah belonged to her great-grandfather, Rav Osher Anshil Jungreis, the Menuchas Osher, who was well known in his time as the "Miracle Rabbi."

The Rebbetzin saw my husband and me davening and pouring out our hearts to Hashem. The Rebbetzin had not long before had hip surgery, and although it was difficult for her to ascend the steps onto the *bimah*, she joined us at the *aron kodesh* and davened for us as well.

I didn't know why, but after we completed our tefillos, I felt very different.

The next day, we received a call from the hospital where the surgery was scheduled. It was a major cancer hospital in New York City. They told us that we needed to come right in and retake the MRI. The new MRI showed that what appeared to be cancer was no longer there. While the doctors at the hospital could not explain or understand what happened, the Rebbetzin said that it was perfectly clear to her that it was an open miracle from Hashem.

It was not just us. The Rebbetzin was always there for anyone who sought her guidance, her comfort, her berachos, and her davening. There was something special about the Rebbetzin's davening that just pierced through the heavens and brought so much good to so many people. We will forever be grateful to the Rebbetzin for caring for us just as she would for her own children.

Nechama Farber relates:

I was originally from Poland. At some point Rabbi Michael Schudrich (my rabbi in Poland) sent me to study at a seminary called Midreshet Rachel in Yerushalayim. As time went on, more and more people began asking me if I was interested in finding a shidduch and getting married.

My standard response was, "I'm not ready." But the truth was, of course I was ready, I just didn't want to have to deal with the whole shidduch process.

Not long afterward one of the girls in the seminary became a kallah and invited me to her wedding. Having been blessed with artistic skills, I drew her a beautiful card filled with blessings for the future.

At the wedding a friend of mine happened to mention that one of the guests was a Rebbetzin visiting from New York.

"She's a big Rebbetzin, a real holy woman! She can give you a berachah!"

In need of all the berachos I could get, I replied, "Let's go over to her."

We approached the Rebbetzin. She gave me a knowing look and her first words to me were, "Are you ready for a shidduch?"

"Yes," I replied. "I am."

Here I'd been pushing shidduchim away anytime anyone asked me, but the second the Rebbetzin threw the question at me, I gave her a yes!

I stood there slightly overwhelmed, thinking, "Oops, that's the first time I said yes. Don't I always say no?"

Without missing a beat, the Rebbetzin goes, "I have someone perfect for you."

I couldn't help asking the Rebbetzin, "How do you know he's perfect for me — you don't even know me?"

She took my hand, looked into my eyes and explained with complete assurance, "I look at your eyes and I see who you are."

Her response shook me.

She told me everything about the boy she wanted me to meet. Lots and lots of details.

"Can you come to New York?"

"I don't think my coming to New York right now is a possibility."

"Okay, give me your contact information and we'll be in touch in two weeks from now."

I gave her a card I had designed with my email address.

Two weeks later I received an email with the words, "Hello from New York!"

My initial thought was that the Rebbetzin had kept her word and sent me an email like she'd promised. But the email was not from the Rebbetzin. It was from the man she wanted me to meet. He included a picture of himself in what turned out to be a really beautiful and thought-out email — where he described my personality through the artwork I had drawn. I read the email and thought it very, very nice.

I liked him and we began communicating with each other. Sometimes my friends asked me how I envisioned the two of us getting together — with him in America and me in Yerushalayim.

"Hashem will bring him here."

The two of us were in touch for a couple of weeks and then he decided to come to Eretz Yisrael so we could meet. We ended up dating for twenty days before getting engaged. Of course we invited the Rebbetzin to our wedding at the Dan Pearl Hotel.

An original portrait of the Rebbetzin by Nechama Farber

She was the first guest to arrive at our wedding. And when I saw her, I broke down and started to cry, thinking about everything she had done for me.

My chassan and I were all on our own. We had no mothers, we had no fathers. As the Rebbetzin and I embraced, she said to me, "You're not only getting a new husband, you're getting a new Ima too."

And since then we call her "Imachke," and she's our Ima/Savta.

It was the Rebbetzin who walked me down to the chuppah, just like any real mother would do. Since then we were in touch every single week, giving me the gift of feeling like I belong somewhere — which is the greatest present you can give someone who doesn't have any family. I feel like I am part of who she was.

I felt like here was this important person who made me feel important too. She has met so many people over her years of service to Klal Yisrael. And somehow she had room in her heart for every one of those people, bringing them into her family and into her life and giving them warmth and love. Maybe because she wasn't just talking to the people she saw, but to their *neshamos* — touching and connecting on the deepest levels possible.

She herself was the most beautiful *neshamah* — a genuine

treasure! Whenever I called her or she called me, she always said, "I am your Ima and you are my children — and I am going to give you a berachah."

I had no one else to give me a berachah, just her, just my Imachke the Rebbetzin — and I loved her so much!

Reuven Rosenthal remembers:

It was 1993 and I was living on the Upper West Side. A friend and I were interested in attending a Jewish singles event. One day we came across an ad in the paper for an event at this place called Hineni, which I had never heard of before.

I knew the very basics. I had heard of Abraham, Isaac and Jacob, I knew there was such a thing as G-d and I knew that you were supposed to celebrate a Pesach Seder once a year. That was pretty much it.

Anyway, we decided to go to the event. At the last second my friend canceled but I chose to go despite his backing out.

On the way out, I picked up a class schedule and the following Thursday night I decided to return and check out the Rebbetzin's lecture — she used to give a Thursday night *parashah* class every week. I attended the class and that was it.

The Rebbetzin's Chumash class in the Hineni Heritage Center

I still remember what she talked about. It was *Parashas Vayeitzei* and she was describing the angels going up and down the ladder in Yaakov Avinu's dream — and I was just blown away by the clear brilliance of what she said (she had a way of making her Torah eminently relevant to the issues in everyone's lives), but also by how warm, loving and motherly she was. People felt that she really cared about them and wanted the best for them.

The Rebbetzin was very accessible to me.

After the class, she'd remain in the room for hours talking to everyone, and I was able to talk to her for as long as I needed to.

One of the greatest things the Rebbetzin did for me was to generously share her distinguished lineage with me. She knew exactly who she was and where she came from, and hearing her speak about her righteous ancestors gave all of us a clear connection to the previous generation — the generation of the pre-war Eastern European world of Torah giants.

That precious connection has helped me immensely through the years, guiding me as I got on the road to learning Torah myself.

And really, the Rebbetzin was the perfect person to do this. How many people came from that generation? And from that kind of family? Her father had been an eminent rav in pre-war Hungary and he was also deeply involved with Hineni.

The Rebbetzin was born with this incredible Jewish feeling that she was able to give over naturally and with an element of such warmth. She was the European Yiddishe bubby to people who had never been exposed to anything like that. This exposure helped me create a genuine Torah outlook that accompanies me through my entire life.

Her deep con- nection to the past made her uniquely suitable to show her

Tapes and CDs of the Rebbetzin's classes disseminated worldwide

students by personal example what it meant to possess a Jewish heart. There are many opportunities to learn and to develop a person's *Yiddishe kup* (a Jewish mind) at different levels. But to develop a Jewish heart — that has to come from someone very special who actually possesses it himself, someone who saw that type of Yiddishkeit and lived it as a child and has the ability to convey what they experienced to other people — and that was Rebbetzin Jungreis.

One of the most important gifts the Rebbetzin gave me was the ability to connect to an authentic tradition! Listening to her, you really felt like you were receiving a true, unadulterated mesorah. There's no question that my first rebbi was the Rebbetzin.

Professor Penina Lester recalls:

On Thursday, May 17, 2007, I began my spiritual journey by attending my first Torah class at Hineni with Rebbetzin Jungreis, along with one of my students. My student, who regularly attended the Rebbetzin's classes, also arranged for me to speak with the Rebbetzin after class so that I could get a blessing prior to my first trip to Israel. The Rebbetzin's words penetrated my heart; I heard the words with my soul. When the Rebbetzin speaks, you listen. She has an incredible presence. She tells stories to make a point.

After class, we met the Rebbetzin in her office. When the Rebbetzin finished telling me what to do when I get to Israel (kiss the ground when you are on Israeli soil; rip your garment when you go to the Kotel for the first time; do not desecrate the Sabbath; keep kosher; pray three times a day; say Psalms; and keep a journal), she also told me that I have a mission to pray for her at the Kotel.

She rose from behind her desk and I walked over to where she was standing and she took my head in her hands and said words of blessing in Hebrew and English. As she held my head in her hands and prayed, my eyes filled with tears (I was crying tears of joy). When she finished praying, she kissed my forehead and both of my cheeks. I knew that my life would never be the same again. I came home to Torah and mitzvos. As the Rebbetzin would say, "and the rest is history."

Lauren Feinberg hails from Los Angeles. Growing up, her mother used to read Rebbetzin Esther Jungreis' books around their Shabbos table. From the time she was a little girl, Lauren had been hearing about "the" Rebbetzin from New York. Arriving in New York to attend Columbia University, Lauren wanted to meet the Rebbetzin — especially in light of the Rebbetzin's reputation as a stellar matchmaker.

> It wasn't long before I was set up with my future husband Daniel. This was exciting for many reasons, one of which was the fact that his family shared an extremely close relationship with the Rebbetzin. This close connection can explain why Daniel chose to take me out on our first date to the Rebbetzin's *shiur*. To me this was a really big deal.

Daniel had been raised on Manhattan's Upper East Side. Through a series of events, he ended up becoming religious and flying to Israel after college. When he returned home, he attended one of the Rebbetzin's classes, which eventually led him to introduce his parents to the Rebbetzin.

In Daniel's words:

> At the time, my parents were very skeptical of my life choices and couldn't understand why I was learning Torah at a yeshivah in Jerusalem. But once they met the Rebbetzin, everything changed. In fact, my father began studying Torah with Rabbi Osher Jungreis, while my mother began coming with me to the Rebbetzin's women's class at Hineni.
>
> I was the only male in the class, but I attended it religiously. Through that class, my mother received her first window into the world of Torah — often touched by the stories and anecdotes the Rebbetzin told. She was especially moved by the Rebbetzin's description of how her father had saved crumbs of bread throughout the week in Bergen-Belsen so that he would be able to give them to his children come Friday night, while painting a verbal picture of how Shabbos had been back home before the horror of the Holocaust began.
>
> My mother was also extremely touched by the way the Rebbetzin described her life with her husband and the inspiration she'd gleaned from his final days at Sloan Kettering. To her, the Rebbetzin was a paradox of a woman — so small and yet so incredibly powerful; soft, yet unbreakable. She was so down to

earth. Able to understand and connect to people with all their flaws. Able to visit the diamond mines in South Africa and meet the people toiling deep below in the mines. The Rebbetzin was able to look them in the eye and tell them of her own suffering, of her own horrific experiences during the Holocaust.

"Our people were once slaves," she told them. "We know very well what it's like to be enslaved to another people."

That was the Rebbetzin, always able to find a common bridge with everyone she met.

In my mother's eyes, Rebbetzin Jungreis was a woman to admire. The depth of her feeling was something out of this world.

My mother and the Rebbetzin ended up becoming good friends, and the Rebbetzin helped her get used to the changes in her life and the fact that her son eventually got engaged to a religious woman and was living a completely Orthodox life. The Rebbetzin was the perfect person to develop this relationship with my parents — bridging the world of authentic Torah Judaism and the modern-day culture of Manhattan's Upper East Side. My family's life was completely altered through the Rebbetzin's efforts.

One day someone suggested a girl named Lauren to me. She sounded good; however, I was eleven years older than Lauren and her mother didn't allow us to meet. I therefore provided her with a list of people she could call for references. When she saw

The Rebbetzin teaching a class around her desk in the Hineni Heritage Center

The Rebbetzin being interviewed on WABC

the Rebbetzin's name on the list — a woman she had never spoken to but whose books she loved — that was the clincher that got me the approval to date her daughter. Basically, it was all because of the Rebbetzin that I was even allowed to meet the person who became my wife, and I'm grateful to her for that as well. In a way, the Rebbetzin was like this fairy godmother flying around and sprinkling golden marriage dust on everyone she touched.

Not long after our dear friends Andrew and Shannon Penson got married, they hosted a dinner/lecture featuring the Rebbetzin at their home. ABC News covered it, referring to her as "The Rebbetzin Matchmaker." At the event they interviewed people, and I ended up being presented on TV as "The Bachelor," explaining what was so special about being set up by the Rebbetzin.

When we had gotten the green light to go out on our first date, I told Lauren that I wanted to take her to a *shiur* given by Rebbetzin Jungreis.

There was a very good and important reason why I chose to do this.

One of the teachings of the Rebbetzin I often heard that made a huge impression on me was: "If a woman can cry from hearing Torah — if her heart is touched and you see her cry — then she has a pure heart." The Rebbetzin's words struck a chord in my heart and I instinctively knew them to be true and brought the girls I was dating to the *shiur*.

With Lauren there was no question. She cried a lot.

Little did I know that she had been hoping to meet the Rebbetzin for years! And so it all came together. Lauren passed the Rebbetzin's "pure heart" test and was able to meet her hero after waiting for so long. It was like the grand crescendo of a beautiful symphony.

Lauren continues:

During the course of our relationship, we would still attend the Rebbetzin's classes together and she would invite us up to her office to meet afterward. There were always platters of cookies and things to nosh on, as we spent time together.

I really feel that the Rebbetzin saw herself as a Bubby to the Jewish people. Anytime she met someone new, she took them under her wing and looked after them — with great humility and absolute selflessness. There was a beautifully quiet way about her — yes, even though she was a powerful speaker and an inspiring personality, she never put herself first. The Rebbetzin was all about serving Hashem's people.

Years passed. Our family grew as our children were born. Often, our visits to Florida would coincide with the Rebbetzin's Shabbatons in Palm Beach. Having the opportunity to spend time with the Rebbetzin was a highlight for us, and that feeling spread to our children as well. The Rebbetzin had a very poetic way of relating her experiences during the Holocaust, and they saw the Rebbetzin as this heroine who rose from the ashes to rebuild a world that was destroyed. They saw her as someone who maintained her faith and loved Hashem and as someone who was incredibly holy, and they admired her no end.

Through their connection and exposure to the Rebbetzin, our children have developed a genuine fascination with the Holocaust. And although most parents today try to shield their children from learning too much about the Holocaust at a young age, we encourage them to study and learn from it. Their connection already exists — it was brought about by the Rebbetzin's sincere and compelling way of discussing this painful topic. They continue to educate themselves in one of the most important chapters of Jewish history — and that is all due to the Rebbetzin and her involvement in our lives.

There was something else I always found unique about the Rebbetzin. Although she was constantly speaking to large groups, there was another side to her that operated on a completely different level. After a speech to a large audience, she always stayed on and wanted to speak with a smaller group where she'd

The Rebbetzin always had room in her heart to give more and more berachos

reflect on what was happening in the world. The Rebbetzin would always gather us together to listen to her innermost thoughts — thoughts which weren't necessarily meant for the larger audiences, but which she still wanted to share with others. For her it was almost as if the party had never happened and now the real party was taking place, as she spoke to us in depth about what was most important to her.

Though after-parties have a different connotation in the general world, the Rebbetzin's after-parties were spiritual journeys that took us to otherworldly places high above whichever venue we were sitting in. The clock struck twelve, and now we were on another journey — in a room that had been filled with hundreds of people a short while before, but was now virtually empty except for our small group. Suddenly she was talking about the direction of the entire world and what her concerns were — be it 9/11 or anti-Semitism in America. She was always afraid that one day there would be another Holocaust and didn't hesitate to voice that fear.

Janie and Bobby Fisher went with the Rebbetzin on a Hineni trip to Israel in the late '90s. As was the Rebbetzin's way, she brought the group to the Kosel the first chance she had — which meant virtually the moment they'd finished unpacking. It was the Fishers' first visit to Israel, and they were very excited to see and feel the Western Wall up close for the first time in their lives. They had already been told back in the States to prepare a shirt to tear when they visited the Kosel for the first time. It was a huge game changer for them.

In Janie's words:

> As we walked across the Kosel Plaza, the Rebbetzin directed the women toward the women's section, and the men to the men's section. My husband had already moved off with the group, when we suddenly heard a siren go off! My heart skipped a beat. I hadn't been expecting to hear a siren and I didn't know what was going on! I was filled with abject terror. At the same time, a part of me recognized the siren (almost as if it was something familiar and I had heard it before, though I never had). Later I found out that there was an unclaimed package that had caused all the panic and confusion — a somewhat common occurrence in Israel.
>
> The Rebbetzin must have seen the look of utter panic on my face, because she grabbed my hand and took me with her toward the entrance of the plaza, leading me the way a mother leads a child. I don't usually get shaken by things, but now I was not myself.
>
> We sat down off to the side in a quiet spot.
>
> The Rebbetzin looked at me and I looked at her and she said, "Both of us have heard that siren before."
>
> "Yes," I said agreeing with her, "but where would I have heard it?"
>
> "In the Holocaust. That's where your *neshamah* heard it. Your *neshamah* feels the pain of past generations. During the

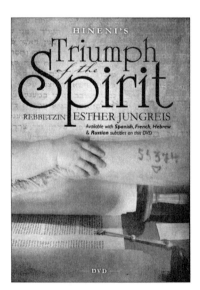

"Triumph of the Spirit" documentary focusing on the Rebbetzin's Holocaust experiences

Paris Theater In Manhattan to Host *Triumph of The Spirit*: The Life of Rebbetzin Esther Jungreis

BY FERN SIDMAN

Holocaust films and literature are, to say the least, depressing and devastating - how else can they be? Rebbetzin Esther Jungreis' new film entitled, "Triumph of the Spirit," however, stands alone in the genre of Holocaust documentaries. While it depicts the Holocaust in all its horror and savage brutality, its dominant theme is hope, faith, and the triumph of the Jewish spirit.

The film demonstrates that the spirit of man is infinitely more powerful than Hitler or his mighty armies and that the flame of faith is more intense then the fires of the crematorium. This long awaited film is a must see for the secular, religious, young and old as it speaks to every heart. While the vintage photos, the music and the images are all captivating, it is Rebbetzin Jungreis' personal story and voice that penetrates the soul and touches the deepest recesses of the heart in this compelling documentary.

In twenty minutes, the Rebbetzin conveys the history of this most satanic period in the annals of mankind in all its horrific detail, but remarkably, at the film's conclusion the audience is left inspired rather than despondent. This was recently evidenced at special screenings at the Pierre Hotel in New York City and at the Sheraton Plaza Hotel in Jerusalem as the audience responded in unison. The Jerusalem screening saw an overflow crowd of over 1000 people and those who could not get a seat sat on the floor. Tears welled in every eye and the hushed silence in the room spoke volumes. The tears and the silence, however, were not tears of despair, but tears of pride - a determination to build a better world. This film dedicates itself

Triumph of the Spirit will premiere for the general public on Tuesday evening, September 22nd at 8:00 p.m. at the Paris Theater in Manhattan.

to re-creating a new generation of Jews who are devoted to G-d and Torah by serving as a joyous inspiration and moral compass on the trajectory of life. "Triumph of the Spirit" can only be defined as an authentic testament to the triumph of the soul in the face of unspeakable adversities. As such, this stellar documentary has been accepted as an entry in the Fort Lauderdale Film Festival and has been entered in over 30 international film festivals.

Rebbetzin Esther Jungreis' personal saga is a welcome and urgently needed contribution to the corpus of films on the history of the Holocaust.

Rebbetzin Esther Jungreis' personal saga is a welcome and urgently needed contribution to the corpus of films on the history of the Holocaust. Among the few survivors of that evil period who can still relate the story it is Rebbetzin Jungreis who has been blessed with the ability to speak to the hearts and souls of our generation. Said Rebbetzin Jungreis, "The screening of this film comes at an important time. Iranian president, Mahmoud Ahmadinejad, the premiere Holocaust denier

and rabid Jew hater may be coming to New York to speak at the same time that this film will be shown. We consider this film to be a counter protest of sorts to the venomous lies that will be spewed forth by this hater of America, Israel and the entire western world."

"Triumph of the Spirit" will premiere for the general public on Tuesday evening, September 22nd at 8:00 p.m. at the Paris Theater in Manhattan. The theater is located at 4 West 58th Street, near 5th Avenue. Following the film, the Rebbetzin will address the audience. For tickets and information, please call Hineni at 212-496-1660 or visit www.hineni.org.vals.

Among the few survivors of that evil period who can still relate the story it is Rebbetzin Jungreis who has been blessed with the ability to speak to the hearts and souls of our generation.

"The screening of this film comes at an important time. Iranian president, Mahmoud Ahmadinejad, the premiere Holocaust denier and rabid Jew hater may be coming to New York to speak at the same time that this film will be shown. We consider this film to be a counter protest of sorts to the venomous lies that will be spewed forth by this hater of America, Israel and the entire western world."

"Triumph of the Spirit" will premiere for the general public on Tuesday evening, September 22nd at 8:00 p.m. at the Paris Theater in Manhattan. The theater is located at 4 West 58th Street, near 5th Avenue. Following the film, the Rebbetzin will address the audience. For tickets and information, please call Hineni at 212-496-1660 or visit Hineni on the web at www.hineni.org.

News report of the New York premiere of "Triumph of the Spirit" at the Paris Theater

Holocaust, that was the siren the Nazis used — a siren that alerted people that their lives were about to change — yet again."

"You recognized all that in my eyes?"

The Rebbetzin nodded. "Yes, I see the pain in your eyes."

Those few words completely changed my life.

US Senator Joseph Lieberman and wife Hadassah with the Rebbetzin at the Washington Capitol Visitor Center premiere of "Triumph of the Spirit"

This chapter has been dedicated in loving memory of Loni Gail
Leah Gittel bat Moshe and Preva Gumora ע"ה
Michael and Cheryl Minikes

CHAPTER THIRTY-SIX

The Little Csenger
Sefer Torah

*R*av Osher Anshil HaLevi Jungreis was Rav Meshulem's father. Rav Osher Anshil passed away and was laid to rest in his town shortly before the Holocaust and the deportation of millions of his brethren. Though he hadn't seen his father in decades, Rav Meshulem never forgot the tzaddik he had known and loved.

Rav Osher Anshil HaLevi,
father of Rav Meshulem

The author of a *sefer* on Shabbos called *Zachor V'Shamor*, Rav Osher Anshil showed his incredible love for the holiest day of the week by bringing proof that the entire Torah is connected to Shabbos. Yet while his Rebbetzin had both her parents, Rav Meshulem Jungreis was left with mere memories of his parents, his mother, Rebbetzin Chaya Sora, having perished in the Holocaust.

That was why he was so happy when one of the members of his shul, a man named Larry Krulik, let him know that he had to travel to Hungary on business.

Hearing this, Rabbi Jungreis asked Larry if he would be willing to make a stop during his trip.

"Where do you want me to go, Rabbi?"

"To a little city called Gyongyos."

"What do you want me to do once I get there?"

"I would appreciate it very much if you would be willing to visit the cemetery and check on my father's gravestone. If you do find it, please recite some Tehillim for my father's *neshamah*. Can you do that for me?"

And Larry agreed.

It took Larry a long time to reach the city of Gyongyos, which was somewhat out of the way. Once there, nobody seemed to know anything about a Jewish cemetery. He didn't give up and asked enough people until one of them helped him find it.

Problem: It was locked.

He asked around, but nobody knew who — if anyone — had the key.

Larry's next stop was the town hall. There he found a clerk who was slightly more helpful, sending him to the home of the sole Jewish

The Rebbetzin at the *kever* of Rav Osher Anshil, the father of Rav Meshulem

Matzeivah of Rav Osher Anshil Jungreis in Gyongyos, Hungary

Becher presented by the Gyongyos Kehillah to Rav Meshulem's brother, Rav Moshe Nosson Nota, upon his engagement and appointment as the Rav of Tokay

inhabitant of Gyongyos, who was also the keeper of the key. Larry introduced himself to the elderly gentleman who opened the door, telling him he had come to Gyongyos on behalf of Rabbi Meshulem Jungreis — son of Rav Osher Anshil.

He could have never expected the outcome of that revelation.

The old man was overcome by emotion, and using Yiddish he clearly hadn't spoken in decades, invited Larry into his simple home. He then climbed up to a high closet and presented Larry with a box that had been hidden on the topmost shelf. He explained that he had been given the box for safekeeping, and was now overjoyed at being able to fulfill his mission.

"This is for your rabbi," the old man said.

Now it was Larry's turn to be overwhelmed, as he pictured Rav Meshulem's face when he would hand him the box. He then asked the old man to accompany him to the cemetery.

"Can you show me Rav Osher Anshil's grave?"

The man nodded.

He took Larry to the cemetery, opened the gate and showed him the gravestone, which had been overturned by vandals. It was surrounded by overgrown weeds and bushes and hadn't been tended to in decades.

Somehow Larry managed to lift the tombstone.

He would never know how he was able to lift such a heavy stone on his own. Underneath, he read the name of Rav Meshulem's father. There was no question that this was the right grave.

After praying at the *kever* and sending the tzaddik regards from his beloved son, Larry took the mysterious box and left Gyongyos.

Imagine the scene when Larry presented Rav Meshulem with the box. The drama was intense. Rav Meshulem opened the box and found a gift beyond all expectation — for the box held a copy of his father's *sefer Zachor V'Shamor*.

Cover and title page of *Sefer Zachor V'Shamor* on Shabbos,
by Rav Osher Anshil HaLevi Jungreis

It was the only copy of the *sefer* still in existence. A testimony to one man's loyalty to his rabbi. At the same time, it was just as much a testimony to the fact that when Hashem wants something to survive — it will.

The Rebbetzin had the *sefer* reprinted and distributed to every member of the Jungreis family, and even far beyond. This was consistent with her deep-rooted connection to the Torah scholarship of her ancestors. Who would have believed that the *sefer* would not only survive, but would be studied by Torah students and scholars for years to come? Was it not a modern-day miracle?

Against all odds, the Jungreis *sefarim* managed to not only survive the flames and persecution, but to emerge triumphant — from decades of solitude — to grace the bookcases of Jewish homes and to be studied by Jewish people who find it difficult to comprehend the enormity of the *sefer's* journey.

But that was only the start of an entire array of Jungreis reunions that would take the family by storm — as many of their most precious belongings miraculously came home to them.

Sometimes one phone call can change a person's life for the better. That's the way it was when the phone rang in the Rebbetzin's house one morning.

"Is this Rebbetzin Jungreis?"

It was an elderly voice speaking.

"Yes, it is," she replied, "and who is this?"

"My name is Dr. Blatt."

It was not a name she recognized.

"Rebbetzin, I have something to show you which I think you will find very interesting! But you must come alone. I live in Manhattan."

The Rebbetzin was taken aback. Most people who called her wanted to ask her a question or were seeking her advice. This was a different type of conversation. What could this individual possibly have to show her?

"I can't come alone," she told the man. "I will ask my husband if he can accompany me to your apartment. But before we go any further, please give me some details as to what you want to show me."

"You're not going to believe this, but I have some items in my possession that belonged to your ancestor the Menuchas Osher."

It was almost impossible to believe that he could be telling the truth. Yes, the Rebbetzin knew that the world was a funny place where amazing things happened every day. And yet, how on earth could this man have obtained Jungreis family possessions? It was especially incredible because the Rebbetzin had just returned from a visit to Csenger where she had spent a lot of time davening at the graves of her ancestors. And now this: a call from a long-ago world.

"Please give me your address."

Dr. Blatt told her the name of the street. She wrote it down. Then she went to find her husband. But when she told him about the strange conversation Rav Meshulem wasn't convinced.

"How do we know this isn't some sort of fake story? Who knows who this man is or what he really wants from us! It's a crazy world out there!"

The Rebbetzin looked at her husband — the man who had been her anchor for so many years — and said, "You're right, we'll be careful. But if he is saying the truth and has managed to obtain some of the Csenger treasures, and is willing to show them to us, surely we have a responsibility to see them for ourselves. How can we possibly turn away from the world of the Zeides?"

Rav Meshulem conceded that his wife was making a good point — and that they couldn't ignore the call. Not if the call was coming from the Csenger dynasty and the magnificent heritage of the distant and not-so-distant Jungreis past. If the door to the world of their ancestors was opening up — could they ignore it and choose to walk away?

Obviously not.

The drive to Manhattan passed quickly, and soon they found themselves standing on the street in front of the man's building. It was a regular Manhattan building, with a typical stone façade. Could such a place possibly be housing the treasures of a bygone world? Could this building contain a time-continuum elevator that would transport them out of New York and straight back to the magic of Csenger?

The man who opened the door was elderly and distinguished. He smiled — a smile that reached his eyes — and he seemed to be a kind individual.

In short order they were seated in his comfortable living room and he told them a truly amazing story.

"I don't know if you've heard about the planned Nazi museum in Czechoslovakia," the doctor began, "but it was meant to be extremely large, grand, and all-encompassing, designed to showcase the items the Nazis had confiscated from the homes of the rabbis and sages all across Europe. The purpose of the museum was to show that although the Jewish nation had once played a major part in Europe's culture, business, religious and political arenas, they were no more."

The man showed Rabbi and Rebbetzin Jungreis beautiful ceremonial pieces that had belonged to some of the most famous rabbis of pre-war Europe. Holding the pieces was like touching history — bridging the gap between the modern world and the world that had existed for so long and which was no more. He then handed them some silver Kiddush cups and candlesticks to examine and invited his guests to read the names that had been carefully etched in the silver.

The silver items bore the names of the Jungreis Zeides of Hungary. And since the Rabbi and his wife were third cousins, this meant that everything in their hands — the precious heirlooms of a vanished world — had belonged to both their ancestors. They

The Csenger Sefer Torah

looked at each other and their eyes glistened with unshed tears. Could this be real? Were they really touching the actual silver Kiddush cups and candelabras that had been used on the Shabbos tables of their Zeides and Bubbas?

But that was not even the most incredible part. Because the next object he showed them was a small Sefer Torah that had belonged to the Menuchas Osher and which had been written by a famous scribe. The Menuchas Osher had the tradition of reviewing the *parashah* of the week from the Sefer Torah itself. In keeping with that tradition, a small ark had been built in the Menuchas Osher's home — and that was where the little Torah scroll resided in solitary splendor throughout the week. It was removed from its home and read on Shabbos before being replaced until the following week.

The Rebbetzin didn't know what to do. She wanted that Sefer Torah. More than she'd wanted anything — ever.

It was theirs. Their heritage. It had belonged to their great-grandfather and should be brought home to its family.

"Can we have this Sefer Torah?" she asked.

"No," Dr. Blatt replied. He didn't waver at all. His no was final.

"What are you planning to do with everything here?"

"I plan on endowing all of these holy objects to a museum in Israel."

"But this scroll belonged to our family!"

He didn't argue.

"That is true. And yet, there is a Jewish law of *yei'ush* (abandonment) that states that when someone believes his belongings are lost and gives up on them, whoever finds them is allowed to keep them. Your family gave up on all these items. You never dreamed that anything remained from your ancestral homes. I was the one who found out about the Nazi museum and I was the one who spent the money to obtain these priceless objets d'art. They are mine, I purchased them legally and I intend to gift them to the museum."

He looked them in the eye as he spoke, sure of himself and his rights, knowledgeable of the law, secure in his interpretation. Still, he felt a little bad on some level, knowing how disappointed they were by his refusal to give them the objects that had graced their family's Shabbos and Seder tables for generations.

Just before they left his home, he showed them a collection of wooden walking canes on which were carved out the names of the Jungreis Zeides. In Europe it was the accepted norm for grand rabbinical figures to use a walking cane when they strolled in the street, and here were still more items that had belonged to them. It hurt their sensitive hearts.

"You can have your Zeides' canes," he told them.

It was as if a rainbow had burst forth from what had previously been a cloudy sky. Color filled the room. To hold one of the Zeide's canes in their hands! What a *zechus*! To think they had arrived empty-handed in Manhattan and were leaving with a tangible connection to their past! It was absolutely incredible, and they were overjoyed.

One of the Jungreis sons was skeptical about the whole story.

"Maybe the man carved out our name on the canes himself? Who says this is all true?"

So the Rebbetzin invited her son to accompany her to Dr. Blatt's home in Manhattan so he could see everything with his own eyes and verify the authenticity of all they had seen and held. Handing his guests the keys to the breakfront, their host invited them to examine every item on display.

The Rebbetzin's son reached inside for a silver Kiddush cup. Removing it, he turned it over and there engraved in the silver was the name of one of his Zeides.

He tried again. Reaching inside once more, he removed another silver cup and examined it as well. The name on the bottom of that cup was of another one of the Jungreis Zeides from back in Hungary. There were over a hundred Kiddush cups in the breakfront — yet somehow the three cups her son chose had each belonged to three different Jungreis Zeides! The same thing occurred when he reached inside and removed a silver candelabra. Once again, the one he chose was engraved with the family name! There was no logic here, no way to explain how the same thing was happening over and over.

But the crown jewel — the greatest treasure of all — was the little Sefer Torah of Csenger.

Mother and son looked at the doctor pleadingly, beseeching him with their eyes. Didn't he understand that the whole story was miraculous? Wasn't he seeing how the Rebbetzin's son instinctively knew which Kiddush cups were theirs? Wasn't he able to grasp that the Zeides themselves were calling out to their grandchildren — begging to be reunited with their descendants after so many decades apart? Didn't he see?

But no. He didn't see.

The Kiddush cups and candlesticks were staying with him. So was the Sefer Torah. They could look at everything. They could even touch. But that was the limit.

In the days leading up to Yom Kippur, Rebbetzin Jungreis had an idea. While it was true that the owner of so many of their family treasures was unwilling to give them back, maybe he would agree to allow them to house the Sefer Torah at Ohr Torah in North Woodmere over Yom Kippur? The Rebbetzin called Dr. Blatt. She promised him that they would return the Torah scroll to him as soon as Yom Kippur was over.

"I don't understand," Dr. Blatt said to her. "The Sefer Torah is *pasul* — it's not kosher. Some of the letters are missing and you won't be able to read from it. So why is it so important that you have it with you at Ohr Torah?"

"Let me put it this way," the Rebbetzin replied, her voice cracking with emotion. "How did this Sefer Torah survive? I'll tell you. It survived — it's around right now — because my grandfather buried it before being sent away to be killed. The reason he buried it in the ground was because he hoped that one day a Jew would discover it and return it to his family. The Nazis dug everywhere. They knew that many people had buried objects worth a lot of money and they wanted everything for themselves. That is why they discovered my Zeide's Sefer Torah.

I don't know when or how, but somewhere along the way, the Torah scroll was damaged and made unusable. And like the remnants of the Luchos (the Tablets on which the Ten Commandments had been inscribed and which Moshe broke when he threw them to the ground upon descending the mountain) that were kept in the Ark due to their holiness even though they were no longer whole — this Sefer Torah deserves the same treatment!

"Give me the unusable scroll that belonged to my family! It is holy — so holy — and it too deserves to occupy a place of honor, in a shul, on the holiest day of the Jewish year!"

She gave it her all — as if she were in a courtroom delivering the closing arguments of a major trial — and by the time she got off the phone, she knew that she had done all that she could. And Dr. Blatt finally agreed to allow Rabbi and Rebbetzin Jungreis to borrow the Torah scroll they loved so much.

And then disaster struck.

Dr. Blatt called their home a few days before Yom Kippur. The Rebbetzin wasn't there and he spoke to Rabbi Jungreis.

"I'm very sorry to change my mind like this," he said, his voice filled with regret, "but I don't feel comfortable with my earlier decision. I can't allow you to borrow the Sefer Torah — even for so short a time and even if you bring it back right after Yom Kippur."

There was nothing the Rabbi could say that would change his mind. The doctor was dead set on keeping the Csenger Sefer Torah in his home and close at hand. When she arrived home from teaching at Hineni, Rav Meshulem told his wife about the phone call and how the Sefer Torah would in fact not be spending Yom Kippur with its family.

The Rebbetzin was unwilling to give in. When she wanted something she was tenacious and would never back down. That's how she was when it came to founding Hineni, her great events at Madison Square Garden, her trips to the army bases in Israel and many other fantastic accomplishments.

"We will go see him in Manhattan. We will try to convince him — we'll give it one more try…"

And off they went.

She would never know how she managed to convince the man to part with the Sefer Torah he cherished so — for he truly loved it — but in the end he agreed to allow them to leave his home, Sefer Torah safely ensconced in their arms. It was a modern-day miracle. When they walked into the house, Rav Meshulem laid the Torah scroll on a tallis and opened it up. Reverently, he rolled the handles apart and peered inside the scroll, his eyes staring lovingly at the ancient parchment. The letters were cracked and faded, the parchment was old and weakened with age; but the scroll opened up to the Yom Kippur Torah reading — and Rabbi Jungreis almost jumped backward in shock. The last time the scroll had been used decades earlier was on Yom Kippur! If this wasn't a sign that the Sefer Torah belonged in North Woodmere for Yom Kippur, what was?

The tears rolled down their cheeks unchecked.

After all, the little Sefer Torah had come home — just in time for the most important day of the year!

How awesome are Your ways, Hashem!

The Csenger Sefer Torah was the most honored guest in Ohr Torah that Yom Kippur. Everyone stared at it in wonder and awe. The children kissed its mantle and stroked it lovingly. It was accorded a truly incredible welcome and given a place of honor in the *aron kodesh.*

The Rebbetzin was true to her word, calling the Torah Scroll's owner on Motza'ei Yom Kippur to inform him that they were about to leave North Woodmere, Sefer Torah in tow.

"You don't have to bring it back," he said.

The Rebbetzin's hand gripped the receiver so hard her knuckles turned white.

"What do you mean?"

"Exactly as I said. You can keep the Sefer Torah."

They were absolutely flabbergasted and couldn't digest what he was telling them. Was this a dream? Were they imagining something that wasn't really true? What on earth was going on?

"I don't understand," she said at last.

"I will explain. I had a dream on Kol Nidrei night. In my dream I was told that I must return the Sefer Torah to you and your family — that it's your inheritance."

"Are you sure?"

"I am. It belongs to you."

Today the little Csenger Sefer Torah has found its home in the *aron kodesh* at the Hineni Heritage Center in Manhattan. The only time the Sefer Torah leaves its current home at Hineni is for Rosh Hashanah and Yom Kippur, when it is taken from its spot in the *aron kodesh* and transported to whichever hotel Hineni is using for their yearly program, where it occupies a place of honor, though it cannot be used. For the rest of the year, however, it is kept in its white mantle — in honor of the first Yom Kippur when it was returned to its family.

One Friday morning Dr. Blatt called the Rebbetzin. The question that he asked her came as an absolute shock.

"Rebbetzin, do you have someone in the family named Slova Chana?"

"Dr. Blatt," the Rebbetzin replied, "can I ask you why you want to know?"

"Certainly. I have a very good reason for wanting to know. I had a dream last night."

The Rebbetzin was extremely taken aback by this revelation. After all, the last time Dr. Blatt had had a dream, Hineni had ended up the recipient of their precious Sefer Torah. This was a man who took his dreams seriously.

"You had another dream?"

"Yes. I dreamt that the candlesticks in my possession belong to someone named Slova Chana and should be given to her. That's why I'm asking if you have anyone related to you with that name. If you do, I want you to drive over to Manhattan immediately."

"My daughter's name is Slova Chana," the Rebbetzin told him.

"Come see me right now. Drive over this second!" He was very emphatic. "I must return these candlesticks to their rightful owner."

So the Rebbetzin called her daughter Slovie and the two of them drove to Dr. Blatt's apartment in the city, where he ceremoniously presented Slovie with the candlesticks from his dream.

And so it came to be that the Rebbetzin and her daughter were reunited with yet another piece of Jungreis history.

Today the four Shabbos candelabras that were rescued from the "Jewish Museum" of Prague burn brightly come Friday night in the Wolff home. In addition there is another candlestick which belonged to Zeide's mother Slova Chana and which was given to Slovie by her great-aunt Elsa (that candlestick was not buried in the shul's courtyard). There is also a very special candlestick that belonged to the Rebbetzin of the Menuchas Osher — the illustrious ancestor of the Jungreis family — and one more *leichter* that belonged to the original Esther Jungreis and that the Rebbetzin bequeathed to her daughter.

Toward the end of the Rebbetzin's life, she asked her daughter Chaya Sora to come to the house, explaining that she had something very important to discuss with her. Taking her into the dining room, the Rebbetzin related the lineage and pedigree of the numerous *leichters* she had been lighting every Friday night for many years, several of which had likewise been returned to her by Dr. Blatt.

The Rebbetzin then asked Chaya Sora to take a piece of paper and write down the names of each of the family's Bubbas and which of the many *leichters* corresponded to that particular grandmother. Chaya

The Rebbetzin's *leichters* from her Bubbas, many of which were returned to the family by Dr. Blatt, always stood ready and prepared for Shabbos.

Sora was to then insert the papers into the openings at the base of every *leichter*.

Today, Chaya Sora lights a candlestick dating back to Rebbetzin Necha, the wife of the Menuchas Osher. She also lights the *leichter* of the Rebbetzin's mother "Mama" — the *leichter* that the Rebbetzin's mother gave to her daughter even before she passed away, telling her that she wanted to see her using it during her lifetime.

Another candlestick from the Menuchas Osher's rebbetzin was given to Rabbi Yisroel and his wife Rivki, as well as the *leichter* that had belonged to the Rebbetzin's grandfather Rav Tzvi Hirsch and his rebbetzin.

Rabbi Osher and his wife Yaffa received a candelabra, another of the precious heirlooms that Dr. Blatt had returned to the family. It had belonged to Rebbetzin Chaya Peril, wife of Rav Moshe Nosson Nota, son and daughter-in-law of the Menuchas Osher. Rabbi Osher also has the menorah of the Menuchas Osher — another priceless piece of history returned to them by Dr. Blatt, a man who gave so much to the Jungreis family.

The Jungreis children's homes are filled with family history, the unique glow of Shabbos candlelight, and the priceless feeling that comes from being connected to those who came before you — golden links in the chain of our mesorah.

Many of the walking sticks/canes that had belonged to the most esteemed of Hungarian Rabbanim were also returned to the Rebbetzin; she davened her every tefillah with them at her side, secure in the knowledge that she was connecting herself to the incredible merits of the tzaddikim from whom she was descended. And when a Jungreis grandchild got married, the Rebbetzin made sure to remind them just before they began their walk to the chuppah that the Zeides would be walking with them.

CHAPTER THIRTY-SEVEN
Seder Night Story

Of all the Yamim Tovim, Pesach always held a certain special significance for the Rebbetzin. There was a reason for this. It was because she had been born on the first Seder night. As far back as she could recall, at every Seder, her father, Rav Avrohom HaLevi Jungreis, would regale the family with the story of his daughter's birth.

"We were just sitting down to the Seder," he would begin, "and Mama, may she be healthy and well for many long years, told us, 'I think that this is the night the baby will come.'"

"My father loved to tell how he quickly dispatched our housekeeper to fetch the midwife," the Rebbetzin would say, "and how the Seder proceeded with intense prayer and trepidation.

"He would lean back in his chair and recall what came next with a great big smile on his holy face.

"'When we opened the door for Eliyahu HaNavi, a cry was heard from the bedroom and the midwife announced, "Mazel tov, Rav Jungreis, you have a beautiful baby girl!"'

"I do not know," the Rebbetzin would continue, "whether I was really born at the specific moment that the door was opened for Eliyahu HaNavi, but it sufficed for me to hear it that way, and my father never grew tired of telling and retelling the tale. Even on those dark nights when we were trapped within the walls of the ghetto or in Bergen-Belsen, when our table was bare and where the saltwater was made with our own tears — even then, my revered father related the story of my birth and made me feel special."

When the Jungreis family reached the blessed shores of America after their harrowing Holocaust experience, Esther's parents enrolled her in Rabbi Levi's Bais Yaakov elementary school in Brownsville. She didn't speak the language, and with hardly any schooling behind her, she had to start with the basics.

One day it was announced that Barton's candy company was running a contest for the most meaningful essay on Pesach and that the winner would be rewarded with several pounds of chocolate. To little Esther, coming from the concentration camps as she did, the whole thing sounded like a dream. Chocolate was a luxury the Jungreis family could hardly afford. But how could she, with her limited broken English, possibly win?

Nevertheless, with the encouragement of her teacher she tried — writing the story of her Pesach birthday, and about how even during the nightmare of the Holocaust, her father never forgot to speak of the moment he opened the door for Eliyahu and heard his daughter's cry.

Amazingly, although her teacher had to make many corrections in her essay's grammar and spelling, she won the contest. The Jungreis children were ecstatic with joy. They had a chocolate feast second to none and happily shared their bounty with family and friends.

"All this occurred many years ago," the Rebbetzin would write in years to come, "but the sound of my father's voice lovingly relating the tale has not faded from memory. As time passed, I married and became a rebbetzin and it was no longer feasible for me to return to my parents' home for Pesach. There were too many responsibilities in our own congregation, and my husband and I had to celebrate the Seder in our own home. We would invite widows and others who were alone, as well as those who came from assimilated backgrounds and had never experienced a real Seder. Yet, although we could no longer join my parents for the Seder, every Pesach my father would remind me of the story of the first Seder night of my life. The story contained a special bond that we shared and neither one of us was willing to allow the memory to fade.

"And so the story was told and retold year after year."

After the Rebbetzin's oldest child Chaya Sora married Rabbi Shlomo Gertzulin in 1977, the Seder took on a different dimension, for soon Rabbi and Rebbetzin Jungreis had grandchildren around their table and the joy of the experience was boundless. But one year, the Rebbetzin's Yom Tov joy turned into a time of anguish and pain. As usual she had been expecting her children and grandchildren. Her preparations were feverish — she wanted everything cooked and baked and the table set so that she would be able to welcome them when they arrived without tension.

Suddenly the phone rang for the hundredth time that day.

"*A gutten Erev Yom Tov,*" she said to the caller.

But the second she heard her brother's voice on the line, Rebbetzin Jungreis knew that something was terribly wrong.

"What's the matter?" she asked him, bracing herself.

"Tatty had a stroke," he replied. "He's not responding. I'm waiting for an ambulance. The doctor will meet us in the emergency room."

For what seemed like an eternity the Rebbetzin couldn't find her voice, until she finally managed to stammer, "I'm coming. I'll meet you there."

After that everything happened very quickly.

The Rebbetzin called Chaya Sora and told her the news, outlining everything that still needed to be done at her home before Yom Tov.

"Ima, don't worry about a thing," Chaya Sora reassured her mother. "I will finish making everything as soon as I get to North Woodmere. Please don't worry. Everything will be fine. Zeide should have a *refuah sheleimah!*"

Rabbi Jungreis was not at home just then. It was his tradition every Erev Shabbos and Erev Yom Tov to visit the sick people in their community, so the Rebbetzin asked her children to relay the news to their father when he returned home.

The Rebbetzin had difficulty speaking when it was time for her to leave. She packed an overnight bag, throwing things inside without thought.

"Ima," her children said to her, "take a Haggadah with you. And a small Seder plate with all the special foods."

Even as they spoke to their mother, they were packing up the charoses and *zeroa* (shankbone), and as they reached for the marror it occurred to the Rebbetzin that this was one Pesach she wouldn't need any marror — because the bitterness was already in her mouth.

Rav Meshulem had arrived home by then and he and the children walked the Rebbetzin to the corner where they waited with her until the taxi arrived. The drive to the hospital was sheer agony. How could this be happening to her father, the *heiliger Zeide*, the tzaddik, the crown of their family, a man who was such a pillar of Klal Yisrael!

The taxi pulled up in front of the hospital and the Rebbetzin raced into the emergency room. There on a stretcher lay her father, unconscious. The doctor still hadn't arrived. Meanwhile the clock was ticking away and her brother had to get back home to his own shul — and the Seder he was running for their mother and his own family.

"Go home," the Rebbetzin told her brother.

"What about you?"

"I will stay here with Tatty."

So commenced a Seder night she would never, ever forget. She sat at her father's bedside the entire night. It was only in the wee hours of the morning that he was finally assigned to a room. In the interim, the Rebbetzin covered a little stand in her father's cubicle with a napkin and placed the makeshift Seder plate on it. A kindly nurse arranged for some electric candles so that she might be able to usher in Yom Tov. She davened from the depths of her soul and cried out to Hashem for help. Then the Rebbetzin took out her Haggadah and began to read aloud. But when she came to the familiar words, "*Ma nishtanah halailah hazeh* — Why is this night different from all other nights," she broke down and began to sob uncontrollably.

Her question echoed in the cold, sterile room. She sat there holding her father's hand, but his eyes remained closed and he gave her no answer.

What would she not have given to hear her father's sweet voice!

This was one Seder night where there would be no "Happy Birthday, *mein heilige kindt*."

But as the Rebbetzin went through the Haggadah page by page, she felt that her father could hear her, and just reciting those timeless words infused her with renewed strength and energy.

As the sun began to rise, Zeide's eyes were still closed. There was still no response. But the mercies of Hashem are many, and as the second Seder night commenced, Zeide opened his eyes — those loving, beautiful eyes — eyes that spoke volumes, eyes filled with love.

"*Es iz Pesach, Tatty, es iz Seder nacht* — It's Pesach, it is Seder night," Esther Jungreis whispered to her father. He nodded and made a supreme effort to speak. The words came painfully and haltingly.

"Estherke," he finally managed to get out. He tried to say something more, but it was very difficult for him. The Rebbetzin strained to hear his words, leaning forward until she distinctly heard him say, "*Lichtige kindt, du bist doch geboren haint bai nacht* — You were born on this night."

It was a special birthday after all.

"*Gut Yom Tov*, Tatty," the Rebbetzin whispered to her beloved father.

He smiled at her — and then they sat and celebrated the second Seder night, father and daughter, the way it had always been.

CHAPTER THIRTY-EIGHT

"V'nafsho Keshurah V'nafsho"

$\mathcal{I}$t was Motza'ei Shabbos Chanukah and all the Jungreis children and grandchildren had just spent Shabbos at their grandparents' home in North Woodmere. Rav Meshulem finished reciting Havdalah and the Rebbetzin rushed for the phone to call her parents.

Zeide — Rav Avrohom HaLevi Jungreis

Mama — Rebbetzin Miriam Jungreis

Matzeivah of Rav Avrohom
HaLevi Jungreis

Even as she dialed, her heart was pounding. Her beloved father's condition had been rapidly deteriorating, and she was anxiously hoping for some reassuring news.

Her mother answered the phone.

In response to her daughter's question, she replied simply, "Tatty is very sick."

"I'm coming right over with my children and grandchildren," the Rebbetzin said.

All plans for the evening were immediately canceled, as the children, grandchildren and great-grandchildren — even the youngest, who was then two — all made their way to Zeide's home. The doctor, a wonderful dear friend, was there.

"I'm sorry to have to tell you this, but time is quickly running out."

The words hung there in the stillness of the room. It was impossible to comprehend that Zeide might be leaving them soon.

The family surrounded the bed of their beloved Zeide. Placing his hand on the head of every child, grandchild and great-grandchild, he gave them each a berachah — then they kissed his hands and washed them with their tears. Everyone said the *Shema* and other appropriate prayers.

As dawn approached, the family helped their Zeide don his tefillin for what would be his final time: the tefillin that had once belonged to the Menuchas Osher and had been given to the Zeide on the day of his bar mitzvah by his father, who perished *al Kiddush Hashem*, sanctifying Hashem's Name, in Auschwitz.

It was time to recite the *viduy* (final prayers).

And then, the tzaddik Rav Avrohom's blessed *neshamah* left his body and ascended to heaven and the family had the *zechus* to close his eyes.

It was the seventh day of Chanukah, Rosh Chodesh Teves 5752/1992, and in the midst of their pain the Rebbetzin understood that they had just been granted an awesome privilege. How special it was that Zeide had left this world like the true tzaddik he was, surrounded by his family, with true love and admiration on the part of his descendants.

Six years earlier, Zeide had recovered from a serious illness. At the time, he'd called his daughter to his side and told her the following words:

"*Lichtige kindt*, my child, my precious light. If something should happen to me, you should never be afraid. My berachah is always with you, in this world and in the World to Come."

Now the Rebbetzin recalled that conversation and felt the tiniest measure of peace within the stormy ocean of her pain.

They read *Parashas Vayigash* on the Shabbos that concluded the *shivah*. Three words jumped out at her from the pages of the Chumash, leapt into her heart and broke her down completely. The three words that opened the floodgate of tears were "*V'nafsho keshurah v'nafsho* — and his soul is bound up with his [child's] soul" (*Bereishis* 44:30).

It was as if Zeide had beseeched the Heavenly Court to be allowed to depart this world specifically at that time, so that his family would be able to find a measure of *nechamah*, comfort, in the words of Torah that they read that week.

Somehow, Zeide had managed to send them all one final message — a final kiss and hug to all the children and family members he loved so very much.

Memories assailed her.

A thick blanket of snow covering the ground in her grandfather's village in Hungary.

"*Follow in my footsteps, lichtige kindt, follow in my footsteps...*"

Her father in Bergen-Belsen feeding them the crumbs he'd saved for Shabbos.

"*You, my precious children, you are the malachim...*"

Her father at Madison Square Garden.

"*Esther, you cannot start the event until every single Jew is allowed inside the arena!*"

The Rebbetzin davening
at the *kever* of her father

Memories. Thousands of them. Such precious, exquisite memories.

The Rebbetzin heard her father's voice once again.

She imagined the *Shechinah* (Divine Presence) on his beautiful face and she found strength.

The strength to comfort and the strength to be comforted.

"V'nafsho keshurah v'nafsho, mein kindt, v'nafsho keshurah v'nafsho."

Part 7
1987-1996

"Hineni" is mentioned in regard to three of our greatest leaders. Avraham Avinu said "Hineni," Yosef HaTzaddik said "Hineni," and Moshe Rabbeinu said it as well.

As one of the first religious women in the world to do kiruv, and following in the footsteps of her illustrious ancestors, Rebbetzin Esther Jungreis is a prime example of the word "Hineni."

Rav Yisroel Meir Lau —
Chief Rabbi of Israel 1993-2003
(Recorded message at the Sheloshim Memorial
Service for the Rebbetzin, September 2016)

Glamour and theatrics fight spiritual genocide — the call comes from a woman who has been called a Jewish Billy Graham.

The Sunday New York Times

A long life is not good enough, but a good life is long enough.

Rav Meshulem Jungreis

CHAPTER THIRTY-NINE
New York Magazine

Michael Beckman first met the Rebbetzin when he was hired to produce a number of fundraising videos for Hineni's dinners and other functions. A filmmaker by profession, Beckman had been producing films for industries and corporations, as well as commercials for luxury brands. His work ranged from global documentaries for the opening "Earth Day" summit in Rio, to working with some of the biggest names in the music industry.

Michael Beckman had a finger in a lot of pies and Hineni used him for all of their technological needs. At some point their relationship took a major leap forward, when he began producing the Rebbetzin's television show for JTV (Jewish Television Network) — recording the Rebbetzin's Torah/*hashkafah* classes to be released on cable television, where they had the potential to literally reach millions of people on a weekly basis.

In the beginning, Michael filmed the Rebbetzin's classes at "KJ" — Kehilath Jeshurun on Manhattan's Upper East Side — which he then edited for television. Eventually, however, he decided to build the Rebbetzin her very own television studio in the Hineni building. The Rebbetzin would deliver an hour-long class for the crowd who had come to hear her and when she was finished, deliver another hour of the same material that was filmed live in her studio, edited by Michael and sent out to JTV.

There were numerous people whose lives were touched by watching the Rebbetzin on TV. While most would remain unknown, there were

The Rebbetzin on her National Jewish Television program with Russian Prisoner of Conscience Yosef Mendelevich, holding tzitzis made and worn by Mendelevich during his 11 years in a Russian prison

those who made it their business to find the Rebbetzin and capture the magic they had witnessed through the screen.

The story of Pat Cayne was a classic example.

Dr. Patricia (Pat) Cayne is a highly educated, sophisticated Manhattanite. She earned a PhD and thought that it would give her satisfaction.

But it didn't, and she couldn't figure out why not.

She reached the point where she realized she needed a spiritual anchor in her life. Pat went from one Manhattan rabbi to another, but no one gave her the answers she was looking for — no one helped her discover the true meaning and purpose of life.

It got to the point where her husband, James (Jimmy) Cayne, suggested that they research and look into Born-Again Christianity. For some reason they didn't get around to it.

And the search continued.

One Sunday afternoon Pat was surfing the channels on her TV set and came across the Rebbetzin giving a Torah class on the National Jewish Television program. The class touched her in a special way. She

The Hineni Show *The Longest Running Torah Program*

VIEW REBBETZIN ESTHER JUNGREIS ON TELEVISION
SUNDAYS – 3:00 P.M. EST
Noon – Pacific Time

CABLE COMPANIES
Ca - Cablevision Systems
Com - Comcast
M/1 - Media One
T/W - Time Warner
ATT - (formerly TCI Cable)

California - (205,000 11H)		Channel
Bakersfield	T/W	55
Palm Springs	T/W	16

Connecticut - (625,000 HH)		Channel
Avon	ATT	51
Berlin	ATT	51
Bloomfield	ATT	51
Bridgeport	Ca	88
Bristol	ATT	51
Branford	ATT	51
Burlington	ATT	51
Darien	Ca	89
East Hartford	ATT	51
East Haven	ATT	51
Easton	Ca	89
Fairfield	Ca	89
Farmington	ATT	51
Greenwich	Ca	89
Guilford	ATT	51
Hamden	Com	51
Hartford	ATT	51
Kent	ATT	51
Madison	ATT	51
Milford	Ca	99
New Britain	ATT	51
New Canaan	Ca	89
New Haven	Com	51
North Haven	ATT	51
Norwalk	Ca	9
Orange	Ca	99
Redding	Ca	89
Simsbury	ATT	51
Stamford	Ca	89
Stratford	Ca	88
West Hartford	ATT	51
West Haven	Com	51
Weston	Ca	89
Westport	Ca	89
Wallingford	ATT	51
Wilton	Ca	89
Windsor	ATT	51
Woodbridge	Ca	99

Florida (310,000 HH)		Channel
Coconut Creek	M/1	19
Deerfield Beach	M/1	19
Ft. Lauderdale	Com	46
Hallandale	Com	46
Hollywood	Com	46
Lakeview	M/1	19
Lauderdale Lakes	M/1	19
Lauderhill	M/1	19
Lighthouse Point	M/1	19
Margate	M/1	19
Miramar	Com	46
Oakland Park	M/1	19
Pembroke Pines	Com	46
Plantation	M/1	19
Pompano Beach	M/1	19
Sunrise	M/1	19
Tamarec	M/1	19
Westin	M/1	19

Maryland (525,000 HH)		Channel
Baltimore	Com	02
Bethesda	Prime	68/38

Chevy Chase	Prime	68/38
Gaithersburg	Prime	68/38
Germantown	Prime	68/38
Pikesville	Com	02
Potomac	Prime	68/38
Rockville	Prime	68/38
Silver Spring	Prime	68/38
Timomium	Com	02
Towson	Com	02
Wheaton	Prime	68/38
White Oak	Prime	68/38

Massachusetts (482,000 HH)		Channel
Boston	Ca	A55
Brookline	Ca	A55
Foxboro	M/1	04
Framingham	Ca	17
Mashpee	M/1	56
Needham	M/1	56
Newton	M/1	56
Watertown	M/1	56
Wellesley	M/1	56
Weston	M/1	56
Whalen	M/1	56

Michigan (165,000 HH)		Channel
(Detroit Suburbs)		
Birmingham	M/1	25
Bloomfield	M/1	25
Hamtramck	M/1	25
Madison Heights	M/1	25
Oak Park	M/1	25
Southfield	M/1	25
West Bloomfield	M/1	25

Minnesota (236,000 HH)		Channel
Bloomington	T/W	46
Eden Prarie	T/W	46
Edina	T/W	34
Minneapolis	T/W	46
Richfield	T/W	46
St. Louis Park	T/W	34

Missouri (192,000 HH)		Channel
Clayton	Charter	6/10
Ladue	Charter	6/10
St. Louis	Charter	6/10
University	City Charter	6/10

New Jersey (225,000 HH)		Channel
Asbury Park	Ca	34
Avon	Ca	34
Bayonne	Ca	39
Belmar	Ca	34
Bradley Park	Ca	34
Brielle	Ca	34
Colt's Neck	Ca	34
Farmingdale	Ca	34
Freehold	Ca	34
Howell	Ca	34
Interlaken	Ca	34
Jackson	Ca	34
Lakewood	Ca	34
Manalapan	Ca	34
Mannesquan	Ca	34
Marlboro	Ca	34
Neptune	Ca	34
Ocean Grove	Ca	34
Ocean Twp.	Ca	34
Sea Girt	Ca	34
Seaside	Ca	34
Spring Lake	Ca	34
Spring Lake Hgts.	Ca	34
Wall Twp.	Ca	34

New York (1,815,000 HH)		Channel
Albany	T/W	18
Bronx	Ca	48
Brooklyn	Ca	48
Manhattan (South)	T/W	51
Nassau County	Ca	25
Saratoga Springs	T/W	18
Suffolk County	T/W	25
Troy	T/W	18

Ohio (472,000 HH)		Channel
Auburn	Ca	50
Bedford	Ca	50
Beechwood	Ca	50
Bambridge	Ca	50
Brecksville	Ca	50
Bedford Heights	Ca	50
Chagrin Falls	Ca	76
Cleveland Heights	Ca	50
Glenwillow	Ca	50
Highland Heights	Ca	50
Gates Mills	Ca	50
Garfield Heights	Ca	50
Cuyahoga Heights	Ca	50
Hunting Valley	Ca	50
Independence	Ca	50
Lyndhurst	Ca	50
Maple Heights	Ca	50
Mayfield Village	Ca	50
Moreland Hills	Ca	50
Northfield Village	Ca	50
Newburgh Heights	Ca	50
Newbury	Ca	50
North Randall	Ca	50
Orange Village	Ca	50
Pepper Pike	Ca	50
Richmond Heights	Ca	50
Shaker Heights	Ca	50
Solon	Ca	50
South Euclid	Ca	50
South Russell	Ca	50
Russell Twp.	Ca	50
University Heights	Ca	50
Valley View	Ca	50
Walton Hills	Ca	50
Warrensville Heights	Ca	50
Willowick	Ca	50
Warrensville Twp.	Ca	50
Austin	Armstrong Utilities	43
Boardman	Armstrong Utilities	43
Canfield	Armstrong Utilities	43
Canton	T/W	11
Columbiana	ATT	36
Hiram	Adelphia	36
Hubbard	County Shenango	23
Ellsworth	Star Cable	05
Kent	ATT	47
Lisbon	Tele-Media Co.	19
Mantua	Alelphia	36
Massillon	Massillon Cable	49
Niles	ATT	19
Newton Falls	ATT	56
Poland	Armstrong Utilities	43
Ravena	ATT	47
Salem	Star Cable	05
Sebring	ATT	40
Sharon	Century Shenango	23
Struthers	Century Ohio	02
Warren	ATT	19
Warren Twp.	Northeast Cable	34
Youngstown	T/W	13

Wisconsin (258,000 HH)		Channel
(Milwaukee/Suburbs)		
Bayside	T/W	95
Brookfield	T/W	95
Brown Deer	T/W	95
Butler	T/W	95
Elm Grove	T/W	95
Fox Point	T/W	95
Glendale	T/W	95
Greendale	T/W	95
Greenfield	T/W	95
Milwaukee	T/W	95
River Hills	T/W	95
Wauwatosa	T/W	95
West Allis	T/W	95
Whitefish Bay	T/W	95

The Hineni Heritage Center   232 West End Avenue New York New York 10023 212.496.1660

Listing of TV channels that carried the Rebbetzin's Chumash class
in hundreds of cities across America

had never experienced a reaction even remotely similar to anything before. Then and there she decided to begin studying Torah with the Rebbetzin, but had no way of making the connection.

Coincidentally (although there are no coincidences), Elsa Haft, a friend of Pat's, was being honored at a Hineni luncheon in The Plaza. Pat was not planning to attend. But when one of her clients could not make her afternoon therapy session, Jimmy asked her to go, because a business associate of his was dating Elsa, and he told Pat that it would mean a lot to him if she went to pay tribute to Elsa. So off she went to The Plaza.

Pat relates:

> I couldn't believe what I saw when I entered the hall. There at the podium was none other than the Torah teacher I had seen on TV. I didn't hesitate for a moment. I went straight up to the Rebbetzin and said, "I just saw you on TV. I want to study one-on-one with you."
>
> "I think it would be best," the Rebbetzin replied, "if you started your learning by attending one of our classes at Hineni."
>
> I didn't give up. You see, I wanted more than that. While I was sure that sitting in the audience at the Rebbetzin's classes would be a wonderful experience, I wanted something private, something intense, something that would be just the two of us.
>
> Now that I knew about Hineni, I showed up at the Center in Manhattan and again asked the Rebbetzin to give me private classes.
>
> "What do you want to learn?"
>
> "I want the knowledge of Solomon. I want to know why I'm here. What should my goals be? What can I hand down to my daughter that will give substance to her life?"
>
> "Do you know who Solomon was?" the Rebbetzin rejoined. "Do you know what the Five Books of Moses are?"
>
> "I do know that I believe in G-d, and I know that I'm Jewish."
>
> We began studying together, and I realized very quickly just how little I really knew, even though I minored in religion while studying at University of Pennsylvania.
>
> The Rebbetzin asked where I wanted to start, and I said at the beginning, from the very first book of the Torah — from *Genesis* (*Bereishis*). For two full years we studied *Genesis* two hours every

Thursday. We made a deal. The Rebbetzin would teach me privately, and I would transcribe everything she said and try to put it into book form.

The first year, I studied with just our tape recorder and a notebook. But eventually, eager to share all this new knowledge with friends, I began inviting them to the Rebbetzin's office. Later, wanting to involve even more women, I opened up my home for a monthly Torah study class, led by the Rebbetzin. The group grew from ten, to twenty, to thirty, to forty, and then to as many as eighty. It was a commitment. We never missed a Wednesday. My life revolved around these classes. Wherever I was — whether in Bloomingdales, restaurants, the hair stylist, Florida — I'd recruit more and more women to join our class. And though I'm not a big social person, I'd go to parties and social events just to spread the word to more and more.

There were the skeptics and even some hostility.

But I persevered. I didn't give up. And they came and came. At one point, just about every Jewish woman in Manhattan knew about The Rebbetzin and "The Pat Cayne Class." In fact, it continued for twenty-seven years.

The Rebbetzin's class led to the wisdom of Torah penetrating into the women's hearts, and gave new meaning to their lives. Many women started going to synagogue, lighting Friday night candles — ON TIME! — and taking on various mitzvos. For many women, the Rebbetzin's class was their lifeline to Judaism. They were able to bring spirituality into their homes, and to convey the beauty of the Torah to their children and grandchildren.

The Rebbetzin taught me fundamental life lessons. She gave me the wherewithal to understand that even when something bad happens in life, it's always for the good… And good does follow. The Rebbetzin also taught me that when you light just one candle, it can kindle many others without diminishing the original light. And that's how spreading the Torah works. You open your home to more and more people to study Torah, and it never diminishes your knowledge.

I still have my notes. And every Friday, I text my grandchildren and give them a one-line lesson from the Rebbetzin's *parashah* teachings. That continues to this day.

For Michael Beckman, working with the Rebbetzin was a wonderful experience. She was dynamic, a truly fantastic speaker, and able to deliver an entire class for the cameras with almost zero need for input from her producer. She was a natural in front of the camera — which meant that Michael had very little editing to do. At the end of the day the show was the Rebbetzin — and the draw of the show was the words of Torah she was sharing, along with some of the stories from her personal life. And so for years on end, Beckman produced the Rebbetzin Jungreis show and sent it out into the world of media content.

Usually they didn't know whether it had an effect on people.

But sometimes they found out that it did.

Sometimes it changed people's lives.

It was the '90s and the Rebbetzin and her Hineni organization were about to enter the world stage in a big way.

For years, Steve Eisenberg has been involved in numerous kiruv programs. Back then, however, he was just a really young man working at Bear Stearns, a major Wall Street firm.

After hearing one of the Rebbetzin's classes, he knew that he wanted to hear more. And so, Steve began attending the Rebbetzin's classes every single Tuesday night.

One day the phone rang at his office.

"Steve Eisenberg."

"Hi, Steve, this is Craig Horowitz. I'm the senior editor at *New York Magazine*."

"What can I do for you?"

"It's like this. Someone gave me your number and recommended I give you a call. I'm writing a piece on assimilation and intermarriage — and they said you would be able to help me with the research for the article. So, Rabbi Eisenberg, can we make a time to get together and have a conversation?"

"I'm not a rabbi," Steve corrected Craig Horowitz.

"Why am I calling you then?"

"I don't know, you called me. But if you're writing an article on intermarriage I can help you. I happen to be very involved in Jewish outreach in Manhattan and I can tell you exactly what's going on in the intermarriage department."

"Well, I don't understand, if you're not a rabbi…"

"You still called the right person."

Craig was not very happy.

Steve sent a silent prayer to G-d asking for the right words.

"Look," he said to Horowitz, "whom were you planning on interviewing for this article?"

"I'm meeting the head of Jewish Federation, I'm meeting the head of Israel Bonds, I'm meeting the head of UJA."

"I'm telling you right now — none of these people has any clue about what's really going on with intermarriage. The ambulance drivers don't know where the hospitals are!"

"I don't understand what you're telling me."

"I know you don't understand," Steve said to the confused writer. "You're going to sit down with the official Jewish leadership — the leadership who has the money and the connections. But they don't know what's really happening in the Jewish world. They may be driving the ambulances, but they don't know where to deliver the patients."

"I still don't understand."

"Do me a favor," Steve said to Horowitz. "When you meet the head of the Federation ask him what he does for his own spirituality. I will tell you the answer right now. He goes to ashrams. But ask him yourself and see what he answers you. And when you meet the other people on your list, ask them what they would do if their child chose to become religious. Ask them how they'd feel if their kid became an Orthodox Jew."

Craig Horowitz brought the conversation to a close a minute later and Steve Eisenberg thought that was the end of it.

It wasn't long before Steve got another call. This time a Chabad rabbi was on the line. He was the Rabbi who'd given Steve's name to the editor of *New York Magazine*.

"How'd the conversation go?" he wanted to know.

"I'll tell you the truth, he called me. When I told him I wasn't a rabbi he stopped being interested in what I had to say."

"So what did you do?"

"I provided him with a list of questions to ask the Jewish leaders he planned on interviewing."

"What kind of questions?"

"I recommended that he ask them if they could tell him the name of Moshe Rabbeinu's mother — and *l'havdil*, Yoshke's mother. Ask them to name the Five Books of Moses and ask them to name five of the Apostles. Ask them to sing one non-Jewish holiday song by heart and one song that religious Jews sing every Friday night. Ask them who wrote *Das Kapital* and who wrote *The Guide to the Perplexed*."

(These comparisons were often mentioned by the Rebbetzin in her classes, challenging her listeners with the idea that they often knew more about other religions and cultures than their own.)

"What was his response to that?"

"He told me that he didn't understand what I was talking about. Then he hung up the phone."

"Well," the Chabad rabbi said, "Hashem runs the world. You did the best you could and whatever is supposed to happen, will."

Steve went to London for a business trip and returned five days later. He was back at his desk when the phone rang. It was Craig Horowitz.

"Steve Eisenberg?"

"Yes?"

"Craig Horowitz. I'd like to meet you."

"Why?"

"I want to meet you."

"How did it go with all the important Jewish leaders?"

"I want to meet you. We'll discuss it then."

They met at the Great American Health Bar.

"How did it go?" Steve asked the editor of *New York Magazine*.

New York Magazine article profiling the Rebbetzin and her Torah class at KJ

"Well, the guy from the Federation — the guy controlling a multi million-dollar 'outreach' budget — goes to ashrams for his spiritual growth, exactly like you said. One of the other leaders said in response to my question as to how they'd react if their child became religious that they'd rather them marry a non-Jew than see their kid become Orthodox. None of them knew who Moses' mother was (surprise, surprise), none of them were able to sing a Shabbos song and none of them knew who wrote *The Guide to the Perplexed*. These are the Jewish American leaders who have been handed the outreach mandate for American Jews — yet they lack basic Jewish knowledge!

And that," Craig finished, "is the reason I have come to you. Whom do you think I should meet with?"

In an interesting turn of events, Craig Horowitz began researching his article a short while after Rav Meshulem Jungreis passed away. At the time, sixty to seventy people a week were attending the Rebbetzin's class in the Hineni building. When she returned to give her class after sitting *shivah*, the number of participants went up by about a third from one week to the next. Maybe people wanted to show solidarity with the Rebbetzin, who had just suffered a loss; but whatever the reason, the numbers jumped exponentially.

When that happened, the Hineni building was bursting at the seams and could no longer accommodate the crowds, as more and more people came to hear the inspirational words of Rebbetzin Esther Jungreis.

The outcome of the much larger crowd meant that the Rebbetzin needed to move her weekly class to a larger venue — which she did. The new location was Kehilath Jeshurun, or "KJ" as it was more popularly known. In the class's new location the numbers jumped yet again, from 100 people to 250-300 attendees.

Steve introduced Craig Horowitz to the Rebbetzin and even brought him to "KJ" to hear a class.

After attending several classes, Craig felt that he had enough material for his article on intermarriage. From that moment, things moved very fast. Craig wrote the article, titling it "Are American Jews Disappearing?" It came out in *New York Magazine*, where it created roiling waves throughout the New York Jewish scene. The article was filled with an appreciation of what Horowitz had seen at "KJ": the class of people who were coming to hear the Rebbetzin speak (he wrote in the article, "You could smell the Prada in the room"); what he heard — the Rebbetzin's Torah; and what he had learned about intermarriage and assimilation.

The article's graphics had a picture of a Jewish star made of sand that was eroding — the outcome of everything he had learned from all the religious people that he interviewed. It ended up being a thoughtful, realistic and well-researched piece by the time it hit the stands. And it was all about Hineni!

When the *New York Magazine* article came out, attendance at the Rebbetzin's *shiur* jumped in one week from three hundred people to one thousand people! In the months that followed, Hineni had to hire a security team to maintain order — there were people lined up outside the shul waiting to get in to the Rebbetzin's *shiur*. It was as if a Torah lecture had taken the place of the city's most popular night club! And it fed on itself every week, with the line of people waiting to get in stretching around the corner.

The people themselves couldn't believe that they were actually spending their Tuesday evenings going to hear a rebbetzin speak. But it was never just a speech. Not at all. She gave serious Chumash classes with authentic Torah messages and didn't mince her words about what

The Rebbetzin teaching a full house at KJ

she expected from the people attending her *shiurim* and what they needed to do to get their lives in order.

Shabbos. Hashem. Torah.

The Rebbetzin made people laugh and cry. She knew how to zero in on the contemporary issues with which young people were grappling. She focused on political, social and relationship issues. She told it like it is.

And yet they'd come back to hear her do it again and again the next week!

The Rebbetzin wasn't intimidated by anyone. Not by the models in the audience or the wealthy people or the children of Park Avenue. Not by the jetsetters and not by those whom many would coin the "down-and-outs of society," who also streamed to Hineni and felt connected to the Rebbetzin and her message. Whenever you went to one of her classes it was like a big melting pot of different types of people. She was the sort of leader who had the ability to unite everyone under one umbrella. She had been around the world and around again — and had seen it all. And the people benefited from her wisdom and understood intuitively that they could not do better for themselves than by spending their evenings in her company.

And so the numbers grew.

From a thousand Jews in the audience, the numbers continued climbing to twelve hundred and fourteen hundred, and eventually there were some weeks when there were close to two thousand professional, upscale, yuppy, good-looking, and successful people — the elite of the secular world — coming to hear words of Torah in the busiest city in America! Against all odds, the Rebbetzin's *shiur* had become "the thing."

One time Steve ran into a young man who told him he was really trying to keep Shabbos and other mitzvos.

"How did you get involved?"

"I met Rebbetzin Jungreis at an event in Denver, Colorado."

"What was the Rebbetzin doing in Denver?"

"She was at a Barnes and Noble for a book signing for her second book — *The Committed Life*."

(After her second book was published, the Rebbetzin embarked on a whirlwind book tour through the largest cities in America — a city a day.)

Book-signing events for
The Committed Life,
The Committed Marriage
and *Life Is a Test*

"What happened?"

"I waited on line to have her sign a copy of the book. When I reached the head of the line and handed her the book, she did something out of the ordinary."

"What do you mean?"

"I mean that instead of saying hello, signing the book and wishing me a good day, she looked me in the eye and said to me right out of the blue, 'Break up with her!'

"'What are you talking about?' I asked, completely taken aback.

"'Break up with your non-Jewish girlfriend,' the Rebbetzin repeated. 'You need a Jewish wife.'"

If you want to be cynical you can say that since a huge percentage of Colorado Jews intermarry, it was a safe bet on the Rebbetzin's side to make that statement. But the truth is, this particular guy was struggling with the fact that he was dating a non-Jew. It was a battle for him and he didn't know what to do. He felt guilty on one hand, but on the other hand, he didn't know how to end the relationship. But the second the Rebbetzin in her incredible wisdom and intuitiveness made her comment to him — he knew that he could do it.

And he did.

He followed through and got involved with Aish HaTorah — another life saved by one of her comments. It was uncanny. The Rebbetzin always knew what to say!

There were many additional pieces to the puzzle that turned Hineni into a household name throughout the '90s.

One of those pieces went by the name of Elisa Kashar Akrongold, a young woman who had moved to New York from Miami. It was Elisa who was able to offer the Rebbetzin the opportunity of an introduction to millions of Americans. And she was repaid for her efforts. Repaid with interest.

This chapter has been dedicated
in memory of the Rebbetzin ע"ה.
We are incredibly grateful for all that she has done
for us and for all the Jewish people.
Bruce and Amy Gelb

CHAPTER FORTY
"Good Morning America"

*E*lisa Kashar moved to New York from Miami in 1997 with years of television experience. In Miami she had worked at the local NBC affiliate. She was good at her job — good enough to win two Emmy awards for shows she had produced. During her time at NBC she worked at a number of different shows: a news show and a show called 20/20, among others. Her experience was varied and extensive. Overall, however, her specialty was consumer investigative reporting.

One story that won her lots of recognition was when her team exposed a scandal at the Miami Dade courthouse in South Florida, where they were able to prove how the people who worked for the municipality were issuing tickets all over the place for any infraction of the rules, while at the same time, they themselves would park in parking spaces reserved for the handicapped — every day and all day long. Elisa won an Emmy for that story; it was quite a story for a local TV station.

She ran another investigation into a whole chain of nursing homes and elder-care facilities, exposing the abuse and the terrible conditions. She won a second Emmy for that story.

When one of the people she worked with in Florida was hired by CBS and moved to New York, he called and asked her if she was interested in leaving Miami and coming to work as a producer at his afternoon talk show.

Short answer, she was.

Elisa was in her twenties at the time, and a friend of hers kept on inviting her to attend a Tuesday night Torah class that was being given by some Rebbetzin.

"No, no, no. That's not for me. I'll meet you after the class."

It just so happened that the Hineni townhouse where the Rebbetzin's classes were being held was located right across the street from Elisa's apartment.

Her friend didn't give up. She asked Elisa again, and she promptly refused.

Six months later the friend called and said, "You have to come with me to this class," and Elisa gave in. It really wasn't a big deal — after all, it was right across the street.

So she went.

The night of her first class was literally a life-changing experience. There were fifteen people in the class, and the Rebbetzin gave her unique and inimitable Torah lesson.

"I could not believe that the things I was hearing were being taken from the Torah."

Elisa was astounded. "That's in the Torah? This is in the Torah? It can't be!"

The Rebbetzin always used to say that every single Jewish person has a *"pintele Yid."* On that night, she turned Elisa's *pintele Yid* into a forest fire! That was it — Elisa was blown away.

It was the first time in her life that anyone had spoken about the Torah to her in a relatable way. Elisa had grown up praying at a huge Conservative Temple in Houston, where they played music and there was no connection with the rabbi. The whole service was more like a show, with no spiritual fulfillment on any level. But what she was hearing at Hineni resonated deeply.

Elisa returned the following week and the week after that.

And she noticed that the class was starting to grow, because everyone was bringing friends. A few weeks later there were twenty-five people. Then next week it jumped to forty participants. Then sixty. It was at that point that they outgrew the Hineni building and the Rebbetzin relocated the class to "KJ," where it jumped to a hundred attendees and then more than doubled again! Suddenly the Rebbetzin's *shiur* was growing so fast, she was having trouble keeping up with her own success!

Although she had left a job in Florida for a more prestigious position at CBS, Elisa would remain there only for a year before moving on to another position, this time at the "Good Morning America" Sunday show on ABC. While there, she was assigned to work on a story about how single twenty- and thirty-year-olds across the United States had begun gravitating to spiritual locations in order to meet other likeminded people. The world of bars, singles clubs and night clubs was falling out of fashion and people were returning to churches and synagogues to further their social lives. It was an interesting trend, and ABC wanted to turn the phenomenon into a major story.

The story interested Elisa Kashar because it was a good story, one that she knew would appeal to ABC's viewership around the country. But there was another reason why she was excited about the story she'd been assigned — and that had to do with the Rebbetzin. Because by then, some fifteen hundred people were coming to hear her speak every Tuesday night — fifteen hundred Jewish singles coming together. After the class was over there was an hour designated for socializing, with the Rebbetzin requiring that anyone who wanted to meet people at the social hour had to first attend her class and learn Torah.

Elisa herself was a regular at the Tuesday *shiur* at "KJ" and during the hour-long Torah class, you could have heard a pin drop — it was so quiet. The Rebbetzin had command of the room in a way that few had. It was mesmerizing to watch the way she spoke, taught and simply

Hundreds listening attentively to the Rebbetzin at KJ

related to the incredibly large crowd that came to see and learn from her. Elisa could think of no better person to interview on the subject of Jewish singles returning to the synagogues of their youth — than the very person who was making that happen!

She called the Rebbetzin.

"It's Elisa Kashar."

"How are you, sweetheart?"

"I'm doing great, Rebbetzin. The reason I'm calling is because I wanted to offer you the opportunity to appear on 'Good Morning America,' as an integral part of the story I'm working on."

"What's the topic of the show you want me on?"

Elisa gave her the rundown.

"I'll be happy to be a part of it."

Thus began a fascinating process: one that afforded Elisa Kashar the opportunity to spend time alone with the Rebbetzin and to get to know her on a personal level.

ABC shot the segment with the Rebbetzin in the "KJ" sanctuary where she held the Tuesday-night class. The interviews were done a few hours prior to the class — one-on-one with the Rebbetzin. The cameras were then moved near the "KJ" entrance where they filmed the hundreds and hundreds and hundreds of people streaming into the building and filing into the sanctuary where they found seats and waited for the Rebbetzin to begin.

The sight of so many obviously prosperous and successful people eagerly rushing into a Torah *shiur* was gripping all on its own, and the cameramen loved the visuals. It was as if the crowd were rushing into a concert hall to hear their favorite musical artist perform. The energy level was high, and the room was filled with positive and enthusiastic vibes from the people filling every seat. Looking at the expressions of the people in the audience, there was no question that there was no place they would have rather been.

When everyone was seated and the Rebbetzin began to speak, the cameras shot footage of the actual class, and that was followed by more filming of the social scene after the class was done. Of course they also made sure to interview some of the people who had been at the class and who attended regularly for their take on what was obviously a transformative experience.

For Elisa there was an added benefit above and beyond the success of the show — and that was the fact that she and the Rebbetzin ended up spending a lot of time together before and during the filming, which led to a real relationship. And like the article in *New York Magazine*, the segment on ABC was yet another piece in the Hineni puzzle, drawing thousands of Jewish people — many of them not religious at all — to hear words of Torah from a Holocaust survivor.

Needless to say, the Rebbetzin was very grateful to Elisa for inviting her to appear on ABC.

Seven months later the Rebbetzin called Elisa.

"Hineni is having its annual dinner in a few months' time," she began, "and I would like you to be one of the young honorees."

Elisa had merely been doing her job as a producer at ABC. She was very happy that her job had afforded her a vehicle through which to showcase what the Rebbetzin was accomplishing at Hineni (the segment brought Hineni huge exposure), but she had never imagined that she would be honored because of her involvement with the organization. The whole thing had just fallen into place, like the most elusive puzzle pieces have a way of doing just when you need them most.

Following the Rebbetzin's Chumash class —
the perfect place for Jewish singles to meet (and where many shidduchim were made!)

"On the evening of the dinner," Elisa said, "I found myself seated at the head table on the dais, speech written and ready to be delivered, the other two honorees seated on the dais as well. The honoree seated closest to me introduced himself. His name was Bruce Akrongold."

Bruce had known the Rebbetzin for years. He and his brother Barry were both extremely close with the Jungreis family in general and the Rebbetzin in particular. And she never ceased to amaze him.

Some of Bruce's fondest memories took place during the Hineni trips to Israel:

> Being on those Hineni trips provided us with the opportunity to interact with the Rebbetzin in an informal setting. She took us to the graves of many great rabbis and gave us living history classes. But for me, everything else paled alongside the trips we used to take with her to the Kosel very late at night. We'd meet her downstairs in the lobby of the Plaza Hotel at about 12:30 or one in the morning. Most people would probably expect to be driven to the Kosel in the middle of the night. But that was not the way the Rebbetzin did it.
>
> We walked.
>
> Our group surrounded her as we walked along the Jerusalem streets, asking her question after question, which she answered

Davening at the Kosel at midnight was part of every Hineni tour

Chapter Forty: "Good Morning America" □ 429

The Rebbetzin overlooking her beloved city of Yerushalayim

in her trademark down-to-earth fashion. It was a very relaxed walk and really special. By the time we arrived at the Kosel it was already very late at night and there weren't a lot of people around. And those who were there were a very interesting and eclectic group, because most "regular" people are at home sleeping at two o'clock in the morning.

Upon arrival, we'd split up, men to one section, women to the other, and everyone would get a chance to daven.

One night we arrived at our usual time, and as I went to daven at the Kosel, I happened to see a man sitting under a table crying hysterically and davening at the same time. I felt bad for the guy because he really seemed to be experiencing a difficult time — he was crying as if his entire world had just been shaken by its very foundations... And I couldn't help wondering if he'd just lost someone close to him and had come to the holiest spot on earth to pray and cry...

Eventually he rose from his spot under the table and I walked over to him.

"You seem to be going through a really terrible time," I said to him. "Is there anything I can do for you?"

"There's nothing you can do for me," he replied.

"But you're sitting and crying under the table," I protested, "and you're doing it as if someone passed away — as if the most terrible thing in the world just occurred!"

"I come here every single night and I sit *shivah* for the Temple," he explained simply.

I had no idea how to respond to that. I had never seen a person cry quite like that before, and the last thing I'd expected was to be told that his tears were not for him at all — but for the Beis HaMikdash! We ended up speaking for a while that evening, and I saw him every night after that, sitting under the table and crying for the Temple, just outside the spot where it had stood for hundreds of years. It was a fascinating nightly encounter.

Of course I told the Rebbetzin about meeting the man, asking her, "What's the story with this guy?"

The Rebbetzin turned to me and said, "You know, Bruce, the people who come to the wall here at this hour — these are not regular people. These are what are called 'People of the Wall.' They don't come here for lighthearted reasons. They are very serious about coming here and praying — they are here for a purpose.

"It could be that he's just an interesting person, sitting on the floor, doing his thing.

"It could also be that this man really does come to the Kosel every night to sit *shivah* for the Temple — and to him it's the most serious thing in the world. And if that's the case and he's sincere about his prayers, he should be treated with the utmost respect."

That story and the Rebbetzin's response stayed with Bruce for years.

On another Hineni trip the Rebbetzin brought the tour to the ancient Jewish cemetery on the Mount of Olives in East Jerusalem. There at the top of the mountain, the Rebbetzin climbed on a large rock to speak to the thirty people on the tour. She then proceeded to describe to them what was going to happen on that very spot at the End of Days.

"This is where it's going to happen! The Mashiach will come from here! All the enemies of the Jewish people will leave the country!"

She was becoming very excited.

"At the end of the Six Day War," she went on, bringing history into the discussion (she loved doing that), "the Jewish people won one of the greatest military victories in the history of warfare. With the help of Hashem we destroyed all the Arab armies in six short days! And after we won, Moshe Dayan went and gave the holiest spot in the world back to the Arabs after we won it during battle! What kind of people win a war, then give back what they won?"

As she spoke, more and more tourists and Arabs began gathering around their group, listening as the Rebbetzin described the Biblical prophecies of the End of Days in the most vivid terminology, until the Arabs began to show signs of restlessness and unhappiness with the verbal picture she was drawing — how there was going to be a bridge from the spot they were standing to the Beis HaMikdash, etc....

Eventually, the soldiers who had accompanied them to the Mount of Olives, realizing that the Arabs were starting to stir themselves up into a restless mob, approached the Rebbetzin and whispered to her, "We're sorry, but you really can't speak this way here. Please get down from the rock immediately. It's time to go."

The Rebbetzin got down — but not before she left her group with the kind of images that last: images of Eliyahu HaNavi blowing the shofar, and Mashiach entering Jerusalem to redeem the Jews, and the return of the nation from around the world. Meanwhile the Arabs bristled and the soldiers grew more nervous. And then all at once, she finished her speech, was helped down to the ground and away they went — back to Jewish Jerusalem.

But the image of the Rebbetzin describing the End of Days would always remain with Bruce Akrongold.

"Bruce and I had a wonderful time getting to know one another at the Hineni dinner," Elisa continued, "where we hit it off immediately. It goes without saying that the Rebbetzin — who must have seen us enjoying our conversation — didn't just leave it at that but actually called Barry Akrongold (the two brothers shared an apartment at that point) at 1:30 in the morning and told him in no uncertain terms that they needed to get the shidduch between Bruce and Elisa off the ground.

"Barry," she said to him, "you have to promise me that you are going to help me get Bruce and Elisa together!"

In the end Bruce did call Elisa the next day and asked her to go out with him. And although Bruce was already serious about Elisa, the Rebbetzin would call him to make sure that he was really following through.

Today Bruce and Elisa are married with four children.

It would be quite accurate to say that the Rebbetzin was really responsible for helping Bruce and Elisa get married.

"And it wasn't just the marriage," Elisa said. "She made an enormous difference in every aspect of our lives, from the way we raise our children, to the amount of Torah we learn and mitzvos that we do."

Not long after her class began taking off, the Rebbetzin invited Elinor (Ellie) Wohl — Joe and Ronne's daughter and a Hineni benefactor — to come see for herself what was happening at Hineni. Ellie came and was extremely impressed. The room was packed, the people were spellbound and motivated, and Ellie walked away really proud of the Rebbetzin and everything she was accomplishing.

That year, Hineni chose to honor Ellie at the Hineni luncheon, which meant that Ellie would have to deliver a speech. Standing before the packed-to-capacity hall, Ellie said, "Ladies, you know how sometimes, you're out, you're busy shopping, your driver takes you to the stores — and you come out of the building, your hands full of packages, and you're looking and looking and thinking to yourself, *Where is the driver? Where is the driver?*"

The entire room nodded. They knew exactly what Ellie was talking about.

"This is what happened to me," she said. "I came out of the Rebbetzin's class. I was searching for my driver but he was nowhere to be found. So I said to myself, 'Okay, I'll go back in and hear the rest of the class.' I walked back inside and who do I see sitting and listening to the Rebbetzin's class — none other than my driver!"

From a class in the Hineni building with fifteen people... to "KJ" with upward of fifteen hundred people... and all the way to a segment on "Good Morning America," Rebbetzin Esther Jungreis went about her business of changing lives, through any and every medium available.

And she succeeded.

CHAPTER FORTY-ONE
A Tale of Two Promises

It was holiday season in Manhattan when a friend first brought Barry Akrongold to hear the Rebbetzin at the Hineni Center and to meet her afterward. The Hineni Center was a happening place. Located in a New York brownstone, it stands self-assuredly between two much taller buildings and beckons to passersby with allure. In the center's early days, the Rebbetzin designed the building as a center/museum/shul. Schools around the tristate area brought their students to meet the Rebbetzin at the Hineni Center on a regular basis, and she turned part of the center into exhibits that were light years ahead of their time.

The Hineni Heritage Center in Manhattan

There was a Holocaust room, something she dubbed "The Jewish Way of Life Room," and another room devoted to Eretz Yisrael. There were multi-media screens playing videos of the Rebbetzin speaking around the globe, and it was quite an experience. Her office, located on the top floor of the building, was a

Groups of all ages learning from the Rebbetzin about their Jewish heritage in the Hineni Museum

The Shabbos exhibit

The Holocaust Studies Exhibit

The Jewish Way of Life Exhibit

The Israel exhibit

The Hineni Multi-Media Museum

comfortable and welcoming spot. There was a picture of the Rebbetzin with President George W. and Laura Bush at the White House Chanukah party, others of her meeting with Ariel Sharon, Menachem Begin and Bibi Netanyahu, and one of her with Rebbetzin Kanievsky.

The Rebbetzin with President George W. and First Lady Laura Bush at the White House

But the prime spot — the section of wall right behind her chair — was reserved for a collage comprised of pictures of all the Zeides. They hung on the wall just behind their granddaughter, peering down at the visitors and making them feel at home.

This was what the Zeides had always done and that was what they did at the Hineni Center as well.

As soon as the Rebbetzin began to speak, Barry realized he'd never heard anything like it before. A serious real estate investor, Barry was used to really listening when people talked, but he'd never seen the sight that met his eyes. There were seventy-five people sitting in the Hineni center, among them thirty women, poised with pens in hand, listening and taking notes on every word the Rebbetzin was saying as if their very lives depended on it (which in some cases wasn't far from the truth).

For Barry, it wasn't just about the Rebbetzin's message — it was more about the fact that there were thirty eligible Jewish women in a room accepting marriage advice (which he found to be really solid) from the woman giving the speech.

Barry was about to leave on a trip to Israel, but he told himself that he would return to Hineni when he got back to New York.

He saw the Rebbetzin again at a different event standing on a chair

talking with charismatic fire, and he
knew just from hearing her speak that
there was nothing in the world able
to hold her back. He approached the
Rebbetzin after her speech and introduced himself. It wasn't long before
Barry Akrongold had become a regular
at the Rebbetzin's "KJ" *shiur*.

Within a short while the Rebbetzin
began getting him more and more
involved in what she was doing. The
Rebbetzin saw Barry Akrongold as a
way of reaching a lot of people — he
was extremely well connected — and she had big plans for him. As for
Barry, he saw her as one of the wisest, most caring and incredible people
he'd ever met and was willing to do just about anything for her.

This translated into Barry writing letters for the Rebbetzin and setting
up appointments for her with people he knew.

"This woman is phenomenal," he'd tell his friends, who, taking his
word for it, went out of their way to meet her and were always favorably
impressed. Being actively involved with the 92nd Street Y, Barry suggested that the Rebbetzin speak to the large groups of Jews who visited
the Y for social purposes.

"Rebbetzin, the Y hosts some of the most famous speakers in the
world on a regular basis," he told her. "They have people from industry,

The Rebbetzin at one of her many lectures at the 92nd Street Y

people from literature — even former presidents have spoken there — and I think you'd make quite a hit!"

The Rebbetzin didn't believe the Y would be interested in hosting her for their members and told him so. Barry, however, was on a mission by that point and said, "Rebbetzin, let me try to set something up."

So Barry called up his friend who ran programming at the Y and told him he had a good idea for a speaker.

"Who do you have in mind?"

"She's a bestselling author and a popular speaker."

"What's her name?"

"Rebbetzin Esther Jungreis."

"The Rebbetzin!" he said excitedly. "Of course we'll take the Rebbetzin! We can't wait for her to come here!"

The Y gave the Rebbetzin a huge auditorium, Barbara brought a van-load of books for a book-signing after the speech, and Barry began arranging these kinds of events for her — very high-profile events — on a regular basis. After conquering the Y, Barry decided that he wanted to showcase the Rebbetzin at some of the major UJA events for their big donors. Eventually UJA did bring her in to speak at a serious event at Napa Valley in California, where she blew the crowd away with a speech about how a person has to make sure to present a smiling face to the outside world regardless of how he feels on the inside.

"Your face is public property," she'd explain. "Put on a smile and make the people around you happy — even if you're not happy, and even if you're not in a good mood. You'll see, before you turn around, your mood will change and you'll feel much better about everything that was bothering you before."

She then told a story (one of her favorites) about a man named Lord George Hell who was an ugly and disfigured person, with a nasty disposition to match his physical appearance. Wanting to convince a young girl that he was a person worth marrying, Lord Hell put on a mask with the face of a kind person. He kept the mask on for a long time, and when he finally removed it, he found that his real face had changed as well — and that he looked like a kind individual, with a smile and a twinkle in his eye.

"It's a funny thing," the Rebbetzin would say, "but people can change their inner feelings, really transform the way they're feeling inside, by putting on a smile — even when they don't feel like smiling at all.

"Why are all of you sitting around all depressed? Jews aren't depressed! When you get up in the morning you should jump out of bed like a lion!"

Needless to say, the speech in Napa Valley went over well.

But Barry had yet another dream. He wanted to introduce the Rebbetzin to the people at AIPAC (American Israel Public Affairs Committee) and have her featured as a keynote speaker at that noteworthy event. He felt it would do everyone there a world of good to listen to a person like Rebbetzin Jungreis — and he knew they would love her and connect to her message. The question was how to get her through the door. AIPAC was a primarily secular organization and wasn't keen to feature religious speakers on their rostrum. Barry wasn't deterred. He knew that if you can't get in the front door, you go in through the back door. At the end of the day, both doors lead to the same place.

Booking a large hotel suite at the AIPAC Conference, Barry hosted a private reception for the Rebbetzin, spreading the message to everyone he knew at the convention that the Rebbetzin was in town and that they were going to want to be there and meet the legendary Rebbetzin Jungreis. As was the case with everything the Rebbetzin did, the catering at their private event was top level, and they shipped in a large crate of the Rebbetzin's books from New York for the long line of people who streamed to meet her and wanted to purchase a copy of *The Committed Life*, which had recently been published.

The Committed Life was a bestseller in its day. It had been endorsed by internationally known names such as John Gray, author of *Men Are from Mars, Women Are from Venus*; and Mark Victor Hansen, coauthor of the #1 *New York Times* bestselling *Chicken Soup for the Soul* series. The Rebbetzin's book was selling like hotcakes and changing people's lives around the country.

At one of the AIPAC conferences, the Rebbetzin crossed paths with one of America's most famous pastors, a man named John Hagee, who was extremely pro-Israel and had thousands and thousands of people coming to hear him at his church in Texas.

"Rebbetzin," he said, greeting her with incredible warmth, "we're so happy to meet you here. My wife watches your Bible television show every single week — she never misses!"

He couldn't do enough for her. It was clear to them that she was in possession of a certain intangible spiritual gift — one which they weren't sure how to relate to, but made them respect her beyond all measure.

The Rebbetzin held court like a queen and was totally at ease as she greeted everyone who made an appearance — seemingly without having to think twice about what to say or do, no matter who they were.

Someone would attempt to trap her with a political question: "Rebbetzin, do you believe that Israel should revert to its Biblical boundaries as written in the Torah?"

She wasn't fazed by those kinds of questions and deftly turned them any way she wanted, leaving the questioner bemused and impressed with her rhetorical abilities. Where others might have blundered, she emerged victorious, engaging would-be critics and drawing them to her side.

Eventually the Rebbetzin's conference room became a hot spot, as many of the most well-known people there came by to see her and have a conversation with the celebrated woman proudly known as "The Rebbetzin."

But she was never really interested in the famous people — that wasn't her goal. One time a young Jewish man from France entered the room — he was looking for a shidduch and had come to meet her. Seconds later she excused herself from whatever conversation she had been in the middle of, and was handing him a signed copy of *The*

The Rebbetzin meeting with Congressman Clarence Long on Capitol Hill

Committed Life, while taking down his number and contact information in her ubiquitous little shidduch notebook. He was young, good-looking and Jewish. This was too important to pass up. There were shidduchim to be made and she couldn't afford to allow him to slip away because she was involved in a conversation with the president of the trade unions or some actor from Hollywood. This was her primary interest: saving the Jewish world, one shidduch at a time.

Making matches between Jewish people who weren't necessarily religious was her greatest pride and joy. Because that meant she had managed to serve as Hashem's messenger once more in stemming the tide of the spiritual Holocaust that was engulfing American Jewry.

Rabbi Tzvi Hersh Weinreb, the Executive Vice-President Emeritus of the Orthodox Union, related an experience that he had with the Rebbetzin on Capitol Hill.

"Some years ago, the Rebbetzin and I were invited, along with some other Jewish leaders, to a meeting with Senator Bill Frist of Tennessee. He was then the majority leader of the United States Senate and a serious candidate for the Republican nomination for President, to succeed George W. Bush. That entire evening calls for a long description, but suffice it to say that the Rebbetzin was the star of the show. She eloquently and movingly spoke of her appreciation of our great democracy and explained how honored she felt, as an immigrant and refugee, to be standing at the epicenter of the American government, in the office of the majority leader, which then stood in a section of the Capitol that was not destroyed by the British in 1812.

"When Senator Frist asked her to say grace, she honored me with the recital of the berachah but reserved for herself the privilege to, in her own words, thank G-d for the religious liberty that Jews, and all others, enjoy in the United States of America. At that moment, just as after every one of her public addresses, there was not a dry eye in the house. I am confident that there will be no dry eyes among all those who recall, now or in the future, her gracious and inspiring presence. May her memory be a blessing."

Barry organized the Rebbetzin Jungreis event at AIPAC for six years running. Just being at AIPAC and walking the floor at the conference

The Rebbetzin with New York senator Alfonse D'Amato

gave the Rebbetzin access to influential and key government people whom she approached to share her opinion.

The people at AIPAC took to her and couldn't help but be impressed — which led to her being invited to deliver the benediction at the AIPAC Conference. AIPAC draws upward of twenty thousand people to its conference, and many of those people were meeting the Rebbetzin, which was Barry's goal: to introduce her to as many people as possible.

And she barely had time for sleep.

She'd talk to people until one or two in the morning. She was indefatigable: defending Israel like a mother lioness defending her cubs, signing yet another book, talking to this one, suggesting a shidduch to that one. Barry's eyes might be closing, but she was still going strong.

Barry Akrongold had met a lot of people through the course of his life and years in business. But he had never met a person who could hold a candle to the Rebbetzin. He saw her as one of the greatest Jews who ever lived, taking all of the hardships that had happened to her throughout her life (and make no mistake, she had her fair share) and using them as a springboard to transform other people's lives. Some people are great speakers, some are great matchmakers, some are great organizers, but she combined it all.

At a certain point Barry's mother was diagnosed with cancer; she lived with the illness for many years. When Barry told the Rebbetzin about his mother's illness, she began calling Mrs. Akrongold every Friday afternoon — she never missed — giving her something to look forward to throughout the week. Barry's mother was on chemotherapy, very sick, but her relationship with the Rebbetzin transcended her illness and suffering, lifting her above what she was experiencing and giving her a spiritual perspective and lifeline to hold onto within the midst of the cloud of never-ending pain.

Here was the Rebbetzin — writing bestselling books, traveling the world on speaking engagements, delivering the benediction at the Republican National Convention, at Madison Square Garden, giving classes at "KJ" for upward of fifteen hundred people a week — and yet, she never, ever ceased doing the myriad individual acts of kindness that made her who she was, and turned her from a charismatic and influential person into The Rebbetzin.

And she did the same for so many people, and their families, their extended families and their friends and their families. How on earth could one person do so much? How was it possible?

Well, for one, she didn't sleep.

But even that isn't the real answer.

Because the amount she accomplished in a twenty-four-hour period was off the charts. People were traveling to see her literally from around the world. There's no exaggeration here — her audience on Tuesday nights was international. One Tuesday Barry met a man from Argentina at the class. The man was astounded by what he'd just experienced.

"Do you people realize how lucky you are to get to hear her speak every week? I flew thirteen hours just to hear this once! You don't know how lucky you are to be able to hear this! We have nothing like this in Argentina!"

The Rebbetzin was focusing simultaneously on the chessed, both large and small, and somehow managing to pull it off. For decades.

Barry's mother was honored at the Hineni luncheon a few months before she passed away. Knowing how many medications his mother was on at the time and afraid she might become confused, Barry jotted down some notes for her.

"I don't need any notes," she told him emphatically, and proceeded to stand at the lectern and deliver the speech of the year. By the time Mrs. Akrongold finished speaking that afternoon there wasn't a dry eye in the house.

"Do you know how lucky we are that we have the Rebbetzin? Do you realize what a great woman she is?"

She went on and on expressing her gratitude to the Rebbetzin and the Jungreis family, and the audience roared its approval.

Mrs. Akrongold was in the hospital that Yom Kippur. After the fast ended, the Rebbetzin got into a car with Barbara and showed up at

Sloan Kettering in a beautiful white dress, direct from the Neilah service. It was ten o'clock in the evening after a long, long day of davening, and Mrs. Akrongold couldn't believe her eyes when the Rebbetzin walked through the door of her room.

But the Rebbetzin didn't just take a seat. She sat down on the patient's bed — as if they were best friends or sisters — and they proceeded to have a heart-to-heart conversation and daven together. She did all this while still managing to keep the atmosphere lighthearted and upbeat.

During the course of the incredibly meaningful conversation that ensued, Mrs. Akrongold began speaking to the Rebbetzin about her son Barry.

"Rebbetzin," she said, "my son takes very good care of me. But I won't deny that I am extremely worried about him."

"What are you worried about?"

"I want to know that he will marry a Jewish girl and have Jewish children."

Here the Rebbetzin took something monumental on her shoulders.

"Do not worry," she reassured the desperately ill patient. "I will do my best to ensure that Barry marries a Jewish girl. You have my word."

"You cannot imagine what that visit meant to my mother," Barry said. "She didn't stop talking about it for the rest of her life, reminding us again and again how the Rebbetzin — looking like an angel, dressed in white from head to toe — had come to see her just a short time after Neilah, after spending the entire day davening on her feet. But she didn't go home to eat and rest. She went to the hospital to make another person's day.

"That was the Rebbetzin."

And so, while Barry was trying his utmost to introduce the Rebbetzin to newer and more far-reaching audiences, the Rebbetzin was trying *her* best to marry him off. He had a goal for her and she had a goal for him. Both wanted the best for the other. It was a beautiful thing.

Sometimes she'd call him up at three in the morning with an idea.

He'd answer the phone and hear the Rebbetzin saying, "Hello, am I waking you?"

"No, Rebbetzin," he'd reply dryly. "I was waiting for your call."

And after trying and trying to find him the right woman — one day the Rebbetzin succeeded.

Rachel Storch grew up in St. Louis. Her family had a strong Jewish identity and was affiliated with an Orthodox shul, but they themselves were not observant. In 2004-5 Rachel began studying with a rabbi at Aish HaTorah in St. Louis, who gave her a copy of *The Committed Life*. The lessons the Rebbetzin wrote in her book and the stories she told exemplified the way Rachel wanted to live her life, and she found that the book truly resonated with her on the deepest level. At the time, Rachel's mother had leukemia — she became sick at the young age of 57 — and she too read it and connected with every word of the book. Mother and daughter had the same reaction. Not content with stopping at liking the book, her mother picked up the phone, called Rachel's brother in New York, and said, "You have got to meet the author of this book! Please go find her and attend her class."

Her brother listened to their mother and went to hear the Rebbetzin speak. When the class was over he waited to meet with the Rebbetzin. It so happened that Rachel's brother was young, good-looking and not

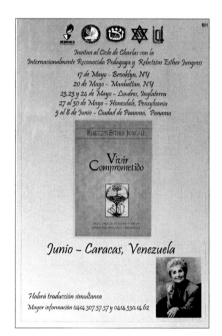

The Rebbetzin's *The Committed Life* book tour in Caracas, Venezuela

The Rebbetzin's *The Committed Life* book tour in Panama

The Committed Life

Russian edition

Hebrew edition

Hungarian edition

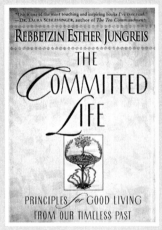

English edition

Spanish edition

Portuguese edition

French edition

married — he was what one might call very eligible — and since he was waiting in line to speak with her, the Rebbetzin naturally assumed that he wanted to speak to her about a shidduch.

However, he explained that he wasn't there for marriage purposes; the reason he'd come to see the Rebbetzin was because his mother was sick. He asked if Rebbetzin Jungreis would be willing to call her, because he just knew that a phone call from the Rebbetzin would make her year.

The Rebbetzin — being the Rebbetzin — called Mrs. Storch that Erev Shabbos, and the two of them developed a close connection due to that conversation. And the Rebbetzin continued calling Mrs. Storch every Erev Shabbos until she passed away two years later. But the Rebbetzin didn't stop there. When Mrs. Storch passed away, the Rebbetzin flew to St. Louis for the funeral and accompanied the Storch family to the cemetery, after which she returned to New York. She then called the family the next day from New York. Everyone gathered in the dining room, they put the Rebbetzin on speaker, and she then gave them a speech that would remain with everyone who heard it, telling them how their mother's *neshamah* was now in their hearts and that it would be a part of them for all eternity.

It was a very, very powerful moment for the Storch family.

The Rebbetzin returned to St. Louis two years later to speak at an event. At that time, Rachel Storch was involved in politics — she was an elected state representative for the 64th District of St. Louis — working in Jefferson City, the state capital of Missouri. Of course, Rachel arranged her schedule to be back in St. Louis for the Rebbetzin's speech. Rachel drove back that night and introduced the Rebbetzin at the event. At the end of the night, the Rebbetzin pulled Rachel aside and said, "There's someone very special I want you to meet."

She then told Rachel all about Barry Akrongold and how she was going to have him call her.

"I just want you to know that when this person calls you, it is not your run-of-the-mill person and you have to take this seriously."

The next day's two-hour drive back to Jefferson City gave Rachel plenty of time to consider the Rebbetzin's words.

"If the Rebbetzin — such an incredible judge of character — is speaking so highly of this person, he must really be somebody special," she said to herself.

Barry called two days later.

Rachel was on her way to participate in a panel discussion when the call came. She parked the car and sat there talking to him, and there was something so warm and kind in his voice that she just didn't want to get off the phone. They had a wonderful conversation, but he was in New York and she was in St. Louis/Jefferson City, so Barry ended the call with, "The next time you're in New York to see your brother, give me a call — I'd love to take you out to dinner."

And they left it at that.

If left to their own devices, it is very possible that Barry Akrongold would still be in New York and Rachel Storch still in Missouri. But because the Rebbetzin was involved, the story moved in a different direction. She called Rachel a few days later and said, "*Sheifelah*, this is too good of an opportunity to miss. You have to fly to New York next week and meet Barry."

If anyone else would have ordered Rachel Storch — elected representative in the State of Missouri — to drop everything and fly to New York to meet a man she had spoken to only once on the phone, she would have, in all probability, continued with her life. But this was the Rebbetzin and she just couldn't say no — even though she was in the middle of work on the budget committee hearings and a million other things. Somehow events had taken on a life of their own, and Rachel Storch found herself on the phone with the travel agent, booking a ticket for New York, where she stayed with her brother.

Barry took her to dinner, as he'd promised. The next day he picked her up again and they went for a walk in Central Park and out for brunch. A few weeks later Barry invited Rachel to spend part of Pesach with his family and she accepted happily, knowing from the constant twinkle in his eye that it would be a wonderful experience, which it was.

Yet while all this was going on, the Rebbetzin wasn't resting.

First she called Barry.

"There's something you have to know about Rachel."

Her tone of voice got him nervous.

"What's that, Rebbetzin?"

"She's a Democrat."

He couldn't help but laugh, relieved that her identification with the Democrats was the whole story.

Then the Rebbetzin called Rachel. Rachel, who was back in Jefferson City, took the call and excused herself from a committee hearing.

"What is it?"

"Rachel, I have to tell you something about Barry."

Butterflies started dancing in her stomach. What had she missed? What bad news was the Rebbetzin about to tell her?

"There's only one problem."

What on earth was the Rebbetzin talking about? Had Barry been married before they met? Did he already have three kids?

"Barry's a Republican."

Rachel was overjoyed, relieved beyond words that that was the major problem the Rebbetzin was referring to.

This was one of the Rebbetzin's ways of helping two amazing people get past their political leanings to focus on what was truly important in a relationship.

But there was another secret that Rebbetzin Jungreis hadn't told either one — and that was the fact that both of their mothers had spoken to her before they died, begging her to find their children a Jewish soul mate. The Rebbetzin, for her part, kept their requests to herself, not informing Barry that Rachel's mother had been sick, or Rachel that Barry's mother had been through a similar experience.

They ended up dating for eleven months — the Rebbetzin helping him to close the deal at two or three in the morning; and Rabbi Yisroel married them in St. Louis (he also officiated at Bruce Akrongold's wedding).

Of course the Rebbetzin came to the wedding.

"Rebbetzin," Barry had said to her, "you know that my mother passed away. I wanted to know if you would be willing to walk me down the aisle."

"I'm not going to walk you down the aisle, but I will walk behind you."

Barry likes to joke that the reason the Rebbetzin wanted to walk behind him was to make sure that he wouldn't run away...

In the end, Barry's father accompanied him down the aisle, with the Rebbetzin walking slightly behind them.

At the wedding, the Rebbetzin delivered a speech "to an audience of one" that the kallah would never forget, explaining how Rachel's mother was going to be with her under the chuppah, the imagery of which evoked the kind of emotion that made both of them break down. Later she would describe how Barry's mother and Rachel's mother danced together under the chuppah.

At the wedding, the Rebbetzin gave Barry and Rachel the most meaningful blessing in the world: telling them that she was going to speak at their son's bris. Barry was fifty and Rachel thirty-seven, yet the Rebbetzin was telling them with all the confidence in the world that there was going to be a bris. And there was — nine months later — and the Rebbetzin spoke, just as she had promised.

And every time the Akrongolds were ready for another child, Rachel and Barry would go speak to the Rebbetzin after her weekly class, and Rachel would ask her for a berachah for a child. The Rebbetzin would give them — she called them "her children" — a beautiful berachah and lay her hand on Rachel's stomach; and three times — year after year — they learned that Rachel was expecting within the month! There was no question in their minds of the tremendous power contained in the delicate hands that foretold the miracle of birth three years in a row.

"It's all you, Rebbetzin," Barry used to tell her, "all you. You bring down the blessing from G-d."

And the Rebbetzin would wave her hand at them and act as if she didn't even know what they were talking about.

If you speak with Barry Akrongold today, he will tell you that he and his wife are the luckiest people in the world — just by virtue of the fact that they merited to spend so much time in the presence of such greatness.

And though they wish they could still speak with the Rebbetzin and ask her for advice, they know that her *neshamah* will always remain in their hearts and souls — and that she will be looking down at them from her lofty spot in Gan Eden.

This chapter has been dedicated
in the merit that the *neshamah* of our beloved Rebbetzin ע״ה
should have an *aliyah* in shamayim, and in the memory of our parents
Deborah Storch ע״ה, Rochelle Akrongold ע״ה, Harold Akrongold ע״ה
and in honor of Gregory Storch
The Storch and Akrongold Families

CHAPTER FORTY-TWO
The Taxi Driver's Rebuke

*S*hannon Penson relates:

The first time I met the Rebbetzin, it was because of my cousin. She had just moved into New York and begged me to go with her to a Jewish singles event.

I didn't really want to go — it wasn't my speed — but I went for my cousin. When we arrived I learned that before you were even allowed to go into the social hall, you had to first listen to a lecture. It was like a condition for permission to get inside. Of course I was very irritated that this was going to be a whole long drawn-out night and that I had to sit through a lecture, when the whole reason I was there in the first place was just for my cousin — and to be honest, I was not looking forward to the lecture.

I went. Begrudgingly.

One thing I couldn't help noticing was that the speaker was talking to a full house. There were hundreds of people in the audience. You don't see that every day.

And as the Rebbetzin was talking, I started to feel like I was on "Candid Camera" and that she was speaking directly to me, since everything she was saying was directly related to what was happening in my life right then.

"This has got to be some kind of joke," I said to myself.

I looked around the room and wondered when everyone sitting there — all 700 of them — were going to jump out of their seats and yell, "Surprise, you're being filmed right now!"

It had to have been planned, because how else could the aristo-cratic lady giving the speech have known everything about me like that! Eventually the speech ended and I walked out of the room on an unbelievable high.

And I said to myself, "You are going back to hear that lady talk."

I returned the next week by myself to learn from the Rebbetzin. I found a seat in the front row and again I was totally moved. It was as if I had just seen the greatest movie in the world and I was so inspired that I almost didn't know what to do with myself. For me, the experience was like that, but on steroids. I couldn't believe what I was hearing.

I returned again and again and again. Not for a party and not with a friend — just by myself, because she was touching a chord inside me, and I knew for the first time in my life that I was hear-ing the truth.

One day the Rebbetzin brought up the concept of Yissachar and Zevulun: Yissachar was the Torah scholar who sat and learned and Zevulun was the businessman who supported him and received a share in the reward of his Torah learning.

When I heard that, I said to myself, "This is a great idea. This will help me cover my bases. I should also support a Torah scholar and get a piece of his reward! It would be like buying a spiritual life insurance."

That was the moment when I approached the Rebbetzin to intro-duce myself. She was so warm — like a mother or a grandmother. She was hugging me, and it just felt like home. A touch on the arm, holding your hand… She kind of hugged you with her words and body language. I had grown up with a warm family, surrounded by love. But the Rebbetzin's love was on a different level — because it was a Yiddishe love and it was intoxicating. I just wanted more of it and to be close to her and to become part of her life.

I remember saying to her, "I really connected to the idea you just discussed in class about supporting the Torah scholar. Where do I sign up?"

"I have a better idea," she replied. "Instead of hiring a rabbi to learn *for* you, *you* will learn with a rabbi," and she asked her son Rabbi Osher to study Torah with me. I did give Hineni a check, but the focus wasn't on the fact that I was giving money in exchange for spiritual merits — but rather that I had begun learning Torah myself!

The Rebbetzin helped make me frum by first bringing home the concept that there is a G-d in this world.

"Did you create yourself? Did you will yourself into being? Can you make your mind stop thinking?"

That was one of her speeches and a way for her to help people understand that there is a Higher Power in the world. Once I grasped that concept, the Rebbetzin went into her next phase about how Hashem Who had created me and made me who I was had also given me a list of things that He wanted me to do.

"You owe Him so much; following His list is the least you can do!"

"What does that mean for me, Rebbetzin?"

"For now, that means when you go out to a restaurant, don't order meat."

"I can do that."

She eased me into things, one step at a time.

"Shannon," she'd say, "you have to live your life wearing Torah glasses."

"Torah glasses?"

"Yes. You need to make a shift in the way you see and relate to the world."

One day I called her daughter Slovie and asked her, "Tell me, how much percentage of your life is Jewish stuff, and how much is secular related?"

"You can't break it down, Shannon," she replied. "It's totally interwoven. The Jewish element plays a major role within every single part of my life. Life is a tapestry, with Judaism part of every stitch."

Slowly but surely, I began wearing Torah glasses. Suddenly life was a whole different picture.

If Shannon's family identified themselves as Reform, Andrew — her husband-to-be — came from a family that wasn't even Reform. They didn't even celebrate his bar mitzvah. He'd had a bris, and occasionally the family celebrated a Pesach Seder with his grandmother, but that was it. Totally enmeshed in single life in Manhattan, he was forty when a friend introduced him to Rebbetzin Jungreis at the annual Hineni dinner. They had a brief conversation, with Andrew giving the Rebbetzin a rundown of his life up until that point. The Rebbetzin then made it very clear to him what type of person she expected him to marry. She made her statement with the kind of authority Andrew rarely encountered, and it made a deep impression on him — especially as he himself was beginning to feel that his earlier lifestyle was no longer the way to go.

At that time, Shannon was the Hineni "announcement girl" — which meant she was the one who would stand in front of the huge crowd at the end of the Rebbetzin's weekly "KJ" class and announce the Hineni schedule for the coming week.

It was Rabbi Osher Jungreis who called Shannon and suggested that she go out with Andrew Penson. Though she had been attending Hineni events for quite a while, this was the first time the Jungreis shadchanim had set her up. Shannon asked no questions, telling herself, "What, you're so busy that you don't have ten minutes to meet someone for a cup of coffee?"

She agreed to the date with no expectations.

On their first date, Shannon set the guidelines.

"I'm interested in a Torah lifestyle," she told Andrew, "and if you're not interested in that kind of lifestyle, there's no reason for us to have a second date."

Andrew's sister was already religious and living in Zichron Yaakov. She had been trying to convince him to take a deeper look at religion for years. Having been exposed to the beautiful family life his sister had created, Andrew was ready to take Shannon seriously when she made it clear what she was looking for in a husband.

Every time Shannon gave birth, the Rebbetzin came to visit her in the hospital, just as she would have done for her own children. Of course, Shannon would let her know what names they were considering for the baby — and the Rebbetzin always had something to say on the subject.

As you've no doubt realized from everything you've read until now, names — more importantly, Jewish names — were a big deal to the Rebbetzin.

Which made the following story all the more special.

One week, the Rebbetzin spent Shabbos at the Pensons' home in Manhattan, along with some of her children. It so happened that Shannon had just experienced an incredible story the day before, and the Rebbetzin would go on to write about it in "The Rebbetzin's Viewpoint," sharing their story with the rest of the Jewish world.

It all began when Shannon made an appointment for her oldest son Yedidya at the orthodontist. For several of their children, Andrew and Shannon gave both Hebrew names and secular names for their American legal documents, such as passports and social security. In school he was always called Yedidya, and at home they alternated between Yedidya and his English name, Jed, mostly referring to him as Jed. As it was his first time at the orthodontist, Shannon had to fill out a bunch of paperwork. When she came to where it said "Name," she asked Yedidya what name he thought she should write down on the paper.

"Just put down Jed," he told her. "The doctor won't know how to pronounce Yedidya."

His words hit Shannon like a punch in the stomach, and she couldn't help thinking, "Here we're baalei teshuvah, yet our son wants me to use Jed on the form! We should have only used Yedidya from the beginning! Now it's too late — he's used to Jed!"

Rather than bringing Yedidya into the jumble of thoughts rolling around her mind, Shannon wrote down "Jed" on the form and they took their seats. They were called in to see the doctor a few minutes later and when the appointment was over, they left the office and took a taxi home.

It was a rainy rush hour in Manhattan when the cab pulled into Park Avenue traffic. This was prior to the days of Uber, and Shannon was just happy she'd been able to flag down a taxi. After they'd been driving for a block, Yedidya tapped his mother on the shoulder and whispered, "Mommy, look at the name of the taxi driver!"

Shannon looked at the little plaque with the driver's name and identification number and couldn't believe her eyes when she saw that his name was Yedidya!

There was no divider in the cab and she said to the big, burly driver, "Excuse me, sir, are you Jewish?"

Turning around, the driver replied roughly, "What's it to you?"

"You don't understand," she said, immediately clarifying where she was coming from with her question. "We're Jewish too, and my son's name is also Yedidya!"

At first the driver didn't react. But at the next light, he stopped, turned around to them and said in his rough voice, "I come from the Old Country, from Russia."

He then put his finger right in front of them, right in the middle of their personal space, pointing directly at them (almost throwing himself over the front seat), as if the message he had to say was the most important thing in the world.

"In Russia we had to fight to keep our Jewish names!"

Looking Yedidya straight in the eye, the driver commented fiercely, *"Never change your Jewish name! You change your name, you change your mazel in life!"*

He wasn't nice and smiley, he was tough and blunt, but he made his point in a way mother and son would never forget.

Needless to say, the two of them were blown away by that little exchange with what had turned out to be their very unorthodox New York cabbie. They got out of the taxi and Yedidya turned to his mother and said, "From now on, my name is Yedidya, and if the doctors can't pronounce it, too bad."

The next morning (it was Friday) Shannon took another taxi and because of what happened the previous evening, she couldn't help but take a glance at the name of her current driver.

It was Yaakov. The name of their second son.

Not Jacob.

Not Jay.

Yaakov.

Shannon took a picture of the name plaque, just in case people didn't believe the story and claimed she was making things up.

That Friday night was beautiful. With the Rebbetzin and her family sitting around their dining room table, Andrew and Shannon related the story of the New York City taxi drivers' names.

Suddenly the Rebbetzin said, "Shannon, what's with you and all the taxis?"'

Shannon didn't know what the Rebbetzin was talking about.

"Don't you remember when Hineni took a trip to Prague ten years ago?"

Suddenly it all came back to them.

"We were already dating at the time of the trip," Shannon said. "Since we were going out at the time, we decided to take a taxi and follow the bus. This way, we'd be able to spend time with the group and have plenty of time to talk as well. When we arrived at the hotel, Andrew looked around him, saw all the men wearing kippot, and realized that he'd left his in the back of the taxi. Turning around, Andrew went running down the street to catch the taxi, banging on the cab when he caught up so that the driver would stop. When the driver stopped the car and Andrew opened the door, he found his kippah, and beneath that — his international cell phone. Had he lost that, it would have been a major inconvenience, since that was his link to his New York office."

When she heard the story the Rebbetzin said, "You see, you ran after Yiddishkeit and Hashem rewarded you in a language you can understand — with a *gashmiyus* (materialistic) answer."

After all the taxi stories/memories, it was time to sit down around the table and make Kiddush, looking forward to enjoying an incredible Shabbos experience with the Rebbetzin. What made it all the more special was the fact that it was Shabbos *Parashas Shemos* where we read the story of Klal Yisrael's sojourn in a foreign land, during which they refused to change their Jewish names. No one at the table was able to get over that particular coincidence.

As for the name on the form in the orthodontist's office — Shannon fixed it the next time she was there. It would be Yedidya and nothing else from that day on.

"I remember hearing people talking about making shidduchim for their children," Andrew said, "and how they were looking for *yichus* (impressive lineage). I looked at Shannon and commented, 'I guess that means they won't be marrying into our family because we don't have *yichus*.'

"It kind of bothered Shannon and she mentioned the incident to the Rebbetzin.

"'But you do have *yichus*,' the Rebbetzin said pointedly. We weren't sure what she meant.

"She came over to our house the next day, carrying a poster of all the illustrious rabbis in her family tree — from the Menuchas Osher down — looked us in the eye and said, '*Kinderlach*, if anyone wants to know what kind of *yichus* you have, tell them one thing: We have Jungreis *yichus!*'

"But she wasn't finished yet. Calling over our children, she showed them the pictures of her Zeides on the poster, and said, 'You see these tzaddikim?'

"They nodded.

"'Those are your grandparents.'

"It was a moment we would never forget."

Shortly before their twin sons' bar mitzvah, Andrew went with the boys and Rabbi Osher Jungreis and his sons to purchase tefillin for Andrew's boys. After Rabbi Osher introduced himself and the *sofer* (scribe) grasped that he was Rebbetzin Jungreis' son, he grew very excited, commenting how special it was to be the son and grandsons of Rebbetzin Jungreis.

Watching this scene, Andrew couldn't help commenting while pointing at his boys, "She is their grandmother as well…"

Osher's sons were a little confused, Andrew's boys were a little confused, but the Rebbetzin used to tell them the same thing all the time, and Andrew understood exactly what she meant. If you make a person religious, it's as if you gave birth to him. So yes, his twins are her grandsons.

She used to say, "I am your spiritual mother, I am your spiritual Bubby."

And she didn't just say it. She got involved.

If the Rebbetzin felt the Pensons needed to do something differently, she had no problem saying, "*Sheifelah*, this isn't our way. You are a Jungreis now."

Rather than her expectations feeling like a burden, they felt good and right. Because it meant she was treating them like one of her own. And that meant becoming family with royalty.

One Shabbos, shortly after they moved in to their new apartment on the West Side of Manhattan, Andrew and Shannon were invited for a Shabbos meal at one of their new neighbors. Sitting together around the table making conversation, their host asked them, "So how would you categorize your *hashkafah* (Jewish worldview)?"

Andrew and Shannon looked at one another and said, "We'll get back to you."

After Shabbos, Shannon called the Rebbetzin with yet another urgent question.

"Rebbetzin, what's our *hashkafah*?"

"You're the Jungreis *hashkafah* — *sheifelah*, you're the Jungreis *hashkafah*."

And so it was.

CHAPTER FORTY-THREE

The Reporter

*L*isa Castleman Glazer was a news correspondent, delivering the news on the air for CBS. She also worked for CNBC Business News. She would also go on to work as a host in the studio for FOX News. Her jobs were extremely high powered and pressurized and demanded that she give of herself from morning till night. If she wanted to do anything for herself, it was very hard to find the time.

Lisa relates:

I was interested in becoming religiously observant before I actually met the Rebbetzin in 1995. By the time we met I had already started learning, but she provided a certain depth to the learning that had been missing until that point. She had achieved a certain type of celebrity status by then because she was referred to by one and all as "The Rebbetzin."

I remember thinking to myself, "But there are a lot of rebbetzins, aren't there?"

Maybe there were a lot of rebbetzins, but Rebbetzin Esther Jungreis was *the* Rebbetzin, and this was an acknowledged fact by one and all, which convinced me that she was probably worth going to hear.

I saw her for the first time at "KJ" on the East Side. The shul was packed with hundreds of young people — as if this was *the* place to be in the city on a Tuesday night, and I was enthusiastic about being there. After all, I'd heard so much about her!

I sat there listening to her relating the story of that week's *parashah* and the true and underlying motivations people have for why they do the things they do, and I remember thinking, "Wow, I'm so lucky that I came specifically this week when she chose to talk about the exact topics that were on my mind!"

I returned to hear the Rebbetzin several weeks later and the same thing happened. She discussed the *parashah* of the week in such a relatable way to what I was experiencing in my own life, and I remember looking around and thinking, "Wait a minute, is everyone else sitting here getting the same feeling that I have, that she's speaking directly to them and that the Torah that she's saying is speaking to them personally?"

It was those Tuesday-night classes with the Rebbetzin that showed me that not only is learning Torah a good thing for people to do — it's our heritage and our link to Sinai — but that the Torah is alive, a living organism, part of life in our times in just the same way that it was right and relevant at Har Sinai.

She was real and honest and there was Torah in her every breath. There was no such thing as partying at Hineni for partying's sake. There were events and gatherings and a good time was had by all — but the fun was presented through a prism of Torah concepts that she imparted in every thought and word.

And even with all her elegance and eloquence she had certain street smarts, too. Sometimes I'd wait in line to speak with her after the class about whatever I was doing right then, be it at the office or maybe about someone I was dating, and she'd say, "Let me tell you something, sweetheart," with this kind of world-weary voice, as if she'd seen everything the world had to offer — twice.

And she was always right.

It was uncanny how on the mark she was.

Later on, I would come to realize that the brilliance I had long recognized inside her had been acquired through her *ruchniyus*, through her spirituality — and it allowed her to operate in a whole different atmosphere. She had endless energy and was never uncomfortable — not in any situation and not with the most secular people. She had no problem looking anyone in the eye and telling them the truth about life.

I remember a class one Thursday night in her office.

One of the people spoke up.

"Rebbetzin, we have challah in our home every Friday night. And it's so great! And Shabbos morning, we get up, we just remember that taste, and we make French toast with the leftover challah!"

I'll never forget her reaction.

She smiled at the woman and said, "Sweetheart, I'm so delighted that you're making Kiddush and eating challah and lighting candles on Friday night, it's so special — you don't know what it means to me, but sweetheart, we don't make French toast on Shabbos — because we don't cook on Shabbos."

There was steel beneath the silken glove.

She wasn't afraid that her words would damage her relationships, because A — she was speaking Torah; and B — she was coming from a place of love. From watching her I learned that when you come from a place of love you can be truthful and never have to feel embarrassed.

When the Rebbetzin did a live interview on FOX News I came down from my office (I was also at FOX then) to make sure I got to see her. The Rebbetzin was being interviewed by a host named Uma, alongside two other people who were live at different locations. After the interview was over, I remember watching how the Rebbetzin emerged from the studio holding the hand of the host — they were talking and the Rebbetzin was holding Uma's hand…

I watched as she said goodbye to her FOX News host: "Sweetheart, it was so nice, thank you."

"Thank you for coming, Rebbetzin."

"No, thank you." So humble and gracious. So classic Rebbetzin Jungreis.

That was the way it was. Everyone loved her. It didn't matter who they were. It didn't matter if they were Jewish, Christian or Muslim. Everyone responded to her warmth and her charm.

By the time I met the Rebbetzin I had come in contact with many frum families and many wonderful children.

But when I got to know the Jungreis children, all four of them, Chaya Sora, Slovie, Rabbi Yisroel and Rabbi Osher, I saw such magnificence. From the first moment that I met her children I remember thinking: This is not like the old days of video, when you would dub one tape to another, you would lose what's called a "generation." What was that? That meant you were losing clarity. Resolution. And if you dubbed from a copy to yet another copy, you lost a little more resolution and a little more clarity.

But with the Rebbetzin's family, the resolution was the same from generation to generation to generation — from children to grandchildren to great-grandchildren. It was the same wisdom and knowledge, the same warmth, the same kindness, and the same spiritual vigor. The essence of who they were just didn't fade. It was like digital video — in the sense that nothing was lost. The clarity and the resolution were all the same!

I learned who the Jungreis family is the hard way when my husband and I had been married for six years without children. And the Rebbetzin would always give me a berachah. Always give me a berachah.

A berachah before I found out I was expecting.

And a berachah after I found out I was expecting.

And more berachos when things became complicated.

She always told me it was going to be fine. *Baruch Hashem*, after six years of marriage we had two sets of twins.

Fast forward many years.

We spent Shavuos at a hotel with the Rebbetzin and many other members of our Hineni family. As the meal was winding down to its conclusion, we approached the Jungreis table to say hello. The Rebbetzin greeted all of us and then noticed that my son was holding a little bag of popcorn in his hands.

"Mmm, popcorn," she said, making it sound as if that bag of popcorn was a delectable delicacy. "I like popcorn; would you give me a taste?"

My son had heard the Rebbetzin speak. He knew she was a very special person and extremely beloved to us.

Smiling at her, he gave her a taste of his popcorn.

"Thank you so much," she said, "that is so good. Would you get me a bag?"

He looked at me, asking me with his eyes if he could run by

himself and get the Rebbetzin a bag of popcorn, and I nodded at him and off he ran, so proud at having been afforded the opportunity to bring her a bag of popcorn. He was back almost immediately, bag of popcorn in hand.

"Thank you so much, sweetheart," she exclaimed, her regal face lit up with her classic radiance. And I knew at that moment that the simple request on her part had shown him that he was a giver and that he could always be a giver. I do not know how much Rebbetzin Esther Jungreis enjoyed popcorn. But I do know that she loved that moment with my son.

Later that day, there was a man in the lobby who was blind. He was searching for a minyan. Having lost his bearings, he asked me if I could direct him to the synagogue. Turning to my son, I said, "Do you want to show this man the way?"

At first he gave me this look: "Mom, I don't know this man! How can I take him — a man who can't see — all by myself?"

I stared back into his eyes.

"It's a kindness," I said, "and you know that's good."

My son led the man by the arm into the sanctuary. I would have to say that I am very proud of our son, but I'm not so sure that he would have been willing to lead the way for a man who was blind, had he not gotten a bag of popcorn for the Rebbetzin a short while earlier. Because she had a way of showing people how to taste the goodness within themselves in her inimitable and infinitely magical way.

That didn't mean she wouldn't give rebuke when necessary. She had no problem looking someone in the eye and telling him that he was on the wrong path and needed to change. At the same time, she saw the good in people — to the point where she allowed them to see it themselves.

I miss her terribly. We miss her terribly. I miss receiving a berachah from her.

But it's not over because I go to Slovie's class on the Upper West Side regularly and she combines her mother's wisdom and stories; and when a person is able to raise children to do what the Jungreis children do — well, I can't help walking away anytime I meet them, thinking, "That's a life well spent."

It's incredible that she was able to do so much for people on the individual level and the communal level — to be invited to the halls of political power, and even address America at the Republican National Convention — yet never once raise her fist in the air and talk about women's liberation. In my mind, she epitomized the *eishes chayil*, the true woman of valor: the woman who was really able to reach her potential, the woman who knew who she was and was completely at peace with herself and her role in society, as a speaker, author, motivator, media personality — and most importantly — daughter, wife, mother and grandmother.

She taught me so much and we owe her more than we can ever repay.

This chapter has been dedicated
in memory of Rebbetzin Esther Jungreis ע"ה
for the Torah she taught, the chessed she did,
and the love she had for every Jew
Anonymous

CHAPTER FORTY-FOUR
Four Mitzvos

*D*ebbie August's mother tried to convince her to study with the Rebbetzin for the longest time. Eventually Debbie gave in. What could she do? It was her mother, after all.

Debby recalls:

My mother was part of the group of women already studying at Pat Cayne's house and wanted me to join.

"Mom," I told her, "I'm twenty-one years old, I just finished college, I have my whole life ahead of me and I'm not ready to jump into Torah learning."

"I'm telling you, you're really going to love it!"

At one point I didn't want to hear about it anymore and I decided I was going to go to one of the classes and just get it over with already. When I arrived, I found that I was by far the youngest one there, and I sat at the back of the room. Later on I would hear one of the Rebbetzin's trademark statements, which was, "When you go to a Torah class there's always going to be at least one thing that Hashem puts in my mouth, so that you want more."

I sat there patiently — sort of listening and trying to be respectful, when suddenly I heard the Rebbetzin say, "It says in the Torah that men are commanded to get married."

My ears perked up and I said to myself, "Wait a minute, it says that in the Torah? Wow, that's really interesting!"

I had had no idea that the Torah even talked about these kinds of things. I thought it was all about the sacrifice of Abraham and Isaac. So I started listening as she explained that there are feminine and masculine commandments in the Torah, and that Hashem felt that men needed to be commanded to get married; otherwise, they would just go along with their lives and never get around to it… Women, on the other hand, had a natural desire to want to get married and didn't need to be commanded to do so.

It was fascinating stuff — suddenly Torah was the coolest thing on earth — and I was hooked. Turns out my mother had been right.

The Rebbetzin really sparked my curiosity and I decided that I needed to hear more of what she had to say. I asked around and found out that she had a small class in her office, and I started attending it by myself. It was very intimate — almost like a private class — and the Rebbetzin took me under her wing. It was warm and wonderful and I loved our 4:30 to 6:30 Thursday-night classes and went religiously.

The Rebbetzin became my spiritual mother. She chose my Hebrew name, Devora — I'd never had one before — and taught me that the Torah is a guidebook to life. She discussed, dissected and explained every *parashah* — and was more than capable of studying one line for two hours straight. She made me feel grateful for my heritage and for what I had in life, and she made me start to see the world in a totally different way. The more I learned from her, the more I began to relate to the world through the lens of "Everything in life comes from Hashem."

I found myself saying, *"Baruch Hashem,"* recognizing that that's where it all came from. Over time I shortened it to "BH" — which caught on, and now my entire family and peer group says "BH" all the time.

Eventually, I went up to the Rebbetzin and I said, "Look, this is really good stuff and we need to make Torah 'cool.'"

"What do you have in mind?"

"We need to get you to speak to people who are my age, because nobody knows that the things you tell us are in the Torah! They don't understand what the Torah is all about!"

And so we established something we called "Hineni Young Leadership," which began in the Hineni building, and we decided to provide food — because we wanted to make sure that people would come…

In the beginning we had to call people and ask them to come. It was my friends and the children of my parents' friends, and it was a pretty small group. But it didn't remain small for long, because people came and returned and brought more friends and they brought their friends, and before we knew what was happening the *shiur* was starting to grow and grow and grow; eventually it moved to "KJ" on 85th Street, expanding and taking on a life of its own, with thousands and thousands of Jewish people learning Torah — and I'm not even talking about all the shidduchim that resulted from the Rebbetzin's weekly *shiur*…

She elevated everything. She would teach for hours on end without eating anything, and then she'd need to make a berachah, so she'd take a tiny bit of food, just to be able to recite a blessing.

Making berachos was always very important to the Rebbetzin. She'd seen this with her own mother, who used to bring a bag stuffed with candies when the Jungreis family went away together for their summer vacations. It wasn't so much a bag — it was more a suitcase, and it was absolutely bulging with lollipops and candies of all kinds. She would sit herself down in the hotel lobby and make an announcement summoning all the children in the hotel to line up for a candy — but first they had to make a berachah and tell her their Hebrew name, and only then were they free to unwrap and enjoy.

It took some time, but eventually I met my husband and we got married. But before we could go to the chuppah, Glenn had to come and meet the Rebbetzin. It was vital that she give her blessing to the match. He came to the Hineni Center to sit in on a class and the Rebbetzin liked him immediately. I'll never forget standing in front of the *aron kodesh* at the Hineni building just before our wedding and the Rebbetzin's blessing to my husband and me on that special day.

At that time the Rebbetzin introduced me to her daughter Slovie, who began teaching classes in my home.

When I learned I was expecting my first child, I decided that I needed to take on a mitzvah. The Rebbetzin used to say that a

Aron kodesh in the shul of the Hineni Heritage Center

person has to get on Jacob's ladder — always growing and never stagnating. I felt an overwhelming amount of gratitude to Hashem that I had been able to conceive so quickly, and I wanted to do something to show my thankfulness to Him. And so I decided that I was going to give up eating pork and shellfish. Some of my relatives thought I was completely crazy — they said, "You shouldn't do things that are so radical" — but I felt so much gratitude that I knew it was totally the right thing to do.

From that point on, there was no turning back.

I ended up having four children, and every time I had another child, I took on another mitzvah (all credit to the Rebbetzin).

Unfortunately it was around this time that her husband, Rabbi Meshulem Jungreis (may his memory be a blessing), passed away. The Rebbetzin would always speak about how kind he was, how he never raised his voice, and how he had such a good *neshamah*, illustrating her words with stories to show exactly what she meant.

And so when my first child was born — it was a son that time — I asked the Rebbetzin's permission to name my baby after her husband, feeling that it was such an incredible honor to do so. I named him Moshe Meshulem, adding the name Moshe because the name was similar to Glenn's mother's name, which was Masha, and because Moshe Rabbeinu was the ultimate leader. As to the name Meshulem, I felt that if my son had just a fraction of the kindness that characterized Rabbi Jungreis, it would be such a blessing!

For my second mitzvah I decided to recite the bedtime *Shema* with him every night.

For my third child — a daughter — I chose to take on the mitzvah of not mixing milk and meat, which I understood was a crucial mitzvah for a Jew to do. (We recently celebrated her bat mitzvah at an all-female party.)

Then I wanted another child and I started praying even more, and then I started keeping kashrus and then I studied more — all steps on Jacob's ladder. I also started hosting what became known as the Hineni Couples Class, which continues in my home until this very day.

But I really wanted to have another girl. Slovie taught me to say the *Nishmas* prayer every day. When she was born Slovie began referring to her as "my *Nishmas* baby."

When we moved into our current home, which I love, I decided that I had to show my *hakaras hatov* (gratitude) to Hashem — which is when I decided to begin keeping a completely kosher kitchen. But as I said before, every single one of those mitzvos would have never become part of my life were it not for the Rebbetzin and the way of life she taught me.

Every Thursday class was another incredible learning experience — and I couldn't believe just how relevant the Torah really was! Every time I went, something touched the *"pintele Yid"* inside me, and I would find myself exclaiming yet again, "I can't believe that this is in the Torah!"

That's the way it went — with more and more people finding out about the Rebbetzin and her magic.

And it made perfect sense, because Torah was "cool" — especially the way the Rebbetzin taught it — and anyone who showed up at the *shiur* even for one time couldn't help but be moved and inspired by what she said. And many times, there were stories and marriages.

That class at "KJ" eventually turned into something that was much, much larger than life — drawing people to it from all over — like bees to honey. It was incredible to watch.

Sometimes there were so many people it was standing room only. At a Torah class!

Every seat was filled downstairs, every seat was filled on the balcony; there were people in the aisles. The door to the lobby was opened and there were people filling the outer area! It was not to be believed. It was as if a *shiur* had become the main attraction in Manhattan, with everyone young, cool, hip, Manhattan-looking and excited to be there.

And you could hear the Rebbetzin telling the same stories again and again, but they made you cry every time you heard them. Because it was the Rebbetzin telling them, and there was something about her eyes and something about her voice — which had the power to cut straight through a person's soul.

I'd call her sometimes right before Yom Kippur and I'd say, "I don't even have the right words to say to you — other than thank you!"

She was always so grateful that I called.

But I never managed to truly express the gratitude that I felt. It was just impossible to convey my emotions. How do you thank a person who changed your life forever?

You really can't, but I did my best, trying to put everything I felt into the words "Thank you."

I think she knew what I felt.

Toward the end of the Rebbetzin's life we were all privileged to receive a blessing from her. It was the most meaningful berachah I ever received because I was afraid that this was the end. I knew that this was the last time she was going to see my family. It wasn't just us there that day. All the people who had been so close to her came to her home, along with all their kids. There were tons of kids there that day.

We drove over to the Rebbetzin's house — my entire family was with me — and it was so, so hard for her, but she wouldn't allow anyone to leave without giving them a beautiful berachah. I'll always remember the way she gave those berachos… and what she said about carrying on her dream and keeping Torah alive.

I will never forget the way she gently placed her hands on

my head — and I listened to every word carefully.

In that final encounter she showed us her spiritual strength. She utilized that final opportunity to share stories with our children — imbuing them with pride in their heritage in her inimitable way.

Day of berachos shortly before the Rebbetzin's passing

These days I'm baking challah every Erev Shabbos — more and more steps up Jacob's ladder, as the Rebbetzin taught — changing us into messengers for Torah to the people around us, who have thanked us for making the Torah life alluring and something they want to be part of. But that all came about because of the Rebbetzin, because she was the one who introduced us to the beauty of Torah in the first place. And every time a group of women gathers in our home to bake challah for Shabbos, thanking me for giving them the opportunity to get involved and feel the warmth, I know that I can direct that thank-you back to Rebbetzin Esther Jungreis, who managed to uncover the hidden sparks in every Jewish person she met.

CHAPTER FORTY-FIVE
"Kumu L'avodas HaBorei"

For many years, the Rebbetzin was invited to speak in South Africa. One year she had a disquieting experience. The Rebbetzin and Barbara Janov flew into Johannesburg with South African Airlines. They were supposed to have been met at the airport and driven to their hotel. The grueling flight from New York to South Africa took fifteen and a half hours. When they deplaned, the Rebbetzin and Barbara were thrilled to be able to stretch their legs. All went well until they arrived at passport control, where they were in for a surprise.

The Rebbetzin had no trouble passing through passport control. Barbara, however — the same Barbara who always accompanied the Rebbetzin with no trouble whatsoever — was stopped by security and not allowed to enter the country. When she asked what the problem was, she was informed that she lacked the blank page in her passport required by South African passport control. Barbara stared at the customs officer in shock.

Poster with the Rebbetzin's itinerary for the South Africa speaking tour

The Rebbetzin addressing a full house in Johannesburg

This was the last thing she'd expected to hear and she wasn't sure how to react.

"I'm sorry," the officer said. "I can't stamp your passport and you will not be able to enter the country."

Barbara couldn't believe what she was hearing.

"I can't understand why this would come up now! Why can't you just find half a page and stamp it?"

"At the risk of repeating myself, it has to be exactly as I said. You need a blank page. You don't have one. Which means I cannot allow you into South Africa."

"Nobody told us this at JFK!"

"They should have told you, because now you're stuck and won't be allowed to enter."

"I have to be allowed in," Barbara protested, beginning to really lose it. "This lady (she pointed at the Rebbetzin) has traveled all the way here from the States to speak. Many people are waiting to hear her. In fact, there's a major welcoming committee outside the airport right now! You have no idea how excited everyone is that she has arrived!"

"She can go. You cannot."

"Excuse me," the Rebbetzin interjected. "I cannot leave the airport without my friend."

"No problem. Neither of you goes in."

The officer wouldn't budge and all arguing was getting them nowhere. Eventually, the officer decided to call her supervisor.

The airline supervisor was a middle-aged Afrikaner. He heard the story, agreed with the passport control agent and motioned for the Rebbetzin and Barbara to follow him into a holding room. Turning around, he told them he'd return soon with a final decision. He then left the room, leaving them behind. There was nothing for them to do; there was nobody to talk to. They were stuck in a foreign country — unable to leave the airport because of some inane technicality!

By now Barbara was prepared to tear the airport apart for putting them through this ordeal. The Rebbetzin, however, had something else on her mind. Glancing at her watch, she saw that she was running out of time to daven Minchah. Soon it would be too late to say the afternoon prayer. Airport or no airport, blank page in the passport or no blank page, there was something more important that she needed to take care of. Without making a big deal about it, she withdrew her siddur from her hand luggage and found a corner of the room to use for her prayers.

The Rebbetzin was engrossed in her prayers when she heard the supervisor returning to the room.

"This is a serious matter," she heard him say. "There's no way we can possibly allow you into the country without stamping a blank page in the passport."

Suddenly the official caught sight of the Rebbetzin standing and swaying in a corner. (If you had seen the Rebbetzin daven, you would understand how it made an impression.)

Turning to Barbara, he said, "What is your friend doing right now?"

"She's praying."

"Now that's a good lady," he exclaimed. "When someone prays, everything has a way of working out!"

It was obvious that he was no longer at peace with his earlier stance and wanted to make amends.

"I'll tell you what," he said at last. "I will hold the airline officials at JFK responsible for this. You are free to go."

They barely had time to process the unexpected deliverance before he uttered one last line.

"You should know," he told them with a smile, "I wasn't even supposed to have been working today. I guess G-d sent me here to help you out — because when people pray, help is forthcoming."

There were to be many noteworthy incidents that happened to the Rebbetzin when she was away from home. Somehow, even the ordinary evolved into the extraordinary — especially when she was on the road.

Back in the early days when the Rebbetzin was launching Hineni, there were numerous challenges: not least the question, how on earth were they going to fill Madison Square Garden? The Rebbetzin decided that she needed to generate interest and went about doing so full speed ahead by speaking at high schools and college campuses. Since she lived in New York, one of the obvious stops was at Queens College, where a large percentage of the students were Jewish.

"If you get fifty kids you'll be lucky," the organizers told the Rebbetzin, but to her great surprise, she found herself speaking to a crowd of more than seven hundred students! Once again, the Rebbetzin had been underestimated. The event didn't go unnoticed, especially since someone called the *New York Post*, which sent a reporter to cover the speech.

The next day a story appeared in the paper about the runaway success of the Rebbetzin from North Woodmere — the writer going so far as to crown her as "The Jewish Billy Graham!"

In all honesty, the Rebbetzin was unhappy about the nickname. But her husband reassured her in his sweet, wise way.

The Rebbetzin in one of South Africa's largest shuls

"It's *bashert*," he said. "It can only help. People who would have never considered listening to a Rebbetzin will now be curious to hear the 'Jewish Billy Graham,' and you will have the chance to kindle the light of Torah in many hearts — hearts which would have otherwise forever remained closed to Hashem."

As always, Rav Meshulem Jungreis was on the mark.

Wherever the Rebbetzin went, people were incredibly excited to meet her in sold-out events, the crowds streaming in as people gathered to hear what the "Jewish Billy Graham" had to say.

This was true even when the Rebbetzin left the shores of America and headed overseas. Here too, the local papers loved using her nickname when writing about her.

On one trip, a local newspaper in South Africa picked up the story from the *New York Post* and put the Rebbetzin's picture on the front page with a headline, "Jewish Billy Graham Arrives from the United States!"

The headline created a major buzz and the speech went from a thing of interest to a must-see event for everyone in the city. Being the Rebbetzin, the story didn't end there, but continued with a fascinating outcome.

At her hotel, the Rebbetzin couldn't help but notice a middle-aged couple sitting by themselves off to the side, seemingly lost in their thoughts. They were surrounded by people, yet completely alone. Looking at them, the Rebbetzin sensed that they were enveloped by a cloud of sadness.

"Tell me," she said to the Jewish owner of the hotel, "what happened to those people? Why are they so sad?"

The hotel owner knew the story and he was ready to provide the details.

He explained that the couple had a son who was somewhat emotionally unstable and worked as a security guard at the local Israeli consulate, making no waves. In those days, terrorism was not yet an overwhelming threat, and it was the perfect job for the young man. Yet the longer the "security guard" worked at the consulate, the more convinced he became that the consulate was vulnerable to a terrorist attack. He shared his concerns with his superiors, who brushed them away. In the end, desperate to prove his point, the guard decided to do something that would call attention to the situation.

With no warning, he feigned an attack on the consulate, called the police and his younger brother, and told them that the consulate was under siege! The guard's brother had no clue that the entire event had been staged by his brother, and he ran to the consulate, desperate to help his sibling whom he truly believed was in grave danger.

There was a shootout with the police and both brothers were arrested.

The media didn't stop rehashing the event, and that was the cause of the sorrow that the Rebbetzin had recognized on the faces of the two people sitting in the hotel lobby. It was the haunted look of the hunted.

"I do not wish to intrude," she said to them, "and if I am, please tell me, but I would like to help you. If you want, I can try to visit your sons."

"They will never let you into the prison," the mother replied.

"Let me try; you never know what can happen in this world."

Morning found the Rebbetzin off to the prison armed with a siddur, Chumash, and a copy of the local paper. The prison loomed up ahead, harsh and forbidding, and she was subjected to intense grilling by security before being allowed inside.

"Who are you?"

Pointing at the newspaper, she introduced herself as the "Jewish Billy Graham" who had come all the way from America.

It made an impression.

A celebrity was in the house.

The guard called his superior officer. The next thing the Rebbetzin knew, the gates were sliding open and she had been given permission to meet with the brother of the consulate operation mastermind.

The young man was in a terrible state of mind. One look in his eyes and the Rebbetzin could discern the extent of his suffering. All he'd wanted to do was protect his brother, and now he seemed to be in trouble for life! He was in a deep state of despair.

"You must never give up hope," the Rebbetzin said to him. "One day you will be free."

He looked at her as if she were out of her mind.

"I'm serious. There was a time in the not-so-long-ago past when I too wondered if I would ever be able to laugh again."

She then shared some of her concentration camp experiences with him.

"Take a good look into the Torah," she urged him. "There is a teaching for every situation."

"Not for me."

"You're wrong. When I say every situation, I mean every situation. There is precedent for your story in the Torah as well."

She could see that he was interested, wanting to know what she was referring to.

"Study the story of Joseph, who found himself in prison — and believe me, his situation was a lot more hopeless than yours. He had been set up. Locked away for no reason. But Joseph never stopped praying to Hashem. And he did this despite the fact that he had no way of knowing that he would one day be appointed viceroy over Egypt. Take a lesson from the story of Joseph and do not lose faith!"

"But it's impossible to find the strength just to get up in the morning! Life is too depressing!"

The Rebbetzin gave the prisoner a practical assignment.

"In the morning when you wake up and feel that you can't bear to face another day in your cell, say three words."

He looked at her, puzzled.

"Three words. These three words will have a major impact on your life. Are you ready? These are the words: '*Kumu l'avodas haBorei* — Rise up to serve the Creator.'

"Find something each and every day with which to serve Hashem. Pray, study Torah and relate to everyone you meet with kindness."

"Who can I relate to? What can I do for anyone if I'm locked away in prison?"

"Who can you relate to in prison? That's a very good question. Lucky for me, I have a very good answer.

"Everyone you meet.

"Who can you do chessed with?

"Same answer. Everyone you meet — from your fellow inmates to the guards to anyone who comes to visit you. Most importantly, you can do chessed with yourself.

"Do not become an angry person! You need to remember that the miracle that occurred with Joseph happened to him because he did not despair — even under the worst and most desperate circumstances. He never lost sight of his father and his responsibility to Hashem. And because he remembered who he was and his ultimate role in life, he was able to rise above the darkness of his prison cell. It is that service that will, *b'ezras Hashem*, bring you your freedom as well very soon.

But you must never forget those three precious words: *'Kumu l'avodas haBorei* — Rise up to serve the Creator.'"

The Rebbetzin finished speaking with the young prisoner and left the prison soon after.

Years later, a stranger approached her after a speech. The room was already almost completely empty. The man's eyes were glistening with tears.

"Rebbetzin," he said to her. "For more than thirty-three years I've been waiting to ask you a question."

Rebbetzin Jungreis looked at him, intrigued.

"What question have you been waiting to ask me for thirty-three years?"

"Which words come first when a Jew wakes up in the morning — *Modeh Ani* or *Kumu l'avodas haBorei*?"

The Rebbetzin stared at him and she knew, without having to ask, that the three words she had given him had helped him escape the darkness of prison with their incredible power. He had used those words to connect with Hashem and had thereby proven that anything is possible — as long as a person maintains his connection with the Creator of the world.

CHAPTER FORTY-SIX
A Perfect Man Prepares

Nobody saw it coming. Nobody had had any inkling of the news that was about to send their entire world into a frenzy. Nobody could have ever guessed that someone who was such a rock, such a pillar of strength and power, would suddenly be snatched from them — without warning.

Rav Meshulem Jungreis went to the doctor's office for what he had imagined to be a routine checkup. Little did he know that he was about to learn a bitter truth. He was a strong man, a healthy man — and yet, the doctor was suddenly sending him for a battery of tests. The next thing he knew, the doctor informed him — in a very serious tone of voice — that he was being sent for an MRI. After the tests were done, the Rabbi returned to the doctor's office.

He was all alone at the moment when the doctor broke the devastating news to him.

"There is a tumor in your colon. It looks malignant."

Rav Meshulem did not lose his natural composure. He didn't blink

Rav Meshulem Jungreis

or start to sweat. His hands weren't shaking. He didn't lose his mind and start to cry. He was a man of Hashem and he trusted Him implicitly. In his mind, whatever was supposed to happen — would.

Amazingly enough, it was he who comforted the doctor instead of the other way around. His faith was like a skyscraper.

"I want to thank you for helping me so many times through the years," he said to his old and trusted friend.

The doctor could barely hold back his tears. He had never seen a man like Rav Meshulem. Doctors see the true face of society. They know people well — seeing them at their best and at their worst. He couldn't get over the Rabbi's reaction. How could a person be so calm after hearing such devastating news!

The doctor could barely focus on what Rabbi Jungreis was telling him.

"Always remember," the Rabbi told his doctor, "always remember that every single thing that happens in this world lies in the hands of G-d."

The doctor nodded in recognition of the unassailable truth and they exchanged one final, frank look before Rabbi Jungreis left the office.

The Rabbi didn't have the luxury of being able to fall apart. He had things to do and prior obligations to keep. One of those was a speech he was about to deliver to the children of the Ohr Torah Hebrew school. He spoke to the children and was his usual beautiful self, smiling gently and praising every child. He then drove over to visit his grandchildren, where he told stories to the younger set and learned Gemara with an older grandson. Once again, he didn't let on that anything was wrong or even slightly amiss.

The doctor, however, called the Rebbetzin and let her know what had happened in his office that afternoon.

From one second to the next, her entire universe shifted.

The Rebbetzin called a specialist with whom she was acquainted, filled him in on the emergency situation, and set up an appointment for the following morning at New York University Hospital.

Unfortunately, the doctor was not going to be the bearer of good news.

"I am sorry to have to say this, but Rabbi Jungreis needs to check in for surgery — immediately!"

Rav Meshulem at a Melaveh Malkah with grandchildren

"I would like to spend the Sabbath with my family and my congregation," Rav Meshulem told the doctor. "Would it make that much of a difference if I check in on Saturday night instead of right now?"

The doctor considered his request.

"That will be fine, Rabbi," he told the patient, "but I don't want you eating anything tomorrow."

And so Rav Meshulem Jungreis — the gentle giant, the man who was always surrounded by children climbing all over him — returned home for his final Shabbos at Ohr Torah, the shul in which he'd invested his heart and soul.

The Rebbetzin called all the children and let them know the situation. All of them wanted to come to North Woodmere to spend Shabbos with their Abba. Everyone knew why they were there and everyone knew that the situation was dire, and yet, they had to be happy. It was Shabbos Kodesh and on Shabbos a Jew is not allowed to be sad. When Rav Meshulem stood up to bless his children that Friday night, a silence descended on the room. Nobody was able to look at anyone else. Each one knew if their eyes met they would dissolve into tears.

Rabbi Osher made Kiddush. He was barely able to make it through without breaking down.

Rav Meshulem and the Rebbetzin with grandchildren at a family wedding

Rav Meshulem sat with his family at the head of the table, singing Shabbos *zemiros* and expounding uplifting Torah ideas that flowed from his lips in a never-ending stream of sanctity. And the children looked at their holy, special father and couldn't believe that he was entering the hospital the following night.

Shabbos morning in North Woodmere.

The Rabbi walked through the main sanctuary of his beloved shul. Nobody looking at their dear Rabbi had even the slightest inkling that there was something deathly wrong with him or that his time with them — his dear friends — was almost up.

Shacharis passed uneventfully.

They finished the Torah reading.

The Sefer Torah was replaced in the *aron kodesh* and then the Rabbi rose to speak. That Shabbos he spoke to his congregation for an hour. He spoke and he spoke. He poured out his heart, begging them to strive for the heavens. He spoke about his love for Eretz Yisrael and particularly the holy city of Chevron, the burial place of our Patriarchs and Matriarchs, and how every Jew needed to strengthen his connection with the Holy Land. He then described his service to the shul for the past 32 years, explaining that the number 32 held the numerical value of the Hebrew word *lev* — heart.

"I have given my entire heart to every single member of my congregation," he told the people sitting there.

It was unquestionably the greatest speech of his life.

Later at the kiddush, he told a few people that he was checking into the hospital.

He told them the news without telling them.

He said it with caring — in his trademark gentle manner — a small, somewhat sad smile playing on his lips.

When the kiddush was over, he bade them all farewell and wished everyone a "Good Shabbos." He then left his shul — the shul he had built way back when North Woodmere had been a spiritual desert.

Oneg Shabbat manual written by Rav Meshulem in 1965 to inspire the congregants of Ohr Torah towards greater Shabbat observance

There were many stories to tell about this unassuming and gentle man.

There was the time he heard that one of his granddaughters in kindergarten was being bullied in school.

"Don't you worry about a thing," he told her. "I will take care of it!"

The next time there was a school production (to which grandparents were invited), Rav Meshulem attended the production clad in full police uniform, including ceremonial cap, white gloves and gleaming badge — the uniform he wore at official police department events. His entrance caused a huge commotion, since every child (and many adults) can't help but get excited when seeing a police officer up close. He took a seat in the audience, but only after making sure that every child realized who his grandchild was and why he was there.

The grandchild never had a problem with the bully again.

Bullies, you see, don't like the police.

That was Rav Meshulem's way: solving issues without a word of reproof to the guilty party.

Rav Meshulem at a granddaughter's kindergarten graduation
in his police uniform

There was so much to talk about, so many memories — so many stories.

He could have boasted to his family about the fact that he'd been ordained a rabbi at the age of eighteen.

He could have talked to them about the fact that he'd been forced into a slave labor battalion — and how he never ate non-kosher food under any circumstances.

He could have told them how he weighed ninety pounds at the time of liberation, and how he used to keep up the spirits of his fellow prisoners by learning Gemara with them from the many sections of Talmud that he knew by heart.

He could have described how he used to wake up at three in the morning to prepare *shiurim* for his fellow inmates, and how he considered it his mission to always bring as many Jews as possible closer to Hashem and His Torah.

He could have made a big deal about the fact that he convinced the Long Island Railroad back in the 1960s to designate a special Purim car on the train to be used for *Megillah* reading, and how while he read the *Megillah*, the Rebbetzin handed out hamantaschen to all the commuters.

He could have described how he visited sick children at the hospital and how he delivered fresh challah on Erev Shabbos to the widows in the community so they would know that someone was thinking of them.

He could have made a big deal over the fact that he served as the spiritual father to the Nassau County Police Department, and how he counseled the officers — from patrolman through commissioner — about Orthodox tradition and how to better understand the Orthodox community and provide for its needs, for which he was awarded a citation for exceptional dedication.

Yet once again, he didn't boast. That wasn't his way.

He could have talked forever.

But he was a quiet, humble man.

It was left to his wife to tell the world about her husband.

She would do just that for the rest of her life.

Rav Meshulem, lovingly known to the grandchildren as "Abba-Zeide"

"The Rebbetzin used to speak in Palm Beach once a year," Cheryl Minikes remembers. "The last time she was there, she was so ill, so frail, using her walker to move slowly down the aisle. And when she finally reached the podium, she delivered the most beautifully moving speech about her husband, Rav Meshulem.

"'He allowed me to be who I was,' she told the assembled. 'I have been so fortunate in my life. I am not well — as you can see — but I will stand here before you as long as I have the strength. Yet I have to give the credit for what I have achieved to my husband, who allowed me and encouraged me to go out and to build Hineni. I will always say that it was because of Rav Meshulem Jungreis that I became who I became.'"

There's no question that the testimony of a wife for her husband is by far the most accurate and authentic. In the Rebbetzin's case, she made no secret of her feelings of gratitude for the beloved tzaddik who had constantly done his best for her.

It wasn't long before Rav Meshulem's illness drove them from NYU to Sloan Kettering. The procedure was supposed to have been minor and he was to have returned home the following day, but things did not go as planned and Rabbi Jungreis never left Sloan Kettering. The procedure that he underwent was not successful and yet another surgery was required that left the Rabbi with an open wound! For the last six weeks of his life, the Rabbi's pain level was excruciating and unbearable, but whenever the doctors or anyone asked him what his scale of pain was from one to ten, he'd reply, "Zero."

He would then whisper quietly, "*Yissurim shel ahavah*, I accept my pain and suffering with love."

One night the phone rang at the Jungreis home. The Rebbetzin answered. Within moments she realized that the person on the other end of the line was not mentally stable. A few more moments of conversation and she learned that her husband used to talk to the mentally disturbed woman on the other end of the line every night without fail.

For anyone else it would have been difficult to be so patient. But for Rav Meshulem it was typical behavior.

The Rebbetzin would have remained at her husband's bedside day and night, but Rav Meshulem insisted that she maintain her normal schedule — go teach her students and continue helping others, even while the walls she had erected around her own life were crumbling onto themselves.

"You must teach Torah," he commanded her, and she listened to him, accepting his advice as she had done throughout their married life.

Every day began and ended at the hospital, morning and evening sandwiching an afternoon of teaching and meeting with people. It was Thursday afternoon and both the Rabbi and his wife had dozed off from sheer exhaustion. Suddenly the Rebbetzin woke with a start. She glanced at her watch and realized that she had to run if she wanted to make her class on time. Grabbing her coat, the Rebbetzin asked the private nurse if she could return to stay with her husband the following day.

"I will pay you tomorrow, if that's okay with you."

It might have been okay with the nurse, but it was not okay with the patient — whose eyes opened and who clearly had something to say.

Paraphrasing a verse (*Vayikra* 19:13), Rav Meshulem commented quietly, "The day workers must be paid on the same day."

In his mind there was no such thing as not paying a worker at exactly the right time. So the Rebbetzin sat down and wrote the nurse a check. Then she bade him farewell and ran off to teach her class.

Rav Meshulem and Rebbetzin Esther

A few days before Rav Meshulem passed away, the Rebbetzin was outside his room waiting, while his nurse cleaned and dressed his wound. Just then Slovie arrived to visit her father. Since the curtains were drawn around the bed, she hesitated for a few seconds, wondering if she should let her father know she was there, or wait.

She still hadn't made a decision when she was shocked to hear the sound of her father sobbing. Slovie stood outside the curtains terribly concerned, and unsure what to do.

"Rabbi," the nurse asked him, her voice filled with concern, "am I hurting you?"

"It's not you," Rav Meshulem replied, reassuring the nurse. "I'm crying because very soon I will have to face my Maker, and what will I say to Him?"

With tears streaming down her cheeks, Slovie left her father to his moment of pain and joined her mother in the solarium, the two of them weeping together for the special man they loved so much, who was slipping away from them second by second.

This chapter has been dedicated
in honor of Mrs. Ina Seaman and
in loving memory of Dr. Charles Seaman ז״ל
Richard Seaman

CHAPTER FORTY-SEVEN

The Bride and Groom Arrive

$\mathcal{M}$any people came to visit Rav Meshulem in the hospital. He spoke words of Torah to them and blessed them with all his heart, the passion clearly visible on his saintly visage. All left inspired and committed to living a better Torah life.

Among them was a young man named David.

The Rabbi and David were extremely close and had been ever since they met.

David Gabay was introduced to the Rebbetzin in a somewhat unusual way. The first time he saw her was on cable television on a Sunday afternoon in 1988. He was watching football — the Jets were on — and at halftime, he began surfing the channels, looking for something to grab his interest until the game resumed.

Suddenly, wham! There she was, an elegant woman — a Rebbetzin, whatever that was — and she was talking about being a Jew and what that meant in the context of life in this day and age. The truth is, he didn't really understand what she was talking about, not being familiar with any Torah concepts. But she was extremely captivating, engaging and articulate, and to his shock, David found himself remaining with the speaker and forgetting about the Jets!

David had grown up in L.A. and wasn't sure what the whole religion thing was about, but when he saw the number and address of Hineni keyed in at the bottom of the screen, he was suddenly infused with a desire to go and find out more. Grabbing a pen, David jotted down the address and phone number of the Center and was finally able to get back to the game. But even after he switched back to the Jets, he was still intrigued by what he'd just encountered.

Since he had never come across anyone discussing Torah on television before, David wasn't sure what to make of it, or whether Hineni was a legitimate Jewish organization.

"Maybe she's a missionary," he thought to himself. On the other hand, she didn't seem like any missionary he'd ever run into. In the end he told himself that he would go hear her for a little bit. If he picked up the wrong vibe he'd be out of there in a minute — and if it was the real thing, he'd stick around and find out more.

He drove in from Westchester County, some twenty-five miles away. Next thing he knew, David was pulling up outside the Hineni Center on West End Avenue. A flight of stairs led up to the entranceway, where two heavy glass doors were continually opened by those who were arriving to hear the Rebbetzin speak.

"Ten or fifteen minutes," he told himself, "and you're out of here."

He parked the car and walked into the building. The Rebbetzin was standing at the front of the room doing her usual "meet and greet." But no matter how many people she'd see, she missed nothing; spotting a new face in the room, she made sure to approach him and introduce herself. From the moment that he met the Rebbetzin, David felt an instant connection he couldn't explain. He felt a sense of friendship with her and an intangible bond which he instinctively knew would remain between the two of them forever.

"Are you Sephardic or an Ashkenazi?"

"I'm a mixed breed," he replied with an easy smile. "My father's Sephardic so I have some traditions from that side — my mother's Ashkenazi."

"Are you religious?"

He didn't really understand the question.

"What do you mean?"

"Do you go to shul?"

"We go once or twice a year."

She heard what he was telling her and recorded every detail in her mind. Then she found him a place to sit.

"You'll sit here," she said to him, motioning him to the second row from the front of the room. And then, for the first time in his life, David Gabay heard a lesson in the weekly Torah portion. He sat there open-mouthed, listening in wonder to the concepts she was explaining. While he'd entered the Center planning to stay no longer than ten or fifteen minutes, a full hour passed and he didn't even know it.

From the first night of their meeting back in the 1980s, David never missed another *shiur*. He attended her classes like clockwork. The Rebbetzin introduced him to Torah study, jump-starting the process that would transport him from the life of an unaffiliated Jew to a life filled with Torah and mitzvos.

But the Rebbetzin didn't stop there. She invited David to North Woodmere for Shabbos, drawing him close to her home, family and community. He'd stay at the Neubergers' and eat at the Rebbetzin's home. That was also when he first met Rav Meshulem Jungreis, who impressed him to no end. The two of them developed a very close relationship, with David walking the Rabbi home from shul on countless Friday nights. The Rabbi and Rebbetzin treated him like family and took a truly active interest in his life. He felt welcome at their home — welcome, warm and cared for.

To the point that he never wanted to leave.

It took David a long time to find a shidduch. Then one day the Rebbetzin introduced him to a girl named Caroline who had become religious through Hineni as well.

That was it. There was no question in either of their minds that both of them had found their soul mate. There was also no question that Rabbi Jungreis would be the one officiating under the chuppah at their wedding. David had walked the Rabbi home for so long. They had had so many conversations. He loved the Rabbi with all his heart and the feelings were mutual. How could anyone else possibly send David off into married life?

No. It had to be Rav Meshulem.

And yet, the Rabbi was growing sicker and sicker. As the days passed, he reached the point where even breathing was difficult. There was no way in the world that he'd be able to officiate at a wedding — even for someone he loved as much as David.

In the end Rav Meshulem asked his son Rabbi Yisroel to officiate in his place.

The day of the wedding was a fine day in most respects. For the Jungreis family it was one of the most difficult days they had ever lived. Every member of the family had come to the hospital, where they surrounded Rav Meshulem in a circle of strength. If it would have been up to Yisroel Jungreis, he would have never left his father's side. How could he leave? What if he missed his father's passing? He was supremely afraid that he would miss his chance to say goodbye at that final moment.

On the other hand, his father had given Yisroel a mission: to take his place at the chuppah.

In the end Yisroel left the room, tears in his eyes. Leaving his father's bedside was one of the most difficult things Yisroel had ever had to do.

He drove to the hall and he conducted the most beautiful wedding imaginable. He didn't stop there. He read a letter his father had written to the new couple. He rose above himself and ran that chuppah with genuine happiness, somehow able to compartmentalize the two very, very different events happening simultaneously in his life. Only after the chuppah was over, after they had escorted the chassan and kallah from the room with dancing, after he'd arranged a minyan for Maariv — after everything was taken care of in a way his father would have approved of — did Yisroel Jungreis make the call to the hospital.

"Abba?"

"Still here, come back as soon as possible. He's waiting for you."

"I'm on my way."

He would make it.

When the wedding was over, the young couple left the hall, ready to go home. They were already on the highway driving toward David's house, when they suddenly looked at one another and said, "We have to go visit Rabbi Jungreis in the hospital right now!"

They got off the highway at the next exit, turned around and drove right back in the opposite direction to the hospital.

And then, suddenly, like a dream — there appeared the most incredible sight in the corridors of Sloan Kettering. In all likelihood it had never been seen before and would probably never be seen again. There was David, walking down the hallway in his tuxedo and bowtie. Gliding beside him — a vision in white — was Caroline in a beautiful wedding dress. They had arrived at the hospital to receive their rabbi's berachah on their wedding night.

The moment they entered his room Rabbi Meshulem Jungreis opened his eyes. Gathering the remaining vestiges of strength he had left, he smiled at the chassan and kallah and whispered, "Mazel tov, my children."

Then and only then were David and Caroline able to begin married life. Their dream had come true. They had been with their rabbi on their wedding day.

Rabbi and Rebbetzin Jungreis had led David from a Jets game to a full-fledged Jewish life, introduced him to his wife and watched as they got married and built a beautiful Jewish home.

And the Rebbetzin cried when they named one of their children Meshulem after the great rabbi who had had such an impact on their lives.

Rav Meshulem Jungreis left this world in the early-morning hours of the second day of Shevat 5756. His family — children and grandchildren — was there, standing by his side at the moment of truth.

In the days before his *petirah*, he blessed every person in the room, and as he did so, he mentioned each and every one by name. He could barely talk by then. Yet somehow, he summoned the last reserves of strength and uttered the words Yaakov Avinu said to his children before leaving this world for the next.

"Hamalach hagoel osi mikol ra… — May the angel who redeems me from all evil…"

These were the words our father Jacob blessed Yosef's children with before he passed away.

As the words issued from his lips, his young grandchildren sang the well-known tune for those words. It was a moment of great import, a moment they would never forget. To the grandchildren, Rav Meshulem was known as "Abba-Zeide," a term first coined by his oldest grandchild, Yosef Dov Gertzulin. Calling him "Abba-Zeide" was a mark of the fatherly love that he possessed and that flowed forth from him for each and every grandchild.

The name of Rav Meshulem Jungreis will live on forever — not only through his children, grandchildren and great-grandchildren — but also through the thousands and thousands of lives that he touched during his sojourn on earth.

Tears streaming down their faces, the Jungreis family said goodbye to their patriarch: the Gentle Giant, the Rabbi, the man with the gracious smile, the Torah scholar, the halachic Jew, the Holocaust survivor and the builder of Torah in North Woodmere.

Two years after Rav Meshulem passed away, the Rebbetzin would leave her home and move closer to her children and grandchildren. When that happened, she would be forced to go through decades of papers and mementoes from the past; to make the decision what to keep, what to give away and what to throw out.

In all their years of marriage, the Rebbetzin and her husband had never exchanged a harsh word. Their relationship had been nothing short of exemplary. There was, however, one area in which the Rebbetzin struggled — the fact that her husband the Rabbi was a major collector. Nothing was ever thrown away, nothing was ever put in the trash. His papers, with voluminous notations, filled many drawers and cabinets.

Yet now, with the move imminent, there was no choice but to take the time to go through the vast assortment of papers. With her children at her side, the Rebbetzin began wading through the endless sea. As they organized their father's documents they felt as though they were carrying on a conversation with their father and grandfather. Every notation was a message, every scribble a thought to be reckoned with. More than anything, it was as though they were only now starting to read Rabbi Jungreis' final will and testament.

The Rebbetzin was the one who came across the sheet of paper.

On it, the Rabbi had written in his beautiful and bold handwriting, "The two most important words to remember: *Thank you.*"

This chapter has been dedicated
in memory of Bella and Moses Gottfriend ע"ה and
Sonia and Albert Gabay ע"ה
David and Caroline Gabay

CHAPTER FORTY-EIGHT
Salute of the Ducks

Rav Meshulem Jungreis passed away in Memorial Sloan Kettering Cancer Center in Manhattan close to three o'clock in the morning on Tuesday, January 23, 1996/2 Shevat. The funeral was slated to take place at Congregation Ohr Torah in Long Island at one o'clock that afternoon, some ten hours later. Between the

The *aron* of Rav Meshulem being carried into Congregation Ohr Torah for the *levayah*

moment of his passing and the beginning of the *levayah*, over two thousand people gathered to pay their final respects to a man who had never sought or requested an iota of *kavod*. On the contrary, throughout his lifetime he'd run from honor time and again. Yet now it was no longer up to him, and the crowds continued to swell outside the shul he'd built up from scratch.

The motorcade escorted the Rabbi from the funeral home in Boro Park to Long Island. People lined the streets to watch as this over twenty-car Nassau County Police motorcade — in their bright orange and blue colors — made its way through the streets of Boro Park for the Rabbi's final journey.

Not only that, the NYPD joined up with the motorcade and shut down the entire Belt Parkway from Brooklyn to the Nassau County line to enable the Rabbi's *levayah* motorcade to travel unimpeded by the normally heavy traffic on this route — a procedure normally reserved for heads of state as they make their way from Kennedy Airport to the City.

It was an amazing sight.

As soon as Rabbi Jungreis was *niftar*, word was sent to Donald Kane, the Police Commissioner of the Nassau County Police Department.

Police Honor Guard saluting their beloved chaplain at the *levayah* of Rav Meshulem Jungreis

Chapter Forty-Eight: Salute of the Ducks □ 497

Aron of Rav Meshulem Jungreis arriving at Ohr Torah

Police Commissioner Kane loved the Rabbi for his warmth, compassion and kindness, and for his unique method of dealing with every member of the police force, whenever they needed his pastoral care and guidance.

The Commissioner had his top Deputy, Lieutenant Daniel Lishansky, contact Rabbi Shlomo Gertzulin to arrange an "Inspector's funeral." Lieutenant Lishansky told him that it normally takes two-three days to arrange all of the logistics for this type of departmental funeral, with all of the attendant ceremony.

"Daniel," Rabbi Shlomo said to the Lieutenant (who happened to be Jewish and was also extremely close to and enamored by the Rabbi), "while the Jungreis family greatly appreciates the honors that the Department wants to bestow upon the Rabbi, Jewish law and tradition mandate that the funeral be expedited, and although it is now about four o'clock in the morning, the funeral will be taking place in just a few hours at Ohr Torah."

The lieutenant of course told him that it would be difficult to arrange a suitable "official" funeral on such short notice, but that they would try their best.

It was a sight to behold outside Ohr Torah at one o'clock.

Hundreds of uniformed police officers, as well as the entire top brass of the County, Village and the Nassau County Police Department, were standing at full attention as the hearse bearing the Rabbi's *aron* arrived at the shul.

It was a lengthy *levayah,* as befitting a rav of his stature, addressed only by rabbanim, roshei yeshivah and family members (requests to have political and governmental officials speak at the *levayah* were politely declined — with an appropriate explanation, of course). And when

Rav Meshulem's police chaplain badge presented to the Rebbetzin by Nassau County Executive Tom Gulotta and Police Commissioner Donald Kane

the *levayah* concluded, they were all still standing there outside, as an

Award presentation to the Rebbetzin by Nassau County Police Department

aerial salute of police helicopters in a "missing-man" formation flew overhead as they bade a final farewell to their beloved chaplain.

Do not think that they were all Jewish policemen; they were not. But it made no difference to them. Rabbi Jungreis was their man, their rabbi, their bridge to G-d, and they had all come to bid him farewell.

As Nassau County Executive Thomas Gulotta said to the family at the funeral, "We will miss his advice and counsel. He was a dear and trusted friend."

The police weren't just paying him lip service. Their Rabbi Jungreis had been promoted through his years on the force to the rank of Inspector, the highest rank below Chief of Department.

Across the street from the Jungreis home on Hungry Harbor Road lies a small lake known as Doxy Pond. It was gated, and Rav Meshulem had the key. That was where the congregation went to recite Tashlich on Rosh Hashanah every year — to the point that this body of water became known as "Tashlich Pond."

Being a loving father and grandfather, Rabbi Jungreis would also open the gate when his own grandchildren came to visit, taking the kids for a walk around the pond. The pond was a place where the Rabbi could meditate in learning and prepare his speeches. It was serene and tranquil, removed from the hustle and bustle, yet close enough that he was just a few minutes away. It was a picturesque spot and he loved it very much, both for the privacy and connection with nature that it afforded him, and for giving him an opportunity to feed the ducks that gathered at the pond. He'd take leftover pieces of Shabbos challah with him and scatter them every few feet. The ducks knew that the tall man with the bright smile always came prepared, and they'd congregate around him.

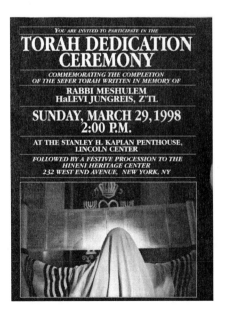

YOU ARE INVITED TO PARTICIPATE IN THE
TORAH DEDICATION CEREMONY
COMMEMORATING THE COMPLETION OF THE SEFER TORAH WRITTEN IN MEMORY OF
RABBI MESHULEM HaLEVI JUNGREIS, Z'TL
SUNDAY, MARCH 29, 1998 2:00 P.M.
AT THE STANLEY H. KAPLAN PENTHOUSE, LINCOLN CENTER
FOLLOWED BY A FESTIVE PROCESSION TO THE HINENI HERITAGE CENTER
232 WEST END AVENUE, NEW YORK, NY

The Rebbetzin and her children remember looking out of the window of the car on the way to the cemetery. There was much to see as they accompanied their father and grandfather on his final journey, among others, the astounding sight of the several hundred police officers who stood at rigid attention.

But then they saw something else, something completely unexpected.

The sight of dozens of ducks standing and watching the procession passing by.

Who could have prepared the Jungreis children and their mother for the unique sight of those ducks? Nobody had ever seen them venture outside the pond's gate before. Yet there they were for the first time anyone could recall, standing at attention on Hungry Harbor Road — dozens of them just standing and watching solemnly, as they paid their final respects to the Rabbi who was so good to them.

When I flew in to the States to write the book about the Rebbetzin, I visited Rav Meshulem's Ohr Torah on Hungry Harbor Road in North Woodmere on the same day that I went to daven at the Rav and Rebbetzin's *kevarim*. Rav Meshulem's portrait is on display in the shul's lobby, and the street outside had been renamed Rabbi Jungreis Way in

One of Rav Meshulem's grandchildren singing at the street-renaming ceremony

At the ceremony renaming the street in front of Ohr Torah as "Rabbi Jungreis Way"

The Rebbetzin with family and elected officials at the street-renaming ceremony

The Rebbetzin speaking at the street-renaming ceremony

honor of the founder and longtime rabbi of North Woodmere's first Orthodox shul.

As we drove away from the shul and passed Doxy Pond, scene of the duck procession at the Rabbi's funeral, I searched the surroundings, trying to see if any ducks were out on the water or waddling on the grass.

I searched in vain. Try as I might, I was unable to see a single duck. Not even one.

This chapter has been dedicated
in memory of our beloved
Abba Zeide זצ״ל and Bubba ע״ה
Rav Meshulem and Rebbetzin Esther Jungreis

Dov Gertzulin and Family

Part 8
1998-2016

Rebbetzin, I want you to know somethin'. Wherever I go — I can't go nowhere without someone talkin' about you. You're becomin' more famous than me, and you know somethin' — it's really startin' to get on my noives!

Jackie Mason

Think about it, Rebbetzin. You, a child of the Holocaust, a survivor of Bergen-Belsen, are flying over Germany right now — in the plane of the President of the United States — on your way back from Jerusalem!

Fred Zeidman,
Chairman, United States Holocaust Memorial
Commission, talking to Rebbetzin Jungreis
aboard Air Force One.

When asked to what he attributed his cousin's phenomenal success, a close relative didn't hesitate or think twice before replying, "Esther's success stemmed from the fact that everything she did, she did with tznius!"

Rav Mordechai Jungreis — the Nikolsburger Rebbe,
Rav of the Woodbourne shul, and a cousin of
Rav Meshulem and Rebbetzin Esther

CHAPTER FORTY-NINE

The Chaim Shlomo Siddur

*A*fter Rabbi Meshulem Jungreis passed away, Slovie told her mother about a house that was for sale around the corner from her house in Lawrence. Now that her husband was no longer the Rabbi of Ohr Torah, Rebbetzin Jungreis didn't consider herself the shul's rebbetzin any longer. It was especially challenging for her to daven in the women's section and see someone else standing at the podium, conducting the services her husband had led for so many decades. Rosh Hashanah and Yom Kippur would never be the same without Rav Meshulem Jungreis at the *amud*. Suddenly Rebbetzin Jungreis felt like a stranger in her shul.

That was why Slovie's suggestion that she move to Lawrence came at the perfect time. Decisive as ever, the Rebbetzin went to see the house, and put in an offer. And not long afterward she left the house that had been her home for so many years, exchanging the old-fashioned ranch house for a small but comfortable, modern home near her children and grandchildren. She converted the garage into an office, and that was where Sharon Weiner, her longtime Hineni bookkeeper, would work every Friday.

Sharon relates:

> I'd be sitting and working in the office, and the Rebbetzin would come down and keep me company, telling me stories about her childhood and about growing up in Europe. She told me about life in the camps and how there was no food, and I listened to her

every word and felt very bad that she had had to go through such terrible times — so unlike my own life, which had always been so calm.

And then my husband was diagnosed with pancreatic cancer and everything turned upside down almost overnight. He was fifty-two years old when it happened, and it was hard to comprehend how someone who had been so alive and vital could become so sick, so quickly. I remember calling the Rebbetzin from the hospital on a Thursday afternoon and telling her the results.

He had gone in for what was supposed to have been a simple gall bladder operation — and it wasn't.

"I don't know where to turn," I said to her. "I don't know what to do."

"You're coming to my house tomorrow," she replied, and when I arrived, she pulled me into her kitchen and told me to sit down.

I sat down.

She then took out her telephone book and proceeded to dial the Chief of Gastrointestinal Oncology Services of Sloan Kettering Hospital in Manhattan. Nobody could believe that the Rebbetzin was not only able to get through to Dr. David Kelsen so quickly but also managed to schedule an appointment for my husband for the following Tuesday.

If you know anything about pancreatic cancer, you will know that it is extremely difficult to treat. But the Rebbetzin met with both of us, looked into our eyes and said, "It is time for us to start to pray."

She then suggested that my husband's name be changed from Shlomo to Chaim Shlomo.

Both my husband and I had had grandparents who were Orthodox Jews and parents who had let religious practices slide. But our current situation was a major wake-up call and my husband decided it was time for him to begin studying Torah with the Rebbetzin. She would call him at his office (he was a principal in the New York City school system), and he'd close the door and learn with her on the phone — giving him the most incredible private Torah lessons in the world! He sat at his big desk and took copious notes of everything she told him, filling up his notebook with Torah thoughts. For the first time in his life, my husband was finally studying Torah — and loving it. But he didn't stop at learning. Within a short time my husband began wearing a yarmulke on his head, as if it were the most natural thing in the world.

Sometimes he'd say to me, "The Rebbetzin has to be one of the brightest people I've ever met!"

And he was a pretty smart person himself.

One day there was a problem with his chemotherapy and they rushed him to the hospital. We were still there when the Rebbetzin came rushing in to see us, later telling me, "You know what got me the most — seeing him sitting up in bed with his yarmulke on and the *sefer* open on his lap. He was reading from the *sefer*! Terribly ill and in the hospital — and learning Torah."

For the next fourteen months — until the cancer decimated his body — he kept up with his learning.

They operated on him at Long Island Jewish Medical Center — but there was nothing they could do for him. The Rebbetzin gave up a lot of time to learn with him and lift his spirits. I never met a person who went without sleep. Literally. I'd come into the house Friday morning and she'd say to me, "What time is it?"

"About a quarter to nine," I'd say.

"Oh."

"Why?"

"I never slept."

She'd spent the entire night on the telephone. The phones never stopped ringing.

I was allowed to interrupt her for anything — except when she was davening in her dining room, something she used to do every day for hours.

Before my husband passed away I was in the hospital. I called my son and told him to get everyone over to the hospital immediately. Then I called my daughter and said, "Arlene, you'd better come right now — it's going to be over in a few hours."

Then I called the Rebbetzin.

Chapter Forty-Nine: The Chaim Shlomo Siddur ☐ 509

"Rebbetzin, they told me it's almost over. I don't know what to do."

She explained to me about closing the eyes and my daughter took his glasses off, and she kept repeating, "Through your having a connection with Hineni, your husband went the right way."

The truth is, that meant more to me than all the money in the world.

Toward the end of her life, the Rebbetzin told me she was ill and asked me not to tell anyone. That was in February and she passed away in August. Before she was *niftar*, she said to me, "I want you to have something to remember me by — and I purchased these siddurim for you."

There were twelve siddurim — one for every member of my family. And the cover of every one of the siddurim was engraved with the words: "Siddur Chinuch Chaim Shlomo," and she inscribed every inside cover with a personal message to the recipient. For example, in the siddur she gave to my son, she'd inscribed an absolutely beautiful message to him about his Dad. She always knew exactly what to write and say. It was uncanny.

Her gift to me/us was incredibly meaningful. The Rebbetzin went out of her way to find the perfect gift. For one thing, it was a chinuch siddur, the ArtScroll educational version of the siddur; and for another thing, that particular edition had been dedicated for the *refuah sheleimah* (complete recovery) of a young man named Chaim Shlomo — which was my husband's name as well. There was no question that it was an absolutely perfect gift! What could possibly be more appropriate or suitable

The Chaim Shlomo Siddur

a present for our family? And I was touched beyond all measure by the fact that she'd gone out of her way to find "The Chaim Shlomo Siddur" from among the numerous siddurim in existence. Her gesture meant the world to me.

CHAPTER FIFTY

Getting on Jackie's Nerves

For many years the Rebbetzin had a dream of holding a Hineni service for the High Holy Days. She knew what an incredible experience it would be for all the people who frequented her classes and were part of Hineni. However, she was the Rebbetzin of Ohr Torah and her place was at her husband's side.

After Rav Meshulem passed away, however, the Rebbetzin and her children felt it was the perfect time to implement her long-awaited dream.

And so it began.

That year (1996) Hineni had its inaugural Rosh Hashanah and Yom Kippur services, hosted by Rebbetzin Esther Jungreis and her four children: Rabbi Yisroel, Rabbi Osher, Chaya Sora and Slovie. It was a phenomenal success from the start, almost as if people had been thirsting for a service of this kind for many years and hadn't even known it.

Now, however, it had become a reality.

There were over five hundred people davening with the Rebbetzin and her family that Rosh Hashanah. The Jungreis family couldn't put out the chairs fast enough. Chaya Sora remembers grabbing chairs from other ballroom and conference rooms, because the ballroom door kept on opening with more people showing up, wanting to participate in the davening. What was so amazing about that Rosh Hashanah service was the fact that so many of the people there would have never even considered attending such a davening a year earlier, and the rest would have never imagined themselves at an Orthodox service. And yet here they

R-L: Rabbi Osher, Rabbi Yisroel and Rabbi Shlomo preparing
for Hineni Yom Kippur davening

were, hearing inspiring messages from Rabbi Yisroel and Rabbi Osher, and listening to Rabbi Shlomo Gertzulin chanting the opening lines of the Mussaf prayer, while they stood on either side of a real *mechitzah* — not a row of ficus or palm trees, but an authentically kosher *mechitzah* — women on one side, men on the other. It was truly a miraculous gathering.

Not only that, the Rebbetzin wouldn't hear of compromising anything when it came to the davening. Some kiruv programs cut out parts of the davening and abridge here or there. Not at the Hineni davening. Here the members of the "kehillah" were part of a service that lasted for many hours — the same as in thousands of other shuls across America. And while the Rebbetzin did of course speak, the speech took place following the conclusion of the services.

One would have imagined that being the Rebbetzin of the shul, she would have elected to sit at the front of the room, but that was not the case. Instead she chose a corner seat near the aisle in the back of the room. People would enter the room and she'd give them a little nod, making it clear that she noticed them and was glad they were there. You had to pass the Rebbetzin's seat on the way in — and that was exactly

Welcoming one and all to the Hineni Yom Kippur program at New York's Essex House Hotel

how she wanted it, because it gave her a way to connect with every single woman attending the davening.

Sitting in the back of the room wasn't easy for her, especially in her later years when she had to make the long walk from the back of the room to the front to deliver her speech at the end of davening. But to her, all the effort was worthwhile, because it allowed her to be "The People's Rebbetzin," and not some untouchable Rebbetzin sitting in all her glory at the front of the room. It was always about her people and what would help make them feel at home, cared for and loved.

In an interesting turn of events, the back of the room became the hot spot because she was there; people had to be convinced to sit in the front, because everyone wanted to be as close as possible to the Rebbetzin.

A few years after the Hineni minyan started, the Plaza was unable to accommodate Hineni, and the Rosh Hashanah/ Yom Kippur services were moved to the Pierre Hotel on Fifth Avenue and 61st Street, and later to the Essex House on Central Park South. And they were really davening.

And it continues to this day.

At a typical Yom Kippur service, people start looking at the clock midway through the day, as they wait for the fast to come to an end. But at the Hineni Yom Kippur davening, there were hundreds of people sitting (or standing, when appropriate) from nine o'clock in the morning until the final shofar blast at the end of the day. Nobody was looking at the clock and nobody was looking to leave. The congregation's absolute immersion in their prayers was breathtaking. The feeling was: "This is where I belong today and I wouldn't want to be anywhere else."

One year, the Hineni davening took place at the Pierre Hotel on Fifth Avenue. It so happened that Reb Yisroel Neuberger's father owned an apartment on the twentieth floor of the hotel. After davening on Rosh Hashanah afternoon — a long, emotionally exhausting davening — Yisroel Neuberger approached Rabbi Shlomo and said, "Would you be able to do me a favor?"

"I'd love to do you a favor. What do you need?"

"Well, as you know, my father lives in this hotel."

Rabbi Shlomo nodded. "Go on."

"My father is ninety-nine years old right now. There's no question in my mind that for at least ninety-five years, my father has not had the opportunity to hear the sound of the shofar. Do you think it would be possible for us to go on upstairs to his apartment so you can blow shofar for him?"

Fulfilling Reb Yisroel Neuberger's request meant a good climb up nineteen flights, but Rabbi Shlomo was more than happy to accede. Together with his son Yosef Dov, Rabbi Osher, Reb Yisroel Neuberger and the shofar, the four climbed flight after flight of stairs until they finally reached the floor where Mr. Neuberger Sr. lived.

They entered the apartment and Reb Yisroel led them into the room where his father was relaxing on a La-Z-Boy recliner.

"Dad, I brought Rabbi Shlomo here and he is going to blow the shofar for you."

Rabbi Shlomo Gertzulin had no idea what to expect or how Roy Neuberger Sr. would react to his son's announcement — but to his relief, the elderly Mr. Neuberger didn't make a thing about it one way or another.

Rabbi Shlomo let forth a *tekiah* and Neuberger Sr. just stared at him, appraising him with unblinking eyes.

"Can you blow another few?" Yisroel Neuberger asked his friend.

Rabbi Shlomo blew another set of thirty. When he finished the set, Neuberger Sr. said enthusiastically, "You did that very well! Please blow some more!"

Rabbi Shlomo was happy to acquiesce to the elderly man's request.

It was clear that Reb Yisroel's father had been moved by the sound of the shofar and was not averse to making it a part of his life. For the next few years, Rabbi Shlomo Gertzulin and Reb Yisroel Neuberger climbed those many flights of stairs after a long Rosh Hashanah davening to give an elderly Jew the opportunity of a lifetime.

At the end of the day — if he was prepared to listen, Rabbi Gertzulin was ready to blow the shofar for him.

Another woman brought her 100-year-old father to hear the shofar on Rosh Hashanah, telling the Jungreis family that he hadn't heard the sound of the shofar for seventy years — since he was thirty years old and the Holocaust broke out.

"My father never wanted to go to shul after the war," she explained to the Rebbetzin, "but I decided it was the right thing for him at this point in his life. Besides, today is his birthday!"

It goes without saying that the Rebbetzin made a huge deal over the 100-year-old birthday celebrant. She made an announcement, telling the assembled how the visitor hadn't heard the shofar for seventy years and how he was finally back — just in time. The men broke into spontaneous song and began to dance around the man, turning a situation that he hadn't wanted into a memory that he would take with him to the World to Come.

There was a single woman who had lived with her mother in Hungary, moving to the States after her mother passed away. She joined the Hineni Rosh Hashanah service, introduced herself to the Rebbetzin and let her know that she was interested in getting married. One thing led to another, with the woman beginning to attend *shiurim* at Hineni and introducing more and more religious changes to her life. Eventually the Rebbetzin set her up and the couple was engaged to be married. But there was something weighing her down and she confided her worries to the Rebbetzin, asking her, "Who will be my mother? Who's going to walk me down the aisle?"

"I cannot be your mother," the Rebbetzin replied, "but I will try to love you as if you were my daughter."

After the wedding the Rebbetzin called her every single Friday, talking to her the way a mother talks to her daughter.

"Vera*," the Rebbetzin would say, "what are you making for Shabbos?"

It was the exact same question mothers around the globe were asking their own daughters.

"You know — soup, chicken, kugel."

One Friday the Rebbetzin called Vera as she did every week and asked her the same question, "What are you making for Shabbos this week?"

There was a resounding silence from the other end of the line. The Rebbetzin sensed the tension and knew a storm was brewing.

"Nothing," Vera answered.

"Nothing?"

"He doesn't deserve to eat! If you would only know what he did to me! I'm not cooking for him!"

The Rebbetzin didn't respond by saying, "Oh, no, what happened?" She didn't say, "*Oy, sheinkeit*, tell me, let me hear all the details!"

When the Rebbetzin spoke, it was with tremendous power.

"Vera, you are making a mistake!"

"What do you mean?"

"When you cook for Shabbos, you are not cooking for your husband. You're cooking for the Shabbos Queen. The Shabbos Queen is on her way to your house and you're not going to prepare anything in her honor?"

Vera pulled herself together and prepared a beautiful Shabbos.

In later years, Vera's husband would say with a smile that that was the best, most delicious Shabbos his wife ever cooked in her life.

Most people would have responded to Vera's opening line by asking for the details of the fight. That would have led to Vera rehashing the entire scenario over and over — which would have only made her more depressed, frustrated and angry. The Rebbetzin stayed far away from that. She didn't ask Vera what her husband had done and she never found out what happened that Friday to make her "daughter" so upset. All the Rebbetzin said was, "You are not cooking for him — you are cooking for the Shabbos Queen."

Once again, the Rebbetzin had known exactly what to say.

Holding a Rosh Hashanah service in an upscale Manhattan hotel can make for interesting scenarios. The rabbis would make a point of walking through the hotel lobby clad in their kittels and talleisim, drawing quite a bit of attention to themselves.

"Rabbi, is today Rosh Hashanah?"

"Are we in the middle of the High Holidays?"

"Yes, it is," they'd reply, before inviting the person asking the question (who had been on a pleasure trip to New York) to come and join the Hineni service. Many times they accepted their offer — and sometimes that first davening literally changed their lives. It was incredible what a small move like wearing your kittel in an upscale hotel lobby with numerous Jewish guests could accomplish!

One particular couple was so moved by the davening that they make a point of flying in to New York from California every single year to join Hineni for Rosh Hashanah!

For one simple reason: Because people recognize the real thing and respond to it.

They'd walk into the room and feel the intensity and seriousness of the people inside. Some of the people there don't even know how to read *aleph-beis*. But nobody talked.

Another couple became religious in their forties. They'd been married for a while and had children — an established family in every sense of the word. Excited by what they'd found at Hineni, the wife tried convincing her mother to attend the davening on Rosh Hashanah and Yom Kippur. The first year she came, she stayed for a few hours in the morning, enjoyed the festive meal following the prayers, and returned home. Clearly, however, the service had had an impact on her, because she returned the next year, taking a room at the hotel and remaining an active participant throughout.

"I have to respect my children," she explained. "This is important to them and I want to be a part of it."

That doesn't mean she became religious. But there's no question that her affiliation with Hineni has had and will have an impact on her life. It would be impossible not to.

It was Rosh Hashanah afternoon and the Hineni contingent was making its way from the hotel where the davening was taking place to the hotel where they were eating. Some years everything happened at the same hotel; other years the meals and davening were split between two locations. As the group of Jewish people walked through the Manhattan streets clad in their Yom Tov finery, they heard a somewhat familiar voice calling out, "Rebbetzin!"

Turning to look in the direction of the voice, Mendy Wolff saw that the voice belonged to none other than internationally acclaimed comedian Jackie Mason.

"Rebbetzin," he repeated himself, "is that you?"

"*Avada*, sure, it's me," she replied, "who else would it be?"

"Rebbetzin, I want you to know somethin'. Wherever I go — I can't go nowhere without someone talkin' about you. You're becomin' more famous than me, and you know somethin' — it's really startin' to get on my noives!"

During her final Rosh Hashanah, the Rebbetzin was in a lot of pain and could barely walk. Of course, she still had to walk from her seat to the stage to speak (her grandson Meshulem supported her), and people still lined up before her for berachos at the end of the davening on Rosh Hashanah night.

As they were walking into shul that night, the Rebbetzin turned to her grandson and said, "Meshulem, do you know how much pain I'm in right now?"

He knew.

"I'm in such tremendous pain, but I can't show people how I feel. That would ruin everyone's mood. I feel like a fire is running through my body right now, but I have to keep a smile on my face and give everyone their berachos like I do every year, so nobody's Rosh Hashanah will be ruined."

And she sat in her chair and smiled at every person in the room. She spoke to them and listened to them with a gracious smile on her face and gave them berachos. Every person walked out of the ballroom in an uplifted Yom Tov mood. She was the Bubba for many of the people at Hineni who never had a Bubba of their own. There was no way in the world she would put a damper on her grandchildren's Rosh Hashanah. So she kept her feelings to herself and almost nobody knew how she really felt.

They walked out of shul happy.

And so did she.

CHAPTER FIFTY-ONE
The Presidential Invite

*F*or years Barry Akrongold was a very active member of a group called The Republican Jewish Coalition, a prominent group of influential Jews who proudly identified themselves as Republicans. One of Barry's good friends was a man by the name of Shelly Kamins, one of the most successful Republican fundraisers. Shelly was based in D.C. and had a close relationship with the Bush family — both with President George H.W. Bush and his son, President George W. Bush. The Akrongolds and Shelly Kamins were good enough friends that he was a guest at Bruce Akrongold's wedding in 2000.

Having made the match between Bruce and Elisa, the Rebbetzin was of course asked to address the crowd at their wedding, and she "knocked the ball way out of the park." That was the first time Shelly met the Rebbetzin. You have to understand: There just aren't many speakers like Rebbetzin Jungreis in the non-Jewish or non-religious Jewish worlds, not in terms of charisma and certainly not in terms of content.

"Where did you find this lady?" Shelly enthused to the Akrongold brothers.

"This is nothing," Barry reassured his friend. "We go listen to the Rebbetzin's Torah classes all the time. She gets better every time you hear her!"

George W. Bush was running for president at that time. Having met the Rebbetzin and instantly grasping her immense abilities of persuasion, Shelly personally asked her if she would be willing to fly down to

Florida to campaign for George W. Bush among the Jewish population of the Sunshine State. As the Rebbetzin was a very concerned citizen who connected with the Republican Party on a host of issues, she was happy to accede to his request. The next thing everyone knew, the Rebbetzin was up on the stage addressing the crowds at a host of rallies. Of course, she was the Rebbetzin and spoke the truth as she saw it without holding back, and the moment she looked at them, the crowd was hers. All they wanted was to hear the Rebbetzin speak. She took full advantage of this and proceeded to deliver speeches replete with Torah *hashkafah* and messages of moral living for our day and age — and the audience loved her.

After her success on the Republican national stage, things began to happen. George W. Bush was someone who considered himself a religious man, and he liked the Rebbetzin. The result: She was asked to speak to members of the Republican Jewish Coalition, who were becoming more and more favorably impressed with the Rebbetzin from North Woodmere.

Thirty-one years after the Rebbetzin first stood on the stage at Madison Square Garden and shook the world with her call of "Hineni," she would be back — this time invited to deliver a religious invocation at the Republican National Convention (this was for George W. Bush's second term as president), which was taking place in the main arena. The event organizers let her know that she had between two to three minutes to deliver her message, and the Rebbetzin smiled and agreed — and then proceeded to speak for at least five minutes at the actual event.

As always, the Rebbetzin did things her way.

Of course the Jungreis children and many of the grandchildren were in attendance. In an exciting turn of events, the Rebbetzin's granddaughters were

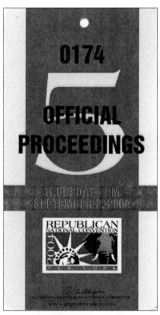

The Rebbetzin's official Republican National Convention credential

The Rebbetzin addressing the Republican National Convention in 2004

seated in the same box at the Garden with President Bush's twin daughters — Jenna and Barbara. Being around the same ages, they had a fine time getting to know one another before the actual event began.

Those familiar with the Rebbetzin's style of speaking know that she spoke from the heart and never from notes. But Convention protocol required the submission of all speeches in writing prior to the actual event. This would turn out to be very positive in the long run, because having committed her benediction to writing, she would be able to respond to the many requests she received for a copy of the text.

Almighty G-d —

We are living at a most challenging time in our history — one that our founding fathers could never have envisioned. Global terror and the breakdown of moral values menace our very lives.

Such threats are not foreign to me. I am a survivor of the Holocaust, a survivor of Bergen-Belsen concentration camp. I have experienced the degradation and the brutality of which man is capable, but I have also experienced the healing balm of faith, the magic of compassion and love which is the bedrock upon which our great Republic was built.

Following a Holocaust memorial address to our armed forces at Fort Hood, Texas, a little girl asked: "Rebbetzin, Ma'am, why didn't you call the army or the police to help you?"

What an American question!

How could I explain to her that in those days of darkness, a uniform was the symbol of torture and murder — that it was only when I encountered American soldiers and police that I discovered that these men in uniform could be trusted, that they are guardians of peace, committed to the protection of the innocent.

How different the world might have been if a man like George W. Bush had been at the helm in those days of darkness.

(The audience went wild when she said those words.)

Following 9/11, it was President Bush's valor and commitment to do battle against the forces of terror and evil that has ensured the safety and security of our nation.

Of all the world's leaders, it was only President Bush who had the courage to raise his voice on behalf of beleaguered Israel and recognize that terror in any part of the world must be eradicated. And just this morning, we were witness to yet another horrific act of terrorism with a bus bombing in Israel. Let us all pause for a moment of silence and prayer in memory of those who were so brutally murdered.

More than hope, our president is determined to triumph over evil, and continues to labor, not only for a safe, secure world, but for an America in which timeless values prevail.

The miracle that is America is not only to be found in her might, but in her spirit, in her faith in G-d, and it was with this faith, with the words of the Psalmist, that President Bush comforted our nation on that day of infamy.

"Gam ki eilech b'gei tzalmaves — Even though I walk through the shadow of the valley of death, I shall fear no evil, for You are with me."

"Kavei el Hashem — Trust in the L-rd."

We place our trust in You, O G-d. We pray to You to heal those who are sick with hatred; and to sensitize the hearts of those who are indifferent to the cries of their brethren.

Teach us, O G-d, to live by Your word in truth, compassion and peace.

G-d bless America, G-d bless our President, and may G-d bless each and every one of you.

"The people in the audience (many of them with an evangelistic worldview) had never heard anyone like the Rebbetzin before," Bruce Akrongold said, "and were ready to follow her up to Mount Sinai, or pretty much anywhere else she would have chosen to lead them. They would have followed her to all ends of the earth — that's how enamored they were by the Rebbetzin from North Woodmere, and they gave her a major ovation anytime she said a great line. And since the speech was replete with great lines, there was a lot of applause."

The response that followed her speech contained the kind of power usually reserved for a presidential nominee and went on and on, refusing to die down, as the crowd acknowledged their agreement with the Rebbetzin's call for morality and belief in G-d to a country that

054
Presidential
Acceptance
Podium Seating

Thursday Evening
September 2, 2004

REPUBLICAN
NATIONAL CONVENTION

CHAIRMAN, REPUBLICAN NATIONAL COMMITTEE
WWW.gopconvention.com

The Rebbetzin's
Podium Seating Badge
for the Presidential
Acceptance at the 2004
Republican National
Convention

had strayed far from the vision of its founding fathers.

President Bush himself was so moved by the Rebbetzin's benediction that he invited her to return on Thursday night to sit on the podium while he gave his acceptance address.

When the phone call came from the White House inviting the Rebbetzin to return to the stage, she was at first very happy, but after reflecting on the matter for a short while, she made a point of informing the person who invited her that she would not be able to shake President Bush's hand, his traditional way of greeting all the leaders seated on the stage.

"That will not be a problem at all," she was told.

And so on the big night, the Rebbetzin waited her turn to greet the President of the United States of America. As he approached her, he did indeed shake hands with every one of the influential people sitting on the stage.

The Rebbetzin addressing the Republican National Convention

Article in the Hebrew language *Mishpacha* magazine profiling the Rebbetzin and her appearance at the podium of the 2004 Republican National Convention

Then he reached the Rebbetzin.

In a marked digression from his interactions with everyone else, President George W. Bush stood before Rebbetzin Esther Jungreis and instead of offering her his hand, placed both hands behind his back, bowed his head and greeted her with extreme cordiality and respect.

In an amusing aside, all the ushers had been briefed as to the Rebbetzin's "special needs" — so when a gentleman took the seat just beside her, an usher was at his side in a second, informing the gentleman that it was preferable for a woman to sit beside her.

The Rebbetzin would laughingly describe the incident as the ushers going *"Lifnim mishuras hadin* — beyond the letter of the law."

The special connection between President Bush and Rebbetzin Jungreis — there was no similar precedent with any Jewish leader — would continue when she was invited by the President in 2008 to be part of his official delegation at the 60-year celebration of the relationship between Israel and the United States.

When President Bush spoke, he made a point of mentioning Abraham, Isaac and Jacob, stressing the richness of the Jewish nation's

Chapter Fifty-One: The Presidential Invite ☐ 525

heritage and noting the fact that the Jewish people were able to retain its faith and belief in G-d despite relentless persecution through the centuries.

After his speech the President made the rounds, taking the time to personally greet each of his guests. When coming face to face with the Rebbetzin, she let him know in no uncertain terms that his message had been an incredible sanctification of G-d's Name — a *Kiddush Hashem* that would go down in history. She then explained to President Bush what a *Kiddush Hashem* is and how important a concept it is. As always, her well-chosen words were accepted by the one to whom she was talking; in this case, the most powerful man in the world.

New York Times profile of the Rebbetzin on the day of her appearance at the Republican National Convention

The Rebbetzin with President George W. and First Lady Laura Bush at the White House

But the Rebbetzin never allowed people — no matter how important — to faze her. The only question on her mind was, what does Hashem want from her interaction with any particular person? And yes, that included the president. So while she honored, revered and respected President Bush immensely, Rebbetzin Esther Jungreis feared only Hashem.

Of course the Rebbetzin was invited by the President and Mrs. Bush to the White House for the annual Chanukah party/menorah lighting ceremony. The invitation gave her an opportunity to speak with the president and to raise any topic she chose, and there were those who urged her to utilize the chance to ask the President for clemency for Jonathan Pollard. Obviously, there was nothing comfortable about broaching such a sensitive topic, especially when she was invited as a guest and was not supposed to make diplomatic waves or rock the boat with political comments.

"Don't bother the President about Jonathan Pollard," many people said. "Don't even mention it. Pollard is a big no-no."

And yet, how could she pass up the opportunity to try to help a

The Rebbetzin with New York Mayors Michael Bloomberg and Ed Koch, along with other dignitaries, in Yerushalayim for the dedication of Yad Vashem's new Holocaust History Museum

fellow Jew who had been imprisoned for so long for helping Klal Yisrael? Was helping Jonathan Pollard not in the category of *pidyon shevuyim*, redeeming those imprisoned?

In the end, the Rebbetzin couldn't stop herself. When she was face to face with the president, she said, "Mr. President, I have one request of you."

He gave her a questioning look.

"Jonathan Pollard."

"Rebbetzin, I heard you," President Bush replied.

She would never know what impact her words had — if any. But that wasn't the point. Because the Rebbetzin was unable to pass up such a golden opportunity just

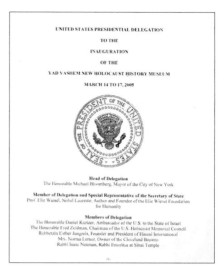

UNITED STATES PRESIDENTIAL DELEGATION
TO THE
INAUGURATION
OF THE
YAD VASHEM NEW HOLOCAUST HISTORY MUSEUM
MARCH 14 TO 17, 2005

Head of Delegation
The Honorable Michael Bloomberg, Mayor of the City of New York

Member of Delegation and Special Representative of the Secretary of State
Prof. Elie Wiesel, Nobel Laureate, Author and Founder of the Elie Wiesel Foundation for Humanity

Members of Delegation
The Honorable Daniel Kurtzer, Ambassador of the U.S. to the State of Israel
The Honorable Fred Zeidman, Chairman of the U.S. Holocaust Memorial Council
Rebbetzin Esther Jungreis, Founder and President of Hineni International
Mrs. Norma Lerner, Owner of the Cleveland Browns
Rabbi Isaac Neuman, Rabbi Emeritus at Sinai Temple

Announcement of a presidential delegation to the inauguration of the Yad Vashem Holocaust History Museum

because it was uncomfortable. Her personal comfort didn't matter. It wasn't about her and it had never been about her.

It was February 2005 and the phone rang in the Rebbetzin's office. The White House was on the line.

Yad Vashem, the Holocaust Memorial Museum in Yerushalayim, had just completed a new wing, and many important dignitaries and heads of state had been invited to attend the dedication ceremony. It went without saying that Yad Vashem sent an invitation to the President of the United States, George W. Bush. Unfortunately, the president was unable to attend

UNITED STATES HOLOCAUST MEMORIAL COUNCIL
In Appreciation

REBBETZIN ESTHER JUNGREIS
2006–2011

Together we have worked to preserve the memory of the Holocaust and honor its victims and survivors. We have pledged to ensure that their legacy helps to confront hate, prevent genocide, promote human dignity, and strengthen democratic values. For your part in fulfilling this pledge as a member of the United States Holocaust Memorial Council, we thank you.

UNITED STATES
HOLOCAUST MEMORIAL MUSEUM

Certificate of Appreciation to the Rebbetzin for serving on the United States Holocaust Memorial Council

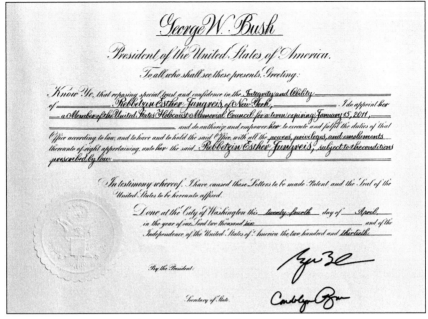

Appointment of the Rebbetzin to the United States Holocaust
Memorial Council signed by President George W. Bush and
Secretary of State Condoleezza "Condi" Rice

and he appointed a seven-person delegation to represent him in
Israel.

Rebbetzin Jungreis was one of the seven.

She was deeply honored to have been chosen to take part in what
would prove to be an extremely moving and inspirational experience.

On the return trip to Andrews Air Force Base in Washington,
Fred Zeidman, Chairman of the United States Holocaust Memorial
Commission, approached the Rebbetzin and said, "Rebbetzin, do you
know where we are right now?"

Rebbetzin Jungreis looked at him in puzzlement, not understanding
what he was getting at.

"Here, take a look," he said to her, pointing to the screen on the wall,
which showed that the presidential plane was flying over Germany. The
Rebbetzin gazed at the map on the wall of the plane and her face took
on a pensive expression.

"Think about it, Rebbetzin," Fred said. "You, a child of the Holocaust,
a survivor of Bergen-Belsen, are flying over Germany right now — in
the plane of the President of the United States — on your way back from
Jerusalem!"

The Rebbetzin meeting with President George W. Bush at the White House

For a moment the Rebbetzin choked up and she had to swallow long and hard before she found her voice.

"Fred," she finally said, "I think about it every day. When I was a child with a shaven head and hot tears rolling down my cheeks, dressed in rags and covered in lice, I didn't dream that I would survive, never mind fly over Germany in the President's plane while coming back from Jerusalem!"

CHAPTER FIFTY-TWO

The Equestrian

Chaim Zev (Howard) Taylor first met the Rebbetzin in March of 1999.

Here is his account:

At the time of our meeting, I could see my forties up ahead and I wanted to get married. I had been in a series of unhealthy relationships and I wanted to find a way to change things for the better. At that time I was a vice president of a very large financial institution in New York City. I lived in Princeton, New Jersey, and commuted to my job in the city; and while on the surface I had everything a person could possibly want, I felt a major lack and an emptiness that wouldn't go away. I had a wonderful job and an active social life, but I was floundering and restless. My father passed away in 1988 at a very young age, and I began asking myself what exactly was the point of life — scared silly because I had no clue.

My one major source of enjoyment and satisfaction in life was my involvement with horse riding — the particular equestrian sport that I did was called "competitive English riding," and I excelled at it. It meant jumping fences on hot-blooded horses in a broad range of terrain around the world, and I absolutely adored it.

For vacations I traveled to the highest-rated courses around the world. There was a famous course in the city of Seville on the southwestern coast of Spain. The area was called Andalusia, the scenery was magnificent and the Andalusian horses were part of the local history. This was the kind of place where the locals had been breeding horses for hundreds of years. Riding an Andalusian horse was almost as good as riding an Arabian steed. You looked at them and there was a smoldering fire in their eyes. You didn't go riding those horses unless you knew what you were doing. It was not a game.

I spent my final horse-riding vacation at a place called Carmona, which is a necropolis — basically a burial ground built by the Romans thousands of years earlier and replete with columns built of stone and a scenic view that was priceless.

As I stood there in the shadows of the Roman necropolis, I heard a voice speaking to my *neshamah*.

"Maybe you should take your next vacation in Israel."

I stood there somewhat disconcerted, trying to figure out where that voice had come from.

It was an interesting if somewhat surreal moment.

A friend of mine, knowing I was looking for a serious relationship with someone Jewish, suggested that I meet Rebbetzin Jungreis, who would be able to help make this happen.

"She gives this incredible class once a week," he said, "and there's like fifteen hundred singles from all over coming to hear her."

"What's it about?"

"Like life wisdom and Jewish thought and lessons from the Bible all mixed together."

I was enthusiastic about the idea and I figured I had nothing to lose.

When I was a little boy my parents used to take me to visit my maternal grandfather, Shlomo ben Chaim HaKohen. He used to put me on his knee and make Kiddush, giving me a taste of the sweet, heavy red wine. Good memories. No doubt he davened for me a lot and eventually it paid off.

I had grown up at the East New York Jewish Center, a Conservative synagogue not far from my home. My only memories from any service I'd ever attended at an Orthodox shul was listening to the rabbi yelling from the pulpit. I have no idea what he was saying — I just remember him yelling. For a ten-year-old, that kind of interaction is not much of a draw, if you know what I mean. I'd gone to Hebrew school and had grown up hearing Bible tales. I knew how to read Hebrew and I was familiar with many of the names and concepts of Judaism. Which meant that while I was connected to Yiddishkeit from a cultural angle, there was nothing going on ritually. I didn't keep the mitzvos or feel a need to do so.

Then I went to hear the Rebbetzin.

It was right after Purim and she was talking about the *parashah* of the week with a depth that I had never been exposed to in my life. As I sat there listening to her that Tuesday night, my mind began churning as I said, "Okay, if she's telling the truth, I'm going to have to give up all the beer dinners with my Princeton WASP friends."

With a name like Howard Taylor, my proclivity for horse-riding, and the fact that I'd even traveled to Ireland for its unique riding courses, people naturally assumed I was Irish. This errone-ous assumption was reinforced when I rode a horse down Fifth Avenue in the St. Patrick's Day Parade. The horse was outfitted with sashes of orange, white and green, the colors of the Irish flag. I had long fit in with that group (even after I made it clear that I was not Irish but Jewish), yet now I suddenly realized that I might have to say goodbye to everything to which I was accustomed.

After the class at "KJ" (Kehilath Jeshurun), I waited to speak to the Rebbetzin. She gave me a big smile. I introduced myself and told her how much I had enjoyed her class.

"It was truly eye-opening for me."

Then I said something which didn't really make sense in the context of the conversation.

"Most people don't even think I'm Jewish."

I then handed her my business card.

The Rebbetzin called me the next day. We talked a little on the phone and she asked me for my Jewish name.

I told her it was Chaim.

"Chaim, I have some people (by people she meant women) whom I want to introduce you to."

I took down the phone numbers.

I called one of them — she was sort of the female version of me — and we dated a few times, but it wasn't for me. The Rebbetzin wasn't fazed and introduced me to other women every week when I attended her *shiur*. She took a special interest in me and I felt unique and honored to be on the receiving end of her magic.

She was a true spiritual leader. So were her kids. They blew me away.

Though I clearly remembered the voice I had heard in the Roman necropolis back in Spain, I wasn't sure that I was ready to travel with a bunch of religious people — voice or no voice. Heaven, however, had other plans for me. Whichever exotic horse-riding location I tried to book was full. All the travel agencies that specialized in the horse-riding world were either offering trips to places I had no interest in, or were filled by the time I made inquiries and tried to book a ticket.

Italy was out.

Bordeaux was out.

Needless to say, I was disappointed. But then one day I opened my mailbox and found a flyer advertising a trip to Israel with Rebbetzin Jungreis. I realized that I would be going to Israel after all — just as the voice had suggested.

Hineni held their annual dinner at the Plaza a short while later. It was so well done, so tasteful. I sat in my seat and just enjoyed being with the people around me. It was a different crowd than I was used to and the difference was palpable. I had met many people in Manhattan who were only interested in taking advantage of other people. I used to refer to them as vampires. But the people who came to that dinner and the people who attended the Hineni events and *shiurim* were of a different caliber completely, and I loved being with them. The Jungreis family was constantly accomplishing amazing things — these were people who were really living their Judaism. I looked around the vast Manhattan ballroom and I said to myself, "You are going to Israel with the Rebbetzin."

In the months leading up to the Israel trip, the Tuesday class stopped being enough for me (I loved it and wanted more) and I added the Thursday class to my weekly schedule. Soon I needed even more than that and I began learning Gemara with Rabbi Osher on Monday nights. My life was being filled with Torah learning and I was suddenly feeling the intangible sense of satisfaction that had constantly eluded me in the past.

It was 1999 and I was learning Torah like a Jew for the first time in my life.

I remember boarding the plane, stowing my luggage above my seat and getting comfortable. I was traveling to Eretz Yisrael for the first time. I had no idea of the significance of Yerushalayim or the Beis HaMikdash. I was barely familiar with Jewish history and our historical connection to our ancient homeland. I was like a baby taking his first steps. Hashem was giving me an opportunity to see Eretz Yisrael. The rest was up to me.

We took off from JFK on one of the old El Al 747 planes. I remember looking across the cabin and seeing the Rebbetzin and Barbara sitting side by side. I watched the Rebbetzin saying Tehillim, an expression of utter bliss on her face — as if she were counting diamonds…

With every word, the Rebbetzin was sending me a message: "I am connected. I am connected. I am part of something much, much bigger than myself, and you can be part of it too!"

Later on I would learn about how Yaakov Avinu recited the *Shema* when he was reunited with Yosef after twenty-two years. The look of serenity and complete immersion in her prayer reminded me of what Yaakov Avinu's prayer must have been like at that crucial moment.

That trip turned out to be the changing point in my life.

On the Shabbos morning after we returned, I woke up and I knew that I had to go to shul. Keeping kosher became important to me. Shabbos took on a deeper meaning. I was becoming a different person and I was growing more and more connected to the Rebbetzin and her family.

As an aside…
Rabbi Yisroel Jungreis relates:
  My mother's Hineni trips to Israel were game-changers for many people.

Avi Dobuler was our tour guide. He had known my mother since he was a young teen — she was the one who got him through the terrible time after his father passed away. He'd meet us at the airport at the beginning of the trip. My mother always made sure to arrive on a flight that landed around sunset. As the setting sun shone rays of orange and red on the mountains leading up to Yerushalayim, my mother would instruct the driver to pull over on the side of the road just beside the words, "Beruchim Haba'im L'Yerushalayim/ Welcome to Jerusalem."

Avi would have a bottle of grape juice and some cake prepared and she would say, "Kinderlach, we're about to enter Yerushalayim. We have to make a berachah."

There was nothing "normal" about those trips.

Friday night, my mother would gather the women together and teach them how to bench licht (light candles). She'd stand in the Plaza explaining to the group the significance of Klal Yisrael's mothers lighting Shabbos candles for thousands of years — and more and more people would pause to listen to her, until the lobby was packed with guests, who wanted nothing more than to hear what she had to say about Shabbos.

After that introduction to Shabbos, the entire group would walk to the Kosel together, enjoying the incredible atmosphere of Shabbos Kodesh in Yerushalayim Ir HaKodesh.

And a big part of the trip was the visit to my great-grandfather

The Rebbetzin leading a Hineni Israel tour

The Rebbetzin spending time with immigrant children during a Hineni tour

Rav Tzvi Hirsch Cohen's kever on Har HaMenuchos. Once every-
one was gathered around the grave, my mother would say, "Heiliger
Zeide, I'm bringing more kinderlach back to Yiddishkeit."

She would then introduce them to him using their Hebrew names
and their mother's Hebrew names. It's a funny thing. Many of the
people who went with my mother on those trips make sure to return
to the Zeide's kever when they visit Eretz Yisrael on their own.

"When Yisroel and I got married," his wife Rivki said, "the two of
us went to Har HaMenuchos to daven at the kevarim, because both
of our grandfathers were buried there. When we arrived, we found,
to our utter surprise, that Rav Tzvi Hirsch and my grandfather
Rav Yosef Freund were buried in extremely close proximity to one
another. When I told the Rebbetzin about our discovery, she said,
"What do you think, this is coincidence? There are no coincidences,
sheinkeit — when it comes to the Bubbas and the Zeides, nothing!"

Chaim Zev returned to Israel with Rebbetzin Jungreis a year later. He
continues the narrative:

By that point in time I was keeping the mitzvos in a committed
fashion, but although I was already wearing a kippah on my head

and putting on tefillin every morning, I still found it difficult to start wearing tzitzis on a daily basis. The idea of having to wear another layer of clothing went against my nature, and I couldn't bring myself to go the final step.

One afternoon during the trip I ventured forth into deepest Meah Shearim where I found a store that sold religious objects. The proprietor engaged me in conversation and we had a nice chat.

"What can I get you?" he asked me at last, and being embarrassed to admit that I was in the market for a tallis kattan, a pair of tzitzis, I told him that I wanted to purchase a regular tallis — even though I wasn't married or even in a serious relationship at the time! I ended up buying both. And I wore my tzitzis from then on.

The second Israel trip was also memorable in my mind for our visit to Amukah — the burial place of the Talmudic sage Yonasan ben Uziel and a place that is frequently visited by people actively searching to get married who come to pray at his grave. The *kever* is located at the bottom of a long winding road, which descends and curves down between the towering trees of the Amukah forests on the outskirts of Tzfas. It is picturesque and incredibly scenic, and the carefully calibrated drive down that narrow road is a worthwhile experience. I davened there with all my heart and got back on the bus feeling as if a load had slipped inexplicably off my shoulders.

It was just a few short weeks after we returned from Israel when the Rebbetzin called me over after a class.

"Chaim," she said, "you're ready to meet a religious girl. This one's beautiful."

I still have the piece of paper that she gave me with my wife's phone number on it.

Her name was Robbie.

I called her and we began to date — dating like two people who kept the Torah and following the halachic rules of interaction between men and women. We talked and we had a connection, and it quickly reached the point where it hurt when we weren't talking to one another.

In a fascinating turn of events, my wife's father was a seventh-generation descendant of the Noam Elimelech and was able to trace his family heritage all the way back to Dovid HaMelech!

Needless to say, my father-in-law wasn't exactly thrilled with the Rebbetzin's shidduch for his daughter. He even called her up and expressed his displeasure with the match.

"I don't know where he was before and I don't know where he'll end up," the Rebbetzin replied, "but I can tell you that right now, he's a very good and real Jew!"

We met at the beginning of August and got engaged after Succos a couple of months later. Our wedding took place on Thanksgiving weekend/Rosh Chodesh Kislev, in the boathouse at Central Park. Rabbi Osher Jungreis took care of the *aufruf* on the Shabbos preceding the wedding. I went to hear the Rebbetzin speak that Shabbos afternoon and there was a family Melaveh Malkah on Motza'ei Shabbos. I was invited to join the family and I accepted the invitation, honored to have been asked.

There, behind closed doors, the Rebbetzin spoke to her family with a sense of urgency and power. It was the same passion and charisma which I'd seen so many times when she spoke in public. Here, however, it was just her family. And yet there was no difference between her public and private personas. There was no show, no drama. She was the same person, no matter where she was, always demanding much from the people around her, but even more from herself. The theme of her speech that night: how it was up to them to take their places in the chain of their ancestors. It made such an impression on me. There's no shortage of phoniness in this world, and there was no question in my mind that the Rebbetzin was the genuine article. She lived what she preached, and that was the source of her power.

Our boathouse wedding took place during the afternoon. That night we left to the airport on a Hineni mission to Israel. It was during the second Intifada and the Rebbetzin was making a very clear statement by choosing to visit specifically at a time when everyone else was staying away. We celebrated a sheva berachos at the General Assembly of the Jewish Federations of North America and in other interesting places. But our favorite sheva berachos was at Café Rimon off Rechov Ben Yehuda. There was a bunch of yeshivah students at the restaurant and we invited them to join us in the festivities and to help make the minyan. The Rebbetzin ordered a bottle of wine and we made the berachos and danced in the middle of Café Rimon, the sound of our singing reverberating through the emptiness of the street outside.

We returned home a few days later. You can imagine my shock and dismay when I heard on the news that a terrorist had just blown up Big Apple Pizza, which was around the corner from where we'd danced a few days earlier, celebrating a new union in Klal Yisrael.

Our wedding took place in the month of Kislev.

By Elul we were the proud parents of a brand-new baby girl whom we named Aviella Rachel.

That Succos we took Aviella Rachel to meet the Rebbetzin for the first time.

Our families have remained close through the years, and I will never forget her Torah and the lessons that she taught me and thousands of others both in the United States and around the world. For many years now the Taylor family has been living in Israel, fulfilling the teachings of the Rebbetzin who taught us to love the Holy Land with all our hearts.

She wasn't just our Rebbetzin: For so many of us at Hineni she was our first rebbi as well.

This chapter has been dedicated
in memory of the Rebbetzin ע״ה

The Bolton Group – Neuberger Berman

CHAPTER FIFTY-THREE

The Struggle

"On the day of 9/11, I was still married to a non-Jewish man."
So Chaya began her story.

We were living in Old Tappan, New Jersey. My husband had a good job, and I was a full-time mommy, taking care of my kids, who were still young. I was living what anyone would consider the absolutely perfect life. My husband was a super-nice Wall Street guy, I lived in a monster house, there were two BMWs parked in the driveway, and we even had a dog. Really, the ultimate dream life for a Jewish American Princess.

My husband was actually down there on 9/11. He worked in the World Financial Center right across the street from the Twin Towers and his office was also destroyed. I didn't know where he was for many hours; but at least he survived, unlike the thousands who perished in the attack against the United States.

In the aftermath of 9/11, I was devastated. For my husband it was bad. He'd been there when the planes crashed into the buildings, had seen people jumping out the windows, seen people on fire — and he himself barely managed to escape. But of the two of us, my reaction was probably stronger, though I hadn't been there at the time of the attack. I started watching the news obsessively; and because the television was always on, I began taking notice of what was happening across the ocean in Israel. At that time, Israel was experiencing a spate of suicide bombings and I found myself thinking, "For the Israelis, it's 9/11 every other day!"

I had never thought that way before. I had never really given any thought to Israel at all. Yet suddenly I found myself thinking about the country halfway across the world all the time. It was as if I had suddenly begun looking at the world through a completely different prism: a prism stressing the fact that Israel was a Jewish State, I myself was a Jewish woman, and that I too needed to stand strong with and for my people in their hour of need.

As an aside…

In the aftermath of 9/11, the Rebbetzin's entire world shifted. She couldn't just allow the monumental event to pass and fade into oblivion. That wasn't her way. Instead of making do with a comment here and there, Rebbetzin Jungreis began calling for worldwide gatherings for teshuvah. She spoke about teshuvah and 9/11 at "KJ," where hundreds lined the streets waiting to get in and hear the Rebbetzin speak. There was not an empty seat — nor a dry eye — in the house.

The Rebbetzin also spoke about 9/11 on the radio and television, and she spoke about it in cities across America and around the world. She refused to allow people's minds to wander away from the terrible event that had occurred, so she spoke about it again and again, urging everyone

Full-page ad in the *New York Times* publicizing the Rebbetzin's Post-9/11 Prayer Works campaign

Hineni "PRAYER WORKS" pin distributed by the Rebbetzin after 9/11

The Rebbetzin took her "Prayer Works" message to cities across America.

she met to respond "to the call of the hour with strength and might."

The Rebbetzin spoke with great emotion about the horrific event that had just unfolded before the very eyes of all humankind. Her message was succinct and direct and it hit people hard — right in the heart. She focused on the Torah message of the struggle between Islam and Judaism.

"If a few diabolical men were able to inflict such terrible destruction upon the mightiest nation on earth, just think what an army of good people can do if their hearts are alight with teshuvah, dedication and love for Torah!"

She would go on to cite four areas in which a tikkun (self-improvement) must be made: tefillah, tznius, mesirus nefesh, and chessed (prayer, modesty, sacrifice for Torah and loving kindness).

It goes without saying that the Rebbetzin's message brought people to tears wherever she went.

For the Rebbetzin, the fact that such a terrible thing had occurred was bad enough. But in her mind, it would have been infinitely worse had the event passed unchallenged, without a mention and without taking something from it.

The Rebbetzin called her 9/11 campaign "Prayer Works." There was a special emphasis on the power

Crowd forming outside Kehilath Jeshurun to hear the Rebbetzin speak after 9/11

of tefillah. A major campaign was undertaken, including placing full-page ads in national newspapers, and distributing many thousands of special pins on which were written the words "Prayer Works." That was the Rebbetzin's unique answer to the day of infamy that claimed so many lives. It was the Rebbetzin's answer to 9/11.

It was classic Rebbetzin Jungreis. One didn't just deal with tragedy — one grew from tragedy.

Chaya continues:

> I didn't really understand how I made the leap from 9/11 to my recognition of Israel's security situation, but the fact is, I felt terrible for having never given any thought to my people's challenges in the past. After thinking about my breakthrough for a while, I decided that I simply had to visit Israel. Trying to figure out how to handle all the feelings inside me, I asked a woman I met at the JCC what to do. She recommended that I get in touch with Chabad.
>
> "They're really great," she said to me. And so I came to meet the rabbi she was referring to — who had a lot of questions for me, as he tried to understand the root of my feelings. At this point it was

all about Zionism. There was no religious aspect.

Having gotten to know the rabbi, I began spending time at the Chabad House. It was a twenty-minute drive from my home and I started attending services there. Overnight, I had become the biggest Zionist imaginable. I would only buy items from Israel and attended Israeli vendor fairs where I purchased all kinds of things I didn't need, due to my desire to support the Israeli economy. I also got involved with a program at my JCC called "Open Hearts, Open Homes," where teenagers who were victims of terrorism would come spend part of the summer in the States at people's homes.

That summer I went on a trip to Israel. The trip was organized by a man named Phil Rosen from the Five Towns, who was active in the Likud Party and AIPAC, which I joined as well. Since we hadn't been involved in giving charity up until that point, my husband was supportive of my desire to help Israel and victims of terror, considering it a worthy and just cause.

I had never even heard of the Five Towns before my trip to Israel, and suddenly I was spending a lot of time with people who were religious. Knowing that the women on the trip would be dressed modestly, I went out and bought skirts and new clothing. From the moment we arrived in Israel, we were on and off of buses and visiting graves and towns around the country, and they were constantly talking about people I had never heard of — like Avraham, Yitzchak and Yaakov.

"Why are they talking about these people non-stop?"

"Who are these people?

Except for having learned how to read Hebrew, I knew nothing of my Jewish heritage, despite the fact that I'd had a bat mitzvah and even read from the Torah.

Everyone else on the trip had been to Israel before. We visited Chevron, Itamar and Beit El in the West Bank and even traveled up north to Afula, and the entire time I was thinking, "This is the most unbelievable trip of my life!"

One morning we pulled up in front of Kever Rachel. There was no gigantic wall at that time, and the guides explained that we needed to jump off the bus and run into the building as fast as we could, because the Arabs could shoot from the nearby buildings…

This Rachel must be really something for us to be risking our lives to come and pray by her grave! What did she do to deserve this from all of us?

And why are we visiting graves all day long?

We stepped into the building, and within minutes I found myself crying hysterically beside Rachel's tomb — the tomb of the Rachel whom I had never heard of before...

There are pivotal moments in everyone's life. Standing in Kever Rachel crying my eyes out, I knew — I just knew — that my life was never going to be the same again!

And yet I had a whole life at home, with numerous secular Jewish friends (my Neiman Marcus crowd) and a really wonderful non-Jewish husband...

I returned home. To my life in Old Tappan, New Jersey.

While walking in midtown Manhattan one day, I saw a bookstore named Eichler's. I went in. I walked up to the man at the counter and said, "I have to tell you, I think I'm interested in becoming more religious. What should I be doing?"

He didn't say a word. Just motioned for me to follow him over to one of the bookcases. Reaching up, he pulled a book off the shelf. I looked at the cover. It was titled *The Jewish Soul on Fire*, and it had been written by someone named Rebbetzin Esther Jungreis.

"*The Jewish Soul on Fire*," I said, reading the words to myself, "that sounds interesting.

I bought the book, started it — and I could not believe what I was reading. I had never in my life heard, read or seen anything like this. I remember taking the Rebbetzin's book with me up to Vermont when my entire family — all my siblings and my parents, all the kids and the wives and husbands — drove out there for a long three-day weekend.

I was lying on the sofa in the living room reading the book, and — *The things she is saying!* — I was crying. At one point I turned to everyone and called out, "You have got to hear this." I read one of the paragraphs out loud — something the Rebbetzin had written about a person's *neshamah* — the tears streaming down my face, and I looked around the room and every person was staring at me, and it was obvious that they were thinking, "What on earth is wrong with her?"

It was at that moment that I knew I was in trouble.

It didn't take me long to discover that the Rebbetzin was not only a writer of fantastic and inspirational books, but that she also gave classes every week in Manhattan. Ecstatic at the idea of meeting her, I began driving in from New Jersey every Tuesday night, to the huge class at "KJ." It didn't matter if it was pouring rain outside — it didn't matter if there was a snowstorm — it didn't matter in the slightest. I never missed her class. I would go to that class, sit there in the room, and it felt to me like I was the only person in the room. She would talk about the *parashah* — and somehow every word was directly connected to whatever was going on in my life right then!

(Later I learned that every person in the room felt the same way.)

There was not one class where I didn't find myself sitting with tears streaming down my face. It was the same thing every time. To me, the Rebbetzin was the most incredible person in the world. The class was my therapy session — it was truly everything.

Here's the "problem" with going to such a class.

When a person goes to a class like that — they start to change. And that was what happened to me. When the Rebbetzin mentioned how a person should buy a Tehillim, I returned to the bookstore and purchased a Tehillim with an English translation. I also started davening at home; and because everyone thought I was crazy, I felt like I had to hide in the closet when I did it. Since I had this big, beautiful walk-in closet, there was plenty of room, but there is something demoralizing about having to daven in the closet — no matter how big it is!

The hardest part of my situation was trying to co-exist in two very different worlds at the same time. I couldn't hang out with my Neiman Marcus crowd and say things like *"Baruch Hashem."* I'm not saying it's impossible, but it's definitely a major challenge. Or when they start talking about one of your friends, it is very difficult to look them in the eye and say, "I'm sorry, I can't talk about Debra or Sheila or Ann, because that's *lashon hara* — harmful speech!"

A few years had gone by and I was becoming frum through Chabad, and even taking my husband with me to many of their events. I also started keeping chalav Yisrael and peeling all my vegetables for Pesach. And still returning to Israel once a year.

And at the same time, I was married to a non-Jew.

I would wait to speak with the Rebbetzin after class was over; and where in other cases she would tell the girls, "Only marry Jewish," here I was already married — with kids — and the situation was extremely complicated.

Of course my family — my Jewish family — tried to hold an intervention for me. My brother, sister, parents — all sitting around the dining room table — pummeling me emotionally for two hours straight about how I'm ruining my marriage and my kids' lives, etc.

It was me against the entire world.

A lot of my friends started to drop me. I had read Yisroel Neuberger's book, and what he had written was incredibly true: how his Jewish bosses were the ones who wouldn't let him find the time to daven during his time in the office, while his non-Jewish bosses were fine with it and even supportive. It was the same with me. My non-Jewish friends would say, "What you're doing is so wonderful," or "Good for you!" while my Jewish friends were saying, "You're nuts! You're losing your mind!"

I remember how one of my friends was arranging a surprise birthday party for her husband on a Friday night. I had just started officially not driving on Friday night.

"I'm sorry," I told her, "but I won't be able to come over."

She could not understand.

"Why can't you come? How are you breaking Shabbos by coming over for a birthday party?"

"Even if I drove over before Shabbos, I won't be able to get home when it's over."

She couldn't grasp the concept.

After that, we just weren't friends anymore.

As for my husband, I think he really, really thought everything I was doing and going through was a phase. And that if he just held on long enough I would come to my senses and revert to being the normal girl he had married.

After a couple of summers of traveling to Israel by myself, I decided it was time for us to go together as a family. My husband thought Israel was great, but his reaction was nothing like mine. I loved him very much and I had been hoping that maybe we could find a way to make things work.

We returned from the trip. School was starting the next day and I had a surprise for him: the fact that I wanted to take our children out of public school and enroll them in local Jewish schools. My daughter was entering fourth grade and my son was going into first.

But here my husband finally drew a line in the sand.

"Absolutely not."

We battled it out in our upstairs laundry room. I remember sitting on the floor crying hysterically for hours and hours — until my face was puffy and my eyes were redder than they'd ever been in my life — but he said, "No, no way, no way!"

We argued the entire night.

In the morning he had to leave for work — and I was still not giving up. In my mind, my children's education was the most important thing — Rebbetzin Jungreis had really drummed that into my head over and over.

"You have to give your kids a Jewish education! You have to give your kids a Jewish education!"

As he was walking out the door, he spat out, *"Fine, do what you want!"*

Seizing his words (words he didn't mean) like a lifejacket, I took the kids and moved them into a Jewish school, which only required the signature of one parent.

When my husband returned home from work that evening, he said, "So how was the kids' first day of school?"

"It was great!"

"Where did they go?"

I told him.

World War III.

"You said I could do what I want," I reminded him. He was not

happy or mollified or even a little bit okay with the situation —
but at that point there wasn't much for him to do. He ended up
giving in — and the kids had an amazing year.

Over the next year and a half, our marriage officially fell apart.
I had reached the point where I was ready to go all the way. I
wanted to live a completely frum life. I did ask him if he would be
willing to consider converting to Judaism.

"What about if I converted Conservative?"

"We need to be living life on the same page."

We ended up moving to a city called Plantation, Florida, trying
to see if we could make it work in a new place. And the best part
about our new life was the fact that I was finally close enough to
the local shul to be able to walk there on Shabbos. He thought that
by moving to Florida, we'd be leaving all the Jewish stuff behind
in New Jersey, but the opposite was true — because, guess what
— there are Chabad Houses in Florida too!

That was it. I was finally completely frum.

We ended up getting divorced. His last words to me were, "You
will see, I am going to do everything I can to make these kids not
religious."

He didn't say that because he was a bad person. But he felt that
I had destroyed our lives. I understood him. There had been times
along the way when I'd felt the same thing. There was a period
when I backed away from religion for a few months, because
I didn't want to lose my life. But that decision only made me
depressed — because once you discover the magic and truth of
Torah and mitzvos, and once you realize that that is the life you
want to lead, nothing is a substitute for it. And so I was willing to
fight to give my children the Jewish education they needed and
deserved if they were to grow up to become proud Jews.

It was a battle. At every stage. From elementary to middle
school and from middle school to high school. But I never gave up.
And I have had the *zechus* to watch my children grow up in the
right schools, and with good *middos* (character traits) and a love
for Hashem. You can't imagine what it's like for me to see my son
walking through the door in his black hat and jacket — a *yeshivah
bachur* in every way; it's just a tremendous berachah.

As for the Rebbetzin, I still have her voice saved on one of my voice mails. I've kept it because I like listening to it from time to time: the voice that gave me the strength to defy society, family and so many pressures, to do what I knew to be right. I still read her books all the time; just pull them off the shelf, sit down on the couch and immerse myself in the Jungreis world, because — you know what? There was never anyone like her, and I am pretty sure there will never be.

This chapter has been dedicated
in memory of our "Torah Bubby" Rebbetzin Esther Jungreis ע"ה
who inspired generations to seek out and cling to our Jewish heritage,
and in honor of her children and grandchildren who continue her legacy
with warmth, wisdom, eloquence and kindness
Paul and Lisa Glazer and Family

CHAPTER FIFTY-FOUR
"Jewish Ammunition"

*R*ebbetzin Blimi Jungreis lives in London, England. Yet despite the fact that she resided across the ocean from her aunt, the two of them still managed to maintain an extremely close relationship. On one of her visits to the States, she was waiting along with her husband, Rav Osher Anshil Jungreis (the Rebbetzin's nephew), in line to go through passport control, when she happened to notice that one of the security officers had a yarmulke on his head.

Turning to her husband, she said, "I really hope we are sent to his counter."

They were.

Standing in front of the customs officer, Rebbetzin Blimi said, "It's so nice to be welcomed into the United States by a Yid wearing a yarmulke on his head!"

He smiled in response to her words and began flipping through their passports. As he stamped her passport he asked her, "Tell me, are you related to Rebbetzin Esther Jungreis?"

Now keep in mind that Rebbetzin Blimi Jungreis has been asked the very same question in all its alternative versions numerous times throughout the years. But this was the first time it had been asked to her by the officer stamping her passport in an international airport — and she was slightly taken aback.

"Yes, I am related to her — Rebbetzin Jungreis is my aunt."

"You should know that the Rebbetzin made me religious."

Once again, she had heard that same line ("the Rebbetzin made me religious") and other versions of it many, many times over the years, but never by a man stamping her passport.

They weren't able to stand around talking — too many people were waiting to get into the U.S. — but he said to her, "Please tell the Rebbetzin that I heard one of her speeches and that's why I became religious."

Rebbetzin Blimi Jungreis couldn't stop herself. Pulling out her phone, she dialed her aunt's number and told her where she was and who she had just met. But that was the Rebbetzin's life. For her, every day was another opportunity to do amazing things, and rare was the day when she didn't see the results of her actions from long before.

You too can achieve this kind of life.

But you have to be a doer like she was. The more you do, the more it all comes back to you at the end.

At a speech in London, the turnout to hear the Rebbetzin was so great that all standing room was taken as well, compelling the overflow to spill out into the lobby. The Rebbetzin realized that if she had any hope of commanding the attention of the people at the back of the hall and in the lobby, she would have to stand on a chair — otherwise they would not be able to see her at all. The Rebbetzin began to speak, and amazingly the crowd was oblivious to the discomfort of their surroundings: the oppressive heat and the terrible crush. Nobody was paying any attention to the discomfort — they were too focused on what she was telling them.

Life Is a Test — English, Hebrew, Spanish and French editions

At the Saatchi shul in St. John's Wood, London, waiting on line for autographed books by the Rebbetzin (at the table on the lower level)

Half an hour into the speech a woman fainted from the extreme heat. She recovered immediately and was taken into the office, where Hatzolah made sure she was fine. Despite this, the crowd would not allow the Rebbetzin to stop the speech, begging her to carry on sharing her words of Torah.

About fifteen minutes later, it happened.

As she was describing the darkness that descended on the world with the advent of the Holocaust, the electricity blew and the entire hall was enveloped in utter darkness. It goes without saying that the heat became even more intense now that the fans had all stopped working. At this point the Rebbetzin felt the time had truly arrived for her to wrap things up, but the people wouldn't allow her to stop talking. In an amazing turn of events, the electricity was only partially off, because her microphone and sound system were

Life Is a Test — Audio edition

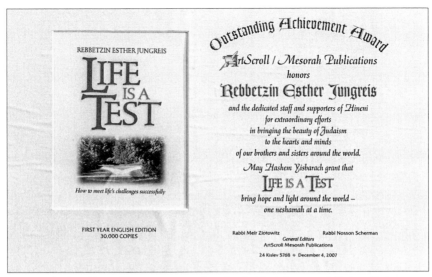

REBBETZIN ESTHER JUNGREIS

LIFE IS A TEST

How to meet life's challenges successfully

FIRST YEAR ENGLISH EDITION
30,000 COPIES

Outstanding Achievement Award

ArtScroll / Mesorah Publications

honors

Rebbetzin Esther Jungreis

*and the dedicated staff and supporters of Hineni
for extraordinary efforts
in bringing the beauty of Judaism
to the hearts and minds
of our brothers and sisters around the world.*

May Hashem Yisbarach grant that

LIFE IS A TEST

*bring hope and light around the world —
one neshamah at a time.*

Rabbi Meir Zlotowitz   Rabbi Nosson Scherman
General Editors
ArtScroll Mesorah Publications

24 Kislev 5768 ✦ December 4, 2007

ArtScroll certificate presented to the Rebbetzin upon *Life Is a Test*
reaching first-year sales volume of 30,000 copies

still working and everyone was able to hear her. There was something extremely poignant hearing the Rebbetzin describe her experiences in Bergen-Belsen while sitting in complete darkness.

But then someone else fainted.

"My dear friends," the Rebbetzin said to the crowd, "I have no doubt that Hashem has witnessed your enormous devotion and *mesirus nefesh* tonight, but in the interest of everyone's health and safety, we must end the program."

Yet many people remained behind even once the speech was over.

The Rebbetzin spoke to every one of them, signing her book, *Life Is a Test*, again and again in the velvety darkness.

It was a night that would forever be remembered by anyone who had the good fortune to be there. As she bade the women of London farewell, the Rebbetzin turned her face toward heaven and said, "Ribono shel Olam, look at us — look at Your people! Who is like Your nation, Israel? Master of the world — do You see how thirsty Your children are to hear the words of Your Torah? Hashem, see who we are!"

One of the Rebbetzin's speeches took place at a shul in Mill Hill, in Northwest London. It was winter time and she arrived with Barbara Janov directly from the airport with all their luggage. Their flight had

Doctor of Humane Letters bestowed upon the Rebbetzin by Touro College
in recognition of her life's work and writings

been delayed, which was why they had no time to drop off their things
and unpack before the speech. The Rebbetzin's friend and student
Frances Jay stowed their coats and luggage in the coat room, and the
Rebbetzin made her way up to the stage where she spoke for nearly an
hour, somehow fresh after the transatlantic flight. Then Frances drove
the Rebbetzin and Barbara to their hotel and bade them a good night's
rest.

The Rebbetzin smiled at her friend and replied, "Frances, I'm not
going to bed just yet. I have to check my email from the office and prepare my column for *The Jewish Press.*"

There was no thought of rest.

Rest and relaxation were reserved for the End of Days.

A private tzedakah luncheon was arranged at the Clarinet Hall in
Stamford Hill, featuring the Rebbetzin as the guest speaker. She arrived
before the speech and Frances waited outside the hall to greet her. Her
taxi pulled up at the hall, but the Rebbetzin didn't get out of the car.
Frances opened the back door of the car, and the Rebbetzin took her
hand and pulled her into the back seat. Frances sat beside her — the
Rebbetzin held her hand the entire time — as she finished reciting her
Tehillim for the day.

When she was done, she gave Frances her usual berachah and apolo-
gized to the driver for making him wait, explaining to him that before
she speaks anywhere, she always has to have help from the Almighty.

The driver smiled in appreciation of her sentiments.

The Rebbetzin spoke at American military bases on many occasions. On one such trip to Fort Hood, Texas, she had no luggage, since she had flown in for the day and was traveling with just a briefcase and her Tehillim. Though there was no conceivable reason why it should have happened, there was a beeping sound as she walked through security.

"Ma'am, can you please put the book down," the security agent asked her, pointing to the soft-cover Tehillim that she had been carrying in her hand.

The Rebbetzin followed instructions, and when she passed through the security scanner for the second time, there was no buzz.

"What is this book?" the agent asked her, puzzled.

"Jewish ammunition," the Rebbetzin replied with a twinkle in her eye. "This is the *Book of Psalms* — which was written by King David," and on the spot she began giving airport security a history lesson on *Sefer Tehillim*. She was a born teacher — it didn't matter where she was:

Signing books for American servicemen at Fort Hood, Texas, the most populous U.S. military installation in the world

The Rebbetzin addressing officers at the Great Lakes Naval Training Center, the largest military installation in Illinois and the largest training station in the U.S. Navy

the airport, an army base or a jail. If there was teaching to be done, the Rebbetzin would do it.

She never stopped giving her all for her people.

It didn't matter what form it took: whether it was a speech to a thousand people, a speech that was being broadcast on national television, or a visit with one person in the hospital.

There was a six-year-old child who was fine one day and struck by a terrible illness the next. The child's grandmother, seeing the toll the illness was taking not only on the boy himself, but also on her son and daughter-in-law, offered to take over for them at her grandson's bedside any time his parents needed to leave the hospital.

"Any time you want," she said, "Zeide and I will drop everything and go to the hospital. If you want to spend Shabbos at home with the other kids, just tell us and we'll be there immediately."

One Erev Shabbos, their children accepted their offer and asked them to stay with their grandson while they returned home.

When the grandfather returned to the hospital after davening on Friday night, he was very excited.

"Rebbetzin Jungreis is in town," he told his wife. "She's spending this Shabbos as a guest speaker at the Park East Synagogue!"

By that point in time their grandson was already in a coma, and his grandmother approached one of the nurses and asked her if it would be okay if she attended services at one of the local synagogues the next morning.

"Can you take over for us for two hours tomorrow morning? I won't have my cellphone with me because it's our Sabbath, but I'll only be away for a short while."

"Of course, sweetheart," the nurse replied, "go and pray — take your time — we'll stand guard while you're away."

"I went to shul that Shabbos morning," the bubby said, "and I found the Rebbetzin in attendance — in all her glory. How I loved that woman! I couldn't believe she was standing right there in front of me, just when I needed her so desperately!"

The truth is, this grandmother had seen the Rebbetzin a short while earlier.

As she would later relate:

Friends of mine, seeing what a wreck I'd become over my sick grandson, had been encouraging me to speak to someone, to unburden my soul.

I agreed with them.

"Who would you want to speak with?"

There was no question in my mind.

"Rebbetzin Esther Jungreis. I have a feeling that a conversation with the Rebbetzin would go a really long way in helping me work things through."

Knowing that I really did need to speak with the Rebbetzin, I got in touch with her daughter Chaya Sora, who arranged for me to meet the Rebbetzin after her Thursday evening class at Hineni.

"Do I need to make an appointment?"

"No. Just go and wait for her and you'll be able to talk to her for as long as you want."

I went to the Hineni Heritage Center, took a seat in the audience and listened to her lecture. After the speech was over, I went upstairs to her office on the top floor and waited until she was able to see me. When I was finally seated across from her — her wide desk between the two of us — I told her that my grandson was very sick, and she gave me berachos for his complete recovery.

"Rebbetzin," I said to her, "though I really wish for the story to turn out the way you're saying, the truth is, my grandson is very sick."

"What's his name?" the Rebbetzin asked me ever so gently.

"Yehudah."

The second she heard his name, she became a walking Sefer Torah, quoting Torah passages showing how Yehudah was a true leader of Klal Yisrael, leading his brothers down into Egypt.

Looking me in the eye, the Rebbetzin said, "You will see that your grandson will be a real Yehudah."

When I arrived home that night I asked my husband to show me the verses she had quoted from the Chumash. I read the words and felt a little better. Just speaking with her was comforting, even though I knew the situation and how little chance there was for a recovery.

All that had occurred a short while before, and now our paths had crossed again. I greeted the Rebbetzin and she asked me what I was doing there.

"I'm staying with my grandson Yehudah in the hospital. It's not far from here."

We were quiet for a few seconds and then I said, "Rebbetzin, it would mean so much to me if you came to see him — not on Shabbos because he's on the sixth floor — but if you could come after Shabbos at some point, I would truly appreciate it!"

"I can't promise," she said.

"Only if you have the time," I told her, and we left it at that, not finalizing any after-Shabbos plans.

That night my husband and I were sitting in our grandson's room after Shabbos, wondering if she would come.

"Don't be disappointed if she doesn't manage to find the time," he said to me, "you know how busy she is."

"I know. If she comes she comes, and that's it."

Half an hour later I got a call from the nurses' station telling me I had a visitor.

"Mrs. Fireworker, there's someone here to see you."

Five minutes later the Rebbetzin swept into the room.

It was so, so good to see her again. She had this incredibly positive energy — it just radiated from her. Just being with her made you smile and feel better about life. She hadn't come empty-handed, carrying a huge chocolate cake she handed to me.

"Really, Rebbetzin, you didn't have to bring cake. Just having you is much more than enough!"

My grandson was lying in his bed when she came into the room, and she walked over to his side. She could see that he was in a coma, as I told her — and she looked at him and started talking to him as if it were the most natural thing in the world.

Introducing herself to him, she said, "My name is Esther Jungreis."

Then she gave him many berachos and alternated between talking to him and to us. Her voice was extremely soothing; there was something about her — something in her voice that just made us feel better. She left a few minutes later, but her visit changed the entire atmosphere.

I called my daughter-in-law a little later and told her about the Rebbetzin's visit and all the berachos she gave our grandson — and that was it.

Two weeks later, our six-year-old grandson passed away. It was the first day of *Parashas Vayigash* — the *parashah* in Chumash that describes the story of Yehudah going down to Egypt and leading the way.

Two days later, my children were sitting *shivah* at their home, when I heard someone call out excitedly, "The Rebbetzin is here!"

It was bitterly cold outside, but she never let anything stop her.

"Rebbetzin, why didn't you tell us that you wanted to come? We would have picked you up and driven you here!"

"No, no, it was no trouble at all. I just returned from my trip and Barbara drove me here."

She spoke to my son and she spoke to my daughter-in-law. I do not know what she told them. But I do know that the fact that she stood at our side in our family's moment of pain will never be forgotten.

And I miss her. I really do.

CHAPTER FIFTY-FIVE
Whisper of Love

Michelle Blistein was a person who would come to mean a great deal to the Rebbetzin and the entire Jungreis family. A successful businesswoman, Michelle had originally become close to the Rebbetzin through her mother, Florence Farber, who had a long-standing relationship with the Rebbetzin, dating back to Zeide's days in East Flatbush. At one point Barbara Janov took ill and was no longer able to be at the Rebbetzin's side 24/7. That was when Michelle totally dedicated herself to assisting the Rebbetzin. She would eventually come to move in with the Rebbetzin for the last three years of her life, accompanying her mentor and friend on all of her travels to far-flung parts of the world. When the Rebbetzin was hospitalized in San Diego after fracturing her hip, Michelle remained at the Rebbetzin's side, waiting for Chaya Sora to fly out to be with her mother until she was able to return to New York.

That was Michelle — another one of the devoted messengers sent by the One Above to help the Rebbetzin fulfill her life's mission.

(In general, the Rebbetzin was extremely blessed when it came to the people who chose to accompany her and stand by her side throughout her life's journey. From Barbara Janov, to Michelle Blistein, to Tzippy Midroni Hersh [her long-time Hineni secretary] and Chaya'le Gordon Deutscher, the Rebbetzin was surrounded by smart and loyal people who loved and revered her and wanted the best for "their Rebbetzin.")

Michelle had a single friend who was living on her own in the city and going through a difficult time. She just didn't feel well. No matter what she tried or how many Advil or Tylenol she took, her body felt worse and worse. She visited a host of doctors, but none of them were able to make the right diagnosis. By the time a doctor finally realized what she had, she was already dealing with advanced-stage cancer. Compounding matters was the fact that she had very poor medical coverage.

"I know that my friend has never come to Hineni," Michelle said to the Rebbetzin, "and I know that you never met her before, but I think it would mean a lot to her to have a visit from someone like yourself."

It goes without saying that the Rebbetzin agreed to visit the sick girl.

The Rebbetzin, being the Rebbetzin, was able to cut straight through all extraneous layers, and the two of them became friends in a very short time. Feeling a close connection to her new friend, the girl decided to unburden herself.

"My hair is beginning to fall out at a rapid pace," she told Rebbetzin Jungreis. "I need to buy a wig or I won't be able to show my face in the street. The problem is that I don't have the money to buy a wig…"

She cried bitterly over her lot in life and the Rebbetzin cried with her.

The Rebbetzin wasted no time (she was actually physically incapable of wasting time); she called up Georgie (a prominent wig designer) who graciously agreed to sponsor a brand new sheitel for the suffering patient.

This was classic Rebbetzin Jungreis in action. People simply couldn't say no to her — it just didn't work. The word "no" was not in her lexicon.

So now they had a wig, but sheitels cannot be worn until they are styled.

Knowing that Georgie had already gone above and beyond by donating a sheitel, the Rebbetzin couldn't ask her to cut and style it too, especially since the girl wasn't well enough to leave her apartment and the stylist would have to come to her.

But the Rebbetzin had *emunah* and knew that everything was going to work out.

She went to visit Michelle's friend again the following day. There was another woman waiting for the elevator when they entered the lobby, and the Rebbetzin greeted her warmly, as was her wont with every person that she encountered.

"How are you?" the Rebbetzin wanted to know.

"I'm fine, and how are you?"

To that question, the Rebbetzin responded with a heartfelt, *"Baruch Hashem."*

"Baruch Hashem — what does that mean?"

"Well, I'm a Rebbetzin," she told the lady, "which means a Jewish Torah teacher — and when someone asks religious Jewish people how we are, we respond with the words *'Baruch Hashem.' Baruch Hashem* means 'Thank G-d.'"

"That's very interesting."

The Rebbetzin smiled and said, "And what do you do?"

"I'm a hair stylist."

"If that's the case," the Rebbetzin told her, "I have a place to take you to right now."

And the hair stylist accompanied the Rebbetzin and Michelle to the sick woman's apartment, where she cut and styled the sheitel to the woman's specifications.

When you lived life with the Rebbetzin's outlook, everything always worked out. You just need to take the initial step — and then watch as Hashem meets you in the middle.

As you can see, visiting the sick was a focal point in the Rebbetzin's life, and she transmitted it to her children. During one particular class on *Parashas Vayeira*, Chaya Sora was expounding on the words, "And Hashem was appearing to him..." — words which are referring to Hashem's visit to Avraham Avinu when he was healing from his bris milah.

"This is a lesson to all of us on the essence of *bikur cholim* (visiting the sick)," she told her class. "Why does the Torah write that Hashem appeared to him (Avraham) and not his actual name? Avraham was such a great person, why wasn't his name mentioned?

"My mother taught me that the reason Avraham's name isn't mentioned in the context of Hashem's visit is so that people shouldn't think that it's only the Avraham Avinus of the world who deserve visitors. No. Every person deserves visitors and to be a recipient of *bikur cholim*.

"There are plenty of 'Mr. Anonymouses' out there, who are sick at home or in a nursing home or a hospital — forgotten about and alone, without any visitors. And that is the lesson the Torah wants to teach us:

that everyone deserves visitors and to be given attention and love and not to be forgotten."

At that moment one of the women in the class spoke up. Her name was Karen*.

"My husband is a Mr. Anonymous."

A shocked silence filled the room.

"Nobody comes to visit him. Nobody comes to see him. He is all alone."

"Tell me about your husband."

"My husband used to work as an nuclear scientist. He is a brilliant man. But he got sick and we had to move from Texas to New York so he could have access to the right medical care. Now he's just lonely and at home without any visitors — all day, every day — and it breaks my heart."

Chaya Sora responded immediately.

"Next week, we will be having our class at your home," she told the woman. "All of us will be visitors for your husband. We are all going to learn Chumash together and he is welcome to join us."

But Karen wasn't convinced.

"You don't understand," she said. "My husband is an atheist and someone who defined himself as an ethical culturist his entire life. He doesn't believe in religion."

"Doesn't matter," Chaya Sora replied. "He's a Jew, he deserves visitors and we will all be there at your house next week."

The following week the entire class met in Karen's apartment, where they discussed the *parashah* of the week. And for the first time in his life, the nuclear scientist who had always classified himself an atheist held a Chumash in his hands, looked inside, and listened to a Torah *shiur*.

The class took place on Wednesday. On Motza'ei Shabbos, Karen called Chaya Sora to let her know that her husband had passed away that Friday night in his sleep. She called again early Sunday morning.

"I just wanted to let you know something. I went to order flowers for the funeral, and when I gave my name to the florist, he turned white — and handed me a card.

"I stood there in the florist shop reading the card and my hands began to shake.

Dear Karen,
Thank you for the Torah class. I love you."

The card had been signed by her husband, and came along with flowers that he'd ordered for her, but hadn't had the opportunity to give her.

"Chaya Sora — holding my husband's card in my hands was like receiving a message from Above."

"Karen," Chaya Sora replied, "because you held that class in your house, your husband died a different man. It could be that he had to wait to have that one mitzvah — of holding a Chumash in his hands and learning Torah — before his passing."

Florence Penkin was a founding member of Ohr Torah. When she was stricken with illness, the doctors told her family members that there was nothing to do for their mother.

"All her organs are shutting down. It's just a matter of time."

Florence lay in the hospital and it really did seem like a matter of days. And then the Rebbetzin came to visit her old friend. After hearing how Florence's body had shut down — how her kidneys were failing and how every one of her systems was systematically closing down — the Rebbetzin remained unfazed.

Giving the family a host of beautiful berachos, she wished Florence well and wished her a *refuah sheleimah.*

 Two weeks later, Florence recovered. There was no way to explain what happened. In a matter of days her kidneys recovered and began functioning, as did the rest of her body. Twenty years later, she is still alive. Her family has no other way to explain the miracle — other than attributing their mother's recovery to the Rebbetzin's berachos. There was nothing else. No other way to explain how a woman on the verge of death recovered without an operation or procedure. There was only the Rebbetzin's berachos — which in her case were clearly enough.

One of the women who regularly attended the Rebbetzin's Chumash class, suddenly and without any warning, began losing her hearing. The situation was becoming progressively worse and the doctors all told her there was nothing to do, that it was just a matter of time until she would be totally deaf.

But she was not willing to give up the fight.

One night after the *shiur*, she waited on line to ask the Rebbetzin for a berachah.

"You need to take upon yourself to say *Shema* every night," the Rebbetzin told her. "And when you do, have in mind that the word *Shema* means to listen and hear — and that you need to be able to listen and hear to learn Torah. Keep in mind that you are accepting the yoke of heaven upon yourself, and Hashem is going to help those ears work."

Suddenly the Rebbetzin told her, "Bend down."

The woman bent down beside the Rebbetzin, with her ear just beside the Rebbetzin's mouth. And then the Rebbetzin began to whisper the words of *Shema* into her ear.

"All of a sudden," the woman later said, "I felt what I can only describe as a whoosh in my ear, and my hearing slowly started to return, eventually returning to full capacity. If that wasn't a miracle, I don't know what is!"

CHAPTER FIFTY-SIX

"T" Is for Tiffany

*I*n 1999, Chaya'le Ilene Gordon didn't even know what it meant to be a Jew. That was the year she and her husband moved back to New York, after having lived in Buffalo and Boston for twenty years. Her husband had been working as a merger manager for his life insurance company, and with their return to the big city he was heavily involved in the merger of five separate offices, one of which was comprised of all Orthodox Jews. Suddenly the Gordons began receiving invitations for Shabbos from the different religious agents. After repeated offers, finally her husband decided to accept an invitation for him and his wife to come and spend the weekend in Boro Park.

"What are we going to do there for an entire weekend?"

"Well," he replied, "we're going to first buy you a really long skirt, then we're going to check into a hotel — we don't have to sleep in their house, but we will have to remain in the area until Saturday night."

"That's crazy! We're going somewhere for dinner and we have to eat lunch at their home and remain in the neighborhood until sundown the next night? Don't you think that's a little strange?"

"Trust me," George Gordon told his wife, "it's going to be good."

Chaya'le remembers:

We packed up Friday afternoon and headed off to the wilds of Boro Park. There we were greeted by our hosts — Shmuel Dovid and Chaya Friedman — at the Avenue Plaza Hotel. They brought us back to their house and when we walked inside, there were children everywhere, all asking, "Ima, where's this?" and, "Ima, where's that?"

The house was flying, but Mrs. Friedman was the calmest person I have ever met in my life, and I said to myself, "There's something strange happening here. Either this woman is on drugs, or…" But I couldn't finish the sentence, because it was like nothing I'd ever encountered…

Slowly the evening started to unfold.

All the children were gathered together to meet us — from the youngest to the oldest still at home — and my husband left to shul with our host. After the men and boys had all filed out, the women went into the dining room to light their candles and I stood in the hallway just watching them. And there was something about that candle-lighting that moved me. As they were lighting I just started to cry. I turned my head so that they wouldn't see and I looked the other way and started counting the number of chairs around the table. Twenty-six people.

"We don't even have twenty-six people for Thanksgiving," I said to myself. "Who are all these people?"

It turned out that Mr. Friedman's parents were coming for dinner, her sister, some of the kids had friends over, someone who was renting their basement apartment…

The men returned from shul and stood around the table singing *Shalom Aleichem.*

Again I felt these stirrings of emotion. I kept on looking at my husband and asking him quietly, "What is going on here?"

My husband didn't have an answer for me. There was no reason he should have had an answer. It was his first time at a Shabbos meal too.

Our host made Kiddush. I then watched all the children walk to their parents for a berachah, and I couldn't help thinking, "This is astounding! Does anyone else know about this?"

Everything that they did was something I'd never seen or witnessed, yet was touching me very deeply at the same time.

I started asking questions. After the fifth question, my husband whispered to me, "Please stop, you're embarrassing me."

"Why am I embarrassing you? This is so new to us!"

Besides, the Friedman family was very eager to answer everything I asked.

But he just said, "Stop it already. Just be cool."

On my way out of the house that night, Chaya Friedman handed me a copy of the Rebbetzin's book, *The Committed Life*.

I started reading the book the minute we entered our room and I couldn't put it down.

"Can you turn off the light, honey?" my husband asked. "I have to meet Sam in the morning."

But I said to him, "Honey, listen to what this lady is writing. This is who we are!"

He looked at me and said, "Please, I'm going to have to get up really soon. Please turn out the light."

In the end I took the book and sat on the floor next to the bathroom, reading by a sliver of light — reading and weeping.

I ended up staying up all night reading it. And the entire time I couldn't help thinking, "All I want to do is meet this woman."

I wanted to know who she was, what she did and what else she could tell me that I didn't know. When Chaya came to pick me up for lunch the next day, I said, "I know I asked you a lot of questions last night and I'm really sorry."

"Are you kidding me?" she shot back, "we love questions! Is there anything else you want to know?"

"Yes, I have two more questions."

"Go ahead, ask."

"What's a Ribbizin," I asked her, mispronouncing the word Rebbetzin by mistake.

"What?"

She was confused, not grasping my question.

"What's a Ribbizin?"

It took her a second.

"Oh, you mean a Rebbetzin."

"Yes, what is a Rebbetzin?"

So she told me what a Rebbetzin is.

"Do you know where I can find her?"

"I think she teaches in Manhattan."

All of a sudden I became extremely happy.

"I live in Manhattan! If she teaches in the city I can find her!"

And so I began attending the Rebbetzin's classes.

One day I heard her say a line that hit me hard and convinced me that I needed to commit to what I knew was the truth.

"We can only survive," the Rebbetzin said, "if we have players. It's great to be a fan in the stands, but if there's nobody on the ball field playing the game, we won't exist. If every stadium was filled to capacity with only fans and there were no players out there hitting the home runs, would there be a game?"

It was at that point that I decided to become committed to joining "Team Torah."

Her love for Torah imbued me with a sense of purpose and responsibility to stop cheering in the stands and to actually join the team.

I wanted to jump right in and change my entire life around, but my husband wasn't that interested in becoming religious and wanted to take things slow. In addition, my children were grown up and not religious — so it was just me, sitting all the way in the back of the cavernous room listening to the Rebbetzin speak. Her voice was like a bird singing songs to me. Many of the words she used were foreign to me, but they resonated in my heart. I felt everything — whether I understood the actual words or knew what to do with them.

I was in.

But I wasn't all the way in because my feet were standing in two different worlds. My husband was not ready to make changes and *shalom bayis* (harmony in the home) was a real challenge.

Eventually, despite himself, George began to change. He loved and was incredibly proud of his Orthodox agents. They were his favorites. They hung out in his office, just for fun. A short while later, two of the agents began bringing rabbis in to learn with him.

One night I went to the Rebbetzin's class at "KJ" and Rabbi Yisroel recognized me from a class that he gave at Bear Stearns.

"Have you ever met my mother?" he asked me.

"No. She's like royalty. I sit in the back of the room."

He brought me up to meet her. There was this long line of

people waiting for *berachos* or just to talk to her at the end of her *shiur*, and he just sort of cut into the front and said, "Ima, I want you to meet somebody who comes to my class."

That was the first time we met.

It wasn't long before the people at Hineni suggested that I join a women's *shiur* the Rebbetzin was giving at the home of Pat Cayne. This meant that I was going to a class at Pat's, hearing Rabbi Yisroel at Bear Stearns, attending the Rebbetzin's *shiur* at "KJ" once a week, and coming to hear the Rebbetzin speak at the Hineni building on Thursday night as well. I was running around like crazy and loving it.

George, meanwhile, was starting to get very nervous, while his agents were getting a real kick out of my interest in a frum lifestyle. We'd sit around the office and I'd ask questions about religion and Torah and they were always extremely happy to answer me. In an interesting turn of events, one of the rabbis whom the agents brought into the office finally got through to my husband and he began putting on tefillin. That was followed by him starting to learn with Rabbi Levi Baumgarten, of Mitzva Tank fame.

The more he learned, the more George started to calm down, as he realized what an incredible world we'd been introduced to.

And then as things were really beginning to fall into place, tragedy struck us when I was diagnosed with cancer. The next few months were a blur of surgery, chemo and radiation. Just as I was finishing with the radiation and starting to feel better, my husband was diagnosed with ALS. It was a very sad time in our lives, but the Jungreis family was incredible, standing at our sides and guiding us through the trials and the tribulations. Their chessed was just extraordinary.

At the same time that he was experiencing the onset of the illness that would claim his life, George agreed to *kasher* the kitchen. He began keeping Shabbos in a serious way. George was growing more and more involved in keeping a Torah life — even though he was already in a wheelchair at the time and could no longer walk on his own.

I lost George a number of years ago. Prior to leaving this world, however, he held the little Csenger Torah that resides in the Hineni sanctuary — a Torah that was saved from the Holocaust in the arms of a man who was saved as well before he left this world.

I remember the moment like yesterday. When everyone was marching with this big float and the new Sefer Torah down Park Avenue, one of the Jungreis rabbis gave my husband the little Hineni Torah and he held it lovingly in his arms the entire way, down Park Avenue to the Safra Synagogue.

I'll never forget the look on his face. It was a look of absolute and indescribable joy! I have a picture of that moment — Sefer Torah in his arms (he was embracing the Torah not only physically but spiritually too) and the Rebbetzin standing beside him, her hands raised above his head, giving him a berachah.

Hineni Torah dedication procession down Park Avenue

George passed away in 2008. The Rebbetzin was with us throughout my husband's long, debilitating and terminal illness, as were her children and grandchildren. She held me close at his funeral and never left my side. As I got to know her better, I discovered that I was one of thousands whom she counseled, consoled and held close. She wasn't just the Rebbetzin, she was a spiritual mother to countless souls.

I lost count of the number of times she gave me berachos.

At first I would thank her for the berachah. Then she taught me the meaning of the word "Amen."

Every time I took leave of her, she would say, "Chaya'le, come here, I have to give you a berachah."

"Rebbetzin," I would reply, "you already gave me a berachah!"

"Chaya'le, you can never have too many berachos!"

If only the Rebbetzin were still here today to give me one more berachah!

In the wake of George's passing, I became extremely close with the Rebbetzin. If she was conducting a Shabbaton, I'd attend. One of the Shabbatons was in Palm Beach, Florida. I remember that the Rebbetzin spoke Friday night, Shabbos morning, Shabbos afternoon — it was wonderful. Sunday morning we were leaving the hotel and I ran into the Rebbetzin and Barbara as they were trying to arrange a ride so that the Rebbetzin could go to pay a *shivah* call to someone in Florida.

"Rebbetzin," I said to her, "I rented a car, I can drive you."

"Are you sure it's not an inconvenience?"

"Not even a little bit."

I drove the Rebbetzin to the *shivah* house and on the way, Barbara received a phone call from Mexico City from people who were trying to arrange for the Rebbetzin to come to speak to their community. I have no idea what made me speak up, but I suddenly found myself saying, "I have never been to Mexico City."

"Do you want to come with me?"

"Really?"

The Rebbetzin smiled at me and said, "I would love for you to come with me."

And so I accompanied the Rebbetzin, Barbara and Michelle to Mexico City. And we all had a very good time together. That was the first of many journeys that we all took. Soon the Rebbetzin dubbed me "Food and Beverage Manager," because I always made sure to bring yogurts, fruits, coffee and cups, so that our rooms had nosh and were fun places to be. We went to Hungary and Paris, Marseilles and Israel. My life was full and the Rebbetzin was my anchor.

We left to Israel together on a Hineni trip in 2009, a year after George passed away. We called the trip "Tears and Prayers," because we just kept on crying — everything we saw and experienced touched us deeply, and our siddurim became soaked with our tears.

When the trip was over, I said to the Rebbetzin, "I can't go home yet. I have to stay here. What can I do with myself in Israel?"

"Would you like to stay here and learn?"

"I would love to stay here and learn!"

Between breakfast and lunch she made some phone calls. She then informed me that she had arranged a meeting for me with Rabbi Yitzchok Shurin over at a seminary called "Midreshet Rachel." She gave me the address and off I went.

Midreshet Rachel was located on a quiet, tree-lined picturesque street in the Kiryat Moshe neighborhood of Jerusalem.

"What can I do for you?" the administrator asked me. He was very friendly and welcoming.

"I want to learn."

"Okay, you're in."

(Wow, good work, Rebbetzin!)

"Where are you going to live while you're here? Most of the girls in the seminary are much younger than you."

I told him that I'd been offered a place to stay for as long as I needed.

"Do you have their phone number?"

I gave him the number. He called and asked for directions to the apartment. Then he looked at me and said, "Come with me."

He walked out the door, made a left, crossed a major boulevard and their apartment was right there! Talk about *hashgachah*!

I stayed there for the rest of the summer, immersing myself in the world of Torah learning. Every morning I'd leave to school with a bag of food like a little girl — it was the cutest thing ever. It was an idyllic time in my life. I studied Hebrew in the morning. There was a Navi class that I loved. But really the entire day was one wonderful thing after the next. And every Tuesday the entire seminary went on a trip around the country.

One day we traveled to the battlefield where Dovid HaMelech fought the giant Goliath. It was hot and the climb was steep and all the young girls were miles ahead of me. And they kept on calling to me, "Come on, Manhattan, you can make it!" (They called me Manhattan.)

And I did.

It was a memorable summer.

When I finally returned home, my feet didn't touch the ground for months.

I think about the Rebbetzin a lot. She was the one who brought me back. I knew nothing when I met her. I grew up in a Jewish family and married a Jewish man, but we had no idea what it meant to live as a Jew. We didn't know about Torah and mitzvos or the meaning of any of the Jewish customs, laws or the holidays. I have a vague memory of my mother lighting candles when I was very young. But as my parents became more and more assimilated and my father made more and more money, the candles were extinguished — and they were only reignited when I began lighting them decades later, after the Rebbetzin showed me what it means to be a Yid and infused my life with Yiddishkeit.

One Friday night the Rebbetzin would be staying in the neighborhood, giving a speech at a shul a few blocks from my home. The shul used to put up their speakers at a nearby hotel, but I said to myself, "Let me ask her if she'd rather stay here."

"Are you sure?"

"Sure I'm sure."

"My daughter and son-in-law are going to be with me."

"No problem, they can come to me too."

We had a wonderful Shabbos in many ways — not least because it led to the Rebbetzin staying at my apartment whenever she was near. It wasn't long before it had become something akin to a second home for her. She'd come for Shabbos and drop in during the week, and our relationship rose to a whole different level. At a certain point, Barbara Janov was no longer able to help the Rebbetzin with her weekly column for *The Jewish Press* and then she'd come to my house almost every Wednesday; we'd have dinner and she'd dictate the article to me. I'd type the article for her on my computer and send it in to the newspaper. It was the rarest of honors.

And every time she left the house, I'd find these Post-it notes with messages like, *"Thank you, Chaya'le, you're precious, I love you. Your Torah Ima."*

A while back Tiffany's came out with a new piece of jewelry, a bracelet. It was called the Tiffany "T" and a group of the Rebbetzin's *talmidos*/students chipped in and bought one for her as a present, along with a note on which we wrote:

"T" — What is "T"?

"T" is Torah

"T" is Tefillah — Prayer, service of the heart

"T" is Tehillim — Psalms

"T" is Talmud — Mishnah and Gemara

"T" is Tekias Shofar — Blowing of the Shofar

"T" is Tzedakah — Charity

"T" is Tznius — Modesty

"T" is Tikkun — Perfection

"T" is Tefillin — Phylacteries

"T" is Tzibbur — Congregation

"T" is Tzaddikim — Righteous People

"T" is Talmid Chacham — Torah Scholars

"T" is Tatty — Father — The One you revere

There are countless other "T"'s, too many to mention. Rebbetzin, we, your talmidos, are so grateful for all you have done for us and for Am Yisrael. Like the links on this bracelet [every link was in the shape of a T], you and your teachings link all of us to Torah and mitzvos. We pray that Hashem grant you a good and long life filled with berachah, mazel and nachas.

We knew we had chosen well when we saw that the Rebbetzin wore the bracelet every day, never taking it off, joining the Hineni diamond pendant she constantly wore around her neck. There was no question in our minds that we had struck gold (though it was made of sterling silver).

My travels with the Rebbetzin took me all around the world and introduced me to many communities throughout the United States. Wherever I went, I felt so blessed to be a part of the Rebbetzin's world. Seeing me standing with her, people would constantly stop and ask me, "Are you the Rebbetzin's daughter?"

In the beginning I would smile and reply, "I'm her Torah daughter."

After several years of getting perplexed looks from the questioners, I started answering, "Yes," because the reality is, I am her spiritual daughter in every way.

One Tuesday evening at "KJ," following the Rebbetzin's Torah class, she called me over.

She said, "Chaya'le, (she always used my Hebrew name), look at this beautiful young girl."

The girl in question was wearing jeans, a long-sleeved T-shirt and boots. She had long brown hair and a beautiful smile, but truthfully, I was wondering what the Rebbetzin was asking me to look at. I soon realized that the Rebbetzin was able to see the *pintele Yid* within each Jew that she met. She then proceeded to tell me the story of how Salomé had read one of her books in French, sent her an email asking if she could meet her if she ever came to New York, and here she was.

The interesting thing is that this 15-year-old girl came all the way from New Caledonia for a dual purpose: to study art techniques with her uncle, a known artist who lived on the Upper East Side, and learn more about her Jewish identity.

Before that night I had never heard of New Caledonia. It's a beautiful French island with white sandy beaches and crystal-clear green-blue waters, situated between Australia and New Zealand. Salomé's parents originated from Paris and wanted to learn more about their Jewish roots. They began by listening to Torah classes on tape and reading books a rabbi from Paris sent them.

The Rebbetzin told me that Salomé was on her school break, and asked me to look after her. I walked her home, gave her my phone number, and before I knew it she had become like a spiritual daughter, staying with me every Shabbos.

The Rebbetzin gave her a Hebrew name, Shulamit. She had a burning desire to pursue a Torah life, so much so that she did not want to go back to New Caledonia. She desperately wanted to attend a Jewish school.

The Rebbetzin spoke to her parents about sending Shulamit to yeshivah. They agreed on one condition: The school had to be French-speaking. The Rebbetzin knew about the Bais Yaakov in French-speaking Montreal that had a program, Achoseinu, that was tailored for girls from the former Soviet Union and Eastern Europe. Why wouldn't they accept a girl from New Caledonia? So the Rebbetzin called the school's dean, Rabbi Shneur Aisenstark, who agreed to meet her. Two days later, Shulamit and I boarded a plane to Montreal.

Rabbi Aisenstark asked her only two questions. "Can you read Hebrew?"

She said, "a little bit." He handed her a *sefer* and she sounded out the Hebrew letters.

A portrait of Rav Meshulem, drawn by Shulamit while still a high school student, and gifted to the Rebbetzin

"Do you know what you just read?"

"No, Rabbi, but I really want to know what I just read."

"You're in," Rabbi Aisenstark said.

Two years later she graduated from Bais Yaakov, going on to seminary in Israel.

Today, Shulamit lives in Eretz Yisrael, is married to a wonderful French-speaking yeshivah student who is learning in kollel, and has two beautiful daughters.

It was just another example of how the Rebbetzin's books have been a spiritual lifeline and transformed the life of yet another beautiful *neshamah*.

During the final years of her life, the Rebbetzin suffered greatly, yet I never saw her lose it. She never complained! Instead she would say, "Hashem, I accept Your judgment with love."

She was remarkable.

She continued drawing me near until the very end. When I would get ready to leave her side, I would kiss her goodbye and walk toward the door.

"Come here, Chaya'le," she'd call me. "I want to give you a berachah."

I would return to her side once again, bend down and bow my head as she raised her hands to bless me. Always, she'd whisper into my ear, "Don't ever forget — you are my daughter!"

As the Rebbetzin brought me closer to a Torah way of life, she introduced me to Chaya Sora and encouraged me to establish a Chumash class in my home. For many years now, we've had a wonderful group of women who gather together to hear Chaya Sora's fascinating *parashah* lessons.

Hashem showed me more kindness when Slovie introduced me to a wonderful man who would become my husband.

Ten years after my first husband was *niftar*, I remarried on Rosh Chodesh Elul 2017. My husband's name is Shimshon Deutscher, and he has four children and a whole bunch of grandchildren. In a fascinating turn of events, the Rebbetzin's yahrtzeit falls on my second husband's birthday, making it clear to me that she had something to do with this.

I reviewed every date with Chaya Sora — like an eighteen-year-old. And then we got engaged and married, and what can I say… Hashem has been so good to me, because today I have finally been blessed with the dream I have wanted for so long — to be an integral part of a beautiful, frum family. I have seen the words of Tehillim come alive for me: "*Moshivi akeres habayis eim habanim semeicha…* — He has turned the barren woman into a happy mother of children."

I had always wanted to have a set of Shas in my house. But for whom?

Today there is a set of Shas here and another one there — *sefarim* and learning and Torah. It's a dream come true.

When I think of my beloved Rebbetzin, my mind always takes me to Yosef HaTzaddik. Yosef was in Egypt surrounded by idol worship, and yet he rose above it all to become Pharaoh's second-in-command. The reason he was able to remain the same Yosef even after all those years was because he saw the image of his father Yaakov before his eyes, reminding him of who he was and what he needed to do.

Today, when I travel the road of life, it's the image of my revered Rebbetzin, my Torah Ima, Rebbetzin Esther Jungreis, that fills my life with berachah, and I am eternally grateful.

This chapter has been dedicated
with great *hakaras hatov* to my Torah Ima, the Rebbetzin ע״ה
who brought a generation of Jews back home —
to Torah, to family, to Hashem
Shimshon and Chayale Deutscher

Part 9
1995-2016

As we became more and more friendly, the Rebbetzin began asking me to introduce her before her speeches. The reason she asked me to introduce her was because I started referring to her as "The Bubby of Klal Yisrael," and she loved that title...

Rabbi Paysach Krohn,
author of the Maggid series

One thing I can tell you, my sheifelah, Hakadosh Baruch Hu is my witness that everything I did was l'sheim Shamayim.

Rebbetzin Esther Jungreis

CHAPTER FIFTY-SEVEN

Visits to a World Long Gone

The Rebbetzin's conscientiousness extended itself to Jewish history as well, and the need for accuracy when anything had to do with who we are as a people. On a trip to Eretz Yisrael, the tour guide arranged for the group to visit a Jerusalem attraction called The Time Elevator. It was just intended to be a filler/fun thing to do between more significant activities. But when the group emerged from the building, she put on her sunglasses — it was a very bright, sunny summer day — and made everyone sit on the steps.

The Rebbetzin addressing a Hineni tour group near the Old City wall

She then expressed her outrage at how the movie had portrayed Yirmiyahu HaNavi (the prophet Jeremiah). She was very *makpid* (stringent) that the honor and authenticity of true Judaism be sustained, and the fact that one of our nation's greatest men had had his honor slighted rankled at her *neshamah* and gave her no rest.

She gave a sizzling rebuke that day, explaining how what they had just witnessed was incorrect and inaccurate — almost begging them not to allow what they had just seen to corrupt the way they thought of Yirmiyahu HaNavi.

On another trip, this time to Theresienstadt — the "model" concentration camp the Germans used for prominent Jewish prisoners and the place to which they would bring the Red Cross to show them how "well" the Jews were being treated — the tour guide, who happened to have been a Jew, said something along the lines of, "The Jews didn't die here at the hands of the Germans, but from natural causes."

The moment she heard that line, there was no stopping her.

"Pardon me," she interrupted the man, "I have to say something. The Jewish prisoners were starving in Theresienstadt and living under terrible conditions! How can you possibly claim that they died of natural causes and not at the hands of the Germans? Are you implying that the Germans weren't at fault for the people who died at Theresienstadt?"

There was no backing down when truth was at stake. She was inevitably gracious and there was no raising her voice. But she would not rest until she clarified the truth.

In the course of touring the Theresienstadt Ghetto, the Rebbetzin and the Hineni group visited "The Hidden Synagogue," a sanctuary that was created by the camp's inmates in a ground-floor storage room behind one of the ghetto's indistinguishable houses. Upon entering the synagogue, all eyes were drawn to a series of murals painted on its walls in 1943 by Reb Asher Berlinger, a German educator, cantor, musician, artist and a truly pious Jew who was known for his deep *emunah* (faith in Hashem). He had been initially sent to the Dachau concentration camp, then to Theresienstadt, and ultimately to his death at the hands of the Nazis in Auschwitz. The verses on the various murals beseech Hashem to mete out His judgment to the wicked, to never forget the plight of the Jews, and proclaim unwavering *emunah* in an undying hope for a brighter future.

The Hidden
Synagogue of
Theresienstadt
Ghetto

Hand-painted
murals on
the walls of
the Hidden
Synagogue in
Theresienstadt

The Rebbetzin and all those present were emotionally overwhelmed by the *pesukim* (verses) on the murals. She then asked her son-in-law Rabbi Shlomo to sing a beautiful tune that had been composed by Rabbi Shmuel Brazil for the verse, *"Habeit miShamayim ur'ei... u'vechol zos Shimcha lo shachachnu...* — [O G-d,] look down from heaven and see... And despite everything we have been through, we have never forgotten Your Name..."

There was not a dry eye in the room, as everyone joined together in an emotional and heart-rending chorus.

As the group left The Hidden Synagogue, they all were awestruck by the ironic juxtaposition — the Nazis had sought to strip the Jews of their human dignity, yet nothing could stop them from showing that their spirit remained strong, their faith fast, and their humanity intact.

All this the Rebbetzin derived from paintings on the wall.

A few years later, the Rebbetzin took a Hineni group on a tour of *kivrei avos* (ancestral graves) in Hungary. On the itinerary was a boat ride on the Danube, Europe's second longest river (after the Volga), which winds its way for more than 1,700 miles past the cities of Vienna, Budapest, and Belgrade, among others. Of most significance to the Rebbetzin was the fact that this river was infused with the blood of thousands of Jews who were murdered by fascist Arrow Cross militiamen in Budapest during December 1944 and January 1945, toward the end of World War II. They were ordered to remove their shoes, and were shot at the edge of the water so that their bodies fell into the river and were carried away.

The Rebbetzin passionately related the tragedy that had befallen so many on that very spot, and that the Danube was filled with Jewish blood. Rabbi Shlomo led the group in reciting the *Kel Maleh Rachamim* memorial prayer for those *kedoshim* (martyrs). The ship's captain brought the ship to a standstill. It was a sight to hear and behold as the Rebbetzin's powerful words and the moving tefillah were broadcast loudly over the ship's public address system for thousands of others to hear, not only on the banks of the river, but on the many other tour boats that were on the water at that time.

The captain then went on to offer his apologies for the indescribable brutality that his countrymen had inflicted upon so many innocent men, women and children during World War II.

"There were times when I accompanied Bubba on her trips to Hungary," Shaindy Wolff Eisenberg recalls. "We would travel for hours at a time in the car to visit *kevarim* around the country — honestly, I couldn't keep up with her — and then when we'd finally arrive at the cemetery, the gate would be locked, but she wouldn't let a locked gate stop her from davening at the graves of the Zeides.

"I'd watch in awe and amusement as my petite grandmother literally sailed over the gates, hoisting herself over the side with what seemed like no effort at all. Then she'd manage to find the *kever* — I remember hearing her calling out joyously, 'I found it, I found it,' from across those overgrown cemeteries. And of course she'd find a way to open the gate and we'd all troop inside, through the dirt and the weeds and the decades of neglect, until we reached the grave of the Zeide, where we'd daven, though none of us could possibly match her intensity and emotion.

"On a different trip, I traveled to Poland with my grandmother on the March of the Living. She was leading a group from South Africa, and things were working out just fine, until she was injured while visiting the Auschwitz concentration camp — hurting herself badly walking through a revolving door and breaking her arm, though nobody knew at the time the extent of the injury.

"I remember being very concerned about her because she was clearly in excruciating pain. But it bothered me more than it bothered her. She kept saying to me, 'I need to carry some of the pain for all my family who were killed in this place.'

"In a way, she was actually happy that she had fallen and hurt herself, because it afforded her the opportunity to participate in her family's pain. Not only was she back in the place where the horrific events had taken place, but she was feeling a small dosage of their suffering, and it was a kind of *nechamah*, a solace in

The Rebbetzin with Hon. April Foley,
U.S. Ambassador to Hungary

The Rebbetzin with the late Chief Rabbi of Romania, Rabbi Moshe Rosen

a way — because now she was part of all those who were no more. I looked at her, and I had the feeling that my grandmother was not with me at that moment — that she had retreated into that special place deep inside her mind, the place where she'd experienced all the trauma of the past, the place she was so good at keeping at bay but was such a major part of her at the same time. There was no question that she carried a heavy burden on her shoulders — the burden of her Bergen-Belsen past and the onus of the survivor.

"Once again, I found myself marveling at the greatness of my Bubba."

On one of the Rebbetzin's Hineni trips to Poland, the tour's theme was feeling the pain of the Jewish people through visiting the concentration camps. Chaya Sora accompanied her mother on that trip. They spent Shabbos in Warsaw, and following davening, the Rebbetzin and Chaya Sora were mingling with the locals. One young Polish Jewish girl, still at her seat in shul, stood out. Her name was Naomi* and there was something very fine and sweet about her — a refinement that made a greater impression considering the fact that she was more or less the only Jewish girl her age in shul. Chaya Sora couldn't help noticing that Naomi was still davening even after everyone else had already finished.

Something about the girl's purity pierced her heart and she decided that she had to go over and speak to her.

After introducing herself, she asked the girl she'd never met, "How is it that a girl like yourself who was raised in Warsaw is spending so much time in shul and davening with such sincerity?"

Naomi responded in a very broken English, telling the American visitor that her dream in life was to become a Bais Yaakov girl.

"Where do you go to school now?"

"The Lauder School. But it's not enough for me. I want more Yiddishkeit. I really want to be frum!"

"If you are really sincere about wanting to be a frum girl, come see me at my hotel after Shabbos and we'll talk."

Naomi showed up later that night, leaving a piece of paper on which she'd written her Jewish name in Hebrew, asking that she not be forgotten.

Extremely taken by Naomi, Chaya Sora called her husband and told him about the girl she had met.

"We have to do something to help this girl!"

"What do you want us to do?"

"We need to give her an opportunity to make her dream of becoming a Bais Yaakov girl come true!"

"Don't get so excited," her husband said, trying to calm his wife. "I'm sure she's a great kid, but does she really know what it means to be a

The Rebbetzin with high school girls in Moscow after distributing the Russian-language edition of *The Committed Life*

Chapter Fifty-Seven: Visits to a World Long Gone □ 591

Bais Yaakov girl? Does she understand what the school will demand of her?"

"I'm telling you, she's really sincere."

"Fine. Before we do anything, let me look into this."

Chaya Sora told the girl she'd be in touch and left Poland soon afterward.

Meanwhile, Rabbi Shlomo contacted Rabbi Chaskel Besser, who was not only on the Presidium of Agudas Yisroel, but was deeply involved in the rebirth of Jewish life in post-Communist Poland. Rabbi Besser put him in touch with the Chief Rabbi of Poland, who was also the Rabbi of the girl's shul. He was happy to confirm that Naomi was the real thing and that her father was one of the only Jews living in Poland who walked the Warsaw streets wearing a black hat.

Chaya Sora remained in touch with Naomi and her parents for the rest of the school year. As summer approached, plans were put in place for Naomi to fly to the States from Poland. Upon arrival, Naomi first stayed with the Gertzulin family, and then spent a month in Chayl Miriam, the teen division of Camp Bnos.

Naomi had told Chaya Sora how difficult it was and how limited her parents were when it came to obtaining kosher food, and wanting to give her guest a good time and a real New York welcome, Chaya Sora took her on a tour of Pomegranate and Glatt Mart. You cannot imagine how excited Naomi was just to walk up and down the aisles of the kosher supermarkets. Her eyes shone with excitement and her smile stretched from ear to ear. She kept on pointing at different items and asking, "Is this kosher? Is that kosher?"

"Everything in the store is kosher, Naomi."

Her smile spread even wider.

But that was just the beginning. Naomi also had her first experience in a kosher pizza store. It is difficult to describe her reaction to that first fresh slice of pizza straight out of the oven, dripping cheese and sauce. Naomi had never tasted anything remotely similar to that first bite of pizza; it would forever be remembered as a kind of "Welcome to Kosher America" experience.

Naomi blended right in at Chayl Miriam, enjoying the most wonderful summer of her life in the Catskill Mountains. She made amazing friends. It was a fantastic experience all around for the girl from Poland.

The problem is, summer comes to an end.

Back in Brooklyn, Naomi was ready to discuss the next step.

"There's a program I heard about called Achoseinu," the brave 15-year-old told her hosts, "based in Montreal, Canada. They have a special program for girls from Eastern Europe. I think that would be the best place for me to go."

Rabbi Gertzulin picked up the phone and called Rabbi Shneur Aisenstark in Montreal (the program was affiliated with his school), and arrangements were made for Naomi to enroll in Bais Yaakov of Montreal.

Naomi was extremely successful at her chosen school in Montreal, completing her high school education. The school placed her at the home of a warm and loving Montreal family, who treated her like their very own daughter. She returned to the Gertzulin home on many school breaks and for many of the Yamim Tovim. Following high school, she went to a seminary in Eretz Yisrael, and when she returned to the States, the Rebbetzin made her shiduch. Today, Naomi and her husband are the proud parents of three beautiful yeshivah and Bais Yaakov children.

And so the story of Naomi — the Jewish girl from Warsaw — came full circle. Another beautiful story in an endless tapestry of stories involving "The Bubby of Klal Yisrael" and her wonderfully caring family, who do things for other people just because they care and want to help. And because their mother raised them that way.

CHAPTER FIFTY-EIGHT

Family First

*R*abbi Tzvi Hersh Weinreb, upon hearing of the *petirah* of the Rebbetzin, wrote:

"Our stay in Israel was interrupted by the news of the demise of Rebbetzin Esther Jungreis *zt"l*. I use the abbreviation for '*zecher tzaddeikes livrachah*' advisedly, because she was indeed a *tzaddeikes*. She founded Hineni and stood at the forefront of the outreach movement long before it became popular, and long before 'kiruv' became a household word.

"I had the privilege of speaking from the same podium as Rebbetzin Jungreis on numerous occasions. She was a tough act to follow. Her speeches were typically emotional but had firm grounding in Torah sources, in her amazing repertoire of chassidic anecdotes, and in the personal relationships she had with her distinguished family.

"She never resorted to the use of the newly devised rabbinic titles which are in vogue among some contemporary women seeking religious validity. She never needed to, because her ability to convey profound and genuine Torah lessons with authority was all she needed to gain credibility and legitimacy. She was proud of her femininity and always dressed modestly but fashionably. As she told me, the titles she was most proud of were 'Mother' and 'Grandmother.'

" 'These titles were good enough for Sarah and Rivkah and Rachel and Leah,' she said. 'Why are they not good enough for today's woman?!' "

Indeed, the Rebbetzin was above all a mother and grandmother, and would always be a Bubba par excellence. Love flowed in a never-ending stream from her heart — down to every child and grandchild. And along with the love came words of gentle reproach when needed. When her daughter-in-law Rivki was expecting her first child, she went through a difficult labor but, not wanting to worry their parents, the young couple kept what was happening to themselves. Right before the baby was born, however, the Rebbetzin found out what had been going on and what a nightmare her children were experiencing.

After everything had calmed down, the Rebbetzin sat her daughter-in-law down and said, "Rivka'la, *sheinkeit*, never, ever do that again!"

"Ima, I didn't want to bother everyone."

"What do you mean? It's not a bother. I have to daven for you and ask the Zeides and the Bubbas in *Shamayim* (Heaven) for assistance. Never do that again! In the future, you must call me to tell me when to daven!"

From that day — through the birth of every child, or any crisis at home, work or school — Rivki called her mother-in-law immediately and asked her to daven, as she did so well.

The Rebbetzin never let her children forget where they came from and who they were. Every Jungreis family member was presented with a beautiful framed collage with the glowing faces of all the Zeides from Hungary. This was the Rebbetzin's most powerful ammunition and she used it well, along with her siddur and Tehillim, whose pages were almost shredded from use and from the copious tears she shed while deeply immersed in prayer day after day.

Every time the Rebbetzin got into the car she would remove her Tehillim from her bag and off she went, reconnecting anew with her past and her holy ancestors. She especially loved saying Chapter 20 seven times, because that was what Zeide had instructed her to say in the name of the Csenger. There were underlined paragraphs and notes in the margins and names of people for whom she needed to daven. Her Tehillim was like an old friend — a friend she carried in her purse and without which she never went anywhere.

And just as she carried that Tehillim with her wherever she went, so it was with every member of her family — and the thousands of people whom she adopted along the way.

At every family simchah, the Rebbetzin would arrive with a bag

The Rebbetzin, Rav Meshulem, Zeide and Mama
with grandchildren and great-grandchildren

in tow. In it was what she called "the family ammunition" — the bag containing the *sefarim* of the Zeides. Among the many *sefarim* were the *Menuchas Osher* from the Csenger, and *Zachor V'Shamor*, which had been written by Rav Meshulem's father, Rav Osher Anshil HaLevi Jungreis. Entering the room where the simchah was taking place, the Rebbetzin would place the bag on the table while proclaiming to the room at large that the Zeides were here with them and that their berachos were with the family at this moment of great joy!

"We have to always remember who we are and where we come from," she'd say with great sincerity and at least a few tears, "and that the Zeides' berachos accompany us at every simchah."

Today the Rebbetzin's tradition still lives on, as the family continues bringing the Zeides' *sefarim* to every family simchah.

While they miss the drama and the Rebbetzin's grand entrance and the way she introduced every new addition to the *mishpachah* to the *sefarim* of the past while saying, "The Zeides are here," at least the *sefarim* are still there.

It went back to a bitterly cold morning in Hungary, when a little girl took a walk through the heavy snow with her father, walking in his footsteps — in the footsteps of the Zeides, in the footsteps of the Zeides for all time.

The Rebbetzin presenting a copy of *The Committed Life*
to New York Mayor Rudy Giuliani at a City Hall Chanukah celebration

Slovie Wolff had a routine prenatal sonogram scheduled while her husband Mendy was overseas on a business trip. During the appointment, she was told that the sonogram indicated that the baby had no heartbeat. With her husband away, there was only one other person in the world Slovie would possibly consider calling at that moment — and that person was her mother.

As it turned out, the Rebbetzin was at HarperCollins that morning, about to sit down at a conference table to sign a contract for her about-to-be-released book, *The Committed Life*.

It was absolutely the last thing she wanted to do, but with no choice, Slovie called her mother's phone. There was no answer.

Hands trembling, Slovie dialed Barbara's cellphone.

"Your mother can't talk right now," Barbara told her, "we're signing the contract at the publisher's office."

"I know," Slovie said, "but it's urgent and I need to speak with her immediately!"

The Rebbetzin got on the phone and Slovie told her the nature of the emergency in a few words. The Rebbetzin didn't hesitate for a second.

"I'm coming over right now."

Before her mother pressed the off button, Slovie heard voices telling her mother, "Rebbetzin, you can't leave now, you're about to sign the contract!"

New York Mayor Rudy Giuliani and Consul General of Israel Shmuel Sisso, applauding the Rebbetzin following her presentation at City Hall

Picking up her pocketbook, the Rebbetzin said, "Let's go, Barbara." Excusing themselves, they left the office and headed directly to Slovie. There the Rebbetzin remained holding her daughter's hand and giving Slovie strength throughout her ordeal.

This was the Rebbetzin's default setting.

If her children needed her she would drop whatever she was doing — and it didn't matter what it was — because they needed her and her children came first.

The Rebbetzin's influence and involvement with each of her children's lives cannot be overstated. It wasn't just that she was always ready to open her house for her children after they had a baby and needed a few weeks of rest. Everything would be ready for them: from a stack of diapers and a baby bathtub to a quiet room with fresh linen, and 'round-the-clock care provided by both parents. That went without saying.

More importantly, when it came to an emotional or medical crisis, the Rebbetzin always knew the right thing to do and say — and that was her greatest gift of all. To her way of thinking, love was all about unconditional giving, and she used to say as proof of what it meant to really love someone, "Look at a nursing mother — just consider it. The more milk she gives, the more milk she has!"

A young couple came to her and said they wanted a divorce.

The Rebbetzin asked them why.

They responded by saying that the love had dried up.

"No way," she said. "Your giving dried up, not the love. The more milk you give, the more you have. The moment you stop giving, that's when it all dries up."

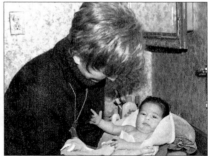

The Rebbetzin was always "hands on" with her grandchildren

Life could be very simple with the Rebbetzin — a simple matter of giving with unconditional love and then watching the incredible results.

"As a little girl visiting her Bubba's house," Shaindy Wolff Eisenberg remembers, "I recall seeing a bowl of grapes on the table. They were appealing-looking grapes and I removed a cluster and ate them. When I finished I began reciting the blessing of *Borei Nefashos*, instead of *Al HaEitz*, which I should have said.

"Bubba was disappointed.

"'That is the wrong *berachah acharonah* (after-blessing),' she told me. On the spot, she sat down with me and taught me the correct berachah so that I would know what to do the next time I ate fruit of the seven species that require the after-berachah of *Al HaEitz*. She was very stringent when it came to matters of halachah in general, and making proper berachos in particular. She washed for every meal. If we were eating at a restaurant she would make sure we knew how important it was to wash for bread, making a *seudah* out of the meal and benching afterward.

She made sure to eat shalosh seudos on Shabbos afternoons — no matter if it was winter and she had just finished eating the day meal a short time before — or during the summer. She was extremely careful to eat Melaveh Malkah, lighting a candle every Motza'ei Shabbos without fail. On Yom Kippur, she'd stand for the entire davening, and fasted every Yom Kippur Kattan.

"As a child and teenager, I used to walk with her to shul on Shabbos. She would be the first to arrive in shul for davening, and we were the last to leave because she had to collect every single siddur, Chumash and even the tissues that people left on the tables.

"'Why are you doing this?' I'd ask my Bubba.

"'It's not respectful to leave the beis medrash in such a mess, and I do not want the non-Jewish cleaning lady to be the one to return the siddurim and Chumashim to their places. This is a job for a Jew.'

"At her *levayah* I stood there after everyone left, overcome by the memory of my grandmother alone in the empty shul, unwilling to leave until every single Chumash was back in its proper place... I could still see her there, moving from shelf to shelf, piles of *sefarim* balanced in her arms..."

The Rebbetzin was renowned for going out of her way to visit people in the hospital. But as much as she visited her students and friends, when it came to her family she was even more involved — if that were possible.

From the birth of her very first grandchild Yosef Dov, through the more recent births of the great-grandchildren, Bubba was a steady and loving presence.

Rabbi Osher and Yaffa had twins who were born prematurely and had to remain in the hospital for two long months. The entire time during the pregnancy, the Rebbetzin made sure to mention the twins whenever she gave a *shiur* and asked everyone to daven for them. She was involved with every particle of her being — her entire self immersed in the desire to see them well enough to bring home from the hospital. She'd go visit them every night at one or two o'clock in the morning, updating their mother when she couldn't be there herself. And nobody glowed like the Rebbetzin when "her" babies finally made it through their front door.

In her later years, the Rebbetzin would spend each Shabbos with a different child. One Motza'ei Shabbos when the twins were six years old, their Bubba announced that she was so proud of them that she was going to write their teacher a note.

Rabbi Osher and Yaffa's twins

My dear Morah Devorah,

A gutte voch. I had the zechus to enjoy Shabbos with my most wonderful grandchildren and beautiful twins — children I am so proud of — Miriam and Rachella. They came to my shiur at the Agudah. They behaved so nicely. They did not make any noise. Everyone was so proud of them. They helped me walk without my cane. They are always at my side. They tell me all the meaningful Torah teachings they learn from Morah Devorah. So thank you for all that.

Miriam and Rachella are just so amazing. They love their friends and their cousins, they share with them and play with them. I thank you for your wonderful chinuch. Tizki l'mitzvos.

Rebbetzin Esther Jungreis

Like many other young marrieds, Yaakov Yosef (JJ) and Rivkie (Gertzulin) Bistricer started off as a kollel couple in Eretz Yisrael. Upon learning that the Rebbetzin was on a speaking tour in Eastern Europe, they excitedly arranged to fly to Hungary for a one-day trip to meet the Rebbetzin and daven at the *kever* of the Csenger Tzaddik. As a newly married couple, nothing more was on their minds at that time than asking for the berachos to build a *bayis ne'eman b'Yisrael* (a faithful home in Israel).

Rivkie and JJ were first *bentched* with three wonderful daughters, and then upon the birth of their son, they could think of no more appropriate name to give him than that of their holy ancestor, Rav Osher Anshil. Today, Ashi takes great pride in seeing a beautiful oil painting of the Csenger Tzaddik, whose name he carries, hanging in the Bistricer home.

"She never acted likes she was a famous person," her grandson Moshe Jungreis recalls. The rest of the grandchildren agreed. Being the grandchildren of Rebbetzin Jungreis held a certain dichotomy. On the one hand, they knew their grandmother was the "coolest lady in the world." On the other hand, she was their Bubba. When someone would ask them, "How it is being Rebbetzin Jungreis' grandchildren?" they would reply, "It's the most normal thing in the world."

Because she was an incredibly normal grandmother.

Moshe used to call and ask to come visit her and she always said, "Of course." At a certain point she said, "Stop calling and just come over" — and that's what he started doing.

"We would talk about anything — politics, dating, and obviously *yichus* and *mishpachah*.

"I remember one time she saw me drinking a can of ginger ale. The next week when I came over, I found thirty cans of ginger ale stocked in the fridge.

"One time Bubba took me with her to Budapest for Shabbos. She was scheduled to speak at one of the grandest shuls in the city. Since her Hungarian was somewhat rusty after so many years, the community provided a translator for her speech. In the middle of the speech, Bubba decided that the translator wasn't relaying her message properly, and she took over, switching from English to Hungarian — just like that. The entire audience started clapping for her — loving the fact that she was willing to address them in a language that she hadn't really spoken for decades.

"It was an eventful trip.

"At some point she didn't feel well and had to be hospitalized while still in Hungary. I remember her lying on the hospital bed, tubes, wires and machines all over the place; but nothing stopped her, that's the way she was. She picked up her phone and called someone she knew — his name was Andre — and arranged for him to take me around to see the sights in Budapest, thinking about me even from her hospital bed!"

"When Bubba would eat at our home in Far Rockaway on Shabbos morning, I'd go pick her up from her house, and as we walked through the streets, there were always people coming over to her — and it didn't matter if it was raining or whatever was going on, she gave them her full attention.

"They'd say to her, 'My father/brother/cousin knows you'; and she had her standard follow-up questions: 'How's he/she/they doing?' — asking it with all her heart and interest, making the person feel like a million dollars.

"Countless times people would approach her and ask, 'Rebbetzin, do you remember me?'

"And she'd look them in the eye and give them her charming, regal smile and reply, 'Of course, you look so familiar!'

"Many times she had no idea who they were yet greeted them like they were her own children.

"'Zeide taught me how to leave a room,' she used to say. 'When we went to the hotel in the summer and I used to accompany him out of the dining room, it took us at least forty-five minutes to get from our table to the dining room door due to Zeide's insistence on stopping at every table to ask the guests how they were doing and where they were from. He didn't stop there. Zeide wasn't satisfied until he knew where everyone's parents were from back in Europe and had heard stories about them and their extended family; by the time he was done, he was best friends with everyone at the hotel.'

"Zeide used to remark that the root of the word *shalom*, peace, is *shaleim*, whole, explaining that you can only bring *shalom* to another if you make them feel *shaleim*."

Growing up watching her father in action, his way became her life

The Rebbetzin enjoying Chol HaMoed with her grandchildren

The Rebbetzin with grandchildren at a family simchah

philosophy as well. She loved him so much and modeled herself after his behavior. Simply speaking, she revered him.

On Friday nights, when the Rebbetzin would be walking home from eating the *seudah* at one of her children's homes, there were invariably teenagers hanging out on the street. She'd always approach them. Most people would quicken their pace and ignore the kids, but not her. On the contrary, she'd stop for a long conversation.

"She was so amazing," one of the teenagers told the Rebbetzin's family. "She was just talking to us as if she were so interested in every facet of our lives!"

They wanted to speak with her, and even when she gave them mussar they didn't want her to leave. She had a way about her and was able to do things nobody else would even attempt.

There were times when she was walking in Israel and girls passed her in the street dressed all in black, with heavy makeup, chains and even tattoos. Nothing fazed her. She'd seen it all — from the hippies in the '60s to the cult members in the '70s to the Wall Street guys in the '80s — and she would wrap her arms around those lost *neshamos* and exclaim, "You look like such a *bas Yisrael*, so beautiful — why cover up your natural uniqueness with a tattoo? You don't need it at all!"

And she'd smile at them and give them a hug and a kiss and they'd walk away feeling good about themselves for the first time in years.

There was no person whom she wouldn't try to help.

She was incapable of ignoring someone in pain. It wasn't in her DNA.

"On the day of my graduation from Darchei Torah," Shmuel Jungreis related, "Bubba sat in the front seat of the car and recited Tehillim all the

Photo of the Rebbetzin's grandchildren presented as a gift to their beloved bubby

way to the auditorium. And she continued reciting Tehillim throughout the graduation — davening and davening for my *hatzlachah* in life. Not only that, before she passed away, she said to me, 'Shmuli, I want you to remember something. Even when Bubba isn't here any longer, she will never forget you and will always be davening for you.'

"That was Bubba — sitting in the hall and praying for me without stop — unceasing prayer as long as the night went on, also promising to go to bat for me in Heaven."

"Bubba loved, absolutely loved, giving presents," Moshe said. "And every time she came to any of her children's homes for Shabbos, everyone would gather around her on Motza'ei Shabbos for the grand gift-giving ceremony. Everyone would line up next to Bubba. She'd be shining, her entire face glowing from within, and she handed out presents to everyone; at moments like those you would have never guessed that the woman sitting at the dining room table, handing out gifts to child after child, was in fact a world-renowned international speaker. During those moments she ceased being the iconic figure of the stage, newspapers and world media and was simply Rebbetzin Esther Jungreis — Bubba, the woman who plastered some of the walls of her house with hundreds of pictures of her children and grandchildren, creating a collage of family members, until not even an inch of free space remained."

"My grandmother used to tell me that she wasn't really a kiruv pioneer," Yaakov Jungreis said, "that it was really her father who gets the credit. She always told us how he became a Rav in Szeged, which was the seat of Reform strength in Hungary. Despite the fact that becoming the Rav in such a city guaranteed him a lifetime of battles, Zeide willingly chose to expose himself to the pain and challenges that would inevitably arrive.

"But as much as she lived in the past, somehow she was completely in the present at the same time. I used to call her every Erev Shabbos, both when I learned in Torah Temimah and when I went out of town to Philly. And every time I told her a *vort*, she would listen, then say, 'Okay, now let me tell you how I answer that question.'

"Bubba was a tremendous *mechadeish* (innovator), constantly coming up with new approaches in Torah. Her mind was sharp and agile, and people sought her out because she always knew what to do.

"When I wanted to leave the Philadelphia yeshivah to go learn in Eretz Yisrael, it became very complicated — everyone had a different opinion about whether I should leave. So I asked my rebbi, who said to me, 'What does your grandmother think?'

" 'My grandmother said I should stay.'

" 'Then I'm not getting involved.'

"When I eventually did go to learn in Eretz Yisrael, Bubba came to visit my Rosh Yeshivah, who later told me how impressed he was by her.

"Bubba demanded perfection from us and held us to a very high standard. Her main message to us — and this was something she focused on constantly — was that we needed to remember where we came from. Every simchah, every *yahrtzeit seudah*, we'd be introduced to the Zeides all over again. There was no such thing as not knowing who you were."

"In a way," her granddaughter Shaindy reflected, "the Rebbetzin was a paradox. She was a beautiful person, and never shy about standing up in front of the world or speaking on television while addressing

America at the Republican National Convention — this was who she was. Everything she wore had to conform completely with the requirements of *tznius,* and at the same time it had to look good, because it was important to her to show every woman she met that it was possible to look good and to take care of oneself and at the same time, to be in line with what halachah demanded of a person.

"I cannot fully explain the paradox that was my grandmother," Shaindy continued, "but in her later years, when I spoke with her on the phone from Eretz Yisrael — it would be late at night in America — she used to cry a lot. She was already much older by then. She'd dispense a lot of berachos and break down crying very easily. There are lines I recall with extreme clarity — as if she said them to me yesterday. This was one of them, a line which she repeated, as if it was vital that I understand what she was telling me:

" 'One thing I can tell you, my *sheifelah* — Hakadosh Baruch Hu is my witness that everything I did was *l'sheim Shamayim* (for the sake of Heaven).'

"She used to cry and repeat that line over and over.

" 'Hashem is my witness, Hashem is my witness that everything I did was *lishmah,* and *lichvod sheim Shamayim.*'

"As she spoke, it was almost as if she were retreating into her own world, reminding herself that everything she did was for the Ribbono shel Olam and for the sake of Heaven."

"With every birth in the family," Yosef Dov Gertzulin related, "Bubba was the first to arrive at the hospital to see how the parents — her grandchildren — were doing, and to give the newborn baby a berachah. When one of our daughters was born prematurely, we had to stay in the NICU for an extended period of time.

"Bubba visited us multiple times.

"But that was just the beginning, because Bubba placed a Tehillim in my daughter's incubator — in a sterile bag, of course — and rested one of Zeide's canes alongside the incubator as well. The nurses were very confused at first — who wouldn't be? But she quickly won them over with her charm.

"*Baruch Hashem,* my daughter made a full recovery."

The Rebbetzin giving
berachos and enjoying time
with great-grandchildren

"I called Bubba on the way to the hospital," her grandson Moshe Wolff relates. "I wanted Bubba to say Tehillim as my wife was in labor with our first child." (This was a given among the children and grandchildren. Everyone wanted Bubba's tefillos.)

"By midnight the baby was born. I called my grandmother with the mazel tov. It was a Thursday evening in New York City. Though Bubba had remained after classes to speak with people, as she usually did, she excused herself, explaining that she was on her way to visit her new great-grandchild. I cannot accurately describe the amazement my wife and I felt as Bubba walked into the recovery room shortly after the birth with my wife's favorite Snapple flavor in hand. There was Bubba holding her newest great-grandchild once again, laughing with the joy at the miracle of seeing yet another fruit of her tree."

But the truth is that the Rebbetzin was somehow always there to greet her newest grandchildren and great-grandchildren no matter where or what time they came into the world. The Rebbetzin was frequently in Israel lecturing and teaching. On one such occasion, Shaindy Wolff Eisenberg gave birth — and what a special treat and honor for her and her husband Rabbi Shlomo that their Bubba was there to hold her newest great-grandchild soon after birth in the Jerusalem hospital!

"I was on the shidduch scene for a long time," her grandson Yosef Jungreis remembers. "Needless to say, my grandmother was always very busy with my shidduchim. Every time we were in one of the hotels, she would pretend that she needed my help to walk around the hotel, while in reality she wanted me to see who was there and if I was interested in going out with anyone at the program. The moment I gave my approval for any girl, my grandmother would make sure to spend time at her family's table talking to the girl and getting to know her family, while developing a feel for the situation. In fact, the last words she ever said to my father (Rabbi Yisroel Jungreis) were, 'What's with Yosef's shidduchim?'"

That's the way it was. Until the very end.

CHAPTER FIFTY-NINE

The Unexpected Bris

*T*uvia Sablosky met the Rebbetzin when he began attending classes at Hineni. On one of his initial visits to Hineni, he had an extensive conversation with the Rebbetzin.

"Thank you for coming back," she said to him. "Tell me your name again."

"Tommy."

"Are you Jewish?"

"Yes."

"Is your mother Jewish?"

"Yes."

"Is your father Jewish?"

"Yes."

"What's your Jewish name?"

"I don't have one."

"What happened to you?"

Tommy explained that his mother had passed away about four months earlier. Immediately, the Rebbetzin responded by saying, "I am going to become your spiritual mother. Did you have a proper bris? The reason I'm asking is because every Jewish baby boy receives a Jewish name at his bris and you don't have one."

"I don't remember that far back," he quipped.

"Look, Tommy, I'm going to introduce you to my son Rabbi Osher and I want you to start attending his Monday evening Chumash *shiur*. You'll begin learning Torah and he'll arrange for you to have a proper bris and to receive a Hebrew name and a pair of tefillin. And when you meet my son, tell him that I think your Jewish name should be Tuvia."

Through the rest of 2008, Tommy followed the Rebbetzin's advice and the relationship became stronger with both the Rebbetzin and her son Rabbi Osher.

Tommy relates:

> Rabbi Osher kept on asking me to come visit his yeshivah in Brooklyn, so we could take care of all the things that needed to be done to turn me into a real Jew, and I kept on telling him that I'd get around to it soon.
>
> I called him up one Sunday morning. It was about ten degrees outside and beautiful, and I said to him, "I'm ready."
>
> "Great," he replied, "meet me in Flatbush."
>
> I parked near the address he'd given me and found his yeshivah building. It was absolutely magnificent. It was large, sprawling and a true monument to Torah learning. Looking at the building, I said to myself, "I knew the Jungreis family is very successful, but I didn't realize they had this kind of an operation going on in Brooklyn!"
>
> Turning to Rabbi Osher, I said, "Rabbi, I didn't realize you had such an impressive yeshivah!"
>
> He smiled and set me straight.
>
> "This yeshivah is called Yeshiva Rabbi Chaim Berlin. It's where *I* learn, where I've been coming to study Torah for much of my life!"
>
> He walked me into the grand edifice and began introducing me to rabbi after rabbi, until I felt like I was back in the 1800s. We learned Torah together for about an hour, at which point he said, "Okay, now it's time for us to go across the street and get you a pair of tefillin at Tiferes Stam."
>
> We left Chaim Berlin, walked across Coney Island Avenue and entered Tiferes Stam, where he introduced me to the owner, Rabbi Pincus. And then five minutes after we entered the store, the door opened and none other than Rabbi Paysach Krohn walked into Tiferes Stam. Immediately, Rabbi Jungreis went over to say hello, telling the world-renowned *maggid*, whom I was meeting for the first time, "Rabbi Krohn, you're just the man we're looking for!"
>
> Rabbi Krohn smiled at Reb Osher and said, "And why is that?"

As an aside …

Rabbi Paysach Krohn, famed speaker and author, became acquainted with the Rebbetzin in her later years, a long time after she established Hineni. Rabbi Krohn came to know the Rebbetzin since the two of them began sharing the stage at many speaking venues. Both of them usually attended the other's speech and both made a point of beginning their speeches by acknowledging the other's presence in the audience.

Rabbi Krohn relates the next part of the story:

> I had met the Rebbetzin at the Homowack Hotel many years ago, and we did some programs together. Both of us spoke for the N'shei Cares Sefirah Program — it was just the two of us then. And then we were both part of an incredibly moving program that took place years later in South Africa, which was titled Sinai Indaba. I don't know how in the world she found the strength to travel all the way to South Africa at that point in her life. But she did, wowing the crowd with her unique speaking abilities and charisma.
>
> I started referring to her as "The Bubby of Klal Yisrael," and she loved that title. I noticed that as she was getting older she started talking to her audiences in a different way. Though she had always been a person who focused on the positive and on the power of making connections to the past (she always talked about her husband, father, grandfather and the Holocaust), as time passed, I began to notice that her tone changed. It was much softer, it was more pleading, almost begging people to connect to their families — as if she were a grandmother talking — someone who realized that she wouldn't be around forever and wanted to give over her message to her children and grandchildren. It seemed to me that that was the way she looked at her audience — like her own family and her own kids — and everything she said was with softness, sensitivity and compassion.
>
> I couldn't help but notice her approach, and that's when I started calling her "The Bubby of Klal Yisrael."
>
> I really believed that she deserved the title, because there was no doubt that she felt a genuine responsibility for her people — she was much older than the people she was speaking to and had a extraordinary amount of life experience to convey — and just like she considered herself everyone's grandmother, the people

she was talking to looked at her the same way.

All this brings me to a truly amazing story in which the Rebbetzin and I each took part.

One Sunday, I happened to find myself in need of a visit to Reb Heshy Pincus' Judaica store Tiferes Stam on Coney Island Avenue in Flatbush. I needed to have my tefillin straps freshly blackened. As I entered the store, I encountered Rabbi Osher Jungreis with a person I had never seen before in my life. The next thing I know, Reb Osher says to me, "Rabbi Krohn, I can't believe that you're here. You're the exact person we were just talking about!"

Understandably my curiosity was piqued by that statement and I waited for an explanation.

"Let me introduce you to my good friend Tommy Sablosky."

"*Shalom Aleichem*, Reb Tommy, it's nice to meet you."

"Rabbi Krohn, Tom has been attending my mother's classes in Manhattan and she arranged for us to learn together. We were learning together for a while and began discussing the fact that every Jew needs his own tefillin. After a while we decided that it was time for him to purchase his own pair — and guess what, we've just come into the store now to make the purchase!"

Of course I wished Tommy a warm mazel tov on the occasion of buying his first pair of tefillin — but just then Reb Osher said something that turned our encounter into something I would never forget.

"Rabbi Krohn, I can't help but point something else out to you — something amazing."

"What's that?"

"Wearing tefillin is an *ois*, a sign for the Jewish people. But there is another *ois* and that is the mitzvah of bris milah. I just think it's so amazing that you, a *mohel*, just happen to be here in the store on the exact day that Tom is purchasing his tefillin, because Tommy needs a little work done by you."

I turned to look at Tom.

"Tell me," I said to him, "did you ever have a kosher bris?"

"I did not."

"Well, then, we should take care of it right now!"

Needless to say, he was taken aback.

"What are you talking about? What do you mean — we should take care of it right now?"

"It just so happens that I have my bris instruments — my 'tool box,' so to speak — in the car right now. If you were circumcised when you were born, all we have to do is *hatafas dam bris* — and then you can purchase a brand-new pair of tefillin and have a kosher bris — both on the same day!"

He looked at me and said with a big smile, "Okay, let's do it!"

Turning to Reb Osher Jungreis, I said, "Look, while I'm doing the *hatafah*, please run outside — I'm sure Reb Heshy can tell you where to go — and buy some cake and wine so we can make a *l'chaim* in honor of the bris."

I couldn't believe this was happening. I ran outside to my car and got my instruments. Heshy Pincus provided a room at the rear of the store, and I explained to Tommy exactly what I was going to do; and just like that, we took care of it, and Tommy — who was really quite bemused by the unexpected turn of events — was the recipient of a completely kosher bris milah!

By the time we were finished in the back room, Rabbi Jungreis had returned with some cake and a bottle of grape juice. I asked Reb Osher and Reb Heshy to gather everyone who happened to be in the store at the time, and then, after filling a cup with grape juice, I recited the berachos one says at a *hatafas dam bris* and Tom was officially renamed Tuvia on the spot.

When it was over, spontaneous singing and dancing erupted in the middle of the store as the members of Klal Yisrael celebrated the fact that Tuvia Sablosky had reached this crucial milestone in life. It was beautiful. You can imagine the *simchah* — especially considering the fact that it was all unplanned and had kind of just fallen into our laps.

It so happens that we hadn't chosen the name Tuvia at random. Tom and the Rebbetzin had discussed the question of his Jewish name a while back and the Rebbetzin had suggested he go with Tuvia. With a new name, a new bris and a new pair of tefillin, Tuvia was beyond excited. So was everyone else in the store who joined in with the celebration, wishing the *baal simchah* "Mazel tov" and taking part in the festive atmosphere.

When the celebration was over, Rabbi Pincus sat Tuvia down and spent a good forty-five minutes teaching him about the mitzvah of wearing tefillin.

"How much does a pair of tefillin cost?" Tuvia wanted to know.

"Prices begin at six hundred dollars and go up to around a thousand dollars for a beautiful pair."

So Tuvia bought his pair of tefillin.

Meanwhile Reb Osher called his mother and said, "Ma, you're never going to believe what's happening at Tiferes Stam! Rabbi Paysach Krohn just 'happened' to walk into the store a few minutes after we came in. I told him about Tommy and he offered to do his bris right here in the store — and Tommy is now officially Tuvia and he just purchased his first pair of tefillin!"

"Do you know what *parashah* it is?" the Rebbetzin asked her son.

"Sure, it's *Parashas Shemos*."

"And who was born in *Parashas Shemos*?"

"Moshe Rabbeinu."

"And what was the name I chose for Tommy? Tuvia — which is another name for Moshe!"

All things considered, it was quite a story! (And that's Rabbi Krohn talking.)

But the story wasn't over. Because when Tuvia got married, one of Tuvia's relatives met the Rebbetzin at the wedding and asked her why she decided to choose the name Tuvia out of all the Jewish names in the world.

Tiferes Stam Judaica Center, location of "The Unexpected Bris"

One might think that the Rebbetzin would have answered that since Tom begins with the letter T and Tuvia begins with the letter T — that it made sense. But that was not her answer.

"I don't know," she replied. "I just thought of that name and felt it was the correct choice for him."

"Rebbetzin," the relative replied, and she was crying, "you have been blessed with prophetic vision!"

"What do you mean?"

"I mean that somehow you managed to choose a name out of all the names in the world that just happened to be the name of Tuvia's grandfather!"

And for years afterward, every time the Rebbetzin and I were the featured speakers at a venue, she always used to tell the audience, "Rabbi Krohn and I have this great story!"

And so that part of Tuvia's story became our story — mine and the Rebbetzin's — and we told and retold it together and alone many times.

Rabbi Krohn continues:

Through the years I had gotten to know the Rebbetzin's husband, Rav Meshulem Jungreis, when our paths crossed at his shul Ohr Torah in North Woodmere. I heard her mention her husband in her speeches numerous times, crediting him as being the anchor of her life.

She used to say that she never moved a step without him, never did anything without his counsel and advice. Her respect for him was awesome — and I do not say this lightly. She spoke about him with such reverence that it was absolutely incredible.

After he passed away it was very difficult for her to look at his *sefarim*. He had a very distinct handwriting, and just looking at it brought home to her how much she missed him. One night Slovie was going through her father's papers (and there were many, because he was never able to throw anything out) and she found a sheet of paper — with a message I like to quote all the time.

On it Rabbi Jungreis had written: *"A long life is not good enough, but a good life is long enough."*

And whenever I tell this story, I make a point of explaining how goodness means giving to others, and how it's not what you amass from a financial perspective — not the real estate or port-folios — but how you changed the lives of the people you came across.

Because, you see, that was really how the Rebbetzin (and yes, her husband and parents) lived. Finding that piece of paper was like a signal from her husband in heaven telling her that she should carry on living as she always had, changing the world each and every day with her kindness and care for everyone she encountered.

Part 10
2012-2016

She wasn't just a yechidah b'dorah — a singularly unique individual in her generation.

She was a yechidah b'kamah doros — a singularly unique individual in many generations!

It must be very lonely for her up in Gan Eden! I cannot imagine who could possibly be sitting in the same row!

An American gadol and Rosh Yeshivah of a major yeshivah speaking to the children at the shivah for the Rebbetzin

As one rav put it very succinctly, there are, baruch Hashem, many wonderful kiruv organizations. Wonderful people being mekarev others. But the Rebbetzin pioneered kiruv. The Rebbetzin pioneered kiruv! She led the way when nobody knew what it meant. And she was so happy to see so many others follow in her footsteps and do more and more.

Rabbi Shlomo Gertzulin at the levayah

CHAPTER SIXTY

The Ballerina

*T*he Rebbetzin broke her hip at a hotel in Encinitas, California. For the first time, the woman who couldn't be stopped simply couldn't move. She was extremely weak, tired and in horrendous pain. But the moment she saw the doctor's name tag and recognized it as a Jewish-sounding name, she shifted from suffering patient to the founder of Hineni. She could no more stop herself from drawing him close to Judaism than she could stop herself from breathing.

Looking at him, she asked a question she'd asked thousands of times before.

"What's your name?"

"Dr. Levine*."

She repeated the question. "No, what's your name?"

No doubt the doctor was thinking that he was dealing with a patient who was suffering from dementia.

"Dr. Levine. Dr. Mark Levine."

"No, what's your real name?" (He stared at her as though he couldn't for the life of him figure out what she wanted.) "Your real name. Your Jewish name. What did your Bubby call you?"

"Moshe," he answered after a long pause.

"What's a Moshe'le like you doing in Encinitas? Do you have children?"

He nodded. "Yes, I have two girls."

"What's going to be with your little girls if you raise them in a place with no other Jews? There is nothing Jewish in this whole town!"

It was true. The only time religious Jews came to the town was Pesach, when there was a program at the local hotel.

It was as if she had completely forgotten about her earlier agony. She proceeded to give the doctor a *shmuess* and he shut his phone and listened and listened and listened. And he returned the next day to examine her again. Of course she took advantage of his return to deliver another *mussar shmuess*. It was the same story every time he showed up in her room. Yet he returned every day for another installment.

It was as if she had an addiction — an addiction for doing kiruv.

As the Rebbetzin was being wheeled into surgery, she davened to Hashem from the bottom of her heart.

"Ribono shel Olam," she begged, "please leave me my mind, so I can continue speaking and being *mechazek* (give strength) and *mekarev* (draw) Klal Yisrael closer to You! I don't mind losing the physical abilities that I once had, but please allow me to keep my mind and my feet so I can continue my mission in life!"

Later, as she became increasingly frail and her children tried convincing her to relinquish the burden she had so willingly accepted upon herself, she wasn't able to obey their directive, explaining that slowing down and stopping to do what she had always done went completely against the tefillah she'd asked of Hashem on her way into the operating theater.

"I cannot sleep. I still have work to do. When my job is over I will sleep."

The hip would need a replacement and a rod — it was a very complicated procedure — and the Rebbetzin was forced to remain in California for far longer than she'd originally imagined when she had been invited for that year's Pesach program. The Rebbetzin — being who she was — didn't rest until she was able to stand on her own two feet again. She followed the doctor's orders and did double of everything he asked her to do.

Finally the big day arrived: the day the Rebbetzin would attempt to walk.

"Okay," the therapist said, "now you're going to walk down the hallway."

The Rebbetzin stood with her walker, a turban on her head accenting her high cheekbones, radiating a timeless and ethereal beauty — the kind of beauty that would remain with her and give her a glow until her final day on earth.

As she stood at the starting point about to begin, the nurses, who loved and admired her, began cheering. One of the nurses called out, "You're our ballerina!"

"Ballerina? Some ballerina I am, with this robe and a turban on my head. What kind of ballerina looks like this?"

Yet she continued repeating the word over and over to herself: "ballerina, ballerina…"

And then she suddenly uttered the word in a whole different way, emphasizing it from another angle.

"*Baal rinah, baal rinah.*" (Master of [your own] happiness.)

She was suddenly triumphant, seizing the silver lining in a dark situation, as she had done throughout her life.

"We all have to go through life being a *baal rinah*. We need to remember that no matter what happens to us we have to smile and remain *b'simchah.*"

Finding the lesson within an untenable situation was inevitable. But who could have guessed that the word ballerina would became the message of the day! It was vintage Rebbetzin Jungreis.

Then, putting the biggest smile on her face, she lifted her feet and began walking down the hallway.

And a cheer went up from the assembled. . .

When the Rebbetzin was finally given the green light to leave the hospital and go home, there was still the question of how she would return to New York — considering that she was in constant pain and unable to sit in a regular airplane seat, even in first class. The doctors told the family that the only way the Rebbetzin would be able to travel was on a private plane, where she would be able to lie down for the duration of the flight. That way she'd be in relative comfort and able to endure a trip she had taken hundreds of times throughout her life.

But now she couldn't.

The woman who had consistently done the impossible had finally shown she was human and had limitations. She didn't like it and she didn't want to accept her new reality, but she understood that the doctors were correct and she'd only be able to travel by private plane.

That was when Mrs. Paula Pilevsky from North Woodmere — the Pilevsky family who had stood at Rabbi and Rebbetzin Jungreis' side from day one, no matter what — came through for her again. Paula and her husband Fred (Ephraim), the patriarch of the family, loved the Rabbi and Rebbetzin, and Paula's next move came as no surprise. Calling her son Phil, Mrs. Pilevsky informed him that the Rebbetzin couldn't possibly take a regular flight and needed different arrangements.

Phil Pilevsky, a successful real estate developer and friend of the Jungreis family, didn't hesitate for a second. After getting off the phone with his mother, he chartered a private jet for the Rebbetzin, which flew her home to the warm embrace of her family.

Many years earlier, Phil Pilevsky had given the Rebbetzin space for a Hineni office when it was time to move her nascent kiruv organization into professional quarters. At that time, Paula Pilevsky called her son and told him what the Rebbetzin needed. Phil called his office and that was that — the Rebbetzin was offered a suite of rooms in one of his buildings on 38th Street and Third Avenue. But that was just the beginning, because Hineni's move from the Rebbetzin's house in North Woodmere to an office in the city would eventually lead to Hineni purchasing a building of its own.

It's like Chazal say, "One mitzvah leads to another."

The Pilevsky family can attest to the truth in that statement.

What was particularly interesting about the Rebbetzin's relationship with the Pilevsky family was the fact that while it began with the family back in North Woodmere, the relationship continued with their children and with their grandchildren. And it's the same way with many of the families who became close to the Rebbetzin and her children.

Once connected — never severed.

The Pilevsky children and grandchildren's close connection to the Torah way of life is a testimony to the extremely close-knit relationship they shared, and Mr. Pilevsky Senior's fierce loyalty to "his" rabbi and rebbetzin. Such behavior does not go unrewarded, and the Ribono shel Olam repaid them manifold with a beautiful *mishpachah*.

The Rebbetzin used to tell her children that Hineni wasn't just an organization, it was the "Hineni *Mishpachah*" (the Hineni family), and the Jungreis children all felt that their mother gave them a wonderful gift: the gift of having many, many siblings and a really big family. And that was their parents' strength even before Hineni, when it was just the shul. Because everyone in the community became part of their house, their lives and their family.

After the Rebbetzin fell and broke her hip, it was the first time people saw her as an ordinary mortal. Until that point she had always been able to do anything she put her mind to. But now she was hurt, and that meant following the serious regimen of exercise that she was assigned. If the doctor told her to do an exercise ten times she did it twenty times. If he told her to do it for five minutes, she did it for fifteen minutes. She did whatever she had to do, because she knew how many people were depending on her to be healthy.

And eventually the Rebbetzin went back to giving classes and counseling and giving advice, and everyone breathed a sigh of relief — but it was premature. Nobody wanted to imagine a world without the Rebbetzin, so they did their best to block out such a possibility from their imagination. But the clock was ticking and her time was almost up.

When the Rebbetzin davened she had the custom of holding on to one of the Zeides' walking sticks. This gave her the feeling that the *zechus* of her holy ancestors was accompanying her tefillos. She lived her life hanging onto the coattails of the Zeides.

And she never, ever stopped reminding her children and grandchildren from whom they were descended. And when a grandchild or great-grandchild wasn't acting in a way that befitted their name, she would tell them, "You are named after a very big tzaddik, and have a lot to live up to. You cannot do whatever you want. You have a responsibility to rise above yourself and be a credit to the tzaddikim who came before you."

The Rebbetzin spoke from her heart. Many times, a child who had no trouble ignoring his own mother had a much more difficult time ignoring her. Even the most rambunctious children couldn't dismiss the message — "You're a Jungreis, act accordingly" — when told it by the Rebbetzin.

And just as she demanded a certain kind of behavior, so did she expect her children and later her grandchildren to go above and beyond, because she knew that they could, and had it in them to do so.

The Rebbetzin's grandchildren singing at a Hineni function

It had begun with the Rebbetzin. But she encouraged all her children to take it further and to spread the magic as far as possible.

At one point, with so many couples attending her *shiurim* and seeking her advice on the subject of the Torah's viewpoint on raising children and chinuch, the Rebbetzin felt that it was time for Slovie to write a book. Slovie, however, struggled with the idea. After all, she had never authored a book before.

But the Rebbetzin quieted her daughter's fears and encouraged her to write the book, even penning the foreword.

"*Sheifelah,*" she'd said, "this is who we are, and this is what we do."

In the end Slovie wrote the book. It was titled *Raising a Child With Soul*.

And she encouraged her sons Rabbi Yisroel and Rabbi Osher to co-author a book on the *parashah* called *Torah for Your Table*, and her daughter Chaya Sora to continue writing inspirational articles.

These were the latest in a long line of Jungreis *sefarim*, spanning the generations: from the scholarly works of the Menuchas Osher back in Hungary to a book on chinuch for Jews living in America today.

Of course, it goes without saying that all the Jungreis children teach various classes for Hineni on a wide range of subjects, reaching all ages: singles, couples and young families.

It's what their mother wanted and what they grew up seeing.

Or in other words, it's what a Jungreis does.

Footsteps, my friends, footsteps of the Zeides.

"It was the same with the younger generation," Shaindy recalls. "Here it wasn't about writing books or teaching classes, but the same principle applied — how can I bring out the best in my family? How can I make them recognize the greatness I see in them?

"Somehow Bubba always knew how to bring out the best in

everyone she encountered. She knew how to give people opportunities they might not have otherwise had. She believed in taking a shy child and training her to stand up in front of a room full of adults to give a speech because she recognized a certain potential in that child for public speaking. The first speeches I gave in public were with Bubba and the groups she led, and she made a big deal about them and even described them in her books — though I am sure they were not that big a deal. But she turned them into a big deal, and in the process I became a person who knew I could speak, which I still do to this day.

"She wanted all her children and grandchildren to have a share in her life work, so she pushed us to get up and sing and teach — to do and to accomplish. She would encourage all of us to stand up at the Shabbatons and give speeches, and we had to babysit on Rosh Hashanah for people's children, and it was really important for her that her grandchildren be involved and continue the work she started. She would send her granddaughter Nechamie to give someone a yarmulke and ask some of the younger grandchildren to sing a song at the meals. Everyone had a job to do — children, grandchildren and later great-grandchildren — from walking around the ballroom with challah and honey on Rosh Hashanah, to singing *zemiros* and performing original skits at various Hineni Yom Tov gatherings."

Meshulem Jungreis, the son of Rabbi Yisroel and Rivki, inspired all who heard him with his beautiful renditions of some of the Rebbetzin's favorite tunes, particularly *"V'zakeini"* and *"Hamalach Hagoel."* Tragically, he passed away at a young age in 2018, and his *kever* is just a few feet away from those of his beloved Bubba and Zeide.

Tziri Salamon used to bring her children to visit their great-grandmother every Erev Shabbos. There were always two new trucks waiting for the boys and presents for the girls.

First everyone received a berachah. Then the presents.

The Rebbetzin and Meshulem

The house was always stocked with the kinds of things that everyone liked. Plenty of ice cream in the freezer. Cupcakes from Zomick's Bakery. And she'd prepare bags of treats for them to take home.

"This is for you," she'd say to Tziri, handing her a bag. "This is for your husband. And this is for the babysitter."

The Rebbetzin never forgot the babysitter.

Taking leave of the Rebbetzin was no simple thing.

She never let anyone go without first giving him or her a berachah — and then another berachah. If a child or grandchild was expecting a baby, she would get another special berachah, with the Rebbetzin's hand placed on the stomach of the expectant mother — just for the baby.

"I used to do the same exact thing with my father," the Rebbetzin would tell her family. "When Zeide was sick, I used to run to his bedside twice a day, whether he was at home or in the hospital. When I arrived, I too would bow my head to receive my father's blessing. The time always passed too quickly and I would have to leave him — inevitably before I was ready to say goodbye.

"When I knew that I had to leave, I would ask him for another berachah. And then, as I stood by the door of his room, about to leave, ready to go, I would turn around and come back to his bedside for just one more blessing.

The Rebbetzin bentching a granddaughter at her wedding

The Rebbetzin bentching a grandson after buying him his tefillin for his bar mitzvah

"'*Gei shoin*,' Mama would shoo me away jokingly, '*vos kimst du tzurik?* (Why are you coming back?)'

"'I want another blessing from Tatte. Just one more.'

"'Enough,' Mama would say. 'Enough.'

"But Zeide would interject, 'You can never have too many berachos.

Mama's *nachas* — with great-grandchildren at a family gathering

As long as you can, you have to *chap* (grab) the berachos...'

"He would then add in plaintive tones, '*Halevai*, if only I myself would still be able to go to my own father for a berachah...'"

Even when she wasn't feeling well, the Rebbetzin would always make sure to walk her children and grandchildren to the door when they were leaving her home. She would stand by the door, waving, until she could no longer see the car. She'd learned this behavior from Zeide, who used to stand outside his home in Canarsie waving goodbye until the visitors were lost from sight.

The children learned to turn on the ignition and leave the driveway as rapidly as possible, knowing that she wouldn't sit down until they were out of sight.

Rav Meshulem and the Rebbetzin at grandchildren and great-grandchildren's *upsherins*

CHAPTER SIXTY-ONE
Hazos Rebbetzin Jungreis?

As a world traveler, the Rebbetzin was once asked in an interview by a Torah magazine what was the most important thing she took along with her on her journeys across the globe.

The Rebbetzin didn't hesitate. There was no question in her mind.

"My Tehillim," she replied simply. "The words of Tehillim can pierce the deepest crevices of our *neshamos* and penetrate the depths of our hearts and minds. If you make saying Tehillim part of your daily life, you will never truly be alone, no matter what happens. And if you learn the words by heart, they will become engraved on your soul. And then when you are inevitably tested by the many challenges and vicissitudes of life, your Tehillim will be there to give you strength when you need it most."

The Rebbetzin was true to her word and recited Tehillim every free moment she had: in the car, on the plane, or at home, surrounded by the *sefarim* on the shelves and the Csenger Zeides' canes. Every word became part of her. They flowed from her tongue with ease; comfortable with her, secure in the knowledge that she loved them and recited them as if they were diamonds, there to be lovingly counted and treasured. How grateful she was that the Tehillim had become such an integral part of her being! Nobody would ever be able to take it from her. Even if her Sefer Tehillim disappeared, the Tehillim itself — the intangible words and message — would forever be a part of her.

That's the way it went throughout her life.

And then the Rebbetzin became ill. And her illness intensified and grew steadily worse, encroaching on her previously healthy body and inching forward as it conquered more and more previously healthy territory.

Suddenly she had a decision to make. Should she go public with her ordeal or keep it private? The Rebbetzin was being faced with a dilemma shared by many people who find themselves ill after a lifetime of good health.

She didn't know what to do.

"If I go public with my illness," she said to herself, "people will ask me a thousand and one questions every time I walk outside. They'll say, 'Rebbetzin, what happened? When? Where? How?'"

She wasn't prepared for that! It felt like an invasion of privacy, and Rebbetzin Jungreis was a very private person — yes, even as an international figure, she was still private about her personal life.

"Then I realized how foolish I was being," she later said. "Why should I go to battle by myself when I have the most magnificent army standing by my side ready for action? The moment you give them the word," she told herself, "your army will be in uniform, massing together at the front lines, ready to do battle for you!"

And so the Rebbetzin elected to go public with the news and called upon her army — her larger family — the Jewish people throughout the world. The war cry was sounded and was heard everywhere. Suddenly the name Esther bas Miriam was heard in shuls and yeshivos worldwide, as the weapons of our people were wielded by all hands. And knowing that her people had come together to daven for her gave the Rebbetzin hope. Because while she had been the one to give hope, faith, succor and courage to multitudes throughout her lifetime, the time had come for the members of her extended family to return the favor and give back to her.

And they did.

On one of the last times the family spent Shavuos at a hotel with the Rebbetzin, her great-granddaughter Miriam Botknecht wouldn't stop begging her great-grandmother to come visit her at home the next day. Trying to entice the Rebbetzin to come, Miriam — who was four at the time — said, "Please come over tomorrow, Bubba. If you do, we'll make an apple kugel together."

In Miriam's mind, promising Bubba that they would make an apple kugel seemed like the ultimate plan to convince her to come for a visit.

After all, hadn't she heard Bubba say on many occasions how much she enjoyed a nice piece of apple kugel, fresh from the oven?

Eventually, having obtained a promise from her great-grandmother to come visit, Miriam dropped the subject and when they left the hotel that night, her parents thought no more of the whole thing.

The next day was Sunday. There was a downpour, with the streets turning into raging rivers. It was so bad that basements around the neighborhood flooded. All of a sudden there came a knock at the door.

Aryeh Botknecht went to see who it was, wondering who would be venturing outside in such weather. He never dreamed that he would see Bubba on his doorstep, after his wife Nechamie called earlier that day to cancel the visit due to the inclement weather. To his shock, he saw the Rebbetzin and Michelle standing on the doorstep, weighed down with the inevitable bags of presents, stickers and erasers…

"Bubba, you didn't have to come out in the rain. Miriam is only a kid. She wouldn't know the difference. You should be home right now!"

But the Rebbetzin was not at home. She was in Flatbush at the home of her grandchildren, because, as she explained to her grandson, "Aryeh, you can't promise a child something and not keep your word to them. Never say, 'It's only a kid.' On the contrary, *because* it's a kid you have to keep your word. Otherwise they will never forget it and it will make an impact on them!"

And so the Rebbetzin and her four-year-old great-granddaughter made a kugel together and the Rebbetzin enjoyed a slice straight out of the oven. And now, a few years later, Miriam remembers the day her great-grandmother braved a vicious storm to come see her, because she had made a promise to a four-year-old, and promises had to be kept — no matter what.

Toward the end of the Rebbetzin's life, she became increasingly frail. This was especially difficult for her since she was a woman who never left home without being elegantly dressed. Yet now, for the first time, she couldn't go anywhere without supporting herself with a walker. It was a terrible blow and she hated the fact that a walker was now part of her life. With no recourse, the Rebbetzin accepted the inevitable, but cringed every time she had to use it to get around.

It was the Rebbetzin's granddaughter Aliza Wolff who came up with an idea she knew her Bubba would love. Aliza decided to decorate her grandmother's walker, turning it into something grand that would reflect her personality and sense of style.

Aliza went to Michael's and purchased the materials she needed to turn that walker into a fashion statement. Covered in crystals and shiny material, the walker looked like something designed by Swarovski. The Rebbetzin loved it. She called it "Bubba's Bling." Now instead of being put off by her walker, the Rebbetzin pushed it in front of her with pride. She'd maneuver it onto a plane and all the passengers would delight in the novelty and ask her where she'd purchased it. From one second to the next, the Rebbetzin's walker had gone from being a liability to an asset. She even used it at the final Hineni dinner she attended, beaming from ear to ear as she pushed that gleaming walker down the aisle to her seat on the dais.

Entering the Rebbetzin's house in those final months was no simple matter. The woman who had never gone anywhere without her heels was barely able to move herself from spot to spot.

Yet as she moved, there was always a *pasuk* on her lips.

One evening her grandson Eli Wolff stood beside her, helping his Bubba over to the couch, when he heard her quoting from *Megillas Rus*, "*Hazos Naomi* — Is this Naomi?" (a reference to what people asked one another when Naomi, Rus' mother-in-law, returned to Eretz Yisrael from Moav, an aged version of her once beautiful and young self).

Then he heard her say, "*Hazos* Rebbetzin Jungreis?"

Turning to Eli, she said, "Please don't remember me like this! Please remember the way I used to be!"

"When I think about my Bubba's plea to me," Eli said, "I do recall her in her younger years, glamorous and striking, but at the same time, I will never forget the way she looked at the end and the constant *mesirus nefesh* she exhibited to keep on fulfilling her mission until her final moments. I remember how she was so careful about keeping halachah. How she insisted on putting on her right shoe first. How she would correct someone if they read a word of Tehillim incorrectly — even if she was half asleep or out of it. I remember everything I saw — and to me, her behavior was incredible, worthy of emulation and something I would never want to forget. Just as Naomi's return from Moav brought about the onset of Mashiach, so too my grandmother's behavior at her weakest moments was something out of this world."

Unique and unforgettable.
Just like her.

In her later years, the Rebbetzin continuously exhorted her audiences to make a commitment to recite the words of the *Shema*.

"You can't ask a person you just met to become *shomer Shabbos*," she would say. "You can't ask them to begin keeping kosher. But you could ask them to recite the special message of *Shema*. It's like Yaakov's ladder; it's a question of taking small steps and climbing rung by rung. So many Yidden were *niftar al Kiddush Hashem* saying those very words. How can they fail to be moved and changed by those holy words?"

Just a few short weeks before the Rebbetzin passed away, she asked Chaya Sora to "please take a pen and pad and write down this important message." It was the message of *Shema Yisrael*.

Many centuries ago we all had a Zeide.
Our Zeide was the most amazing man.
His face shone like sunshine.
His eyes sparkled like two brilliant diamonds.

Our Zeide was Yaakov Avinu — our father Jacob.
Zeide Yaakov was so remarkable that one day,
Hashem sent an angel to change his name to Yisrael.
Time passed, and the day came when Hashem sent a message to our Zeide:

Worldwide *Shema Yisrael* Initiative, in memory of the Rebbetzin

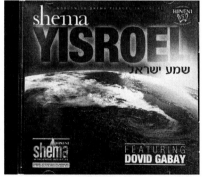

Shema recording, commissioned especially for the Worldwide *Shema Yisrael* Initiative

It's time to come home. Join Me up here.
Zeide Yisrael called for all of his children and grandchildren to gather around him quickly before he embarked on his final journey. Zeide Yisrael wanted to say something, but he lacked the strength to do so.

But his sons could feel what was on their Zeide's heart, and they understood his wishes. And so, in unison, they cried out:
"SHEMA YISRAEL HASHEM ELOKEINU HASHEM ECHAD — HEAR O ISRAEL ..."

Their Shema Yisrael was so powerful that it took on the form of the TREE OF SHEMA YISRAEL.

With time, a turbulent storm came and the beautiful Shema Yisrael leaves that were attached to the tree slowly but steadily began falling and blowing all over the world.

But the leaves never forgot their identity. Although the Shema Yisrael leaves were trampled upon, swept away into the oceans, and even burned by so many, no one could take away their inner strength and potency.

The eternal words of Shema Yisrael remained forever attached to these dispersed leaves; the song remained in their souls, and ultimately the leaves found their way back to the tree.

We, the Jewish people, sing the song of Shema Yisrael.
It takes us back to the days of our father Yaakov — Jacob.
We, the Jewish people, are an eternal people, even if we have forgotten our past.
The Shema Yisrael helps us reconnect, and our Heavenly Father promises us:
Say Shema Yisrael, and then the unbelievable will happen —
the Shema Yisrael tree will bloom again.

On Tuesday evening, March 15, 2016, just a few months before the Rebbetzin would pass away, the Hineni organization paid tribute to the

Rebbetzin to commemorate 50 years of her pioneering outreach activities. It was an emotional evening. There was a packed house. Hundreds of people whose lives had been touched and transformed by the Rebbetzin were there. And when the Rebbetzin rose to speak (in what was to be her final speech) there wasn't a dry eye in the room. Everyone was overwhelmed by an indescribable emotion just looking at this remarkable woman who had given her entire life for Am Yisrael.

Hineni's 50th Anniversary Dinner tribute to the Rebbetzin

The Rebbetzin was frail and weak, supported at the podium by her two daughters, Chaya Sora and Slovie. And she used that last speech of her life to implore everyone in attendance to take up her call to bring the words of *Shema Yisrael* to the entire Jewish world. "*Shema Yisrael* is our credo, our anthem, that which enabled us to survive the centuries," cried out the Rebbetzin. "It is forever engraved upon our hearts, upon our souls. As long as Am Yisrael says *Shema Yisrael*, Hashem will help. Hashem is the *Shomer Yisrael*, the guardian of Israel, and He will never forsake His nation who recite *Shema Yisrael*. Tonight, we will start an awakening for all our people."

Rebbetzin Jungreis really understood the concept of helping people take things step by step, and in her mind, one of the most effective first steps a person could take was to recite the *Shema*. It was the words and message of *Shema Yisrael* that served as the theme for the first major Hineni event at Madison Square Garden in 1973, and the words and message of *Shema Yisrael* that served as the focus of the final speech she ever gave. In essence, *Shema Yisrael* bookended her life's work.

When the Rebbetzin became very ill at the end of her life, her children accompanied her to the doctor's office. During the consultation, the doctor asked the patient to please step into one of the other rooms to be examined.

The Rebbetzin asked Slovie to come with her.

Sitting together waiting for the doctor to come in, Rebbetzin Jungreis turned to her daughter and said, "I have just one fear and one tefillah."

"What's that, Mommy?"

"I just want to be able to continue doing for others, and if I can't... This is my whole life. I daven that *loh niga larik, v'lo neled labehalah*, that I did not struggle in vain nor produce for futility" (from the morning prayers).

The two of them returned to the doctor's office a few minutes later and he delivered the very difficult piece of news to the patient.

Looking at the Rebbetzin, he asked, "Do you have any questions?"

Esther Jungreis took a tissue, dabbed at her eyes and replied, "I just have one question.

"Can I still go on teaching Torah? That's what I do. That's my whole life. Will I be able to carry on teaching?"

"You can do whatever you feel you can do," he answered her, with sympathy and wisdom.

"That's all I need to hear."

Later on, she asked all her children to keep the flame burning and her life's work alive.

Along the same lines, at the 50th Anniversary Hineni dinner she told all her Hineni children that she was leaving them a gift — her biological children.

She would always remain an educator, a teacher and disseminator of Torah, until her final day on earth. When the Rebbetzin first moved to Lawrence from North Woodmere after Rav Meshulem passed away, she was invited to deliver a *Shabbos Mevorchim shiur* to the women of Lawrence and Far Rockaway at the Agudah of Long Island. It was a different kind of *shiur* than what she normally gave — a different level and focus — and the Agudah was packed every time she spoke. With her children and grandchildren accompanying her down Reads Lane and into the shul, the Rebbetzin would take her place in front of the *aron kodesh*, while the women overflowed the beis medrash. She would then proceed to deliver an incredible *shiur*, hitting the nail on the head every time. No matter how many times she spoke at the Agudah, the crowds never diminished in number — they only increased.

Of course, there were some men who couldn't help themselves and hid in the women's section to listen to her speak (the phenomenon of men hiding in the *ezras nashim* to hear her speak didn't just happen at the Agudah, and who could blame them — it was Rebbetzin Jungreis, after all…).

Hakaras hatov, showing gratitude, always played a significant role in the Rebbetzin's life. Rebbetzin Goldie Jungreis reminisces that when her husband, Rabbi Binyomin, the Rebbetzin's brother, was hospitalized, the Rebbetzin came to visit every day armed with all kinds of goodies for the nursing staff. It was very important to her to always give thanks to those who helped her, Hineni, or any member of her family. Likewise, whenever the Rebbetzin would go see any of the many doctors who took care of her, particularly toward the end of her life, she always made sure to bring along freshly baked challah and cakes that she would distribute to the doctors and nurses with a smile.

Still giving.

Always giving.

Even at the end.

Sometimes, when one of her children would tell their mother that they were tired, she'd reply, "There's only one person in the entire Torah who we know was tired — do you know who that was?"

"No, Mommy, who?"

"It was Esav."

That was the end of the conversation.

When her children would tell her that she needed to sleep more, she'd reply, "I did sleep."

"When?" they'd ask.

"Last night."

"But you slept only for two hours!"

"I sleep fast."

And what do you say to that?

One of the Rebbetzin's cousins, Rav Mordechai Jungreis, the Nikolsburger Rebbe and the Rav of the Woodbourne shul, commented about the Rebbetzin's sleeping habits (or lack thereof) that people who experienced the Holocaust couldn't sleep. Being the chosen few to escape the inferno, the survivors felt they had to be doing something with every minute.

"It was like they had been given a mission and couldn't waste any time."

Rav Mordechai had something else to add as well.

When asked to what he attributed his cousin's phenomenal success, this close relative didn't hesitate or think twice before replying, "Esther's success stemmed from the fact that everything she did, she did with *tznius*!"

As her illness progressed, the Rebbetzin would still present her grandchildren with a positive message when they left her on Motza'ei Shabbos, telling them, "You know I'm going to have to approve of your kallah and that I will be dancing up a storm at your wedding…"

As her strength further diminished, she changed her message and began telling her grandsons, "If Hashem calls for me before your weddings, you should always know I will be watching and waving from the window in Heaven, watching over you wherever you go and whatever happens."

At the end of her life, the Rebbetzin was in and out of the hospital on a frequent basis. Once when she returned home, her son Rabbi Osher invited a friend of his who lived in the neighborhood, Dovid Bodenheim, to come say hello.

"Dovid," the Rebbetzin said when she caught sight of his familiar face, "I just met this nurse in the hospital who I thought might be a good shidduch for you."

Dovid was incredibly moved by her thoughtfulness. Her stays in the hospital were no vacation. She was in terrible pain the entire time. And yet, she remained true to form — managing to forget about her own physical pain while thinking about other people and their needs.

Sometimes she would ask Chaya Sora to bring her a drink. Chaya

Sora knew that her mother didn't really want or need the drink — but she did want to give her precious daughter another opportunity to fulfill the mitzvah of *kibbud eim*, honoring one's mother. Sometimes she'd say to her daughter, "Let's say Tehillim together."

"I used to read the Tehillim," Chaya Sora said, "and there were times when I was very tired and made a mistake with the pronunciation, and my mother corrected me without the Tehillim in front of her and despite being sick. She didn't need me to say the Tehillim for her — she knew everything in her head and she never forgot her *pesukim*. But that was a last gift from her to me — a chance for me to have one more mitzvah."

During one of her final visits to her grandmother, Tziri Salamon found the Rebbetzin in bed, crying.

Alarmed, Tziri asked, "Bubba, what's the matter? What's wrong? Should I call Ellie?" (Ellie, Tziri's husband, is a doctor and served as the "managing director" of the Rebbetzin's medical team.)

"I don't feel well enough today to say my Tehillim or to daven. There are so many people I have to daven for, but I'm too sick to daven for them right now..."

She was sobbing.

"It's okay, Bubba, you don't have to daven for them right now."

"It's not okay. How can I not daven for these people? This one is sick and another has marital problems..."

She would not be consoled over the fact that she couldn't find the strength to daven for all the people who so needed her tefillos.

When her grandson Eli Wolff came to make Havdalah for the Rebbetzin toward the end of her life, they'd spend precious hours together.

"After I made Havdalah for Bubba, we'd sing '*Eliyahu HaNavi*' together, and then she'd say '*ah gutte voch* for Shlomo and Chaya Sora, *ah gutte voch* for Yisroel and Rivki, *ah gutte voch* for Oshie and Yaffa, *ah gutte voch* for Tatty and Mommy,' and mention the name of every one of their children and grandchildren."

Later on there were times when she asked him for a drink.

"Sometimes I went to bring Bubba a glass of water and she was dizzy and had difficulty speaking when I walked away from her, but when I returned and it was time to make the berachah, she summoned all her reserves of inner strength. I'd watch her sit up straight, and recite the berachah with complete concentration. It was an extraordinary sight!

"A second later she would slip away again. But never when she needed to make a berachah. Then she was 'all there'!"

During her final days in the hospital, the Rebbetzin was attended to by a frum nurse. After they had gotten to know one another a little better, the nurse shyly made a request.

"Can I ask the Rebbetzin for a berachah to find a chassan?"

The Rebbetzin was terribly weak at the time, but a frum girl had asked her for a berachah and she was more than happy to oblige, thrilled to still have the opportunity to give someone a berachah even at that stage in her life. Of course the moment she gave a berachah to one nurse, word spread, and more and more nurses made their way to the Rebbetzin's room, all seeking blessings from the holy woman who was still holding court from her hospital bed.

The Rebbetzin had no strength any more. Gone were the days of going with no sleep and unceasing travel. But she looked at her life as a mission — and according to her mission statement she was a Rebbetzin, and a Rebbetzin gave berachos and eased people's pain. Summoning every last vestige of whatever energy she had left, the Rebbetzin blessed the nurses until every last one had received a berachah — a berachah that brought a genuine smile to their lips and peace to their hearts.

On the day of the *sheloshim* (the nurse didn't know the significance of the day), the original nurse who first approached the Rebbetzin for a berachah became a kallah.

This story was completely in keeping with the Rebbetzin's character.

In one of the final interviews the Rebbetzin gave, the interviewer asked her, "What do you want it to say on your gravestone?"

Her answer was short and to the point.

"I want it to say two words: *I cared.*"

Testimony to her sentiment would come in thick and fast during *shivah*, when hundreds and hundreds of people came to visit the family, to comfort them and to share personal stories of how the Rebbetzin had impacted their lives. Many of those people were complete strangers to the Jungreis family — complete strangers who credited their mother with having altered their lives forever.

One day a postcard arrived in the mail. On it was a picture of a beautiful family with many children. On the back of the postcard the sender wrote, "I went to one of your mother's speeches many years ago and became religious as a result. This is a picture of my family."

More *einiklach* for the Rebbetzin who cared.

CHAPTER SIXTY-TWO

The Zeide's *Yaaleh*

And then everything sped up. It was almost over. The entire Jungreis family assembled at Maimonides Medical Center in Boro Park — children and grandchildren; everyone was there. There was a minyan around the Rebbetzin's bed when her *neshamah* left this world. On the walls of her hospital room, the family had hung pictures of the Menuchas Osher, Zeide and Rav Meshulem Jungreis.

And then as her *neshamah* was departing, as it was wafting out of her holy body and upward toward heaven, the family began softly singing the songs of the tefillos (prayers) that the Rebbetzin had loved so much. Despite their tears, the children and grandchildren sang with their broken hearts. Their voices filled the room with the lyrics of "*Hamalach Hagoel*" (May the angel who redeems me...), "*Shema Yisrael*," and other tunes.

One of the most beautiful of all the songs was the *niggun* Zeide used for the *piyyut* of *Yaaleh* on Kol Nidrei night. It was a song that the Rebbetzin loved with all her heart, and it was the perfect song to accompany her soul as it left this world. Zeide had taught this tune to Rabbi Shlomo, and now he led the family in singing this *niggun* that was normally sung but once a year, on Yom Kippur, and now once again at the bedside of a holy *tzaddeikes* — the queen mother known as "The Rebbetzin" all across the world.

Rebbetzin Esther Jungreis had an incredible look of peace on her face as she ended her earthly journey and commenced with the next stage, onward and upward, eager to be reunited with her beloved husband, parents, and all the Zeides and Bubbas from the past — all anxiously waiting to be with their Esther again.

That was how she left, encircled within the holy warmth of the very tune she and her family had used year after year to bring Jewish people back to their Creator.

Rebbetzin Jungreis was *niftar* on the 19th of Av 5776/August 23, 2016, during the week of *Parashas Eikev, Shabbos Mevorchim* — the very same week decades earlier when she first delivered her "Eikev/Footsteps" Shabbos afternoon speech at the Pine View Hotel in the Catskill Mountains way back in 1973. That was the speech that led her from the mountains to the ballroom at Terrace on the Park, to her kitchen table, to Joe and Ronne Wohl and to the moment when she walked out onto the stage at Madison Square Garden and uttered the legendary words, *"You are a Jew!"*

Her *levayah* took place at the Agudath Israel of Long Island, where the *aron* was brought into the shul and placed on a table before the *aron kodesh* — in the exact spot where she'd addressed the women of Far Rockaway and Lawrence every *Shabbos Mevorchim* for many years.

The Rebbetzin's *levayah*

The *maspidim* spoke of her accomplishments, of the many great things that she did throughout her life. But in truth, no matter what anyone said, they could not possibly do justice to such a woman. For without question she was larger than life, and her essence couldn't be captured in a speech, article or video.

From the grand stage at Madison Square Garden to her final moments on earth, Rebbetzin Esther Jungreis had come full circle. The journey was done.

But in truth it was only beginning.

Here is interred

A VIRTUOUS WOMAN OF VALOR

Renowned For her accomplishments and good deeds

REBBETZIN ESTHER JUNGREIS, *a"h*

Wife of the illustrious Rabbi and scholar
HaRav Meshulem HaLevi, *zt"l*
Rav of Congregation Ohr Torah, North Woodmere, NY

Daughter of the distinguished sage
HaRav Avraham HaLevi Jungreis, *zt"l*
Leader of the Rabbinical Court of Szeged, Hungary
and
Rebbetzin Miriam Jungreis, *a"h* –
Daughter of HaRav Tzvi Hirsh Cohen, zt"l –
Leader of the Rabbinical Court of Deretchkeh, Hungary

A descendant of the holy dynasty of the
MENUCHAS OSHER of CSENGER, *zt"l*

Love for every Jew burned deeply within her heart
She stretched out her hand to the weak and infirm
The Torah of lovingkindness and compassion was on her tongue

The HINENI movement which she founded,
was her splendor and majesty
She endeavored to bring Jews closer to HaShem and His Torah
For bringing so many couples together, her reward is immense

Her prayers for every Jew were beyond comprehension
She treasured and honored her revered parents and ancestors
She imbued in her descendants respect for their holy forefathers
She was singular in her generation
in the measure of what one human being can accomplish
Her blessings for every individual and all Jews
were driven by a deep sense of connection

Her memory shall forever be etched in the hearts
of her descendants, disciples and admirers

Departed with a good name at the age of 80 years
During the week of the Torah portion of Ekev
19th day of Menachem Av 5776

• **MAY HER SOUL BE BOUND UP IN THE ETERNAL LIFE** •

The Rebbetzin's *matzeivah* and English translation of the inscription

The *matzeivos* of Zeide, Mama, Rav Meshulem and the Rebbetzin

This chapter has been dedicated
in honor of the Jungreis, Gertzulin and Wolff Families
Jill Roberts

Chapter Sixty-Two: The Zeide's *Yaaleh* □ 649

Afterword

And so we have arrived at the end of the book: the incredible story of a young girl, a young refugee who arrived in the United States and proceeded to make a difference.

The curtain is lowered — the story has been told.

After walking in her beloved father's footsteps through the deep snow of her Zeide's Hungarian village, Esther Jungreis would go on to create footsteps of her own — giving future generations of Jews the ability to walk through the deep snow of their own day and age, helping them with their challenges and difficulties on both a personal and communal level.

From smuggling medicine to the Hungarian Jewish prisoners as a tiny girl, to the darkest nights lying on her bunk in Bergen-Belsen; from the crowded Brooklyn neighborhood teeming with immigrants, to the earliest classes given to the irreligious American children by Zeide — which she translated into English — she would never stop doing, teaching and connecting with people.

From trying to move to Eretz Yisrael and being forced to return to the States due to illness; from getting married to her cousin Rav Meshulem and establishing a community in North Woodmere, the Rebbetzin never took a vacation from her involvement with her people.

From fifty years of columns in *The Jewish Press*, to the sloping lawns of Camp Naarah; to years of *shiurim* in the Syrian community, to summers spent at the Pine View Hotel, the Rebbetzin was continually gearing up for the big moment, the moment when her entire life would change forever.

From a sold-out crowd at Hineni's "Shema Yisrael" rally at Madison Square Garden, to an endless array of meetings, encounters, lectures and classes with members of Klal Yisrael around the globe; to the message of *Shema Yisrael* at the last Hineni dinner she attended, Rebbetzin Jungreis would never rest — not for a second.

It mattered not at all if the venue was a flight from Oregon, a speech in a dusty, sun-drenched square in a Ramle prison, a meeting with Prime Minister Menachem Begin, or a Chanukah party at the White House with President and Mrs. Bush — the Rebbetzin would utilize every opportunity presented to her to make a *Kiddush Hashem* to the best of her considerable abilities.

She would go on to bring *chizuk* to thousands of Israeli soldiers, visit war-torn Lebanon, hear the *Megillah* reading on the roof of *Kever Yissachar* and Zevulun, address thousands at Jerusalem's Binyanei Ha'uma, distribute recordings of her speeches around the world, write four runaway bestselling books, be invited as a guest on national television, host her own television/Chumash show teaching Torah to millions, never cease crisscrossing the globe — and somehow find the time and energy to raise her own beautiful family, and to serve as a role model of what it means to be an amazing wife, mother and daughter.

The ripples of everything she has done have spread farther and farther — with hundreds of thousands of Jewish people positively affected by her — by the Rebbetzin.

Was it anything less than miraculous that nobody challenged her in a serious way? Was it anything less than a miracle that she received clear and powerful berachos from the greatest *gedolim* of America endorsing her work and giving her a mandate to carry on? From Rav Moshe Feinstein to the Satmar Rebbe, from Rav Henkin to Rav Soloveitchik, all agreed and stated that Rebbetzin Jungreis should be encouraged and endorsed and supported.

They supported her with no controversy.

From Rav Moshe promising to send his *bachurim* to help Hineni at Madison Square Garden, to the Satmar Rebbetzin sponsoring a thousand yarmulkes for Israeli soldiers, the Rebbetzin proved to be a uniquely unifying source for Klal Yisrael — welcomed, revered and listened to from the magnificent homes of Cape Town in South Africa to the crowded and congested alleyways of Bnei Brak.

It was a true miracle — but more importantly it was a testimony to the words she repeated so many times:

"Everything I did was for the sake of Heaven."

And from Klal Yisrael's response to her, it seems that Heaven agreed.

If you feel that you have come to know the Rebbetzin after reading this book, you will have understood that she was very meticulous in everything that she did, and was never one to leave any "i" undotted, or "t" uncrossed. And so it was in her final written missive to her family… written in her own handwriting on Motza'ei Yom Kippur ten months before her *petirah*.

The Rebbetzin's true essence came out in her will. Despite traveling the four corners of the world, meeting *gedolei Yisrael*, presidents, prime ministers, internationally successful businesspeople, and people of every description and achievement, nothing — nothing — meant more to her than seeing her children, grandchildren and great-grandchildren follow in the footsteps of her ancestors.

Her family read the Rebbetzin's *tzavaah* (will) and wiped the tears from their eyes as they reflected yet again on how blessed they had been to have had her in their lives.

From the Rebbetzin's Final Will and Testament

I am your mother who lives and breathes for you. You are the meaning of my life, and I thank you for all the *nachas* you have given me. I daven that you have *nachas* from all of your *doros* (generations). As Zeide said after finding out that he was the sole survivor of all the great tzaddikim after the Holocaust, *"Ich beit nur eine zach… az aleh meine doros zolen bleiben bei Torah…* — I ask only one thing… that all my generations should remain committed to Torah."

I created Hineni many years ago with one purpose in mind — to bring Am Yisrael back to Hashem. It was a revolutionary idea — I did not have much support, but moved ahead with the berachos of my holy *tatte*, Abba, and the *gedolim* of our generation. Hashem opened many gates to me and Hineni changed the Jewish world.

Today, there are many baal teshuvah movements, but *baruch Hashem* we were the first.

When I started Hineni you were young children and teenagers. The concept may have seemed foreign to you. *Baruch Hashem* you have become leaders and movers of Hineni, and I thank Hashem for that, because that gives me much *nachas*.

I conclude with Zeide's words, which are inscribed in my heart and *neshamah*: *Ich bin imer mit eink* (I am forever with you) *meine lichtiger kinder* (my precious children), *in di velt un in yener velt* (in this world and in the eternal world).

V'nafsho keshurah v'nafsho.

Ima

The Rebbetzin's mission continues through her children

I would like to conclude this epic book with one final, very touching story.

Rav Tzvi Hirsch Cohen, the Rebbetzin's grandfather, lived a long life filled with Torah, chessed and peacemaking. He was a true tzaddik in every respect. If you visited his home, you would find him sitting and learning from the *sefarim* he loved so much. They were his life, his beloved children and his passion — and he loved them with all his heart.

As he grew older and weaker, his eyesight failed him and he could no longer make out the words written in the pages of his *sefarim*. And yet, Rav Tzvi Hirsch refused to leave them on the shelves of the bookcase, keeping them in front of him though he couldn't read from them any longer. He needed them on his table, needed to touch them, to feel the ancient words and caress the pages he loved with all his heart.

One day the call came. The call the Rebbetzin had been dreading.

Her Zeide was leaving them. He was almost gone.

Rabbi and Rebbetzin Jungreis grabbed their four children and ran. By the time they arrived, their beloved Zeide was semi-conscious.

The Rebbetzin made her way to her Zeide. He was lying in bed. He was still there with them and yet he wasn't there anymore. There and not there. His two feet were firmly planted in separate worlds.

The author at the *kever* of the Rebbetzin

"Zeide, it is I," Esther said. "I have brought my children. Look, Zeide, they are all here. Bless them, Zeide, please, Zeide, bless them!"

Slowly Rav Tzvi Hirsch opened his eyes.

He could barely talk by then. He could barely lift his arm at all. Somehow, he managed to place a hand on each of their heads. How did he do it? She would never know.

She could see that there was something on his mind. He

wanted something. But he could no longer make himself understood.

Esther knew that if there was anyone in the world who would understand, who would know what he wanted, it would be her father.

Rav Avrohom HaLevi Jungreis leaned in close to Rav Tzvi Hirsch's holy mouth. To the dear face of his holy father-in-law. He listened closely. When his daughter caught sight of his face she could see the traces of tears.

"Zeide wishes to be carried to the bookcase so that he might say farewell to his beloved life partners, the holy books of the Torah."

And so it was.

And so he said goodbye.

The Menuchas Osher of Csenger gave her strength; her grandfather Rav Tzvi Hirsch Cohen was a powerful role model; her father Rav Avrohom HaLevi gave her endless encouragement; her husband Rav Meshulem was her rock and anchor; her mother Rebbetzin Miriam gave her support, running her home when she was on the road; her children Chaya Sora, Yisroel, Slovie and Osher Anshil gave their mother

A newspaper captures the essence of the Rebbetzin

unconditional love — and her students gave her the ability to teach Torah to Klal Yisrael.

Very few have ever accomplished what she did.

May her memory serve as a blessing and may she forever be remembered as **"The Rebbetzin."**

IN MEMORY OF – לזכר נשמת

Rebbetzin Esther Jungreis ע״ה

AUGUST 23, 2016 — 19 Av 5776

The New York Times

Esther Jungreis, 80, Who Led Secular Jews to Study Torah

By WILLIAM GRIMES

Esther Jungreis, a charismatic speaker and teacher whose enormously popular revival-style assemblies urged secular Jews to study Torah and embrace traditional religious values, died on Tuesday in Brooklyn. She was 80.

The cause was complications of pneumonia, her son-in-law, Rabbi Shlomo Gertzulin, said.

Ms. Jungreis (pronounced YOUNG-rice), a Hungarian Jew who spent several months in the Bergen-Belsen concentration camp as a child, was often called "the Jewish Billy Graham," and her artfully staged rallies, with theatrical lighting and musical accompaniment, were in fact inspired by Mr. Graham's Christian crusades.

She styled herself "rebbetzin," the Yiddish honor bestowed on wives of rabbis. Her husband, Rabbi Theodore Jungreis, led the Congregation Ohr Torah, an Orthodox synagogue in North Woodmere, N.Y., on Long Island.

But the title understated her role. In "American Judaism: A History" (2005), Jon...

A charismatic speaker and teacher who became known as the Jewish Billy Graham.

Sarna wrote that "to some of her followers she functioned as a full-fledged rabbi in almost everything but name."

Alarmed at the threats to Judaism posed by assimilation, secularism and the rise of religious cults, Rebbetzin Jungreis held a rally attended by 10,000 people at the Felt Forum in Madison Square Garden in 1973 to inspire a Jewish awakening. She also founded an outreach organization, Hineni, its name — Hebrew for "I am here" — alluding to Abraham's answer when called upon by God in Genesis.

The organization offered classes in the Torah and social mixers at which Jewish singles could find one another. As its ... der Rebbetzin Jungreis ad-... ... around

---

the United States and abroad and, beginning in 1982, broadcast a weekly half-hour Torah program, "Hineni," on National Jewish Television.

Her style was impassioned, her message urgent. She routinely called the threat of assimilation "a spiritual Holocaust." Onstage, she would exhort and scold, admonish and warn, tugging at the heartstrings with both hands, distraught at the erosion of Jewish identity and religious devotion.

"We have a generation that has surpassed expectations in every field," she told The New York Times in 1997. "But when it comes to the Torah, we — the people of the book — we have Jewish illiterates." It was her life's mission to correct this state of affairs.

Esther Naomi Jungreis was born on April 27, 1936, in Szeged, Hungary, to Abraham Jungreisz, a rabbi descended from a long line of rabbis, and the former Miriam Cohen.

In June 1944, as mass deportations of Hungary's Jews gathered momentum, Esther, along with her parents and her two brothers, was put on a train bound for Auschwitz. Although the family

---

did not realize it, an aunt in Budapest had placed their names on the passenger list of a special train traveling from Budapest to Switzerland, organized by Rudolf Kastner, a founder of the Jewish Aid and Rescue Committee. Mr. Kastner had bribed Adolf Eichmann to allow some 1,800 Jews to escape the country.

On reaching Budapest, the family was transferred to the Kastner train, which, for unknown reasons, was diverted to Bergen-Belsen. Esther and her family remained there as inmates for six months — she was prisoner No. 5357 — before being released and traveling on to a refugee camp in Caux, Switzerland.

The family emigrated to the United States and settled in a basement apartment in the East Flatbush section of Brooklyn. Her father started a shul and yeshiva in the Canarsie neighborhood. She recounted the events of her childhood in her first book, "The Jewish Soul on Fire" (1982), which wove her life story together with her religious views.

Esther received a yeshiva education at the Bais Yaakov School for Girls, then studied in Israel with the biblical scholar Nechama Leibowitz. On returning to the United States, she married a distant cousin, Theodore Jungreis, also a Hungarian refugee, in 1955.

After moving to Long Island, the couple founded both the North Woodmere Jewish Center and Congregation Ohr Torah in 1963, and Rebbetzin Jungreis began developing her speaking style by lecturing to Jewish groups and presiding over Torah lunches.

Hearing her speak at a hotel in the Catskills in the early 1960s, the editor of The Jewish Press invited her to write an advice column,

---

"Rebbetzin's Viewpoint." It ran for the next 45 years. Her last column appeared on Aug. 19.

She is survived by her two brothers, Jacob, a rabbi, and Benjamin; two sons, Yisroel and Osher, both rabbis; two daughters, Chaya Sora Gertzulin and Slovi Wolff; 23 grandchildren; and 32 great-grandchildren. Her husband died in 1996.

Initially, Hineni offered classes and social events in the Canarsie shul, but over the years it expanded its reach, establishing offices in Jerusalem and elsewhere. In 1989, Rebbetzin Jungreis opened the Hineni Heritage Center on the Upper West Side of Manhattan, where it houses a multimedia museum and offers Torah classes, singles events and religious services on High Holy Days.

To apply the lessons of Torah to modern life, Rebbetzin Jungreis

---

wrote the self-help books "The Committed Life: Principles for Good Living From Our Timeless Past" (1998), "The Committed Marriage: A Guide to Finding a Soul Mate and Building a Relationship Through Timeless Biblical Wisdom" (2002) and "Life Is a Test: How to Meet Life's Challenges Successfully" (2006).

Her aim, she said, was to bring secular Jews home to their religion, but not to any specific form of it. "There is not one page in Torah that says anything about being Orthodox or Reform," she told Malka Drucker, the author of "White Fire: A Portrait of Women Spiritual Leaders in America" (2002). "These modern-day manifestations have only created disharmony. I believe that every Jew is a Jew; we have one Shabbat, one God, one Torah and one faith."

The Rebbetzin genuinely believed that the Torah was everyone's heritage.